The Economic History of the Caribbean since the Napoleonic Wars

This book examines the economic history of the Caribbean in the 200 years since the Napoleonic Wars and is the first such analysis to span the whole region. It is divided into three parts, each centered around a particular case study: the first focuses on the nineteenth century ('The Age of Free Trade'); the second considers the period up to 1960 ('The Age of Preferences'); and the final section concerns the half century from the Cuban Revolution to the present ('The Age of Globalisation'). The study makes use of a specially constructed database to observe trends across the whole region and chart the progress of nearly thirty individual countries. Its findings challenge many long-standing assumptions about the region, and its in-depth case studies shed new light on the history of three countries in particular, namely, Belize, Cuba and Haiti.

Victor Bulmer-Thomas is Emeritus Professor of Economics at the University of London and Honorary Research Fellow with the University's Institute for the Study of the Americas. He is also a Senior Distinguished Fellow of the School of Advanced Study at London University and an Associate Fellow in the Americas Programme at Chatham House, where he was Director from 2001 to 2006; he was Director of the Institute of Latin American Studies, London University, from 1992 to 1998. His publications include *The Economic History of Latin America since Independence* (2nd ed., 2003), *The Political Economy of Central America since 1920* (1987) and *Input-Output Analysis for Developing Countries* (1982). He is also coeditor of *The Cambridge Economic History of Latin America* (2006).

The Economic History of the Caribbean since the Napoleonic Wars

VICTOR BULMER-THOMAS

University of London

 CAMBRIDGE
UNIVERSITY PRESS

CAMBRIDGE UNIVERSITY PRESS
Cambridge, New York, Melbourne, Madrid, Cape Town,
Singapore, São Paulo, Delhi, Mexico City

Cambridge University Press
32 Avenue of the Americas, New York, NY 10013-2473, USA

www.cambridge.org
Information on this title: www.cambridge.org/9780521145602

First published 2012

Printed in the United States of America

A catalog record for this publication is available from the British Library.

Library of Congress Cataloging in Publication data

Bulmer-Thomas, V.
The economic history of the Caribbean since the Napoleonic wars / Victor Bulmer-Thomas.
   p. cm.
Includes bibliographical references and index.
ISBN 978-0-521-19889-9 – ISBN 978-0-521-14560-2 (pbk.)
   1. Caribbean Area – Commerce – History.   2. Caribbean Area – Economic conditions.   I. Title.
HF3312.B85   2012
330.9729–dc23   2011023537

ISBN 978-0-521-19889-9 Hardback
ISBN 978-0-521-14560-2 Paperback

Additional resources for this publication at http://www.cambridge.org/9780521145602

For Barbara

Contents

List of Figures

x

List of Tables

Preface

This book has had a long gestation period. The final phase began in 2007, after I retired as Director of Chatham House. However, its intellectual origins go back to 1998, when I retired as Director of the University of London's Institute of Latin American Studies. This was when I started a research project with other scholars on the causes of the wide spread of income per head between Caribbean countries in the twentieth century. That research project resulted in a first attempt at a database covering the whole Caribbean and led to a special issue of the journal *Integration & Trade* (September 2001). However, the research stopped as soon as I became Director of Chatham House.

Yet, in a very real sense, the origins of this book can be traced to 1966–7 when I was a secondary school teacher in Belize (at that time called British Honduras). This was my first exposure to the Caribbean, and it gave me a lifelong interest in the region even though I spent the first decades of my academic career as a specialist on Latin America. After writing economic histories of Central America (*The Political Economy of Central America since 1920*) and of Latin America (*The Economic History of Latin America since Independence*), it seemed only natural to turn my hand to an economic history of the Caribbean.

It proved to be more challenging than I had expected. Pulling together data for the thirty countries of the Caribbean over a period covering two centuries was not easy. And yet the further I advanced, the more intriguing the research project became. Not only was I able to build time series for the Caribbean as a whole that had never been seen before, but I was also able to cast a sceptical eye over the secondary literature on many individual countries in the light of the new empirical evidence itself. This has allowed me to develop a new approach to the economic history of several Caribbean countries, not just the region as a whole. The most important of these form the three case studies in this book (Haiti, Belize and Cuba).

This book is intended to help those inside the region acquire a better grasp of its economic history and to provide a framework for those outside the

Caribbean who wish to learn more about its past. The Caribbean is largely ignored today by governments and peoples outside the region itself. That is very different from the position 200 years ago, when it was central to the concerns of many important states. The decline in interest is understandable, but it has gone too far. In the last two centuries the Caribbean has had a habit of springing surprises on the world, starting with the successful slave revolt in Haiti leading to independence in 1804, and knowledge of the region's economic history is a first step in building greater understanding.

I cannot list here all those who have helped me in writing this book, but I owe a special debt of gratitude to all the librarians around the world who helped me track down specialist material. I am also very grateful to Florida International University for allowing me to spend part of each year from 2007 to 2010 as a visiting professor and giving me the time to devote to research. Finally, I would like to thank the Caribbean Development Bank and the Tinker Foundation for the financial support that has made it possible to use color printing in this book.

List of Abbreviations

ABC	Aruba, Bonaire and Curaçao
ACP	African, Caribbean and Pacific
ACS	Association of Caribbean States
ALBA	Alianza Bolivariana para los Pueblos de Nuestra América
BEC	Belize Estate and Produce Company
BG$	British Guiana Dollar
BH$	British Honduran Dollar
BLS	Bureau of Labor Statistics
BNdH	Banque Nationale d'Haiti
BNRdH	Banque Nationale de la République d'Haiti
BVI	British Virgin Islands
BWI$	British West Indian Dollar
CAFTA	Central American Free Trade Agreement
CAP	Common Agricultural Policy
CARIBCAN	Caribbean-Canada Trade Agreement
CARICOM	Caribbean Community
CARIFORUM	Caribbean Forum
CARIFTA	Caribbean Free Trade Association
CBERA	Caribbean Basin Economic Recovery Act
CBI	Caribbean Basin Initiative
CBR	Crude Birth Rate
CD&W	Colonial Development & Welfare
CDB	Caribbean Development Bank
CDR	Crude Death Rate
CEPAL	Comisión Económica para América Latina y el Caribe
CET	Common External Tariff
CMCF	CARICOM Multilateral Clearing Facility
CO_2	Carbon Dioxide
COM	Collectivité d'Outre-Mer
COMECON	Council for Mutual Economic Assistance

CSA	Commonwealth Sugar Agreement
CSME	CARICOM Single Market and Economy
CTO	Caribbean Tourism Organization
CUC	Cuban Convertible Peso
CXC	Caribbean Examinations Council
d	Old British penny (240d is one pound sterling)
DFQF	Duty-Free Quota-Free
DLOC	Digital Library of the Caribbean
DOM	Département d'Outre-Mer
DOTS	Direction of Trade Statistics
DR	Dominican Republic
D.S.	Dutch Standard
DUA	Domestic Use Agriculture
DVI	Danish Virgin Islands
EBA	Everything But Arms
EC	European Community
ECCB	Eastern Caribbean Central Bank
ECCU	Eastern Caribbean Currency Union
ECLA	Economic Commission for Latin America
ECLAC	Economic Commission for Latin America and the Caribbean
ECU	European Currency Unit
EEC	European Economic Community
EFTA	European Free Trade Area
EPA	Economic Partnership Agreement
EPZ	Export Processing Zone
ERP	Effective Rate of Protection
EU	European Union
EXA	Export Agriculture
FAO	Food and Agriculture Organization
FAOSTAT	Food and Agriculture Organization Statistical Database
FATF	Financial Action Task Force
FTAA	Free Trade Area of the Americas
G-7	Group of Seven
G-8	Group of Eight
GATT	General Agreement on Tariffs and Trade
GDP	Gross Domestic Product
GNI	Gross National Income
GNP	Gross National Product
GSP	Generalized System of Preferences
HFCS	High-Fructose Corn Syrup
HIPC	Highly Indebted Poor Countries
HOPE	Haitian Hemispheric Opportunity through Partnership Encouragement
IBC	International Business Company
IBRD	International Bank for Reconstruction and Development

IDB	Inter-American Development Bank
IFS	International Financial Statistics
ILO	International Labour Organization
INIE	Instituto Nacional de Investigación Económica
INRA	Instituto Nacional de Reforma Agraria
INSEE	Institut National de la Statistique et des Etudes Economiques
IRS	Internal Revenue Service
ISA	International Sugar Agreement
ISAg	Import-Substituting Agriculture
ISI	Import-Substituting Industrialization
ITO	International Trade Organization
ITT	Income Terms of Trade
JUCEPLAN	Cuban Central Planning Board
lb	Pound weight
LCU	Local Currency Unit
LDC	Less Developed Country
MDG	Millennium Development Goal
MFA	Multifibre Arrangement
MFN	Most-Favoured Nation
MINUSTAH	United Nations Stabilization Mission in Haiti
MNC	Multinational Corporation
MOxLAD	Montevideo-Oxford Latin American Economic Database
MT	Metric Ton
NAFTA	North American Free Trade Agreement
NBTT	Net Barter Terms of Trade
NTB	Nontariff Barrier
OAS	Organization of American States
OECD	Organisation of Economic Cooperation and Development
OECS	Organisation of Eastern Caribbean States
ONE	Oficina Nacional de Estadísticas
OPEC	Organization of Petroleum Exporting Countries
PAU	Pan-American Union
PDVSA	Petróleos de Venezuela, S.A.
PEA	Population Economically Active
PP	Parliamentary Papers
PPP	Purchasing Power Parity
PTA	Preferential Trade Agreement
RNM	Regional Negotiating Machinery
SALA	Statistical Abstract for Latin America
SEM	Single European Market
SITC	Standard International Trade Classification
STABEX	System of Stabilization of Export Earnings
STUSECO	Stichting ter bevordering van de Studie van de Surinaamse Economie

SYSMIN	System of Stabilization of Export Earnings from Mining Products
TIEA	Tax Information Exchange Agreement
UBPC	Union of Banana Producing Countries
UFCO	United Fruit Company
UK	United Kingdom
UN	United Nations
UNCTAD	United Nations Conference on Trade and Development
UND	United Nations Database
UNNA	United Nations National Accounts
UNSY	United Nations Statistical Yearbook
UNWTO	United Nations World Tourism Organization
UNYITS	United Nations Yearbook of International Trade Statistics
US	United States
USSR	Union of Soviet Socialist Republics
USVI	United States Virgin Islands
VAT	Value-Added Tax
WDI	World Development Indicators
WTO	World Trade Organization

I

Introduction

Many general histories of the Caribbean have been written since the arrival of the Europeans in 1492. There have also been a number of economic histories covering the age when sugar was 'king' and the colonial possessions generated huge rents for their imperial masters. Yet since the Napoleonic Wars ended in 1815 little has been written on the economic history of the region as a whole, although there have been some excellent studies of individual countries.[1]

There are various reasons for this. For many countries, but not all, the nineteenth century was seen as a period of decline, and therefore the region was considered unworthy of serious attention by economic historians. The data for the different territories are not easily comparable and are hard to access in some cases. As a result, scholars have tended to focus on subregions – such as the British West Indies before independence or the French-speaking territories. For British, Dutch and French scholars, other colonies outside the Caribbean have attracted much more interest. Scholarship in different parts of the world has paid attention to the economic development of Cuba and Puerto Rico, but the rest of the Caribbean has generally attracted much less interest from the same researchers. The first independent countries – Haiti and to a much smaller extent the Dominican Republic – have generated monographs and articles published inside and outside those countries, but comparatively little of this has focused on their economies.

This book is therefore designed to fill a gap in the economic history of the region. It covers the period from the end of the Napoleonic Wars to the present. The story starts at a time when Haiti had already become independent, when the slave trade had started to be abolished and when Spain was strengthening its grip on its Caribbean colonies, having lost its mainland Latin American ones. The vast majority of countries were still British, Dutch, French or Scandinavian colonies, but in every case the old order was changing, and an uncertain future was beckoning.

---

[1] These are referenced mainly in the Notes on A., B., C., and D. tables.

The end of the Napoleonic Wars was the moment when transfers of sovereignty among colonial powers were coming to an end. There would still be a few – notably Spain to the United States in the case of Puerto Rico – but in most cases the transitions from now on would be to independent states. Military conflicts became less common, but the few that did take place caused much destruction. The quantity and quality of statistics in all countries improved as the nineteenth century advanced, and it becomes possible to detect trends and cycles that were previously obscured by a lack of comparable data.

The economic history of the Caribbean in the twentieth century has also been notable in two ways that have not perhaps received sufficient attention. First, the cycles that had so marked the nineteenth century did not disappear, but they started to take place around a rising trend. As a result, the Caribbean has reached a level of average income that is high by the standards of developing regions. Indeed, many countries now have income per head comparable to that of rich countries. Thus, the problem of production has become much less acute, and for many countries the principal problems now revolve around distribution, employment and sovereignty.

Second, the primary products with which the region has been so intimately associated – especially sugar – have become much less important because all countries have switched exports from agricultural commodities to mining, energy, manufactured goods, and services. Indeed, the Caribbean is the region of the world most specialised in service exports and is likely to remain so. This creates opportunities that are not available to other parts of the world, but these are still not properly understood.

Everyone is agreed that the Caribbean is a region, but there is no unanimity about the countries it embraces. The term 'Caribbean' is derived from the Spanish word for one of the indigenous peoples the *conquistadores* found on their arrival, but it did not define a region until much later.[2] A definition based only on language or colonial origin is clearly too parochial, but it is still common for books on the countries that were once British colonies to carry the word 'Caribbean' in the title without any qualification.

The **narrowest** acceptable definition includes all the islands that are not part of mainland states.[3] This is a natural derivation from the ancient concept of the Antilles, the islands divided into Greater and Lesser according to size and geography.[4] This has the advantage of simplicity and has been used by many

---

[2] According to Gaztambide-Geigel (1996), the expression 'Caribbean' only became common at the end of the nineteenth century.

[3] This definition excludes islands such as the Florida Keys (part of the US) in the north and Margarita (part of Venezuela) in the south. It also excludes islands belonging to Colombia, Honduras, Nicaragua and Panama in the west.

[4] The Greater Antilles comprise the large islands to the north (Cuba, Hispaniola, Puerto Rico and Jamaica). The Lesser Antilles are all the others (often divided into Leeward and Windward islands).

authors.[5] However, it leaves out the littoral states that share much in common with the islands in terms of history, culture and economic experience.

The **widest** acceptable definition includes all the littoral states from Mexico to Venezuela and the three Guianas.[6] This is very similar to the membership of the Association of Caribbean States (ACS).[7] It is also close to the concept of the Caribbean Basin promoted by the United States in the 1980s.[8] However, both definitions are much too broad for purposes of Caribbean economic history because they include some countries that are essentially part of Latin America (e.g. Guatemala) or whose intercourse with the island Caribbean has been minimal (e.g. El Salvador).

Some littoral countries have been virtual islands and should be included in a study of the Caribbean. These are Belize on the Caribbean coast of Central America and the three Guianas on the northern coast of South America (today called Guyana, Suriname, and Guyane, or French Guiana). It is true that **parts** of other countries – especially Costa Rica, Honduras and Nicaragua – have had for much of their economic history more connections with the island Caribbean than with the mainland. However, it is statistically impossible to separate these parts in the areas that matter. The definition of the Caribbean used here is therefore all the islands, Belize and the three Guianas – what has been called the insular Caribbean.[9]

This is nearly thirty countries and can be unwieldy. It is therefore necessary for many purposes to aggregate them into subregions. Some scholars have chosen to aggregate by size or geography, others by language, and still others by colonial origin. Aggregations by economic activity can also be found. A further complication is that in an economic history covering 200 years, the most appropriate type of aggregation will change over time.

The aggregation used in this book is by constitutional status.[10] Thus, the independent countries are first separated from the nonindependent ones, and the latter are grouped in terms of the metropolitan power with ultimate responsibility for defence and foreign affairs. The independent countries, however, are not all lumped together, because this would be unworkable today. Haiti and the Dominican Republic – the two countries that form the island of Hispaniola – form one subregion in all periods. Cuba is kept separate after

---

[5] For a recent example, see Higman (2011).

[6] There is even a definition based on 'plantation America' that embraces the southern US and parts of Brazil (see Wagley, 1960), but this is too unwieldy to be operational.

[7] The ACS was established in 1994 and has twenty-five member and four associate states, but it excludes Puerto Rico, the US Virgin Islands and most of the British Overseas Territories. See Serbin (1994).

[8] The notion of a Caribbean Basin was revived by US President Ronald Reagan (1981–9) to provide a means of rewarding friends and punishing enemies at a time of political upheaval in the region. It has therefore acquired a geopolitical meaning.

[9] See Girvan (2005), p. 305.

[10] The database allows countries to be grouped together in other ways if desired.

it became independent because it is such a large part of the Caribbean as a whole. The other sovereign states are included together after they gained their independence.[11]

In addition to aggregating countries into subregions, it is necessary to divide the two centuries since the Napoleonic Wars into subperiods. It is common in economic histories to use the notion of a 'long' or 'short' century depending on the cycles of growth or depression, and this approach is used here. The end of the nineteenth century coincided with the Spanish-American War in 1898. This marked the end of Spain as a colonial power in the Caribbean and the rise of a United States based on an empire that included territories and neocolonies. It is therefore an appropriate moment to end the first part of the book, which therefore runs from 1810–20 to 1900 – the short nineteenth century. Because this period coincided with the end of mercantilism in all countries and a reduction in trade restrictions of most kinds, Part I is also described as 'The Age of Free Trade'.

The second part of the book runs from 1900 to 1960. The end year is influenced by three considerations. First, it is a convenient moment to mark the beginning of the shift from economies based overwhelmingly on primary products to economies based largely on services. Second, it is the year soon after which many countries acquired formal independence. Third, it follows the triumph of the Cuban Revolution that has played such a large part in perceptions of the contemporary Caribbean. Because this period coincides with the introduction of imperial preference by the United States and by its reintroduction in the case of the UK, Part II is described as 'The Age of Preferences'.

The final part of the book runs from 1960 to the end of the first decade of the twenty-first century. This is a period when the region has been subject to rapid structural change, with which it has at times struggled to cope. The importance of traditional agricultural commodities, such as sugar, has dramatically declined while minerals and manufacturing exports have grown in importance. Overshadowing these changes, however, has been the rise of service exports that now exceed merchandise exports by value in most countries. Because this period coincides with the liberalisation of capital flows, the accelerated transfer of technology and the shift of economic power from the west to the east, Part III is described as 'The Age of Globalisation'. It is also the period when thirteen countries won independence to join the three – Haiti, Dominican Republic and Cuba – that were already sovereign.

These three time periods have then been used in the preparation of the database for this book. (Throughout the database the US dollar ($) is used as the unit of account.) The first part (1810–20 to 1900) is a mixture of annual and decennial data (A. tables), with the demographic data mainly given annually, but other data are given at ten-year intervals, starting in 1820 based on three-year

---

[11] Because they all became members of the Caribbean Community, they are aggregated as 'CARICOM'.

averages and ending in 1900.[12] This is the period when only Haiti was independent for the whole time and the Dominican Republic for part of it.[13] Other countries have then been grouped into British, Dutch, French and Scandinavian colonies. There is also a special database for Haiti (B. tables) based on annual data in view of the importance of a better understanding of the evolution of the Haitian economy in the nineteenth century.

The second part of the database (1900–60) consists entirely of annual entries (C. tables) – the subregions are Hispaniola (as before), Cuba (now independent)[14] and other countries grouped by the responsible metropolitan power for most of the period.[15] However, in recognition of the constitutional changes in many countries, I use the word 'dependencies' rather than 'colonies' in describing the subregions.[16] The final part of the database (1960–2008) also consists of annual entries (D. tables), and the subgroupings are now Hispaniola and Cuba (as before), CARICOM (i.e. the other independent countries), and the British, Dutch and French territories.[17]

Haitian independence and the Napoleonic Wars changed the political landscape, but it did not change the prevailing economic outlook. The Caribbean was still subject to the mercantilist policies practiced by the imperial powers, according to which the colonies enjoyed special privileges for their exports to the metropolis in return for restrictions on trade with other countries and favourable treatment of metropolitan imports. Even Haiti, despite gaining its independence in 1804, was made subject to these rules of the international game – first with Britain and later with France.[18] Adam Smith's *The Wealth of Nations* may have been first published in 1776, but it had little resonance in the Caribbean even fifty years later. Among the colonies, only a handful of ports in Dutch and Scandinavian possessions were free to import from any source.[19]

---

[12] The final year (1900) is not, however, a three-year average in order to make it compatible with later entries in the database.

[13] The Dominican Republic was briefly independent in 1821 and again from 1844 to 1861. It then became a Spanish colony before winning its independence for the third time in 1865.

[14] Cuban independence is usually dated from the end of the first US occupation in 1902. However, because Cuba is such a large part of the Caribbean, I have chosen not to aggregate it with the other independent countries at this time.

[15] I have therefore labeled the Virgin Islands 'US' rather than 'Scandinavian' because the transfer from Denmark took place in 1917.

[16] Even this may not satisfy the purists, because the French 'dependencies' became part of metropolitan France in 1946.

[17] Haiti and Montserrat (a British Overseas Territory) are members of CARICOM, but the former is included here in Hispaniola and the latter in British territories.

[18] See Chapter 7.

[19] At the end of the Napoleonic Wars, the most important were St Thomas (part of the Danish Virgin Islands), Curaçao (part of the Dutch Antilles) and Gustavia on the Swedish island of St Barthélemy. These ports could import freely, but other countries restricted their exports, and many goods ended up as contraband – including weapons sold to the revolutionary forces in South America.

The final abolition of the slave trade by the European powers, starting with Denmark in 1803,[20] did not change the prevailing orthodoxy in favour of mercantilism. Gradually, however, the heavy-handed restrictions and monopolist practices of mercantilism gave way to a new orthodoxy based on imperial preference. Spain, for example, gave its Caribbean colonies in 1818 the right to trade with all countries but imposed a four-tier tariff on their imports that favoured Spanish goods in Spanish ships.[21] French recognition in 1825 of Haitian independence led to a two-tier tariff that favoured exports from France. The United States, with no colonial possessions in the Caribbean, was therefore frustrated in its efforts to export its growing surpluses to countries that generally purchased their imports from farther afield.

The emancipation of the slaves in the European colonies started with the British possessions in 1834. By the time emancipation was completed in Spain nearly fifty years later, the prevailing orthodoxy had changed once again. Britain, Holland and the Scandinavian countries had eliminated imperial preference, and the independent countries had adopted uniform tariff systems. The door was open for the United States to export to the Caribbean the goods that would pay for its ever increasing imports. The trade pattern of the Caribbean for the next century was starting to take shape.

Whether operating under mercantilism, imperial preference or free trade, the Caribbean countries were expected to export primary products. As in mainland Latin American countries, these resources were then used to buy a range of manufactured goods whose local production was not encouraged by the prevailing orthodoxy. However, the small size of all Caribbean countries – physically in most cases and demographically in all – meant that export specialisation in a small number of products was taken to a very high level. As a result, many imports consisted of foodstuffs to feed the growing population. Thus, the Caribbean both exported **and** imported primary products, making calculations of the net barter terms of trade more complicated than in mainland Latin America.

The first chink in orthodox thinking came – appropriately enough – in Haiti. The leaders of the country in the first three decades following independence did all in their power to revive the export sector after the ravages of the revolutionary war. Their efforts to reestablish sugar exports, however, would fail, and the country came to depend on other commodities – especially coffee.[22] The need for diversification was apparent to many Haitian thinkers, and a lively debate began in the 1880s that revolved around the merits of industrialisation based on the substitution of imports. The first steps were taken to promote local manufacturing, but they were very timid, and the experiment had failed by the time of the US occupation in 1915.

---

[20] France abolished slavery, and therefore also the slave trade, in 1794, but it was restored in 1802. Slavery and the slave trade had been abolished in Haiti in 1793.
[21] The highest tariff band was reserved for foreign goods in foreign ships.
[22] See Chapter 7.

Policy in other countries was based on the need to promote exports of primary products, but domestic and foreign elites were aware of the dangers of monoculture – the dependence of export earnings on a single commodity.[23] Following a long period of low sugar prices, the British government had established a Royal Commission in 1896 to provide policy recommendations.[24] However, the hands of the Norman Commission – as it became known – were largely tied by the UK's laissez-faire practices at the time, and the only substantial change recommended was land grants to small farmers to reduce the power of the estates.

More significant was the reaction of Cuban intellectuals to the extreme specialisation of the island in sugar following the reciprocal trade treaty with the United States in 1903. This took two forms. First was the condemnation of sugar dependence on economic, social and political grounds, which found its most articulate expression in Ramiro Guerra y Sánchez's *Azúcar y Población en las Antillas*. First published in 1927, it was a devastating critique of what could go wrong in a society that had put all its eggs in one basket. The second was the recognition that not all export commodities are the same and that each one can have a different impact. This found expression in Fernando Ortiz's *Contrapunteo cubano del tabaco y el azúcar*, which was first published in 1940 and drew attention to the differential impact on Cuba of sugar and tobacco.

Ortiz's book might have opened up a fruitful line of research into what today would be called the 'commodity lottery'.[25] However, it was rapidly overtaken by another event in the Caribbean that would have greater influence on economic thinking. This was 'Operation Bootstrap' in Puerto Rico, which launched the rapid industrialisation of the US territory from the 1940s onwards, taking advantage of the island's privileged access to the US mainland and fiscal concessions from the local and federal governments. Furthermore, with the island's constitutional transition in 1952 to *estado libre asociado*, Puerto Rico was seen by many as offering a model for the future of the rest of the Caribbean.

One of those dazzled by the Puerto Rican experience was Sir Arthur Lewis, the Nobel-laureate, who was born in St Lucia and enjoyed a distinguished career in economics inside and outside the region.[26] From the 1930s onwards, Lewis had recognised the bankruptcy of an economic model based on a small range of agricultural exports that could not provide employment for the expanding labour force.[27] Industrialisation seemed to provide the answer. However, Lewis recognised that manufacturing could not be based only on the domestic market, as was happening in many mainland Latin American countries, or on export only to the United States, as was the case in Puerto Rico. At a time when federation was under discussion, he called for a customs union of

[23] On the establishment of monoculture in the British colonies, see Ward (1988), chap. 2.
[24] See Report of the West India Royal Commission (1897).
[25] See Bulmer-Thomas (2003), p. 43.
[26] For an excellent biography of Lewis, see Tignor (2006).
[27] See Lewis (1977).

Caribbean countries to promote intraregional manufactured exports.[28] More controversially, he was pessimistic about the capacity of local elites to provide the investment required and recommended policies that would encourage foreign capital – as in Puerto Rico – to take the lead.

This made Lewis deeply unpopular with many of the nationalist thinkers that emerged after the Second World War. Indeed, one of them dismissed the model proposed by Lewis as 'industrialization by invitation' – a soubriquet that quickly caught on in the popular imagination.[29] These intellectuals were much more inspired by the structuralists that had formed around Raúl Prebisch in the UN Economic Commission for Latin America (ECLA) and that would later lead to the dependency school.[30] Both theories started from the global nature of the economic system and emphasised the subordinate role played within it by the developing countries as a result of unequal relations between the metropolitan countries and the rest of the world.

That Caribbean countries had been caught up in a global design not of their own making since the arrival of the Europeans was hardly in doubt. Furthermore, it was obvious to all that the Caribbean was frequently disadvantaged by the operations of a world system in which policy was largely determined at the centre. At the heart of the relationship between the Caribbean periphery and the metropolitan countries, according to some, were the estates producing the traditional commodities for export, such as sugar. This line of thinking led in the 1960s to the Plantation School, whose most forceful exponents came from the newly independent countries of the British Caribbean.[31]

The Plantation School placed the sugar estate based on slavery at the centre of its analysis.[32] This was then modified to take account of the end of slavery in the nineteenth century while keeping the estate at the core of the theory. However, the Plantation School was launched just at the time that many Caribbean countries were making the transition from commodity to service exports. The analysis had to be modified again, but claiming that the new exports were no more than 'quasi-staples' did nothing to change the essential elements of the model because they were still controlled by foreigners. What mattered was to gain control of the economy through radical policies that favoured nationalisation, expropriation and indigenisation.

The Plantation School had some influence on economic policy in a number of countries. Yet it was in Cuba that the nationalist agenda acquired its greatest expression. This had nothing to do with the Plantation School, but it had a great deal to do with Marxism. These two theories therefore co-existed side by side in the Caribbean in an uneasy relationship, yet there was a great deal of

---

[28] See Lewis (1950).

[29] The expression was first used by Lloyd Best. See Meeks and Girvan (2010), p. 224.

[30] ECLA, or ECLAC as it would later be called when a number of Caribbean countries joined, was established within the UN system in 1948 and quickly established a reputation under Prebisch for heterodox thinking. See Dosman (2008).

[31] See Meeks and Girvan (2010), chap. 1.

[32] See Best and Levitt (2009).

respect of each for the other. However, the failure of the radical experiments in Grenada, Guyana and Jamaica in the 1970s and 1980s undermined the Plantation School, leaving Cuban socialism as the preferred model for many on the left in the Caribbean.[33]

Others inside and outside the region had watched these developments with great unease. The business community in some countries fought back and found intellectual comfort in the neoliberal model that began to take shape in the 1980s. The collapse of the Soviet Union (USSR) did not destroy the Cuban Revolution, but it undermined the attractions of socialism in the Caribbean and left the field clear for policy recommendations based on free markets and private-sector initiatives. The international financial institutions took the lead, and the World Bank captured the new mood and orthodoxy with *A Time to Choose*, published in 2005. Its title was a provocative response to the 1992 Report of the West India Commission titled *A Time for Action*.[34]

Yet neoliberalism would in turn falter with the financial crisis un-leashed across many parts of the world by the collapse of the subprime mort-gage market in the United States in 2008. The Caribbean was affected in many ways, and the impact was made worse by a series of frauds perpetrated by foreign financiers.[35] The result was an intellectual vacuum in which both con-servative and radical theories had become discredited and where policy had become ideologically rudderless. This was not necessarily a disaster, but it did mean that 'muddling through' became the order of the day in most countries.

This book is not based exclusively on any of the established theories of development for the Caribbean. Instead, it takes its inspiration from a series of ideas that begins with the recognition that the Caribbean has, since the arrival of the Europeans, slotted into a world system in which a small number of metropolitan countries have had an enormous influence as a result of their policies and economic performance. These countries, referred to in this book as the 'core', have changed over time. However, the importance of the core as a whole has not changed and needs to be the starting point for any economic history of the Caribbean.

The reason why the core has been so crucial is that the Caribbean economies have relied on exports to the rest of the world as their main engine of growth. Thus, the ratio of exports to Gross Domestic Product (GDP) is very high by international standards, and most of these exports are sold outside the region. The main market is the core, and therefore the consumption patterns of a small number of countries have had a very large influence on economic performance

---

[33] On Marxist thinking in the Caribbean more generally, see Morrissey (1981).

[34] The West India Commission had been established by CARICOM heads of government in 1989, and the report carried numerous policy recommendations to take integration of the region to a new level. See West India Commission (1992). The World Bank had never been enthusiastic about regional integration, and its 2005 report must be seen in this light.

[35] The most notorious has been Sir Allen Stanford. His company, Stanford Financial Group, collapsed in 2009, leaving in its wake a series of financial disasters.

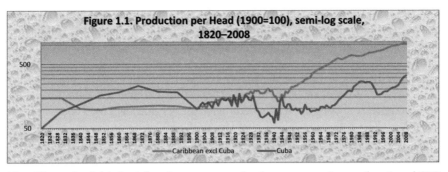

Figure 1.1. Production per Head (1900=100), semi-log scale, 1820–2008

Note: The production index is based on exports per head at constant prices until 1960 and GDP per head at constant prices thereafter. Years before 1900 are based on decennial data with gaps filled by interpolation.

Source: Derived from Tables A.1a, A.14, C.1, C.9, D.1 and D.19.

in the Caribbean. As these consumption habits have changed, the Caribbean has had to adapt in order to survive.

It is not just the consumption patterns of the core that have mattered. It is also the core's commercial policies. From mercantilism to imperial preference and free trade, the Caribbean countries have been caught up in a web of policies adopted by core countries that have had an enormous impact on income and employment. In the past, the instrument with the greatest impact was the tariff, but today it is just as likely to be the exchange rate or fiscal policy. A change in the basis for taxing airline flights in the core, for example, can have a major impact on visitor arrivals in the Caribbean. The core's consumption patterns and commercial policies then set the framework in which exports took place in the Caribbean and this, in turn, influenced other forms of production.

Before the Napoleonic Wars, many parts of the Caribbean had achieved a high level of output per head. This was based on an extreme level of specialisation in exports where land was owned by a few and labour was coerced, and thus the distribution of income was highly unequal. Nevertheless, by international standards, average income was high because Caribbean countries slotted into a colonial system based on specialisation in a small number of products with high labour productivity. The abolition of the slave trade, the emancipation of the slaves and the end of various colonial privileges then caused a crisis of production in some parts of the Caribbean. Cuba was at first exempt, but in the rest of the Caribbean the fall in production per head did not end until the middle of the nineteenth century, and it was not until the twentieth century that output per head started its upward trend again (see Figure 1.1).

Cuba, always among the largest of the Caribbean economies, at first followed a different path. The slave trade continued – albeit illegally – until after the US Civil War (1861–5), and exports per head at constant prices rose rapidly

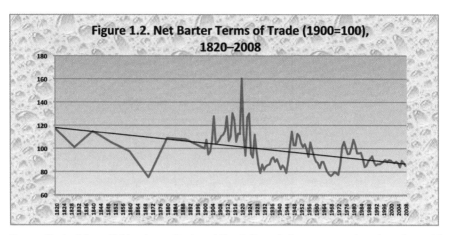

Figure 1.2. Net Barter Terms of Trade (1900=100), 1820–2008

Source: Derived from Tables A.31, C.26, and D.16. Years before 1900 are based on decennial data with gaps filled by interpolation.

until the 1870s (see Figure 1.1). The productive apparatus of the island survived the First War of Independence (1868–78) but not the Second (1895–8), and exports per head declined sharply in the 1890s. Thus, Cuba followed a different path than did the rest of the Caribbean before 1870, and it did so in parts of the twentieth century as well. It is therefore sometimes necessary to distinguish between the Caribbean with or without Cuba when making international comparisons.

In Table 1.1 the growth of exports in the region is compared with their growth in other parts of the world since 1870 (before this the data for other regions are incomplete). We may observe an initial period (1870–1913) when performance in the Caribbean lagged seriously behind every other region, followed by another cycle (1913–50) when almost the opposite was true. From 1950 to 1973, Caribbean export performance was slightly below the world average, but it was above it if Cuba is excluded. From 1973 to 1998, export performance was in line with other regions, and there was a convergence across the world towards the mean.

The core–periphery relationship in the theory of economic development is often assumed to mask a deterioration in the net barter terms of trade (NBTT). The Prebisch-Singer hypothesis, for example, predicts a secular decline in the NBTT based on the assumption that the periphery exports commodities and imports manufactured goods. The Caribbean NBTT has exhibited a mild deterioration since 1820 (see Figure 1.2), but this does not fit easily with the cycles in the region's economies (see Figure 1.1). Furthermore, the fall in the NBTT in certain periods (e.g. 1850–70) has had less to do with the fall in export prices and more to do with the rise in the price of imports – some of which were themselves commodities. One is left with the strong impression that the NBTT is a rather blunt instrument for diagnosing the performance of

TABLE 1.1. *Export Growth at Current Prices (% per year), 1870–1998*

Years	Western Europe	Western Offshoots	E. Europe & USSR	Latin America	Asia	Africa	World	Caribbean	Caribbean Excl Cuba
1870–1913	2.81	4.16	3.25	4.12	3.21	4.45	3.21	1.83	1.68
1913–50	2.00	4.27	3.83	3.77	2.65	4.47	2.99	4.08	4.43
1950–73	11.70	8.90	11.18	6.32	11.66	7.51	10.39	8.78	11.11
1973–98	8.87	9.07	6.68	10.49	11.78	6.58	9.27	8.44	8.94
1870–1998	5.29	5.98	5.47	5.63	6.15	5.41	5.57	4.98	5.52

Note: Caribbean exports after 1960 include services. USSR after 1991 is the former countries of the Soviet Union. Other regions as defined by Maddison (2001).

Source: Caribbean growth rates derived from Tables A.11, C.8, and D.8. Other regions derived from Maddison (2001) where the last year reported is 1998.

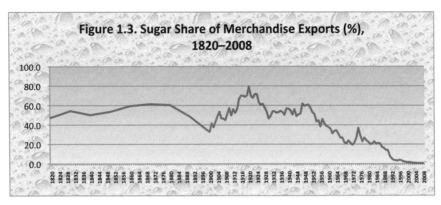

Figure 1.3. Sugar Share of Merchandise Exports (%), 1820–2008

Note: Merchandise exports include re-exports but exclude services. Years before 1900 are based on decennial data with gaps filled by interpolation.

Source: Derived from Tables A.13, A.17, C.8, C.12, D.5 and D.6.

the aggregate Caribbean economy in the last 200 years, although – as we shall see – the NBTT has much more utility when applied to individual countries.

Caribbean production has always relied heavily on exports, which have been concentrated in a small number of commodities. The most important of these has been sugar, but its importance has varied greatly over the last 200 years. In the nineteenth century its contribution to merchandise exports tended to fluctuate between 50 and 60 per cent until the collapse of sugar prices in the 1880s and the shrinking of the Cuban economy in the 1890s (see Figure 1.3). In the first two decades of the twentieth century, its share doubled from one-third to two-thirds, with a brief moment (1920) when sugar accounted for 80 per cent of Caribbean exports. At that point, sugar really was 'king', but since then there has been a steady decline in its importance. Today, sugar represents less than 1 per cent of merchandise exports – and an even lower share if total exports (including services) are used as the point of comparison.

Today, as 200 years ago, output per head in the Caribbean compares favourably with other parts of the developing world. The Caribbean consists mainly of countries that are either 'high' or 'middle' income, with only Haiti regularly classified as 'low' income.[36] The problem of production has not been 'solved', but in most cases it is less acute than the difficulties in achieving a fairer distribution of income, high employment and real sovereignty. Caribbean countries have generally found ways of increasing output at a rate faster than population growth, but they have been much less successful at achieving these other goals.

The problem of income and wealth distribution is a long-standing one. When St-Domingue (modern Haiti) was acclaimed as the richest colony in the world,[37] its average income concealed a huge disparity between the owners of large estates and the enslaved majority. The emancipation of the slaves

[36] These are the categories used by the World Bank.
[37] See Lacerte (1993), p. 42.

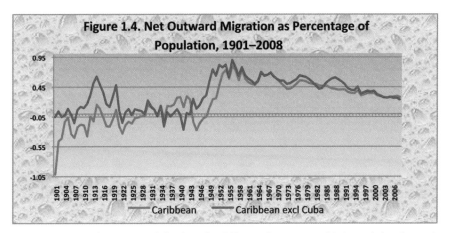

Figure 1.4. Net Outward Migration as Percentage of Population, 1901–2008

Note: Net outward migration defined as the difference between net births and the change in population.
Source: Derived from Tables C.1, C.2, C.3, D.1, D.2 and D.3.

throughout the Caribbean improved the distribution of income, but it still left large inequalities. In Jamaica, the decline in the importance of absentee plantation owners allowed the colony to offset a fall in production against an increase in the proportion of income that stayed in the country.[38] Yet everywhere – even in independent Haiti and the Dominican Republic – assets were unequally distributed as a result not only of land concentration but also unequal access to education and political influence.

Although income inequality in the Caribbean is similar to that in some other parts of the world, it has one peculiarity. This is the large gap in some countries between GDP and Gross National Income (GNI). The extreme case today is Puerto Rico, where GNI is only two-thirds of GDP as a result of the high share of income that accrues to foreign companies. Yet it has been a problem over the whole period as a result of high levels of absentee ownership and/or foreign investment. Caribbean countries have sometimes increased production only to find that the main beneficiaries are economies outside the region.

By contrast, the problem of employment is relatively recent. For most of the nineteenth century the Caribbean experienced a shortage of labour that manifested itself in the slave trade, indentured labour and net inward migration of free labour. This started to change in the 1880s after the fall in sugar prices, and by the start of the twentieth century there was net outward migration from the Caribbean, if Cuba is excluded (see Figure 1.4). By the middle of the century, the net flow was outwards, even if Cuba is included, and it has remained that way subsequently in every single year. Population growth has therefore been much lower than if there had been no migration.

[38] See Eisner (1961), p. 262.

Net outward migration on this scale is a sign of serious disequilibrium in the labour market. It was lamented by Sir Arthur Lewis, whose model of a dual economy took as its starting point high levels of underemployment in the traditional sector.[39] Disguised unemployment was in fact one of the main arguments Lewis used in favour of industrialisation on the grounds that only manufacturing could create the jobs to employ new entrants to the labour force. Yet industry has remained a minor source of jobs, most of which now occur in the service sector, and unemployment is now as much a scourge on Caribbean societies as underemployment – if not more so.

The final problem the Caribbean has had to face is that of real sovereignty – both political and economic. It took forty years from Haiti's declaration of independence before there was another sovereign state in the region. It took nearly sixty years before there was a third (Cuba), and another sixty before there were others. Yet even today only just over half the countries of the Caribbean are nominally sovereign, the remainder having opted for constitutional arrangements that range from full integration into the metropolis (e.g. Martinique) to self-governing colonies (e.g. Cayman Islands).[40] These arrangements are still fluid even though the option of independence has lost its appeal, and the last Caribbean country to become a sovereign state was in 1983.[41]

The nonindependent countries are not responsible for their own foreign affairs and are subject to various forms of metropolitan interference (these disadvantages have to be set against certain benefits that flow from nonindependent status, such as metropolitan citizenship and numerous transfers and subsidies). Yet the independent countries also have sovereignty problems as a result of their participation in a global system in which not all states are equal. Haiti was the first to experience the capacity of core states to bully nominally sovereign countries in the Caribbean, but it was by no means the last. The restricted nature of state sovereignty in the Caribbean was a cornerstone of the Plantation School, and it remains a serious problem today.

This brief account of the problems the Caribbean has faced, and continues to face, suggests that there may be trade-offs among production, distribution, employment and sovereignty. These are illustrated schematically in Table 1.2. The goals are listed in the column and the trade-offs in the row. Puerto Rico, for example, assigned strategic importance to increasing production after 1940 through industrialisation, but it had to accept a deterioration in distribution. Trinidad & Tobago also prioritised production in its oil and gas industry, but

---

[39] See Lewis (1954). This famous article, however, was inspired more by Lewis' experience in Africa and Asia than the Caribbean. See Tignor (2006), chap. 3.

[40] There are five British dependencies, two Dutch (at least until October 2010), two US, and three French Départements d'Outre-Mer (DOMs). Since 2007, there have also been two French Collectivités d'Outre-Mer (COMs).

[41] This was St Kitts & Nevis.

TABLE 1.2. *Trade-Offs in the Caribbean between Production, Distribution, Employment and Sovereignty*

	Production	Distribution	Employment	Sovereignty
Production		Cuba (1960s); Guyana (1970s)	Cuba (1990s)	Haiti (19th century)
Distribution	Puerto Rico (>1940)		Dominican Republic (>1980)	Haiti (20th century)
Employment	Trinidad & Tobago (>1970)	Martinique and Guadeloupe (>1970)		Jamaica (>1970)
Sovereignty	French Guiana (>1960); Cayman Islands (>1960)	British Virgin Islands (>1980)	Turks & Caicos Islands; Aruba	

it had to accept relatively high levels of unemployment after 1970. Similarly, the high growth of production in French Guiana and the Cayman Islands, to name just two, has only been possible as a result of the sacrifice of formal sovereignty.

Not all countries have always given priority to production. Cuba, for example, in the 1960s and Guyana in the 1970s attached huge importance to improving distribution, but the result was a lower level of output than might otherwise have been achieved. A relatively equal distribution of income in Guadeloupe and Martinique has been an objective for many years, but it has been associated with high levels of unemployment. Similarly, the British Virgin Islands has an income distribution that is much better than most, but it would probably not have been possible as an independent country.

Some countries have prioritised employment. Cuba was determined to avoid high levels of unemployment in the 1990s, and production may have suffered as a consequence. The Dominican Republic, by contrast, sustained high levels of employment through a wage policy that has damaged income distribution. In addition, a small number of nonindependent countries, such as the Turks & Caicos Islands, and Aruba, have achieved lower rates of unemployment than would have probably happened as independent states.

The final trade-off involves those countries that gave priority to sovereignty. Haiti in the nineteenth century was so determined to avoid recolonisation that its constitution heavily restricted foreign ownership. As a result, production grew more slowly than it might otherwise have done. Haiti then fell under US occupation for twenty years (1915–34), and it was subsequently so determined to avoid a repeat that domestic elites were allowed to capture the state apparatus. This generated economic rents and led to a deterioration in income

distribution. Jamaica also attached great importance to the issue of sovereignty in the 1970s and paid a heavy price in terms of an increase in unemployment.

Trade-offs cannot be avoided in economics, and the Caribbean is therefore not unique. Yet some economic policies are better than others at alleviating the cost. If it is still true that the countries of the Caribbean are destined to live from exports, the domestic market being too small to justify self-sufficiency or high levels of import substitution, it is certainly **not** the case that all exports are the same. One of the lessons of this book is the importance of export diversification. The second is a recognition that services in general provide a more secure future than commodity exports. The third is that services themselves are not homogeneous, and some are much more beneficial to the domestic economy than others. And just as Fernando Ortiz emphasised the difference in Cuba between sugar and tobacco,[42] policy in the Caribbean today needs to distinguish between those exports that imply high levels of foreign ownership and those that do not.

There is a great deal of pessimism in the Caribbean today – just as there was in the 1930s, 1890s and even earlier. The region has struggled to find the correct policy responses to globalisation, is increasingly marginal to the interests of most core countries, is mostly too 'rich' to qualify for aid flows or debt relief, and has failed to build the institutions it knows are required. Some of this pessimism is justified, but much of it is not. The Caribbean still has advantages that other less fortunate regions lack and is in a position to resolve many of its problems itself. Whether it does so depends in part on drawing the right lessons from its own historical experience.

---

[42] See Ortiz (1940).

PART I

THE CARIBBEAN IN THE AGE OF FREE TRADE

From the Napoleonic Wars to 1900

2

The Core and the Caribbean

From the beginning of European colonisation, the Caribbean economies depended on foreign trade for their growth and development. The domestic market was very small and import substitution actively discouraged. Yet the countries with which they could engage in commerce were strictly limited in number as a result of consumption patterns for tropical products and imperial trade restrictions. Thus, a small number of states (the core) came to exercise an overwhelming influence on the economic fortunes of the Caribbean countries.

What happened in these core countries – in terms of economic performance, structure and policy – is crucial for a proper understanding of the Caribbean periphery. The standard of living – indeed, the very survival – of the Caribbean countries depended on the opportunities for trade with the core states. There were no exceptions, but Haiti in the nineteenth century is misleadingly often cited as one (the Haitian case is reviewed in detail in Chapter 7). This was not just a matter of trade policy in the core, but it also depended on the evolution of the core economies themselves and their changing trade patterns.

Before the French Revolution began in 1789, the Caribbean played a critical part in the tropical trade of the imperial European powers. Caribbean colonies provided a high proportion of the tropical products imported by the core, and capitalists with Caribbean interests exercised a significant influence on external trade and policies towards slavery. This changed with the spread of European imperialism to countries in Asia, Africa, the Middle East and eventually the Pacific. The once dominant position of the Caribbean in the European colonial empires had altered completely by the end of the nineteenth century and was never recaptured. Indeed, the Caribbean became increasingly marginal to the economic development of the European core states, but the latter remained of huge importance for the economic development of the Caribbean.

At the end of the Napoleonic Wars in 1815, the core consisted of those powers in Europe with Caribbean colonies (Denmark, France, Holland, Spain, Sweden and the UK), together with the United States. By the end of the nineteenth century, however, Germany was firmly established as a core country,

despite its lack of colonial ties to the Caribbean. Austria-Hungary, Japan, Italy, the Ottoman Empire and Russia were also major powers by the end of the nineteenth century, but their contact with the Caribbean was so minor that they need not be considered as part of the core. Thus, the core never consisted of more than eight countries, and for much of the century was as few as seven, because Germany did not join the core until after unification in 1871 and Sweden had ceased to be part of it following the return of its one Caribbean colony (St Barthélemy) to France in 1878.[1]

These core countries were not of equal importance for the Caribbean economies. The Napoleonic Wars and the rise of the Latin American republics left Spain much less powerful than it had been, yet it was able to retain Cuba and Puerto Rico.[2] The United States struggled at first to reestablish the trade links that had been so important between the different British possessions before the Declaration of Independence in 1776. The UK, on the other hand, was greatly strengthened. The British decision to return to France, Holland and Spain only some of those possessions occupied during hostilities left the UK in a dominant position. Britain, it could be said with little argument, was the hegemonic member of the core at the start of the 'short nineteenth century'.[3]

By the end of the century, the ranking within the core had been reversed. Spain had almost ceased to be an imperial power, and Denmark would not be one for much longer. France and Holland were secure in their Caribbean possessions, but the latter's once dominant position in the trade and investment of its colonies had diminished. Germany had established a strong trading relationship with the two independent countries of the Caribbean (Haiti and the Dominican Republic) and was developing links elsewhere. The UK was still the most important European colonial power in the region. Yet the hegemonic position it had established at the end of the Napoleonic Wars had ended.

This was because of the expansion of US economic and political power. The conclusion of the Spanish-American War in 1898, with the cession by Spain of Puerto Rico to the United States and the end of its sovereignty over Cuba,[4] brought to a logical conclusion a process that had begun with the Louisiana Purchase in 1803. The United States was now the hegemon, and the other members of the core – however grudgingly – duly recognised the new geopolitical realities. From now on the fortunes of Caribbean countries would

[1] Guadeloupe had also been a Swedish colony, following its transfer in 1813 when it was occupied by Britain, but this was very brief because the UK reversed this decision the following year at the Treaty of Paris.

[2] The eastern part of Hispaniola was also nominally Spanish from 1809, when France was ousted as the colonial power, until 1821 when independence was first declared. Haiti annexed the eastern part in 1822.

[3] This is the term I give to the period from the end of the Napoleonic Wars in 1815 to the loss by Spain of its last colonies in the Americas in 1898. See Chapter 1.

[4] Under the 1899 Treaty of Paris, Spain 'relinquished' its title to Cuba and ceded Puerto Rico to the US. See Lloyd Jones (1936), p. 28.

increasingly be tied to developments in North America rather than Europe, even where the colonial power was European.

US economic progress differed in important respects from that in the European core. From mid-century onwards, the development of the United States strongly favoured inward-looking development with tariffs to match. Although the growth of the US economy was a huge bonus for the Caribbean, US commercial policy often caused difficulties.[5] Where Caribbean countries produced goods that complemented domestic US production or where domestic US capacity could not keep pace with the growth of demand, geographical proximity ensured that they would be well placed to take advantage. Where the exportable surplus of the Caribbean countries competed with domestic output in the United States, it was a different story. US tariffs, the highest among the core by the end of the century, were increasingly designed to provide protection rather than revenue, and they played this role to great effect.

2.1. GEOPOLITICS IN THE CORE

The UK came out of the Napoleonic Wars as the strongest of the European powers. Having seized numerous Caribbean territories from Denmark, France, Holland and Spain during hostilities, the UK was in a strong negotiating position at the postwar peace conferences. The Virgin Islands – St Thomas, St John, and St Croix – were returned to Denmark, but St Lucia was taken from the French, Trinidad from the Spanish, and Berbice, Demerara, and Essequibo were taken from the Dutch. Elsewhere territories were returned to their former colonial masters, while the British settlement in the Bay of Honduras quietly expanded far beyond the limits set by treaty with Spain in 1786.[6]

British imperial ambitions at the Congress of Vienna in 1815 were not limited to the Caribbean. Ceylon and the Cape of Good Hope, conquered during hostilities, were taken by treaty from Holland, and Mauritius and the Seychelles were taken from France. The British presence on the west coast of Africa expanded through the creation of Crown colonies in Gambia and Sierra Leone. Yet the greatest threat to the once dominant position of the Caribbean in the British Empire was the expansion of British influence south of the Himalayas. By the end of hostilities, Britain was the preeminent European power on the Indian subcontinent.[7]

[5] So did commercial policy in the European core, but the US was the fastest growing market, and therefore what happened in the US was of special importance.
[6] The first resident British superintendent arrived in 1786, but it would not be until 1862 that the settlement at the Bay of Honduras became the British colony of British Honduras (today Belize). See Humphreys (1961), pp. 10–14.
[7] Portugal retained a small foothold in Goa, and France held onto a number of trading posts, such as Pondicherry.

Although the Caribbean was to decline in importance for the UK, that was not yet how it was seen by British contemporaries. Within a short period after 1815, the UK was anticipating the need for further territorial acquisitions in the area for strategic rather than commercial reasons.[8] This was because of the possibility of an interoceanic canal, which – it was widely assumed – would be built through Nicaragua. In anticipation of this, the Bay Islands (off the coast of Honduras) became a British colony, Mosquitia (the Caribbean coast of Honduras and Nicaragua) was recognised as an independent country (its kings were crowned in Belize),[9] and Tigre Island in the Gulf of Fonseca (on the Pacific side of the isthmus) was temporarily occupied. The weak states of Central America, established after the collapse of the Central American Federation in 1838, were in no position to resist.

British imperial expansion was not welcomed by the United States, although at first there was little that it could do to resist. The United States may have become a quasi-Caribbean power for the first time in 1803 with the purchase of Louisiana from France, but the Napoleonic Wars and the initially tense relationship between Britain and its former North American colonies limited the scope for US action. Britain discouraged trade between the US and the British Caribbean territories, the United States imposed a trade embargo on the UK in 1808,[10] and the two countries went to war in 1812.

US scope for action changed rapidly first with the end of hostilities in 1814 and second with the purchase of East Florida from Spain in 1819. Because West Florida had been taken by force from Spain during the Napoleonic Wars, the United States now had a tropical or subtropical coastline stretching from the Mexican border to the lands adjoining the strategic Florida channel. The republic was finally in a stronger position to assert its authority and to challenge European imperial ambitions. That authority was put to the test with the Monroe Doctrine in 1823. Fearful of an attempt by European powers to capitalise on Spanish weakness in the Americas, demonstrated so visibly by the collapse of Spanish power on mainland Latin America, the Monroe Doctrine was a unilateral attempt to restrain the other imperial powers – principally in the Caribbean region – while reserving the option of annexation for the United States itself.[11]

Of particular concern for the United States were Spain's remaining Caribbean possessions (Cuba and Puerto Rico) together with the eastern part of

---

[8] See Williams (1916), Chapter 2.

[9] Needless to say, no other country accepted the fiction of an independent Mosquitia.

[10] The Embargo Act, passed at the end of 1807, banned all exports to Europe. However, it was aimed in particular at the UK in response to British seizure of US ships on the high seas. See Bailey (1964), pp. 122–9.

[11] There is a vast literature on the Monroe Doctrine. See Perkins (1937) for its application to the Caribbean.

Hispaniola[12] – reoccupied in 1822 by Haiti.[13] Other European powers did toy with the idea of annexing the eastern part of Hispaniola themselves, so it was not difficult for the United States to imagine that they might have similar designs on Cuba (Puerto Rico was smaller and less strategically important). This was unacceptable to the United States, several of whose leaders had voiced ambitions with regard to Cuba within a few years of independence.

The Monroe Doctrine was not at first taken seriously by European leaders (the Austrian Chancellor Metternich was particularly contemptuous), but a crude balance of power ensured that Cuba and Puerto Rico remained Spanish. The prospect of an interoceanic canal, however, required more vigorous diplomatic action by the United States. The territorial gains made in the Mexican War had converted the United States into a continental power by the end of the 1840s, and the new realities were recognised by Great Britain in the Clayton-Bulwer Treaty of 1850. This obliged the UK to relinquish all of its isthmian possessions except the settlement in the Bay of Honduras[14] and to acknowledge that no foreign power would have exclusive control of any canal that might be built.

A treaty with Colombia in 1846 paved the way for the US-built railway across the isthmus of Panama a few years later. This project temporarily reduced the need for an interoceanic canal, allowing the United States to refocus its ambitions on expanding its influence in the Caribbean. Cuba was again the main centre of attention (the southern states hoped to expand the territory of the United States through the incorporation of the island's slave economy) even as the northern states cast an eye towards the Dominican Republic,[15]

---

[12] 'Hispaniola' was the English version of the name given to the island by Columbus in 1492. It fell out of use until it was revived by the US Hydrographic Department in the 1930s (see Montague, 1940). It is not ideal, but it is frequently necessary to have one name to describe the territory that embraces two countries, and other words are confusing. 'Haiti' is an Amerindian word that originally described the whole island, but by the end of the nineteenth century it referred only to the western part, and 'Santo Domingo' in the nineteenth century could mean either the eastern part or the whole island ('San Domingo' was a corruption of Santo Domingo used by US officials).

[13] Haiti occupied Santo Domingo in 1805, which at the time was a French colony (Spain had ceded it to France in 1795). However, a Dominican uprising in 1808–9 reestablished Spanish control. A further revolt in 1821 led to the creation of the 'Independent State of Spanish Haiti'. This in turn led to the Haitian invasion and occupation of 1822, which only ended in 1844 when Dominican nationalists finally secured independence and established the Dominican Republic. See Moya Pons (1998).

[14] The treaty was so vaguely worded that Britain thought it could keep all its Central American possessions, and the US thought the UK should relinquish all of them. The eventual compromise left Britain in charge of Belize only, while the Bay Islands and Mosquitia were abandoned in 1860.

[15] A number of countries have changed names in the Caribbean in the last 200 years. To avoid confusion, I generally use one name only (see Notes on A. Tables). The Dominican Republic is a very good example, because it went through various changes of name in the nineteenth century.

which had secured its independence from Haiti in 1844 and offered perhaps the finest harbour facilities in the Caribbean at Samaná Bay.

The outbreak of the Civil War in 1861 temporarily put on hold US ambitions in the Caribbean – a situation that European powers were quick to exploit. A joint British, French and Spanish *démarche* towards Mexico led to the disastrous French invasion under the Hapsburg Maximilian in 1862, and Spain reoccupied the Dominican Republic the previous year (at the invitation – it should be stressed – of its political leaders). Great Britain turned the settlement at the Bay of Honduras into the colony of British Honduras at the same time, following a boundary treaty with Guatemala.[16]

European powers generally favoured the South in the Civil War, despite the continuation of slavery, because of their need for cotton and their hope that an independent Confederation would diminish the North's growing power. None of them felt confident enough, however, to recognise the Confederation as a sovereign state, and their hesitation may have saved them from subsequent retribution. The United States that emerged from the Civil War was soon to become the dominant power in the Caribbean, with a readiness to use diplomacy, coercion and military force to secure its national interests in the region.

The end of the US Civil War (1865) was swiftly followed by Spanish withdrawal from the Dominican Republic and French defeat in Mexico. By 1867, the year in which Alaska was purchased from Russia, the United States had opened negotiations with Denmark for the acquisition of its Caribbean territories, but this would be blocked by the US Senate (the Danish parliament and the few people allowed to vote on the Danish Caribbean islands were strongly in favour). A few years later, the US government succeeded in taking out a long lease on Samaná Bay in the Dominican Republic, but a change of government on the island led to its abrogation within a matter of months.[17]

Cuba and Puerto Rico, however, remained the great prizes that eluded the United States. The abolition of slavery after the Civil War removed the South's interest in controlling these Spanish islands where slavery still operated, but their geostrategic importance steadily increased for the United States as the prospect of an interoceanic canal came closer. Although overtures to Spain for the acquisition of Cuba (always more important in US eyes than Puerto Rico) were consistently rebuffed, the First War of Independence (1868–78) even raised the prospect of a Cuban republic friendly to US interests being created without the need for US intervention.

[16] The Anglo-Guatemalan Treaty of 1859 established the boundary, and the former British settlement at the Bay of Honduras became a colony in 1862. However, the 1863 Additional Convention between Britain and Guatemala was never ratified. Guatemala subsequently took the view that this nullified the 1859 treaty. See Dobson (1973), pp. 202–13.

[17] See Martínez-Fernández (1994), p. 225. In 1870 the US had come very close to annexing the Dominican Republic and was only prevented from doing so by an unfavourable vote in the US Senate (see Tansill (1938)).

The outbreak of the Second War of Independence in 1895 was to change the situation dramatically. US entry into the war in 1898 quickly secured the defeat of Spain and provided the United States with a major expansion of its offshore empire. Puerto Rico was annexed, but Cuba was allowed to become nominally independent in 1902 after its political elite had accepted the humiliating Platt Amendment, which provided the United States with the right to intervene and granted indefinite leases on coaling stations and naval bases in different parts of the island (including Guantánamo Bay).

By now the hegemonic position of the United States was obvious to all, and Great Britain accepted the inevitable with the signing of the Hay-Pauncefote Treaty in 1901. This provided for exclusive US control of any future interoceanic canal, a change from the Clayton-Bulwer Treaty, which was becoming increasingly urgent for the United States as the prospect of construction in either Nicaragua or Panama came closer. Anglo-American rivalry in the Caribbean did not entirely end with the new treaty, but it played a much smaller part and allowed the UK to concentrate on the competition with Germany and its imperial interests in other parts of the world that were now eclipsing the Caribbean in importance.

The Napoleonic Wars curtailed French imperial ambitions in the Caribbean sharply. The slave revolt in St-Domingue (modern Haiti) in 1791 could not be suppressed, despite the huge loss of life by French troops, and by the end of 1803 Napoleon had been forced to accept that the French presence had ended.[18] Indeed, it was this defeat – not formally acknowledged until 1825 when the independence of Haiti was recognised by France – that persuaded Napoleon to sell Louisiana to the United States, despite the fact that Napoleon had only recently persuaded the Spanish king to exchange it for French possessions elsewhere. By 1815, the French presence had been reduced to the islands of Guadeloupe and Martinique together with the commercially much less important Cayenne (French Guiana).

French interest temporarily revived in the 1870s, despite the earlier fiasco in Mexico, as a result of Ferdinand de Lesseps' interest in constructing a canal in Panama following his great engineering triumph at Suez. Perhaps in anticipation of the need for additional territories for geostrategic reasons, the French government took back from Sweden the small island of St Barthélemy in 1878 (it had been French until 1784),[19] and the next year de Lesseps obtained the concession from Colombia that he needed to begin work on the canal. By the end of the 1880s, however, the project had collapsed, and French dreams for

---

[18] The 1791 slave revolt was followed by a ferocious fight for territorial control of St-Domingue involving Britain, France, Spain and the former slaves themselves. The British abandoned the island in 1798, but Napoleon sent his brother-in-law General LeClerc to reestablish French sovereignty (he arrived early in 1802). About 50,000 of the 58,000 French troops died in the unsuccessful effort. See Moya Pons (1985), pp. 239–45, and McNeill (2010), pp. 251–67.

[19] France always insisted that it had not 'bought' the island on the somewhat specious grounds that the money it paid was to be used by Sweden to construct a hospital for the care of those Swedish officials that remained.

a Caribbean renaissance ended with it. By that time, in any case, France had
acquired a vast empire in Africa, starting with Algeria in 1830, and possessions in Indochina and the Pacific that far exceeded the Caribbean colonies in
importance.

Dutch imperial interest had also switched away from the Caribbean by the
end of the nineteenth century – to Southeast Asia. Deprived of its profitable
plantations in the western Guianas by Britain at the end of the Napoleonic
Wars, Holland was fortunate in being allowed to keep Suriname. Elsewhere,
Dutch interests were confined to three small islands off the coast of South
America (Aruba, Bonaire and Curaçao – ABC) and three of the Leeward islands
(St Eustatius, Saba and Sint Maarten – the last shared with France).[20] These
six islands, the Dutch Antilles, had survived mainly as centres of contraband
before the Napoleonic Wars, and thus their prospects dimmed with the gradual
elimination of trade restrictions in the nineteenth century.[21] Much the same
was true of the three Danish islands (St Croix, St John and St Thomas), and
this helps to explain the interest of the Danish government in their sale to the
United States (finally accomplished in 1916).[22]

The survival of the Spanish Empire in the Caribbean after 1815 was very
much because of the unwillingness of other powers – including the United
States – to allow a different country to gain control of Cuba and Puerto Rico.
For a long time, anti-Spanish activity on the islands focused on annexation by
the United States rather than independence, but this changed after the US Civil
War. The commercial success of both islands (especially Cuba) led Spain to
cling tenaciously to the last of its hemispheric possessions, and the outcome
of the Second War of Independence was still in doubt until the United States
entered the fray. At that point, Spanish defeat was assured, and 400 years of
Spanish colonialism in the Caribbean came to an end, leaving Spain with an
assortment of African colonies of limited commercial value.

For Germany, interest in the Caribbean came late. Not until unification
under Bismarck in 1871 did Prussia, the most important part of the German
Federation, show much interest in transoceanic colonies, but this changed rapidly in the next three decades. A toehold was established in the Pacific before
Germany finally succeeded in carving out a substantial empire in sub-Saharan
Africa. By the 1890s, Germany was an imperial power to be reckoned with,
and Britain in particular was careful to avoid imperial clashes with a major
commercial rival.

---

[20] Because of the transatlantic route taken by Dutch sailing ships, the three islands in the Leewards
were described in Holland (but nowhere else) as being in the Windwards, and the ABC islands
were known as the Leewards.

[21] For much of the first half of the nineteenth century, these islands were administered from Suriname, a reflection of the greater commercial importance of the mainland colony. See Goslinga
(1990), p. 153.

[22] On the transfer of the Danish West Indies to the US, see Tansill (1932).

Although the legitimacy of the Monroe Doctrine was never accepted by Germany, its Caribbean ambitions were limited by the difficulty of finding territories that were not already under the control of other European powers. Inevitably, therefore, German interest in the Caribbean was drawn to the island of Hispaniola, where a German commercial presence became significant by the end of the century and where the weak states of Haiti and the Dominican Republic could be subjected to coercive diplomacy. This, however, excited the suspicions of the United States, whose government sent frequent messages to Berlin to remind Germany of the dangers of precipitate action. This seems to have had the desired effect because – despite much US paranoia with regard to Hispaniola, Venezuela and even Cuba – the archival record suggests that Germany did not in the end harbour serious imperial ambitions in the Caribbean.[23]

In the eight decades between the end of the Napoleonic Wars and the Spanish-American War, the Caribbean had lost much of its commercial and geostrategic importance for the European colonial powers. However, its importance for the United States had greatly increased and would do so even more following the opening of the Panama Canal in 1914. The Monroe Doctrine, mocked by many European leaders when it was first pronounced, embodied this change by the end of the nineteenth century. The new geopolitical reality was to prove uncomfortable for the independent Caribbean states (Cuba, the Dominican Republic, Haiti). European colonies in the Caribbean had less fear of military intervention, but their economic fortunes were increasingly determined by their links with the colossus to the north.

2.2. GROWTH AND DEVELOPMENT IN THE CORE

At the end of the Napoleonic Wars, the core economies were not the biggest in the world. China in 1820 had a GDP that was several times the size of even the largest core country.[24] Yet the direct impact of China on the Caribbean was negligible; its economy was stagnant, its external trade small, and almost all of its imports came from Europe and the rest of Asia. India also had a larger GDP in 1820 than any member of the core, and its economy was at least growing in the nineteenth century.[25] Indian exports competed with those from the Caribbean by virtue of their low prices and the use of nonslave labour. However, almost none of India's imports came from the region. In the nineteenth century the most important link between these two Asian giants and the Caribbean was in fact provided by the export of indentured labour.[26]

---

[23] There is no doubt, however, that the purchase of the Danish Virgin Islands in 1916 was precipitated by US fear of German occupation of Denmark in the First World War.

[24] Maddison (2003) estimates the size of China's GDP in 1820 at $228.6 billion (1990 prices) compared with $36.2 billion for the UK (the largest core economy at the time).

[25] India's GDP in 1820 is estimated at $111.4 billion – see Maddison (2003). This had risen to $204 billion by 1913.

[26] Indentured labour from China and India is examined in more detail in Chapter 3.

Many of the countries undergoing industrialisation in the nineteenth century – Austria-Hungary, Japan, Italy and Russia – also had little or no contact
with the Caribbean. Furthermore, although not insignificant in terms of population and economic growth, these countries showed little interest in establishing
links. Their need for tropical products could be met more cheaply elsewhere,
and the market for their nascent industries was either domestic or in neighbouring countries. The small markets of the Caribbean provided little attraction for
these countries, and their geostrategic interests tended to lie in other regions.

What mattered therefore for the export-orientated economies of the Caribbean was growth and development in the small number of states constituting
the core. During the nineteenth century, the core experienced a modest demographic expansion as a result of higher living standards and advances in medical
science. For the core as a whole, this demographic expansion averaged just over
1 per cent per year during each half of the century. This may not sound like
much, but it was sufficient to increase the population of the core from 85 million in 1800 to 243 million in 1900. Coupled with rapid urbanisation in the
core, this implied a significant increase in the demand for tropical products,
even without allowing for the additional demand created by an increase in
income per head.

The demographic expansion of the core as a whole conceals significant
variations between the eight countries. The country with the slowest rate of
growth was France, where the population rose by only 0.35 per cent per year
over the whole century (see Table 2.1). Given the semiclosed trading system
operated by France with its colonies, this was a matter of considerable concern
for French Guiana, Guadeloupe and Martinique. Spain was also a country
with very low population growth, and, like France, the rate of growth dropped
in the second half of the century (see Table 2.1). However, Spain had ceased
to apply a truly mercantilist system to its Caribbean colonies even before the
Napoleonic Wars, and therefore the impact of its slow population growth on
Cuba and Puerto Rico was less severe.

By far the fastest growing part of the core was the United States. From a
population of a little over 5 million in 1800, the country had expanded to reach
76 million a century later. This rapid growth, 2.7 per cent a year (see Table
2.1), was made possible by a high level of net inward migration, with most of
the immigrants coming from other parts of the core. At the end of the century,
the population of the United States was still small in relation to China or India,
but it now constituted nearly one-third of the core compared with only 6 per
cent in 1800. As the core country closest geographically to the Caribbean, this
was highly significant.

Demographic expansion in the core was only part of the story. Growth
of the core economies depended also on productivity gains. The GDP in the
core countries from 1820 onwards is shown in Figure 2.1. In the first period
(1820–50), the core country with the slowest growth was Spain. This was not
surprising, however, given the loss of all of its mainland American colonies,
the disruptions caused by the Napoleonic Wars and the political upheavals

TABLE 2.1. *Core Population Growth Rates (% per year), 1800–1900*

Years	Denmark	France	Germany	Holland	Spain	Sweden	UK	US	Core Total
1800–50	0.85	0.52	1.04	1.14	0.69	0.99	1.12	3.0	1.06
1850–1900	1.08	0.18	0.93	1.09	0.44	0.78	0.81	2.4	1.05
1800–1900	0.97	0.35	0.99	1.12	0.57	0.86	0.96	2.7	1.05

Source: Derived from Mitchell (2007) and Mitchell (2007a).

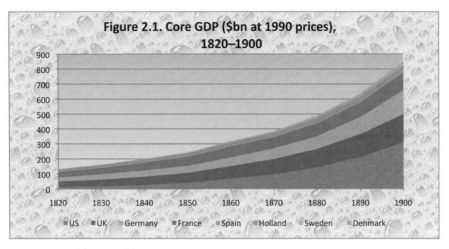

Figure 2.1. Core GDP ($bn at 1990 prices), 1820–1900

Source: Derived from Maddison (2003).

associated with the Carlist wars after 1833.[27] Sweden also grew slowly in this period, but this mattered less to the Caribbean given its tenuous links to Scandinavia.

The core country with the fastest GDP growth in the first period was the United States (see Table 2.2) – so much so that it was the only core country whose annual growth rate (4.18%) exceeded the mean rate for the core (2.05%). Even so, the US economy was still less than 20 per cent of the total core in 1850, with France, Germany and the UK all having larger GDPs (see Figure 2.1).

In the second period (1850–1900), the core rate of annual growth accelerated to 2.53 per cent (see Table 2.2). Once again the United States was the only country whose rate of growth (4.07%) exceeded the mean for the core, but Germany's rate of growth (2.46%) came close. Thus, the fastest growing core economies were the two that had no formal colonial links with the region in the short nineteenth century. Furthermore, the United States had overtaken the UK as the biggest core economy by 1880, and Germany had overtaken France by then to become the third largest (see Figure 2.1). On the eve of the Spanish-American War, when the United States still had no Caribbean colonies, Germany and the United States represented over 50 per cent of the core's GDP. By 1900 the US economy alone represented nearly 40 per cent of the core. The figure for the UK, the second-largest core economy, was just over 20 per cent.

The growth of the core economies generated increased demand for traditional tropical products (e.g. sugar) along with demand for new products (e.g. bananas). However, the structure of the core economies was also changing as a result of industrialisation. Starting in Great Britain before the Napoleonic Wars, industrialisation spread in the first half of the nineteenth century to

---

[27] On domestic upheavals in Spain at this time, see Carr (1975).

TABLE 2.2. *Core GDP Growth Rates (% per year), 1820–1900*

Years	Denmark	France	Germany	Holland	Spain	Sweden	UK	US	Core Total
1820–1850	1.98	1.66	1.97	1.81	0.89	1.24	1.88	4.18	2.05
1850–1900	2.16	1.41	2.46	1.76	1.46	2.17	2.17	4.07	2.53
1820–1900	2.09	1.50	2.28	1.78	1.25	1.82	2.06	4.11	2.35

Source: Derived from Maddison (2003).

France, Germany and the United States to be followed by the other members
of the core in the second half. Industrialisation required raw materials, particularly coal, cotton and iron ore, and in many core countries these needed to be
imported.

Trade was the main link between the core and the Caribbean throughout the
short nineteenth century. Furthermore, the capacity of the Caribbean countries
to import from the core depended almost entirely on the willingness of the core
to import from the Caribbean (the reverse was not true). Thus, the growth
of the core's imports (at current prices) provides a first approximation of the
scope for export expansion by the Caribbean periphery. Table 2.3 provides
the evidence, and the final column estimates import growth for the world as a
whole.

There were wide variations in import growth among the core and, indeed,
during the course of the century. For core countries for which data are available, import growth speeded up in the second half of the century, with one
minor exception (Denmark). This was caused partly by the acceleration in
GDP growth rates (see Table 2.2), partly by the impact of declining tariffs
(with the exception of the United States) and partly by the impact of changing
economic structure through industrialisation.

We may now compare the relationship between import growth and GDP
growth. This comparison needs to take into account that the GDP growth rates
in Table 2.2 are at constant prices, but the import growth rates in Table 2.3
are at current prices. Nevertheless, for the century as a whole, price movements
were small, and the comparison may therefore be legitimate.

In the first half of the century, for which we have data for six countries,
we find there were only three countries (Denmark, Spain and Sweden) where
import growth exceeded GDP growth. In two of the other three countries (UK
and United States), import growth was far below GDP growth, and in the third
(France) import growth was a little below GDP growth. In the second half
of the century, however, where we have data for all eight core countries, all
but one had import growth above GDP growth, and in most cases the import
growth rate far exceeded the GDP growth rate.

The one exception was the United States. Notwithstanding rapid economic
growth, net inward migration and industrialisation, US import growth fell
below its GDP growth in both halves of the nineteenth century. Furthermore,
in the second half of the century – when the US economy became the biggest in
the world – the growth of US imports was the slowest of all the core countries,
despite the fact that it had by far the fastest GDP growth.[28] Because the UK
had the second slowest rate of growth of imports in the second half of the
century (see Table 2.3), the Caribbean faced a major challenge because these

[28] At current prices, US imports as a proportion of GDP fell from 6.6% in 1850 to 4.5% in the
period 1899–1908. In constant dollars (1860 prices), the ratio fell from 7.5% to 5% over the
same period. See Lipsey (2000), table 15.3, p. 691.

TABLE 2.3. *Core Import Growth (% per year), 1800–1900 (3-year averages)*

Years	Denmark	France	Germany	Holland	Spain	Sweden	UK	US	World
1800–1850	8.3(a)	1.46	na	na	1.56(a)	3.1(b)	0.95	2.93(a)	2.67(c)
1850–1900	3.7	3.64	3.32 (d)	8.45	3.84	9.35	3.21	3.12	2.62(e)
1800–1900	5.42(a)	2.54	na	na	2.98(a)	4.63(b)	2.07	3.04(a)	2.65

Note: (a) Starts at 1820; (b) starts at 1830; (c) ends at 1860; (d) starts at 1860; (e) starts at 1880.
Source: Mitchell (2007) and Mitchell (2007a); world data from Woodruff (1967).

two countries – UK and United States – had such a vast influence on export prospects from the region.

2.3. TRADE AND TARIFF POLICY IN THE CORE

In the mid-eighteenth century, before the Seven Years' War (1756–63), all European imperial powers practised a system of commerce widely known as mercantilism.[29] Although full of exceptions, the objective of mercantilism was the accumulation of specie (gold and silver) through a balance of trade surplus. The means to achieve this included laws that restricted the carrying of trade to subjects of the imperial power – a single buyer (the imperial power) for the exports of the colonies, and a single seller (again the imperial power) for the imports into the colonies. Trade with the colonies could include other imperial possessions as long as they were part of the same empire.

In the case of the Caribbean colonies, mercantilism required that all their exports be sold directly to the imperial power in Europe or to the 'mother' country's colonies in the Americas.[30] Imports were expected to come either directly from the imperial power or to be supplied by colonies in the Americas. Shipping was to be provided by subjects of the imperial power, based either in Europe or in the colonies. In the mid-eighteenth century, mercantilism therefore permitted a triangular trade between colonies in the Americas and Europe. French colonies in the Caribbean, for example, could obtain part of their import needs from French North America, provided that the goods travelled in ships owned by French subjects. Similarly, a large proportion of the exports of the British North American colonies consisted of consumer goods sold to the British West Indies.[31]

Mercantilism, the subject in 1776 of a devastating critique by Adam Smith in *The Wealth of Nations*, was dismantled in the short nineteenth century in four stages, but some of the core countries never went beyond the first two. The final outcome, never completely achieved, was unrestricted free trade. The first stage was the designation of certain cities as free ports and the abrogation of the laws restricting the transport of goods to imperial subjects (these laws were known in Great Britain as the Navigation Acts, but all other imperial powers had equivalent legislation). This was 'freedom to trade', but not 'free trade'. The second stage was the reduction of tariffs from the very high levels in force at the end of the Napoleonic Wars. The third stage was the abolition of imperial preference, so that the tariff structure no longer favoured colonial imports. The final stage was the elimination of tariffs altogether.

The country that came closest to unrestricted free trade in the nineteenth century was the UK. This was a consequence of Britain being the leader in terms of industrialisation among the core countries and therefore not requiring

---

[29] On the basic principles of mercantilism, see Brezis (2003), pp. 482–5.
[30] 'Mother' refers to the colonial or former colonial power. See Chapter 1 and Notes on A. Tables.
[31] For the years 1768–72, this figure has been estimated at 29%. See Lipsey (2000), p. 686.

tariff protection for the development of its manufacturing sector. At the same time, the UK was changing politically, and thus the industrialists, with their preference for low or zero tariffs, were gaining at the expense of the agrarian interests, who favoured high tariffs on competing imports. Finally, the growing sophistication of the British economy meant that the fiscal system was no longer so dependent on income from taxes on trade.

The first step in the UK was repeal of the Navigation Acts, finally achieved in 1849. This meant that goods could now be transported by foreign ships not just to the UK, but also to the colonies. At the same time, the UK revised downwards its tariff rates from their previous high levels. However, it was not until 1846 that the UK took the momentous step of repealing the Corn Laws and abolishing tariffs on grains. This measure, which split the Conservative Party, had been demanded by manufacturers in order to reduce the price of wage goods and keep British industry competitive. It would lead to a massive increase in grain imports – first from Russia and later from North America (principally the United States), followed by Australia.

The repeal of the Corn Laws did not eliminate all tariffs. However, in the next eight years (1846–54), the UK phased out imperial preference, so import duties on other goods (including sugar) no longer favoured the colonies. At the same time, tariffs were reduced further as Great Britain began its long march towards free trade. This was most nearly achieved in the 1870s, when almost all import duties were abolished. The British era of zero or low tariffs, unique among the core countries, lasted with a few exceptions until the First World War. However, it became increasingly controversial. The growing competition in manufacturing from France, Germany and the United States led to calls from British industrialists for the reintroduction of tariff protection, and these calls were taken up by sections of the political class from the 1890s onwards.[32]

It must be clearly understood that British trade policy in the nineteenth century did not mean the abolition of tariffs in the colonies. On the contrary, the income from tariffs was so important (up to 90 per cent of colonial revenue), and the desire that the colonies should not be a drain on the imperial purse so strong, that the abolition of tariffs in the colonies was never an option. Colonial tariffs in the Caribbean were designed to maximise revenue. Tariffs did not normally favour British imports after mid-century, but imperial preferences started to appear towards the very end of the century. Subject to these constraints, British colonies – in the Caribbean and elsewhere – were generally free to buy their imports from the cheapest source and, of course, to sell their exports wherever they chose.

The smaller members of the core (Denmark, Holland and Sweden) never progressed as far as the UK towards unrestricted free trade, but they did allow freedom to trade. This was largely because of the needs of their nascent industrialists for at least some tariff protection throughout the nineteenth century.

---

[32] Their undisputed leader was Joseph Chamberlain, an industrialist himself, who was a strong advocate of imperial preference.

However, their small size made it difficult, if not impossible, to apply mercantilism strictly even in the eighteenth century. Thus, as early as 1764, Denmark declared the trade of St John and St Thomas in the Danish West Indies with other foreign colonies in the Americas to be open to the ships of all nations. This was extended three years later to trade with Europe. Unrestricted trade between St Croix (the third Danish island) and the rest of the world was finally adopted in 1833. Tariffs were reduced, but a mild form of imperial preference remained in force throughout the nineteenth century.

The opening of the Danish Virgin Islands[33] to freedom of trade took place before their occupation by Britain in the Napoleonic Wars. Two of the Dutch islands (St Eustatius and Curaçao) were also free ports.[34] However, Curaçao had thrived on contraband with South America, and this declined after the independence of the southern republics. This led the Dutch king in 1826 to abolish all tariffs in Curaçao in the hope of recapturing the trade with South America.[35] Yet Curaçao never fully recovered its role in the entrepôt trade, and the trade declined further when Venezuela in the 1870s imposed a surcharge on imports from the Dutch Antilles, which was not eliminated until the twentieth century.[36]

Suriname was also subject to British occupation during the Napoleonic Wars, but mercantilist principles had been breached even earlier. Despite legal restrictions, Suriname established strong trade relations with the United States, and these continued during hostilities. Holland owed its survival as a sovereign country at the Congress of Vienna to the UK and was in no position – either politically or economically – to reimpose mercantilism on its South American colony. Suriname was now open to trade with all nations, but Holland was still able to impose a form of imperial preference.[37]

The Swedish island of St Barthélemy had no natural resources of any significance, but it had one good harbour (Gustavia). Under Swedish rule, it therefore engaged in entrepôt trade, concentrating on the import of slaves for sale elsewhere in the Americas. By 1790, St Barthélemy had become a free port with a tax system designed to favour Swedish ships. The slave trade saw a jump in the island's population from 224 in 1750 (while still under French rule) to 4,016 in 1830. The end of the slave trade undermined the basis of the island's economy,

---

33 Denmark referred to its Caribbean colony as the 'Danish West Indies'. However, for reasons explained in the Notes on A. Tables, I will from now on refer to them as the 'Danish Virgin Islands'.

34 In *The Wealth of Nations* (1776), Adam Smith had favourably compared freedom of trade on these two islands with mercantilism elsewhere in the Caribbean.

35 See van Soest (1978), pp. 4–5. However, the tariffs were replaced with a 'safety duty' that reestablished tariffs under another name.

36 The Curaçao authorities had made the mistake of appearing to back the wrong side in an uprising in Venezuela against President Guzmán Blanco.

37 The Dutch colonies, however, were not finally freed from mercantilism until 1848. See Goslinga (1990), p. 228.

however, and the population had slumped to 2,390 in 1872[38] – shortly before the transfer of the island to France.

The French shift towards free trade was a much more complicated affair. The French Revolution had begun the process of sweeping away the restrictive legislation associated with mercantilism, but two decades of hostilities – including Napoleon's continental blockade – effectively created an infinite tariff behind which French industry thrived. This protectionist system included the promotion of the beet sugar industry, which rapidly filled the gap left by the collapse of cane sugar exports from Haiti.

The infinite tariff ended with the cessation of hostilities in 1815, but the restored Bourbon monarchy quickly increased duties to provide protection against imports. Tariffs were even raised on cane sugar imports from the Caribbean in order to protect the beet sugar industry. It was not until the reign of Napoleon III (1851–70) that France moderated its tariff levels through a series of trade treaties. Subsequently, the Third Republic witnessed a ferocious twenty-year battle between protectionists and free traders that culminated in the Méline tariff in 1892. This introduced minimum and maximum tariffs for the same product designed to favour countries that granted France Most-Favoured Nation (MFN) treatment. Yet tariffs remained generally high and included agricultural products in deference to the demands of French agrarian interests.[39]

No country had applied mercantilist principles more rigorously than Spain. These, it is true, were undermined both by contraband trade and by the weak position of Spain in many eighteenth-century peace negotiations with rival European powers. The brief British occupation of Havana in 1762, however, provided the most important breach in the mercantilist wall. Cuba was never able to revert to the closed trading system under which it had operated before, and the same was true of Puerto Rico. Indeed, in 1818 Spain introduced freedom to trade for its colonies in the Caribbean with dramatic effects. As early as 1820, 36 per cent of Cuban sugar was exported to the United States at a time when sugar accounted for 80 per cent of exports.[40]

Spanish tariffs remained high during the nineteenth century, but these were moderated by a system of imperial preferences. However, following the 1890 McKinley tariff, Spain signed the Foster-Canovas Treaty with the United States on behalf of its Caribbean colonies, which gave tariff preferences to the United States in return for concessions on US raw sugar imports.[41] By this time, the United States was already the most important trade partner for Cuba and Puerto Rico, having overtaken the UK by the middle of the century. US tariff policy then changed again in 1894, and heavy duties were reimposed on the

---

[38] See Table A.1.
[39] On French commercial policy, see Clapham (1968), pp. 260–5.
[40] See Schroeder (1982), p. 413.
[41] This is analysed in detail in Taussig (1967), pp. 304–16.

Spanish colonies. Spain therefore ended the tariff concessions for the United
States in Cuba and Puerto Rico.[42]

The German confederation that emerged from the Napoleonic Wars quickly
evolved into two competing customs unions – a northern one dominated by
Prussia and a southern one dominated by Bavaria. It was not until 1833 that
a joint customs union (*Zollverein*) could be formed of which Prussia was by
far the most important member. In order to keep the *Zollverein* independent
of Austria (at that time the most powerful state in central Europe), Prussian
political economy favoured a modest common external tariff because Austria
had some of the highest tariffs in the world.[43] Thus, the Prussian-dominated
German confederation came closest to the UK in terms of the pursuit of unrestricted free trade.

Prussian political economy changed after victories in war against Austria
(1866) and France (1870). The German Federation founded in 1871 no longer
feared Austrian expansion, but its eastern farmers became increasingly wary
of competition from Russia and the United States. At the same time, Bismarck
needed to increase revenues from indirect taxes in order to provide adequate
income for the central authority in the Federation. In 1879, a new tariff policy
was therefore adopted that was much more protectionist. Known as the mar-
riage of iron and rye, the new trade and tariff policy combined protection for
farmers and industrialists with subsidies for a number of exporters. Further
tariff increases were introduced in the 1880s, but the impact of these were
moderated by the trade treaties negotiated by Caprivi, Bismarck's successor as
German chancellor.[44]

The Declaration of Independence in 1776 may have brought an end to the
British Navigation Acts and other restrictions on trade for the thirteen colonies,
but the US government remained a strong defender of tariffs throughout the
nineteenth century. The first act of the federal government in 1789 was to pass
a tariff law, even before Alexander Hamilton's famous report in defence of
protection for manufacturing, and measures were also adopted to favour US
shipping in coastal and international trade.

Because the federal government was heavily dependent for much of the nineteenth century on income from tariffs, import duties could not be set at prohibitive levels. Similarly, the tension between the northern states that favoured
high protective tariffs for industry and the southern states that specialised in
raw materials helped to moderate upward pressure on import duties. However,
the victory of the North in the Civil War gave a huge advantage to the protectionists, and tariffs drifted upwards. The McKinley tariff in 1890 was blatantly
protectionist, and duties rose further in 1894 and 1897. It is estimated that

---

[42] The start of the Second War of Independence in 1895 is often linked to these changes.

[43] It was assumed by the German Chancellor Bismarck – correctly, as it turned out – that Austria
would object to joining any customs union that required it to lower its tariffs. See Clapham
(1968), pp. 314–16.

[44] See Henderson (1975), pp. 212–24.

at the beginning of the next century the average duty on British manufactures imported into the United States was 73 per cent.[45]

The McKinley tariff also introduced for the first time the principle of reciprocity. This allowed the US president (the authority having been given to the president by Congress itself) to impose higher duties on imports if the country exporting them was deemed to be taxing imports from the United States unfairly. This use of trade diplomacy, suspended in 1894, was reinstated in the 1897 tariff act and became a powerful instrument in US commercial policy. The United States also copied the European example of trade treaties designed to lower tariffs on a reciprocal basis. In 1892 alone, treaties of this nature were signed with eight countries, including Great Britain (acting on behalf of Jamaica, Trinidad, Barbados and British Guiana), Spain (on behalf of Cuba and Puerto Rico) and the Dominican Republic.[46]

2.4. THE ABOLITION OF THE SLAVE TRADE AND SLAVE EMANCIPATION

At the beginning of the nineteenth century, there was no aspect of trade policy more controversial than the trade in slaves. However, the slave trade was not just an issue of commercial policy. It was also a crucial component of the Caribbean labour market, and at the same time slaves represented one of the most important assets in the process of capital accumulation. Last, of course, it was a humanitarian issue.

The arguments for and against the slave trade were not the same as the arguments for and against slavery. Those in favour of the slave trade were always in favour of slavery, and many of those who argued against the slave trade also opposed slavery. However, there were influential voices in the core countries that were in favour of an end to the slave trade, but not to slavery. That is why the chronological gap between abolition (end of the slave trade) and emancipation (end of slavery) was so extended in a number of countries.

The case **against** the slave trade was partly humanitarian and partly economic. The former needs no further elaboration, but the latter does. The transportation of slaves was expensive, and there was a very high mortality rate; the fixed and variable costs of forts on the African coast, maintained at public expense, needed to be taken into account; Africa, Asia and the Pacific could provide the tropical products imported by the core from the Caribbean at lower cost without the need for the slave trade.

The case **for** the slave trade was both economic and political. Death rates exceeded birth rates among the Caribbean slave populations, and thus the labour supply could only be maintained through net inward migration. No labour other than that provided by African slaves was available; even if it were, it would be too expensive. The slave trade reduced the risks of slave

---

[45] See Clapham (1968), p. 322.
[46] See Taussig (1967), pp. 279–82.

rebellions, because it made it more difficult for the slaves to communicate with each other and establish bonds of solidarity. And, of course, the slave trade was often extremely profitable.

The first core country permanently to abolish the slave trade was Denmark. Legislation was passed in 1792. This was principally for economic reasons. The cost to Denmark of maintaining West African forts was seen as prohibitive, and two of the three Danish Virgin Islands (St John and St Thomas) specialised in entrepôt trade rather than the production of commodities – thus slavery was less important. Abolition itself was delayed until 1 January 1803, so plantation owners (mainly in St Croix) had ample time to increase the supply of slaves on the islands.[47] Even after 1803, Danish planters were usually able to obtain (illegally) additional slaves through St Barthélemy or Curaçao if needed.

Legislation was also introduced in the British parliament in 1792 to end the slave trade, but – unlike in Denmark – it was defeated. The humanitarian case was not fully accepted, and the economic arguments against the slave trade had been undermined by the slave revolt on St-Domingue the previous year. This had reduced the supply of cane sugar on the world market, pushing up prices and raising the prospect of a new era of prosperity on the British sugar islands. The plantation interests, strongly represented in Parliament, were able to carry the day.

It was not until 1807 that the British parliament passed legislation to abolish the slave trade. High sugar prices were no doubt one factor. However, the delay may also have been caused by the parlous state of the British armed forces at the outbreak of hostilities with France in 1793. The continuation of the slave trade allowed Great Britain to form African regiments in the West Indies, releasing British soldiers for duties elsewhere. It was only after the defeat of the French navy at Trafalgar in 1805 that the British West Indies became safe from naval attack.[48]

The legislation introduced in 1807 outlawed the transatlantic slave trade from March 1808. It was now seen as imperative to end the slave trade elsewhere in order not to disadvantage British plantation owners in the Caribbean. The United Kingdom (as it became in 1802 with the incorporation of Ireland) was in no position in the middle of the Napoleonic Wars to enforce an international ban on the slave trade. However, the federal government in the United States also ended the slave trade in 1808 (legislation having passed Congress the previous year). The southern states, where slavery was concentrated, raised little objection because – uniquely in the Americas – the birth rate exceeded the death rate among the slave populations. Thus, abolition of the slave trade did not pose such a big threat to slavery in the United States, and, in any case, an illegal slave trade into the southern states continued for many decades.

Towards the end of the Napoleonic Wars there were four core countries still legally engaged in the slave trade to the Caribbean: France, Holland, Spain

---

[47] See Dookhan (1974), pp. 134–7.
[48] This hypothesis is developed at length by Buckley (1998), pp. 128–44.

and Sweden (the participation of Brazil and Portugal in the slave trade – not finally ended until 1851 – need not concern us here). Both Holland, dependent on British support for the recovery of its sovereignty, and Sweden agreed to end the slave trade shortly before the end of hostilities. At the Treaty of Paris in 1814, Louis XVIII conceded the end of the French slave trade in five years, but he was forced to offer an immediate cessation the following year during Napoleon's Hundred Days. Spain reluctantly agreed to stop the slave trade in 1817 in return for £400,000 in compensation from the UK.[49]

Unfortunately, these diplomatic agreements turned out to be almost worthless. Both the slave trade and slave-produced commodities continued to be highly profitable in many parts of the Caribbean. The trade in slaves to Cuba was particularly important, and there are some suggestions that internationally more slaves were traded across the Atlantic in the 1840s than in any previous decade. Britain, with the largest navy in the world, turned to coercion in order to suppress the trade. Armed with the right of search through bilateral treaties, the British navy policed the African coast and boarded suspicious vessels. It was not, however, until the last slaves entered Cuba in the 1870s that the Caribbean slave trade finally came to an end.

The emancipation of the slaves in the Caribbean was an equally tortuous process. Adam Smith in 1776 had questioned the institution of slavery not only on humanitarian grounds, but also for reasons of cost. Yet slave-grown products could still be highly profitable in the nineteenth century in the southern United States and the Caribbean islands. Furthermore, it was widely assumed that emancipation would lead to a drastic reduction in the labour force available for plantation agriculture because the freed slaves would refuse to work for their former masters. And emancipation implied a massive drop in the value of capital assets unless compensation came into play.

Among the core countries, slavery was first abolished in some of the northern US states (Vermont in 1777 and Massachusetts in 1780 leading the way).[50] However, it was the slave revolt in St-Domingue in 1791 that marked the first break with slavery in the Caribbean. By the time the French revolutionary government abolished slavery on the island in 1793, slavery had effectively ended in St-Domingue. The declaration of independence by Haiti on 1 January 1804 marked the definitive end to slavery on the western side of Hispaniola, and slavery was also ended in the east during the subsequent Haitian occupation (the Dominican Republic would not restore it following independence from Haiti in 1844).

Despite efforts to persuade the former slaves to continue working on the sugar plantations, Haitian sugar exports had virtually ended within two decades of independence. This was a powerful argument used by the anti-emancipationists to delay legislation to end slavery. Furthermore, compensation implied a huge fiscal burden on core economies while import duties on

---

[49] See Bethell (1970), p. 20.
[50] See Engerman (2000), p. 336.

slave-grown products brought in valuable revenue. It was many years, therefore, before any of the core countries introduced legislation to outlaw slavery, despite all the efforts of the antislavery societies.

The UK finally passed a law against slavery in 1833. By this time, tropical products – once only available in the Caribbean – could be easily imported from other parts of the British Empire where slavery was not in use. At the same time, political reform had drastically reduced the influence of the West Indian plantocracy, whose profits had also declined as a result of increased competition.[51] Emancipation was to take effect in 1834 – but with an 'apprenticeship' system designed to keep the former slaves attached to the land for several more years. This system, slavery in all but name, was finally ended in 1838. Yet Britain remained dependent on slave-grown cotton from the southern United States until the end of the Civil War and continued to import slave-grown products from Brazil and Cuba until emancipation in the 1880s.

Although Caribbean slavery was of minor importance for Sweden (there were only 1,387 slaves on St Barthélemy in 1830), it was not until 1847 that it was brought to an end. Denmark had tinkered with the issue of emancipation from the 1830s, but the issue of compensation proved to be an obstacle. It was not until the slave revolt of 1848 on St Croix that the Danish authorities took any action, emancipating all slaves with immediate effect in all the Virgin Islands.[52] France did so in the same year. Slavery was not the main issue in the political and social upheavals in Paris in 1848, but it was certainly a factor and emancipation was one of the first acts of the Second Republic.[53] Holland, less affected by the revolutionary atmosphere in continental Europe in 1848 and anxious to protect the planters in Suriname, finally followed in 1863.[54]

Slavery in the southern states was only one of the causes of the US Civil War, but once hostilities broke out it was inevitable that President Lincoln would declare slaves in the rebel states to be free in order to undermine the Southern economy and drive a wedge between owners and slaves. This he did in 1862 (effective 1 January 1863), but it was not until the ratification of the Thirteenth Amendment in December 1865, after the end of the Civil War, that Lincoln's proclamation could take effect everywhere in the United States. From that point on, slavery in the Caribbean – hitherto tolerated by the federal government – would face strong US opposition.

Spain, the only core country that had still not abolished slavery, passed the Moret Law in 1870, granting freedom to all children of slaves born subsequently. This was followed by emancipation in Puerto Rico in 1873, where free labour had always been more important than slave labour. Spain could not afford to alienate the Cuban planters during the First War of Independence

[51] This decline in profitability is a key part of the thesis of Eric Williams that slavery was abolished in the British colonies primarily for economic reasons. See Williams (1944).
[52] See Dookhan (1974), pp. 175–8.
[53] See McCloy (1966), pp. 145–8.
[54] See Goslinga (1990), chap. 7.

(1868–78), and the slave owners were able to delay matters further after hostilities ended. Slavery finally ended on the island in 1880, yet it continued for another six years under the name of the *patronato* (similar to apprenticeship in the British colonies). This brought to an end nearly 400 years of slave labour in the Caribbean.

3

From Scarce to Surplus Labour in the Caribbean

In the first half of the nineteenth century, virtually all Caribbean countries were experiencing scarce labour – a chronic condition in which the demand for labour exceeded the supply of free workers at the prevailing wage rates and where coercion (mainly through slavery) and net inward migration (including the slave trade) were used to close the gap. By the end of the century, the situation had completely reversed. Most countries now suffered from surplus labour, with the supply at prevailing wage rates exceeding the demand. The disequilibrium in the labour market then led to substantial net outward migration from the surplus labour countries rather than to falling wage rates.

Throughout the century, therefore, the imbalance between supply and demand in the labour market was met mainly through quantity adjustments rather than changes in wage rates. When the demand exceeded the supply, this implied net **inward** migration, with the slave trade – despite legal restrictions – dominating labour inflows in the first half of the century. In the second half, indentured labour from Africa, Asia, Europe and even Mexico came to be the most important form of inward migration, with wage rates fixed during the period of indenture. When the supply of labour eventually exceeded the demand, net **outward** migration took place, with the migrants going either to those countries in the Caribbean still facing labour shortages (especially Cuba) or to the Caribbean periphery (Panama, the eastern coast of Central America and southern Florida).[1]

Some inward migration involved free labour (particularly from mainland Spain and the Canary Islands to Cuba). The indentured labourers also became free at the end of their period of indenture, assuming they did not return to their countries of origin (three out of four are estimated to have stayed in

---

[1] Panama was not an independent country in the nineteenth century; it was still a province of Colombia.

the Caribbean).[2] And the slaves eventually won their freedom after the abolition of slavery. However, it would be a mistake to imagine that the end of slavery brought about a truly free market in labour. Coercion rather than the offer of higher wage rates was the dominant response by employers and the state to labour shortages. The ex-slaves themselves were subject to a period of 'apprenticeship' that could last as long as ten years. Restrictions were placed on access to land in an attempt to ensure an adequate supply of labour for the plantations. Vagrancy laws were commonplace, and the internal movement of labour from one province to another was also restricted in some countries.

The first section of this chapter looks at population change throughout the Caribbean, which is the result of births, deaths and net migration. The second examines the twin issues of the abolition of the slave trade and slave emancipation. The third section is concerned with the coercion of labour after the end of slavery, and the fourth looks at inward migration – especially indentured labour. The final section of the chapter examines the connected issues of surplus labour, free labour and wage rates.

3.1. POPULATION CHANGE

The shift from scarce to surplus labour in the nineteenth century came about principally for two reasons. The supply of labour increased in all countries as a result of an acceleration in the growth of population, and the demand for labour in the last two decades of the century stagnated in most countries because of the crisis in the sugar cane industry (see Chapter 4). Only the most efficient sugar cane producers were able to increase output after the fall in prices that took place following the surge in sugar beet production. These two forces were much more powerful than others, such as the rise in education, which, ceteris paribus, tended to reduce the supply of labour because it meant that a growing proportion of the population attended school, and the growth of a small-scale peasantry that presented the ex-slaves with an alternative to wage employment.

The demographic figures tell a compelling story (see Figure 3.1). The population of the Caribbean rose by nearly 45 per cent between 1810 and 1850 and by 95 per cent between 1850 and 1900. The decennial growth increased from 6 per cent in the 1810s to 13 per cent in the 1890s.[3] The Spanish colonies, it is true, suffered a decline in the annual growth rate[4] as a result of the

---

[2] These are rough figures. However, in the case of Indian migration to the British Caribbean (the most important form of indentured labour), we have more precise figures; between 1838 and 1918 there were 429,623 arrivals and 111,303 returns. See Look Lai (1993), table 6, p. 276, and table 10, p. 279.

[3] Derived from Table A.1.

[4] From 1.66% before 1850 to 1.15% between 1850 and 1900. Derived from Table A.1.

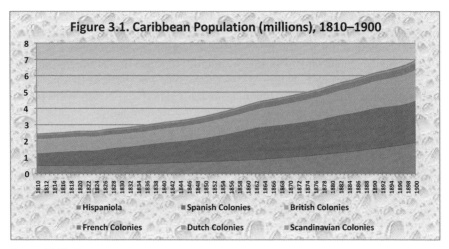

Figure 3.1. Caribbean Population (millions), 1810–1900

■ Hispaniola ■ Spanish Colonies ■ British Colonies ■ French Colonies ■ Dutch Colonies ■ Scandinavian Colonies

Source: Table A.1.

final suppression of the slave trade, and the Scandinavian colonies, where net outward migration was important, experienced a **fall** in population throughout the second half of the century. However, Hispaniola, the British, French and Dutch colonies all experienced an acceleration in their population growth rates.[5]

Population growth can accelerate through a combination of rising birth rates, falling death rates and changes in net migration. Birth rates in the Caribbean were fairly stable, but death rates started to fall as the century advanced, despite the occasional pandemic (cholera, smallpox and yellow fever were particularly virulent in the 1840s and 1850s).[6] Thus, much of the **increase** in the rate of growth of population can be attributed to falling death rates. An increase in net inward migration was much less important. Indeed, many countries experienced net **outward** migration in the second half of the century.

The demand for labour was derived from the performance of the economy (driven by the export sector). This is the subject of Chapter 4 onwards. We may note here, however, that only a handful of countries were able to expand the export sector after 1880, and thus the demand for labour tended to stagnate or even shrink in the last two decades of the century. By then a growing proportion of the population was attending school, but it was still small (see Figure 3.2). In the British colonies as a whole it had risen from little more than 1 per cent in

[5] For the British colonies, the annual growth rose by a factor of 6 (from 0.23% before 1850 to 1.35% between 1850 and 1900). Derived from Table A.1.
[6] Crude Birth Rates in Table A.3 are expressed as the number of births per thousand of the population. Crude Death Rates in Table A.4 are expressed in the same way. In these tables the numbers are colour-coded to take account of the slave population – see Notes on A. Tables.

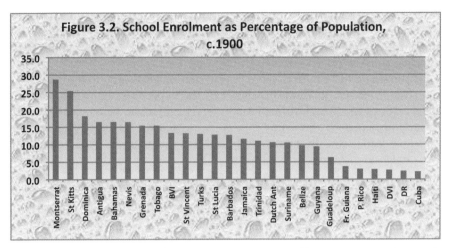

Figure 3.2. School Enrolment as Percentage of Population, c.1900

Note: The figures are for 1900 in all cases except Dominican Republic (1883), Puerto Rico (1883), Danish Virgin Islands (1886), Guadeloupe (1888), Cuba (1889) and Haiti (1895).
Source: Derived from Tables A.1 and A.7.

the 1830s to over 12 per cent by 1900.[7] In the independent countries and the Spanish and Scandinavian colonies it was between 2 and 3 per cent as the short nineteenth century ended, a little higher in the French colonies, and around 10 per cent in the Dutch colonies.[8] School attendance did not increase enough to reverse the shift from scarce to surplus labour in most countries.

Some structural change had taken place in the nineteenth century, but the labour force was still overwhelmingly rural, and the market for rural labour was mainly focused on the plantation. The rural labour force outside the plantation was employed in the peasant economy producing a small marketed surplus – usually for sale in the domestic market.[9] These workers were therefore on the margins of the wage labour market, but at certain times their participation was crucial. In the small urban labour market, domestic service was generally the largest source of employment, followed by trade and distribution.

As surplus labour replaced scarce labour, the need for coercion by employers and the state diminished. Starting in the towns, a free market in labour gradually spread to the rest of the economy until by the end of the century even the plantations were able to secure most of their labour requirements without

[7] School attendance numbers in Table A.7 are based on pupils registered. Average school attendance was much lower, with actual attendance varying between half and two-thirds. This suggests that school attendance did not necessarily prevent at least partial participation in the labour force by pupils.
[8] This is based on those countries in Table A.7 for which data have been collected.
[9] But not always. Much of the bananas, coffee, cacao, arrowroot and other spices exported from the Caribbean in the second half of the nineteenth century came from the small-scale peasantry.

resorting to coercion. Yet nominal wage rates remained very stable even during the period of surplus labour (see the last section of this chapter), and thus the standard of living was determined more by the amount of work on offer and the change in the price level than by the wage rate itself.

Throughout the century, there was a fierce debate about the impact of the cost of labour on the profitability of the export sector, particularly the sugar industry.[10] Yet it turned out that sugar could be profitable under slavery sustained by the traffic in slaves (e.g. Cuba), under slavery without the slave trade (e.g. the French Antilles), with coercion (e.g. Barbados) and with indentured labour (e.g. Guyana). The difference in the cost of labour that each of these systems implied was a much less important determinant of profitability than the change in the price received from the importing countries. However, the size of profits was influenced by the level of output in the export sector. As we shall see, the sugar industry – particularly in the years immediately after emancipation – was sometimes unable to secure all the workers required for optimum production. Quantity, not the wage rate, was the defining feature of the labour market in the nineteenth century.

3.2. SLAVERY AND THE ILLEGAL TRAFFIC IN SLAVES

Coerced labour took many forms, of which the most extreme was slavery. Before the nineteenth century, the Crude Death Rate (CDR) had invariably exceeded the Crude Birth Rate (CBR) among the slave population in Caribbean countries.[11] Thus, slavery was intimately associated with the traffic in slaves because it was widely assumed that the slave population would disappear without it. Because the male slaves caught in the slave traffic outnumbered the females, this became a self-fulfilling prophecy.

Those campaigning against the slave trade in Europe argued that, in the absence of forced migration through trafficking, the planters would have to treat their slaves better, and this would improve the net birth rate. They also pointed out that, in the absence of the trade, the gender imbalance would correct itself over time, leading in turn to an increase in births. The planters rejected these arguments and insisted that the end of the traffic in slaves would spell disaster because not only would the slave population decline, but the cost of labour would rise, rendering their activities unprofitable.[12]

---

[10] The debate had actually started even earlier with the publication of Adam Smith's *The Wealth of Nations* in 1776. Smith argued that slavery would always be economically less efficient than free labour.

[11] For the British colonies, see Ward (1988), chap. 5.

[12] Before abolition, the planters argued that slavery without the traffic would be very expensive. After abolition of the trade, but before slave emancipation, they would argue that slave labour was cheap in comparison to 'free labour'. For the case of the British colonies, see Sewell (1861), p. 29.

What might happen to the size of the slave population was therefore an empirical question that should have been settled by its growth – positive or negative – after the abolition of the slave trade. However, in many colonies the transatlantic slave traffic continued long after legislation was introduced to abolish it. Indeed, the last shipments of slaves (to Cuba) were not made until the 1870s.[13] And even where the transatlantic trade ended, as in the case of the British colonies in 1808, there was still a legal and illegal intra-Caribbean trade in slaves for many years (see below in this section). Thus, the growth in the slave population continued to be affected by migration even after abolition of the slave trade.

The reasons for this have much to do with the conviction of the planters that only the traffic could profitably sustain their activities, but it was also made possible by the venality of local officials and a lack of commitment by governments in Europe, Brazil and the United States. Denmark had led the way in abolishing the slave trade, introducing legislation in 1792 that would end it ten years later in order to give the planters plenty of time to obtain through trafficking increased supplies of slaves and a better gender balance. However, Denmark lacked the resources to suppress the slave trade elsewhere. The United States, which had agreed to allow the traffic in slaves to continue for another twenty years when debating its new federal constitution in the 1780s, duly abolished it in 1807, with effect from 1808.[14] Yet the United States would remain a country with slave states until 1865;[15] its commitment to suppressing the trade was minimal and the eastern seaports even in the nonslave states continued to play a key role in the traffic.

The UK was the third country to pass legislation abolishing the trade in slaves, with effect from March 1808.[16] This did not immediately end the British trade, because the movement of slaves between British colonies remained legal under certain circumstances until 1830.[17] This loophole was of great importance for Guyana[18] and Trinidad because these colonies were chronically short

---

[13] See Santamaría and García (2004), p. 79.

[14] The bill abolishing the slave trade was signed into law by President Jefferson on 2 March 1807, with effect from 1 January 1808. See Thomas (1997), pp. 551–2.

[15] President Lincoln's proclamation freeing the slaves in rebel states took effect from 1 January 1863. However, the Civil War meant that this had no effect until the surrender of the South. The Thirteenth Amendment outlawing slavery in the US was finally passed in December 1865.

[16] The bill abolishing the slave trade received the royal assent on 25 March 1807, a few weeks after similar legislation in the US. However, it was still legal for British citizens to land slaves in the Caribbean until 1 March 1808, provided the ships had cleared British ports before 1 May 1807. See Ragatz (1928), p. 276.

[17] After 1824 it was only legal if those transported were domestic servants in attendance on their masters. See Ragatz (1928), p. 433.

[18] I have chosen to use one name as far as possible to describe a country even when its name changed over the period after 1810. Guyana is the name given on independence to the colony of British Guiana formed in 1831 from the merger of two former Dutch colonies: Demerara & Essequibo and Berbice. For further details, see Notes on A. Tables.

of slaves at the end of the Napoleonic Wars.[19] The British transatlantic slave trade, however, did end in 1808, and slaves caught in British ships by the British navy off the coast of West Africa were usually taken to Sierra Leone and set free.[20]

By the end of the Napoleonic Wars, it was clear to the British authorities that a major international effort would be required to persuade other countries to join them if the traffic in slaves was to come to an end. Without an international embargo on the slave trade, it was claimed, planters in the British Caribbean colonies would face unfair competition, and the UK would be in the embarrassing position of importing products whose profitability might depend on the traffic in slaves. Starting in 1814, therefore, the UK launched an international campaign that would not end until the last slaves crossed the Atlantic in the 1870s.

Sweden,[21] whose Caribbean colonies had all been occupied by the British, agreed in 1813 to end the traffic in slaves immediately. The Anglo-Dutch Treaty of 1818 committed Holland to suppress the slave trade (agreement in principle had been reached in 1814), and Anglo-Dutch courts were established in Sierra Leone and Suriname to ensure compliance.[22] France, like Holland, agreed in principle to end the trade in 1814, but it secured a grace period of five years.[23] The suppression of the French trade was reconfirmed in the Anglo-French Treaty of 1818. Yet the French government, aware that its planters had been denied access to a new supply of slaves by the British occupations, made no effort to end the traffic in slaves until the signing of a new Anglo-French Treaty in 1831. Even then the transatlantic slave trade to the French colonies probably did not end completely, but it operated under increasingly severe restrictions.

---

[19] Legislation had been introduced in 1805 in the British parliament banning the import of slaves for new estates while hostilities continued in those territories, such as Guyana, St Lucia and Trinidad, occupied during the Napoleonic Wars. The annual importation of slaves for existing estates was restricted to 3% of the slave labour force. Thus, the intracolonial trade from 1814, when hostilities ended, to 1830 was a crucial way for the slave populations of those colonies to be legally increased. See Ragatz (1928), p. 278. For the case of Trinidad, see Brereton (1981), pp. 54–6. See also Eltis (1972).

[20] Sierra Leone had been purchased as a home for ex-slaves in 1787. It became a British colony a few years later. See Thomas (1997), pp. 497–9. In 1820, Liberia was established by the United States with a similar purpose.

[21] In 1813, Guadeloupe – then under British occupation – had been transferred to Sweden. The following year, at the Treaty of Paris, the UK changed its mind and returned the island to France, paying an indemnity to Sweden in compensation. This left the island of St Barthélemy, once again, as the only Swedish possession in the Caribbean.

[22] On the Anglo-Dutch courts, see Emmer (1998), chap. 5. By the time the courts were wound up in the 1830s, twenty-three ship captains had been charged with illegal trading. See Thomas (1997), pp. 612–13.

[23] Napoleon had decreed the end of the slave trade during his brief return from exile in 1814–15, but this had no impact.

That left the Iberian peninsula, and Britain's problems with Spain and Portugal (and later with Brazil) have been studied in depth.[24] Suffice it to say that the first Anglo-Spanish Treaty in 1817, committing Spain to end the traffic by 1820, had no effect; the second in 1835 was not much better; and it was not until 1845 that the Spanish government introduced legislation that made trafficking a criminal offence. This was enough to slow the traffic to Puerto Rico to a trickle, but it was not enough to stop the far more lucrative trade to Cuba.[25]

The traffic in slaves was the largest source of inward migration before 1850, and it remained of some significance even after that. Because the trade was illegal, we have no exact figures on its scale.[26] However, various scholars have prepared estimates of slave imports after abolition that make a compelling case for its importance.[27] At least eight countries were still importing slaves a decade after the Napoleonic Wars ended.[28] These included Guyana, Trinidad and all the French and Spanish colonies. Despite the presence of the Anglo-Dutch Court at Paramaribo, slaves were still being imported into Suriname until 1826.[29] By contrast, a sharp fall in the slave population in the Dutch Antilles probably came about because some slaves were **sold** to other islands in the Caribbean.[30] Intra-Caribbean imports ended in the British colonies by 1830, and all imports in the French colonies the following year. By the end of the 1840s, slave imports had ended in Puerto Rico,[31] leaving Cuba as the only Caribbean country still heavily engaged in the traffic.

Expressed as a percentage of population (see Table 3.1), slave imports were highly significant in the first decade after the Napoleonic Wars. Indeed, they

---

[24] On negotiations with Spain to end the trade, see Murray (1980). On negotiations with Portugal and Brazil, see Bethell (1970).

[25] Portuguese participation in the slave traffic to Brazil had effectively ended by 1840. Brazilian participation continued for another decade. However, this trade does not appear to have had any significant spillover effects on the Caribbean.

[26] The British consuls in the Caribbean did provide some estimates of the illegal slave traffic. For Cuba, see Murray (1980), table 6, p. 111.

[27] Because the change in the slave population must be due to net births, manumissions and the traffic in slaves, it is also possible to estimate **net** slave imports (purchases less sales) after making certain assumptions about the other variables. This method of calculating the traffic in slaves has the advantage of estimating slave migration from all sources – transatlantic and intra-Caribbean. It can also be used to identify those Caribbean countries where slaves were exported to neighbouring countries – a much neglected topic.

[28] For details, see Table A.5.

[29] See Emmer (1998), p. 122.

[30] These are my estimates based on the methodology outlined in note 27. The Dutch had in fact granted Curaçao, the most important of the Dutch Antilles, the right to export slaves in 1832. See Dorsey (2003), pp. 184–5.

[31] This was less because of greater vigilance by Puerto Rican officials than the high cost of importing slaves in an economy desperately short of working capital. See Dietz (1986), p. 38. There is also a suggestion that Puerto Rico was selling slaves (to Cuba) after the mid-1840s. See Kiple (1970), pp. 157–8.

TABLE 3.1. *Slave Imports as Percentage of Population, 1817–1873*

	Cuba	Puerto Rico	Guyana	Trinidad	French Guiana	Guade-loupe	Martinique	Suriname
1817	4.5	0.4	0.7	1.4	2.0	0.8	0.5	1.7
1824	1.0	0.6	0.7	1.4	9.6	3.7	2.7	1.7
1834	1.8	0.6						
1844	1.0	0.1						
1854	1.1							
1864	0.5							
1873	0.1							

Source: Derived from Tables A.1 and A.5.

represented nearly 10 per cent of the population in French Guiana in 1824. Slave imports into Guyana and Trinidad were even more important than into Puerto Rico as a percentage of population until the trade ended. Annual slave imports represented over 1 per cent of the population in Cuba until the 1860s.[32] From 1815 until the trade finally ended, it is estimated that 660,000 slaves had been imported, with most of these coming from outside the Caribbean.[33]

While the traffic in slaves was gradually being outlawed by international treaty and greater vigilance by the authorities on both sides of the Atlantic, the institution of slavery itself was also coming under attack. Abolished first in St-Domingue in 1793 and in all the French colonies the following year, it was reintroduced by Napoleon in 1802 everywhere except Haiti, where French authority had collapsed. At the end of the Napoleonic Wars, slaves still represented half the total population of the Caribbean (see Figure 3.3), and this ratio increases to 60 per cent if we exclude Hispaniola (Haiti and the Dominican Republic), where slavery had ceased to exist.

Most Caribbean slaves at the end of the Napoleonic Wars were to be found in the British colonies, where they represented over 80 per cent of the population until emancipation.[34] The ratio was very similar at that time in the Danish, Dutch, French and Scandinavian colonies, but it did decline slowly as the century advanced (see Figure 3.3). It was only in the Spanish colonies, the Dutch Antilles and St Barthélemy that most of the population was nonslave.[35]

[32] The slaves were required primarily as plantation workers. Because almost all trafficked slaves were of working age and the plantation workers were about 25% of the population, the annual traffic in slaves would have represented around 3% to 4% of the plantation labour force in Cuba before the US Civil War. By any standards, this is a very high figure.
[33] See Table A.5.
[34] In Trinidad, the ratio of slaves to the total population fell below 50% after 1831, but slaves probably still constituted more than 50% of the labour force.
[35] Once the slave trade was suppressed by Sweden, St Barthélemy had little economic value, because its principal function had been as an entrepôt for the purchase and sale of slaves. It is very probable that some of the decline in the slave population before emancipation in 1847

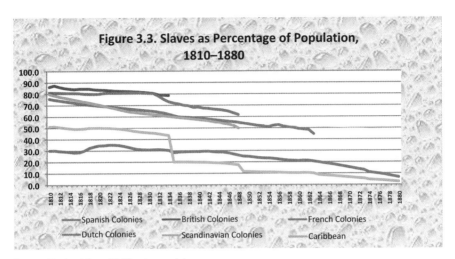

Figure 3.3. Slaves as Percentage of Population, 1810–1880

Spanish Colonies — British Colonies — French Colonies
Dutch Colonies — Scandinavian Colonies — Caribbean

Source: Derived from Tables A.1 and A.2.

Cuba and Puerto Rico may have been majority nonslave, but this was a reflection of their backward economic status in the eighteenth century. And the ratio of slave to nonslave population at first rose in both countries, rising above 40 per cent in Cuba in the 1820s before falling below 30 per cent in the 1850s. This was low by comparison with the British, Danish, Dutch and French colonies, but the qualitative impact of slavery was far greater than these figures imply. Slavery was the key mode of employment in the dynamic plantation sector, on which Cuba's economic success depended. And without that success, Cuba would have been unable to attract nonslave workers from Europe and the rest of the Caribbean. Although the slave population was even lower in Puerto Rico (it never exceeded 12 per cent), the same arguments apply. The expansion of the sugar economy in the first half of the century was dependent on slave labour.

As the traffic in slaves gradually came to a halt, the change in the size of the slave population came to depend more and more on slave births and deaths. Vital statistics suggest that the abolitionists were only partially correct about the impact of the end of the slave trade on slave demographics. In 1820, slave births exceeded deaths in only six British colonies.[36] Ten years later, this was true of more colonies. Yet for the British colonies as a whole, there was no improvement between 1820 and 1830. Although the birth rate rose, the death rate rose also, and deaths still exceeded births. Jamaica, the largest British

---

was from the export of slaves to other islands. See, e.g., Chinea (2005), pp. 80–1, for details on St Barthélemy emigrants to Puerto Rico.

[36] These were Anguilla, Bahamas, Barbados, Belize, Cayman Islands and the Turks & Caicos Islands. See Tables A.3 and A.4.

colony, even went backwards, with a rise in the death rate and no change in the birth rate.

In other countries – the statistics are less complete – it was generally the case that slave births did not exceed slave deaths even after the end of the slave trade. By the end of the slave period, deaths still marginally exceeded births in Guadeloupe and Martinique and massively so in French Guiana. In Curaçao (the main island in the Dutch Antilles), the slave birth rate **was** almost twice the slave death rate in the 1840s. However, this was not the case in Suriname, a much more important colony, where slave births never exceeded deaths.[37] In Cuba, the gender imbalance caused by the slave trade made it almost inevitable that slave deaths would exceed births, as indeed happened, but in Puerto Rico slave births did outstrip deaths in at least one province by the 1860s.[38] In the Scandinavian colonies, slave deaths exceeded births on the eve of abolition.[39] In no colony, with the exception of the Dutch Antilles where slavery was not of great importance, could the slave owners rely on natural growth to sustain the slave population.

Thus, the abolition of the slave trade was bound eventually to undermine the institution of slavery itself – and this duly happened. British emancipation occurred in 1834, after which a sharp drop took place in the proportion of the Caribbean population that was slave (see Figure 3.3). This was followed by Sweden in 1847, Denmark in 1848[40] and France in the same year. In Holland, emancipation took another fifteen years,[41] but the Spanish colonies still held out. The passage of the Moret Law in 1870, freeing all children of slaves born after the law's publication in Cuba and Puerto Rico, ensured that the institution would eventually end.[42] However, slavery was not formally abolished until 1873 in Puerto Rico and 1880 in Cuba. At that time, Cuban slaves still accounted for 10 per cent of the island's population.[43]

Emancipation may have brought an end to slavery in a juridical sense, but it generally continued for a few more years by other means under a different name. The apprenticeship system in the British colonies was intended to last

---

[37] Even during the period of state supervision, after the end of slavery in 1863, deaths usually exceeded births among the emancipated population. See van Lier (1971), p. 188.
[38] This province was Ponce, an important sugar-producing region. See Curet (1980), p. 217.
[39] For the Danish Virgin Islands, see Johansen (1981), who concludes on the basis of a very detailed study that the slave CDR was 50 and the slave CBR was 40 in the 1840s. For St Barthélemy, see Hyrenius (1977), who comes to the conclusion that slave births and deaths were roughly equal in the 1840s.
[40] The decision by the Danish authorities to abolish slavery in the Danish Virgin Islands was taken after the slaves of St Croix had liberated themselves. See Dookhan (1974).
[41] Except in Sint Maarten, where emancipation occurred in 1848 – shortly after the French slaves were emancipated on the rest of the island. Without emancipation, it was assumed, the slaves would have fled across the border.
[42] The Moret Law also freed all slaves over sixty. See Figueroa (2005), p. 114.
[43] Derived from Tables A.1 and A.2.

until 1840,[44] but it had collapsed by 1838.[45] The Danish and French colonies tried various schemes to tie the ex-slaves to the plantations in the 1850s, with limited success (see next section). The Dutch introduced a ten-year period of state supervision in Suriname, and thus slavery did not truly end until 1873.[46] Puerto Rico limited the freedom of the ex-slaves (*libertos*) for another three years after emancipation, and Cuba did the same through the *patronato* for six years.[47] Thus, the apprenticeship period ended in 1876 in Puerto Rico and in 1886 in Cuba.[48]

3.3. COERCION WITHOUT SLAVERY

Emancipation did not mean the end of coercion. On the contrary, the scarcity of labour in most countries was even more acute because the ex-slaves could now leave the plantations. If that happened on a very large scale, export agriculture would go into decline and the foundations of the Caribbean economy would collapse. Preventing this from happening was therefore crucial not only from the point of view of the planters, but also of the state. Export agriculture paid for imports, and foreign trade provided directly and indirectly the public revenue out of which all government activities were financed.

A shortage of labour should lead to an increase in wage rates in a normal labour market. This happened in the United States in the first half of the nineteenth century, in Argentina in the second half and in Australia at the start of the new century. Higher wage rates can always be justified if labour productivity is rising at the same rate. This will happen if new investments are being made in laboursaving technology. The scarce labour countries in the Caribbean, however, either lacked access to capital or were insufficiently profitable to self-finance new investments. It was also an article of faith among the planters, based in part on experience immediately after emancipation, that the supply curve of labour was so inelastic that only huge increases in wage rates could clear the market.

The result was a series of policies designed to tie labour to the plantations and prevent the emergence of a large class of free workers. These policies met with some success to the extent that very few plantations collapsed because of

---

[44] The apprenticeship period was set at six years for field slaves and four years for all others. See Green (1976), p. 121.

[45] In Antigua, there was no apprenticeship period, and slavery ended in 1834.

[46] See van Lier (1971), chap. 7.

[47] The *patrocinados* in Cuba have been well researched. See, e.g., Scott (1985), chap. 7.

[48] It is often said that slavery did not end in Cuba (and therefore the Caribbean) until 1886. In practice, that may well have been true. However, the *patronato* system in Cuba was similar to the apprenticeship system in the British colonies and the state supervision system in Suriname. In the interests of consistency, therefore, we should regard 1880 as marking the legal end of slavery in Cuba because emancipation for the British and Dutch colonies is always given as 1834 and 1863 respectively.

a shortage of labour.[49] However, they did not prevent the gradual emergence of a class of workers who – if not strictly free – were no longer dependent on the plantation for their main source of livelihood. These were the peasants or proto-peasants, who exploited the new opportunities after emancipation to acquire access to land through title, tenure, share-cropping or squatting and who produced mainly for themselves and the domestic market.[50] Many also participated in the plantation economy as the most efficient means of raising the cash income needed to buy essentials and pay taxes.[51]

As the country where slavery had first ended, it is not surprising that Haiti was also the first to apply coercive measures to ensure that the ex-slaves continued to work on the plantations. Dessalines, from the earliest days of independence (1 January 1804), was determined to prevent the elimination of export agriculture, because without it the Haitian state was not expected to survive.[52] These policies met with some success, and, as we shall see in Chapter 7, export agriculture in Haiti did not collapse. Indeed, it is estimated that by the time Dessalines was assassinated in October 1806, between two-thirds and nine-tenths of the land had been brought under state control, keeping the former slaves attached to the plantations and preventing the emergence of a small-scale peasantry.[53]

The political rivalries that followed the death of Dessalines led to the division of Haiti. Christophe in the north maintained the land policy of Dessalines, and the large estates producing for export survived with labour provided by the former slaves. Pétion in the south, however, in greater need of political support, tolerated the drift of the ex-slaves away from the plantations and the establishment of a small-scale peasantry. The large estates were not expropriated, but they found it increasingly difficult to obtain the labour they needed. Following the reunification of Haiti in 1820 under Boyer, Pétion's successor in the south, the big estates in the north began to crumble. The *Code Rural* of 1826 was a draconian measure to deal with the problem of labour scarcity by forcing everyone except public officials and members of certain professions to work the land in an effort to protect the plantations. However, the state was too weak to enforce it.[54]

---

[49] Labour shortages, however, could reduce output below the profit-maximising level.

[50] The origins of this proto-peasantry can be found in slavery, because it was in the interest of the planters to allow slaves access to provision grounds for growing at least some of their own food. See, e.g., the chapters by Hall, Beckles, Tomich and Mintz in section 11 of Shepherd and Beckles (1993). See also Craton (1997) and Marshall (1968), pp. 1–14.

[51] Imperial governments throughout the world have always known that imposing taxes payable in cash on the peasantry was an efficient way of ensuring a labour supply to the nonpeasant economy.

[52] See Rotberg (1971), p. 54. In fact, Dessalines simply reestablished the coercive policies adopted by Toussaint L'Ouverture in 1799.

[53] See Moya Pons (1985), pp. 181–2.

[54] One of the reasons was the reduced threat of invasion, following recognition of Haitian independence by France in 1825. Military discipline subsequently declined, and the soldiers themselves became interested in acquiring small plots of land. See Moya Pons (1985), pp. 194–6.

With a negligible export sector at the end of the Napoleonic Wars, the Dominican Republic did not need to coerce labour to the same extent. The modest labour demands of the tobacco, timber and cattle sectors could be met easily enough, and the natural growth of the population provided an expanding labour force from early in the nineteenth century. During unification with Haiti (1822–44), Boyer had repeatedly tried to introduce the Haitian system of land titling based on French law and had promoted export agriculture, but without success.[55] When the country finally became independent in 1844, however, it quickly moved to adopt the same coercive measures.[56] When these proved insufficient, particularly after the rise of the sugar industry towards the end of the century, the labour demands of export agriculture were met principally through immigration.[57]

In the British colonies after emancipation, compensation for the end of slavery had resulted in payment of £20 million to the planters, a huge sum by any standards, but most of this was absorbed by debts owed to merchants and other creditors.[58] Capital for raising productivity was scarce – even scarcer than labour – and the planters were desperate to avoid a rise in wage rates that might have driven them out of business.[59] At the same time, the planters needed to be sure that workers were available to meet the seasonal needs of export agriculture. Coercion was therefore seen by the planters and colonial governments as the only option.

The first step had been the apprenticeship system, but this was only temporary and had ended everywhere by 1838. The next few years were often chaotic, and planters were in some cases forced to raise wage rates temporarily in order to secure the labour that they needed (even so, production fell in many colonies).[60] Wage labour taught the planters to distinguish between their needs for permanent and temporary labour (a distinction that had not been necessary under slavery), so it was the planters more than the ex-slaves who underwent an apprenticeship. By the 1850s – where labour was scarce – coercion was helping the planters to meet their seasonal demands. Where coercion was not sufficient, inward migration (see next section) was filling the gap.

---

[55] Boyer, who was overthrown in March 1843, had targeted the system of *terrenos comuneros* in the eastern part of the island in order both to modernise agriculture and to encourage small-scale ownership. To some extent, however, these were contradictory aims, and he was unable to achieve them. See Moya Pons (1985), pp. 186–94.

[56] See Vega (1977), who outlines the three laws introduced between 1847 and 1849 to deal with the shortage of labour.

[57] The investment of US capital in the sugar industry was the main cause of these changes. It also triggered a change in land titling practices in the Dominican Republic, because foreign investors wanted to be secure in their property rights.

[58] See Green (1976), pp. 118–21.

[59] Wage rates did rise at first, but in most colonies they had been brought back to previous levels by 1850. See last section of this chapter.

[60] This is the origin of the planters' belief in a backward-bending supply curve of labour – higher wage rates leading to a reduction in labour supply because cash needs could be met with fewer hours worked.

The key to coercion in the British colonies was restrictions on access to land. Where land was scarce, as in the old sugar colonies, this was relatively easy to do. The ex-slaves in Anguilla, Antigua, Barbados, Montserrat, Nevis and St Kitts had little option but to offer their services to the plantation owners in return for accommodation and access to their own provision grounds. Yet this did not necessarily rule out the emergence of a small-scale peasantry. In Barbados, where export agriculture continued to expand after emancipation and labour shortages were avoided, proprietors with less than five acres increased from 1,100 in 1844 to 3,537 fifteen years later.[61]

In some British colonies, the solution to the land and labour problem was found in sharecropping. On St Lucia, where the French *metairie* system was well established before it became a British colony in 1815, the planters secured the labour that they needed through sharecropping, and output expanded. The planters in Tobago did the same, but output failed to increase (capital and labour were moving to Trinidad). In the Bahamas, sharecropping was also common, but this had more to do with the unprofitability of estates and the inability of the plantation owners to pay wages in cash.[62]

Where land was relatively abundant, other measures were usually needed if the ex-slaves were to continue to work in export agriculture. In Guyana and Trinidad, the colonial government set a high minimum acreage for purchase and introduced other measures to discourage the establishment of a small-scale peasantry independent of the estates.[63] These measures were not very successful, but it did not necessarily spell disaster for the large landowners because the plantations remained the key source of cash income for the peasantry. The same happened in Jamaica. The sale of crown lands discriminated against the growth of a small-scale peasantry, and subterfuge had to be used to circumvent restrictions on access to land.[64] However, many of the peasant villages were close to the plantations, and labour services continued to be provided on an occasional basis.[65]

Emancipation in the Swedish colony of St Barthélemy accelerated the process of economic decline. In the following decades, many of the island's inhabitants (both former slaves and others) left for other islands.[66] In the Danish Virgin Islands, where emancipation was won by slave action, the authorities were quick to impose coercive measures to reduce the risk of labour shortages on

---

[61] See Sewell (1861), p. 39.
[62] On sharecropping in the British colonies generally, see Marshall (1965). For Nevis, see Dyde (2005), pp. 171–3; and for the Bahamas, see Johnson (1996), chap. 5.
[63] In Guyana, the minimum parcel of Crown land for purchase was set at 100 acres. See Adamson (1972), p. 35.
[64] The Baptist church was heavily involved in these subterfuges. See Eisner (1961), pp. 210–13, and Hall (2002).
[65] Hall (1959) provides an excellent study of the relationship between the peasantry and the estates. See especially chap. 5.
[66] Many settled in the Danish Virgin Islands, where they gave their name to a suburb of Charlotte Amalie.

the plantations. Annual labour contracts were made obligatory from October 1849, and there was only one month in the year (August) when workers could give notice. Payments for even the smallest tasks were specified in the labour law in order to avoid a sharp rise in wages, and absence from work was punished severely.[67] These measures were so unpopular that a major revolt took place on St Croix in 1878, during the month when the annual contract was due for renewal.

In the French colonies, as in the Danish, vagrancy was seen as a key problem, and steps were taken to prevent it. Workers were issued a passbook, which was updated each month by the employer. In this way the authorities could tell if a worker had been in regular employment. If not, (s)he would be charged under the antivagrancy laws. In addition, workers were issued an internal passport to make it more difficult to leave the plantation and find work elsewhere.[68] And yet, despite these draconian measures, a small-scale peasantry did emerge, producing for the domestic market while still linked to the plantations through occasional labour services. As in the other colonies, the plantation owners discovered that their need for a permanent labour force was much more modest than under slavery and that temporary labour needs could be met by small-scale proprietors, provided that they remained in the cash economy.

Slavery ended late in the Dutch colonies, and the period of 'state supervision' extended it by ten years to 1873 in Suriname. In the Dutch Antilles, the labour needs of export agriculture were so modest that a free market in labour had already developed by the time of emancipation, but in Suriname the high death rate among all classes of workers created a chronic problem of labour scarcity. Furthermore, the state was unable to prevent the ex-slaves from leaving the estates in large numbers, and the labour shortage became even more acute. Peasant villages, separate from the maroon communities that had been in existence for decades, began to emerge with some links to the plantations.[69] However, many of the ex-slaves moved to Paramaribo, which accounted for over one-third of the population in the 1870s. The Dutch authorities, therefore, increasingly relied on inward migration to meet the labour needs of the estates.

In the Spanish colonies, the authorities faced a different problem long before the end of slavery. A small-scale peasantry in Puerto Rico had become established before the nineteenth century as a consequence of the absence of export-led growth. With the expansion of export agriculture under slavery in the nineteenth century, the colonial state needed to coerce labour out of peasant farming and onto the plantations. This was done, as in the French colonies, through antivagrancy laws. The first Puerto Rican law was passed in 1838, and

---

[67] See Knox (1852), pp. 248–55, where the 1849 labour law is reprinted.

[68] For Martinique, see Brown (2002). For Guadeloupe and Martinique, see Blérald (1986), pp. 99–105, and Renard (1993).

[69] The Dutch government even encouraged this process by opening farm settlements in proximity to the plantations. See van Lier (1971), p. 227.

this was strengthened in 1849.[70] Movement of workers from one province to another was also restricted through the introduction of an internal passport. The system was only ended in 1873, at the same time as emancipation.[71] By then, the natural growth of the population was increasing the labour supply at least as fast as the growth of labour demand.

The boom in export agriculture in Cuba created a chronic labour shortage that neither slavery nor the slave trade nor coercion could fully resolve.[72] Indeed, despite massive inward migration, Cuba was still a labour-scarce country well into the twentieth century. Yet output rose steadily because the plantation and sugar mill owners economised on the use of labour through new techniques of production. The priority given to the labour needs of the big estates, however, worked against the growth of a small-scale peasantry. Much of Cuba's food requirements were met through imports, a feature of the Cuban economy that has remained important to this day.

Coercion during the period of labour scarcity was designed to ensure that the plantations responsible for export agriculture should not be subject to labour shortages. The measures adopted – however brutal – were generally effective. Export agriculture did decline in some countries, but for the Caribbean as a whole it did not (see Chapter 5). Where it did decline, as in Jamaica and Suriname, labour scarcity was only part of the problem. In Suriname, many planters used emancipation and the compensation paid as a convenient moment to abandon their estates, leading to a decline in output, and in Jamaica it was as much a shortage of capital as labour that explained the fall in sugar output.

The coercion of labour did not prevent a small-scale peasantry from emerging. Sometimes this was because of the difficulty in enforcing coercive labour laws, as in Haiti, but more generally it was from the recognition that large-scale and small-scale agriculture were not necessarily opposed. Only the maroon and Amerindian communities in the Guianas could truly be said to have escaped the nexus of the plantation. Workers in most rural villages were still dependent on the demand for labour from the estates to meet their needs for cash income. This may not have been the reserve army of labour that many plantation owners would have preferred, but it was certainly preferable to acute labour shortages. And for those countries where it was still insufficient, there was always the option of inward migration.

3.4. INWARD MIGRATION

The combination of rising net births, especially after the 1850s, and coercion of the ex-slaves did not eliminate the scarcity of labour. In many countries, especially those where the death rate remained high and where a small-scale

---

[70] See Mintz (1974), chap. 3. See also Dietz (1986), pp. 42–7.

[71] See Figueroa (2005), chap. 5.

[72] Postemancipation labour scarcity and the coercive measures used by the state to resolve it are discussed in Scott (1985), chap. 9.

peasantry had emerged on the margins of the plantation economy, the labour shortage remained. Planters saw a bigger labour force as necessary not only for their own seasonal requirements, but also as a means of holding down wage rates. Their interest therefore turned to immigration schemes that could be used to replace the trade in slaves. The two inward migrations – slave and nonslave – even occurred at the same time in a few countries (notably Cuba).

The most important form of inward migration after the slave trade was indentured labour. These workers were required to work at a set wage rate for a fixed number of years and were therefore subject to coercion with very limited rights during the period of indenture.[73] They could then either return home, reindenture themselves or leave the plantations. Most chose the last course and became free workers. However, those that stayed usually sought to join the small-scale peasantry.[74] They did not therefore truly constitute a reserve army of labour, and the planters could not rely on them for their labour needs.

Because there was a major imbalance between male and female workers among indentured labourers, net births were often negative. In the 1850s, for example, deaths were ten times more numerous than births in Guadeloupe.[75] Because planters did not meet all the costs of the schemes, indenture depended on a government subsidy that diverted public revenue and imposed a tax burden on everyone.[76] Indentured labour therefore turned out to be an expensive, inefficient and inhumane way of tackling labour scarcity. After the first few years, the planters needed an enormous flow of indentured workers to secure a modest increase in the labour available for their estates.

As a result of its notoriety, much of the focus on inward migration has been almost exclusively on indentured labour. Yet there were many other types of inward migration. And, just as today, not all migrants stayed in their country of destination. What matters, therefore, in terms of economic analysis is migration from all sources adjusted for those that returned (net inward migration) expressed as a proportion of the population. Because net migration is the difference between population change and net births, it is possible to estimate it for most countries after 1850 (and for some before).[77]

One of the first countries that adopted a deliberate policy of encouraging nonslave inward migration was Haiti. In the early 1820s, 6,000 free blacks from the United States migrated to the island, encouraged by President Boyer's offer of land and other inducements. We do not know how many stayed, but

---

[73] The wage rate was fixed, but workers were only paid for the work performed. Because the rate was set per 'task' per day, the planter would not pay the rate if the 'task' had failed to be completed in the day. See Tinker (1993), pp. 183–7.

[74] One of the main attractions of staying was the chance to acquire land. This was usually beyond their possibilities if they returned to their countries of origin. In the case of Indian workers, see Look Lai (1993), chap. 8.

[75] See Blérald (1986), p. 225.

[76] The costs of indenture could run as high as 40% of public expenditure in some years. See Laurence (1994), pp. 528–9, for the case of Guyana.

[77] See Table A.6.

many settled in the area around Samaná Bay in what became the Dominican Republic after 1844.[78] As Haitians left the estates and started to form a small-scale peasant sector, other efforts were made to attract free black labour. Between 1860 and 1862, for example, James Redpath – a US immigrant from Scotland – worked tirelessly, if not very successfully, to bring free black colonists from the United States to Haiti.[79] More successful were the efforts of Haitian governments to attract settlers from other parts of the Caribbean.[80]

In other countries, inward migration was at first spontaneous rather than state-supported and involved intra-Caribbean movements of people. Free labour and owners of capital (in some cases with slaves) came to Puerto Rico even before the end of the slave trade, and the same was true of Cuba.[81] And the flows could go in reverse. During the First War of Independence (1868–78), many Cubans fled to the Dominican Republic.[82] An even larger number left the island during the Second War of Independence (1895–8), but most of these went back to Spain.[83] Haitians started to migrate to the Dominican Republic towards the end of the century, but the major outflow took place after 1900.

In the British Caribbean, the flows at first went from one British colony to another, although Trinidad also recorded over 2,000 Venezuelans in its 1871 census.[84] As early as 1851, the Guyanese census found 4,925 people that had been born in Barbados and 4,353 in the rest of the British West Indies (out of a total population of 135,994).[85] Barbados, where net births turned positive even before emancipation,[86] had become a surplus labour country early on, and most of these workers did not return. Others, however, came and went in a circular flow that was often linked to the crop harvest. The British authorities discouraged the outflow of workers from scarce labour countries, but they could not stop it.

Until the slave trade was finally ended, the colonial powers and the United States had to deal with the question of the *emancipados*. These were Africans taken illegally for slavery to the Caribbean and Brazil but recaptured before they could be sold. By the 1860s, their numbers had reached almost 150,000. They were taken either to Sierra Leone, if the ships carrying them were caught by the British navy near the West African coast, or to St Helena if intercepted in the South Atlantic. If captured in the Caribbean, they were usually taken to

[78] See Stephens (1974), pp. 40–71.
[79] See Boyd (1955). Redpath himself wrote a guide to Haiti. See Redpath (1861).
[80] The population was estimated by foreign consuls to include 3,000 of these Caribbean immigrants in the 1890s.
[81] For Puerto Rico, see Chinea (2005).
[82] See Lluberes Navarro (1978).
[83] See Santamaría and García (2004), p. 252.
[84] Trinidad also attracted a small number of free blacks from the US. See Brereton (1981), p. 97.
[85] See Moore (1987), p. 44.
[86] Higman (1984), p. 307, estimates that the net births among the slave population had become positive as early as 1810.

Havana to be dealt with by the mixed commission court.[87] Those that stayed in Cuba, and those sent to Puerto Rico, were supposed to become indentured labourers. However, it is widely assumed that many were reenslaved.[88]

Some of the *emancipados* taken to Havana were eventually sent to British colonies as indentured workers. By 1838, nearly 5,000 had been taken to the Bahamas where they worked alongside the slaves and were often only paid in rations.[89] The woodcutters in Belize in 1834 petitioned the authorities for 1,800 *emancipados* and received 459 two years later.[90] Most, however, went to the sugar-producing colonies. There they joined others who had been legally recruited in Africa after 1834. From then until 1867, nearly 40,000 Africans arrived in the British Caribbean.[91] Most of these indentured workers went to Guyana, Jamaica and Trinidad. The 1851 Guyana census, for example, listed 7,168 'immigrant Africans'.

In the French colonies, slavery ended in 1848, and the ex-slaves – as elsewhere – did what they could to leave the plantations. Following the restoration of the monarchy three years later, the French authorities approved a very cynical system for resolving the labour shortage in their Caribbean colonies. This was the purchase of slaves on the coast of Africa, who were then 'liberated' as indentured workers in the French colonies – often for periods as long as fourteen years. This scheme came to an end with the Anglo-French Convention of 1861, under which the French state renounced the recruitment of these *rachetés* workers in return for access to indentured labourers in British India (the supply of such workers from French India was too small to meet the needs of the French colonies).[92]

Indentured labour in the Caribbean has a long history, with English and French workers coming to European colonies as early as the seventeenth century. The 'push' factor was agricultural surplus labour in the metropolitan countries, and the 'pull' factor was labour scarcity in the Caribbean. What was different about indenture in the nineteenth century was the source countries of the workers and the huge scale of the inward migration. In addition to labour from Africa, indentured workers came in the thousands from China, India, Java and Madeira and in smaller numbers from the Yucatán peninsula and even Japan.

The Madeirans, Portuguese by nationality, started to arrive in the British Caribbean as indentured labourers in the 1830s. By far the most important destination was Guyana, but many other British colonies received them. Despite high death rates among the first immigrants, the numbers emigrating accelerated in the 1840s following a severe famine in Madeira. In the next decade,

---

[87] This had been established by treaty between Britain and Spain as part of the effort to suppress the illegal slave trade.

[88] See Murray (1980), pp. 279–80.

[89] See Johnson (1996), pp. 54–7.

[90] See Bolland (2001), pp. 603–4.

[91] See Look Lai (1993), table 5, p. 276.

[92] See Schmidt (1990), pp. 24–5.

the French colonies also began to receive indentured workers from Madeira. Altogether nearly 41,000 Madeirans went to the British colonies (32,000 to Guyana), with perhaps another 9,000 going elsewhere. For a small Atlantic island, this was an outmigration equivalent to what happened in Ireland after the potato famine in the 1840s.[93]

Chinese indentured workers were brought to Cuba in 1848, when slavery and the traffic in slaves were still very important. The number of arrivals then accelerated after 1853. The Chinese authorities, however, became increasingly concerned about their treatment, and the last migrants arrived in 1874.[94] By then, over 140,000 had left for Cuba, about 10 per cent dying on the voyage.[95] Because so few were female,[96] the net birth rate of these migrants was negative, and the Cuban census of 1899 recorded only 14,863.[97] Very few of these migrants to Cuba returned to China, and they gradually became absorbed into the general population.

Chinese indentured labour in the British Caribbean began in 1852, but it was never very large (it ended in the 1880s).[98] Most went to Guyana, with much smaller numbers entering Trinidad, Jamaica and Belize.[99] Migration from Java (a Dutch colony) into Suriname began in 1888. These workers were mainly of Chinese descent and came in sufficient numbers to play a significant part in the life of the colony in the twentieth century.[100] A much smaller number of Chinese indentured workers came to the French colonies.

Given the state of Chinese agriculture in the nineteenth century and its vast rural population, there was no shortage of potential workers. And the entrepôt ports of Hong Kong and Macao provided a convenient point of exit. However, the Chinese authorities were troubled by the reports of bad treatment and the high death rates; thus the metropolitan powers – Britain, France and Holland – came to look to British India as the main source of their indentured labour. In the case of the British colonies, a staggering 429,623 indentured workers

---

[93] Madeira had played a leading role in establishing the sugar plantation as a central part of the European economy in the fifteenth century. The population had expanded through immigration until sugar ceased to be profitable.

[94] The migration was suspended while an investigation was carried out on behalf of the Chinese emperor. This damning report was completed in 1876 and can be found in the Cuba Commission Report (1993).

[95] See Turner (1974).

[96] In the 1861 census, there were 34,771 males and only 57 females. See López (2006), table 5.1, p. 95.

[97] Among their number was the father of Wilfredo Lam, the great twentieth-century Cuban painter.

[98] It was suspended in 1866 following a dispute over an article in the Kung Convention between China, Britain and France. The article concerned the terms of repatriation. The dispute was eventually settled in 1872, and a small number of indentured labourers arrived in the British Caribbean in the next decade. See Look Lai (1998), p. 14.

[99] Antigua also received 100 Chinese in 1863, landed from a French vessel stranded off the coast. See Look Lai (1993), p. 276.

[100] See Hoefte (1998), pp. 60–70.

arrived from the 1830s until the scheme stopped during the First World War.[101] If we add those who came to the French colonies from British and French India and those who came to Suriname from British India, the number is close to 500,000.[102]

Guyana was the most important destination, with over half of all the indentured Indian labourers in British colonies. After 1865, the numbers arriving each quinquennium did not drop below 20,000 until the second half of the 1890s. And yet Guyana still suffered from scarce labour. This was partly because some returned to India (the inflow in the 1880s was over 44,000, but nearly 18,000 left), partly because the Indians left the plantations at the end of the period of indenture, and partly because the net births were so low (the CDR among the Indo-Guyanese never fell below 30).[103] The next most important destination was Trinidad, followed – at some distance – by Jamaica. These three countries accounted for 98 per cent of all Indian indentured workers arriving in the British Caribbean.[104]

Indian indentured workers started arriving in the French colonies in the early 1850s. They came from the French enclaves on the Indian subcontinent (such as Pondicherry). Over 10,000 had reached Martinique in the first decade.[105] Yet the supply from French India was too limited to meet the needs of the planters, and after 1861 most of the indentured workers came from British India before the scheme closed in the 1880s (1870s in French Guiana). By that time, over 42,000 Indians (from British and French India) had entered Guadeloupe, and yet the population of Indian descent was less than 16,000 in the 1890s.[106] The reason was not so much return migration as the extraordinary high CDR (68 in the 1850s, 77 in the 1860s and above 40 in the 1870s and 1880s).[107] One is left with the strong impression that the scheme was extremely costly in human and economic terms with very little benefit for the colonial economies. Only the subsidy provided by the colonial governments made it privately profitable.

The planters in Suriname were denied access to indentured workers from British India until towards the end of the period of state supervision. From that moment (1873) until the end of the century, about 25,000 arrived. Migration

---

[101] See Look Lai (1993), table 6, p. 276. It was ended in 1917 following a request of the Indian government, which was concerned over reports about the treatment of Indian migrants in the Caribbean.

[102] On Indian migration to French Guiana, see Mam-Lam-Fouck (2002), p. 64; to Martinique and Guadeloupe, see Renard (1993), pp. 161–9; and to Suriname, see Hoefte (1998). There were also 321 indentured labourers taken to the Danish Virgin Islands in 1862, but this experiment was not repeated. See Sircar (1971).

[103] CBRs and CDRs for the Indian migrants at different periods can be found in the Guyanese census for 1911.

[104] See Look Lai (1993), table 6, p. 276.

[105] See Brown (2002), p. 319.

[106] See Blérald (1986), p. 225. The total number reaching Martinique was smaller, at 25,509. See Vertovec (1995), p. 59. The Indian population in Martinique peaked at 13,189 in 1880 and had fallen to 4,793 by 1895.

[107] Derived from Blérald (1986), p. 225.

continued until 1917, but from the 1890s onwards the number of Javanese exceeded the number of Indians (Javanese migration went on until the Second World War). Return migration was low among the Indians and even lower among the Javanese. In addition, the arrival of the indentured labourers coincided with an improvement in public health in Suriname. The immigrant population was therefore able to increase through natural growth.[108]

The migration of free labour from outside the Caribbean was important mainly in the Spanish colonies, where workers and their families arrived in large numbers at different points in the century.[109] The first wave, in the 1820s, followed the proclamation of the *Real Cédula de Gracias* at the end of the Napoleonic Wars and involved not only Spaniards, but also many others from the rest of the Caribbean.[110] The second wave was in the 1850s when Spain followed a deliberate policy of white immigration to ensure racial 'balance' in its Caribbean colonies. The third wave, affecting only Cuba, was in the 1880s and 1890s. In this period, over 500,000 Spaniards came to Cuba, but most had left the island by the end of the century. Indeed, the net flow was negative in the second half of the 1890s.[111]

In Figure 3.4, net migration is shown for a sample of countries. Net inward migration (excluding the slave trade) accounted for more than 1 per cent of the population in several countries, a high figure by any standards. Cuba was not one of those countries, but it must be remembered that for most of the nineteenth century, the most important form of migration to Cuba was the illegal slave trade and that many of the nonslaves that arrived freely subsequently left. Among the British colonies, net inward migration as a proportion of the population regularly exceeded 2 per cent in Guyana and Trinidad. Net inward migration also exceeded 1 per cent on many occasions in Guadeloupe and Suriname.[112] Barbados, on the other hand, had net **outward** migration in every decade.

Immigration was so important in the nineteenth century that it changed forever the ethnic character of the population. In addition to the slaves transported illegally (800,000 after the Napoleonic Wars), there were perhaps another 100,000 migrants from Africa who landed as *emancipados*, *rachetés* workers

---

[108] See Hoefte (1998), p. 62.

[109] Free labour, as opposed to indentured labour, was not very important in numerical terms in the British, French or Dutch colonies. However, the tiny population of Belize expanded rapidly at several moments in the nineteenth century as a result of migrations from Guatemala and Mexico. These were free workers, but most came as refugees. See Shoman (2011). Free blacks from the US also came to Trinidad in small numbers before the end of slavery (those going to Haiti have already been mentioned).

[110] This law, promulgated in Puerto Rico in 1815 and in Cuba two years later, was intended to encourage capital and labour to migrate to the Spanish colonies and to provide greater security for investment.

[111] See Santamaría and García (2004), pp. 245–60.

[112] There were also occasional periods of high inward migration into the Bahamas (1836–40 and 1850s) and Belize (before 1860). See Table A.6.

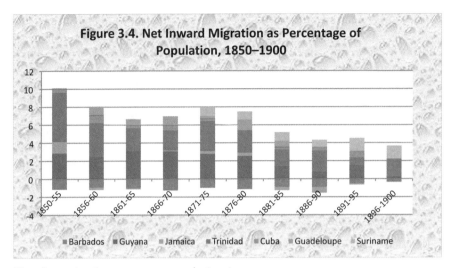

Figure 3.4. Net Inward Migration as Percentage of Population, 1850–1900

Note: A negative sign means net outward migration.
Source: Table A.6.

or indentured labourers. There were 500,000 indentured workers from British and French India and 200,000 from China and Java.[113] Perhaps 60,000 Madeirans came to the Caribbean (we know that 41,000 went to the British colonies),[114] and the number of Spaniards was probably close to 600,000 (it was 500,000 to Cuba alone in the last two decades of the century). If we also add the free blacks from the United States and a smaller number of whites, the Venezuelans who went to the neighbouring British colonies, the Mexicans who went to Cuba and Belize and Europeans other than those from Portugal and Spain, we reach a grand total of 2.3 million in a region that had a population of 2.5 million in 1810.

3.5. SURPLUS LABOUR, FREE LABOUR AND WAGE RATES

The transition from scarce to surplus labour in the nineteenth-century Caribbean was a lengthy process. It took many decades for improved public health, falling death rates, rising birth rates (sometimes) and inward migration to have an impact on the supply of labour. Yet by the 1890s, there were only a small number of countries – notably Cuba, Guyana, Suriname and Trinidad – where labour was still scarce. Elsewhere, labour coercion was in decline because employers were generally able to secure the workers they needed through the normal operations of the labour market.

---

[113] Some of these Indians and Javanese, however, came after 1900.
[114] See Look Lai (1993), table 5, p. 276. In addition, some Madeirans went to the Spanish, French and Dutch colonies.

After emancipation in the different colonies, planters had started to show more interest in laboursaving technological change. These innovations had made little economic sense during the period of slavery, but they became much more relevant in a wage labour setting. What held back the introduction of new technology in most countries was lack of access to credit, with the result that the demand for labour per unit of output did not fall very fast. As long as production was rising, the demand for labour therefore tended to increase. However, the crisis in the Caribbean sugar cane industry in the last two decades of the century (see Chapter 5) halted the rise in output in many countries and accelerated the introduction of laboursaving technologies in others. Surplus labour now became the norm in the Caribbean.

Surplus labour began early in a few countries. In Barbados, the former slaves started to leave the island immediately after the end of the apprenticeship period, and thousands had made their way to other colonies by mid-century. Yet there was still no shortage of labour, and the planters were able to increase output. In the Cayman Islands, after the end of the apprenticeship period, perhaps a quarter of the adult population left immediately for Bermuda and the Bay Islands off the coast of Honduras.[115] And the Bahamas lost over 5 per cent of its population in the 1840s, because opportunities for squatting were reduced by the movement to establish a system of labour tenancy and sharecropping.[116]

After mid-century, net outward migration spread to other countries.[117] Among the British colonies, Anguilla, Antigua, Bahamas, Barbados, the Virgin Islands, Dominica, Grenada, Montserrat, Nevis, St Kitts, St Lucia, St Vincent and the Turks & Caicos Islands all regularly experienced net outward migration. The same was true in Tobago, where many workers and planters moved to Trinidad to take advantage of the fertile lands that were now available. Jamaica turned from net inward to net outward migration in the 1880s.[118] By then most British colonies were experiencing surplus labour, a situation that has prevailed to this day. The only exceptions of note were Guyana and Trinidad.

Among the French colonies, net migration inwards had ceased by the end of the 1880s, and Guadeloupe experienced net outward migration after 1885. The population of the Scandinavian colonies steadily declined after 1850 – partly as a result of outward migration. The Dutch Antilles lost population through outward migration in the last two decades of the century, and the process started earlier in some of the islands.[119] Even in the Spanish colonies,

---

[115] See Craton (2003), chap. 6. The Bay Islands were a British colony until 1860.
[116] See Johnson (1996), chap. 5.
[117] See Table A.6.
[118] See Table A.6. See also Eisner (1961), pp. 140–51.
[119] The small island of Saba experienced its first wave of emigration, mainly to the US, in the 1870s. See Hartog (1975), p. 76.

outward migration took place in the 1890s, driven mainly by economics in Puerto Rico and by war (after 1895) in Cuba.

Where did the migrants go? Those countries where the sugar industry continued to flourish – Cuba, Guyana, Trinidad – remained important destinations for migrants (the sugar industry in Puerto Rico had stopped its spectacular growth in the 1860s). Jamaicans, in particular, were leaving for Cuba from the 1880s onwards. US investment in sugar mills in the Dominican Republic at the end of the century also created a strong demand for labour that could not be met locally. As many as 3,000 migrants are estimated to have come to the Dominican Republic in 1890 alone.[120]

Outside of the island economies, the Panama railway in the 1850s provided a new opportunity.[121] Many Barbadians took full advantage of this, even if they later returned to their island home. The French project to construct a canal across Panama in the 1880s depended heavily on imported labour from all parts of the Caribbean, especially Jamaica.[122] In that same decade, railway construction in Costa Rica and the associated rise of the banana industry on its Caribbean coast provided further opportunities.[123] By the last decades of the century, job opportunities in Florida were attracting migrants from the Caribbean, with Bahamanians settling first at Key West and later at Coconut Grove in Miami, and migrants from Cuba going to Key West and later Tampa. Puerto Ricans (and Cubans) even began to migrate to New York before the century ended.

Surplus labour meant that employers and the state no longer needed to rely on coercion to secure the labour they needed. Indentured labour was no longer necessary where surplus labour prevailed, and restrictions on access to land could also be eased. Antivagrancy laws, internal passports and other coercive instruments may have remained on the statute books, but they no longer needed to be applied with the same rigour. A labour force that was surplus to requirement – as demonstrated by net outward migration – could be relied on to fill any job vacancies at prevailing wage rates without the need for the coercive measures on which planters had relied earlier in the century.

Surplus labour meant that labour increasingly became 'free'. Even in the days of slavery, some labour had been free, and the end of slavery increased the number of workers who were not subject to coercion. Yet a glance at the occupational structure of the Caribbean (see Table 3.2) in the second half of the nineteenth century shows how little had changed since the beginning of the 1800s. The most important occupation by far was that of labourer, followed by mainly female occupations, such as domestic servants, dressmakers

---

[120] See Moya Pons (2007), p. 300.

[121] Completed in 1855, the construction of the Panama railway by US investors was only possible as a result of the import of Caribbean labour. See Petras (1988), chap. 3.

[122] This project failed through lack of finance, not a shortage of labour. When the project was restarted in 1904 with US capital, it would again depend on Caribbean labour. See Petras (1988), chap. 4.

[123] The first Jamaicans arrived in Costa Rica in the 1870s. See Chomsky (1996), chap. 1.

TABLE 3.2. *Occupational Structure in the Caribbean (%):*
Selected Countries

Country	Year	Labourers	Domestics	Laundry Workers
Cuba	1861	91.0(a)	na	na
	1899	57.7	22.8(b)	3.6
Guyana	1861	70.4	9.1	na
	1871	71.8	6.2	na
Jamaica	1844	71.5	12.8	na
	1891	62.8	13.5	na
Suriname	1887	66.1(c)	5.2	4.3
	1899	69.8(c)	3.9	2.7
Trinidad	1861	63.9	4.6	na
	1881	62.4	5.5	4.3

Note: (a) the sum of *trabajadores, industriales y jornaleros*; (b) *servicios
domésticos y personales*; (c) includes small farmers and workers in the
gold industry.

Source: For Cuba, Instituto de Investigaciones Estadísticas (1988); for
Guyana and Trinidad, *Parliamentary Papers*; for Jamaica, Eisner (1961);
and for Suriname, *Surinaamsche Almanak*.

and laundry workers. Other occupations, such as public officials, teachers, mechanics and shopkeepers, were of minor importance. Securing a sufficient supply of **unskilled** labourers was the overwhelming concern of the Caribbean elite in the nineteenth century.

The labourers, who dominated the employment structure in all countries, were mainly employed on the plantations. And the plantation underpinned the whole economy. Its exports paid for imports, which provided the public revenue from which the basic functions of government were financed. Securing labour for the plantations was therefore seen by the planters and their state representatives as the sine qua non for survival. The traffic in slaves may have gradually given way to other forms of coercion, but the goal remained the same: to ensure an adequate supply of labour for the key sector of the economy. Only with the advent of surplus labour could the free operation of the labour market be relied upon to achieve this.

I have argued in this chapter that the labour market adjusted mainly through quantities rather than wage rates. The 'stickiness' of wage rates can be explained by the traffic in slaves, coercion and net migration (particularly indentured labour). It was also because granting access to land was often a more effective inducement to secure labour services than wages – thus labour shortages could just as easily be addressed by changing the terms on which those without title could work the land as by changing wage rates. Indeed, increasing wage rates could be perverse. Employers and state representatives in the Caribbean regularly referred to what today we would call a 'backward-bending supply curve of labour', by which is meant a reduction in the labour services offered

as the wage rate rose (workers being presumed to have a target income for cash and a higher wage rate allowing them to reach it with fewer hours worked).

After the end of slavery, the terms on which labour would be made available – especially for the export sector where slavery had been so crucial – had to be negotiated immediately. The first country to face this issue was Haiti, where coercion – tying the workers to the land – was seen as indispensable by the country's new rulers. The regulations may have been widely ignored, but there is no evidence of rising wage rates in the first decades after emancipation, when the export sector in Haiti was being reestablished. Access to estate lands in return for labour services was the primary means of inducement, and the same appears to have been true in the Dominican Republic. And when labour scarcity became acute in the Dominican Republic at the end of the century, it was tackled through inward migration – not through an increase in wage rates.

Yet it would be misleading to suggest that wage rate variations played no role at all. Antigua was the first British colony to address the issue, because the island's House of Assembly chose to abolish slavery in 1834 without the period of apprenticeship that all other British colonies adopted. A Contract Act was introduced, valid for one year, under which wages were set at 6d sterling per day, estate cottages were provided rent-free with small gardens, and medical services continued to be provided by the planters. Because most land was held in estates, it was assumed all the ex-slaves would have no choice but to sign contracts and accept the 'going wage'. However, within one year the estate labour force had fallen to two-thirds of its level under slavery, and by 1842 the wage rate had risen to 9d and by 1845 to 12d (double its level a decade earlier).[124] These wage rate increases caused panic among the planters, and a sustained campaign was launched to reduce them. By 1850, wage rates for estate workers were back to their level in 1835 and – with minor fluctuations (see Table A.8) – stayed at that level for the rest of the century.

The other British colonies, where apprenticeship ended in 1838, had a similar experience. Wage rates did rise at first,[125] because the ex-slaves held out for better terms and inward migration took many years to have an impact.[126] In these first few years, there was indeed a tendency for the labour market to clear through wage rates. However, as in Antigua, it did not last. By 1850, wage rates for estate workers had fallen everywhere compared with a decade earlier and were very stable for the rest of the century (see Figure 3.5). In Barbados, for example, the daily wage (8d) was the same in 1870 as in 1838 (the year of emancipation) and had only risen to 10d by 1900. Even Guyana and Trinidad (the scarce-labour countries par excellence) saw little improvement as a result of the downward pressure exerted by inward migration after 1850.

[124] See Hall (1971), chap. 3.
[125] The wage rate was usually set per task rather than per day.
[126] See Rivière (1972), passim.

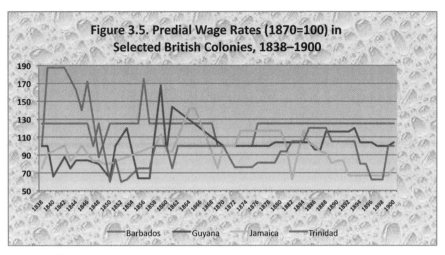

Source: Table A.8.

What did vary were the estate wage rates **across** the different British colonies. At the end of the 1840s, rates varied from 25d and 20d per day in Trinidad and Guyana, respectively, to a low of 6–7d in Antigua, Barbados, Montserrat and Tobago. with Dominica, Jamaica, Nevis, St Kitts, St Lucia and St Vincent somewhere in the middle.[127] In 1870, rates still varied from 8d per day in Barbados to 25d in Guyana. Trinidad (20d) was the closest to Guyana, Jamaica was in the middle (18d) and Dominica and Grenada (both 9d) were at the bottom with Barbados. This range of wage rates barely altered through the century after emancipation, suggesting that coercion and migration were very powerful in preventing the labour market from clearing through the price mechanism.

Coercion and inward migration were intended mainly to help the estates secure the labour needed for export agriculture. It might be assumed, therefore, that wage rates for skilled workers ('trades') would be more flexible, rising and falling according to supply and demand. Using data for the British colonies, there is not much evidence that this was the case.[128] Wage rates were very stable in most countries, and in some cases extremely so (in Barbados the daily wage – 30d – was the same in 1900 as in 1838!). Once the 'going rate' had been established in postslavery British colonies, net migration coupled with market inertia conspired to keep the nominal rates unchanged.

The inertia in nominal wage rates caused living standards to rise when prices were falling and to fall when prices were rising. A cost-of-living index constructed for Jamaica suggested that prices were falling from emancipation

---

[127] See Rivière (1972), p. 29.
[128] See Table A.9.

until 1850, rising until 1870 and remained stationary thereafter.[129] A cost-of-living index constructed using wholesale prices in the core shows similar trends, except that they imply a fall in prices after 1870.[130]

The numbers are not robust enough to draw very firm conclusions, but they do suggest that the first few years after emancipation were favourable for workers (rising wage rates and falling prices). This is the period when planters' complaints about labour supply reached a peak, leading them to economise on the use of labour and to promote immigration schemes. The period between 1850 and 1870 was very unfavourable (stagnant or falling wage rates and rising prices); it is surely no accident that these years coincided with some of the most violent social explosions in the Caribbean, such as the Morant Bay rebellion in Jamaica in 1865.[131] Finally, the period after 1870 was associated with constant or modestly rising real wage rates. However, wage rates in this period were not necessarily a guide to total wage earnings, because the amount of work on offer was affected by the commodity cycle. The crisis in the sugar industry led to a sharp reduction in labour requirements – riots were common.[132]

In the French and Danish colonies after emancipation, wage rates appear to have been even less important in clearing the market than in the British Caribbean. The labour laws in the Danish Virgin Islands specified in great detail the wage rate for every task, and labour services in the French Antilles were secured largely through varying the terms on which the ex-slaves were granted access to land (sharecropping being common).[133] In the Dutch colony of Suriname, indentured labour was introduced so quickly after the end of state supervision in 1873 that there does not seem to have been even the brief spike in wage rates that took place in the British colonies after the end of the apprenticeship period.[134]

Emancipation may have been delayed longer in the Spanish Caribbean than elsewhere, but – unlike the case of the other European colonies – slaves were never a majority of the labour force. Thus, the issue of securing an adequate supply of nonslave labour had arisen early in the nineteenth century. This was especially problematic outside the sugar estates (unskilled labour was predominantly slave in the sugar industry). In Puerto Rico, in the first half of the century, labour was secured primarily through access to land, with the *agregados* entitled to settle on estates in return for various labour services. Following the

---

[129] See Eisner (1961), pp. 376–7.
[130] I have used core wholesale prices to approximate import prices for each country (see Table A.30).
[131] On the Morant Bay uprising, see Green (1976), chap. 13. See also Heuman (1994).
[132] There were frequent complaints in Guyana, for example, about the lack of estate work on offer at prevailing wage rates in the last two decades of the century. See Rodney (1981), chap. 2.
[133] By the end of the century, wage rates for estate workers were as little as 15 to 19 US cents per day (see Hill, 1898, p. 356). This was the sterling equivalent of around 9d and was therefore lower even than Barbados.
[134] On wage rates in Curaçao, see Römer (1981), chap. 2.

1849 law designed to force the *agregados* to become *jornaleros*, wage labour became more important. It was not until the end of slavery in 1873, however, that wage rates started to increase. In the coffee-growing regions, neither coercion nor migration appears to have been able to prevent a steady rise in wage rates up to the end of the century.[135]

In Cuba, where the *patronato* did not end until 1886, wage rates started to play a role at a much earlier stage. Indeed, a wage index has been constructed for the island starting in 1872.[136] As in the British colonies, nominal wage rates did not show much variation before the Second War of Independence (1895–8). However, the cost-of-living index showed a decline over this period, implying an increase in real wage rates. Undoubtedly, this was one of the factors encouraging inward migration from other parts of the Caribbean and from Spain and the Canary Islands. Because Cuba was the country with the most severe labour shortage in the Caribbean, it would not be surprising if variations in real wage rates – if not nominal wage rates – played at least some part in clearing the labour market, even if it was less important than quantity adjustments.

[135] See Bergad (1983a), pp. 83–100.
[136] See Santamaría and García (2004), cuadro II.22, pp. 354–6. The interested reader should note, however, that the index of real wages and the index of nominal wages have been put in the wrong order.

4

Global Commodity Trade and Its Implications for the Caribbean

The Caribbean economies, at the start of the nineteenth century, bore all the hallmarks of 300 years of European colonialism. The indigenous population had been wiped out by war or disease and replaced by a labour force whose main activity was the production of commodities for export. The land was either devoted to exports or to products such as ground provisions and cattle-grazing that supported exports indirectly. The capital was invested either directly in the export sector or in the infrastructure needed to bring the main commodities to market. Only in the Spanish colonies – Cuba and Puerto Rico – was there a significant small-scale peasantry concentrating on the domestic market, and this was a consequence of imperial neglect rather than a deliberate policy of encouraging an internal market.

No other region of the world was so specialised in exports. The mainland colonies of Latin America had also been subjected to 300 years of colonial exploitation, but many of them had large indigenous or *mestizo* populations engaged in agricultural production for themselves or for the internal market. The same was true of the African and Asian economies, whether they were independent, such as Ethiopia and Thailand, recently colonised, such as Natal in South Africa and Bengal in India, or long-standing European colonies, such as the Philippines. Only the Caribbean had economies where virtually all factors of production were devoted either directly or indirectly to exports.

The export sector is therefore the key to understanding the Caribbean economies in the nineteenth century, and its analysis forms the basis of this and the next chapter. In order to do so, I have constructed a database at decennial intervals covering volumes, prices and values of the leading commodities for all countries. This is contained in the Statistical Appendix.[1] These tables

---

[1] Table A.10 contains the commodity volume and value data for each country. The Notes on A. Tables explain the methodology and give sources. All values are in US dollars ($) unless otherwise specified.

distinguish, as far as possible, between domestic exports and re-exports in order that the underlying trends are not distorted by the entrepôt trade.

In this chapter, I first offer a snapshot of the Caribbean economies in 1820 following the end of the Napoleonic Wars. This identifies the ten leading commodities that accounted for over 95 per cent of domestic exports by value at that time. It is these commodities, together with a couple that would be added later, that would largely determine the evolution of the Caribbean economies over the course of the century, and their international market conditions are explored in the second section of the chapter. This is followed by an examination of changes in core trade policies towards these products. The chapter closes with an analysis of world prices and technical change for the leading commodities.

4.1. CARIBBEAN EXPORTS IN 1820

The disruptions in the Caribbean associated with the Napoleonic Wars ended long before hostilities ceased – French naval power was destroyed in 1805 at the Battle of Trafalgar, and the British navy reigned supreme. The remaining problems were the US trade embargo imposed in 1808 onwards and the impact of war between the UK and the United States from 1812 to 1814. By 1820, production of the main commodities had recovered in most countries. The main exception was the sugar industry in Haiti, where efforts by the leadership of the newly independent country to revive the industry largely failed.[2]

Exports can be measured in current or constant prices. I have used 1860 prices for the constant price series because this is midway between the beginning (1820) and the end (1900) of the nineteenth-century series. They can also be expressed as domestic or merchandise, the difference being accounted for by re-exports. Treating re-exports in the same way as domestic exports can be very misleading, but at the same time they should not be ignored completely. Because the entrepôt trade is the export of a service, I have calculated its value as 10 per cent of re-exports and added it to domestic exports in some cases. Exports can also be expressed in per capita terms.[3]

Domestic exports from the Caribbean reached $70 million in 1820 at current prices, and re-exports were valued at nearly $8 million. Merchandise exports were therefore nearly $80 million.[4] Expressed at constant (1860) prices, they were actually lower in 1820 because prices of the main commodities fell on average between 1820 and 1860.[5] These numbers may seem low, but the United

---

[2] The Haitian story is told in more detail in Chapter 7. The sugar industry did not disappear completely, but it was limited in the main to supplying the domestic market and producing molasses for the manufacture of rum.

[3] Using the population figures in Table A.1a.

[4] See Table A.11 for domestic exports, Table A.12 for re-exports and Table A.13 for merchandise exports.

[5] Domestic exports at 1860 prices (see Table A.14) were valued at $55 million.

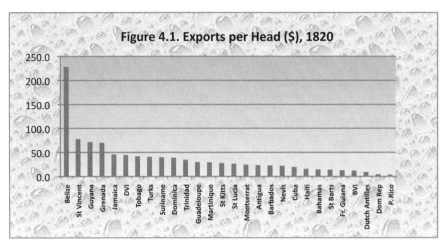

Note: Exports are defined as domestic exports plus 10% of re-exports.
Source: Derived from Tables A.1a, A.11 and A.12.

States in 1820 had domestic exports at current prices of only $52 million and re-exports of $18 million.[6] At the time, the US population was 9.6 million compared to 2.6 million in the Caribbean.[7] So the Caribbean, with about one-quarter of the US population, exceeded US domestic exports by about one-third.

When expressed in per capita terms, the scale of Caribbean export specialisation is even more striking. The United States in 1820 had domestic exports per head of $5.4, but the figure in the Caribbean was $26.6.[8] If we add 10 per cent of re-exports to domestic exports, the figures rise to $5.6 for the United States and $26.9 for the Caribbean. If it is argued that the United States was already moving away from export-led growth, with more emphasis on the internal market and less on exports,[9] it should be pointed out that even in Latin America in 1830 (ten years later) exports per head in Argentina, Brazil and Mexico were only $2.0, $4.4 and $1.8, respectively.[10]

Of course, not all Caribbean countries had such high levels of domestic exports per head. The range was enormous – from a low of $3.5 in Puerto Rico to a high of $217 in Belize. The results for all countries, this time including 10 per cent of re-exports, are given in Figure 4.1. The lowest levels were recorded by those countries that had been neglected by the colonial powers.

[6] See Carter (2006), vol. 5.
[7] For the US, see Carter (2006), vol. 1; for the Caribbean, see Table A.1.
[8] For the US, derived from Carter (2006), vol. 1 and vol. 5. For the Caribbean, derived from Table A.1a and Table A.11.
[9] Even this is not strictly true, because exports as a share of US GDP only started to fall after mid-century.
[10] See Prados de la Escosura (2006), p. 490.

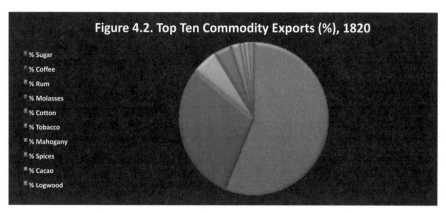

Figure 4.2. Top Ten Commodity Exports (%), 1820

% Sugar
% Coffee
% Rum
% Molasses
% Cotton
% Tobacco
% Mahogany
% Spices
% Cacao
% Logwood

Source: Derived from Table A.18.

These included Cuba, the Dominican Republic and Puerto Rico, although Cuba had started to receive much more attention; French Guiana; the Dutch Antilles; and the Swedish colony of St Barthélemy, whose prosperity, like the islands of the Dutch Antilles, had depended on an entrepôt trade, which was much diminished after the Napoleonic Wars. Two British colonies (the Bahamas and the British Virgin Islands) also had low exports per head. The former depended heavily on re-exports, and the latter had never truly prospered as a sugar colony.

At the other end of the spectrum, with exports per head close to or well above the Caribbean average, were Suriname, the Danish Virgin Islands and a variety of British colonies. These included the long-established colony of Jamaica and the newly established one of Guyana. Pride of place, however, in Figure 4.1 goes to Belize, whose tiny population was dedicated to timber exports and the entrepôt trade with Central America and whose exports per head in 1820 were by far the highest in the Caribbean.[11]

It is often assumed that Haitian exports collapsed even before independence in 1804. As Figure 4.1 shows, this was not the case. Of course, exports and exports per head were far lower in 1820 than 1790, before the revolutionary war began, but this is hardly surprising. As St-Domingue, Haiti had been an artificial construct in which all factors of production were dedicated to exports – by force in the case of labour – with a highly protected market in France. What is interesting therefore about Figure 4.1 is its demonstration that an export sector **had** survived in Haiti despite the upheavals of the revolutionary war, independence and the loss of the protected French market. Indeed, Haitian exports per head in 1820 were only a little lower than those of Cuba.

The Caribbean economies had been developed as colonies to serve the needs of the European imperial powers. Over the years, sugar had come to be the leading export for the region as a whole. This is confirmed by Figure 4.2, which shows that sugar alone accounted for more than 50 per cent of the

[11] This is one reason why Belize is made a case study in Chapter 11.

value of domestic exports at current prices in 1820.[12] There is a convention that molasses and rum should be added to this figure on the grounds that they are derived from sugar. This, however, is misleading. Molasses, it is true, is a by-product of sugar production, but its price moved independently of sugar (see section 4 of this chapter), and it could be either exported (usually to make rum) or sold domestically for rum or as a cattle-feed. Rum, on the other hand, is not even a by-product of sugar and should always be treated as a separate commodity.[13]

After sugar, by far the most important export commodity in 1820 was coffee (see Figure 4.2). This was produced by many Caribbean countries and had been a staple export for many years. It represented nearly 30 per cent of domestic exports by value; thus sugar and coffee combined accounted for over 80 per cent of the total. Coffee was followed – at some distance – by rum and molasses, bringing the cumulative total for these four products to just under 90 per cent. The other principal exports in Figure 4.2 were all relatively minor in 1820. Cotton, grown in many islands and the Guianas, accounted for nearly 2 per cent, and tobacco leaf – grown mainly in the Spanish colonies and the Dominican Republic[14] – for nearly 1 per cent. That left logwood (a dyewood) and mahogany, which were exported by only a few countries, cacao[15] (exported by many countries) and spices. Other exports, such as cigars and gold, were not yet in the top ten by value.

These ten products accounted for nearly 95 per cent of all domestic exports in 1820. All, with the exception of cotton, would remain important contributors to domestic exports throughout the nineteenth century, but other exports would be added to the list. The remaining exports were sometimes important for individual countries, but not for the Caribbean as a whole. They included the ginger and pimento exported from Jamaica, sponges and dyewoods from the Bahamas, hides from the Dominican Republic, arrowroot (a starch powder) from St Vincent, annatto (a food colouring) from French Guiana, cattle and livestock from the British Virgin Islands, salt from the Turks & Caicos Islands and pineapples from St Barthélemy.

The seventeen British colonies[16] were the major source of Caribbean exports in 1820, accounting for 55 per cent of all domestic exports and a much higher

---

[12] See Table A.17 for the numbers.

[13] Rum is derived from sugarcane, but it is not a by-product because the volume of production is determined independently of the output of sugar.

[14] As Santo Domingo, the Dominican Republic was a Spanish colony in 1820. However, as explained in the Notes on A. Tables, I have reserved the term 'Spanish colonies' for Cuba and Puerto Rico only.

[15] I prefer 'cacao' to 'cocoa' to describe Caribbean exports in order to avoid confusion with the processed product. It is also botanically correct.

[16] In Chapter 3, where demographic trends are examined, I was able to distinguish nineteen British colonies. In this and subsequent chapters in Part I, the number is reduced to seventeen because it is impossible to separate Anguilla from St Kitts and the Cayman Islands from Jamaica in the trade data (see Notes on A. Tables). The population data for Anguilla and the Cayman Islands have therefore been added to St Kitts and Jamaica, respectively, in order to calculate exports per head. See Table A.1a.

proportion of re-exports. They were followed by the two Spanish colonies (Cuba and Puerto Rico), with nearly 20 per cent, Hispaniola (Haiti and the Dominican Republic), with nearly 10 per cent, the three French colonies, with 9 per cent, and the remainder divided between the two Dutch and the two Scandinavian colonies. This was, however, the high point of British colonialism in the Caribbean. As we shall see in the next chapter, the British share would fall sharply during the course of the nineteenth century – it would never recover.

Nearly half of all domestic exports from the British colonies came from one country – Jamaica. This jewel in the British crown was responsible for one-quarter of all Caribbean domestic exports in 1820, and the exports were diversified. Sugar may have been the most important commodity, but coffee, ginger, pimento, logwood, molasses and rum – to name only a few – were also significant. Second in importance – with 18 per cent of the total – was Cuba, whose exports were also diversified (the age of sugar monoculture would come later). Third – at some distance – was Guyana, whose exports came from the three former Dutch colonies of Demerara, Essequibo and Berbice. Fourth was Haiti, with 9 per cent of the Caribbean's domestic exports, derived principally from coffee, but also cotton, logwood and cacao. Only the smallest countries of the Caribbean, such as Montserrat and Nevis, were at this stage victims of monoculture.[17]

Trade ties to the imperial country remained strong in 1820.[18] Over 80 per cent of exports from the French colonies went to France. For the British colonies, the share of exports going to the UK was nearly 75 per cent, and for the Dutch colonies the share going to Holland was nearly 80 per cent. Denmark and Sweden also absorbed a high share of the domestic exports of their Caribbean colonies. Spain, on the other hand, liberalised trade with Cuba and Puerto Rico after the Seven Years' War (1756–63) and again after the Napoleonic Wars. As a result, the share of exports going to Spain from the Spanish colonies in 1820 was less than 40 per cent.

For the United States, keen to reestablish its strong trading links with the Caribbean destroyed by the War of Independence, these colonial ties were a major impediment.[19] Its best hope in 1820 lay with the Spanish and Scandinavian colonies and Hispaniola.[20] In Chapter 5, we shall examine the geographical trade patterns in the Caribbean. Here we may note that the United States in 1820 was already purchasing nearly 15 per cent of exports from the Spanish colonies, despite the discriminatory tariffs imposed by Spain favouring metropolitan ties (see section 3 in this chapter). And in Haiti, the only part

[17] See Table A.10.
[18] See Table A.22, which records the share of exports going to the 'mother' country.
[19] The share of exports going to the US is given in Table A.20.
[20] The Bahamas, which included the Turks & Caicos Islands until 1848, also offered opportunities as a result of their geographical proximity and their ability to supply US ships with salt.

of the Caribbean where the United States could be said to face a level playing field, exports to the United States reached 36 per cent of the total in 1820.[21]

Even economies specialised in exports have nonexport sectors. We know much less about the nonexport sectors in the Caribbean in 1820 than we do about exports, but we do have a detailed picture of Jamaica a decade later in 1832.[22] Although exports accounted for over 40 per cent of GDP at current prices, an additional 20 per cent came from food production for local consumption and over 10 per cent from ownership of houses. Only 6 per cent came from manufacturing and the same from public administration, with a slightly lower share from wholesale and retail distribution. Services, including domestic service, provided the missing entries.

Jamaica may have been the most important Caribbean economy in 1820, at least based on the value of its domestic exports, but its structure is likely to have been representative of most of the other countries. So it is fairly safe to assume that exports accounted for at least 40 per cent of GDP almost everywhere at that time.[23] Given the close ties between exports on the one hand and ground provisions, distribution, housing and public administration on the other, it is not unreasonable to argue that the key to economic performance in the nineteenth-century Caribbean lay with the export sector.

4.2. DEMAND FOR AND SUPPLY OF LEADING COMMODITIES

We have seen that the ten leading export commodities in 1820 accounted for nearly 95 per cent of all domestic exports by value. In the second half of the nineteenth century, they would be joined by two others – bananas and gold. Together, these twelve commodities accounted for over 90 per cent of domestic exports by value in almost all years. In constant (1860) prices, however, the share remained over 95 per cent for the whole period.[24] The economic fortunes of the Caribbean in the nineteenth century were therefore intimately linked to the international markets in these dozen products.

Of the external factors that shaped the environment in which the leading Caribbean commodities were traded, five were of especial importance: demand and supply, which will be considered in this section; core commercial policies, which will be explored in the next section; prices and technological change, which will be examined in the final section. Of course, none of this is predetermined, and a country could fail to respond to favourable external conditions or indeed could rise above unfavourable ones. These other – internal – factors

---

[21] The playing field was not level for Haiti, however, because its sailors were not infrequently thrown into gaol in southern US ports by virtue of their colour. This led Haiti in the 1830s to impose discriminatory tariffs on the US. See Turnbull (1840), p. 69.

[22] See Eisner (1961), pp. 25–42.

[23] In Haiti the share was probably lower, but the export sector – as we have seen – was still important in 1820.

[24] All these data are in Table A.18, which records the shares of domestic exports for the Caribbean at current and constant prices.

will be considered in the next chapter, but here we are concerned only with the external environment.

The twelve leading commodities were all based on natural resources. Some – such as tobacco leaf, coffee and cacao – were primary products in the purest sense; others – such as sugar and rum – were really manufactured products, but they are often described as primary. Cigars were clearly manufactured, capable of being branded and the product of an industry whose output was not homogeneous. On the other hand, tobacco leaf from Cuba – especially from the *vuelta abajo*[25] – sold at a substantial premium versus other types of tobacco, so that even 'pure' primary products were not always homogeneous. It is therefore important not to oversimplify in any analysis of the international markets in which these products were sold.

Global demand rose rapidly for many of the leading Caribbean commodities in the nineteenth century. If we divide the period into two (1820–60 and 1860–1900), demand was strong in the first period for all the commodities on which we have satisfactory data and stronger in the second.[26] With population in the core countries rising at 1 per cent per year and income per head also growing at around 1 per cent (see Chapter 2), an annual increase in core import demand for commodities in excess of 2 per cent implied an income elasticity in excess of unity.[27] This was the case for many commodities of special interest to the Caribbean.

Sugar, the most important Caribbean export throughout the period, was perhaps the star performer. The annual increase in global demand (see Figure 4.3) rose from 3.7 per cent in the first period to 4 per cent in the second.[28] The consumption figures for individual core countries tell a similar story. It rose from 17 lbs per person per year in the UK in the 1820s to nearly 40 lbs in the 1860s and around 80 lbs in 1900.[29] In the United States, sugar imports went from 60 million lbs in 1821 to nearly 700 million in 1860 and over 4 billion in 1900.[30] At first, increased consumption could be attributed to direct

---

[25] This part of Cuba, so named from its similarity on a map to the lower part of an ecclesiastical arch, had been recognised for centuries as capable of producing tobacco leaf of a finer quality than anywhere else in the world. See Stubbs (1985), p. 15. It was also an area unsuitable for sugarcane.

[26] Ideally, we would have consistent data on global import growth for the commodities of interest to the Caribbean. Figures on global export growth are acceptable as a proxy for global import growth, but in the case of raw cotton (up to 1860) and tobacco I have used US exports because the US supplied such a high proportion of the total.

[27] Income elasticity is measured as the percentage increase in the quantity demanded divided by the percentage increase in real income.

[28] Global import demand has here been approximated by global production (excluding production for domestic use in British India). For figures on world sugar imports and exports in 1900, see Chalmin (1990), p. 15, table 1.10.

[29] See Deerr (1949), vol. 2, p. 532.

[30] See Carter (2006), vol. 5. These figures imply consumption of imported sugar per person of 6 lbs in the 1820s, 22 lbs in the 1860s and 52 lbs in 1900. These figures, however, do not

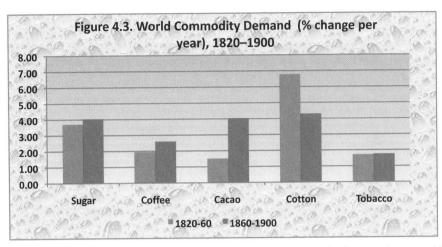

Note: Global demand has been approximated as follows: for sugar, the figures refer to world production (excluding Indian domestic consumption). The numbers are derived from Moreno Fraginals (1978), vol. 3, p. 35, for 1820–40 and Chalmin (1990), p. 8, for 1850–1900. For coffee, the figures refer to world exports and are derived from Thurber (1881) for 1820–70 and Holloway (1980) for later years. For cacao, the figures refer to global exports and are derived from Clarence-Smith (2000), app. 2. For tobacco, the figures refer to US exports only and are derived from Carter (2006), vol. 5. For cotton, the figures for 1820–65 are also from Carter (2006) and refer to US exports only, but the figures for 1865–1900 are from Lewis (1978), app. 3, p. 277, and refer to world production.

use by households, but towards the end of the century the food processing industry became an increasingly important source of demand for sugar in all the core countries.[31]

The second most important commodity for the Caribbean in 1820 was coffee, and there the story was similar – if not so spectacular. The annual increase in global demand (see Figure 4.3) rose from 1.9 per cent in the first period to 2.6 per cent in the second. Coffee, therefore, was also an income-elastic good – at least in the second half of the century – and consumption per head rose steadily in all core countries. What was once a luxury commodity became over the course of the century a staple of the metropolitan diet. By the last quarter of the century, consumption per head exceeded 10 lbs per year in several northern European countries and was only a little lower in the United States.[32] In those nations still addicted to tea, however, the consumption of

take into account sugar grown in the US itself. This would add another 10 lbs to the total in 1900.

[31] UK imports of sugar in 1900 were 1,649,000 tons, and industrial sugar consumption in that year was around 650,000 tons. See Chalmin (1990), pp. 14–15.

[32] It had reached 10 lbs per head by 1900, however. See Uribe (1954), p. 38.

coffee lagged behind. In the UK, for example, it reached only 1 lb per head around 1880.[33]

The other leading commodities for which global demand soared in the nineteenth century included cacao, cotton and tobacco (see Figure 4.3). Consumption of cacao rose slowly in the first period, when it was used primarily as a beverage by households. However, the rise of the chocolate industry changed all that, and the derived demand for cacao soared. Spain led the way until 1890 with the highest consumption per head in Europe, but the UK started to catch up with consumption per head rising sixfold in the four decades after 1870, and Germany and France also increased consumption. US consumption per head also rose, but it was still far below the levels in the core European countries by 1900.[34]

The demand for raw cotton was derived from the textile and clothing industry, which expanded rapidly in the nineteenth century. Indeed, cotton-based products were almost always income-elastic in this period; thus the growth of raw cotton exports was very fast. The industry in Britain, albeit at the expense in part of the Indian textile and clothing industry, led the field, but other core countries were quick to follow. Tobacco growth was not so spectacular, but the growing demand for cigars and later cigarettes in the nineteenth century raised consumption per head to previously unheard of levels. Consumption per head in the second period rose by 56 per cent in the UK, 24 per cent in France and 23 per cent in Germany. However, US consumption per head rose by 240 per cent in these years, jumping from 1.8 lbs in the years after the Civil War to over 5 lbs by 1900.[35]

The two new Caribbean exports – bananas and gold – that came on stream in the second half of the nineteenth century also performed well in terms of global demand. Gold benefitted greatly from the demonetisation of silver in the 1870s and the switch to the gold standard by a growing number of countries. Bananas, at least in the United States, went from luxury status to an article of everyday consumption in the last few decades of the nineteenth century. By 1900, exports from Latin America and the Caribbean were estimated at 20.1 million bunches, and it is safe to assume that most of this went to the United States.[36]

The global demand for commodities of interest to the Caribbean was therefore generally favourable, but there were a few disappointments. The demand for rum as measured by imports was weak. British imports, for example, actually fell in the two decades after 1830. By the end of the first period, the UK

---

[33] Consumption figures for the main core countries can be found in Thurber (1881), p. 241.

[34] Figures on chocolate consumption can be found in Clarence-Smith (2000), pp. 10–31. Per capita figures can be derived from his figures in table 3.7, p. 56.

[35] See Jacobstein (1907), p. 44. By the end of the century, US consumption per head was one of the highest in the world (Belgium was a little higher) and nearly three times higher than the UK.

[36] See Lloyd Jones (1931), p. 139.

was importing annually less than one-third of a gallon per person, and much of this was re-exported.[37] French consumption of rum was boosted temporarily by the diseases that struck its wine industry, but by the end of the century consumption per head was less than a litre per head.[38] And US rum consumption, as with spirits generally, was held back by the spread of the Temperance movement.

If the demand environment facing Caribbean exporters was generally benign, the same could not be said for supply. As a region specialised in exports from the beginning of European colonisation, the Caribbean was always going to be vulnerable to the rise of new sources of supply with lower costs and better access to the markets of Europe. As we shall see, this was indeed the case. However, the Caribbean faced an additional problem on the supply side through the emergence of products that could be easily substituted for the region's output. By the end of the nineteenth century, these two threats were causing problems for most countries in the Caribbean.

The problem was particularly acute for the Caribbean cane sugar exporters. With over 80 per cent of world sugar demand still being met by Caribbean exports in 1820, it was physically impossible for the region to maintain market share as global imports surged. Cane sugar exports expanded rapidly throughout the British empire, starting in Mauritius and spreading to British India, Natal in South Africa and Queensland in Australia. Dutch demand far outstripped the ability of Suriname to meet domestic consumption, which was able to supply less than 10 per cent of requirements even in 1860, and the Netherlands East Indies emerged as a far more important source of supply. The French Caribbean colonies could not match the growth of cane sugar exports in other parts of the French empire, such as Réunion, and French colonial supply as a whole failed to keep pace with French demand.

The European core countries could not produce sugar from cane themselves.[39] However, the United States **could**, and domestic production rose rapidly in Louisiana after 1820, reaching a peak in the first year of the Civil War. Domestic output then fell with the abolition of slavery, but the United States found a new source of cane sugar in the Hawaiian Islands, which became 'domestic' after the incorporation of Hawaii as a territory in 1898.

The Caribbean could probably have coped with the rise of new cane sugar producers. The market was growing rapidly, and there were profits to be made by all suppliers. However, the emergence of beet sugar posed a very different threat. Although the industry had existed since the late eighteenth century

---

[37] By the end of the second period in 1900 consumption per head was down to one-tenth of a gallon. See Smith (2005), p. 208, for this and other rum consumption figures.

[38] See Smith (2005), pp. 208–14.

[39] That is not strictly true, because sugarcane can be, and was, grown in the Atlantic islands belonging to Spain and Portugal. The European sugar industry had actually started in these islands – the Canaries, Madeira and the Azores – but they were not dynamic sources of supply in the nineteenth century.

and had been promoted during the Napoleonic Wars, beet sugar – a perfect substitute for cane sugar – did not gain a major foothold on the European continent until Russian grain exports drove grain prices down and led farmers in Western and Central Europe to search for alternative crops. As a result, and helped by tax policies (see section 3 of this chapter), beet sugar represented 20 per cent of world sugar production by 1860.

Even this might have been manageable for the Caribbean. However, a further fall in grain prices after the US Civil War provoked by the rise in exports from the North American prairies and the South American pampas encouraged European farmers to expand beet sugar production. The fiscal system of many European powers encouraged output growth, and the spectacular rise of the beet sugar industry dates from this period. By 1870 beet sugar had captured 35 per cent of the global sugar market and 60 per cent by 1890.[40] Cane sugar, yet alone Caribbean cane sugar, was very much in second place.

Caribbean coffee exports represented 28 per cent of world imports in 1820 – not as high a share as in the case of sugar, but still very significant. The European core countries promoted the industry in their colonies outside the Caribbean, but it was in the independent countries of Latin America where the main expansion took place. Coffee production and exports became established in Central America and Colombia and rose rapidly in Brazil – so much so that by 1880, nearly 60 per cent of world production was located there. Even the abolition of slavery in 1888 had no effect on the seemingly inexorable expansion of Brazilian coffee. By 1900, Brazil was responsible for 75 per cent of the world's output.[41]

In the late eighteenth century, the Caribbean was the major exporter of raw cotton. It had been overtaken by the United States as early as 1800,[42] but by 1820 it was still a major source of imports for the core countries. The Caribbean faced ferocious competition in subsequent years because the United States came to dominate the global export trade with slave-grown cotton. The abolition of slavery in the United States might have provided a new opportunity for Caribbean exporters. However, the opening of the Suez Canal in 1869 provided a big boost to cotton exports from Egypt, because transport costs to the all-important European market were slashed.[43]

Cotton had no close substitute at this time. This was not the case, however, for some of the other leading Caribbean commodities (beet sugar has already been mentioned). Cigars could be produced in the core countries using imported leaf tobacco, and this was a special threat to Cuba because the United States, Germany and Russia aggressively promoted import substitution.[44] Logwood,

---

[40] See Chalmin (1990), p. 8.
[41] See Holloway (1980), p. 175.
[42] See Farnie (1979), p. 14.
[43] At the end of the century, the US still accounted for over 60% of world exports, with British India supplying nearly 15% and Egypt 10%.
[44] Import substitution in cigars in the core did at least promote tobacco leaf exports from the Caribbean.

used as a natural dye in the textile and clothing industry, faced competition towards the end of the century from synthetic dyes produced by the chemical industry,[45] while mahogany remained vulnerable to competition from cheaper timbers, such as cedar and pine (the threat from plastics and other materials came later). And rum could always be manufactured in the core countries using imported molasses – another case of import substitution that was of special importance in the United States.

The supply side could also be favourable to the Caribbean, and the cacao market offered an illustration of how global forces could work to its advantage. In 1820, Caribbean exports represented 13.3 per cent of global imports – a not insignificant figure. Yet despite the encouragement given to the cacao industry in the newly independent countries of Latin America, particularly Ecuador, and the emergence of new sources of supply in European colonies such as São Tomé & Principe, the Caribbean more than held its own. This was a 'win-win' situation where the growth of global demand was fast enough to allow new sources of competition without undermining Caribbean suppliers.[46]

In fact, the Caribbean nearly trebled its global market share in cacao in the nineteenth century. This was perhaps the first demonstration after the Napoleonic Wars of the opportunities for diversification based on a 'traditional' export in response to global market opportunities. Gold, on the other hand, demonstrated how the Caribbean could break into an established market on the basis of a 'new' product.[47] And bananas taught a third lesson: the opportunities for the Caribbean to develop nontraditional exports on the basis of changing consumer tastes in the core.

Encouraging though this might have been, it could not disguise the fact that during the nineteenth century the Caribbean lost market share in its main exports. The most spectacular case was sugar (see Figure 4.4), where the share fell from over 80 per cent to under 10 per cent. Much of this was caused by the rise of beet sugar, but even if the analysis is confined to cane sugar, the loss of market share was still severe.[48] In the case of coffee, the second most important export at the beginning of the period, the share went from nearly 30 per cent in 1820 to around 5 per cent in 1900, so the loss of market share in the two leading exports was dramatic. Last, the Caribbean's market share in cotton (not shown in Figure 4.4) had virtually disappeared by 1900. It was only in cacao and tobacco leaf that the Caribbean gained market share in a commodity already exported in 1820.

---

[45] A synthetic substitute for logwood was first made in Germany in 1869, but it was not commercially viable until the 1890s.

[46] See Clarence-Smith (2000), chap. 2.

[47] It is perhaps ironic to describe gold as 'new' in the Caribbean context, when it had provided the original justification for European settlement at the end of the fifteenth century. However, that early period of gold exploitation had ended almost everywhere in the Caribbean long before the Napoleonic Wars.

[48] The share was over 80% in 1820 (see Moreno Fraginals (1978), vol. 3, cuadro 1), but had fallen to around 25% in 1900 (see Chalmin, 1990, p. 8).

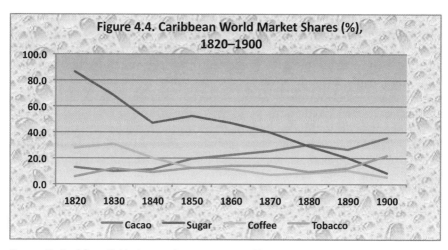

Figure 4.4. Caribbean World Market Shares (%), 1820–1900

Source: Derived from Table A.10 and same sources as Figure 4.3.

4.3. MARKET ACCESS IN THE CORE

In Chapter 2.3, the commercial policies of the core countries were outlined in general terms. Tariff rates and excise duties[49] were designed first to favour colonial over foreign products and second to favour domestic products over colonial ones. They were also designed to ensure that as much as possible of the value added associated with the processing of commodities was carried out in the core countries. In this section, we examine the impact of these policies on the twelve leading commodities exported by the Caribbean in the nineteenth century.

The commercial policies of the core had intended and unintended consequences. This is in the nature of tax systems that have discriminatory features. It is common, for example, in the literature to read of the distinction between 'protective' tariffs, designed to promote domestic production, and 'revenue' tariffs, whose main purpose was to raise government income. However, for the Caribbean countries the distinction was rather artificial. A revenue tariff applied in the core that discriminated between colonial and foreign supply favoured production in one set of Caribbean countries and harmed production in all the others. For the Caribbean, virtually all core tariffs and most of the excise duties had a discriminatory element.

---

[49] Tariff rates apply only to imports of goods, but excise duties are placed on a good whether it is produced domestically or imported. An excise duty applied to a good whose domestic production was negligible therefore had much the same impact as an import tariff.

At the end of the Napoleonic Wars, Caribbean exports were affected not just by import tariffs and excise duties in the core,[50] but also by quantitative restrictions. Some of these involved trade between the Spanish colonies in the Caribbean and the former Spanish colonies on the mainland, but these had largely been resolved by the 1830s. France at first imposed restrictions on imports from Haiti, but these were ended by treaty in 1825 when France secured preferential trade with its former colony.[51] Most of the quantitative restrictions, however, involved navigation laws applied by the core countries, and this is why the proportion of trade going to the 'mother' country was so high at the beginning of the period (see Chapter 5.1). Navigation laws were gradually ended by the core when Holland finally dropped remaining restrictions in 1848,[52] the UK in 1849 and France in 1860.

If the quantitative restrictions had largely ended by the second half of the nineteenth century, the same was not true of the discriminatory tariffs and duties. With only a few exceptions, core countries favoured colonial over foreign products throughout the period, and core countries almost always favoured domestic over foreign production. France and Spain not only favoured colonial over foreign commodities, but also used the tariff system to favour their own merchant navies.[53] The UK ended discrimination in favour of colonial exports in 1854, and Holland shortly afterwards, but both still used discriminatory tariffs to encourage processing of commodities in the core. Even after 1874, when many British import duties were scrapped, those that remained tended to favour processing in the UK.[54]

The United States and Germany, both members of the core (see Chapter 2), did not have colonies until late in the nineteenth century. Both, however, used the tariff system aggressively – as we shall see – to favour the processing of commodities domestically.[55] Furthermore, the United States became de facto a colonial power earlier than is often realised. The preference given to Hawaii by the 1876 trade treaty not only encouraged sugar exports from the Pacific

[50] The Caribbean countries themselves applied export duties in many cases, which were not neutral between the different exportable commodities and therefore affected the volume of exports of the different products.

[51] Haiti lowered export and import duties by 50% on trade with France. See Chapter 7.

[52] It had ended them for Curaçao and St Eustatius much earlier. See van Soest (1978), pp. 4–5.

[53] In theory, this led to a fourfold tariff on each commodity (colonial on 'mother' ships; foreign on colonial ships; foreign on foreign ships; and colonial on foreign ships). In addition, France and Spain often taxed the same commodity differently depending on the colony from which it came.

[54] In 1881, when Britain was supposed to be practising an extreme version of free trade, the average tariff rate was 6% using 1881 weights, 10% using 1854 weights and 13% using 1841 weights. See Nye (2007), p. 6. The revenue from tariffs still yielded between 20% and 30% of British government income in the last two decades of the century. See Nye (2007), p. 101.

[55] Under Bismarck, Germany tried to use the tariff system to favour colonial over foreign production, but German colonial exports never reached a level that threatened commodity exports from the Caribbean.

islands, but also discriminated against sugar imports from the Caribbean. By contrast, the trade treaty with Spain in 1892 (see below in this section) encouraged sugar imports from Cuba and Puerto Rico, but at the expense of sugar imports from other parts of the Caribbean.

The twelve leading commodities in the nineteenth century Caribbean (see previous section) were all affected differently by the commercial policies of the core. Gold was not taxed at all (except for export duties in the producing countries) and was therefore sold in a global marketplace where international arbitrage by and large equalised the price in all countries. Bananas were not produced in the core, and the main importer (the United States) did not differentiate between colonial and foreign imports. Raw cotton and timber (logwood and mahogany) were major imported inputs for the European core, so they were taxed either lightly or not at all in order not to burden the processing industries.[56]

The controversies surrounding core commercial policies towards the Caribbean therefore tended to focus on three kinds of commodities. The first was illustrated by sugar, which as cane sugar could only be produced in colonies or foreign countries (beet sugar could be grown domestically) and which could be refined in the core whatever its source as raw sugar. The second was illustrated by tobacco, which as tobacco leaf could be grown in colonies, foreign countries or domestically and which as manufactured tobacco could be produced in the core. The third was exemplified by cacao, coffee and molasses, which could not normally be produced in the core, but which could be refined and processed into other manufactured products, such as chocolate and rum.[57] Each of these will be considered in turn.

Because sugar was at first exported from almost all the Caribbean countries, it was natural that the core used tariffs to discriminate between foreign and colonial sugar. In the 1820s, for example, French and Spanish tariffs on sugar were twice as high on foreign as on colonial sugar. However, the core countries also taxed sugar from their colonies at different rates. It was only in 1825 that Mauritian sugar was admitted to the UK on the same terms as sugar from British Caribbean colonies and not until 1836 that sugar from British India received the same treatment.[58]

Where the productive capacity of the colonies exceeded the absorptive capacity of the mother country, the colonial tariff was less important than the tariff applied by other members of the core. This was the case for Cuba and Puerto Rico, for whom the United States became a more important market than Spain at an early stage despite the fact that sugarcane was grown in the southern states (mainly Louisiana, but also Texas). Before the Civil War, the US sugar tariff had a strong protective element, and production had risen rapidly in

---

[56] Cotton may have been produced in (and exported from) the US, but the country was the world's cheapest source and therefore had no fear of imports.

[57] The instant coffee industry would come later.

[58] See Deerr (1949), vol. 1, pp. 56, 184.

Louisiana. However, demand grew even more rapidly, so Cuba and Puerto Rico were not unduly disadvantaged.

The defeat of the Confederacy in the Civil War and the subsequent initial decline of the raw sugar industry in Louisiana meant that the US raw sugar tariff remained moderate until the 1880s. By then, not only was the United States the principal importer of Cuban sugar, but Cuban sugar was also the main source of US supply. This period coincided with the rise of monopoly capital and the emergence of a sugar trust, which came to dominate the refining of raw sugar.[59] The trust looked to import raw sugar at the cheapest possible price, and this was reflected in the McKinley tariff of 1890, which eliminated the tariff on raw sugar imports.[60] This privilege was only open to countries whose tariffs on US imports were judged not to be 'unjust or unreasonable', so Spain was obliged to sign the Foster-Canovas Treaty with the United States in 1892 on behalf of Cuba and Puerto Rico that lowered tariffs on US goods.[61]

Caribbean sugar exporters were given very little time to adjust to the McKinley tariff. In 1894, the Wilson Act reimposed duties on raw sugar and scrapped the reciprocity clauses.[62] This was a big blow to those Caribbean sugar exporters dependent on the US market. The Dingley Act in 1897 then confirmed the duties on sugar,[63] reestablished reciprocity and raised countervailing duties on sugar deemed to be subsidised by the payment of bounties (see below in this section). Cuba, following the Spanish-American War, was able to negotiate a 20 per cent reduction in the sugar tariff in the commercial treaty of 1903.[64] By then, Puerto Rican exports (including sugar) were entering the United States duty-free as part of the island's colonial status.[65]

In the first half of the nineteenth century, Caribbean colonies – with the exception of Cuba and Puerto Rico – exported sugar almost exclusively to the 'mother' country in Europe as a result of discriminatory tariffs. French Guiana, Guadeloupe and Martinique exported their sugar to France, Suriname to Holland and the Danish Virgin Islands to Denmark. This was also true of the British Caribbean colonies, but from the 1840s British sugar policy began to change. For a brief period (1844–6) the sugar tariffs discriminated against

---

[59] See Heston (1987), pp. 52–3.
[60] Southern producers were compensated by payment of a bounty (subsidy) designed to protect them from the full impact of the tariff reduction. The McKinley tariff also introduced for the first time a small countervailing duty on bounty-fed sugar from Europe.
[61] The Dominican Republic, by now a major sugar exporter to the US, did the same as did the UK on behalf of its main Caribbean colonies. Haiti, however, was less fortunate. By refusing to enter into a reciprocal treaty, it incurred higher US import tariffs on her principal exports.
[62] For the first time, the US imposed an ad valorem rather than specific tariff. Needless to say, the duty on refined sugar was higher than the duty on raw sugar. See Taussig (1931).
[63] The Dingley Act, however, reverted to a specific tariff on sugar rather than the ad valorem rate introduced in 1894. See Taussig (1931).
[64] This was not, however, because of the reciprocity clauses of the 1897 tariff, but because of Cuba's new semicolonial status, which required special treatment by the US. See Jenks (1928), pp. 132–40.
[65] See Clark (1930), p. 410.

slave-grown sugar, but in the following eight years they were changed again to equalise the tariffs on foreign and colonial raw sugar (refined sugar, as always, paid a higher tariff).[66] Because the UK was by far the biggest market in Europe, this had a huge impact on the sugar trade.

At first it was cane sugar producers outside the British Empire that took advantage of tariff equalisation. By the late 1850s, however, beet sugar from continental Europe was being sold in the UK for the first time. This industry had been stimulated by tax discrimination in its favour, but its growth was relatively modest until entry to the vast UK market became possible. Exporters of beet sugar had always received a drawback on any duties paid on raw sugar imports, but the formula used allowed them to keep for themselves any improvements in yield. As a result, the drawback increasingly included a subsidy element known as a bounty. Gradually, these bounties began to be paid directly rather than indirectly, and thus the sugar exported was to all intents being dumped. As a result, beet sugar began its remarkable ascendance. This process accelerated when the UK scrapped the tariff on raw sugar altogether in 1874.[67]

Continental governments became increasingly concerned at the fiscal burden implied by the bounties paid to beet sugar exporters, but all attempts to negotiate an international agreement faltered in the face of British reluctance to end a scheme that effectively subsidised the British consumer at the continental taxpayers' expense. Cane sugar exporters, particularly those in the Caribbean, watched with concern as prices drifted downwards and then collapsed after 1883. Yet it was not until 1903, following the signing of the Brussels Convention in 1902, that the payment of export bounties to beet sugar finally came to an end.[68] Only the most efficient producers in the Caribbean were able to adjust to the lower prices after 1883, and this required major investments in plants and machinery.[69]

With the exception of the French colonies at the beginning of the period, sugar refining was always carried out in the core. Tobacco, however, was a different story, and the production and export of manufactured tobacco flourished in parts of the Caribbean before 1860. The United States remained the world's major exporter of tobacco leaf, as it had been since colonial times, but the European core could produce it and so could European colonies outside the Caribbean. Thus, Caribbean exporters were potentially at risk both in the export of tobacco leaf and in the export of manufactured tobacco.

---

[66] See Deerr (1949), vol. 2, chap. 27.

[67] There is an enormous literature on this topic. See, e.g., Beachey (1957), Deerr (1949) and Galloway (1989).

[68] This was the first international commodity agreement, but it would prove to be short-lived – it had effectively collapsed by 1908. The text is given in Prinsen (1909), pp. 371–7.

[69] On the international negotiations culminating in the Brussels Convention, see Deerr (1949), vol. 2, chap. 30.

Germany strongly promoted the production of tobacco leaf and encouraged the production and export of manufactured tobacco. Other European countries, and Japan, made the manufacture and sale of tobacco products a government monopoly. Yet the biggest threat to the Caribbean tobacco industry came from the United States as a result of the discriminatory tariffs in favour of tobacco manufactures.[70] From 1860 onwards, the Caribbean tobacco industry was increasingly transferred to the United States because the export of all but the finest cigars became increasingly unprofitable. By 1890, with the formation of the tobacco trust, the Caribbean industry was at a severe disadvantage.[71]

The biggest loser from this was Cuba. Instead of exporting cigars, Cuba found itself increasingly exporting tobacco leaf from which others would make cigars. At one point, the colonial government even considered banning the export of tobacco leaf in order to protect the cigar industry, but it was too late. From the end of the Civil War, the United States imposed a tax on cigar imports of at least 5 US cents. This was equivalent to an ad valorem tariff of at least 100 per cent on most cigars.[72] It succeeded in replacing German cigar imports with domestic production and eliminated a large part of the Cuban cigar industry. Many skilled Cuban workers followed the industry to the mainland United States, where it flourished in Florida.

Cacao, coffee and molasses are traditional Caribbean exports, whose evolution was affected by commercial policies in the core. Coffee, being a beverage of final consumption, was often subject to high rates of taxation. It was still subject to import duties in the UK during the period of so-called free trade after 1874. Levels of consumption per head in the core tended to be inversely related to the rate of taxation. Holland, for example, where consumption per head was among the highest in the world, imposed no import duties by the end of the century, but in Spain a high tariff kept consumption per head at low levels.[73] The United States eliminated its import duty on coffee in 1872, and consumption per head rose accordingly.[74]

Prices rose and fell in line with supply and demand conditions, but they were not primarily affected by commercial policies in the core. Instead, overproduction in Brazil – the world's largest producer and exporter – drove prices down in the 1890s to levels at which exports were unprofitable in the Caribbean. Thus, the two Caribbean commodities (sugar and coffee), which in 1820 accounted for over 80 per cent of exports, were both facing major crises at the end of the century as a result of price collapse. The 1906 Taubaté

---

[70] See Stubbs (1985), pp. 19–20.
[71] On the formation of the tobacco trust, see Jacobstein (1907), chap. 4.
[72] See Jacobstein (1907), chaps. 6 and 7.
[73] See Thurber (1881), pp. 214–15.
[74] The US first eliminated the coffee import tax in 1832, but reimposed it in 1861 at the start of the Civil War. A table showing the rate of tariff from 1825 onwards is given in Thurber (1881), p. 229.

agreement, the first coffee valorisation scheme, was designed to bring prices back to previous levels.[75]

Much the same pattern applied to cacao, but there was no price collapse at the end of the century. Import duties varied greatly and largely determined consumption per head. Holland and the United States eliminated import duties on cacao beans at an early stage, and France and Spain imposed a discriminatory tax in favour of their colonies.[76] As with coffee, the UK continued to tax the import of cacao even during the era of 'free trade'. Because cacao – unlike tobacco – was not processed in the Caribbean, the rise of the chocolate industry stimulated exports. Switzerland, where the import duty was close to zero by the end of the century, became a major market when it emerged as the world's leading exporter of eating chocolate. Holland was the leading exporter of chocolate powder.

Molasses and rum are the final products to be considered here. Because rum can be made in the core, it was always vulnerable to discriminatory tariffs. This was particularly true in the United States, which switched after the Napoleonic Wars to importing molasses from the Caribbean in order to make rum domestically. Cuba from the 1870s may have made the finest rum in the world, but what it exported to the United States was mainly molasses.[77] This switch was underpinned by changes in tariff rates, which made rum exports uneconomic. The UK, however, moved in the opposite direction in order to compensate British Caribbean sugar exporters at least partially for the end of discriminatory tariffs. As a result, rum exports surged from some parts of the British Caribbean. France also adjusted import duties on rum to encourage Caribbean exports at a time of declining sugar prices.

4.4. COMMODITY PRICES AND TECHNOLOGICAL CHANGE

Of all the centuries to be specialised in primary product exports, the nineteenth was probably the best. Demand for many commodities was growing strongly, income elasticities were high, navigation laws were in decline, trade barriers in the core countries were coming down, transport costs were falling and trusts and cartels among the importers only began to have a negative impact on exporters at the very end of the century.

Supply, however, was increasing outside the Caribbean, with new countries entering the market and established ones raising output. Because the Caribbean was a price-taker for virtually all products (the main exceptions were the finest Cuban cigars), this could undermine the profitability of the region's exports, unless price falls could be matched by reductions in costs. That in turn

---

[75] On the Taubaté agreement, named after a town in the state of São Paulo, see Holloway (1975). It is sometimes described as an international commodity agreement, but in truth it was a unilateral policy adopted by the main producer state in Brazil.

[76] See Clarence-Smith (2000), p. 57.

[77] See Smith (2005), p. 217.

might require investments in new techniques of production. Thus, prices and technological change are the subject of this section.

Of the twelve commodities that accounted for virtually all the Caribbean's exports in the nineteenth century, two – Cuban cigars and gold – need not concern us here. Cuban cigars[78] were of such a high quality that the product was branded and manufacturers became price-makers. Gold, on the other hand, was effectively fixed in price under the gold standard to which most of the core adhered.[79] Thus, the prices of particular interest are the remaining ten: sugar, molasses, rum, coffee, cacao, cotton, tobacco leaf, logwood, mahogany and bananas.

From the 1870s onwards, the revolution in shipping forced down international transport costs, driving a wedge between the trends in export (*fob*) and import (*cif*) prices. For goods crossing the Atlantic from the Caribbean to core Europe, the impact was particularly dramatic (less so for goods going to the eastern seaboard of the United States). In choosing reference prices for the ten commodities, I have therefore used export unit values for leading world producers or US import unit values wherever possible. The reader should be aware, however, that no commodities were truly homogeneous. Even raw sugar, for example, was subject to sixteen different classifications, and therefore prices, during the period of the Dutch Standard.[80]

The issues of importance to the Caribbean were the volatility of prices, the correlation of commodity prices and the long-run trends. If the trend was downwards, this required a reduction in unit costs. However, price cycles around a constant or rising trend might still require investments in new technology, because suppliers could not be sure how quickly low prices would correct themselves. Thus, the ability to adjust unit costs of production in the short run was important for almost all commodity producers.

We can begin with the volatility of prices estimated by the Coefficient of Variation (see Figure 4.5).[81] The highest figure was found in the case of cotton as measured by the US export unit value. However, US cotton prices soared in the Civil War, when the supply from the southern states was disrupted. Using the Brazilian export unit value, the volatility was still high (prices also rose rapidly in the early 1860s), but it was about half that of US cotton. The second-highest volatility was found in the case of cacao, where the lag between planting and first crop could be as long as seven years, leading to periods of

---

[78] The quality had been raised in response to the high specific tariffs on imported cigars imposed by a number of core countries. Only the most expensive cigars were now profitable to export.

[79] The US came off the gold standard at the beginning of the Civil War. This temporarily raised the price of gold in dollar terms, and the US dollar deviated from its gold parity to sterling and other core currencies. The US returned to the gold standard de facto in 1873 and de jure in 1879.

[80] The Dutch Standard (D.S.) was adopted in 1864 as a way of setting import tariffs according to the degree of refinement of the raw sugar. Each sugar under the D.S. differed in price from the others. See Deerr (1949), vol. 2, p. 505.

[81] The Coefficient of Variation is the standard deviation divided by the mean.

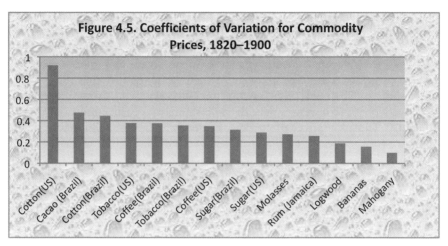

Note: Sugar (US) and coffee (US) are US import unit values (1821–1900); sugar (Brazil), coffee (Brazil), cotton (Brazil), cacao (Brazil) and tobacco (Brazil) are Brazilian export unit values (1821–1900); molasses is Martinique export unit value (1820–1900); rum is Jamaica price *cif* London (1830–1900) and Martinique export unit value (1820–30), spliced to make one series; logwood is Martinique export unit value (1820–1900); mahogany is based on Belize decennial export unit values (1830–1900); and bananas are export unit values for Jamaica (1880–1900).
Source: For the US, Carter (2006); for Brazil, IBGE (1987); for Martinique, *Annuaire de la Martinique* (1936); for Jamaica, Eisner (1961); and for Barbados and Belize, *Parliamentary Papers*.

under- and oversupply. This was also a big problem for coffee and even tobacco leaf. Volatility was less serious a problem in the case of sugar, where the lag between planting and harvest was much shorter.

Price volatility was therefore a major issue for commodity exporters, but it should always be remembered that prices could go above their long-term average as well as fall below it. Commodity prices were cyclical, but no one could be sure how long the cycles would last. Some commodities could be stored, and this was often the first line of response to low prices (this may explain the relatively low volatility of logwood and mahogany, for example).[82]

By contrast, the correlation of commodity prices seems to have been less of a problem (see Table 4.1). The highest (positive) correlations invariably involved bananas (see final row of Table 4.1), but this refers only to the last two decades of the nineteenth century, when most commodity prices were falling in unison, and therefore the correlation is a little spurious. By contrast, the correlations between the prices of sugar, molasses and rum were very low. Rum was a manufactured good that in many cases was subject to branding. It could also be stored (and aged) very easily. Molasses was used for different purposes, and

---

[82] The low volatility for bananas was because of the short period (twenty years) for which we have prices (banana exports in significant volume had to await the transport revolution after 1870, because bananas are a highly perishable commodity).

TABLE 4.1. *Correlation Coefficients for Commodity Prices, c.1820–1900*

	Sugar	Molasses	Rum	Coffee	Cacao	Cotton	Tobacco	Logwood	Mahogany
Sugar	1								
Molasses	0.15	1							
Rum	0.21	0.23	1						
Coffee	0.11	0.29	−0.07	1					
Cacao	−0.35	0.44	−0.12	0.32	1				
Cotton	0.15	0.08	0.001	0.12	0.14	1			
Tobacco	−0.01	0.24	0.09	0.15	0.40	0.85	1		
Logwood	0.17	0.23	−0.29	0.37	−0.01	−0.16	−0.12	1	
Mahogany	0.53	−0.43	0.20	−0.40	−0.76	−0.15	−0.37	−0.15	1
Bananas	0.68	0.53	0.52	−0.10	0.63	0.74	0.30	−0.28	−0.12

Note: Sugar, tobacco and coffee are US import unit values; cotton is US export unit value; others as for Figure 4.5.

its price and quality varied accordingly (the lowest price was for molasses used as animal feed, the highest for the raw material to make best-quality rum).

There were also negative price correlations, but untangling cause and effect is difficult. It did mean, however, that in a period of falling prices for leading commodities in the Caribbean (e.g. sugar), there were other prices (e.g. for cacao) that might be rising. On the other hand, the price correlation of the two leading commodities in the Caribbean in 1820 (sugar and coffee) was positive. This meant that a period of falling prices for one commodity was associated with falling prices for the other.

We turn now to the long-term price trends. At first, the picture is discouraging. If we take the five-year average at the start of the period (c.1820)[83] and compare it with the five-year average at the end of the period (c.1900),[84] we may note that the annual percentage change over the whole period was only positive for two (cacao and tobacco), unchanged for one (molasses) and falling for all others (see Table 4.2). However, the beginning of the period (c.1820) was a period of exceptionally high prices caused by the failure of supply to adjust to the rise in demand at the end of the Napoleonic Wars. When the long-run trend is taken using ordinary least squares (see Table 4.2), the results are of less concern. Prices were still falling in the case of five commodities, but only three of these were significant (sugar, rum, mahogany).[85] One price (logwood) exhibited virtually no change. The long-run rise in price for the other four commodities was not significant for two (coffee and molasses), but it **was** for cacao and tobacco. Thus, it could **not** be argued that the price trends facing the Caribbean in the nineteenth century were generally unfavourable.

The commodity where the downward trend in prices was most significant was raw sugar. This was true whether we look at the annual percentage decline over the period 1820 to 1900 (−1.2%) or whether we look at the slope of the regression line (−0.037). Furthermore, the negative slope was highly significant. In Figure 4.6, the sugar price is shown along with the regression line, and it makes little difference which series is used to plot the sugar price.[86] The series used here (the US import unit value) shows the initial decline following the high prices at the start of the 1820s, the subsequent volatility around a declining trend and the collapse in the 1880s, from which no recovery took place.

Because raw sugar was the most important single commodity export from the Caribbean in the nineteenth century, the long-run decline in its nominal price was a major challenge. Yet the success of some countries in adjusting to this downward trend suggested that there were ways in which unit costs could be reduced. Indeed, sugar was perhaps the Caribbean commodity most subject

---

[83] Where possible, I have used 1818–22 as the starting point.
[84] In general, I have used 1898–1902 as the end point.
[85] If we omit bananas, for which the period (1880–1900) is so much shorter than for the others.
[86] Figure 4.6 uses the US import unit value for sugar, but the results are very similar for other series, such as the Brazilian export unit value.

TABLE 4.2. *Price Trends for Leading Commodities, c.1820–1900*

	Sugar	Molasses	Rum	Coffee	Cacao	Cotton	Tobacco	Logwood	Mahogany	Bananas
Slope	−0.037	0.055	−0.279	0.023	0.111	−0.019	0.035	0.000	−0.021	−0.757
t-statistic	9.334	2.350	3.090	1.275	10.757	0.306	2.241	0.007	11.91	5.905
r2	0.521	0.065	0.107	0.020	0.591	0.001	0.059	0.000	0.666	0.624
%age per year	−1.2	0	−0.44	−1.18	0.91	−1.01	0.26	−0.36	−0.38	−1.51

Note: 'Slope' refers to the coefficient when the commodity price is regressed against time. The final row is the annual percentage change in price using a five-year average for the beginning and end of the period.

101

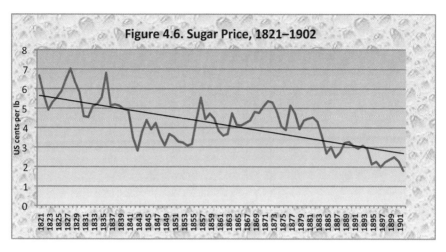

Source: Sugar price (US imports) derived from Carter (2006), vol. 3.

to technological change in the nineteenth century, starting with the cane yield itself and moving on to the different stages of the production process.

Sugarcane production was never mechanised in the nineteenth century, being always cut by hand, but the yield was greatly affected by fertilizer. Although the importation of guano and other natural fertilizers was always expensive, there were other options, including using the guano deposits in the Caribbean itself. Costs could also be cut through the practice of ratooning, avoiding the need for yearly planting, but yields did then fall off in subsequent years.[87]

More dramatic reduction in costs could be achieved in the production process at various stages. The machinery used to crush the cane was constantly being improved; the shift from open pan to vacuum pan techniques in the evaporation process was a major advance; the methods used to clarify the juice and reduce impurities was also subject to regular technical improvements; and the introduction of the railway made possible the separation of the sugar factory (*central*) from the sugarcane estates. This gave rise to major economies of scale with a consequent fall in the unit cost of production for those countries where the process was most advanced.[88]

Other commodities were also subject to economies of scale, but none to the same extent as sugar. Machinery for removing the outer layers of the coffee berry was subject to regular improvement,[89] Eli Whitney's cotton gin made possible the separation of the lint from the seed by mechanical means,[90] drying techniques for tobacco leaf improved and sawmills for shaping mahogany

[87] See Galloway (1989), pp. 13–15.
[88] See Moreno Fraginals (1978), vol. 1, chap. 5.
[89] See Thurber (1881), pp. 8–18.
[90] See Mokyr (2003), vol. 2, p. 25.

were always being upgraded. Molasses and rum could be improved in quality through simple technical changes,[91] and the transport revolution in shipping and railways transformed the economics of the banana industry.[92]

Exporters therefore faced a choice of technique that in general allowed them to maintain competitiveness in the face of volatile or even falling prices. It was only the collapse of sugar prices in the 1880s and coffee prices in the 1890s that imposed an almost insuperable problem for sugar exporters in the Caribbean, and even then some managed to adjust. However, all these technical changes cost money, and this meant access to credit. The survival and prosperity of the Caribbean might have depended on an adequate supply of labour at the beginning of the nineteenth century, but by the end it was likely to depend just as much – if not more so – on the smooth operation of financial markets (see Chapter 6).

[91] See Smith (2005), chap. 3.
[92] See Kepner and Soothill (1935), chap. 2.

5

Caribbean Foreign Trade

In this chapter we look first at the evolution of exports by value and volume over the course of the nineteenth century and the changing commodity structure. New 'nontraditional' exports would make their appearance, but not all survived until 1900. All the traditional exports, however, were still being exported at the end of the century. We shall also see how the commodity structure changed, with some big winners and losers and a handful whose share remained roughly the same.

Exports create income, which is spent in a variety of ways: on consumption, intermediate and capital goods, for the payment of interest on loans, for the repatriation of profits and in export duties to the tax authorities. In very 'open' economies – and all the Caribbean countries fitted this description in the nineteenth century – imported goods constitute a high proportion of final expenditure (public and private), and thus import performance is also a useful guide to living standards.

If exports and imports were always the same, a detailed examination of imports could be brief. However, imports deviated from exports for numerous reasons. In the colonial Caribbean, for example, a large part of exports accrued to absentee landlords whose priority was often the repatriation of profits. As the repatriation of earnings from exports changed, the amount available for imports also altered.[1] An analysis of imports can therefore reveal a great deal, so the first section of the chapter also looks at their evolution and structure.

Section 2 examines the geographical pattern of trade, distinguishing between the United States, the UK and the 'mother' country (the last two being the same in the case of the British colonies) and provides a snapshot of intra-Caribbean trade at different periods. By the end of the nineteenth century, the United States had become the main trade partner for the Caribbean, despite the fact

---

[1] A high proportion of exports in Jamaica in 1832 constituted repatriated profits. With the decline of absentee landlords after slave emancipation, exports fell, but imports did not fall nearly as fast because less income needed to be repatriated. See Eisner (1961), chap. 13.

that its imports were growing more slowly than other members of the core, and would continue to do so thereafter. This section shows how this happened and which countries were most affected.

Prices for exported commodities were volatile in the nineteenth century, but so were the prices of imported goods. Furthermore, import prices did not move in line with export prices. Thus, exports could buy a larger or smaller quantity of imports depending on price movements. Because import prices were generally falling in the nineteenth century, particularly for textiles that constituted such a large part of the total import bill, exports and imports in real terms could be very different. Section 3 explores these issues, including measurement of the net barter terms of trade (NBTT) and the income terms of trade.

The final section of the chapter looks at domestic exports per head at constant prices during the course of the century by region, subregion and country. In the absence of national accounts statistics for any part of the nineteenth century for most countries (Cuba, Guyana and Jamaica are partial exceptions – see Chapter 6), exports per head are one of the best proxies that we have for living standards in the Caribbean, because the export sector was so highly correlated with everything else.

5.1. TRADE STRUCTURE

By 1820 the Caribbean had largely recovered from the disruptions of the Napoleonic Wars. However, labour was still scarce, the slave trade either had become or was becoming illegal and the commercial policies of the imperial countries would soon cease to favour the region. Indeed, European interest in the Caribbean was starting to decline because other opportunities for colonial expansion presented themselves. Of the core countries, the United States was the keenest to expand its commercial presence in the region, but it was held back by trade and shipping restrictions imposed by other members of the core on their Caribbean colonies.

Exports experienced three phases in the nineteenth century. The first, lasting until 1850, was marked by stagnation in the volume and value[2] of domestic exports (see Figure 5.1). In the first decade (1820–30) this was not so surprising because exports had been boosted by high commodity prices at the end of the Napoleonic Wars – particularly for sugar and coffee. However, the disappointing performance continued for another two decades despite an increase in the sugar price in the 1830s.[3] Indeed, the **volume** of exports actually fell between 1830 and 1840 (see Figure 5.1).

The volume of domestic exports (but not the value) started to increase in the 1840s. This marked the beginning of the second phase, in which exports

[2] The volume of exports is proxied by their value at 1860 prices. See Notes on A. Tables for their derivation.
[3] See Figure 4.6.

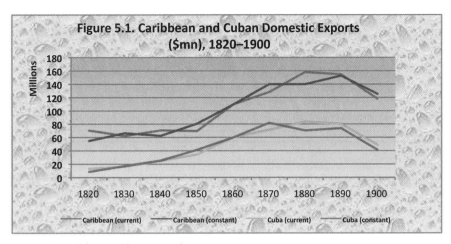

Figure 5.1. Caribbean and Cuban Domestic Exports ($mn), 1820–1900

Source: Derived from Tables A.11 and A.14.

surged. In this second phase, lasting three decades in the case of the value of exports, the annual rate of increase reached 2.8 per cent.[4] For the volume of exports, the second phase lasted longer (fifty years), but the annual rate of increase was lower (1.8%).[5] These were respectable figures, even if they were not enough to preserve global market share.[6] The peak was reached around 1880 in the case of the value of exports, after which the fall in the price of first sugar and then coffee caused major difficulties (see Chapter 4). The **volume** of domestic exports, however, did not reach its peak until 1890 (see Figure 5.1).

The third phase was marked by absolute and relative decline for the Caribbean. While world exports were rising in volume and value, Caribbean exports were plunging. The fall in the value of domestic exports from their peak in 1880 was severe – a drop of a quarter in two decades. For the volume of exports the decline was less severe, but it was concentrated in one decade (1890–1900). Exports were now back to the level of the 1860s.

The sugar price was widely blamed for this decline, but it was also because of the disruptive impact of Spain's unsuccessful attempt to hold on to its last remaining American colonies. This becomes clear when the value of Cuban domestic exports at current and constant prices are plotted alongside those of the Caribbean as a whole (see Figure 5.1). By the mid-nineteenth century, Cuba accounted for roughly half of all Caribbean exports, so what happened on the island had a huge impact on the Caribbean as a whole. Cuban exports started falling in volume terms after 1870 and in value terms after 1880, with

---

[4] Derived from Table A.11.
[5] Derived from Table A.14.
[6] Using Woodruff (1967), Maddison (2001), and Table A.11, we can estimate the Caribbean world market share at 4.9% in 1840, 2.9% in 1860, 2.1% in 1880 and 1.2% in 1900.

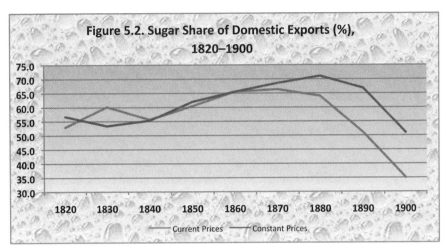

Figure 5.2. Sugar Share of Domestic Exports (%), 1820–1900

Source: Table A.18.

the decline concentrated in the 1890s. This had less to do with the price of sugar and more to do with the Second War of Independence.

The value of Caribbean exports exceeded those of the United States in 1820 (see Chapter 4.1). By 1830, export expansion in the United States and stagnation in the Caribbean meant they were roughly equal. By 1850, the value of US domestic exports was double that of the Caribbean, and the gap was never closed, despite the disruption in the 1860s of the Civil War. By the end of the century, US domestic exports would be twelve times greater than those of the Caribbean.[7]

Given the extraordinary dynamism of the US economy in the nineteenth century, it is perhaps not surprising that Caribbean exports were eclipsed by their northern neighbour. However, the Caribbean did hold its own against other regions and countries. As late as 1870, for example, Caribbean exports were still larger than those of any single Latin American country, greater than those of Australia, Canada, China and South Africa and equal to those of smaller European countries, such as Belgium and Switzerland.[8] It was not until the end of the century that the Caribbean was overtaken by the larger Latin American countries and by most European countries.[9]

It has been said that the Caribbean was so specialised in sugar that no other export mattered. This is not correct. Figure 5.2 shows the sugar share of domestic exports at current and constant prices. Sugar represented just over half of domestic exports in 1820, rising to a peak of 66 per cent in 1870 at current prices and over 70 per cent in 1880 at constant prices. By the end of

[7] Derived from Table A.11 and Carter (2006), vol. 5, pp. 499–500.
[8] See Maddison (2001), pp. 359–60.
[9] See Mitchell (2007) and Mitchell (2007a).

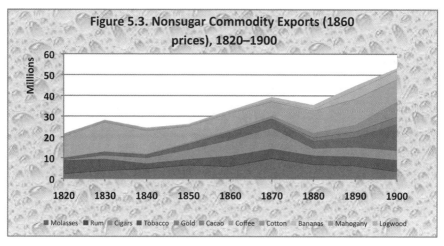

the century, however, the sugar share had fallen to little more than one-third of domestic exports by value. This was a consequence of the sharp fall in sugar prices after 1883 (at constant prices, the share was close to 50 per cent in 1900).

These are high proportions, but it still left plenty of scope for the main nonsugar exports. There were nine such products in 1820 (molasses, rum, cotton, cacao, coffee, logwood, mahogany, tobacco leaf and cigars) and eleven in 1900 (bananas and gold were added to the list). In addition, some nontraditional exports came and went during the century. And, among the 'other' commodities that completed the export list were some that were crucial for particular countries, even if they did not contribute much to Caribbean exports as a whole.

The performance of nonsugar exports is shown in Figure 5.3 at constant prices.[10] The leading nonsugar export in 1820 was coffee. The Caribbean had been a pioneer in the export of coffee in the eighteenth century[11] and accounted for a high share of total world trade at the end of the Napoleonic Wars (see Chapter 4). At that time, Hispaniola, the Spanish colonies and the British colonies each accounted for about 30 per cent of total Caribbean exports of coffee (the remaining 10 per cent came from the French and Dutch colonies).[12] Coffee, however, was and still is a labour-intensive product, and this led to

[10] The performance of nonsugar exports in current prices is much more volatile as a result of price changes. The interested reader, however, will find the data in Table A.17.
[11] It was being grown and exported from the French Antilles as early as the 1720s. See Thurber (1881), p. 137.
[12] Derived from the country export data in Table A.10.

competition with sugar. Because coffee was not usually as profitable as sugar, many planters switched from one to the other in response.[13]

The one area where coffee remained popular throughout the nineteenth century was Haiti. The peasantry found it ideal for their purposes. Indeed, Haiti retained its place as one of the world's leading coffee exporters throughout the nineteenth century,[14] and by 1870 it was responsible for around 70 per cent of Caribbean coffee exports. At that moment, it also began its spectacular rise in Puerto Rico.[15] From then on, almost all Caribbean coffee came from these two countries, but a small amount of Blue Mountain coffee from Jamaica continued to be exported and always commanded a substantial premium on the world market.[16]

As a result of these changes, coffee retained an important place in Caribbean exports in the nineteenth century – at least at constant prices.[17] Cotton, however, declined steadily throughout the period and never recovered. The quality of the sea-island cotton grown in the Caribbean was not in doubt, but the textile industry in Europe preferred to import the cheaper short-staple cotton grown in the southern United States and Brazil. Caribbean exporters found it difficult to cut costs to compete with this slave-grown cotton, even in those countries where slavery still functioned.

US and Brazilian cotton exports were potentially vulnerable to European antislavery campaigns, and a British campaign to discriminate against slave-grown imports did indeed result in a new tariff law in 1844. However, this tariff applied only to sugar, and in any case it was swept aside by the movement for free trade in less than two years. From then on, the British import of raw cotton from all sources was free. By the end of the century, the little cotton still exported from the Caribbean came mainly from Haiti (around 80 per cent) with the remainder from the British colonies.

Tobacco products contributed relatively little to Caribbean exports in 1820 (see Figure 5.3). However, both tobacco leaf and cigar exports rose rapidly thereafter as a result of consumption growth in the core. Tariffs on imports of manufactured tobacco, always an issue, became especially problematic after mid-century. Cigar exports hit a peak in the 1860s and then declined in volume.[18] Tobacco leaf exports faced much lower tariffs (zero in some cases) and ironically benefited from the discrimination against cigar imports because

---

[13] See Thomas (1971), pp. 131–2, for the case of nineteenth-century Cuba.

[14] See Thurber (1881), pp. 240–2; and Chapter 7 herein.

[15] See Bergad (1983), chap. 3.

[16] No one was quite certain why this was the case, but as early as 1880 it was said, "The fine selections of Jamaica coffee command an extreme price on the London market, where the variety is highly prized for its very fine cup qualities" (Thurber 1881, p. 142).

[17] Less so at current prices as a result of the price decline at the end of the century. See Chapter 4.

[18] Not, however, in value. Tariff discrimination by core countries made only the finest cigar exports profitable, so the unit price rose steeply.

the core countries needed to import leaf to manufacture tobacco products.[19] Despite discriminatory tariffs, cigarette exports[20] from Cuba jumped from 9 million packs in 1859 to 40 million in 1890.[21] This was impressive considering that by then the American Tobacco Trust (ATC) held exclusive rights over the all-important Bonsack machine used for rolling cigarettes and was responsible for 90 per cent of US cigarette sales.[22]

Among the traditional exports, cacao performed strongly in the nineteenth century (see Figure 5.3). The region's share of world cacao exports may have been small in 1820 (see Chapter 4), but many Caribbean countries produced it. The world's biggest exporters (Brazil, Ecuador and Venezuela) relied on burning forests to expand production.[23] This option was not so easily available in the Caribbean, but on the larger islands and the mainland countries there were still virgin lands that could be used. However, cacao had one huge advantage for Caribbean countries. Production did not exhibit economies of scale, so it was ideally suited for smallholders.[24] This is one reason why it prospered in the Caribbean after the end of slavery.

The nontraditional exports in the century included bananas and gold. Both performed strongly in the last decades of the century (see Figure 5.3). Bananas had been exported from Cuba to the eastern seaboard of the United States even in the days of sailing boats.[25] The arrival of the steamship brought in other Caribbean suppliers.[26] From 1880 onwards, the expansion of Caribbean banana exports was very rapid indeed. Banana exports by value in 1900 were more important than either molasses or rum. It provided employment for many smallholders, and the industry stayed out of the grip of monopoly capital until the end of the century.[27] Unlike bananas, very few countries produced gold for export, but in those that did expansion was rapid after 1870. Indeed, gold contributed almost as much to total Caribbean exports in 1900 as bananas.

Mention must also be made of some of the minor exports not shown in Figure 5.3. In 1820, these consisted largely of various types of fruit and spices along with hides and honey. Cuba started to export copper in the 1830s, and Guyana did the same for rice (neither would survive to the end of the century). Trinidad

---

[19] In Cuba the value of cigar exports was twice that of tobacco leaf in 1859. By 1890 it was the other way round. See Stubbs (1985), p. 18.

[20] Cigarette exports are included in 'other' exports in the statistical appendix.

[21] See Stubbs (1985), p. 16.

[22] The Bonsack, first invented in 1881, was capable of producing up to 1,000 cigarettes a minute. It replaced the Susini, invented by a Cuban and shown at the Paris Trade Exhibition in 1867. See Stubbs (1985), pp. 2–3.

[23] See Clarence-Smith (2000), chap. 6.

[24] See Clarence-Smith (2000), pp. 125–6.

[25] See Santamaría and García (2004), pp. 142–57.

[26] This story has frequently been told. See, e.g., Lloyd Jones (1931), pp. 132–3.

[27] The first full year in which the United Fruit Company (UFCO) would operate was 1900 (it had been formed in 1899 from the merger of many banana companies). This vertically integrated colossus would come to have a major impact on many Caribbean countries, but this was not yet apparent in 1900. See Kepner and Soothill (1935), pp. 34–5.

exported tar from the famous asphalt lake for the first time in the 1840s, and the Bahamas began the export trade in sponges in the 1850s. Coconuts became an important export in several countries in the 1860s, and Grenada had become a leading exporter of nutmeg by 1870. The decline of sugar in the last two decades saw a concerted effort at diversification, including lime juice products in several British colonies (especially Dominica and Montserrat), processed pineapples in the Bahamas, gum and rice in Suriname and straw hats in the Dutch Antilles.

The structure of Caribbean exports therefore changed during the century. Sugar has already been discussed (see Figure 5.2). Here we concentrate on the share of nonsugar exports.[28] If we compare the beginning and end of the period, coffee, cotton, molasses, rum and mahogany declined in importance whether we estimate the proportions at current or constant prices. Furthermore, the fall was virtually uninterrupted in the case of cotton and coffee. The commodities whose shares **increased** when comparing the beginning and end of the period were tobacco leaf, cigars, cacao, bananas, gold and logwood.

The biggest 'loser' over the whole period was coffee. The main 'winner' was tobacco (leaf and manufactured) followed by cacao and bananas. Other than gold, no minerals of any importance were exported at the end of the century, the copper boom in Cuba having ended in the 1870s. Finally, service exports – so important today – were negligible. Only a small number of tourists reached the Caribbean even in the northern hemisphere winter months, and other service exports were not yet of any importance.[29] It was a relatively simple export structure, even if it was more diversified than is commonly thought.

As we will see in the next chapter, there was very little manufacturing in the Caribbean in the nineteenth century (excluding the processing of natural resources) and import-substituting industrialisation (ISI) was also very limited. Under these circumstances, we might expect the composition of imports not to change much over the course of the century. Imports would then reflect the essential needs of society for consumer goods (such as food, beverages and clothing), intermediate goods (such as fuel and lumber) and capital goods (all of which had to be imported in the absence of a capital goods industry).

Broadly speaking, this is what happened. However, the composition of imports was affected in a modest way by three factors. First, in those countries with rising living standards (e.g. Cuba and Trinidad), we would expect the income elasticity of import demand to favour luxuries over essentials. Second, if income distribution became less unequal (e.g. Jamaica), we might expect the reverse with a **decline** in the importance of luxury imports. Third, changes in relative prices would alter the composition of imports provided that the price elasticity of demand for all imported goods was not unity.

---

[28] The data can be found in Table A.18.

[29] For a study of the Jamaican tourist industry from its origins in the nineteenth century, see Taylor (1993).

TABLE 5.1. *Composition of Imports, c.1900 (%)*

Country	Food (c)	Beverages	Clothing	Shoes (b)	Fuel	Lumber	Hardware
Haiti (a)	52.6	na	18.6	1.4	0.9	5.1	1.4
Cuba	55.1	10.0	19.5	5.6	0.5	na	7.4
Puerto Rico	39.9	5.2	28.2	6.7	0.5	3.7	10.4
Barbados	36.9	1.0	14.6	1.9	3.6	4.2	2.7
Guyana	28.9	2.0	12.0	1.4	1.4	2.0	8.4
Jamaica	23.1	2.1	18.0	3.5	3.4	4.2	3.8
Trinidad	19.2	1.7	15.2	2.3	0.5	2.2	5.9
Fr. Guiana	34.7	14.6	6.8	1.8	na	na	18.7
DVI (d)	14.8	10.3	13.7	3.3	30.3	1.7	2.7

Note: (a) Figures refer to 1886–7 and are based on imports from US only; (b) all leather products have been included here; (c) including livestock; (d) DVI=Danish Virgin Islands.
Source: For Haiti, Marte (1984); for British Colonies, *Parliamentary Papers*; for other countries, US Consular Reports in *Commercial Relations of the United States with Foreign Countries* (various years).

The final effect seems to have been particularly important. Clothing, for example, accounted for a much higher proportion of imports in the early part of the century than at the end. Because there was no textile industry of any importance in the Caribbean (except Puerto Rico) even in 1900, we can make the plausible assumption that the lower share of clothing in imports was due to the fall in the relative price of textiles. Essentially, the productivity gains in the textile industries of the core countries were being passed on to the Caribbean in the form of lower prices at a time when the price elasticity of demand for textiles was low.

It is not possible to show the composition of imports for all countries. However, by the end of the century consuls representing core countries were preparing detailed reports on imports in a number of Caribbean countries for their home governments, and these can be used to supplement the information from official trade statistics. They also provide insights into the comparative advantage of the core countries in supplying different kinds of goods.

The composition of imports around 1900 is shown for a number of countries in Table 5.1. It indicates the continuing importance of consumer goods imports even if these are limited in Table 5.1 to food, beverages, clothing and shoes.[30] Intermediate goods, limited here to fuel and lumber,[31] were much less important, but the role of St Thomas as a coaling station is reflected in the importance of fuel imports for the Danish Virgin Islands. 'Hardware' is a catchall that includes machinery and other products.[32]

[30] Other consumer goods are either included in 'hardware' or are not shown (e.g. soap and tobacco).
[31] Another intermediate good was manure, which represented around 10% of merchandise imports in Barbados and a little less in Guyana.
[32] The capital goods imports of Cuba, the Dominican Republic and Haiti from the UK, US and Germany are given in Tafunell (2007), table 4.

The main change in the composition of imports from earlier in the century was the decline in the importance of clothing. Around 1830, for example, clothing imports represented between 25 and 45 per cent of the merchandise imports of the British colonies listed in Table 5.1[33] – much higher than the proportion in 1900. Britain was still the main supplier of clothing (not just to the British colonies),[34] but it was losing ground to the United States and other core countries in the supply of other goods. The United States was the dominant supplier of foodstuffs (especially flour), and France performed well in silks and beverages. Germany was rapidly gaining ground in hardware, including machinery.

5.2. TRADE PATTERNS

The links between the Caribbean countries and the colonial powers were as strong as ever in 1820. Nearly 75 per cent of British Caribbean exports went to the 'mother' country; for the French, Dutch and Scandinavian colonies the figure was around 80 per cent.[35] For these Caribbean colonies, the United States was still a very minor market, but it did take nearly 14 per cent of exports from the Spanish colonies.[36] This was not only because of geographical proximity, but also the inability of Spain to absorb the growing volume of sugar exports from Cuba and Puerto Rico.

The market for Hispaniola's exports was more complicated. Haiti had declared independence in 1804 following the final victory over the French at the end of the previous year, but it had not yet (i.e. in 1820) been recognised by any country. In the eastern part of the island, Spain was nominally the colonial power. However, Haiti claimed the whole island on the basis of the 1795 Basel Treaty, under which Spain had ceded its rights to France, and in 1822 it would reunite the island by force (there was a brief interlude in 1821–2 when the eastern part was independent).

The absence of formal colonial ties in Hispaniola therefore provided the United States with an excellent opportunity to reestablish its trade links with the Caribbean (these had been disrupted by the War of Independence because the British still refused to grant her former colonies the same rights they had enjoyed during colonial rule). It is not surprising therefore that exports to the United States from Hispaniola in 1820 exceeded one-third of the total.[37] The US share of exports from Hispaniola was much higher than the US share of the European colonies. In the case of the British colonies, where all sorts of restrictions on trade with the United States still applied, the share was only

---

[33] For Jamaica the figure was 45.9%, for Trinidad 39.6%, for Barbados 27.3% and for Guyana 25.5%.

[34] Nearly half of Cuban imports from Britain in 1900 were clothing compared with 5.8% for the US and 36.7% for Spain. See *Commercial Relations of the United States with Foreign Countries 1900* (1901).

[35] See Tables A.21 and A.22.

[36] See Table A.20.

[37] See Table A.20.

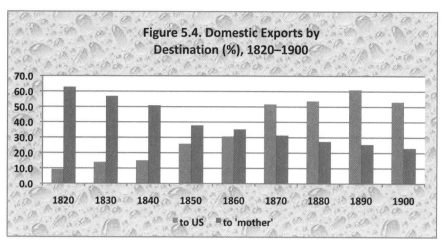

Figure 5.4. Domestic Exports by Destination (%), 1820–1900

Source: Tables A.20 and A.22.

2.9 per cent.[38] With one exception, the 'mother' country remained the dominant market for Caribbean exports up to the middle of the century. The core countries still applied draconian trade restrictions against foreign countries, which were reinforced by navigation laws. Indeed, in the case of the British and French colonies, the share of exports going to the imperial power was higher in 1850 than it had been in 1820 (84 and 90 per cent respectively). Even in Hispaniola, the share of exports going to the 'mother' countries was very high.[39] Furthermore, as Haitian exports became concentrated more and more on coffee, the French market became increasingly important.[40]

The one exception was the Spanish colonies, where the importance of the 'mother' country as a destination for exports declined from nearly 40 per cent in 1820 to little more than 10 per cent by mid-century.[41] The productive power of the sugar industry, particularly in Cuba, far outstripped the absorptive capacity of Spain. Only the United States was in a position to replace Spain, and, despite the fact that the Spanish colonies had no special trading privileges, the US share of exports had jumped to nearly 40 per cent by 1850 (the mirror image of the Spanish decline). Because the exports of the Spanish colonies grew so rapidly, it is no surprise that the US share of total Caribbean exports had reached 25 per cent by the middle of the century (see Figure 5.4).

---

[38] See Table A.20. In 1826, Britain – having tolerated limited commerce with its Caribbean colonies – imposed a total ban on trade with the US, but this was rescinded in 1830. See Bailey (1964), p. 194.

[39] As explained in the Notes on A. Tables, France is regarded as the 'mother' for Haiti, and Spain for the Dominican Republic.

[40] France recognised Haiti in 1825 and secured various trading privileges in return, but Haiti only gained access to the French market on the same terms as other foreign countries.

[41] See Table A.22.

Considering the restrictions still in place on exports to the United States, this 25 per cent share was impressive. It was still lower than the British share, which was purchasing one-third of all Caribbean exports (down from 50 per cent in 1820). However, the UK had not yet completed the equalisation of duties on imports from colonial and noncolonial sources and had only just phased out its highly restrictive Navigation Acts. Exports from the Caribbean to the United States also represented some 10 per cent of US imports by 1850.[42] Thus, although the trade links with the Caribbean were becoming **less** important for the European powers, they were becoming **more** important for the United States.

The rise of the United States as the dominant trade partner for the Caribbean accelerated after the Civil War. From 1870 onwards (see Figure 5.4), the share of Caribbean exports destined for the United States averaged between 50 and 60 per cent. The 'mother' country was steadily squeezed, its share of exports falling from nearly two-thirds in 1820 to one-third in 1870 and just over 20 per cent in 1900 (see Figure 5.4). France, it is true, retained its dominant position as the main destination for exports from its three Caribbean colonies (French Guiana, Guadeloupe and Martinique),[43] but only a small part of total Caribbean exports went to France.

The growing dependence on the US market for Caribbean exports had many causes. Geographical proximity certainly helped – transport costs were so much lower. US tariffs on some commodities of special interest to the Caribbean, such as coffee, were zero for part of the period. Even in the case of sugar, where the United States applied a tariff to protect domestic production, exports to the United States were more profitable than to most European countries, and the US market was growing rapidly. That is why sugar exporters in British, Danish and Dutch colonies increasingly switched from the 'mother' country to the United States. And in the Dominican Republic, the rise of sugar exports from the 1870s onwards was intimately associated with the US market.

The main reason, however, for the rise to prominence of the United States was the dependence of the Spanish colonies on the US market. By 1870, three-quarters of all their exports were destined for the United States, and this would rise to 80 per cent by 1890.[44] US leverage was demonstrated in the McKinley tariff of that year, because sugar was admitted free of duty for the first time, provided that the exporting country was judged not to be discriminating against US imports. The threat of high sugar duties was more than enough to persuade most sugar exporting countries to ease tariffs on US goods. The United States

---

[42] Caribbean exports to the US in 1850 were $17.9 million (derived from Tables A.11 and A.20). Total US imports (see Carter, 2006, vol. 5) were $178 million (*cif*), which I have estimated at $160 million (*fob*).

[43] France may have ended the *exclusif* in 1860, but it still retained a tight grip on trade with its colonies as a result of tariff preferences. Even in 1900, over 90% of Caribbean colonial exports went to France (see Table A.22).

[44] See Table A.20.

introduced a new tariff law in 1894, once again subjecting sugar to a tariff, and it was one of the factors leading to the Cuban revolt against Spain.

The decline of Cuban sugar exports during the Second War of Independence (1895–8) was the main reason for the fall in the US share of Caribbean exports between 1890 and 1900 (see Figure 5.4). However, the United States still took over 50 per cent of all Caribbean exports, and by then it was receiving nearly half of all exports even from the British colonies (the UK still took one-third). By the end of the century, the United States was clearly the hegemonic power in the Caribbean.

The United States and 'mother' accounted for up to 90 per cent of Caribbean domestic exports in the century (see Figure 5.4). The other destinations were mainly Canada, Latin America and the rest of Europe (principally Germany). When re-exports are taken into account – especially important for Belize, the Danish Virgin Islands and the Dutch Antilles – the structure of exports changes a little. In 1840, for example, nearly 3 per cent of merchandise exports from the British colonies was going to non-British parts of the Caribbean (the Spanish colonies were the biggest market). This share fell in subsequent years, but exports (mainly re-exports) among the British colonies became more important, reaching 6.3 per cent of merchandise exports in 1860 before falling to 4.2 per cent in 1880.[45]

These are not large proportions, but it is a salutary reminder that 'intra-Caribbean' trade did not begin with regional integration in the 1960s. Indeed, when the flows of goods are added to the migrations of people, the Caribbean was probably at least as integrated in the second half of the nineteenth century as it was a century later. Yet the export relationships that really mattered were those with the core countries: the United States, the 'mother' country and – in a few cases – Germany. That pattern would prevail throughout most of the twentieth century.

The absence of ISI and a high level of imports per head meant that the Caribbean remained an important market despite the small size of its population. The core European countries had little problem with the diversification of Caribbean exports away from the 'mother' country, but they fought hard to keep market share when it came to Caribbean imports. After the repeal of navigation laws, they came to rely more heavily on preferential tariffs by their colonies. There was no disguising the fact, however, that the United States was the closest source and – especially after the Civil War – in a position to supply the Caribbean with its import needs across a wide spectrum of goods.

The United States also saw the Caribbean as a natural marketplace for its exports not only by virtue of its geographical proximity but also by virtue

---

[45] These trade flows are not shown in the Statistical Appendix, but they can be derived from *Statistical tables relating to the Colonial and other Possessions of the United Kingdom* (various years).

of 'manifest destiny'.[46] Furthermore, the United States could always point to an earlier age (before its independence) when the thirteen colonies had been a major supplier of goods to the British Caribbean. Finally, the fact that the United States was taking an increasing share of exports from the Caribbean gave US authorities the leverage they needed first to remove discrimination against imports from the United States and second to demand preferential tariffs.

The rise of the United States as the principal source of imports may have been inevitable, but it did not necessarily look like that in 1820. The colonial powers were still dominant in the Caribbean import trade, helped by numerous trade restrictions on imports from noncolonial sources. France and Holland provided 70 per cent of the imports of their Caribbean colonies, and Britain had over 60 per cent of the market in the British colonies.[47] Despite refusing to recognise Haiti's independence until 1825, France was still responsible for 17 per cent of Haitian imports in 1820. Spain took a while to reestablish its position after the Napoleonic Wars, but by 1830 it was responsible for one-third of the imports of its Caribbean colonies (Cuba and Puerto Rico), with a complicated tariff structure that favoured Spanish goods in Spanish ships over all other kinds of imports.[48]

The United States, by contrast, struggled at first to gain a foothold in the Caribbean import trade. Its share of the important British colonial market in 1820 was only 5 per cent.[49] It did slightly better in the other colonial markets, but its greatest success was in Hispaniola where the absence of trade restrictions allowed the United States to provide nearly half of all imports in 1820. This could not be maintained, however, because the 1825 treaty leading to French recognition gave the former colonial power trading privileges.[50] Even when these were withdrawn after 1830, this did not at first benefit the United States, because its refusal to recognise Haitian independence was bitterly resented.[51]

The United States slowly made gains at the expense of the 'mother' country, despite the trade restrictions and discriminatory tariffs that the colonial countries imposed. By 1850 its share of Caribbean imports had reached just over 20 per cent (see Figure 5.5). In the next decade, the United States import share rose significantly, helped by a much better performance in the Spanish colonies

---

[46] This doctrine had been promulgated openly in the 1840s, but it had been reflected in public pronouncements towards Cuba much earlier. See Bailey (1964), pp. 285–8.

[47] See Tables A.28 and A.29.

[48] The tariff on imported flour was particularly skewed to favour Spain and discriminate against the US.

[49] See Table A.27. Even this low share was quite an achievement given the obstacles imposed by the British authorities.

[50] See Chapter 7.

[51] The US finally recognised Haiti's independence in 1862 – the same year that President Lincoln had announced that slavery would be ended in the rebel states. See Logan (1941), chap. 10.

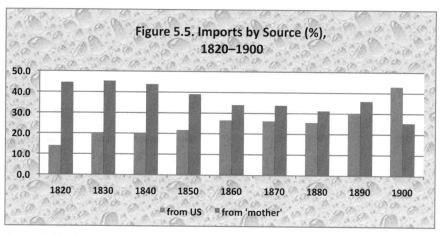

Source: Tables A.27 and A.29.

and the end of navigation laws elsewhere. This share had fallen back modestly by 1870 as a result of the disruptions of the Civil War and the fact that US goods had risen in price much faster than those of the other core countries. However, the United States recovered its position in the 1870s and was once again responsible for 50 per cent of the imports of Hispaniola by 1880.[52]

It was at this point that the United States really began to flex its muscles.[53] Taking advantage of its dominant position in the market for Cuban exports, the United States explored with a reluctant Spain the option of a trade agreement that would have given it tariff preferences in the Spanish colonies. This was anathema to the other colonial powers, who protested vigorously. The United States withdrew the proposal but once again went on the offensive in 1890 with the passage of the McKinley tariff.[54] This granted presidential authority to negotiate tariff reductions with those countries deemed to be taxing US imports more heavily than the United States was taxing their exports.

Because this was the case for almost all Caribbean countries (they depended heavily on the revenue from the import tariff, so their average tariff on US imports was much higher than the average US tariff on their exports), this gave the US authorities enormous leverage – of which they took full advantage. Within two years, the Dominican Republic, Spain (on behalf of its colonies) and Britain (on behalf of its) had implemented tariff reductions on US imports.[55]

[52] See Table A.27.
[53] As early as 1869 the US had expressed concern about the low level of its exports to Latin America and the Caribbean. See Pletcher (1977) and Pletcher (1998). The new, more aggressive policy was in response to the imbalance between US imports from and exports to the region.
[54] See Chapter 3.
[55] For negotiations with the Dominican Republic, see Dodd (1974).

Haiti, however, resisted and was punished with draconian tax increases on its exports to the United States.[56]

The McKinley tariff was replaced in 1894, and many of the tariff reductions adopted by Caribbean countries went into reverse. However, the rise of the United States could not be stopped. By 1900 it was responsible for 43 per cent of all Caribbean imports (see Figure 5.5). Its share was highest in Hispaniola (nearly 60 per cent), followed by the Spanish and Scandinavian colonies (nearly 50 per cent), the British and Dutch colonies (around one-third) and just over one-quarter in the French ones.[57] If it were not for its weakness in the crucial textile trade, where Britain in particular remained strong, the United States share would have been even higher.

The mirror image of the rise of the United States was the decline in the importance of the imperial countries. The 'mother' countries saw their share fall from 45 per cent in 1820 to one-quarter in 1900 (see Figure 5.5). Yet this was a respectable performance, a tribute to the enduring colonial links established by Britain and France in particular. Indeed, France in 1900 was still supplying nearly 50 per cent of the import needs of its Caribbean colonies and even held a 10 per cent market share in Haiti.[58] Similarly, from 1860 to 1900 the British colonies bought over 40 per cent of their imports from the UK, and as late as 1900 Britain was supplying over 20 per cent of all Caribbean imports, thanks to a continued strong presence in Cuba.[59]

5.3. THE TERMS OF TRADE

Changes in the terms of trade are often described as a windfall. When an energy exporter today, for example, sees a sharp rise or fall in the price of oil, great attention is paid to the transfer of resources to or from the country in question. The change in the size of this transfer is likely to determine the rise or fall of national income much more than the change in the volume of exports.

For exporters of commodities, whose prices are inherently volatile, this transfer of resources is such a normal state of affairs that it is perhaps misleading to describe it as a windfall. Certainly, commodity exporters in the Caribbean in the nineteenth century were accustomed to a world in which prices could double or halve in a short period according to international market conditions. Coping with such volatility was part of their survival strategies.

Movements in the Net Barter Terms of Trade (the price of exports divided by the price of imports) may have been a zero-sum game at the global level. However, changes could operate for or against a particular country for very long periods. There was no expectation or requirement that – at the country level – the Net Barter Terms of Trade (NBTT) need balance out over time.

[56] See Montague (1940), pp. 166–7.
[57] See Table A.27.
[58] See Table A.29, where the 'mother' for Haiti is France.
[59] See Table A.28.

Furthermore, the Income Terms of Trade (ITT) – NBTT adjusted for the change in the volume of exports – was not even a zero-sum game at the global level. All countries could in theory experience a gain (or indeed loss) in the ITT whatever happened to the NBTT.

To calculate the NBTT and ITT, we need for each country estimates of changes in export prices, import prices and the volume of exports.[60] Export prices were discussed in some detail in Chapter 4. Using time series on leading commodities from all over the world, we were able to explore the changes in prices of the commodities of most importance for the Caribbean. Here, however, we need to go further because the price of interest is the unit value of exports for each Caribbean country. We may start with the unit value of each commodity exported from the Caribbean. By summing the value of each commodity exported by all countries and dividing by the volume (at 1860 prices), we obtain a 'price' for each commodity exported from the Caribbean from 1820 to 1900. These prices are weighted averages, with the weights determined by the importance of each country in the commodity total. Thus, towards the end of the century, the sugar 'price' reflects in particular the weight given to Cuba (the largest exporter), the coffee 'price' the weights given to Haiti and Puerto Rico, the cacao price the weight given to the Dominican Republic and so on.[61]

These Caribbean commodity price movements are very revealing.[62] We may observe, for example, the fall in the sugar price from its peak in 1820, the dramatic decline in the price of cotton and the more modest falls in the prices of logwood and mahogany. The volatility of the coffee price, falling sharply at first (1820–50), then rising (1850–90) and finally collapsing (1890–1900), is also clear. However, commodity price movements could also be favourable for the Caribbean. There was a rise in the price of tobacco leaf, cigars and cacao and stability in the prices of bananas and gold.

This means that the export unit value for any country will depend on the commodity composition and the weights given to the different products. It is then possible to construct a unit value of exports for each country from 1820 to 1900 by dividing the value of exports of the principal commodities by their volume.[63] This shows that export unit values for countries tended to fall over the century from their peak in 1820, but there were periods of rising prices (1830–40, 1850–60, 1870–80) around the downward trend.

Export unit values for the different subregions and the Caribbean as a whole are shown in Table 5.2. The sharp fall between 1820 and 1830 in Hispaniola

---

[60] These are provided in Tables A.15, A.30 and A.16, respectively, and the data have also been aggregated to produce estimates of the terms of trade for each subregion in the Caribbean and for the Caribbean as a whole.

[61] The weights change each decade depending on the importance of countries in each commodity export.

[62] See Table A.19.

[63] Using the country data in Table A.10. The results are shown in Table A.15.

TABLE 5.2. *Export Unit Values for Caribbean and Subregions (1860=100),*
1820–1900

	Hispaniola	Spanish Colonies	British Colonies	French Colonies	Dutch Colonies	Scandinavian Colonies	Caribbean
1820	218.6	134.6	115.0	111.3	148.0	177.7	126.0
1830	75.5	87.0	97.7	86.3	93.7	156.0	92.1
1840	91.0	99.4	152.3	85.9	107.5	142.9	111.6
1850	79.8	82.4	90.4	87.2	90.6	127.8	85.0
1860	100.0	100.0	100.0	100.0	100.0	100.0	100.0
1870	89.0	85.6	104.0	94.9	100.8	114.1	90.7
1880	131.2	110.8	102.7	96.1	113.1	130.8	109.1
1890	116.5	96.2	87.5	82.4	105.1	104.8	94.7
1900	71.8	98.1	81.6	91.1	98.4	63.4	87.6

Source: Table A.15.

was caused above all by the decline in the coffee price for Haiti.[64] This had been exceptionally high in 1820, when the world market was still suffering from shortages induced by the upheavals of the Napoleonic Wars. The spike in the export unit value in the British colonies in 1840, by contrast, was due to the recovery of sugar prices in the British market following the emancipation of the slaves and the decline in the volume of sugar exports. The collapse in the export price of the Scandinavian colonies after 1880 was due to the sharp fall in the price of sugar received by the Danish Virgin Islands (its only domestic export of importance).

Perhaps the most surprising feature of Table 5.2 is the modest decline in the export unit value after 1880, despite the sharp fall in the sugar price. Hispaniola, it is true, was badly affected, but this had as much to do with the fall in coffee prices in Haiti (after 1890) as with the fall in sugar prices in the Dominican Republic. However, diversification away from sugar helped other subregions avoid the full impact of falling sugar prices. The decline in the export unit value of the British colonies, for example, was moderated by the diversification away from sugar towards other commodities (e.g. bananas, lime juice and cacao), whose prices either remained the same or even rose. Similarly, the export unit value of the Spanish colonies[65] was helped by the rise in relative importance of the tobacco industry (leaf and cigars), whose prices were rising at the same time that sugar prices were falling. Indeed, the export unit value of the Spanish colonies was almost as high in 1900 as it had been in 1860.

If commodity export prices had fallen from their peak at the beginning of the century, so had import prices. Furthermore, the long-run decline in core wholesale prices (used here as a proxy for Caribbean import prices) may not

[64] Haitian exports were far more important than those of the Dominican Republic and would remain so until the end of the nineteenth century.
[65] Heavily influenced by Cuba, whose exports were much more important than those of Puerto Rico.

TABLE 5.3. *Import Price Indices for Jamaica, 1830–1890*

Year	Based on Import Unit Values	Based on Core Wholesale Prices
c.1830/1850	−15%	−11.4%
1850/1870	+44.3%	+49.3%
1870/1890	−23.3%	−25.4%

Source: Eisner (1961), p. 375, for import unit values, and Table A.30 for core wholesale prices.

fully capture the fall because the transport revolution after 1870 was driving down shipping costs so rapidly. It is hard to be sure about this. However, we can use estimates of Jamaican import prices based on *cif* import unit values and compare it with those using core wholesale prices. The results (see Table 5.3) are sufficiently similar to suggest that no great injustice is done by using core wholesale prices.

Because so much of final expenditure in the Caribbean consisted of imported goods, we can also check estimates of import unit values by reference to the domestic price level. The British colonies all published prices for articles of common consumption. They show a similar trend to the import unit values based on core wholesale prices.[66] For Cuba we also have a detailed estimate of domestic prices from 1872 to 1897, showing a steep fall of 37.4 per cent, while the import price index from 1870 to 1900 fell by 23.8 per cent.[67] Given the rise in Cuban prices that must surely have taken place between 1897 and 1900 in war and its aftermath, these results seem broadly compatible.

We are now in a position to show the NBTT using the export and import unit values outlined above in this section (see Figure 5.6).[68] From 1820 to 1830 many countries experienced a decline as commodity prices fell back from their postwar peaks (import unit values also fell, but not usually by as much). Between 1830 and 1860, the NBTT first rose and then fell without any major deterioration. Between 1860 and 1870, however, the increase in import unit values led to a significant fall in the NBTT. This was reversed after 1870 as core prices fell. Finally, the NBTT declined after 1880 during the period when sugar and coffee prices in particular were in retreat.

The Spanish, French, British and Dutch colonies ended the century with the NBTT higher than in 1860. The performance of the British colonies was particularly noteworthy because it was widely assumed by contemporaries that the NBTT had deteriorated in line with the sugar price. The reasons why this

[66] I have constructed crude price indices based on ten articles of popular consumption, but the results are not given here.
[67] See Santamaría and García (2004), cuadro II.19, p. 351.
[68] The detailed results are given in the Statistical Appendix for each country and subregion. See Table A.31.

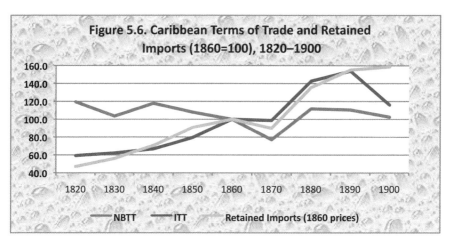

Figure 5.6. Caribbean Terms of Trade and Retained Imports (1860=100), 1820–1900

NBTT — ITT — Retained Imports (1860 prices)

Source: Derived from Tables A.26, A.31 and A.32.

was not necessarily the case have been outlined above.[69] Those British colonies that failed to diversify away from sugar (such as Antigua, Barbados and St Kitts) **did** experience a decline in their NBTT. Those that diversified, including the Bahamas, Dominica, Grenada, Jamaica and Trinidad, reaped a reward in terms of higher NBTT.

The domestic exports of the Dutch colonies were dominated by Suriname. After the period of state supervision (1863–73), there was a shift of resources away from sugar to other crops. Some of these were produced by smallholders for the domestic market. However, exports became much more diversified, with a range of commodities at the end of the century that included balata,[70] rice, gold and bananas along with a much larger volume of cacao. The prices of these commodities held up well after 1870 at a time when import prices were falling. As a result, Suriname's NBTT stood at 116.5 in 1900 (1860=100) – higher than at any time after the peak in 1820.

The NBTT of the Spanish colonies was heavily influenced by what happened in Cuba. There was a sharp fall from 1820 to 1830 when sugar prices fell, followed by three decades of relative stability before a sharp decline between 1860 and 1870 when import prices – particularly from the United States – soared. The NBTT, however, recovered quickly and ended the century above its level in 1860, despite the fall in the price of sugar.[71] Puerto Rico was also

[69] Using a different set of import and export price indices, Eisner (1961) also found an improvement in Jamaica's NBTT between 1870 and 1890, which is similar (+39% compared with +48%). See Eisner (1961), p. 375; and Table A.31.

[70] Balata was the gum obtained from tapping rubber trees. It was used, among other purposes, by telegraph companies to coat submarine cables.

[71] An alternative estimate has been made of the NBTT of Cuba for the years 1826 to 1884 by Linda and Richard Salvucci. See Salvucci and Salvucci (2000), pp. 197–222. The trend of their series and mine is similar in 1830–40, but it diverges thereafter. In particular, their series shows

affected adversely by the sharp rise in US prices in the 1860s, but the shift from sugar to coffee contributed to a big improvement in the NBTT between 1870 and 1890.

The ITT adjust the NBTT for the change in the volume of exports.[72] From 1820 to 1850, only two subregions (Hispaniola and the Spanish colonies) were able to expand the volume of exports. The other groups all suffered a decline, with the British colonies particularly adversely affected. However, the expansion in the Spanish colonies was so substantial that it more than compensated for the fall in the volume of exports in the other colonies. As a result, the Caribbean as a whole enjoyed an increase in the volume of exports of nearly 50 per cent.

From 1850 onwards, the volume of exports rose almost continuously in all subregions (except the Dutch colonies) until 1890. In that year, for the Caribbean as a whole, the volume was nearly three times larger than in 1820 and almost twice as large as in 1850. Even in the last decade of the century, the volume of exports rose in Hispaniola, thanks to the dramatic increase in exports from the Dominican Republic, and in the Dutch colonies as a result of export diversification in Suriname. Elsewhere between 1890 and 1900, however, the volume stagnated (British colonies) or declined (Spanish, French and Scandinavian colonies). Indeed, the decline in Cuba, the most important Caribbean exporter by far, was so severe that the volume for the Caribbean as a whole fell by nearly 20 per cent in that decade.

From this it is easy to guess what happened to the ITT. For the Caribbean as a whole (see Figure 5.6), they rose fairly steadily after 1820 before falling sharply between 1890 and 1900. This was also the pattern in the Spanish colonies. For the British and French colonies, they fell between 1820 and 1850 and then recovered steeply, but for the Dutch and Scandinavian colonies the improvement was delayed until after 1870. In Hispaniola there was deterioration in the ITT between 1820 and 1830, but from then onwards there was an improvement in every decade except between 1860 and 1870.

The ITT can also be expressed as the value of exports divided by the price of imports. They therefore measure the volume of imports that can be purchased for a given value of exports. If exports and imports were always equal, the ITT should then give us the same results as retained imports at constant prices.[73] This is the third line shown in Figure 5.6, and it does indeed show a similar

---

a sharp fall between 1850 and 1860, and mine is stable, but theirs is stable between 1870 and 1880, when mine shows a sharp increase. It is not possible to establish precisely the reasons for this divergence, but I find it hard to accept a sharp fall between 1850 and 1860, when the London price of sugar actually rose. It is also difficult to reconcile stability of the NBTT between 1870 and 1880 with the fall in core wholesale prices (including in the US). Nonetheless, this comparison should serve as a warning that the Cuban data are not – and never will be – as precise as we would like.

[72] The volume figures are given in Table A.16 and the income terms of trade in Table A.32.
[73] See Table A.26.

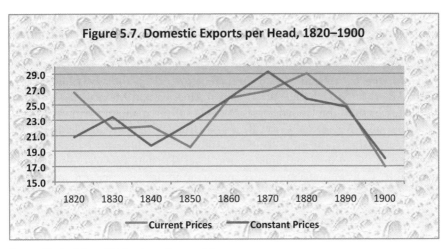

Figure 5.7. Domestic Exports per Head, 1820–1900

Source: Derived from Tables A.1a, A.11 and A.14.

trend to the ITT, except between 1890 and 1900 when it moved in the opposite direction. This was mainly because of postwar reconstruction in Cuba, when imports soared.

5.4. DOMESTIC EXPORTS PER HEAD

We now look at domestic exports per head, starting with the Caribbean as a whole and working our way down to the individual countries. Because population growth rates varied so much over time and across countries, some of the results in terms of exports per head are quite surprising. Many countries had an unimpressive performance in terms of domestic exports. However, if the population was declining, then exports per head could still perform well. On the other hand, the countries with the fastest population growth needed to expand exports rapidly merely to keep exports per head constant.

Domestic exports per head for the Caribbean as a whole are shown in Figure 5.7 in both constant and current prices. Because of the high price of many commodities in 1820, the figure was higher at current than at constant prices, but the reverse was true in 1900, when the sugar and coffee prices in particular were so low. In general, however, the two series do not differ by much.[74] The trends are similar to the three phases (identified in section 1 above) for domestic exports as a whole: flat or declining until 1840–50, rising until 1870–80 and declining steeply thereafter. The main difference is that the decline set in after 1880, even for the series at constant prices as a result of the rise in population.

[74] In the rest of this section, I generally use the constant price series at 1860 prices.

The trend of domestic exports per head over the whole period (1820–1900) was distinctly unimpressive. After all, the value at both current and constant prices was lower in 1900 than in 1820. And yet the Caribbean still compared favourably with other countries and regions at the end of the period. The figure for the Caribbean ($16.9 at current prices) in 1900 was higher than South America ($14), higher than Central America and Mexico ($6) and only a little lower than the United States ($18).[75] Of the mainland Latin American countries, only Argentina, Costa Rica and Uruguay had a higher figure.[76]

Not surprisingly, the mean for the Caribbean as a whole hides a great deal of variation at the subregional and country level. Turning first to the subregions (see Table 5.4), we may note once again the impressive performance of the Spanish colonies – at least until 1870. Domestic exports per head, among the lowest in 1820, had overtaken the British colonies by 1840 and all other subregions by 1850. However, their decline after 1870 was almost as spectacular as their previous ascent. Domestic exports per head in 1900 in the Spanish colonies were once again lower than in the British, Dutch, French and Scandinavian colonies.

The British colonies followed a more familiar path. Starting at a high level in 1820, when slavery had taken export specialisation to its greatest extreme, domestic exports per head at constant prices collapsed in the next two decades. A modest recovery started in the 1840s, but exports per head never regained the 1820 peak. A similar pattern occurred in the Dutch and French colonies, except that exports per head at first rose. This was followed by a sharp decline. The French colonies were the first to recover and had surpassed the previous peak level of exports by 1880, after which another decline took place.

Hispaniola took a different road. Although the absolute level of exports was high, domestic exports per head were the lowest in the Caribbean in 1820 and remained so in every decade of the century. This was a consequence of the large population and the existence of a land frontier that provided at least some alternative opportunities for the labour force other than exports. Despite a high level of volatility, domestic exports per head did rise modestly over the whole period (1820–1900), in contrast to most other subregions. Indeed, taking the period as a whole, exports per head only rose faster in the Spanish colonies (see Table 5.4).

The ranking of the twenty-eight countries in 1820 was shown in Figure 4.1 at current prices. At constant (1860) prices, the top ten countries were still mainly British colonies.[77] This was an indication of how far the British had taken export specialisation and how little they had been disrupted by the

---

[75] The US figure is derived from Carter (2006), vol. 1 (population) and vol. 5 (exports). The figures for mainland Latin America are derived from the Montivideo-Oxford Latin American Economic History Database (hereafter MOxLAD).

[76] See MOxLAD.

[77] The ranking at constant prices (derived from Tables A.1a and A.14) is similar with Belize still in first position and Puerto Rico last.

TABLE 5.4. *Domestic Exports per Head (at 1860 prices), 1820–1900*

	Hispaniola	Spanish Colonies	British Colonies	French Colonies	Dutch Colonies	Scandinavian Colonies	Caribbean
1820	6.4	10.1	38.4	25.3	23.9	21.5	20.8
1830	9.4	19.1	34.8	30.8	31.7	22.2	23.4
1840	8.1	24.4	18.4	25.7	29.4	18.9	19.7
1850	8.0	32.7	20.7	15.2	22.9	14.1	22.6
1860	8.7	35.7	23.3	23.0	21.7	14.7	25.8
1870	6.8	43.8	25.1	28.0	15.2	9.4	29.2
1880	8.0	36.0	23.5	33.7	17.9	16.4	25.7
1890	8.3	34.0	25.1	29.6	15.2	29.0	24.7
1900	10.8	19.1	22.2	22.7	20.6	27.9	18.0
% per year							
1820–1860	0.8	3.2	−1.2	−0.2	−0.2	−0.9	0.5
1860–1900	0.6	−1.6	−0.1	0.0	−0.1	1.6	−0.9
1820–1900	0.7	0.8	−0.7	−0.1	−0.2	0.3	−0.2

Source: Derived from Tables A.1a and A.14.

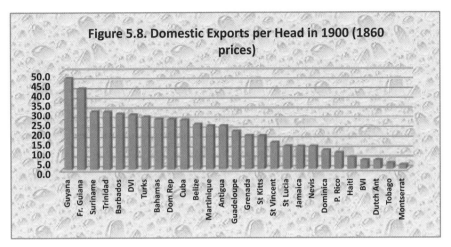

Source: Derived from Tables A.1a and A.14.

Napoleonic Wars compared with their European rivals. By contrast, the bottom ten countries included the two Spanish colonies (Cuba and Puerto Rico) and the two countries of Hispaniola (Haiti and the Dominican Republic).

In the next four decades, these rankings would alter. The disastrous performance of many British colonies, the recovery in the French colonies after 1850 and the spectacular performance of the Spanish colonies led to a sharp change in fortune. Jamaica had fallen by 1860 into the bottom quartile, and Belize had gone from first to twelfth.[78] Cuba was now ranked first, narrowly ahead of Guyana, where exports had started to recover after 1840 and where the plantation owners were investing in the new technologies needed to reduce costs in the sugar industry.

The rankings would change again by the end of the century (see Figure 5.8). Guyana was now ranked first[79] with French Guiana second, where a gold rush had eclipsed almost all other exports. Suriname and Trinidad were third and fourth respectively as a result of export diversification (particularly into cacao). Cuba had slipped to tenth, but the Dominican Republic, last in 1860, had jumped to ninth. The lowest positions in the rankings were taken by three British colonies (Montserrat, Tobago and the British Virgin Islands), where almost nothing had taken the place of the abandoned sugar plantations, and by the Dutch Antilles, where re-exports were much more important than commodities.

It is not possible to comment in detail on the export performance of all countries, but some do merit special consideration. In closing this chapter, I focus on Cuba, Jamaica and the Dominican Republic. These three countries

[78] Belize's decline is examined in Chapter 11.
[79] Guyana was exporting gold, and this helped to offset the damage done to domestic exports by the decline of the sugar industry.

offer contrasting performances from among the different subregions. They were also three of the largest economies in the nineteenth century.

Despite the decline after 1870, pride of place in terms of export performance must go to Cuba. This was largely because of the transformation of the sugar industry. Cuba was not the first country in the Caribbean to adopt the *central*,[80] but in almost all other respects it was a pioneer in new methods of processing cane into sugar. The first railway in Latin America and the Caribbean was constructed in Cuba in 1837 and was used to transport cane from the estates to the mills.[81] The steam engine was widely adopted in sugar mills by 1860.[82] The vacuum pan, which improved the separation of molasses and increased the yield from cane, and new grinding machines found a receptive market in Cuba.[83] Finally, the spread of the *central* after 1870, although it hastened the entry of US capital and generated massive underemployment among cane cutters for much of the year, reduced labour requirements per ton of sugar and eased the transition to a postslavery society.[84]

Finance was readily available for all these innovations in Cuba. The interlocking nature of the merchant class, the slave traders and the sugar planters generated substantial profits that could be ploughed back into new investments without undercutting the luxurious lifestyle of the elite.[85] Financial institutions in Cuba developed on the back of these developments, and funds were available for those that needed to borrow.[86] And Cuba remained an attractive investment destination for Spanish capitalists. Until the First War of Independence, Cuba was growing much faster than the Spanish economy, funds could be borrowed in Spain and the colonial state favoured Spanish over foreign investors.[87]

Yet Cuba's transformation was about much more than sugar. The tobacco industry, for example, despite all the restrictions imposed by the core in the form of discriminatory tariffs, was hugely important. In addition to the tobacco leaf and cigars that Cuba exported were cigarettes manufactured in factories using the latest machines. By 1900, the value of this 'minor' export exceeded $3 million, which meant that cigarettes alone were more important than the

---

[80] That honour belongs to Guadeloupe, where a *central* (a large sugar mill able to process cane from many surrounding estates) was established in 1845. See Deerr (1949), vol. 1, p. 235.

[81] See Santamaría and García (2004), pp. 177–8.

[82] By that time, 72% of the mills were steam-powered, and they produced 90% of the sugar crop. See Dye (1998), p. 31.

[83] All this is described in detail in Moreno Fraginals (1978), vol. 1.

[84] See Thomas (1971), chap. 23, and Moreno Fraginals (1978), vol. 2, pp. 177–89.

[85] On the interlocking nature of this elite, see Thomas (1971), chap. 9.

[86] See Santamaría and García (2004), pp. 210–16.

[87] A frequently asked question is why Puerto Rico did not mirror Cuba's development in view of the two islands' similarities. The sugar industry did expand rapidly in Puerto Rico, but it was never as profitable, and the investment funds needed to cut costs after 1870 were not as widely available as in Cuba. It was coffee, not sugar, that expanded rapidly in Puerto Rico in the last few decades of the century, and this was related to its lower capital requirements. See Bergad (1983), chaps. 3 and 4.

domestic exports of most Caribbean countries.[88] In that year, the current price value of all tobacco exports reached $26 million – greater than sugar, molasses and rum combined.[89]

Cuba's decline began after 1870 because of the prolonged First War of Independence (1868–78), the fall in the sugar price after 1883 and the difficulties facing its tobacco exports as a result of protectionism in the core. However, the fall of the Cuban economy was concentrated in the 1890s, beginning with the Wilson tariff in 1894 that removed the privileged access to the US market that Cuba had enjoyed under the McKinley tariff. The Second War of Independence (1895–8) then caused heavy disruption to the economy, because some of the fiercest fighting was in the main sugar-producing regions. There was also terrible destruction of livestock and much damage to infrastructure.

Jamaica's export performance was not the worst in the Caribbean, but it came close. The sugar industry went into decline even before 1820 and – except for a brief revival in the 1850s – the volume of sugar exports fell in every decade until the end of the century. Some planters made an attempt to reduce costs by introducing new technologies, but they were overwhelmed by the much more numerous members of their class that simply abandoned their estates and left the island.[90] Unlike in Barbados, yet alone Cuba, the planter class in Jamaica did not feel any great affinity with the island and was more interested in pursuing the new opportunities that were opening up elsewhere in the British Empire and in the UK itself.

Jamaican exports had always been diversified. Even in 1820, the export list included many products other than sugar, molasses and rum. These products – for example, coffee, cacao, logwood, ginger and pimento – continued to be exported throughout the century, and some even expanded.[91] All were helped by the interest of those ex-slaves now settled in villages in finding products that could generate a cash income and avoid the need to depend exclusively on the plantations. However, the expansion of these products could not fully compensate for the decline of sugar.

The one crop that did finally replace sugar in importance was bananas. The export trade began in the 1870s,[92] and expansion was rapid on the north of the island. Sugar estates were sold and replanted with bananas. The smallholders in the villages were also able to take part. Boats arrived regularly to collect

---

[88] Only seven countries in 1900 had domestic exports at current prices that exceeded the value of Cuban cigarette exports.

[89] See Instituto de Historia de Cuba (1998).

[90] See Eisner (1961), pp. 198–9. On those estates that adopted new technologies, however, costs fell sharply. Indeed, the Royal Commission of 1897 reported that costs per unit of production were lower in Jamaica than anywhere else in the British West Indies. See Lobdell (1972), p. 48.

[91] See Table A.10. For annual data, see Eisner (1961), pp. 240–4.

[92] This followed the speculative voyage of Captain Baker in 1871, when he took a consignment of bananas to Boston. This is often portrayed as marking the beginning of the Caribbean export trade, but Cuba had in fact been exporting bananas to the East Coast of the US for at least twenty years. See Santamaría and García (2004), pp. 264–74.

shipments, and Port Antonio was built especially to accommodate the new trade. By 1890, banana exports by value exceeded sugar, and in 1900 they were nearly four times greater. Prices had fallen from their peak, but nothing like as much as in the case of sugar.

Jamaica's exports, it is often said, suffered from the 'flight' of the ex-slaves from the plantations to the villages after the end of the emancipation period. This is very misleading. Plantation owners in other countries, as we saw in Chapter 3, were able to secure labour through various coercive measures (including indentured labour), and it is hard to believe that Jamaican planters were uniquely squeamish about the adoption of harsh methods. Other countries, notably Guadeloupe, Guyana, Martinique and Trinidad, also experienced the rise of a small-scale peasantry after emancipation, but their sugar industries did not suffer to the same extent. It is difficult to escape the conclusion that a large part of the Jamaican planter class was simply not interested in making the investments required to reduce costs at a time of falling prices.[93]

The final country to be examined here is the Dominican Republic. In 1820, this country was one of the poorest in the Caribbean. Still nominally a Spanish colony, it exported a small amount of timber, tobacco and hides. The absence of clear title, estate boundaries and enforcement mechanisms, coupled with the threat of Haitian invasion after independence in 1844, meant that the timber was overexploited and the cattle were allowed to run wild. Cigar exports could not compete after the imposition of discriminatory tariffs by core countries and declined sharply after 1850. And yet the Dominican Republic ended the century as one of the more dynamic exporters in the Caribbean. The tobacco industry underwent various improvements, helped by the reduction in costs made possible by investments in railways.[94] The sugar industry was reestablished in the 1870s, and exports expanded rapidly. The cacao and coffee industries were revived around the same time, and the Dominican Republic had become one of the world's leading exporters of cacao by 1900.[95] Finally, the banana industry took root in the 1890s. And even the export of hides recovered because the cattle industry was subject to modernisation.

The catalyst in all this was the emigration of Cuban capitalists to the Dominican Republic during the First War of Independence. It was their knowledge and expertise that helped to establish a modern sugar industry based on the latest technologies and having access to virgin lands. Furthermore, by the mid-1870s the threat of Haitian invasion had finally ended. The Spanish annexation (1861–5), reactionary though it was in many ways, helped to accelerate the adoption of clearer property rights and stronger enforcement mechanisms for settling disputes. Population growth had also relieved the problem of labour scarcity, and by the 1890s the country would start to attract immigrants without the need for coercion.

[93] See Lobdell (1972).
[94] See Baud (1995), chap. 2.
[95] See Clarence-Smith (2000), p. 150.

The Dominican Republic, however, was one of the first Caribbean countries to be brought within the US informal empire that would soon dominate the region. Cuba may have been the first choice for the United States by reason of its proximity, but the existence of slavery made annexation politically impossible for the United States after the Civil War. The financially penurious governments in the Dominican Republic were an easier target. Samaná Bay had a special strategic attraction for US administrations from President Grant's (1869–77) onwards. Indeed, the Dominican Republic came within a whisker of being annexed by the United States in 1870.[96] Privileged access to the US market under the reciprocal trade treaty that followed the 1890 McKinley tariff was the spur for US investments in the sugar industry and related infrastructure developments in railways, ports and harbours.[97]

These three countries illustrate the complexities of the Caribbean in the century and emphasise the need to avoid sweeping generalisations. Cuba, the star performer in terms of exports, was a Spanish colony in which slavery had survived later than anywhere else. Jamaica was a British colony where the export sector went into steep decline after emancipation, but Barbados – another British colony – enjoyed a period of sustained growth after a brief fall. The Dominican Republic performed very badly at the beginning and very well at the end, even though it was independent for most of the period. No single variable (e.g. slavery, commodity prices or political status) is able to explain the variety of experiences of the Caribbean in the nineteenth century.

[96] See Martínez-Fernández (1994), pp. 165–70. See also Tansill (1938), Montague (1940), Logan (1941) and Welles (1928).
[97] In an early example of dollar diplomacy, the US-controlled San [sic] Domingo Improvement Co. took over the debts owed to the Dutch financier Westendorp in 1892 in return for numerous privileges. See Domínguez (1986) and Knight (1928).

6

The Domestic Economy in the Caribbean

The previous two chapters have been concerned with foreign trade and in particular the export sector. In this chapter we look at the domestic economy. Although the Caribbean countries had taken export specialisation to its highest level, there were still many activities that were geared to the home market. Some of these were complementary to the export sector, but a few competed with imports. With the exception of public administration, there is a deficiency of data on the domestic economy. There are no countries, for example, that published a series on industrial output, no regular figures for housing starts and very little on financial services. We therefore have to proceed on the basis of partial data, pieced together from different sources and checked against other evidence.

The first section of the chapter is concerned with the production of goods and services by the private sector for the domestic economy. By far the most important activity was Domestic Use Agriculture (DUA), that is, agricultural goods produced either for autoconsumption or for sale in the home market. These goods were perishable and therefore could not be easily imported at a time of sailing ships. In some countries, there was also a thriving fishing industry geared to the home market.

Industrial output, excluding that large part dedicated to the processing of raw materials for export, was a mixture of mining, artisan output and import-substituting manufacturing. The latter was still very small even in 1900, but the artisan sector included several important occupations. Mineral production for the home market was not of great importance, but it existed everywhere and provided raw materials for construction. The industrial sector did not employ a large share of the labour force. Outside the agricultural sector, the most important occupations were all in services. These included making clothes, washing garments and domestic service – all occupations in which women figured prominently. By contrast, financial services were not a big employer in any country, but the sector was a key one in view of the dependence of so many activities on credit.

The second section of the chapter examines the development of infrastructure. We cannot speak of a railway age in the Caribbean, but the larger countries (and some of the smaller ones) began to develop a network that helped to reduce transport costs. The financing of the railways, however, was difficult, and this held back their development. Other infrastructure developments worthy of note were telegraph and telephone lines, ports, roads and canals.

Public finance is the subject of the third section of the chapter. We have at least some data on government revenue for all countries, and we can observe its dependence on taxes on trade. Public expenditure was a very small part of the economy in the nineteenth century, but it was of growing importance in the areas of health and education as the century advanced. Expenditure on debt service was modest in the colonies, but the independent countries – Haiti and the Dominican Republic – had high levels of indebtedness and often had difficulties in meeting their commitments.

The final section of the chapter brings together indicators that are closely correlated with GDP to measure macroeconomic performance. This is not by any means a perfect substitute for detailed estimates of national accounts, but it gives a rough guide to the ranking of subregions and countries in the century and the variance in living standards between them. The results are also compared with the four countries for which we have some GDP data.

6.1. GOODS AND SERVICES FOR THE HOME MARKET

All economies specialising in exports have a range of activities that are not part of the export sector. Some of these complement the export activities themselves. Examples in the nineteenth-century Caribbean included the raising of draught animals for work on the sugarcane estates and livestock to produce meat for the labour force. Other activities had no direct connection with the export sector. These included the numerous retail outlets that served the population in towns and villages.

The most important nonexport activity in the Caribbean was DUA. In the slave economies, the slaves needed to be fed, and importing was expensive. That is why the slaves were obliged to produce ground provisions and permitted on occasions to sell any surplus in the local markets. The skills developed, brought in many cases from Africa, gave rise to what has been termed a 'proto-peasantry'.[1] With emancipation, many of the former slaves left the estates and established 'free' villages where they could choose what to produce. This process was particularly important in those countries where the export sector had left the interior largely untouched.[2] These countries included Guadeloupe,

---

[1] See Mintz (1974).
[2] If the interior was not mountainous, as in Barbados, it was usually developed for the purposes of the export sector.

Guyana, Haiti, Jamaica, Martinique, Suriname and Trinidad.[3] Not surprisingly, especially in the early days after the end of slavery, the former slaves concentrated on agricultural goods they could either consume themselves or sell locally.[4]

In the Spanish colonies, including in this case the Dominican Republic, the export sector was much less important at the start of the nineteenth century. Many of the descendants of the settlers, an ethnically mixed group, had retreated into the interior to raise crops and livestock for their own use and for the small home market. The development of the export sector in the century was a severe challenge for these workers, because both their land and labour was needed by the plantations.[5] This peasantry, new and old, lived on smallholdings and produced to a large extent for the home market, but the plantations were large estates producing mainly for export. It is easy therefore to fall into the trap of assuming that 'small-scale' is synonymous with DUA and 'large-scale' with Export Agriculture (EXA). This, however, is a mistake. Although most large-scale activities were geared to the foreign market,[6] the smallholdings (those up to 50 acres) became increasingly involved in export products.[7] Examples – there are many others – are spices in Grenada, cacao in Suriname and bananas in Jamaica and Martinique.

The growth of the free villages has been well researched.[8] The ground provisions produced under slavery remained a staple, and gradually the new peasants tried their hand at exports. However, there seems to have been little attempt at import-substituting agriculture. The tariffs on imported foodstuffs were not designed to encourage production for the home market, and the structure of imports hardly changed at all during the century. Perhaps the main exception is rice in Suriname, which initially competed with imports but went on to become an export staple.[9] The small-scale peasantry always operated in the shadow of the plantation.[10] The land was often made available on condition that labour services would continue to be provided to the plantations or taxes would be imposed that could only be paid through wage labour on the estates.[11] Even when the peasantry were squatters or had bought land at some

---

[3] With the exception of Trinidad, these were also countries with a long history of *marronage*, but the emancipated slaves did not usually join the maroon communities.

[4] In Jamaica, it has been estimated that in 1850 ground provisions and animal products represented 89% of the output of the free villages. See Eisner (1961), p. 235.

[5] For the case of Puerto Rico, see Mintz (1974), chap. 3.

[6] The main exceptions were the large cattle ranches ('pens' in Jamaica) selling to the home market.

[7] In Jamaica, the importance of export crops in the value of peasant production had risen from 11% in 1850 to 23% in 1890. At that point the peasantry accounted for nearly 40% of the value of exports. See Eisner (1961), pp. 234–5.

[8] For Guyana, see Adamson (1972); for Jamaica, see Hall (1959) and Monteith (2000); for Suriname, see van Lier (1971).

[9] See Panday (1959).

[10] The main exception is Haiti, where both EXA and DUA came largely from small-scale agriculture in the second half of the nineteenth century. See Chapter 7.

[11] See Chapter 3.

distance from the estates, the prices at which they could sell their produce reflected general economic conditions, and these rose or fell with the fortunes of the export sector. In the Spanish colonies and the Dominican Republic, the squeeze on the peasantry was directly in proportion to the profitability of the export sector.[12]

The peasantry did make use of such things as Friendly and Benevolent Societies to save and borrow, but credit was generally scarce. As a result, Eisner's assumption for Jamaica that labour productivity on farms geared to the home market did not rise is probably justified and can be generalised to other countries.[13] When land and labour productivity rose, it was more associated with the switch to export crops, where returns were much greater. The output of DUA was not stagnant, but it seems to have grown at only the same rate as population. If it had grown faster, we would expect to see a big change in the structure of imports, and that did not happen.

Agriculture accounted for the bulk of the labour force. However, although agriculture (both EXA and DUA) was by far the most important contributor to employment in percentage terms, it still exhibited a marked difference from country to country. Caribbean agriculture was subject to the 'iron law' of economics in which there was an inverse relationship between income per head and the proportion of the labour force in agriculture. Thus, Cuba – one of the richest Caribbean countries in 1900 (see section 4 below) – had a share of around 50 per cent at the end of the century, in Jamaica and Puerto Rico it was over 60 per cent and in Haiti it was probably closer to 80 per cent.

The nonagricultural occupations were very varied. In some countries, fishing thrived, and new coastal villages were established after emancipation to serve the domestic and in some cases intra-island trade.[14] However, fresh fish appears not to have substituted for the salt fish imported from Canada and the northeastern seaboard of the United States,[15] but rather to have supplemented the limited diet on which the former slaves had depended. Mining employment, outside of the export enclaves, was much less important and was limited mainly to the extraction of materials for some buildings and infrastructure projects.

The other activities – all secondary and tertiary – were dominated by services (see Table 6.1). The most important was usually domestic service. This activity, primarily but by no means entirely female,[16] accounted for around one-quarter of all nonprimary jobs in Jamaica and Puerto Rico. In the richer Cuba, it was lower (17.6%). This was to be expected because higher income per head

---

[12] The spectacular growth of the sugar industry in the last three decades of the century, for example, turned many smallholders in the Dominican Republic into wage labourers. See Gómez (1979).

[13] See Eisner (1961), pp. 289–95.

[14] For the case of Jamaica, see Higman (2005).

[15] The structure of imports throughout the century shows the continued importance of imported fish (which had to be salted to preserve it).

[16] It was 55% female in Cuba and 67.5% female in Puerto Rico.

TABLE 6.1. *Secondary and Tertiary Occupational Structure, c.1900 (%)*

Country Year	Cuba 1899	Puerto Rico 1899	Jamaica 1890	Trinidad 1881	Suriname 1897
Services					
Domestic Service	17.6	23.3	25.9	16.3	20.6
Trade	20.1	7.4	4.9	9.3	10.0
Laundry	9.4	14.5	10.2	12.7	14.5
Sales	6.2	3.9	2.2	4.9	na
Teachers	1.1	0.7	1.7	1.2	na
Sailors	2.0	1.4	2.0	5.2 (a)	1.9
Artisan					
Carpenters	6.0	4.4	9.0	(b)	16.8
Tailors	5.0	5.8	21.9	22.0	10.2
Shoemakers	2.7	1.5	1.7	(b)	2.1
Masons	2.8	1.1	2.4	(b)	1.4
Bakers	2.3	2.0	na	(b)	na
Mechanics	2.0	0.3	1.2	(b)	0.8
Manufacturing					
Cigars	10.3	3.2			

Note: (a) includes fishermen; (b) the total for all these categories is 24.5%; the numbers express the different occupations as a percentage of all nonprimary jobs. It therefore excludes mining, fishing and agriculture.

Source: For Cuba, Santamaría and García (2004); for Puerto Rico, Sanger, Gannett, and Willcox (1900); for Jamaica, Eisner (1961); for Trinidad, *Statistical tables relating to the Colonial and other Possessions of the United Kingdom* (1883); for Suriname, *Surinaamsche Almanak* (1899).

creates new employment opportunities outside the home.[17] Trade and laundry services were also very important (the first was dominated by men and the second by women).[18] Other tertiary activities such as teaching were much less important.[19]

Turning to secondary activities, we may note in Table 6.1 the importance of a series of artisan occupations: carpenters, masons, shoemakers, tailors, bakers and mechanics. These were skilled jobs producing products that in theory competed with imports. However, in the nineteenth century – not just in the Caribbean – many of these products were what today we would call 'nontraded'. The raw materials to make shoes, clothes, confectionery and so on may have been imported, but the final products generally were not. These

[17] In Jamaica, Eisner observed a big jump in domestic service employment after 1870 that she attributes – almost certainly correctly – to the **lack** of employment opportunities elsewhere. See Eisner (1961), p. 164.
[18] Trade was 99.1% male in Cuba and 86.7% male in Puerto Rico. Laundry was 94.4% female in Cuba and 98.6% female in Puerto Rico.
[19] The gender division of teaching in Cuba was 44.5% male and 55.5% female.

skilled workers competed with each other rather than with foreign suppliers, and they usually lived in towns.[20]

There was also a manufacturing sector, but data are scarce. For Cuba, not surprisingly, the most important manufacturing occupation was cigar production (see Table 6.1). This, however, included exports. Employment in manufacturing establishments producing for the home market was very small, but it did increase in importance in the last decades of the century. Most of these activities were nontraded and therefore did not compete with imports. However, some did, and they therefore represent the first examples of ISI. A good example is provided by a soap factory established in Port-au-Prince in the 1880s.[21] Soap in Haiti, as in all Caribbean countries, was an important item of foreign trade, frequently accounting for as much as 2 per cent of all imports. By eliminating the import tariff on the raw materials needed to make soap while maintaining or even increasing it on the finished product, the Haitian government was able to create a high rate of effective protection[22] that led to the establishment of a soap industry in the country for the first time.

Other examples of ISI are not hard to find. In 1910 Jamaica still had surviving eight factories that were in existence in 1890. In the 1910 census, however, there were sixty-two factories, so it is safe to assume that at least some of these had been established in the 1890s. They covered activities such as beer and ale, manufactured tobacco and leather products. Jamaica was even processing logwood into a dye, albeit for export.[23] In Guadeloupe, consular reports at the end of the century noted the existence of two ice factories, a manure factory, a steam cooperage, two tanneries, a soap works, a match factory and a flour mill.[24]

Not surprisingly, given its population size and income per head, it was in Cuba that we find the best examples of modern manufacturing geared to the domestic market. By the end of the century, there were over 200 factories that could be said to compete with imports.[25] Over half of these were in drinks and packaging, but there were also printing works, oil refineries, soap and candle works, rope and match factories, flour and paper mills. Indeed,

---

[20] A rare occupational census was taken in 1875 for Puerto Plata, the second city of the Dominican Republic. It shows the importance of a broad range of skilled crafts, including silversmiths and jewellers. See Franco (1999).

[21] See *Commercial Relations of the United States with Foreign Countries for the Years 1882 and 1883* (1884), p. 467.

[22] The Effective Rate of Protection (ERP) measures the increase in value added for manufacturers as a result of the impact of the tariff system on the price of inputs and outputs. It therefore differs from the **nominal** rate of protection that is simply measured by the tariff rate. See Corden (1971), pp. 30–5.

[23] See Eisner (1961), pp. 255–6.

[24] See *Commercial Relations of the United States with Foreign Countries for the Year 1900* (1901), p. 160. The ice factories clearly did not compete with imports, but the others did.

[25] See Santamaría and García (2004), p. 279. This list excludes some factories in the food industry, so the number of factories competing with imports was probably even higher.

the 1899 census carried out during the US occupation listed around 84,000 workers in the industrial sector, of which 60,000 were **not** employed in the cigar or cigarette business.[26] This was 14.5 per cent of the total labour force (10.3 per cent if we exclude the tobacco industry).

The development of Cuban manufacturing geared to the domestic market would no doubt have been greater if the tariff system had done more to favour ISI. Tariffs, as everywhere else in the Caribbean, were designed to maximise revenue, not provide protection, but tariffs were reduced in 1882 in Cuba with a compensating rise in the tax on manufacturing activities.[27] They were also constructed to give preference to the import of manufactured goods from Spain, which is why the Cuban market remained so important for Spanish industry until the end of the colonial era. US-manufactured imports were also boosted by the 1892 reciprocal trade treaty that Spain had signed on behalf of its Caribbean colonies in order to secure tariff preferences in the US market.

Some nonprimary sectors hardly figured at all in the employment figures, but they still played a major role. The most important of these sectors was financial services. This activity was not as specialised as it is today with merchants, landowners and the church (especially in the Spanish colonies) all contributing to the supply of credit. However, banking came early to the Caribbean. The pioneer was the Bank van de Nederlandse Antillen in Curaçao in the Dutch Antilles, founded in 1828 and still in existence today.[28] The Bank of Jamaica was established in 1836, and the British Guiana Bank was established in the same year.[29] The Colonial Bank of the West Indies, which served many of the British colonies and would become Barclays Bank in 1925,[30] was founded in 1837. A bank was established in Guadeloupe as early as 1826, but it subsequently failed.[31] However, banks were successfully established in all three French colonies in 1851 following emancipation. The Bank of St Thomas served the needs of the entrepôt trade in the Danish Virgin Islands for decades before its bankruptcy in 1898.

Cuba, as so often, was among the earliest and had the most developed financial sector, despite the fact that so much borrowing and lending went unrecorded through informal channels. The Banco Español de Fernando VII was founded in 1832, but it closed soon after. Several banks were founded in the 1840s, and the semipublic Banco Español de la Habana, with responsibility

---

[26] Not all of these would have been employed in factories; many would have been artisans.
[27] See Santamaría and García (2004), p. 281.
[28] See van Soest (1978). Following the dissolution of the Netherlands Antilles in October 2010, the name of the bank was changed to Centrale Bank Van Curaçao en Sint Maarten.
[29] The Planters' Bank was established in Jamaica in 1839, giving the colony a third bank in only a few years. See Eisner (1961), p. 196.
[30] See Monteith (2008). See also Aspinall (1912), p. 361.
[31] See Buffon (1979), pp. 122–33.

for note issue, was founded in 1856. The Banco Hispano Colonial started in the First War of Independence. These banks arose in response to the needs of the export sector, but some of their lending went to firms selling in the domestic market.[32]

The independent countries – Haiti and the Dominican Republic – faced bigger obstacles than the colonies in creating modern financial services. Their efforts to establish paper currencies had been undermined by repeated devaluations (see section 3 below), and thus there was no confidence in *fiat* money. It was not until 1881 therefore that the Banque Nationale d'Haiti was established, with a remit close to that of a central bank, but it was in fact controlled by French investors.[33] The Dominican Republic granted a concession to a French syndicate a few years later to establish a National Bank of Santo Domingo, but it was not a success.[34] Paper money in the Dominican Republic was outlawed in 1896, and the US dollar became legal tender shortly thereafter.

Financial services tend to develop in line with income per head, thus bank deposits per head can sometimes be a good proxy for the ranking of countries in terms of living standards. We do not have data for all the Caribbean, but the figures for Guadeloupe and Puerto Rico may be used by way of illustration. In Guadeloupe, a relatively prosperous country, bank deposits per head were $60 in 1892–3.[35] In poorer Puerto Rico, bank deposits per head were around $2 per head in the year of the US occupation (1898). Within ten years, however, this figure had jumped to $6.[36] This was more in line with what was observed in other middle-income Latin American countries.[37]

The British colonies provided information on savings by households in government-controlled institutions. When expressed in per capita terms, the amount was modest – around $5 per head in Antigua, Barbados, Guyana and Trinidad.[38] However, these figures do not include deposits held in commercial banks or the value of deposits held outside the Caribbean by the wealthier inhabitants. More significant, therefore, is the **proportion** of the population that was using these savings accounts (see Figure 6.1), because it was typically only those of modest means who used them. This ranged from 1 to 7 per cent, reaching a maximum in Guyana and Barbados, where it represented around one-third of all households.[39] This can be considered a high figure for the time.

---

[32] On banking in Cuba, see Santamaría and García (2004), pp. 210–11.

[33] See Rotberg (1971) p. 111.

[34] The bank soon fell into dispute with President Heureaux, and the concession was transferred to the US-controlled San [*sic*] Domingo Improvement Company in 1895. See Welles (1928), vol. 2, pp. 499–508.

[35] See Buffon (1979), p. 207.

[36] Bank deposits in 1908 are given in Clark (1930), p. 376. Population figures are from Table C.1.

[37] See Bulmer-Thomas (2003), p. 98.

[38] It was lower elsewhere: $3 in Jamaica, falling to less than $1 in Nevis, Grenada and Tobago.

[39] Assuming each household had two adults and three children and a maximum of one account per household.

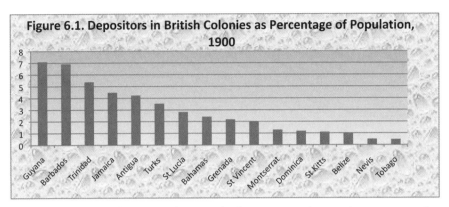

Figure 6.1. Depositors in British Colonies as Percentage of Population, 1900

Note: There is no entry for the British Virgin Islands in Figure 6.1 because there were no savings deposits facilities.
Source: Derived from Table A.1 and *Statistical tables relating to the Colonial and other Possessions of the United Kingdom* (1901).

6.2. INFRASTRUCTURE

Infrastructure development did not play the same role in the Caribbean as it did in other parts of the periphery for various reasons. The small size of most countries and the proximity of the sea meant that there were fewer difficulties faced by exporters than was the case in, say, the interior of Brazil. The main towns were nearly always ports, and they had long ago established connections with international markets. Coastal trade was a realistic alternative to inland communication in moving goods from one part of the country to another. Finally, some countries – notably the three Guianas and Belize – had river systems that served communication needs quite well.

Yet infrastructure development was still important. First, the large countries of the Greater Antilles (Cuba, Dominican Republic, Haiti, Jamaica and Puerto Rico) could not limit development to a narrow coastal strip and therefore needed internal communications to open up the hinterland. Second, one of the most effective ways to counter a fall in export commodity prices was to reduce transport costs through investment in infrastructure. Third, shifts in the composition of exports required changes in infrastructure to prevent the emergence of supply-side bottlenecks.

Infrastructure in the nineteenth-century global economy is commonly associated with the railway. And yet, with one exception, we cannot speak of a 'railway age' in the Caribbean. The exception is Cuba, which not only pioneered railway construction but also dominated the Caribbean railway network throughout the century (see Figure 6.2).[40] Indeed, until the 1880s Cuban

---

[40] There is a large literature on Cuban railways. See, e.g., Zanetti and García (1998).

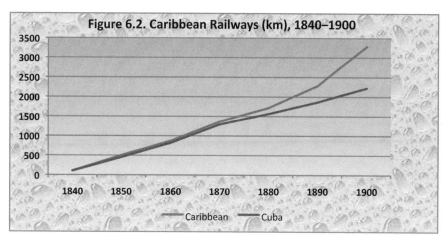

Source: For Cuba, Santamaría and García (2004); for British colonies, *Statistical tables relating to the Colonial and other Possessions of the United Kingdom* (various years); for all other countries, Mitchell (2007).

railways were almost synonymous with Caribbean railways because the network outside of Cuba was so small.

The first proposal for a Cuban railway was put forward in 1830, and a short track was opened starting from Havana in 1837. With the opening of a line in Massachusetts in the same year, Cuba could rightly lay claim with the United States to have the first railway in the Americas. In the next year the railway reached Güines, and sugar could now be transported quickly and cheaply to port with a substantial saving in cost.[41] This line, built at public expense, was privatised a few years later. From then on the railway network would largely be in the hands of private-sector companies.[42]

The reasons for Cuba's precocity are not hard to find. The explosive growth of the sugar industry demanded new lands, and these were farther and farther from the main ports. The railways therefore started by following the development of the sugar industry, spreading out from the area around Havana to the west and centre of the island (the tobacco growers to the west also benefitted, of course). However, the railway network also reinforced the concentration of the sugar industry in the western half of the island. The eastern provinces may have had ample land at their disposal, but transport costs were now much higher than in the west and centre because the sugar still had to travel by road.

If sugar prices had stayed high, this might not have mattered. The sugar industry would have flourished in the eastern provinces, and the railway

---

[41] Before the railway the cost of carrying a box of sugar by mule or oxen from Güines to Havana was $12.50. After the railway was opened, the cost fell to $1.25. See Thomas (1971), p. 123.
[42] See Santamaría and García (2004), pp. 297–305.

network would have eventually reached it. However, the secular decline in the sugar price meant that only those sugar estates with access to the rail network could reduce costs to maintain profitability. And many estate owners took this process one step further, following the introduction of the *central*, by constructing railway tracks on their estates that were not open to the public. Thus, railways – private and public – reinforced the geographical concentration of export agriculture in the western half of the island.

Other countries where the sugar industry prospered – even with falling world prices – did not invest so heavily in railways. A Spanish company received a contract in 1888 to encircle the whole of Puerto Rico with a 453-kilometre (km) railway, and the Spanish government guaranteed a return of 8 per cent. By 1892 the company had built three sections with 190 km of track but then ran out of funds, and the contract was cancelled.[43] Guyana started a railway network in the 1840s, but it remained minuscule until the 1890s.[44] Barbados and Trinidad built their small networks in the last two decades of the century.

Jamaica, one of the countries where sugar did **not** prosper in the century, started railway construction as early as 1843, but the costs were underestimated, and the network had only reached 42 km by 1870. The rise of the banana industry, however, required a more dynamic response, and the government took over the private-sector operations in 1879.[45] By the end of the century, the network had reached nearly 300 km and crossed the island from south to north. This was still very small for an island of Jamaica's size and might have been a serious deterrent to export diversification were it not for investment in public roads. These had been woefully neglected under the old assembly government, but they would be a priority after Jamaica became a Crown colony in 1865. By the end of the century Jamaica had nearly 6,000 km of all-weather roads.[46]

The other two countries of the Greater Antilles were Haiti and the Dominican Republic. In both countries export growth was hampered by a lack of infrastructure, making the development of improved communications a priority. The dependence of Haiti on coffee was in part a consequence of the difficulty of establishing nontraditional exports in the absence of roads and railways. Similarly, the dependence for so long of the Dominican Republic on tobacco and timber was a reflection in part of the high cost of transportation for other commodities. Haiti had tried to resolve the problem at various times in its history, but without satisfaction. Foreign investment, as elsewhere in the Caribbean, was essential for the success of any major infrastructure venture,

[43] See Dinwiddie (1899), pp. 68–71.
[44] Only 34 km were in existence as late as 1890. It grew, however, to 151 km by 1900.
[45] See Eisner (1961), p. 179. The West India Improvement Company was then given 70,000 acres of Crown land to induce new private sector investment. See Hill (1898), p. 217.
[46] These were described by one contemporary in the following glowing terms: '[Jamaica has] roads such as no country district in the United States possesses, – which are built to grade, splendidly macadamized, well drained and cared for'. See Hill (1898), p. 217.

and concessions were issued. However, these invariably were sold on to the highest bidder in a game of musical chairs that ended only when the concession was cancelled or the government sued for breach of contract.[47] A railway contract was granted in 1876 to a US concessionaire, but it was so poorly handled that construction never went beyond the city limits, and it operated instead as a tramline in the capital Port-au-Prince.

By 1900 there were still only 37 km of railway in Haiti, and for all intents and purposes the network played no part in the development of the export sector.[48] Haiti did have ports, at least nine able to handle international trade, but transport to those ports from the interior was exceedingly costly. As late as 1900, for example, it took two days by horseback to travel the short distance of 62 km from Port-au-Prince to Jacmel across the mountains or three days by coastal vessels. It took four days on horseback to go 288 km from the capital to the second city of Cap Haitien.[49]

The Dominican Republic, recognising the need to lower transport costs for the tobacco industry in the fertile province of the Cibao, granted a railway concession in 1882 to a Scottish entrepreneur. Although described as the Samaná–Santiago railway, the line never reached either Samaná or Santiago. However, by 1887 it joined the town of Sánchez with La Vega, not only benefitting the tobacco growers of that region, as had been intended, but also providing an outlet for the cacao and coffee, whose production was then able to expand rapidly.[50]

The success of this venture, despite not being completed as planned, led the government to seek a foreign loan from the Dutch house of Westendorp & Co. to finance the construction of a second line from Puerto Plata to Samaná. The line was duly completed by 1897, but not before Westendorp & Co. had transferred its interests to the San Domingo Improvement Company.[51] Because Westendorp in 1888 (see next section) had acquired responsibility for collecting the customs revenues of the Dominican Republic, this meant that a US company was now for the first time playing a decisive role in the internal affairs of the country.[52]

The two railways certainly helped the Dominican Republic to expand its exports in the last years of the century, but far too many of the concessions granted by the government for infrastructure projects came to nothing because

---

[47] See Montague (1940), p. 199.
[48] Haiti did, however, have an aerial railway built in 1898 to carry dyewood from the mountains to Port-au-Paix on the coast.
[49] See Montague (1940), p. 198n12.
[50] See Baud (1995), chap. 2.
[51] See Domínguez (1986), p. 108.
[52] The San Domingo Improvement Company (SDIC) should not be confused with the Santo Domingo Company established in 1869 by two US concessionaires of dubious reputation. See Tansill (1938), p. 345. The SDIC was set up in 1892 with the specific purpose of taking over Westendorp's interests in the Dominican Republic. See Knight (1928), p. 20.

of the unscrupulous nature of the concessionaires and the cupidity of government officials. Indeed, the situation was so bad that it inspired this remarkable quote from the US consul in Santo Domingo:

[the concessionaires were] adventurers who are dissipated, dishonest, and immoral, who came to have a good time generally, spending freely in the gambling dens and drinking saloons the hard earned cash of some capitalist, and who return to the United States bankrupt with some exaggerated statement detrimental to the interest of both countries to cover up their own debauchery.[53]

The other countries of the Caribbean did not suffer so badly from the lack of railway infrastructure for the reasons mentioned. Public roads, for example in Martinique, were sometimes quite adequate, and this helped to keep transport costs at moderate levels. In Belize, almost all commodities exported went first by river. On the small islands, goods could be taken from the farm to the port without incurring heavy costs because of the short distances involved. Where transport was required, the commodities could often travel by coastal routes before being shipped abroad. Some of the Caribbean ports were sadly neglected, but most were good natural harbours – some were outstanding.[54] Dredging became more common in the last two decades of the century and helped to ease congestion and lower costs.[55]

The telegraphic cable came early to the Caribbean, but it took some time to spread.[56] The first cable from Havana to Key West off the Florida coast was laid in 1867 by the US-owned International Ocean Telegraph Company. Two years later the West India and Panama Telegraph Company was founded in London, but it was a few years before logistical and administrative problems were resolved, and the first cables were laid linking some of the British colonies with the outside world. A French company brought the cable to Guadeloupe, Martinique and French Guiana in the 1880s, with connections to Suriname, the Dominican Republic and Haiti. The Caribbean was then linked to South America through Curaçao.[57] When a cable between Haiti and the United States was laid in 1896, the Caribbean network was largely complete.

Barbados, where the absence of mountains makes communications relatively easy, had built a telegraphic network of nearly 100 km by 1884. Jamaica had constructed over 1,000 km by 1890. Other countries did the same. Telephone lines developed soon after, and Trinidad had an impressive 760 km by

---

[53] See Welles (1928), vol. 1, p. 466. A similar statement could easily have been made about the foreign concessionaires in Haiti.

[54] The finest were Charlotte Amalie in St Thomas, Samaná Bay in the Dominican Republic, Môle St Nicholas in Haiti and several in Cuba, including Guantánamo Bay. All were coveted by the core countries, and this contributed to geopolitical rivalries in the nineteenth century.

[55] Santo Domingo in the Dominican Republic and San Juan in Puerto Rico benefitted greatly from dredging works in the last years of the century.

[56] See Ahvenaien (1996), passim, and Maurer (2001).

[57] See van Socst (1978), p. 171.

1900. Neither the telegraph nor the telephone had the same impact on costs as railways, but they helped exporters greatly by providing up-to-date prices. Because markets were still quite segmented and arbitrage much slower to work than today, knowledge of daily commodity prices could be very beneficial.[58]

Canals did not play the same part in the Caribbean as they did in the industrialising countries. Indeed, only Cuba made much use of them.[59] However, Guyana and Suriname invested heavily in dykes and dams to recover land from the sea and to protect plantations from flooding. These were massive infrastructure projects, and they built on the expertise of the Dutch settlers, who had used their knowledge of polders in the Netherlands to pioneer land reclamation in their South American colonies.[60]

6.3. PUBLIC FINANCE

The nineteenth-century Caribbean economies, like those in the rest of the Americas, were based on systems that relied on the private sector to provide the vast bulk of goods and services. Nevertheless, there were some activities and functions that were always undertaken at least in part by the state. These included public administration, judicial services, public works, education and health.[61] In addition, some countries were expected to contribute funds to the metropolitan countries, and others had to maintain large armed forces, and subsidies were often paid to the church. Where the government had acquired public debt, there was also the need to meet debt-service payments.[62]

These public-sector activities probably amounted to no more than 5 per cent of GDP in the first half of the century, and it is unlikely that they exceeded 10 per cent anywhere even by the end.[63] Nevertheless, they still had to be financed, and raising sufficient revenue to meet the needs of public expenditure was – as it still is today – a major issue. The taxes that were not too expensive or difficult to collect (customs duties) were the most volatile,[64] and therefore public revenue was difficult to predict. Price changes also affected the real value of public revenue and also the volume of public services that could be supported.

[58] Henry Havemeyer, who controlled the American Sugar Refining Company, is said to have set the price of sugar in his office every morning at 10 A.M. between 1893 and 1898. This information was then relayed to the Caribbean by telegraph and telephone. See Moya Pons (2007), p. 282.

[59] See Santamaría and García (2004), pp. 172–7.

[60] For Guyana, see Rodney (1981), chap. 1.

[61] Only judicial services were a state monopoly. Even tax collection could be outsourced (as happened in the Dominican Republic from 1888 onwards).

[62] As we shall see, this debt could be both internal and external.

[63] Eisner's pathbreaking work on nineteenth-century Jamaica suggests that the share of the public sector in GDP varied between 4.8% (1832) and 7.9% (1890). See Eisner (1961), p. 359. It is unlikely to have been very different elsewhere.

[64] Customs duties rose and fell in line with the volume and value of imports and exports.

TABLE 6.2. *Public Revenue per Head (1860 prices), 1820–1900*

| | Hispaniola | Colonies: | | | | | Caribbean |
		Spanish	British	French	Dutch	Scandinavian	
1820	1.9	4.2	3.5	2.7	6.4	4.2	3.5
1830	1.5	10.5	4.3	3.8	6.5	5.4	6.1
1840	2.2	11.2	3.2	4.3	6.1	5.7	6.4
1850	2.5	11.5	4.5	5.4	7.3	8.8	7.2
1860	3.0	11.5	4.6	5.3	5.0	9.9	7.4
1870	2.1	13.9	4.8	4.7	4.2	8.5	8.3
1880	4.5	21.2	6.2	6.0	5.7	9.8	12.2
1890	6.4	13.4	8.1	8.9	8.8	10.0	10.0
1900	4.0	8.8	8.7	7.9	9.7	9.6	7.4
% per year							
1820–60	1.2	2.5	0.7	1.7	−0.6	2.2	1.9
1860–1900	0.7	−0.7	1.6	1.0	1.7	−0.1	0.0
1820–1900	0.9	0.9	1.1	1.4	0.5	1.0	0.9

Source: Derived from Tables A.1a and A.34.

For the Caribbean as a whole, public revenue increased in each decade until 1880.[65] Taking 1820 as the starting point, it rose nearly sixfold over this period at an annual average rate of 3.2 per cent. It then fell in the subsequent two decades, because the decline in the value of foreign trade took its toll on customs receipts. However, the decline was mainly focused on the Spanish colonies (especially Cuba). The British, French and Dutch colonies managed to increase public revenue even after 1880, and the independent countries did so between 1880 and 1890.

These figures do not take account of population growth or price changes. It is easy to adjust public revenue for population, but it is harder to do so for prices because we do not have domestic price indices for all countries. However, given the open nature of Caribbean economies, it is likely that domestic prices will have tracked import prices quite closely. I have therefore used the import price index for each country[66] to adjust public revenue and express it at constant (1860) prices.[67] Because import prices were generally falling after 1870, this raises the value of public revenue in real terms for the period from 1870 to 1900.[68]

The results are given in Table 6.2 for the subregions. Public revenue per head at 1860 prices varied from \$1.9 (Hispaniola) to \$6.4 (Dutch colonies) in 1820. At the level of individual countries, of course, there was even more variance. The highest by far was Belize (\$12.8), where the tiny population sustained an

---

[65] See Table A.33.
[66] See Table A.30.
[67] See Table A.34.
[68] It lowers it, of course, in 1820 when import prices were high and about to fall.

enormous entrepôt trade with Central America that boosted public revenue. The lowest figures (around $1) were also found among some of the poorer British colonies, because so much trade was still with the UK, whose imports were not heavily taxed.

The growth of foreign trade in the Spanish colonies after 1820 quickly pushed public revenue per head above $10 (see Table 6.2). This had surged above $20 by 1880, but this was in part because of the heavy burden that the Spanish government was imposing at the time on its Caribbean colonies in order to finance transfers to the metropolis (see below in this section). By the end of the century, public revenue per head was very similar in the European colonies, with the independent countries collecting about half as much per head of population.[69]

There were essentially three sources of public revenue: nontrade taxes, export duties and import tariffs. The nontrade taxes were a motley collection of fees, licences and taxes on property. Property included not just land, houses and livestock but also slaves. In the British colonies the poll tax on slaves had been an important source of revenue. In Haiti – at least in the north – nontrade taxes came mainly from land as a result of the legislation passed after independence to preserve the large estates. With the demise of the large estates and the impact of currency depreciation,[70] the income from nontrade taxes had withered by the end of the 1840s. Nontrade taxes were especially important in the Dutch and Scandinavian colonies because the entrepôt trade discouraged the authorities from imposing high import tariffs or export duties.

Export duties were very important for some countries. In Haiti almost half of public revenue after 1850 came from them.[71] The Haitian duty on coffee and logwood exports was a specific tax, and therefore the income generated was more stable than the revenue from imports, much of which was derived from ad valorem tariffs.[72] Some British colonies, such as Barbados, were required by the metropolis to impose export duties; others (e.g. Guyana) were entirely exempt.[73] Re-exports were nearly always exempt.

The most important single source of revenue, however, was the income from import tariffs. This was because of its relative ease of collection, and the fact

---

[69] As usual, there was much greater variance at the country level. French Guiana, where public revenue was boosted by gold exports, collected nearly $21 per head in 1900 (at 1860 prices), but the British Virgin Islands could only manage a paltry $2.5 (derived from Tables A.1a and A.34).

[70] The land tax was collected in the national currency, so the real value of receipts was wiped out by inflation. See Chapter 7.

[71] President Soulouque (1847–59) had tried to make foreign trade a state monopoly. This failed, but he did introduce a tax in kind on coffee (the main export) that consisted of withholding 20% of the crop delivered at the ports for export. See Chapter 7.

[72] However, the export tax in Haiti – after the ending of the tax in kind in 1860 – was payable in hard currency. Because it did not fall in line with world coffee prices, it came to represent a higher share of the value of coffee exports.

[73] This difference in the treatment of British colonies went back to the eighteenth century when export duties were imposed by Britain to help pay for wars. New colonies, such as Guyana, faced no such obligations.

TABLE 6.3. *Average Tariff Rates (%), 1850–1900*

	Hispaniola	Colonies:					Caribbean
		Spanish	British	French	Dutch	Scandinavian	
1850	20.5	20.6	9.5	4.3	7.1	4.1	14.3
1860	21.0	19.2	11.4	4.3	5.4	4.6	14.6
1870	24.4	33.9	12.0	4.5	9.4	5.1	21.9
1880	31.1	33.9	11.4	4.1	12.4	9.1	23.2
1890	38.3	23.3	13.9	6.5	14.1	8.2	19.7
1900	36.1	14.9	17.6	5.9	18.7	11.1	16.4

Source: Table A.36.

that it could be passed on to the consumer. Regressive it may have been, but this counted for little among the authorities – colonial and others – in their search for a secure source of income. Tariffs were set to maximise revenue, not generally to provide protection. Furthermore, they could not be set too high because this would have the effect of encouraging contraband.

Navigation laws at first restricted imports from countries other than the metropolis, but the 'mother' country was either exempt from tariffs or received preferential treatment. This limited the revenue that could be generated from import duties, and the average tariff rate (expressed as the ratio of import duties to retained imports) was very modest in 1820. As the century advanced, however, the average tariff rate increased – especially in the independent countries – and from 1870 onwards was starting to provide a modest degree of protection.[74] This is no doubt why the beginnings of ISI date from this period. Table 6.3 gives the weighted average tariff rate for the subregions from 1850 onwards.

The value of public expenditure (both total and per capita) was similar to public revenue for the simple reason that colonial budgetary procedures did not allow large deficits (the independent countries could run deficits, but financing them without inflation was extremely difficult). It was not until the end of the century, following the collapse of sugar prices in the 1880s and social unrest in the 1890s, that the British relaxed budgetary restrictions and started to provide subsidies to their Caribbean colonies. The French, Dutch and Scandinavian authorities did so earlier for their Caribbean colonies.[75]

The structure of public expenditure varied greatly depending on the countries concerned and the period. Almost nothing was devoted to health before 1850, despite the prevalence of epidemics such as cholera and yellow fever. From

[74] Tariffs fell sharply in the (former) Spanish colonies in 1900. The US, as the occupying power, was able to set import duties at a much lower rate than before. However, the average rate had already peaked in 1880 when Spain was extracting the maximum possible from its Caribbean colonies. See Santamaría and García (2004), p. 216.

[75] The annual Dutch subsidy to Suriname and the Dutch Antilles from 1867 onwards is given in Plante (1918), pp. 4, 10, 11. Both colonies, however, regularly received subsidies even before that.

then on, there was a serious attempt in many countries to reduce mortality through increased public expenditure.[76] This included not only the building and staffing of public hospitals, but also public works to improve drainage and sewage disposal. The British colonies, for example, devoted nearly 8 per cent of their budgets on average to health spending in 1900.[77]

Public health received very little attention in the Spanish colonies. Indeed, the US occupation force expressed shock at the sanitary conditions they found.[78] After making due allowance for the hyperbole and self-justification associated with all occupying forces, it would seem that there was some justification in the complaints. The CDR in Havana in 1898 was nearly 90, not all of which could be attributed to the closing stages of the war.[79] Much of the problem was attributed to the poor quality of sanitation, so public works under the occupying force gave emphasis to sewage treatment and waste disposal.

Education was also neglected in the Spanish colonies, with spending on education in Cuba before the war estimated at barely 1 per cent of public expenditure.[80] However, this was not true of the independent countries. Haiti devoted about 5 per cent of its budget to education as early as 1850 (the proportion was similar in the Dominican Republic). From then on, the share devoted to education in Haiti steadily rose, reaching 10 per cent by 1890.[81] The quality of the education provided could be questioned, especially in rural areas, but there was no doubt that the ruling classes attached some importance to education, and the training of the Haitian elite – including higher education in France – was a priority.[82]

Public spending on education in the Dutch and French colonies acquired much greater importance as the century advanced. Indeed, it is estimated that 25 per cent of the budget in Guadeloupe was devoted to education in the 1890s,[83] and the proportion of the population receiving education in 1900 in the French and Dutch colonies was high.[84] This was similar to the proportion in the British colonies, but this was largely because of the presence in the latter of

---

[76] For the cases of the British, French and Spanish colonies, see Boyce (1910).

[77] In the two most important British colonies (Jamaica and Guyana) it was only 6%. By contrast, it was nearly 20% in Antigua.

[78] Robert Porter, sent by President McKinley to report on Cuba, wrote of Havana: '[It] is viler than words can express; and the vileness has slopped over until her harbour is a veritable cesspool, whose waters are deadly and whose bottom is so covered with filth that ships will not drop their anchor in it, because it is necessary to clean and disinfect them before they can be taken on board.' See Porter (1899), p. 109.

[79] The CDR in 1898 in some other cities was even higher. See Porter (1899), pp. 110–21.

[80] See Porter (1899), p. 380. This figure does not, however, include spending on public education by local government.

[81] See the Notes on B. Tables for the sources of these figures.

[82] In Haiti, following the *concordat* with the Vatican in 1860, the Catholic Church was heavily involved in education – especially at the primary level. See Rotberg (1971), p. 101. The public sector budget therefore only covers a part of what was spent on education.

[83] See Hill (1898), p. 341.

[84] See Table A.7.

so many church schools. The share of public expenditure devoted to education in the British colonies was only 6.7 per cent at the end of the century (less than what was spent on public health).[85]

Spending on the military, as might be expected, was high in the independent countries.[86] However, it was also high in the Spanish colonies – especially Cuba – because Spain expected the colonists to pay for the Spanish troops stationed on the islands. Military spending was around 30 per cent of public expenditure in 1890 in Cuba.[87] In the other colonies, it was very low. Indeed, spending on the militia was only 1 per cent in the British colonies in 1900.[88] Some of the British colonies were receiving subsidies from the metropolis by the end of the century, and so were the French Antilles. The Dutch provided a subsidy for their Caribbean colonies in most years, as did Sweden for St Barthélemy from the 1830s (before that the subsidy went the other way).[89] However, the biggest subsidy was the one paid by the Spanish colonies to Spain. In the case of Cuba, this rose from around 8.5 per cent of public spending in 1830 to nearly 50 per cent in 1880.[90] This was an enormous figure and helps to explain why Cuba needed to generate such a large public revenue in that year.

By this time, Cuban transfers to Spain had come to include debt-service payments. This debt, which was cancelled on Cuban independence,[91] was largely fictitious because Cuba was simply assigned responsibility for various metropolitan expenses over which she had no control (these included the military campaigns in Mexico and the Dominican Republic in 1861 and the administration of Fernando Poo off the coast of Africa).[92]

The public external debts acquired by the independent countries were equally dubious. Haiti had to live for decades with the evil consequences of the indemnity imposed by France in 1825.[93] By the early 1870s, Haiti was almost free of debt, but it then unwisely contracted new loans in 1874 and 1875 – much of which it never received. The same happened with a loan taken in 1896. The Dominican Republic stayed free of external debt until 1869, when it began a

---

[85] There were, as so often, big differences among the colonies: around 10% in Barbados, Dominica and Grenada against a miserly 6% in Guyana and Jamaica.

[86] It was nearly one-quarter of the budget in Haiti from 1860 onwards (see Table B.10). Before that it was even higher. In the Dominican Republic in the 1880s, despite the reduced threat of Haitian invasion, it reached nearly 40%.

[87] See Santamaría and García (2004), p. 332.

[88] Derived from *Statistical tables relating to the Colonial and other Possessions of the United Kingdom* (1901).

[89] See Notes on A. Tables.

[90] These figures are obtained by comparing the estimates on transfers in Santamaría and García (2004), p. 218, with public spending in Table A.37.

[91] This was one of the conditions imposed on Spain by the US in the 1898 peace treaty.

[92] See Santamaría and García (2004), p. 219.

[93] Strictly speaking, the $30,000,000 indemnity was not a debt. However, Haiti had to borrow $6,000,000 in 1825 just to meet the first annual payment. See Chapter 7.

long and tragic history of indebtedness with the Hartmont loan.[94] Its inability punctually to meet debt-service payments, despite the fraudulent nature of much of the debt acquired, led first to foreign control of the revenue from customs and eventually to the US customs receivership in 1905.[95]

The external loans acquired by Haiti and the Dominican Republic were always a last resort. Before that, everything possible had been done to finance budgets internally, including printing paper money. The result had usually been monetary chaos and a collapse of the exchange rate.[96] Yet the public liabilities remained, leaving a large stock of internal debt. When added to the external debt, the two countries were highly indebted, and total debt service absorbed a large share of public expenditure.[97]

The colonies faced much greater restrictions on issuing paper money. An early attempt to establish modern banking in Guadeloupe in the 1820s failed, but the colonial banks set up in the three French colonies after emancipation were a model of sobriety. Paper money, backed by gold, was widely accepted.[98] The same was true of the other colonies, but the note issue in Cuba to finance the First War of Independence did lead to inflation.[99] The British government required its Caribbean colonies to operate a highly restrictive currency board system in which the note issue had to be backed 100 per cent by gold.[100]

The note issue was never able to eliminate the severe shortage of currency. Belize adopted the silver coins of its neighbours as its legal tender for many years, and Peruvian and Chilean coins also circulated widely.[101] Cuba, along with many other Caribbean countries, imported Mexican silver coins to ease the shortage.[102] The Dominican Republic even adopted the US dollar as its currency in 1900 after legislation had banned the issue of paper money. In the Scandinavian and Dutch colonies, a wide variety of coins circulated. The same was true of the Spanish colonies, where the US authorities were left with the difficult task of finding conversion rates to the US dollar at the start of the occupation.[103]

---

[94] Hartmont was a financial scoundrel who took advantage of Dominican naivety. See Knight (1928), Welles (1928) and Tansill (1938).

[95] The house of Westendorp took over what was left of the Hartmont loan in 1888 and received in return the right to collect customs duties. Westendorp transferred all its right and obligations to the San Domingo Improvement Company in 1892, paving the way for complete US control of Dominican finances in 1905. See Schoenrich (1918), pp. 355–8.

[96] In the Haitian Civil War at the end of the 1860s, the Haitian gourd had fallen to 4,000 to the US dollar (it had been quoted at 3.0 in the early 1820s). President Saget (1870–74), however, largely succeeded in restoring the health of the monetary system. It remained relatively stable until the fall in coffee prices in the 1890s. See International Bureau of the American Republics (1893).

[97] For Haiti, see Blancpain (2001). For the Dominican Republic, see Schoenrich (1918).

[98] For a case study of the Banque de la Guadeloupe, see Buffon (1979).

[99] See Santamaría and García (2004), p. 345.

[100] On the currency board system in the British colonies, see Colonial Office (1950).

[101] See Chapter 11.

[102] See Santamaría and García (2004), pp. 220–2.

[103] For Puerto Rico, see Dietz (1986), p. 91n37; for Cuba, see Porter (1899), pp. 190–203.

6.4. MACROECONOMIC PERFORMANCE

There are estimates of GDP for only four countries in the nineteenth century. Furthermore, these are point estimates at long intervals. In the absence of more comprehensive data, it is therefore necessary to measure macroeconomic performance using a series of proxies from which annual growth rates at constant prices can be derived along with ordinal rankings of countries in terms of living standards. That is the purpose of this section.

The easiest proxy to construct refers to final expenditure per head at constant prices.[104] Because so much of investment and private consumption was imported, we may use the retained value of imports at 1860 prices to measure these two components.[105] Public consumption can be approximated by government spending at 1860 prices,[106] and domestic exports at 1860 prices are a close proxy for exports of goods and services in final expenditure.[107] Finally, we need to add 10 per cent of re-exports to capture the entrepôt trade in view of its importance for some countries.[108] The sum of all these variables can then be considered a proxy for final expenditure, and we can then calculate the growth rate of final expenditure per head at constant prices by dividing by population. By way of comparison, the same metric can be shown at current prices.

For the Caribbean as a whole, the results are shown in Figure 6.3 for different time intervals. The first two are forty-year periods (1820–60; 1860–1900), and the next is for the whole period (1820–1900). Figure 6.3 shows very clearly a modest but positive performance in the first four decades of the century at both current and constant prices. Final expenditure per head at constant prices increased at 0.7 per cent annually, and at current prices it rose at a more modest rate (0.4%). The figures may appear very low by modern standards, but they were not by any means disastrous and probably not too far out of line with what was happening in mainland Latin America. Given what had occurred in Jamaica (the largest economy in 1820), this was a creditable performance.

What was disastrous was the collapse in the second period (see Figure 6.3), all of which was concentrated in the last two decades of the century. Final expenditure per head fell in both current and constant prices. This virtually wiped out all the gains before 1860. Final expenditure per head from 1820 to 1900 was therefore almost stationary (the annual growth rate was a miserly +0.2 per cent at constant prices and negative at current prices). The last

---

[104] Final expenditure is the sum of private consumption, public consumption, investment and exports less imports.

[105] See Table A.26. Eisner (1961) shows that private spending (consumption plus investment) in Jamaica was roughly four times imports at constant prices in the century. I have therefore multiplied retained imports at 1860 prices by a factor of 3.0 (thus netting out imports themselves) as a rough guide to the importance of private spending in final expenditure in the Caribbean.

[106] See Table A.34.

[107] See Table A.14.

[108] Re-exports (Table A.12) are expressed at current prices because there is no satisfactory way of converting them to 1860 prices.

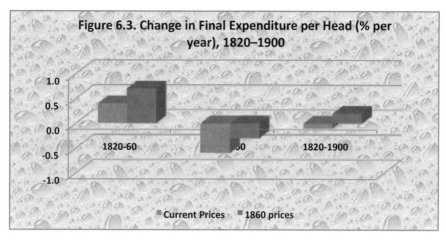

Source: Derived from Tables A.1a, A.11, A.12, A.14, A.23, A.25, A.26, A.37 and A.38.

TABLE 6.4. *Annual Change (%) in Final Expenditure per Head at 1860 Prices by Subregions, 1820–1900*

	Hispaniola	Colonies:				
		Spanish	British	French	Dutch	Scandinavian
1820–60	0.2	2.2	−0.5	0.9	−0.2	−0.3
1860–1900	−0.5	−0.2	0.1	−0.2	0.8	0.0
1820–1900	−0.1	1.0	−0.2	0.4	0.3	−0.2

Source: Derived from same tables as for Figure 6.3.

part of the century, especially after 1880, was therefore calamitous for the Caribbean.

When we focus on the growth of final expenditure per head at constant prices for the subregions (see Table 6.4), we find a similar picture. The annual growth in the first period (1820–60) was generally positive and very fast in the Spanish colonies (it was negative only in the British, Dutch and Scandinavian colonies). By contrast, it was negative or very low in the second period (1860–1900) almost everywhere. For the period as a whole, the performance was disappointing everywhere – except the Spanish colonies, where rapid growth in the first four decades helped to compensate for the poor performance at the end of the century.

From the previous chapters we know that performance at the country level could also differ significantly from performance at the subregional level – yet alone the regional level. We could then analyse growth rates of final expenditure per head at constant prices for all countries. However, country growth rates have one big drawback – they do not allow us to rank countries in terms of absolute performance and therefore to draw inferences about the standard of living.

Finding out who were the richest and poorest countries has always been a source of fascination for economic historians. In the absence of any precise method of cardinal ranking, we must therefore proceed on the basis of ranking countries ordinally. This is done by bringing together the same four indicators (domestic exports, re-exports, retained imports and public expenditure) and dividing by population to obtain a rough measure of final expenditure per head.[109] The results allow us to rank all countries in each decade from 1820 on the basis of a metric that is also likely to be highly correlated with income per head.[110]

The top quartile in each decade are shown in Table 6.5. In 1820 they were all British colonies except the Danish Virgin Islands (DVI).[111] Belize headed the list and would do so in 1830.[112] The tiny Turks & Caicos Islands ('Turks') was second with a thriving re-export trade and sales of salt to passing US ships. The new British colonies of Guyana and Trinidad were already fourth and sixth respectively in 1820 and would remain in the top quartile for the rest of the century. On the other hand, St Vincent and Jamaica (fifth and seventh respectively in 1820) would soon drop out of the top quartile.

Cuba appeared in the top quartile for the first time in 1840 and would then be in the top four for the rest of the century, but it was never ranked first. The Danish Virgin Islands, where the entrepôt trade was so important, stayed in the top quartile for most of the century until after 1890. Guadeloupe and Martinique occasionally figured in the top quartile, but the star performer among the French colonies was French Guiana. This previously unsuccessful colony started to export gold in 1857 and was ranked first in most years from 1870 onwards. The only Dutch colony to figure in the top quartile was Suriname, which finally entered in 1900 as a result of successful export diversification.[113]

The bottom quartile in the rankings is shown in Table 6.6. The lowest-ranked country in 1820 was Puerto Rico, which did not escape from the bottom quartile until 1840. The second lowest in 1820 was the Dominican Republic (DR), which remained in the bottom quartile throughout the century.[114] Haiti

---

[109] As before (see note 105, above), retained imports are multiplied by a factor of 3.0 and re-exports by 0.1. This time, however, current prices are used as the purpose is to rank countries in each decennial year.

[110] The correlation in 1900, for example, between the ranking of countries using final expenditure per head and the ranking using exports per head (domestic exports plus 10% of re-exports) is 0.903.

[111] Because there are twenty-eight countries, the top quartile shows only seven countries. Martinique (a French colony) and Suriname (a Dutch one) were eighth and ninth respectively.

[112] Scholars of nineteenth-century Belize will not be surprised by this. Under the treaties with Spain signed in 1783 and 1786, Belize was prevented from producing for the home market. Thus, almost all those enumerated in the census (Amerindians were not included until later) were engaged in the export trades, where labour productivity was highest. In addition, Belize benefitted in the first half of the century from the large re-export trade to Central America, which swelled public revenue. See Chapter 11.

[113] Suriname's ranking, however, is flattered by high levels of subsidies from the metropolis (included in public expenditure).

[114] The Dominican Republic escaped the bottom quartile in 1900 at constant prices, but the fall in commodity prices in the 1890s damaged its ranking at current prices.

TABLE 6.5. *Final Expenditure per Head at Current Prices: Top Quartile Country Rankings, 1820–1900*

	First	Second	Third	Fourth	Fifth	Sixth	Seventh
1820	Belize	Turks	DVI	Guyana	St Vincent	Trinidad	Jamaica
1830	Belize	DVI	Guyana	Turks	Tobago	St Vincent	Trinidad
1840	Guyana	Belize	Turks	Trinidad	Tobago	DVI	Cuba
1850	Trinidad	Guyana	Cuba	Belize	DVI	St. Vincent	Turks
1860	Trinidad	Guyana	Cuba	Fr. Guiana	Turks	Guadeloupe	DVI
1870	Fr. Guiana	Guyana	Trinidad	Cuba	Martinique	St Kitts	Turks
1880	Trinidad	Fr. Guiana	Cuba	Guyana	Martinique	Guadeloupe	DVI
1890	Fr. Guiana	Trinidad	Cuba	DVI	Belize	Guyana	Turks
1900	Fr. Guiana	Cuba	Turks	Trinidad	Suriname	Bahamas	Guyana

Source: Derived from Tables A.1a, A.11, A.12, A.25 and A.37.

TABLE 6.6. *Final Expenditure per Head at Current Prices: Bottom Quartile Country Rankings, 1820–1900*

	Seventh	Sixth	Fifth	Fourth	Third	Second	First
1820	Montserrat	Fr. Guiana	Haiti	Dutch Antilles	BVI	DR	Puerto Rico
1830	Montserrat	Nevis	Puerto Rico	Dutch Antilles	Haiti	BVI	DR
1840	Barbados	St Barts	Jamaica	Haiti	Dutch Antilles	BVI	DR
1850	St Lucia	Nevis	Haiti	St Barts	Montserrat	DR	BVI
1860	Dominica	Montserrat	Jamaica	Haiti	St Barts	DR	BVI
1870	Dutch Antilles	Jamaica	Dominica	DR	Haiti	St Barts	BVI
1880	Montserrat	Dutch Antilles	Jamaica	Dominica	Haiti	DR	BVI
1890	Dutch Antilles	Dominica	Montserrat	Haiti	DR	Tobago	BVI
1900	Puerto Rico	Montserrat	DR	Nevis	Haiti	BVI	Tobago

Note: 'First' is lowest in the rankings.
Source: Derived from same tables as for Table 6.5.

was also in the bottom quartile throughout the century, but it was never ranked lowest. St Barthélemy joined the bottom quartile in 1840 and would remain there, despite subsidies from Sweden, until its transfer to France. The Dutch Antilles, where domestic exports were negligible and where the entrepôt trade declined in importance, was in the bottom quartile for most of the century, despite subsidies from Holland.

Even before slave emancipation, some British colonies had very low rankings. The British Virgin Islands (BVI), which had never done very well even in the golden age of sugar, was never out of the bottom quartile and was ranked last in five out of nine decennial years. Montserrat, dependent at first on a sugar industry that failed to attract new investment, also had very undistinguished rankings. Tobago started well (it was in the top quartile in 1830 and 1840), but the migration of labour and capital to Trinidad left it at the bottom by 1900.[115] The other laggards among the British colonies were Barbados (1840 only), Dominica, Jamaica, Nevis and St Lucia (1850 only).

The rankings suggest we should be extremely cautious about jumping to conclusions about the causes of success and failure. Independence, as in the case of Haiti and the Dominican Republic, was clearly not a panacea. Market access for exports for the independent countries was at first more difficult, imports failed to grow rapidly and public revenue (much of which had to be spent on the military and debt service) rose only modestly. Haiti did not do as badly as is often alleged (see next chapter), but its performance was hardly stellar, and the Dominican Republic performed poorly until the very end of the century.

On the other hand, colonial status could be a mixed blessing because for every 'star' there was usually a 'dud'. Spain, driven out of its mainland colonies, may have concentrated its energies on Cuba, but it then sucked resources out of the 'ever faithful' island through discriminatory tariffs, debt-service payments and other transfers of dubious legality. Still, Cuba did at least perform well in the rankings. Puerto Rico, by contrast, was largely neglected and paid the price through annexation to the United States in 1898. Suriname received considerable attention (and subsidies) from Holland, and by the end of the century it was performing moderately well, but the Dutch Antilles failed to expand its export capacity significantly despite metropolitan support.[116]

The high rankings of Guyana and Trinidad may have been helped by the importance attached to these colonies by the imperial power, but the low rankings of the British Virgin Islands, Dominica, Montserrat, Nevis, St Lucia and Tobago were in part from metropolitan neglect. Jamaica, on the other hand,

---

[115] Tobago by then had merged with Trinidad to form the unified colony of Trinidad & Tobago. The method for separating the two countries in 1900 is explained in the Notes on A. Tables.

[116] Holland even tried to sell Curaçao to Venezuela, but without success – Venezuela did not see why it should buy what it considered was already its own.

had only itself to blame for its spectacular fall from grace. The planter class was not willing to make the investments needed, and the legislative assembly before the Morant Bay rebellion in 1865 acted in a very shortsighted manner. Crown colony rule after 1865 went some way towards correcting these failings, and Jamaica's ranking started to improve (it dropped out of the bottom quartile after 1880).

The rankings by country of final expenditure per head reveal a great deal about the workings of the Caribbean economy in the short nineteenth century. French Guiana went from close to the bottom to the top as a result of the commodity lottery.[117] Barbados, often considered the quintessential successful sugar colony, had fallen to twenty-second by 1840 following emancipation. By 1880, however, it was ranked eighth – helped by the absence of labour shortages and new investments in the sugar industry. Also of interest is the close ranking at all times of the two French islands (Guadeloupe and Martinique), rarely separated by more than one or two places. On the other hand, Puerto Rico always lagged behind Cuba and never achieved a ranking higher than fourteenth (in 1880).

We can end this chapter by comparing our results with the four Caribbean countries for which GDP data have been constructed. Jamaica experienced a sharp decline in GDP per head from 1832 to 1850, followed by a period of stagnation to 1870 and a very small increase by 1890.[118] Guyana, with a GDP per head in 1830 already much higher than Jamaica, also suffered a decline in the two decades before 1850, but not as steep as in the case of Jamaica.[119] GDP per head in 1870 then showed a small rise followed by another increase by 1890.[120] Cuba enjoyed a sharp rise in GDP per head between 1830 and 1860 and another big increase by 1890 before falling in the next decade.[121] Puerto Rico had a GDP per head that was virtually unchanged between 1830 and 1890.[122] All these estimates are broadly consistent with the ordinal rankings derived from the Statistical Appendix based on final expenditure per head.

[117] This was based on the export of gold from 1857 onwards.
[118] See Eisner (1961), p. 119. I have used my estimates of population in converting Eisner's estimates to GDP per head.
[119] See Moohr (1972), p. 589. Moohr's figures (at 1913 prices) can be used to estimate GDP per head in Guyana in 1832 at $112.4 compared with a Jamaican figure (at 1910 prices) of $73. In my rankings for 1830 at constant prices, Guyana is second and Jamaica thirteenth.
[120] See Moohr (1971), p. 281. The actual figures (1913 prices) for GDP per head are $112.4 (1832), $99.2 (1852), $102.1 (1872) and $108 (1892).
[121] See Santamaría and García (2004), p. 376, and Santamaría (2005).
[122] See Lavallé, Naranjo and Santamaría (2002).

7

Haiti

From Independence to US Occupation

This chapter, the last in Part I, is devoted to Haiti; it is unusual for two reasons. First, although other chapters stopped at the end of the nineteenth century, this one ends with the US invasion in 1915. The period immediately preceding the US occupation, which lasted until 1934, was a crucial period in Haitian economic history and has to be included here. Second, it is the only chapter in Part I devoted to a single country – this requires an explanation.

Haiti was the first independent country in the Caribbean and, with the exception of the Dominican Republic,[1] would remain the only independent country for the whole of the nineteenth century. Thus, it is of interest to see how an independent country fared in comparison with the surrounding colonies. Second, modern interpretations of Haiti tend to be based on a misunderstanding of its performance before the US invasion, it being often incorrectly assumed that Haiti was the poorest country in the region from independence onwards.[2]

Decolonisation today is generally seen in a positive light, because it is expected to increase the resources open to a country, allow for greater national control over the instruments of economic policy and improve the chances of exploiting the opportunities created by the international division of labour. However, the situation was not so clear-cut in earlier times. The United States, for example, struggled for many years after the War of Independence (1775–1783) to regain the trading position in the Caribbean it had previously enjoyed as thirteen British colonies. The Navigation Acts and tariff discrimination held back its development, and hostility with the UK at the beginning of the

---

[1] Leaving aside the few months in 1821–2 when it declared independence from Spain, the Dominican Republic was independent from 1844 to 1861 and again from 1865 onwards. This is about half of the century, but Haiti was independent for virtually the whole of it.

[2] The database I have constructed for Haiti (see Tables B.1–B.10) is designed to provide a more objective basis for evaluating the country's economic performance up to 1915.

nineteenth century led first to President Jefferson's imposition of a trade embargo and later to outright hostilities in the War of 1812.[3]

At least the United States won recognition of its independence at an early stage, allowing the new republic to sign international treaties. Great Britain, the defeated colonial power, recognised US independence within a few months of the end of hostilities, and no reparations were demanded by Great Britain. France, the traditional enemy of Great Britain, had supported the independence movement enthusiastically and welcomed the emergence of a republic in the Americas, despite its own monarchical system and its possession of colonies close to the United States. Haiti, as we shall see, was not so fortunate.

We have seen in previous chapters that Haiti was not the economic failure that it has become today. Its domestic exports were among the most important in the Caribbean, being exceeded in 1820 only by Cuba, Guyana and Jamaica. The subsequent collapse of Jamaican exports left Haiti as the third most important Caribbean exporter for part of the nineteenth century. Its exports exceeded those of the Dominican Republic throughout the century and those of Puerto Rico in parts of it. With exports concentrated on coffee, it was also for most of the century the world's fourth largest exporter of a commodity whose global consumption was steadily rising.[4]

It is true that in per capita terms Haiti's performance was much less impressive – it had a large population in comparison with most other Caribbean countries (only Cuba was bigger). However, its exports per head were never the lowest in the Caribbean, being either third, fourth or fifth from the bottom in all years after 1820 (see Table 6.6). Furthermore, it was not until after 1890 that Haitian exports dropped sharply in absolute terms. This drop was a consequence primarily of the collapse in coffee prices as a result of the overproduction in Brazil in the 1890s.[5]

Until that moment, Haitian exports per head had averaged around 40 per cent of Caribbean exports per head (see Figure 7.1) – not good, but certainly not a disaster. However, following the 1890s collapse in coffee prices the ratio fell below 30 per cent.[6] Furthermore, it continued to fall and – despite a brief rise before the First World War (1914–18) when coffee prices jumped, a much more modest improvement during the latter stages of the US occupation (1915–34) and a short upturn during the Korean War (1950–3) – had slipped below 10

[3] A number of Haitians volunteered to help the US defeat the British in this war.

[4] Haiti was actually the third most important coffee exporter, behind Brazil and the Dutch East Indies, until it was overtaken by Venezuela in the 1880s. See Clarence-Smith and Topik (2003), app.

[5] High tariffs were also imposed by the US in 1892 on Haiti's main exports as punishment for the country's refusal to sign a reciprocal trade treaty that would have deprived the government of much of its income from import duties.

[6] The nadir was 1915, the year of the US invasion, when a poor coffee harvest, low coffee prices, the disruption of exports to Europe caused by the First World War and Haitian political instability reduced the ratio to 5.1%.

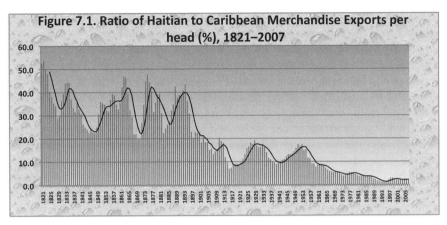

Figure 7.1. Ratio of Haitian to Caribbean Merchandise Exports per head (%), 1821–2007

Note: The decennial data for the Caribbean in Table A.13 have been interpolated for intervening years. The data are 3-year averages and the trend line is a five-period moving average.
Source: Derived from Tables A.1, A.13, B.1, B.3, C.1, C.8, D.1 and D.6.

per cent by 1960. Subsequently, it fell to its current level of around 2 per cent of the Caribbean average.[7] Thus, the Haitian economy entered a downward spiral in the 1890s from which it has never recovered.

This chapter attempts to explain why this was so. Scholars have argued incessantly over whether the causes of Haitian backwardness were mainly internal or external. There is no simple answer, because the causes were complex and both internal and external elements were clearly present. However, there is no doubt that Haiti faced an extraordinarily hostile external environment in the nineteenth century. In responding to this environment, Haitians made decisions that may have been rational at the time but that had negative long-term consequences. The cumulative effect of these decisions was to create an economy that was extremely vulnerable to external shocks, such as the coffee price fall in the 1890s, but which lacked the capacity to respond.

The downward spiral, once it started, was not inevitable, but extreme political instability in the years immediately before the First World War and the US occupation thereafter made it very difficult to reverse. The United States put its own interests far above those of its Haitian protectorate. The inevitable reaction to the occupation then created the ideological movement from which François Duvalier would emerge triumphant in 1957. Haiti's current nightmare can be traced to that moment.

This chapter begins with the relations of Haiti with the core. It is not a pretty story, but it needs to be told. There follows an examination of Haitian exports that goes beyond what was possible in the previous chapters. This is followed

[7] The final year in Figure 7.1 is an average of 2006–2008; thus it does not take account of the impact on exports of the devastating earthquake in January 2010.

by an analysis of public finance that – far more than foreign trade – was the Achilles heel of the Haitian model. The final section asks, When and why did Haiti fall behind?

7.1. HAITI AND THE CORE

Although Denmark, Holland and Sweden despatched consuls to Haiti in 1826, following France's recognition of the country's independence the previous year, these three countries played only a very small part in Haitian development thereafter. Thus, the 'core' in this context refers to its other five members (France, Germany, Spain, the UK and the United States). All these countries played a large part in independent Haiti's early history.

The Haitian declaration of independence on 1 January 1804 was greeted with a deafening silence by the rest of the world. Far from being welcomed, it was seen as a threat by all those countries still engaged in the slave trade. Haitian independence also occurred in the middle of the Napoleonic Wars, when national interests were even more ruthlessly pursued than usual. The United States, for example, anxious to maintain good relations with France at a time when relations with Britain were tense, imposed a trade embargo on Haiti in 1806 at the request of Napoleon.[8] Because trade with France was also very difficult,[9] Haiti began its independent life effectively cut off from two of its most important markets.[10] In these years, virtually the only market open to Haiti was Great Britain, where Haiti had to compete with British colonies on unequal terms. Seen in this light, the decline in the value of Haitian exports compared with the colonial period is perhaps not so surprising.[11]

The end of the Napoleonic Wars provided an opportunity for the core to normalise its relations with Haiti. Instead, however, the Treaty of Paris in 1814 and the Congress of Vienna in 1815 made no mention of Haitian independence,

---

[8] See Montague (1940), p. 45. This embargo, in place until 1809, occurred at a particularly unfortunate time in the history of Haiti because it was imposed a few months before the country split into two parts following the assassination of Dessalines in September 1806: a northern part, the State of Haiti, ruled by Henri Christophe that became the Kingdom of Haiti in 1811 and survived until Christophe's death in 1820; and a southern part, the Republic of Haiti, ruled by Alexandre Pétion, who died in 1818 and was replaced as president by Jean-Pierre Boyer. The two parts were reunited as a republic at the end of 1820 under President Boyer, who then annexed the eastern part of the island in 1822.

[9] Franco-Haitian trade was theoretically impossible for three reasons. First, France did not permit it; second, the Napoleonic continental blockade undermined it; and third, the Kingdom of Haiti under Henri Christophe (the northern part of Haiti) banned it. However, in practice there was some trade as a result of the use of neutral flags to transport French and Haitian goods.

[10] The US trade embargo on Haiti ended in 1809 as part of the reaction against President Jefferson's general trade embargo rather than out of special concern for Haiti. See Logan (1941), pp. 176–83.

[11] Hundreds of books and articles have marvelled at the value of exports from St-Domingue (modern Haiti) and have lamented their subsequent decline immediately after independence, conveniently forgetting that colonial exports were based on forced labour and entered France on preferential terms. See, e.g., Lepelletier (1846), vol. 1, pp. 56–78.

referring instead to the return to France of all its former colonies other than those listed (e.g. St Lucia and Tobago). The implication was that the core, and no doubt other states such as Russia, expected France in due course to try to reestablish sovereignty over Haiti. Indeed, this was the case. Talleyrand, the French foreign minister, signed a secret agreement with Britain at the Congress of Vienna under which the UK was guaranteed access to Haitian ports in the event of a successful French recolonisation.[12] This did not, however, stop the UK from pressuring the Republic of Haiti under Pétion to reduce by half the import duties on British goods at a time when the republic had become heavily dependent on this source of income.[13]

The first French mission was despatched to the Republic of Haiti (the southern part ruled by President Pétion) in 1814 with orders to reestablish French sovereignty but also secret instructions that included the reimposition of slavery.[14] The mission failed, but not before Pétion had made the potentially fatal admission that Haiti might be prepared to pay an indemnity in return for recognition of its independence. A second French mission in 1816 also ended in failure because France was still determined to regain sovereignty and neither the republic governed by Pétion nor the kingdom ruled by Christophe was prepared to consider such a step.[15]

The next opportunity for the core to normalise its relations with Haiti came in the early 1820s, following the independence of much of Spanish and Portuguese America from the Iberian colonial powers. The United States was the first to recognise their independence, followed soon after by the UK. The latter, however, still refused to accept an independent Haiti on the specious grounds that it could not do so ahead of France, ignoring the fact that it had recognised the independence of the Latin American republics without waiting for Spain – the former colonial power – to do so. This so enraged President Boyer, under whom Haiti had once again become united in 1820, that he cancelled the trade privileges granted by Pétion to the UK in 1814.[16]

With the United States the issue of Haitian independence was affected above all by slavery. Anxious to include the United States in the Pan-American Congress of 1826, where the issue of Haitian recognition by the mainland American republics was on the agenda, Simón Bolívar did not invite Haiti to participate, despite the generous support he had received on more than one occasion from Pétion a decade earlier.[17] This sensitivity to US concerns on the part of Bolívar

---

[12] See Blancpain (2001), p. 43.
[13] At the time the tariff rate was 10%, so British imports entered at 5%. See Mackenzie (1830), vol. 2, p. 275.
[14] See Griggs (1952), pp. 57–59.
[15] On the second French mission, see Griggs (1952), pp. 60–1.
[16] Boyer admittedly had additional reasons for cancelling the British trade privileges because he had just been forced to offer the same privileges to France and could ill afford to extend tax concessions to two such important trade partners. See section 2 below.
[17] See Bellegarde (1953), pp. 121–2. Bolívar received a welcome and assistance from Pétion in 1816. See Lynch (2006), p. 97.

turned out to be completely wasted because the US delegation arrived too late to participate, having spent so long arguing over what position to take.[18] In the event, US recognition of Haitian independence was delayed until 1862. This was shortly before the abolition of slavery and after the outbreak of the US Civil War, when the slave states were no longer able to block legislation in Congress.[19] A treaty of commerce duly followed in 1864.[20]

Nonrecognition by the core did not rule out trade relations. However, it did pose a potential threat because there was always the possibility of a challenge to Haiti's territorial integrity. The Haitian state from the very start was therefore highly militarised, with a standing army under Boyer in the mid-1820s estimated at 32,000.[21] In comparison to the size of the population, this must have been one of the larger armies in the world, and it had to be financed.[22] As we shall see in section 3 below, the Haitian armed forces (army and navy) absorbed around 50 per cent of public revenue in the first decades of independence. The size of this army was a direct consequence of nonrecognition by the core, because otherwise it could have – and no doubt would have – been much reduced following reunification of the republic in 1820.[23]

In addition to requiring a large army, the hostility of the core created the need for a national guard composed of all adult males. This military reserve, for such it was, could be called upon at short notice to defend the territory of the fledgling state, and individuals might be required to move far from their homes. The militarised nature of society then helps us to understand one of the fundamental changes in Haiti after the end of colonisation because estate labour was extremely scarce and peasant labour could be disrupted at any time. Under these circumstances it is hardly surprising that Haitian exports shifted from sugar and cotton to coffee and timber because the labour requirements of the last two commodities – combined with the absence of capital – were much more compatible with the militarised nature of society.[24]

---

[18] See Logan (1941), pp. 222–9
[19] See Montague (1940), p. 86.
[20] See Turnier (1955), chap. 5.
[21] See Nicholls (1979), p. 68, who draws on figures in Mackenzie (1830), vol. 2, p. 201.
[22] There is an interesting exchange of letters between Christophe and Thomas Clarkson in 1819–20 on the prospects for reducing the size of the military to increase the labour force for agriculture. See Griggs (1952), p. 187.
[23] Boyer annexed the eastern part of the island in 1822 with a force of 12,000. The Haitian presence (1822–44) in the eastern part is often described as an 'occupation', but it was largely peaceful and initially welcomed by many Dominicans (it only became unpopular when Boyer tried to impose Haitian land and labour laws). See Franklin (1828), pp. 238–9. It cannot therefore be claimed that Boyer maintained a large army purely for internal reasons. The external threat weighed heavily on him throughout his presidency.
[24] It has been repeated ad nauseam that Haitians refused to have anything to do with sugar (and to a lesser extent cotton) because of its association with slavery. However, I do not accept this. Coffee and logwood were also associated with slavery, but they rapidly became the mainstay of the Haitian economy. Furthermore, although sugar exports eventually collapsed, sugarcane production did not and was used to supply the domestic market with molasses (used as a sweetener) and rum (tafia) without the need for imports. Finally, as soon as well-paid

The hostility of the core is accepted by most scholars as an explanation for high levels of military expenditure in the early days. However, very few accept that there was a need for a large army after French recognition of independence in 1825. Yet the territorial integrity of Haiti remained under threat long after French recognition, culminating ninety years later in the US military occupation. As we shall see, the size of the armed forces was reduced, but the military still absorbed around 25 per cent of the budget from 1860s onwards. This was a heavy burden for Haiti to bear, but there was not much choice if Haiti wished to remain independent (and in the end it was not even sufficient).

French recognition in 1825, imposed at the barrel of a gun,[25] was grudging and unjust because of the indemnity imposed (see section 3 below). Because there was little chance of Haiti being able to comply with the terms of the indemnity, there was the continued risk of French intervention. It was not until 1838 that a renegotiation of the indemnity provided for improved – but still harsh – terms and less risk of intervention. This was also the moment when the UK finally recognised the independence of Haiti as a sovereign state, having sent only a consul in 1826.[26]

Under different circumstances this might have been an opportunity for Haiti to move away from its militaristic society, whose armed forces placed such a heavy burden on the public revenue. However, developments in the eastern part of the island precluded this. First, Spain – the colonial power before the Haitian annexation – had never renounced its claims to Santo Domingo and saw in the French indemnity a possible opportunity to impose similar terms for recognition. A Spanish naval mission arrived in Haiti in 1842 with hostile purpose, but Boyer was eventually able to diffuse the situation.[27] The incident might even have led to a rapprochement with Spain. However, natural disaster struck Haiti the same year. An earthquake caused enormous damage, Cap Haitien was completely destroyed and Boyer was forced into exile in 1843.[28] Within a year the eastern part of the island had declared independence.[29]

The independence of the Dominican Republic made it inevitable that Haiti would keep a large standing army for two reasons. First, it felt obliged under

---

opportunities to work in sugar plantations emerged in Cuba and the Dominican Republic from the 1890s onwards, Haitians emigrated in the thousands.

[25] Baron Mackau sailed into Port-au-Prince at the head of a naval fleet carrying the *Ordonnance* setting out the conditions for recognising Haitian independence. Because it was already signed by Charles X, the French king, there was no opportunity for negotiation. Boyer has never been forgiven by many Haitians for agreeing to French recognition on the humiliating terms laid down, but the alternative was bombardment. If he made the wrong choice (and he did), he at least avoided a conflict that might have plunged Haiti into more years of war.

[26] It is sometimes assumed that the mere despatch of a consul is equivalent to recognition, but in international law this is not the case. Haiti, however, regarded a consular presence as de facto recognition.

[27] See Ardouin (1853–60), vol. 11, pp. 229–34.

[28] See Léger (1907), pp. 190–1.

[29] See Moya Pons (1998), chap. 7.

its constitution to seek the reconquest of the eastern part of this island.[30] This was attempted unsuccessfully by President Soulouque (1847–59) on two occasions.[31] Second, Haiti anticipated (correctly) that the Dominican Republic would be a weak state that might fall prey to outside powers. A foreign power in the eastern part of the island would be a constant threat to the territorial integrity of the western republic and so, once again, the shrinking of the armed forces was postponed.

For their part, the Dominicans had no confidence in their ability to survive as an independent state in the face of the Haitian territorial claim and sought instead the security of annexation by a member of the core. In this respect the Dominicans were exceedingly promiscuous, seeking the intervention at different times of France, Spain, the UK and the United States. It was Spain, however, that acted first, recolonising Santo Domingo in 1861 following an invitation from the Dominican president.[32] The Haitians immediately gave military help to the opponents of Spanish annexation and came close to war with Spain itself.

Spain was driven out in 1865, and the first treaty between Haiti and the Dominican Republic was signed in 1867, but the Haitian congress refused to ratify it.[33] However, far from being the prelude to improved security and demilitarisation, it was immediately followed in 1869 by a plan of annexation of the eastern part of the island by the United States, with the connivance of the Dominican president. Had this plan succeeded (it failed to garner the necessary two-thirds majority in the US Senate),[34] there is no doubt that it would only have been a matter of time before Haiti was engaged in an existential struggle for its own survival as an independent state. Instead, following the collapse of President Grant's dream of annexation, Haiti duly signed a definitive treaty with the Dominican Republic in 1874, although the boundaries between the two countries were only finally settled in 1935.[35]

---

[30] When Spain signed a peace treaty with France in 1795, it ceded the eastern part of the island. Thus, the France from which Haiti declared its independence in 1804 had been the colonial power for all Hispaniola. That is why all Haitian constitutions up to the recognition of Dominican independence give the territory as the whole island. The fact that Spanish settlers had won back control of the eastern part of the island from France in 1809 and that this had been recognised by France in 1814 was not considered by Haiti to be of any relevance.

[31] Soulouque, who was crowned Emperor Faustin I two years after becoming president, invaded the eastern part first in 1849 and again in 1855. After this, three members of the core – France, UK and US – combined forces to ensure that no further attempt was made. Soulouque is widely disparaged as militarily incompetent, but his two campaigns did ensure that productive areas on the frontier retained by Spain in 1697 would be incorporated into Haiti by the 1874 boundary treaty. See Bellegarde (1953), pp. 162–3.

[32] See Moya Pons (1998).

[33] See Léger (1907), p. 224.

[34] It failed primarily because of the opposition of Senator Charles Sumner, who consistently supported Haiti during his political career.

[35] The 1874 treaty was known as the Treaty of Amity, Commerce and Navigation. See Léger (1907), p. 224.

Despite this important change on the island, Haiti could still not relax. Following the Franco-Prussian War in 1870, Germany – now unified – began to show its strength and to explore for the first time the possibility of acquiring overseas colonies. In 1872 German gunboats arrived at Port-au-Prince to demand immediate payment of claims by two German citizens arising from the Haitian Civil War a few years earlier.[36] Because the cost of the naval mission to Haiti far exceeded the value of the claims, it is unlikely that this was the real purpose.[37] The Haitian government was subjected to another illustration of German military prowess in 1897 over an equally trivial incident that strongly suggested a more geostrategic purpose.[38]

Before its own civil war (1861–5), the United States had not shown much interest in controlling Haitian territory. The most serious incident occurred in 1857 when a US citizen claimed Ile de Navase (Navassa Island) under the 1856 Guano Islands Act.[39] This island, declared to be part of Haitian territory in all subsequent constitutions, was unoccupied at the time. The Haitian navy tried to expel the individuals involved, but the United States held on to the island and later built a lighthouse. It remains US territory today despite its proximity to Haiti.[40] This was the first in a long line of disputes involving Haiti's islands in which the core exploited its superior military power at the expense of the republic.[41]

After 1865, the United States became much more acquisitive. The rise of US naval power, the attempted construction of a Panama Canal by the French in the 1880s and the rivalry between the core states themselves made the control of naval and coaling stations in the Caribbean a geostrategic necessity. In Môle St Nicholas, Haiti had one of the four finest natural harbours in the region and one that was coveted by the core. Having failed to secure Samaná Bay in the Dominican Republic through annexation or lease, thwarted by the US

[36] Captain Batsh of the German navy seized two Haitian warships without even waiting for the reply of the Haitian government to his demand for payment. See Douyon (2004), p. 119–20.

[37] The claims were for a total of $15,000, so it is safe to assume that the German navy had not been sent thousands of miles for that purpose alone.

[38] This was known as the Lüders incident. A German citizen of Haitian descent had been imprisoned following due process, but the German navy demanded his release and payment of an indemnity. See Montague (1940), pp. 178–9. Modern archival research suggests that Germany was not in fact seeking colonies in the Caribbean, but the Haitians can be forgiven for not seeing it in that way at the time.

[39] This law stated: 'whenever a citizen of the United States discovers a deposit of guano on any island ... not within the lawful jurisdiction of any other Government, and not occupied by the citizens of any other government ... and occupies the same, such island ... may ... be considered as appertaining to the United States.' See Montague (1940), pp. 61–5.

[40] Ile de Navase is thirty miles from the coast of Haiti. It is now known as a US minor outlying island, of which there are nine, and most of which have a similar history to Navassa Island.

[41] One of the most serious was the Maunder incident, under which Great Britain threatened to bombard Haiti because the government had cancelled a concession to a British subject for exploitation of the Ile de la Tortue (Tortuga Island). See Léger (1907), pp. 230–1. The incident was particularly sensitive for Haiti because Mrs. Maunder, who made the claim as a widow, was the granddaughter of Boyer.

Senate in its efforts to acquire St Thomas in the Danish Virgin Islands and unable at this stage to acquire Guantánamo Bay because of Spanish control of Cuba, the United States focused on Môle St Nicholas as the most suitable candidate. Haiti refused to cave into US pressure and was punished in 1892 by the application of harsh tariffs on the main US imports from Haiti.[42] The efforts by the United States under President Harrison to secure Môle St Nicholas have been described as 'one of the more unsavoury episodes in the history of American diplomacy'.[43]

Haiti ended the nineteenth century as an independent country, but it had been a struggle. The need for a large army had drained the public purse while giving serving presidents a means of delaying or blocking the peaceful transfer of power. No excuses should be made for the occasionally selfish, irresponsible and corrupt behaviour of some Haitian politicians in the nineteenth century, but it would be dishonest not to recognise that the core played a very negative role in this process. The core also exploited Haitian relative weakness by pursuing an endless stream of financial claims on behalf of its citizens that were usually grossly inflated and sometimes outrageous.[44] And because the government had to service an enormous debt, Haitian public finances (net of debt-service payments) were deeply unsatisfactory and below what was required to support many state responsibilities (see section 3 below). The only solution to this conundrum was through an expansion of exports, because in Haiti – as elsewhere in Latin America and the Caribbean – exports paid for imports, and foreign trade provided the bulk of public revenue. It is to this we now turn.

7.2. THE EXPORT SECTOR

The first Haitian leaders, from Toussaint to Boyer, understood very clearly that the survival of the state[45] depended on the recovery of the export sector after the ravages of the war of independence. In this, as we shall see, they had some success. Subsequent leaders also recognised that the development of Haiti depended in large part on the long-run growth of the export sector, and policies were indeed adopted to promote exports. However, these leaders struggled to balance the budget. For reasons that will become clear later, Haitian public finance depended very heavily on export taxes. Thus, there was a tension between the short-run needs of public finance and the long-run requirements of export growth. In this struggle, the short run tended to prevail, and exports were burdened with taxes that undermined the long-run goal of export promotion.

---

[42] Ostensibly, the duties were imposed because Haiti had failed to reach a reciprocal trade agreement with the US as permitted under the McKinley tariff, but everyone knew the real reason.

[43] See Montague (1940), p. 162.

[44] See section 3. These claims are well explored in Douyon (2004), pp. 118–26, under the very appropriate subheading 'Les Actes de Piraterie et les Réclamations Etrangères'.

[45] Strictly speaking, Haiti was not an independent state until the declaration of independence by Dessalines on 1 January 1804, but under Toussaint it was a state in all but name.

If there was little alternative to export promotion,[46] Haiti was no different from other countries in the region (including the United States before 1860). However, in one respect – the average size of landholdings – Haiti differed greatly. The multitude of small farms and the small number of large estates made Haiti by the end of the nineteenth century different from most other countries in Latin America and the Caribbean.[47] Exports of agricultural – and to a lesser extent timber[48] – products therefore came to depend on the Haitian peasantry, whose access to capital (financial and human) was severely restricted.

It was not always so. Under Toussaint, Dessalines and Christophe (until just before his death), the large-scale estate was favoured, land grants below a certain size were prohibited and foreigners ('whites' in the 1805 constitution)[49] were prevented from owning real estate, and therefore the large landowners were Haitians. To ensure an adequate labour supply for these big estates, labour laws made vagrancy a crime. The workers on the estates received a quarter of the produce, and the landlord received half. Dessalines went even further than Toussaint and banned the cutting of timber on the grounds that it might prejudice the supply of labour to the large estates.[50] Exports of traditional commodities, including sugar, started to recover – albeit from a very low base.[51]

The state received the remaining quarter of the farm output and, under Christophe, this contribution together with a land tax was sufficient to meet the needs of the government for defence, public works and even education.[52] However, because the estates were producing commodities destined in many cases for shipment abroad, the land tax under Christophe in effect began the practice of taxing exports. When prices were high and the tax moderate it was

[46] Some Haitians did emphasise the need for national self-sufficiency in agriculture and even industrialisation, but this never acquired much support. See Nicholls (1974), pp. 14–18, and Joachim (1979), pp. 172–9.

[47] Not all, of course. Costa Rica, like Haiti subject to a shortage of labour and unable to attract much international migration, had developed an agricultural export sector based largely on small farms until the entry of the banana companies in the last part of the nineteenth century.

[48] Timber was cut and sold for export by the peasantry, but from 1860 large concessions were given to foreigners for timber extraction.

[49] The ban on whites became a ban on foreigners in the 1843 constitution. It did not, however, apply to those blacks who came to Haiti from the US and other parts of the Caribbean.

[50] See Turnier (1955), chap. 3.

[51] From their high point in 1789 (95.6 million [long] lbs), raw sugar exports fell to virtually zero at the time of independence. They had recovered to 5.4 million lbs in 1818, most of which came from the north. In the case of coffee, exports had reached 76.8 million (long) lbs in 1789 before collapsing in the next fifteen years. They had recovered to 26 million lbs in 1818, most of which came from the south. See Barros (1984), vol. 1, pp. 198, 341.

[52] The Kingdom of Haiti under Christophe was much admired by many foreign visitors because of its achievements (especially education), but it was really a feudal system based on coerced labour that was hugely unpopular with the mass of the population. Perhaps it is no surprise that Christophe was a great admirer of the Russian emperor, whose system of serfdom resembled the Kingdom of Haiti in some respects.

not so serious, but when prices were low and the tax high it became a major barrier to export expansion.

In the Republic of Haiti, under Pétion, a different model was followed. A law of 1809 removed the restriction on selling land in small parcels, and a large number of small grants were made by the government. Others simply voted with their feet, squatting on land that belonged either to the state or purchasing small plots from the remaining estate owners. Under these circumstances it is not surprising that the export of sugar collapsed under Pétion, but coffee recovered, and logwood – no longer forbidden – prospered. However, Pétion also came to depend heavily on taxes on exports to balance the budget, because the state's share of one-quarter was suppressed[53] (instead, workers on large estates were now allowed to keep half the produce).

Boyer, who succeeded Pétion in 1818 and then Christophe in 1820, at first allowed both agricultural models to continue.[54] However, following the imposition of the French indemnity in 1825 and the contraction of a loan to pay for the first instalment (see section 3 below), he favoured the large estates on the grounds that only they could ensure the expansion of exports on which debt service would depend. The *Code Rural* of 1826 was as draconian as other measures in the Caribbean to coerce labour to work for the large estates, but it had the opposite effect. Because the only way for most Haitians to escape the vagrancy provisions of the *Code* was to be a small farmer, the process of squatting and purchasing of small plots accelerated. By 1839, it is estimated that there were 46,610 small farms in Haiti.[55] By the time Boyer was forced from office in 1843, sugar had ceased to be an export of any importance, and agricultural output had come to depend on the small-scale peasantry combined with sharecropping on the large estates by small gangs of labourers who had control over the product mix.[56]

Boyer had lowered export taxes in 1825, before the imposition of the French indemnity, in an effort to stimulate exports. He then abolished them altogether

---

[53] See Benoit (1954a), p. 32ff. Pétion raised export taxes no less than four times between 1808 and 1817.

[54] Boyer made a number of small grants from state lands at the beginning of his term, but he did not break up the large estates in the north – or, indeed, those that remained in the south – and was keen to preserve them.

[55] See Candler (1842), p. 122. If Candler is right in assuming that the average farm had five inhabitants, and if we also assume that all these farms were in the western part of the island, this would imply a landowning peasant population of about 250,000 out of a Haitian population of 500,000 (see Table A.1). The remainder of the labouring population either worked for wages in rural areas, in sharecropping gangs or in towns.

[56] The large estates had not disappeared, but it was increasingly difficult for the owners to obtain wage labour. They had therefore in many cases subcontracted the work to different gangs of labourers with an agreed division of the output (typically 50/50). This was like sharecropping in other parts of the Caribbean, but with one major difference: the sharecroppers rather than the landlord decided what to produce.

in 1827.[57] This bold move was partly to encourage exports but also to mitigate the damaging effect of the 50 per cent reduction in export duty he had been forced to concede to France.[58] Unfortunately, the demands of public finance obliged Boyer to reintroduce a specific duty on exports in 1835, and he added an additional burden ('droit de wharfage y pesage') in the same year. Any good this might have done to government revenue was undone by the depreciation of the national currency, because the export taxes were paid in paper gourdes.[59] By 1843, the value of the paper gourde had dropped by one-third (see section 3 below).

The depreciation of the currency accelerated under the four presidents that succeeded Boyer in quick succession.[60] The export tax was first abolished (1843) and then reestablished (1845). When Soulouque became president in 1847, the paper gourde had so depreciated[61] that the real value of the export tax had collapsed. Soulouque therefore imposed a tax of 20 per cent on coffee payable in kind by growers, with the state then selling its share to exporters at a market rate. Hugely unpopular with the peasants and exporters alike, it did at least ensure that government revenue moved more or less in line with the value of coffee exports.

By the time Soulouque was forced from office in January 1859, the gourde had fallen to 30 to the dollar, so there was little point in reimposing an export tax payable in national currency. Instead, President Geffrard (1859–67) in 1860 made the export tax payable in hard currency for the first time. Because the tax was specific, its ad valorem equivalent depended on the evolution of the prices of the main commodities (principally coffee and logwood). After a period of confusion during a civil war (1867–9), when President Salnave reimposed payment in kind, the export taxes were fixed in August 1870. The duty on coffee was set at $2.50 per 100 lbs in 1870, that on logwood at $1.50 per 1,000 lbs, and there were also duties imposed on most of the minor commodities, such as cacao and cotton.[62] However, the export tax on coffee – by far the most important – was steadily increased and had reached $3.86 by 1889.[63]

This was a heavy burden for coffee producers, and it was made worse by various other taxes that applied to exports when they left port. When coffee

---

[57] See Benoit (1954a), p. 33, who is an invaluable source for the export tax in this period of Haitian history.

[58] It might be argued that half a loaf was better than no loaf. However, many ships started to call at Haitian ports carrying the French flag in order to avail themselves of the French tax concession, even though the exports were not destined for France. See Turnier (1955), pp. 123–6.

[59] The reasons for the depreciation will be explained in the next section.

[60] This period (1843–7) was turbulent, but it should not be exaggerated. Two of the four presidents died in office of natural causes. See Léger (1907), pp. 192–9.

[61] By 1847 it was valued around 14 to the dollar. See section 3.

[62] These are long lbs. They can be converted to the short lbs used in the US and the UK by multiplying by 1.083. See the Notes on B. Tables.

[63] This meant that the burden of all export taxes on coffee could easily exceed 100% of the net export price.

prices were high, the burden was – just about – bearable, but it became almost insupportable when prices fell. Furthermore, Haitian coffee was not only taxed heavily in Haiti. It was also taxed heavily in France – its main market – where Haitian coffee received much less favourable treatment than coffee imported from French colonies.[64] It was not until 1904, following the Haitian-French treaty of commerce, that Haitian coffee received any preferential treatment in the French market, and even then France only agreed to apply the minimum rather than the maximum tax rate.[65] Haitian coffee entered the British and US markets free of tariff in most years, but these were much less important markets, except in the early years of the nineteenth century.[66]

Under these circumstances, it might seem surprising that there was any growth at all in Haitian exports in the century after independence. However, as we shall now see, there was growth, in both volume and value, although neither ultimately was able to keep pace with population growth. Furthermore, exports had come to depend far too heavily on one crop (coffee), whose price declined sharply from the 1890s onwards as a result of Brazilian overproduction. Thus, Haiti went into the twentieth century with an export sector that was too small to support the growing needs of public finance, and it was so dependent on one product that it was vulnerable to price movements, over which the country had no control.

The four products that collectively determined the value of Haitian exports in the century before the US invasion were coffee, cotton, cacao and logwood.[67] We will examine each in turn, but we should first note the virtual disappearance of other products from the export list. From 1822 to 1844, when the island was united, exports included tobacco, but this came almost entirely from the eastern part of the island, and I have therefore allocated them to the Dominican Republic. The same was true of timber other than logwood, but there were some exports from Haiti of mahogany, gayac (*lignum vitae*) and fustic (Brazilwood) after the separation of the two countries in 1844. However, the value of these exports (except logwood) was never significant.

Raw sugar exports had ceased to be of any importance by the end of Boyer's term. Attempts were made to revive them under different presidents, notably Geffrard and Salomon (1879–88), and sugar exports were even exempt from

---

[64] Joachim (1972), p. 1520, has a table showing French imports of coffee between 1860 and 1890 and the import duties payable. The tax rate in these years averaged 74% of the *cif* value of coffee imports.

[65] Inspired by the tariff concessions the US had secured from trade partners under the 1890 McKinley tariff, France had moved in 1892 to a system of minimum and maximum tariffs. To benefit from the minimum tariff, partners had to extend to France tariff reductions and other privileges. Not to be outdone, Germany then demanded the same treatment and imposed taxes on Haitian exports until trade privileges were extended to Germany under the 1908 Haitian-German treaty. See Turnier (1955), pp. 210–11.

[66] Haiti, having refused to sign a reciprocal trade treaty with the US in 1892, was then subject to a tariff of 3 US cents per lb until the status quo ante was restored by the Wilson tariff in 1894.

[67] The combined value of these four products as a share of total exports averaged 95%. See the Notes on B. Tables.

taxation for much of the time, but the key constraint was the lack of capital needed to reestablish the industry with modern technology (without which costs would be too high). Sugarcane production may have been labour-intensive, but cane **sugar** production for export was capital-intensive and also demanded sophisticated infrastructure. Shortages of labour, capital and infrastructure made it inevitable that Haiti would cease to be an exporter of sugar. The export industry only started to recover after the First World War, when the United States as the occupying force was able to force through legislation that permitted foreigners to own land, dispossess small farmers and build the necessary infrastructure. At that point, US capital entered the sugar industry, and exports started again (even then they did not prosper).

Haitian coffee (*Arabica*) was considered to be of excellent quality. It was noted in particular for its aroma. After independence, it was sold at first mainly to the UK and the United States, but consumers in those countries gradually came to prefer the cheaper coffee produced by Brazil, Colombia, Central America and a handful of European colonies. With the opening once again of the French market in 1825, Haitian coffee came to depend increasingly on the more discerning consumers of continental Europe (especially the Germans, to whom Haitian coffee was re-exported from France), who were prepared to pay a premium for quality coffee. About 60 to 70 per cent of the Haitian coffee crop was normally sold in this way.

Haitian coffee trees flourished above 300 metres in the south, the main growing region, but in the north they could grow at sea level. It was cultivated under shade and produced organically. The Haitian peasantry did not in general plant the coffee trees, relying instead on natural growth from fallen berries, but occasional weeding and thinning was essential. The coffee was harvested between October and February and was at first prepared for export on the farms themselves in the following manner:[68] 'After drying on the special patio, or even on the ground, the pulp is generally removed by hand in a wooden pestle, then the beans are deparchmented [*sic*] and more or less sorted before offering for sale.' This method of preparing coffee for export, although widely disparaged by foreign visitors, was reasonably well suited to the Haitian environment. However, as the market became more specialised, Haitian growers were penalised for their failure to separate the lowest grades of coffee from the highest. Tackling this problem required machinery and a greater division of labour between the grower and the exporter. This process was underway by the early 1880s, helped by measures taken by President Salomon. Thus, the US consul in 1884 could write as follows:[69]

To procure for Haytian coffee the very latest improvements in the preparation, thus allowing it to compete advantageously with other sorts, and acquire the rank which from its natural superiority is its due, central mills . . . are beginning to be established

---

[68] See Tea and Coffee Trade Journal (1935), vol. 68, p. 103.
[69] See *Commercial Relations of the United States with Foreign Countries in the Year 1883* (1884), vol. 2, p. 468.

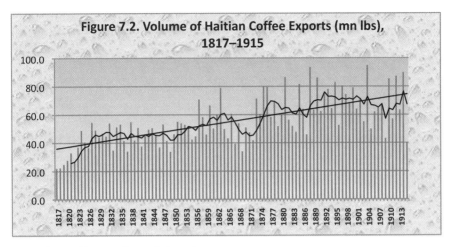

Figure 7.2. Volume of Haitian Coffee Exports (mn lbs), 1817–1915

Note: The trend line is a five-period moving average.
Source: Table B.2.

in the principal coffee-growing centers.... Thus the grower, who by his very primitive mode of preparation was losing at least one-third of his crop, will now obtain one-half more of money value as the result of his toil.

Coffee preparation, especially before the introduction of central mills, provided only modest scope for an increase in yield. The volume of coffee exports therefore depended largely on the ability to expand the supply of labour and land in response to growing demand. Because the population in rural areas increased, and there was no shortage of land suitable for coffee growing, it is not surprising that the volume of coffee exports did rise (see Figure 7.2). The annual figures fluctuated greatly because of seasonal conditions and world prices, and exports were clearly affected by periods of great political upheaval, such as the second half of the 1860s, but the upward trend is clear from the moving average.

Logwood, from which a natural dye is obtained, was the second most important Haitian export for most of the nineteenth century.[70] Although the peasantry was at first forbidden to cut it, the volume of exports expanded rapidly after Boyer (1818–43), under whom restrictions had continued.[71] Much of it was sold to the United States, but it was also sold to the UK, where it was regarded as superior to Jamaican logwood. The volume of exports, however, peaked around 1880 (see Figure 7.3). By then the forests had been

[70] In 1879–80, Haiti was also by far the world's most important exporter of logwood, with two-thirds of the market. See Turnier (1955), p. 155.
[71] Boyer had drawn attention to 'the pernicious custom which many people have contracted of abandoning work on estates and devoting themselves to cutting wood that does not belong to them.' See Nicholls (1974), p. 8.

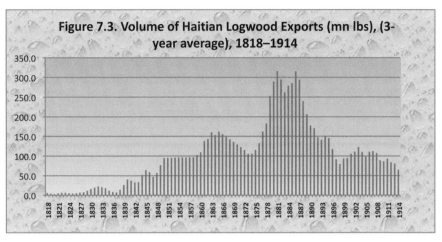

Source: Table B.2.

largely cleared of logwood, and contemporaries noted that in subsequent years a large proportion of exports consisted of roots rather than trees.[72]

The sea-island cotton exported from Haiti, as elsewhere in the Caribbean, was not competitive with US cotton. However, exports from large and small farms continued at very modest levels until the outbreak of the US Civil War. The rise in cotton prices and the promotional measures taken by President Geffrard stimulated exports. Haiti – like so many other countries – was unable to compete when prices returned to more normal levels after the US Civil War. Exports fluctuated in subsequent decades, but did not return to their level of the mid-1860s.[73]

Haitian cacao, unlike coffee, was not especially valued for its aroma or taste, and exports languished at low levels for most of the nineteenth century.[74] Exports only started to accelerate after 1880 in response both to higher prices and to the cacao boom in the Dominican Republic. However, the rise of cacao exports was modest compared with what happened in the neighbouring country, for several reasons, even though cacao, like coffee, can be grown successfully on small estates. First, Haitian infrastructure – especially railways – was progressing much less rapidly than in the Dominican Republic, and, second, cacao exports were much more heavily taxed. Nevertheless, the development of the industry meant that the value of cacao exports was equal in importance to logwood by 1900.

---

[72] Logwood exports were also threatened by synthetic dyes produced commercially in the German chemical industry from the 1890s onwards, but by then the industry had already begun its decline in Haiti as a result of deforestation.

[73] See Table B.2.

[74] See Table B.2.

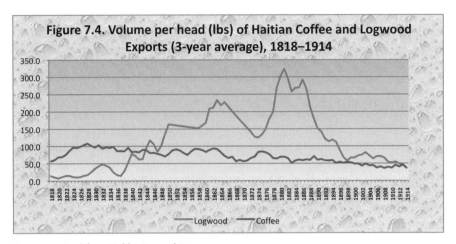

Figure 7.4. Volume per head (lbs) of Haitian Coffee and Logwood Exports (3-year average), 1818–1914

Source: Derived from Tables B.1 and B.2.

For economic development to take place, the volume of exports must normally expand by more than the rate of increase of population. This did happen in the case of cacao and cotton,[75] but it did not consistently happen in the case of logwood and coffee (see Figure 7.4). Because of its importance to overall exports, the decline in the volume of coffee exports per head after 1890 was particularly serious. Given the dependence of public finance on foreign trade and the dependence of imports on exports, this meant that the Haitian development model was only viable if the terms of trade improved. This depended primarily on the price of exports and, in particular, on the price of coffee. It is to this that we now turn.

Haitian coffee may have commanded a premium, but the price still depended on the world market, where Brazil was the dominant supplier. What happened in Brazil therefore had a large bearing on the price of Haitian coffee. However, the price received by Haitians (growers and merchants) was also affected by the export taxes applied in Haiti and the import tariffs applied by France. The French (and German) consumer was able to discriminate between Haitian and other coffees, but the demand curve was not vertical. Thus, part of the export and import taxes was born by the Haitian producer through a reduction in the price received by growers. Because the import tariff was largely unchanged, it was the increase in the coffee export tax and Brazilian market conditions that had the most impact.

Coffee prices fluctuated throughout the nineteenth century, but the prices in different markets were highly correlated. After a brief civil war in the early 1890s, Brazilian prices fell sharply, dragging down with them Haitian and other prices. This price decline would continue with only brief interruptions until just before the First World War. The consequences for all coffee exporters

---

[75] This can be derived from Tables B.1 and B.2.

were bad, but for Haiti they were catastrophic. The value of coffee exports declined, bringing with it inevitably a decline in the value of all exports.[76] What happened then was determined by public finance, to which we now turn.

7.3. PUBLIC FINANCE

Public finance is not normally a subject that generates great interest. Indeed, for many Caribbean countries in the nineteenth century it was not a major determinant of success or failure. For Haiti, however, as an independent country, it was absolutely crucial. It proved to be the weakest point of the Haitian model and, in the end, contributed perhaps more than any other factor to the series of events that culminated in the US occupation in 1915. We will first explore the evolution of public revenue and then the pattern of expenditure.

By the time Boyer reunited the country at the end of 1820, Haiti had developed a tax system that was reasonably diversified. The principal sources of income were taxes on imports, of which the ad valorem tariff was by far the most important.[77] This had been introduced by Dessalines in 1806 at 10 per cent, raised to 12 per cent by Boyer in 1819 and to 16 per cent in 1827, when it applied to the whole island.[78] The yield had been undermined by the preferences conceded to the British in 1814[79] and to the French in 1825,[80] but Boyer soon put a stop to both[81] and added an additional 10 per cent on the import tariffs applied to US ships in 1829.[82]

The other taxes on trade were export duties, which did not apply to all products and which were in any case suspended from 1827 to 1835. In both cases, imports and exports, there were also various minor taxes based on tonnage and wharfage. The contribution of all these trade taxes to public

---

[76] My estimates of the value of Haitian exports are given in Tables B.2 and B.3. See also Notes on B. Tables, which explains the methodology behind the estimates.

[77] A small number of specific tariffs were introduced in 1820, but these were designed to protect rather than to generate income. See Benoit (1954a), pp. 55–6.

[78] See Benoit (1954a), pp. 55–6. Pétion had maintained the import duties, but Christophe had scrapped them, relying principally on the land tax and rents from state lands. See Nicholls (1974), p. 5.

[79] Pétion, despite the huge loss of income implied, had agreed in 1814 to a reduction on import duties on British goods from 10% to 5%. See Mackenzie (1830), vol. 2, p. 275. When Boyer raised the tariff rate to 12%, the British rate went to 7%.

[80] One of the clauses of the *Ordonnance* of Charles X, to which Boyer agreed, was a 50% reduction on all customs duties (import and export) in perpetuity.

[81] Boyer cancelled the British preference in 1825 at the same time he accepted the French preference. If he had not done so, most of Haiti's imports would have paid a much reduced tariff. The French preference was cancelled unilaterally in 1827 when it became clear that other countries were exploiting the French flag to introduce imports to Haiti at half the full rate.

[82] This was in response to the refusal of the US to recognise the independence of Haiti. The surcharge was finally dropped in 1850, despite the fact that the US had still not recognised Haiti. See Nicholls (1974), p. 14.

revenue in Boyer's presidency was around 50 per cent.[83] The other half of public revenue came from the land tax, rent and sale of state lands, sale of patents, stamp duties and so on.[84] Of these the land tax, which had been adopted by Christophe and by Pétion, was the most important.

All taxes at first were paid in the national currency (gourdes). Before the introduction of paper money in 1826, the money supply was based on coins (specie) so that in theory the gourde was equivalent to US or Spanish dollars. In practice, however, a shortage of specie had obliged Pétion to debase the coinage by reducing its metallic content, and the problem was exacerbated by counterfeit money introduced from outside.[85] By the time Boyer reunited the country, the exchange rate of the gourde to the dollar was estimated to be only 3 to 1.[86] Faced with an acute shortage of currency in 1826 (see below in this section), Boyer then introduced paper money that – not being backed by hard currency – caused a further slide in the currency.[87] Boyer therefore decreed in 1835 that import duties must be paid in hard currency, but all other taxes could still be paid in gourdes.

At this point Haiti began its painful experience with two currencies, which did not end until the 1870s.[88] As the fall of the gourde continued, the dollar value of those taxes collected in national currency declined further and further. By the end of the 1840s, when the exchange rate was 14 to 1, the only tax of importance had become import duties, because these were collected in hard currency. A change had to be made, and in 1850 President Soulouque (by then Emperor Faustin I) made the export tax on coffee payable in kind at 20 per cent.[89] This rescued public revenue, but the yield from the other taxes – particularly the land tax – generated very little income by the end of the 1850s because the exchange rate had fallen to 30 to 1.

In 1860, Geffrard, who had replaced Soulouque in January 1859, introduced an export tax payable in hard currency. At first, it was applied only to coffee and logwood (the two main commodities). The export tax on coffee payable in kind

---

[83] In 1837 it was 52.3% (of which 33.3% came from import taxes and 19% from export taxes). See Benoit (1954a), p. 22.

[84] For 1837, each tax is itemised in Marte (1984), p. 108.

[85] See Turnier (1955), pp. 278–9. The first debasement in 1811 reduced the value by 18%. Two years later, Pétion introduced a new money (*serpent*), ostensibly at par with the US and Spanish dollar but with a much lower metallic content, and thus its intrinsic value was only one-third.

[86] See International Bureau of the American Republics (1893), p. 96. See also the Notes on B. Tables, where the Haitian exchange rate to the dollar is discussed in more detail.

[87] It also made counterfeiting easier, and many false notes were introduced from outside. One of the most notorious counterfeiters was a Frenchman, Charles Touzalin, who was caught red-handed. This did not stop the French consul, M. Lavasseur, from protesting vigorously and threatening to break off diplomatic relations if Touzalin was not released. See Ardouin (1853–60), vol. 11, pp. 146–51.

[88] The Dominican Republic suffered a similar fate starting with independence in 1844. In both cases there are ominous parallels with Cuba following the legalisation of the US dollar in 1993.

[89] Soulouque also created a series of state monopolies involving foreign trade, but most of these had to be withdrawn in the face of strong opposition from the foreign merchants who dominated the import-export firms. See Bernardin (1999), pp. 84–6, and Nicholls (1974), pp. 13–14.

was then scrapped. Nearly 100 per cent of public revenue came from customs duties. Other taxes were levied, but – being paid in national currency – the yield was extremely small. By the time the land tax was abolished in 1870, when the exchange rate had fallen to 4,000 to 1, it had ceased to have any purpose. Soon after, the gourde was withdrawn from circulation, and Haiti depended largely on foreign currencies until the introduction of the (new) gourde in 1880 at par with the US dollar.

From this point onwards, despite its dependence on customs duties that made the country very vulnerable to a fall in coffee prices,[90] public revenue might have been sufficient in Haiti if the state had not faced an increase in expenditure on debt service, claims from foreigners and the need to withdraw paper money (see below in this section). In order to meet these additional expenditures, the Haitian government increased the scale of customs duties (all payable in hard currency) rather than try to diversify the tax base. These increases were then earmarked for various purposes, principally debt-service charges, so that the Haitian people hardly benefited at all.

The increases in export taxes have been described in the previous section.[91] The ad valorem import duty remained unchanged at 16 per cent, but a surcharge of 10 per cent was applied in 1863. This was followed a few years later by another surcharge of 10 per cent to meet the claims arising from the 1867–9 Haitian Civil War. There was then a surcharge of 25 per cent in 1872 to pay for the withdrawal of paper money. Then in 1876 all these surcharges were replaced with a new one of 50 per cent, which applied to all taxes on imports (not just the ad valorem duties). Finally, in 1883 an additional surcharge of 33 1/3 per cent was introduced. If we compute the average tariff rate by dividing estimated import duties by imports,[92] we find that it had risen to 35 per cent by the 1880s, and it stayed there until the tariff reform of 1905, when the average rate was temporarily reduced.[93] In these years, no one can fault Haiti for its tax effort, because the government was clearly taxing imports (and exports) very heavily.[94]

Haitian governments may have been able to set the rate of taxes on trade, but they could not control world prices. When coffee prices started to fall

[90] A fall in coffee prices, unless matched by an equivalent increase in volume, reduced the value of exports because coffee was the main export. In turn, this reduced the value of imports. Although the export duties were specific, the bulk of the import duties were ad valorem, so customs duties and public revenue would then decline.

[91] Nearly all these increases were hypothecated and tied to the payment of debt service or claims by foreigners. This made it very difficult for the state to lower export duties, but they had reached dangerously high levels by the 1880s.

[92] To do this, I took the import tariffs in those years for which we have data (see Table B.9) and divided by my estimates of imports in Table B.6. See also Table A.36.

[93] This tariff reform banned the importation of certain products that competed with local production, reduced tariffs on capital goods and articles on essential consumption and raised taxes on some luxury goods. See Benoit (1954a), p. 57.

[94] In 1904, Haiti had conceded import preferences to France as part of the Franco-Haitian treaty of commerce. It did the same for Germany in 1908. However, by this time the US was supplying about 70% of imports, so the impact on tariff collection of these preferences was not so serious.

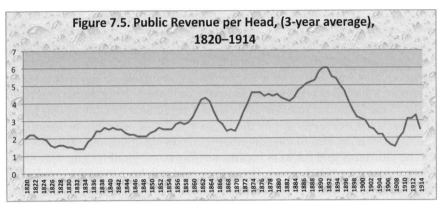

Figure 7.5. Public Revenue per Head, (3-year average), 1820–1914

Source: Derived from Tables B.1 and B.9.

in the 1890s, public finances in Haiti deteriorated. Customs duties could not be raised further (they were already at – if not beyond – the rates needed to maximise revenues), and exports could not be diversified because of the absence of infrastructure, the shortage of capital and the lack of education among the peasantry. In the two decades before the US invasion, Haitian governments resorted with increasing frequency and desperation to internal debt, including the issue of paper money not backed by reserves. Public revenue itself, still almost entirely dependent on customs duties, declined, and the fall was even sharper when expressed in per capita terms (see Figure 7.5). The recovery in coffee prices brought about a brief respite before the First World War, but it was too little and too late to save Haiti from foreign intervention.

Haiti's public expenditure was dominated at first, for reasons explained in section 1 above, by the need for a large standing army. This absorbed about half the budget in the first decade of Boyer's rule. The size of the armed forces was reduced to around 20,000 under Geffrard in the 1860s and perhaps to 16,000 under Salomon in the 1880s.[95] This allowed expenditure on the military to fall below 25 per cent of the budget. However, internal political instability and the ever-present external threat meant that further reductions in the military share of the budget were not possible.[96] Military spending stayed close to 25 per cent until the US occupation.[97]

The armed forces may have absorbed 50 per cent of the budget in the early 1820s, but at least Haiti had no debt to service. This changed when the

[95] See St. John (1889), p. 310.
[96] Geffrard had tried in the 1860s to secure a guarantee of Haitian neutrality from the core, which might have allowed for a major reduction in the size of the armed forces. The European states expressed some interest, but the US – having imperial ambitions of its own following the Civil War – opposed it and the proposal lapsed. See Montague (1940), p. 97.
[97] See Table B.10. There is a case to be made that Haitian military spending was actually too small because it failed to deter the core from its abuse of power and ultimately could not prevent the US from invading in 1915.

French fleet arrived in the harbour of Port-au-Prince in April 1825 carrying the *Ordonnance* of Charles X. Boyer's unwise decision to accept the terms set out by the French king[98] had terrible long-term consequences for Haiti. A loan was contracted in Paris for 30 million francs to pay the first annual instalment. However, this was subject to a 20 per cent commission, so Boyer was forced to impose a special tax on Haitian citizens to pay the balance due to France for the first year (6 million francs).[99] When this proved unsuccessful, he was forced to ransack the treasury and pay the balance in coins, draining the country of specie and forcing him to introduce paper money the following year.

The indemnity and the loan became known as the 'double debt', but it was not a debt in the usual sense. The money had not been used for productive purposes, which would have created the resources from which the debt could be serviced, but was instead a subsidy to the French state that then passed it on to the former slave owners and their descendants. The French authorities presented figures suggesting that the indemnity was compensation for expro-priation of French property, and it was duly itemised, but in practice they had estimated Haiti's annual exports in 1823 (30 million francs), deducted 50 per cent for costs of production and amortised the balance over ten years to reach the magic figure of 150 million francs. Essentially, it was a cynical exercise to extract the maximum subsidy that they thought Haiti could pay.[100]

The double debt was enormously unpopular in Haiti, and there was even an attempted uprising. Wisely, Boyer defaulted on the second and subsequent instalments of the indemnity and made no interest payments on the loan.[101] He also abolished export duties, in effect depriving France of its 50 per cent pref-erence, and also cancelled the reduction of French privileges on import tariffs. However, he did not repudiate the double debt and, after several unsuccessful negotiations, agreed to new terms in 1838.[102] It is from this moment, rather than 1825, that Haiti became burdened with external debt-service payments,

[98] These included payment of an indemnity of 150 million French francs ($30 million) payable in five annual instalments and a reduction of 50% in customs duties on both exports and imports. Thus, the French king imposed an enormous burden on Haiti while simultaneously depriving the young republic of the means to pay it.

[99] The tax was enforced in Port-au-Prince, but Cap Haitien only paid half, and elsewhere nothing at all was raised. See Lacerte (1981), p. 505. It did, however, have one desirable side effect because the Chamber of Representatives had to provide in 1826 an estimate of population on which the per capita tax could be based. This figure, 432,042 for the whole island and 351,819 for Haiti itself, was very different from the inflated census figure of 1824 and is the one found in Mackenzie (1830).

[100] Although disastrous for Haiti, the indemnity brought almost no benefit to the former slave owners and their descendants. There were 25,838 beneficiaries, and the annual payments by Haiti often yielded no more than a few francs for each family. Fairly typical was the case of Jean-Louis Lonchamp, whose family of eleven members received 85 francs ($17) in 1841 to cover the three years from 1838–40. This works out at 51.5 US cents per year per family member. See Blancpain (2001), p. 77.

[101] Curiously, the French government did meet the interest payments on the loan in 1826 and 1827, so it did not go into default until 1828. See Blancpain (2001), p. 67.

[102] The details are given in the Notes on B. Tables.

because up to that point the only disbursement had been a single off-budget payment for 5.3 million francs ($1 million) in specie.

Although payments were occasionally suspended, particularly during 1843–8 and 1867–9, Haiti regularly serviced the double debt and finally paid it off in December 1883.[103] However, in 1874 – as part of its efforts to restructure the monetary system – the republic took out its first true foreign loan. The amount received, after the usual enormous commissions, was small, and President Domingue (1874–6) in the following year was persuaded by his vice president, Septimus Rameau, to take out a much bigger loan (again from French bankers). The fraud involved in this so-called Domingue loan was enormous, on both the Haitian and French side, and President Salomon made renegotiation a priority. This he did with some success, but the fact of the matter is that Haiti ended up servicing a large external debt that had brought virtually no benefit to the country. Much the same happened in 1896 and 1910, with two French loans designed in theory to retire the previous debts on more favourable terms, but in practice they left Haiti with a big increase in indebtedness, a rise in debt-service costs and nothing to show for it in terms of productive investments.[104]

The third major item of public expenditure was debt service on the internal debt.[105] From an early stage in its independent history, the Haitian government had borrowed from those in the private sector with capital (usually merchants). Some of these were Haitians, others were foreigners, but in all cases the loans were treated as internal. Haitian governments were not as punctilious in meeting the service charges on the internal debt as they were with the external debt, and the terms therefore tended to become over time financially more onerous and politically more disadvantageous for the government.[106] Foreign lenders were always ready to involve their consuls and exploit their leverage over Haitian governments to improve their economic position. This is one reason why there was such a large foreign presence among merchant houses by the time of the US invasion.[107]

The cost of internal debt servicing was at first manageable. However, following the 1867–9 Haitian Civil War, it became a major burden. The stock of internal debt, when converted to US dollars, had become as big as the stock of

---

[103] See Brière (2006), p. 132.

[104] These four loans – 1874, 1875, 1896 and 1910 – have been analysed at great length by others. See, e.g., Firmin (1905), pp. 438–50, Vincent (1939), pp. 12–16 and Blancpain (2001), chaps. 4 and 5.

[105] Technically the internal debt included the issues of paper money, but because no interest was paid we can ignore it.

[106] Rates of interest could be as high as 1% per month on these loans, and repayment was often required in hard currency. Lenders also became involved in the financing of coups d'état and normally received commercial advantage if they were successful. See Plummer (1988), chap. 2.

[107] See Plummer (1988), p. 56. Another reason was their ability to raise funds more cheaply outside Haiti than the Haitian-owned businesses.

external debt by 1890.[108] In 1900, therefore, an effort was made to consolidate the domestic interest-bearing debt on more favourable terms. This Consolidation Loan, as it became known, was carried out with the participation of the Banque Nationale d'Haiti (see below in this section), but it was done in such a fraudulent manner that the Haitian government was left worse off.[109] Because coffee prices remained low and the country's external credit was exhausted, the Haitian government resorted to internal debt on more and more onerous terms.[110]

Haitian law restricted ownership of land and retail sales to Haitian citizens. These restrictions, however, were progressively lifted.[111] Yet, the ban still allowed plenty of scope for foreigners in wholesale activities, import-export houses and timber concessions. In addition, a large number of traders had emigrated to Haiti from the Ottoman Empire by the end of the nineteenth century and had successfully, if illegally, circumvented the ban on retailing.[112] Finally, the Banque Nationale d'Haiti had even been allowed to participate in the land mortgage market, and several foreign-owned public utilities and infrastructure companies were established under President Hyppolite (1889–96).

Foreign business interests, present even in the earliest days of independence, became more pervasive, and Haitian governments started to face a trickle of financial claims from foreign residents, and even some nonresidents, arising from alleged damage to property, cancellation of contracts or false arrest. Gradually this trickle became a stream. These claims were pursued with great vigour by the relevant consuls and their governments with little concern for natural justice.[113] In the face of threats of gunboat diplomacy, Haiti often had

---

[108]   This did, however, include the issues of paper money. See International Bureau of the American Republics (1893), p. 111.

[109]   President Nord-Alexis (1902–8) was left to clean up the mess. Despite being an octogenarian, he prosecuted the case with such vigour that several of those culpable – including foreigners – were eventually punished. See Blancpain (2001), pp. 115–39. However, Haiti's ability to service its internal debt remained very fragile.

[110]   In 1914, the year before the US invasion, an internal loan was raised with a commission of 52%, i.e. the government only received 48% of what it was contracted to pay. See Blancpain (2001).

[111]   The prohibitions on foreigners had been relaxed by two laws in 1860, which allowed those married to Haitians to acquire real estate and also permitted foreigners to gain timber and mineral concessions. Then in 1883 a law was passed giving Haitian nationality to companies formed in Haiti but owned by foreigners provided that they were engaged in exporting agricultural products. See Joachim (1979), pp. 176–7. Finally, naturalisation was made easier under President Hyppolite (1889–96).

[112]   These immigrants, estimated by Turnier (1955) at 10,000–15,000 in 1905, were called Syrians, but they were by no means all from modern-day Syria. Some acquired British, French, German and even US citizenship despite arriving on passports issued by the Ottoman Empire, and others became naturalised Haitians. They were subject to a campaign of xenophobia, culminating in the law of 1904 that restricted their entry and made naturalisation more difficult. See Turnier (1955), chap. 6.

[113]   Some of these claims were so outrageous that one can only wonder at the brazenness of foreign governments in pursuing them. The most notorious case involved a slave trader, Antonio

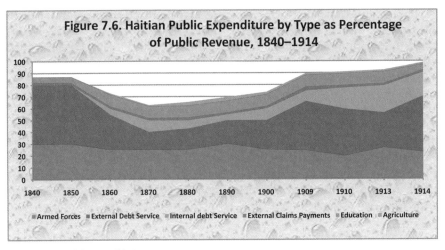

Figure 7.6. Haitian Public Expenditure by Type as Percentage of Public Revenue, 1840–1914

Source: Derived from Table B.10.

no choice but to pay. It has been estimated that in the period up to 1880, Haiti paid $16 million to settle these claims and a further $2.5 million up to 1902.[114] The monetary value of these claims, despite their often frivolous nature, accelerated till the US invasion and constituted another drain on the public finances.[115]

Expenditure on the military, debt service and external claims left little room for anything else (see Figure 7.6). Indeed, the fact that as much as 10 per cent of the budget went to public education from 1860 to 1913 must be regarded as a major achievement. However, it was not enough to make any real inroads into Haitian illiteracy, which remained above 90 per cent of the adult population.[116] The proportion spent on agriculture was even lower, never exceeding 3 per cent, and most of that was absorbed by the salaries of officials. Still, at least agriculture figured in the budget. There was almost nothing for public works, and thus Haiti was entirely dependent on private capital for the development of financial institutions, public utilities and infrastructure projects. In practice, private capital meant foreign capital because the funding and expertise for these projects was not available locally.

Pelletier, who had become a naturalised US citizen and who was sentenced in 1861 for trying to capture slaves in Haiti for sale in Cuba. The US State Department only dropped the case in 1886. See Léger (1907), pp. 232–5.

[114] See Joachim (1979), p. 187.

[115] The outstanding claims were examined by a Claims Commission set up by the US after 1915. After careful examination of each claim, with a total value of $21 million, they recommended settlement of $2.8 million – a reduction of nearly 90%. See Balch (1927), pp. 46–8.

[116] The figures on pupils at school are given in Table A.9. Haitian education – public and private – is discussed in detail in Logan (1930), Rotberg (1971) and Lundahl (1979).

Haitian governments, aware of these constraints, had given priority to the establishment of a national bank since Geffrard's presidency. However, it was not until 1881 that the project was achieved.[117] This French-owned bank, the Banque Nationale d'Haiti (BNdH), combined some of the functions of a state treasury with those of a central and commercial bank. However, it did not lend long-term for productive purposes, so its contribution to economic development was minimal. It was restructured in 1910 as the Banque Nationale de la République d'Haiti (BNRdH), with an infusion of US and German capital giving it some additional powers. In particular, it received the customs duties as they were paid and was only required to remit them to the Haitian government at the end of the fiscal year (September 30). Under an informal arrangement, money needed by the Haitian government was then advanced on a short-term basis until the customs duties were received.

Aware that the Haitian government ran the risk of default on a debt, most of which was owed to foreigners inside or outside the country, the United States resolved to gain control of Haitian finances as it had done in Cuba, the Dominican Republic, Nicaragua, Panama and Puerto Rico in order to eliminate any risk of European intervention. In collusion – it would seem – with the BNRdH, a plan was hatched under which the bank announced it was withdrawing from its agreement with the government on 1 October 1914, the first day of the new fiscal year. This time the bank refused to honour the informal arrangements for advancing short-term money, but it was not required to hand over the customs duties until the end of the fiscal year. The Haitian state was insolvent, and the United States drew up plans for the invasion.[118] The murder of 168 political prisoners during the uprising against President Guillaume-Sam was the final trigger.[119]

7.4. WHEN AND WHY DID HAITI FALL BEHIND?

We have already seen in Figure 7.1 that Haiti's position relative to the rest of the Caribbean did not deteriorate seriously until after 1890. Indeed, if we

---

[117] An offer in 1874 to establish a bank by a US citizen, A. H. Lazare, had been accepted, but he failed to provide the funds. Needless to say, this did not stop him or the US government from pursuing a claim against the Haitian state for breach of contract. See Léger (1907), pp. 231–2.

[118] To ensure that the Haitian government remained insolvent, the US marines arrived in December 1914 and removed $500,000 from the vaults of the BNRdH to New York on the specious grounds that these funds were pledged to the withdrawal of paper money and might be used by the government for other purposes. See Balch (1927), pp. 17–18.

[119] This gruesome episode in Haitian political history, in which President Guillaume-Sam was dragged out of the French legation and torn limb from limb, and the US occupation itself, have been the subject of numerous books and articles. See, e.g., Schmidt (1971).

exclude Cuba (the star performer in the Caribbean up to that point and the largest economy), the Haitian relative position looks even better. The volume of exports, as we shall see, expanded at a sufficient rate nearly to keep pace with population growth, and thus exports per head at constant prices were roughly the same in the 1880s as they were in the 1820s. This was disappointing in comparison with Cuba, but much better than what had happened in Jamaica and many other parts of the Caribbean.

This may seem surprising to those who assumed – in the absence of any data – that debt dependence, political instability, restrictions on foreigners and a shortage of capital in the nineteenth century had led to an absolute decline in the economy. All these factors were present, but they did not undermine a Haitian model based on small-scale agriculture and the export of coffee. Debt dependence was a terrible burden, but the Haitian state had adapted. Political instability was mainly an intra-elites struggle and only caused major economic disruptions during brief periods (especially 1843–7, 1867–9 and 1882–4). The restrictions on foreigners were in large part lifted by 1890, and Haiti was not alone in facing a scarcity of capital.

Yet Haiti did fall behind and by 1910 was lagging all the Americas – not just the Caribbean. In Table 7.1, we can measure Haiti's performance against other groups (including the Dominican Republic) not only in terms of the standard economic indicators such as exports per head, but also in terms of infrastructure. Haiti by this time – only two decades after 1890, when its performance was still satisfactory – had the lowest foreign trade per head, the lowest budget figures, the smallest infrastructure per head and one of the highest rates of per capita indebtedness.[120] The only indicator where Haiti scored highest was the man-land ratio, but we cannot yet speak of an absolute shortage of land.[121]

The comparison with the Dominican Republic was particularly galling for the Haitians. As late as 1880, Haiti had outperformed its neighbour on all counts.[122] Furthermore, the Dominican government had defaulted on its first foreign loan in 1874, but Haiti had punctually serviced her external debts. Yet, thirty years later, it was the other way round. The Dominicans had benefitted hugely from the influx of Cubans during and after the First War of Independence, the sugar and cacao industries had expanded rapidly, infrastructure had

[120] It was exceeded only by South America, where Argentina's debt per capita was enormous. However, Argentina at least had an impressive railway network to show for it. Haiti had nothing.
[121] The Haitian population in 1910 (nearly 1,700,000) was less than one-fifth of what it is today. The US occupation authorities estimated that as late as the 1920s the Haitian government owned half the total area of the country and that much of this was unused. See Millspaugh (1929), p. 561.
[122] Exports per head, for example, in 1880 were $11.8 in Haiti compared with $6.2 in the Dominican Republic (derived from Tables A.1a and A.11).

TABLE 7.1. *Comparative Indicators of Haitian Performance, c.1910*

Country or Region	Imports per Head US Dollars	Exports per Head US Dollars	Revenue per Head US Dollars	Debt per Head US Dollars	Railroad Miles per 10,000 People	Telegraph Miles per 10,000 People	Post Offices per 10,000 People	Population per Square Mile
Haiti	4.3	4.8	2.3	28.9	0.4	0.7	0.5	152.8
Dominican Republic	8.7	14.8	6.5	20.0	2.2	15.3	1.2	35.9
Caribbean	25.4	29.1	8.1	25.4	8.0	20.5	2.0	25.9
South America	14.3	17.1	7.8	32.7	8.6	40.1	2.1	8.2
Central America	6.0	6.0	3.6	10.4	2.6	19.2	1.9	28.4

Source: The population, foreign trade and budget figures for Haiti, the Dominican Republic and the Caribbean are derived from Tables C.1, C.6, C.18 and C.28 for 1910 (3-year averages). The other figures are from the *Statistical Abstract of the United States* (1911) and refer to c.1910. In *Statistical Abstract of the United States*, the Caribbean (excluding Haiti) is the sum of Cuba, Dutch colonies and the Dominican Republic. South America is ten republics, and Central America is six republics (including Panama).

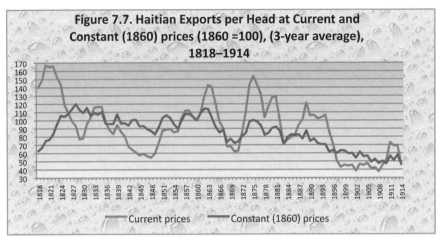

Figure 7.7. Haitian Exports per Head at Current and Constant (1860) prices (1860 =100), (3-year average), 1818–1914

Source: Derived from Tables B.1 and B.3.

improved and the US Customs Receivership, imposed in 1905, had coincided with a big increase in public revenue.[123]

We can therefore state with some accuracy that it was between 1890 and 1910 that Haiti fell behind, and this is also borne out by Figure 7.1. Turning our attention therefore to why this happened, we need to start with exports per head in terms of both volumes and values. Taking 1860 as the base year, we can show both indicators in one graph for the century before the US invasion, and this is done in Figure 7.7. As already mentioned, the volume of exports per head, as measured by the three-year moving average, exhibits a modest downward trend (after the initial rise in the 1820s) until 1890, after which there is a precipitate decline. The value of exports per head is – not surprisingly in view of the fluctuations in coffee prices – much less stable before 1890, but it also begins to decline sharply after 1890, falling by two-thirds by the time of the US occupation.

The decline in the volume of exports per head began with the fall in logwood (see section 2 above). This was partly because of the heavy burden of export duties, but the main reason almost certainly was logging at an unsustainable rate over a prolonged period. Because coffee exports were so much more important than logwood, the volume of exports **per head** did not at first suffer unduly. However, the volume of coffee exports started to fall after 1890 as a result of high export duties and falling world prices. The absolute decline in coffee exports was not enormous, but population growth meant that the volume of exports per head fell much more sharply. The fall in coffee prices

---

[123] In the Dominican Republic – as in Haiti – nearly 100% of public revenue came from customs duties. Foreign trade had been increasing rapidly since the 1880s, and the US Customs Receivership also reduced the opportunities for graft and corruption.

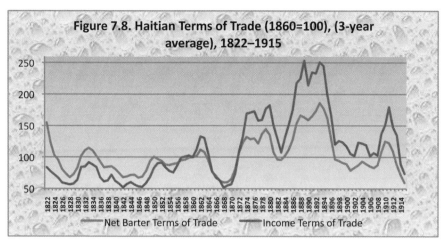

Source: Table B.8.

from the 1890s onwards was only reversed just before the First World War. At the same time, import prices were rising, so the net barter terms of trade went sharply into decline. Because the volume of exports was also falling, the income terms of trade fell faster (see Figure 7.8). This should have been the signal for a reallocation of resources from coffee to other export products whose prices were not falling. However, we have also seen that import tariffs were very high in this period of Haitian economic history, so it was also a signal for a reallocation of resources away from exports towards import-substituting agriculture and industry.

That some reallocations of resources took place cannot be denied. The export of cacao, whose price in world products was exceptionally high in these years, increased. The import of some provisions from the United States (notably fish and pork fat) fell,[124] and so – for a time – did soap imports following the opening of a factory in Port-au-Prince. However, these were little more than drops in the ocean. The Haitian economy, it would seem, was not able to respond to these price signals from the market with the flexibility required. The reasons for this are complex, but the main responsibility was surely the lack of infrastructure. Haiti lacked roads, and there were only sixty-four miles of railway lines in the country in 1910.[125]

This brings us back to the problem of public revenue, the scourge of Haitian governments from the time of independence. The fall in the volume of exports

[124] See Turnier (1955), p. 341.

[125] This was no doubt one reason why the government of President Simon agreed in 1910 to the (in)famous McDonald railway concession, in which vast swathes of land for agriculture were made available on either side of the track from Port-au-Prince to Cap Haitien, the state guaranteed a minimum return on capital and export duties were waived. See Plummer (1988), p. 159.

reduced income from export taxes, the fall in the value of exports reduced imports, and this in return led to a decline in income from import tariffs. Customs duties were effectively the only source of income for the Haitian state, so public revenue and public revenue per head went into decline after 1890 (see Figure 7.5), and at the same time debt-service costs rose. The short-term solution was debt default; the long-term one was diversification of the tax base. Haiti did neither, which begs the question why.

Haiti had a very good case for debt default – much better than the other Latin American republics (including the Dominican Republic), who had all defaulted at one time or another on their external debt obligations. Indeed, it is something of a mystery why Haiti did not do so. There may have been the – not unreasonable – fear of foreign intervention. There was also a great sense of pride among the elite (one suspects much less among the masses) that Haiti had met its external obligations. The main reason, however, was probably the fear of commercial retaliation, because the debt was owed to French creditors and most of the exports went to France. Yet Haiti would have been much better off defaulting and using the resources saved to spend on public works. Interestingly, one of the first acts of the US authorities after the occupation in 1915 was to suspend debt-service payments![126]

Haiti had begun its independent life with a diversified tax base, but this had withered away by the end of the 1840s as a result of the depreciation of the gourde (see section 3 above). A shift from customs duties in the 1890s would have meant the reintroduction of a land tax, because 90 per cent of the population lived in rural areas and agriculture was the main economic activity. Yet by 1890, the Haitian state lacked the capacity to impose such a tax, and its political class was too dependent on the *piquets* in the south and the *cacos* in the north.[127] In the end, the Haitian state opted for loans from the merchant class, but these came with so many conditions that the government was worse off. The cost of the loans was astronomical, and the state became even weaker. When the United States invaded in 1915, only one soldier was prepared to exchange fire in defence of the homeland.

Many explanations have been advanced for the collapse of the Haitian model, but no author has had access to a database as detailed as the one I have constructed for Haiti. This does not answer all the questions, but it does make it easier to answer some of them. It is therefore of interest to review some of the earlier hypotheses[128] in the light of the findings here. Many Haitian writers, and some foreigners, have emphasised colour, but the rivalries between

---

[126] They were resumed in 1919. See Balch (1927), p. 38.

[127] The process by which the peasantry had been formed into these militias is central to Haitian political history. See, e.g., Nicholls (1979), pp. 77–8.

[128] I omit the sensationalist explanations that have been put forward in English since time immemorial. The first foreign visitors, notably the Quaker missionary John Candler, had some useful insights, but by the time of Spenser St. John this approach had been abandoned in favour of outrageous distortions that played well with a credulous foreign audience (unfortunately, St. John (1889) still has to be used because he is the only source for some quantitative data).

blacks and mulattoes cannot logically explain the tolerable performance until 1890 and the decline thereafter. It is true that Haitians were very sensitive to colour before the US occupation. However, in this period the United States was even more obsessed with race, the British with class and the Indians with caste. It is not at all obvious that Haiti was held back by colour any more than the United States was by race or the British by class or India by caste – India did not prosper, but this was much more because of imperialism than the caste system.[129]

There was also a serious debate in Haiti in the last part of the nineteenth century about the restrictions on foreigners. However, these restrictions had become much less of an issue following the changes introduced first by President Geffrard and then by President Salomon. By the 1890s, there was nothing to stop nonresident foreigners from forming companies and acquiring concessions. It is true it was still difficult for foreigners to acquire land for agricultural purposes (that is partly why the McDonald concession in 1910 – see note 125 – was so unpopular), but these restrictions usually did not apply to those foreigners who were resident in Haiti. This group dominated import-export and wholesale trade, held numerous concessions in timber and minerals extraction and controlled the financial system. And by 1900 the ban on foreigners in retail trade had been circumvented by the 'Syrians'.

Finally, there was in Haiti – as in other parts of Latin America – a serious debate throughout the century about the merits of self-sufficiency in agriculture and industrialisation versus dependence on exports. Edmund Paul was a particularly powerful advocate of autonomy and strongly defended the restrictions on foreigners.[130] However, the dependence of the Haitian budget on customs duties meant that politically this was never a real option even though it might have made economic sense. Haiti, after 1890, was exporting coffee at falling prices in order to import many agricultural and some industrial goods that it could perfectly well have produced itself. And escaping from dependence on foreign trade became even more difficult when so much of the customs duties were earmarked to pay debt service and other claims to foreigners.

With the benefit of hindsight, Haiti made many mistakes before the US occupation. It should not have offered tax concessions to the British in 1814. It should not have submitted to the French terms for recognition in 1825. It should not have accepted the terms offered to reschedule the double debt in 1838. It should not have taken out the loans in 1874, 1875, 1896 and 1910 on the terms that it did. It should not have given additional budgetary

One has to read the contemporary literature in French and German or consular reports to gain a more accurate account of Haiti in these years.

[129] It is also said that Haiti suffered from extreme political instability. However, if we ignore 1843–7 when there were four presidents and treat Christophe and Pétion as one, there were fifteen presidents between 1804 and 1911 – an average of nearly seven years each. The four years before the US invasion were, of course, quite different – Haiti had no less than five presidents.

[130] There is a good summary of this debate in Nicholls (1974).

powers to the Banque Nationale de la République d'Haiti in 1910. However, all independent countries make mistakes, and none of these errors of judgement was in itself suicidal. Haiti was undone by a combination of imperialist intrigue by the United States, abusive behaviour by other members of the core and an economic model that was too dependent on coffee and customs duties.

PART II

THE CARIBBEAN IN THE AGE OF PREFERENCES

From 1900 to 1960

8

The Core and the Caribbean

This chapter explores the relationship between the core and the Caribbean from 1900 to 1960. This is roughly the period from the end of the Spanish-American War to the arrival of Fidel Castro on the international stage. Both the beginning and end of this period are therefore intimately associated with Cuba, but the island is also crucial to understanding so much that happened in the economic evolution of the Caribbean in the intervening years. Under US rather than Spanish tutelage, a nominally independent Cuba would remain a huge component of the Caribbean economy; thus what happened in the region as a whole was often determined by what happened in Cuba.

The period from 1900 to 1960 began and ended with a decade of world growth in output, employment and international trade. By contrast, the intervening four decades were marked by extreme volatility that included two world wars, a quasi-world conflict (the Korean War), a major slump (the Great Depression), several minor slumps (1920–1, 1937–8, 1948–9), a spectacular commodity price rise (1919–20), the collapse of the gold standard in the 1930s and the embedding of inflation from 1940 onwards into the global system. The impact of all this on the Caribbean is explored in section 1.

The rest of the chapter explores the relationship between the Caribbean and the different parts of the core. This starts with the United States (section 2), which had acquired its first Caribbean colony by 1900 (Puerto Rico), would soon acquire three quasi-colonies in the Greater Antilles through either treaty or occupation or both (Cuba, Dominican Republic and Haiti) and in 1916 purchased the Danish Virgin Islands to obtain a second colony. These five territories may have been only a minority of the Caribbean countries, but they provided the United States with an exceptional stake in the region.

The most important European power remained the UK throughout the period, and its relationship with the Caribbean is explored in section 3. The

UK may have yielded to the United States in Central America,[1] but it fought tenaciously to preserve a privileged position in its Caribbean colonies. Through a return to imperial preference after the First World War and judicious use of tied aid after the Second World War, the UK was in fact able to strengthen its position in the British Caribbean at the expense of other members of the core, but it eventually had to accept the desire for independence among the colonial people themselves.

The final section is devoted to the relationship between the remainder of the core and the Caribbean, which now excluded the Scandinavian countries but included Canada. The most dramatic change was in the case of France, whose colonial ties were temporarily severed in the Second World War to be replaced in 1946 by full incorporation into the metropolis through *départementalisation*. Not even the former colonists themselves could have anticipated the extraordinary changes this would eventually bring. And for Holland – another member of the core – the Second World War set in motion a chain of events in its Caribbean colonies that would also have far-reaching consequences.

8.1. THE WORLD ECONOMY

By 1900 Sweden had dropped out of the core, and Denmark would do so in the First World War, thereby ending a 250-year Scandinavian colonial presence in the Caribbean.[2] Spain also no longer had Caribbean colonies, but it retained strong ties, and thousands of Spaniards – including Fidel Castro's father – migrated to Cuba once the US occupation ended.[3] The one new member of the core was Canada, which had adopted a system of preferential tariffs in favour of the British Caribbean in 1897. This led to the redirection of the trade of many British colonies towards Canada and made it the core's newest member, despite the small initial size of its economy.[4]

The seven core countries (Canada, France, Germany, Holland, Spain, UK and the United States) may have been responsible for less than 60 per cent of world trade before the First World War,[5] but they received a much higher share of Caribbean exports. Even when we limit it to the exports going to the United States, the UK and the 'mother' country, the core imported around 80 per cent of Caribbean exports in the first five decades.[6] If we add to this the

[1] The Hay-Pauncefote Treaty (1901) was the moment the UK recognised the inevitable and accepted that any future isthmian canal would be controlled by the US. See Williams (1916).
[2] It had begun in 1671 with the formation of the Danish West India Company. See Westergaard (1917), chap. 1.
[3] Spain therefore is still treated as part of the core and as the 'mother' for Cuba and the Dominican Republic in this period. The 'mother' for Puerto Rico, however, changed to the US.
[4] The Canadian economy grew fast in this period, and its imports exceeded those of some other members of the core by the 1950s.
[5] In 1913 their share of world exports was 55%. See Maddison (2003), pp. 359–60.
[6] Derived from Tables C.15–C.17, but deducting the US and UK from Table C.17 to avoid double counting.

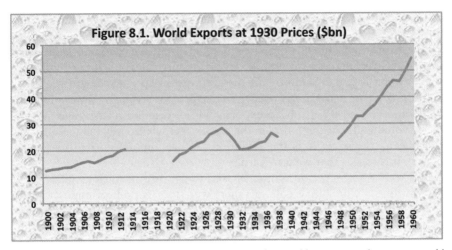

Figure 8.1. World Exports at 1930 Prices ($bn)

Source: Derived from United Nations (2009), assuming that world exports are the same as world imports and converting from 1953 to 1930 prices.

exports of all Caribbean countries to Canada and Germany along with the exports of each country to core members other than Canada, Germany, the UK, the United States and 'mother',[7] the figure is likely to have been closer to 90 per cent.

The umbilical link between the core and the Caribbean continued to be provided by commodity trade and the associated inward investments throughout this period. This would change after 1950 as a result of service exports, but until the end of the Second World War – and in most cases even later – the volume and value of commodity exports determined imports, public revenue and expenditure and ultimately employment and wages. Twenty commodities (see Chapter 9) accounted for over 90 per cent of Caribbean domestic exports. What mattered, therefore, is how these responded to changes in world imports.

The turbulent nature of the period is captured in Figure 8.1, which shows global exports at constant prices. This series, a proxy for the volume of world imports,[8] began well enough with almost uninterrupted growth until the eve of the First World War. Rather like a game of snakes and ladders, the series started again in 1921 at a much lower level. A period of spectacular growth then occurred that reached a peak in 1929, to be followed by another collapse until the bottom of the cycle in 1932. From then until the Second World War, trade expanded, but the brief recession of 1937–8 took its toll. When the series started again in 1948, it was at roughly the same level, but the 'missing years' are generally assumed to have been marked by a steep decline until the middle

---

[7] For example, Cuban exports to France.

[8] In theory, world exports and imports should equal each other. In practice, there is always a difference, but it tends to be small in proportionate terms.

of the war and a recovery thereafter.[9] What followed was then the beginning of the 'golden age' of postwar growth.

The series in Figure 8.1 provides a rough framework for all subsequent analysis. Given that the volume of world imports in 1948 was roughly the same as in 1913, it would be unrealistic to expect spectacular growth in the volume of Caribbean exports over the same period. Similarly, it would be disappointing indeed if Caribbean exports did not respond to the huge increase in the volume of world imports in the 1950s. Yet what really mattered for the Caribbean, as always, was the evolution of core imports during this crucial period. It is to this that we now turn.

In Table 8.1 the period is first broken down into its various phases. For the world as a whole (first column) there were four periods of import growth (1900–13, 1921–9, 1932–8, 1948–60) and three of decline (1913–21, 1929–32, 1938–48). For the period as a whole (1900–60), there was an increase in the volume of world imports of 341 per cent – respectable under the circumstances. When we examine the volume of core imports over this same long period, there were two countries that exceeded the world average (Canada and the United States), one that equalled it (Germany) and four that underperformed (France, Holland, Spain and the UK). The European colonies in the Caribbean therefore had the misfortune of being tied to metropoles whose imports underperformed the world average.

When we now superimpose the volume of Caribbean domestic exports[10] on the same period, we may observe an interesting pattern. In the run-up to the First World War, Caribbean exports exceeded the world average with a performance that paralleled US imports (all at constant prices). From that point onwards, Caribbean exports outperformed the world in the downward phase of the cycle and underperformed in the upward phase. In one case (1938–48), the volume of Caribbean exports actually increased while world imports fell. In financial market terminology, the Caribbean became after 1913 a defensive stock, performing well in a bear market and badly in a bull one. Fortunately for the Caribbean, the process was not symmetric, and the Caribbean actually managed a modest increase in its share of world imports from 1900 to 1960.[11]

If this post-1913 pattern had been observed for Latin America, it would probably have been attributed to Engel's law: exports of commodities for which the income elasticity of demand in the core is less than one leads to a less than proportionate increase in demand in the upswing and a smaller decline in the downswing. Yet in the case of the Caribbean, a marginal region in terms of world trade, this is only relevant in the final phase (1948–60). Indeed, in the first phase (1900–13) the volume of Caribbean exports grew faster than world

---

[9] For those members of the core for which we have accurate data, the low point for imports was 1942. For the US, see Carter (2006), vol. 5, p. 501.

[10] Proxied by domestic exports at constant (1930) prices. See Table C.9.

[11] Measured at constant prices, this rose from 1.1% in 1900 to 1.9% in 1960.

TABLE 8.1. *Trade Growth (%) at 1930 Prices: Core Imports and Caribbean Exports, 1900–1960*

Years	World	US	Germany	France	UK	Holland	Canada	Spain	Caribbean
1900/13	64.8	81.3	62.2	54.9	21.1	70.5	207.1	46.1	89.3
1913/21	−21.8	11.0	−61.5	−17.2	−37.3	−73.8	−20.3	−21.7	−1.5
1921/29	77.6	74.6	138.7	62.6	101.0	57.0	121.2	80.7	62.3
1929/32	−28.7	−39.9	−30.2	−12.5	−9.7	−18.2	−53.9	−30.4	−12.1
1932/38	23.7	16.8	13.9	−10.1	20.0	6.7	48.5	−62.7	4.7
1938/48	−3.5	48.2	−14.4	7.0	−21.0	−16.5	78.2	0	47.7
1948/60	126.6	77.3	331.3	101.9	67.7	193.5	78.8	241.1	80.0
1900/60	341.1	548.4	338.2	254.3	119.2	50.3	1080.8	82.6	640.7

Note: World imports based on world exports and converted from 1953 to 1930 base. Import deflators for Canada, France, Germany and Holland based on US before 1913. German imports in 1948 are estimated. For Spain, end year is 1958.

Source: United Nations (2009) for World, Germany, France, UK, Canada and Holland. Carter (2006), vol. 3, for US; and Prados de la Escosura (2003) for Spain.

imports, but the main commodity exports (e.g. sugar) were already subject to income elasticities of less than unity in most cases.

In fact, special factors were in operation in each phase. Consider the first downswing (1913–21), which encompasses not only the First World War, but also the commodity boom (1919–20) and slump (1920–21) that followed. The Caribbean registered only a small drop (1.5%) in the volume of its exports thanks to strong demand for its export commodities from the United States during the war, when alternative sources of supply were disrupted, and from Europe afterwards. Thus, despite the decline in demand for its leading commodities during the war from much of Europe[12] (especially Germany), the Caribbean was able to ride out this particular storm quite successfully. The same was true, only even more so, in the 1938–48 downswing.

The first phase (1900–13) had taken place under the gold standard. When this was suspended during the First World War, it was assumed by all the belligerents that the system would be restored at the end of hostilities. However, the war was much longer than anticipated, and it was accompanied, and (briefly) followed by, a period of inflation. This made the restoration of the gold standard highly problematic because some countries could only return to the prewar priorities by deflating – an uncomfortable process at the best of times. France's dismal performance in the 1920s is widely attributed to this problem, and France did not even return to gold at the prewar parity because the currency collapse had been so severe during and after hostilities.[13] Only those Caribbean countries that shared a currency with France (French Guiana, Guadeloupe and Martinique) were unaffected by this exchange rate turmoil, but they still suffered from slow French import growth.

The human and physical cost of the First World War in Europe was terrible, despite the fact that some countries, including the core countries Holland and Spain, remained neutral.[14] The United States, neutral until the last eighteen months, was less affected and emerged as a net creditor with a stronger stake in the world system than before. Yet the United States was not yet ready to assume a responsible global leadership role and also failed to understand that its domestic actions were now likely to have greater international impact than before. Reconstruction was complicated by the desire of the victors to punish the losers, particularly Germany and Austria, and the unwillingness of the United States – the only country in a position to do so – to provide aid and credit on generous terms. The United States insisted on full payment of wartime

---

[12] Banana exports were particularly vulnerable, because they were regarded as nonessential and shipping space was therefore diverted to other uses. In the Second World War, for example, the UK suspended banana shipments at the start of hostilities and only restarted commercial imports in December 1945.

[13] France had stabilised her currency by the end of 1926, but it did not formally return to the gold standard until 1928 (at a rate of 25.5 per US dollar compared with 5.18 before the First World War).

[14] On war damage, see Aldcroft (1993), pp. 6–10.

debts even from its allies, who in turn demanded reparations from Germany in order to pay the United States.[15]

In this poisonous atmosphere the interests of the Caribbean were completely ignored.[16] The colonists who had volunteered for military service were treated badly on their return.[17] Yet the imperial powers were far from ready to relax their grip on their Caribbean colonies. When the gold standard finally collapsed in the Great Depression,[18] competitive devaluations among the core, increased tariffs and other trade barriers led to a vicious cycle in which international trade collapsed. The core responded with increased domestic protection and imperial preference – Britain now formally adopting and widening a system that it had introduced in 1919. How this was done will be examined in the next three sections, but it was universal and put those Caribbean countries outside any preferential system, such as the Dominican Republic, at a disadvantage.

The leading export from the Caribbean throughout this period was sugar (see Chapter 9), which had long suffered from subsidised beet sugar, trade discrimination and segmented markets. The 1902 Brussels Convention was supposed to deal with the problems, but it was never very effective.[19] In addition, in 1903 the United States had agreed to a reciprocal trade treaty with Cuba, which inter alia granted the island's sugar a 20 per cent reduction on the full US import tariff (see next section). Modest though this sounded, the combination of low-cost Cuban sugar, US direct investments and geographical proximity had driven almost all full-tariff sugar out of the US market within one decade. The rest of the Caribbean, except the US colonies, simply had to look elsewhere.

Fortunately for them, disruption to the beet sugar industry in Europe during the First World War meant that they did not need to look very hard. However, the revival of beet sugar after hostilities ended, and the increase in cane sugar capacity around the world soon created a problem of excess supply. Cuba responded unilaterally in the 1920s with export cuts, but it was not enough.[20] In 1931, several countries, including Cuba, signed the Chadbourne Agreement to distribute lower quotas, but the arrangement was overwhelmed by the fall

---

[15] See Aldcroft (1993), pp. 19–22.
[16] At the lengthy negotiations at the end of the war leading to the Treaty of Versailles (1919), Cuba was the only Caribbean country present; the region was hardly discussed at all because the US occupations of Haiti and the Dominican Republic were a source of great embarrassment to President Wilson. See MacMillan (2001), pp. 17–18.
[17] In one case (Belize) this led to a serious riot. See Shoman (2011), pp. 134–5.
[18] What had actually been reestablished after the First World War was a gold exchange standard rather than a gold standard. Most countries (US, UK and France were the main exceptions) were not required to convert all monetary assets into gold on demand and only had to preserve the gold parity of the exchange rate.
[19] The Brussels Convention did not include all countries and failed to discipline even those that had signed. See Prinsen (1909).
[20] See Heston (1987), pp. 79–82.

in world demand.[21] A second attempt would be made in 1937 when the International Sugar Agreement (ISA) was ratified, but this was suspended as soon as the Second World War started.[22]

Three years earlier, in 1934, the United States had introduced a system of import quotas that would turn out to be far more significant for the Caribbean than the ISA. In drawing up these quotas each year, the interests of US beet and cane sugar growers came first and foreign suppliers last.[23] This system within a generation increased the share of domestic sugar in US consumption from 42 to 65 per cent.[24] The United States had also found a commercial weapon by which country behaviour could be influenced in its favour (or so it thought until Cuba's quota was ended in July 1960 with spectacular, if unanticipated, consequences).

The Second World War was not at all a repeat of the previous conflict from the point of view of the Caribbean. First, the war came to the very shores of the Caribbean through German submarine activity, the opening of US bases, the stationing of Allied troops to guard oil facilities in the Dutch colonies (after the fall of Holland in May 1940) and the uncertainty over the loyalties of the French colonies after the fall of France in June of the same year.[25] Second, the war entrenched inflationary expectations that – as in the core itself – never subsequently disappeared. Third, the nationalist movements were able to exploit the vacuum created by the weakness of European imperial powers and build on the successes of the labour struggles in the 1930s.[26]

The final phase (1948–60) of this period began with the reconstruction of the European core, helped by the Marshall Plan, and the reductions in trade barriers for manufactured goods under the auspices of the General Agreement on Tariffs and Trade (GATT) launched in 1947.[27] Cuba was the only Caribbean country to take part in GATT[28] and was rewarded when Havana became the host city in November 1947 for the negotiations expected to lead to an International Trade Organisation (ITO) – the third pillar of the Bretton Woods system agreed in principle in 1944 alongside the International Bank for Reconstruction and Development (World Bank) and the International Monetary Fund (IMF).[29]

---

[21] See Swerling (1949), pp. 42–5.
[22] The ISA was suspended in 1939 and abandoned in 1942. It would not be restarted until 1953. See Cushion (2010).
[23] Nearly half the US states grew beet or cane sugar, giving sugar a large domestic constituency in Congress. See Heston (1987), p. 26.
[24] See Heston (1987), p. 508.
[25] See Füllberg-Stolberg (2004).
[26] See Bryan (2004), pp. 141–64.
[27] See Scammell (1980).
[28] Cuba's participation was driven by its anxiety to preserve its preferential access to the US market at a time when Most-Favoured Nation (MFN) status was becoming the norm in international trade. The only other countries eligible to attend were Haiti and the Dominican Republic.
[29] On the establishment of the Bretton Woods institutions, especially the IMF, see Horsefield (1969), vol. 1. The three independent countries duly joined the IMF and World Bank, but Haiti

Developing countries, not only in the Caribbean, had great hopes for the ITO. The Havana Charter, signed on 24 March 1948 by fifty-seven countries (including Cuba, Haiti and the Dominican Republic), included agriculture and manufacturing in its scope and promised to tear down barriers to trade in primary products.[30] Yet the ITO was stillborn because the US Senate refused to ratify the Havana Charter, and other countries, including the UK, then suspended the ratification process. European countries would now start among themselves the process of reducing trade barriers that led in 1958 to the formation of the European Economic Community (EEC) and the European Free Trade Area (EFTA).[31]

The reduction in trade barriers outside Europe was left to GATT. This 'temporary' institution did a superb job in lowering trade barriers among the core and in helping to lift living standards. Employment and incomes in the core soared, and new opportunities for consumption were made available. These included mass international tourism that – combined with the growth of air travel – meant that the Caribbean was now accessible to more than a handful of wealthy individuals in the crucial winter months. Service exports, although still much less important than commodity exports, would rise rapidly.

The postwar Caribbean was therefore very different from what had gone before. The march towards decolonisation in the British colonies was irreversible, and autonomy gained further momentum in the Dutch and US ones. The French colonies moved in the opposite direction, but *départementalisation* did not preclude some autonomy. The US customs receiverships had come to an end in Hispaniola, but the Dominican Republic remained in the grip of Trujillo, and Haiti would slide into dictatorship after 1957 when François Duvalier was elected. Only sugar-dependent Cuba appeared to be truly stuck in a time warp, ruled by a ruthless army officer with apparent US support, and even that would change before the period ended.

8.2. THE UNITED STATES AND THE CARIBBEAN

The brief Spanish-American War in 1898[32] catapulted the United States into an imperial role in the Caribbean that had long been anticipated by outside observers. The United States was still not a global power of the first order,[33] but the continental frontier no longer existed, US productive forces had outstripped the capacity of the domestic market to absorb them and a surplus of savings was

did not do so until 1953. The other Caribbean countries were not in theory eligible to join, but the Netherlands Antilles **did** attend the Bretton Woods Conference despite its dependent status.

[30] Article 16, 2c also specifically exempted the preferences in force between the US and Cuba from MFN treatment. See Department of State (1948).

[31] The UK did not join the six-member EEC and instead established EFTA as a rival organisation.

[32] War was declared in April and had ended by August. See Thomas (1971), pp. 381–404.

[33] New York was not yet a serious rival to London as a financial centre, and the value of US trade was still below that of its main European competitors.

available for investment elsewhere.[34] Furthermore, the public mood – hostile to foreign ventures in the first generation after the US Civil War – had now changed. US governments were now ready for a colonial role, even if some US citizens were still uncomfortable with the notion of imperialism, and there was no better place – indeed, almost no other place[35] – to start than the Caribbean.

The imperial experiment would begin with Cuba, an island on which US leaders had cast covetous eyes since Jefferson and John Quincy Adams almost a century before.[36] To the early interest based on geography and trade had been added the need for naval and coaling stations, as the prospect of an interoceanic canal through Nicaragua or Panama came closer.[37] Cuba was also the largest economy by far in the Caribbean, and its sugar and tobacco industries – not to mention its minerals – had already attracted interest from US investors.[38] In addition, Cuba needed to be under US tutelage in order to make sure that no European rival controlled it.[39]

Yet Cuba could not become a colony. The Teller Resolution in the US Senate just before the commencement of the Spanish-American War had committed the United States to an independent Cuba.[40] Even if this obstacle could be overcome, Cuban sugar was a direct competitor of beet and cane sugar producers on the mainland, who would be destroyed if Cuba was fully inside the US tariff wall. Much the same could be said of the US tobacco industry, whose development owed so much to high tariffs on imports from Cuba of manufactured products. Thus, the United States needed to find a third way for Cuba – neither independence nor colony – that would satisfy all these competing needs.

The answer was found in two pieces of legislation. The first was the Platt Amendment, adopted by the US Senate in 1901 and incorporated as

[34] On the transition from the US as a capital importing to exporting nation, see Wilkins (1970) and Wilkins (1974).

[35] The US had already started to play a colonial role in the Pacific, had intervened along with the European powers in China and would acquire its first Asian colony (the Philippines) at the end of the Spanish-American War. Yet the republic could expect serious resistance from Europe if it tried to expand its imperial stake in these regions, and the US navy was not strong enough to be assured of victory in the case of war.

[36] Adams in 1823 had written to the US minister in Spain saying: 'There are laws of political as well as of physical gravitation; and if an apple, severed by the tempest from its native tree, cannot choose but fall to the ground, Cuba, forcibly disjoined from its unnatural connection with Spain and incapable of self-support, can gravitate only toward the North American Union, which, by the same law of nature, cannot cast her off from its bosom.' See Jenks (1928), p. 7.

[37] It was not clear through which country the canal would be built until Panama seceded from Colombia in 1903 and became effectively a US protectorate.

[38] The most important of these investors was Edwin Atkins, who had developed a large business empire based on sugar even before the Spanish-American War. See Atkins (1926) for his memoirs.

[39] European countries used the same argument based on preemption to expand their empires in Africa, Asia and the Middle East.

[40] See Thomas (1971), p. 376.

an appendix word for word into the Cuban Constitution in the same year.[41] The Platt Amendment gave the United States all the rights of an imperial power with none of the obligations. The United States was free to intervene whenever it chose, to select bases for its navy, to ensure fiscal probity and to act as final arbiter on all issues of mutual interest.[42] It so influenced the bilateral relationship that even after its repeal in 1934, no subsequent Cuban government until 1959 felt secure without approval from the United States.[43]

The second piece of legislation was the reciprocal treaty signed in 1902 but not ratified until the end of 1903. This gave each country preferential access to the other's market. However, for Cuba the preference was effectively limited to 20 per cent on two products (sugar and tobacco) because other products of interest to Cuba were either excluded or were duty-free, while for the United States virtually all goods were covered, and some received much greater preferential treatment than 20 per cent.[44]

However unfair to Cuba this might seem, US lawmakers had done their homework. In the first two decades of the century the small preference on sugar would transform the sugar industry in Cuba at the expense of other export activities,[45] and the treaty helped to turn Cuba into a main field for US investment, not just in the Caribbean but in Latin America as a whole.[46] Just as important, it did not cripple the domestic US sugar industry because Cuba's expansion took place at the expense of full-duty sugar from elsewhere.[47]

Despite the absence of a rebel movement against Spain, Puerto Rico had been occupied by US troops in July 1898. The autonomy granted to the island by Spain in 1897 was therefore short-lived because the US military authorities – just as in Cuba – set out to reorganise the economic, social and political life of the country now baptised 'Porto Rico'.[48] Its small sugar industry, in decline since 1860,[49] posed no threat at first to mainland growers, and its principal product (coffee) was not in competition with US interests. No commitments had been made by US lawmakers in favour of independence, and, with the

---

[41] The eight articles of the Platt Amendment can be found in Jenks (1928), pp. 78–9. The Platt Amendment was also included in the Permanent Treaty agreed to between the two countries in 1903.

[42] Article I, for example, stated that 'the Government of Cuba shall never enter into any treaty . . . with any foreign power . . . which will impair . . . the independence of Cuba.'

[43] The government of President Grau in 1934 collapsed because the US did not recognise it – even after the repeal of the Platt Amendment.

[44] The asymmetry became even worse after a decade when Cuban sugar exports displaced full-duty imports from the US market. At that point the Cuban preference essentially disappeared because almost no sugar paid the full tariff.

[45] Sugar went from 32.2% of domestic exports in 1900 to over 80% by 1915. See Table C.5.

[46] By 1927 US investments in Cuba ($1.5 billion) were the same as in Mexico. The next country in importance was Argentina ($0.6 billion). See Winkler (1928), p. 278.

[47] By 1912 only 8% of US sugar imports paid full duty, and these entered only in the months after the end of the Cuban sugar harvest.

[48] Its name would not be changed back to Puerto Rico until 1934.

[49] Sugar exports peaked by value in 1860, but they did not peak by volume until 1880. See Table A.10.

passage of the Foweraker Act in 1900, the island became the first US colony in the Caribbean. However, its inhabitants would not become US citizens until the passage of the Jones Act in 1917.[50]

The Foweraker Act had established the institutions of the new colony, but not the economic policy of the United States towards the island (the army of occupation had temporarily granted Puerto Rico a reduction of 85 per cent on the full US tariff). This was only settled in 1901 when Puerto Rico was brought fully inside the US tariff wall. A well-intentioned law was also passed restricting landholdings to 500 acres.[51] However, when it became clear this might deter potential US investors, it was quietly ignored by the new colonial authorities. With no tariffs and quotas (until 1934), a wave of US investment then entered the island. Puerto Rico once again specialised in sugar, but it remained at the mercy of US domestic sugar policy. When sugar quotas were established for the island in 1934, the industry – already hit by two hurricanes – stagnated, and unemployment soared.

The sugar industry never regained its dynamism, and an alternative model was needed. The first attempt was the Chardón Plan designed to break up the big sugar estates and distribute the land to small farmers, but it failed.[52] The solution was eventually found in the manipulation of the federal tax system to favour manufactured exports on the island (see next chapter). With the passage of Public Law 600 in 1950, the way was paved for Puerto Rico to become an *estado libre asociado* in 1952.[53] In theory this ended its colonial status, but in practice it did not.[54] Puerto Rico also remained without a vote in the US Congress, where its fate would often be determined.

The US government had hoped to expand its Caribbean empire by purchasing the Virgin Islands from Denmark in 1902, but this offer was rejected by the Danish parliament.[55] Nothing then happened until the First World War, when the issue became urgent in case a belligerent Germany chose to overpower a neutral Denmark, acquiring Caribbean colonies in the process.[56] A much improved offer was accepted by Denmark in 1916, and the islands became a US colony the following year.[57] All inhabitants became US citizens, and the three islands – St Thomas, St John and St Croix – immediately gained unrestricted access to the US market.

---

[50] The Jones Act conferred citizenship, but Puerto Ricans still could not vote in US federal elections.

[51] See Heston (1987), pp. 54–5.

[52] See Dietz (1986), pp. 149–54

[53] See Carr (1984), pp. 76–80.

[54] Puerto Rico could have no foreign policy of its own and was therefore unable to participate in international organisations.

[55] Perhaps this was revenge for the rejection by the US Senate in 1867 of the Danish offer to sell the islands. See Tansill (1932), chap. 6.

[56] There was no reason to believe that Germany did plan to attack Denmark, but war makes countries particularly suspicious of each other's motives.

[57] The US paid $25 million compared with the $5 million offered in 1902. See Tansill (1932), p. 343.

The economic attractions of the Virgin Islands in 1917 were much less than those of Puerto Rico in 1898, but St Thomas did at least have one of the finest harbours in the Caribbean. Not surprisingly, therefore, the US Navy Department was responsible at first for colonial administration.[58] When the colony was handed over to the Department of the Interior in 1931, and the first civilian governor was appointed, the sugar-dependent economy was in terrible shape. By 1934, as part of the New Deal, the islands underwent a colonial experiment in which a state-owned enterprise (the Virgin Islands Company)[59] became the principal employer, producing sugar, molasses and rum and later branching out into banking, tourism and public utilities.

The final part of the jigsaw was provided by Hispaniola. As in the case of Puerto Rico and the Virgin Islands, it was not primarily economic opportunities that brought the Dominican Republic and Haiti inside the imperial umbrella. This time it was President Theodore Roosevelt's reinterpretation of the Monroe Doctrine for the twentieth century that provided the justification for US intervention.[60] Within a year of enunciating his famous Corollary in 1904, and two years after the beginning of the Panamanian adventure,[61] the Dominican Republic had become subject to a Customs Receivership, giving the United States complete control over the country's finances and public debt.[62] Haiti was to suffer the same fate following the US invasion in 1915.[63] Financial engineering then ensured that the external debt would be owed principally to US bankers – thus European powers would have no reason to meddle.[64] At this point the Caribbean appeared to have gone backwards politically because there were now no truly sovereign and independent countries.[65]

The Dominican Republic was occupied militarily from 1916 to 1924 and Haiti from 1915 to 1934.[66] Yet their status as US protectorates continued much longer because the customs receiverships could not be ended until all the external debt had been paid off. The United States therefore had financial

---

[58] What is surprising, given the importance of sugar, is that the Navy Chaplain in 1924 was put in charge of the newly established Department of Agriculture. See Dookhan (1972), p. 55.

[59] It later became known as the Virgin Islands Corporation. See Lewis (1972), p. 116.

[60] The Roosevelt Corollary stated that the US had an obligation to intervene in countries at risk in order to ensure that other powers had no reason to violate the Monroe Doctrine. See Munro (1964), p. 65.

[61] The recognition of Panama in 1903 by the US led rapidly to a treaty giving the US exclusive control over the Panama Canal, finally opened in 1914.

[62] The Customs Receivership began in April 1905, but without US congressional approval. This was only forthcoming in 1907. See Knight (1928), chap. 4. Although the US only controlled customs duties, these amounted to 99% of public revenue at the start of the receivership. The proportion subsequently fell, and the Dominicans had to resist an attempt by the US during the occupation to extend the receivership to all taxes.

[63] US powers were embodied in five treaty services that included health, public works and the police along with a financial adviser and the customs receivership. See Munro (1974), p. 73.

[64] The debts were refinanced by US banks, which then became the main creditors.

[65] In theory there were three independent countries – Cuba, the Dominican Republic and Haiti – but all were neocolonies for much of this period.

[66] On the Dominican occupation, see Calder (1984); on the Haitian, see Schmidt (1971).

control of the Dominican Republic from 1905 to 1941 and of Haiti from 1915 until 1947.[67] As a result, neither country defaulted on the external debt in the difficult years of the 1930s, and yet they were never brought inside the US tariff wall[68] – and both benefitted only marginally from the US sugar quotas issued from 1934 onwards. It is of course true that protectorate status brought inward investment (mainly from the United States) that might not otherwise have materialised.[69] However, these investments paled in significance against those US investments going not only to Cuba and the US colonies, but also to other parts of the Caribbean.

These other parts were all European colonies, and the United States, except in the Second World War, did not in general receive preferential treatment. However, US investors exporting to the UK from British colonies benefitted from imperial preference, and the 1938 Anglo-American Trade Agreement put restrictions on which commodities the UK could tax preferentially.[70] The areas of special interest to US investors included banana exports from Jamaica, asphalt and petroleum exports from Trinidad & Tobago and bauxite from Suriname.[71] Perhaps the most important investment of all, however, was the US oil refinery on Aruba. This had been completed by Standard Oil in 1929, a few years after the establishment of the Royal Dutch Shell refinery on Curaçao.[72] These mineral investments had strategic and economic value, and thus the Caribbean would acquire a special importance for the United States in wartime.

By the end of the nineteenth century, even before acquiring an empire, the United States was responsible for over 50 per cent of Caribbean exports and supplied more than 40 per cent of all imports. Thanks in large part to the imperial architecture put in place in the first decade of the twentieth century, these proportions rose sharply (see Figure 8.2). The disruption to trade across the Atlantic caused by the First World War made the Caribbean even more dependent on US imports (they exceeded 70 per cent of the total by 1917). A peak was reached in 1919 when the US dismantled wartime controls on sugar

[67] For the Dominican Republic, see Atkins and Wilson (1998), pp. 71–2. For Haiti, see Lundahl (1979), pp. 373–4.
[68] Under the receivership, the US rewrote the Dominican tariff twice. The first occasion was in 1909 and was designed to maximise revenue in order to hasten the repayment of the public external debt. The second occasion was 1919 when tariffs were lowered and the US changed the terms on which the debt had to be repaid in order to lengthen the period of the receivership (it could not end until the debt was paid off).
[69] The US forced Haiti to adopt a new constitution in 1918 (Franklin Roosevelt would later boast – incorrectly – that he had drafted it), which repealed the restrictions on land purchases by foreigners. Some US companies took advantage of this to establish large estates at the expense of small farmers, but the results were very modest.
[70] See Russell (1947), p. 34.
[71] See Winkler (1928), pp. 210, 220–1, 271–3.
[72] Standard Oil had bought out the Lago and Oil Transport Co., which was the first to invest in Aruba. The Curaçao refinery had been built by the Anglo-Dutch Shell Co. between 1924 and 1926. See van Soest (1978), pp. 228–31 and Goslinga (1990), pp. 574–95.

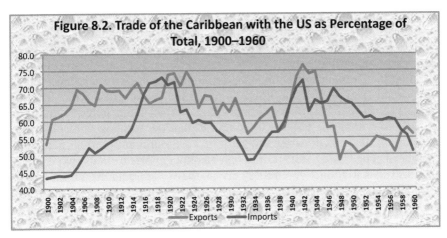

Figure 8.2. Trade of the Caribbean with the US as Percentage of Total, 1900–1960

Source: Tables C.15 and C.22.

and other commodities.[73] Caribbean exports soared, and only the United States was in a position to respond to the region's demand for additional goods.

From this point onwards, the US share of Caribbean trade started to fall because increased US trade barriers in 1921 and 1922 took their toll on commodity exports. In 1934, however, the Cuba Reciprocity Act was revised, giving the United States even bigger preferences in the all-important Cuban market, and Cuban import capacity rose as a result of both the sugar quota under the Jones-Costigan Act of the same year and the introduction of a quota for Cuban tobacco.[74] Foreign suppliers – Japanese and European – were squeezed out, and the US share of the Cuban market (still by far the biggest in the Caribbean) increased. This trend continued in the Second World War, when trade across the Atlantic was once again disrupted.

The United States had become an imperial power, but it never accepted the full range of colonial responsibilities in the countries where it exercised tutelage. The worst affected were Cuba and the two protectorates on Hispaniola, but even the two colonies (Puerto Rico and the US Virgin Islands) did not escape unscathed. With the notable exception of the Second World War, it also failed to understand – or chose to ignore – that domestic US policy could have an enormous impact not only on those territories where the United States held sway but also in the European colonies.

The first illustration of all this in the twentieth century was the 1903 reciprocal trade treaty with Cuba and the abolition of tariffs on imports from Puerto Rico. Cuba's share of US sugar imports in 1901 had been 28 per cent, but the

---

[73] The US had established an Equalization Board to centralise purchases during the war, but all controls were lifted in November 1919.

[74] The revised Reciprocity Act gave Cuba a quota of 18% of all tobacco used in the manufacture of US cigars. See Thomas (1971), p. 694.

share of Puerto Rico was 2.5 per cent.[75] In the next decade, the promotion of domestic US sugar (beet and cane) left imports largely unchanged,[76] but the two former Spanish colonies – along with Hawaii and the Philippines – had squeezed out almost all other sources. Exporters in other Caribbean countries, including the Dominican Republic, had to look elsewhere for markets.

A second example was the Volstead Act at the end of 1919, which marked the start of nearly fifteen years of Prohibition in the United States.[77] No better example of a domestic policy can be found than the banning of alcohol consumption in the United States, and yet it had profound implications across the Caribbean. The United States could ban alcohol exports from its two colonies (Puerto Rico had in fact voted to go dry in 1918),[78] forcing the Virgin Islands to switch quickly from rum to bay rum exports,[79] but to ban it from elsewhere was much more difficult. It was not until 1926, when a convention was signed with Cuba designed to prevent smuggling,[80] that the United States was able to curtail rum exports from the island, but by then Prohibition had given a huge boost to Cuban tourism whereby the rum industry as a whole did not suffer unduly.[81]

The British and French authorities turned a blind eye at first to the implications of the Volstead Act. Indeed, re-exports from the Bahamas, Belize and many other colonies soared.[82] St Pierre and Miquelon, two French territories at the mouth of the St Lawrence River in Canada, suddenly emerged as major export destinations for the British and French colonies. The boom only ended when both Britain and France signed conventions, in 1924 and 1927 respectively, discouraging smuggling and allowing US Customs to stop and search suspected vessels outside US territorial waters.[83] By the end of the 1920s, the export of rum and molasses to the United States – legally through Canada or illegally through smuggling – was in serious decline.[84]

The Caribbean adjusted nimbly to US Prohibition, exploiting loopholes and taking advantage of whatever opportunities presented themselves. Avoiding the impact of US domestic policies in the Great Depression was another matter altogether. The Smoot-Hawley tariff in 1930 applied to dutiable imports from

---

[75] Sugar export figures from Table C.5. US sugar imports from Carter (2006), vol. 5.

[76] They fell from 4 billion lbs in 1900 to 3.9 billion in 1910 before rising to 4.5 billion on the eve of war. See Carter (2006), vol. 5, p. 554.

[77] The Eighteenth Amendment had passed in January 1919. However, the enabling legislation embodied in the Volstead Act was not passed until October.

[78] The Jones Act had given Puerto Ricans the opportunity to express a view on the sale of alcoholic beverages. They did so in July 1917, and the colony went dry in March 1918. See Dietz (1986), p. 97n55.

[79] Bay rum mixes bay leaves and alcohol, but because it was not a beverage, it was legal.

[80] See Jones (1933), pp. 113–28.

[81] For rum exports from Cuba in this period, see Table C.5.

[82] See Table C.7. The Bahamas was particularly involved in re-exports.

[83] See Jones (1933), chaps. 3 and 6.

[84] Re-exports, which included whisky and other alcoholic beverages not produced in the Caribbean, also declined. See Table C.7.

all Caribbean countries (it excluded Puerto Rico and the US Virgin Islands).[85] In particular, it applied to sugar – Senator Smoot had vigorously promoted US domestic sugar interests in the 1920s.[86] Domestic sugar production was rescued, but sugar imports started to decline from their peak in 1929.[87]

The New Deal brought a new approach, and the Jones-Costigan Act of 1934 ushered in the era of US sugar import quotas. Even Puerto Rico and the US Virgin Islands were affected. Sugar exporters in the US imperial space were now squeezed between stagnant US consumption, rising domestic production (behind the higher tariff wall) and falling imports. However, quotas under both the Jones-Costigan Act and the revised Cuba Reciprocity Act led to improved prices for Cuban sugar and tobacco and a revival in her foreign trade. Other Caribbean sugar exporters faced insuperable barriers in the US market and had to look elsewhere if they had not done so already.

US interest in the Caribbean rose sharply with the Second World War. Even before the country entered the war in December 1941, the United States had established a military presence in several British colonies,[88] sent troops to the Dutch colonies to protect strategic assets[89] and was keeping a watchful eye on the French colonies in case their resources should fall into the hands of Germany.[90] Inter-American economic assistance extended to the increased purchase of commodity exports from the Caribbean, and sugar quotas were suspended. Rum exports boomed as whisky production in the United States was curtailed.[91] By 1942 the United States was responsible for nearly 80 per cent of all Caribbean trade (see Figure 8.2), a proportion that proved to be the high point of the whole period considered here and will almost certainly never be reached again.

More normal trading conditions returned after the war. US sugar quotas were restored in 1948[92] but failed to keep pace with the rise in Caribbean production. Cuba was soon desperate for new markets (indeed, it sold 500,000 tons in 1955–6 to the Soviet Union at prices well below those in the world

---

[85] The Smoot-Hawley tariff is widely blamed for accelerating and deepening the world recession that was already under way. It aimed to protect US industry against imports from all sources.

[86] Senator Smoot, who came from a sugar state, had successfully pushed for tariff increases in 1921 and 1922.

[87] They would not surpass the 1929 peak again until 1970. See Carter (2006), vol. 5.

[88] This was the famous 'destroyers for bases' deal under which President Roosevelt provided Britain with fifty old destroyers in return for ninety-nine-year leases on military bases and the right to station troops in Antigua, Bahamas, Guyana, Jamaica, St Lucia and Trinidad. Outright sale of land for military bases was also agreed to in Bermuda and Newfoundland. See Füllberg-Stolberg (2004).

[89] Troops were despatched to the bauxite mines in Suriname and the oil refineries in the Dutch Antilles to protect the installations from sabotage.

[90] The French island colonies were particularly problematic because Admiral Robert controlled not only a large part of the French navy but also a considerable part of France's gold reserves. See Roberts (1942).

[91] The increases in rum exports during the middle of the war from Cuba and the US Virgin Islands were spectacular. See Table C.5.

[92] They had been suspended at the beginning of hostilities.

market). The two US colonies (Puerto Rico and the US Virgin Islands) remained completely dependent on the US market for both imports and exports.[93] Cuba, the Dominican Republic and Haiti all tried hard to diversify their markets, with some success.[94] The European countries were able to lure their colonies back into the imperial fold after the war as a result of both preferential tariffs and as a consequence of dollar scarcity.

The US share of Caribbean trade fell after the war, despite the fact that many commodities, such as bananas and bauxite, enjoyed duty-free entry into a US economy that was booming. Indeed, the US share ended in 1960 at roughly the same ratio as in 1900 (see Figure 8.2). Given the dominant – not to say hegemonic – position of the United States in the Caribbean during this period, this might seem puzzling. However, the explanation was quite simple. US trade with Cuba was always the most important part of US trade with the Caribbean. So the US share of Caribbean trade was positively correlated with both the US share of Cuban trade[95] and the Cuban share of Caribbean trade. The Cuban economy – locked into quotas for the principal exports – stagnated in the 1950s while at the same time Cuba managed to reduce modestly its dependence on the US market. It is not so surprising, therefore, that the US share of Caribbean trade declined after the Second World War.

8.3. THE UK AND THE CARIBBEAN

Although the UK had been displaced by the United States as the most important trade partner for the Caribbean, it was still in second place in 1900 with nearly 20 per cent.[96] Despite the absence of imperial preference, it remained the main supplier of the British dependencies,[97] was responsible for 16 per cent of Cuban imports and about half as much of the less important market of Hispaniola. Only in the French and Dutch dependencies was British trade of negligible importance, and this was because of the impact of discriminatory tariffs in the former and cultural ties with Holland in the latter.

The Caribbean was therefore of some importance in British trade, and the government was bound to look with mixed feelings at the rise of US imperialism in the region after 1898. The strategic argument, accepting US dominance in the former Spanish colonies and in Hispaniola in return for concentrating

---

[93] Over 90% of their exports went to the US, and over 80% of their imports came from the US in almost all years up to (and beyond) 1960. See Tables C.15 and C.22.

[94] Hispaniola ended the period with the same share of imports from the US (nearly 60%) as in 1900. However, the Haitian export share going to the US had risen because France was no longer such a crucial market.

[95] The correlation coefficient between the share of US Cuban and Caribbean imports between 1900 and 1960 is +0.895.

[96] Britain supplied 20.5% of all imports and took 15.8% of domestic exports in 1900. See Tables C.16 and C.23.

[97] The US, however, was the most important export market for the British colonies in 1900, with nearly 50%. See Table C.15.

naval resources closer to home to combat the challenge from Germany, may have been settled.[98] However, the UK still hoped for an 'open door' in those countries whose commercial policies were not controlled by rival European states.

The 1903 Reciprocity Act between Cuba and the United States was therefore something of a shock. It would have been hard enough, in view of geographical proximity, for the UK to compete with the United States even without preferences. With them – it was widely assumed – it would be almost impossible. The British representative in Cuba therefore did all he could to dissuade the Cuban government from ratifying the treaty.[99] When this failed, he drafted a trade treaty that would not have given the UK equal preferences to the United States, but it was more in the nature of damage limitation. The United States, however, made sure that the Cuban government did not sign.[100]

Yet British trade with Cuba did not collapse, because it was based fundamentally on two products (textiles and rice) in which the UK could compete despite preferences.[101] Indeed, the British share of Cuban imports did not drop below 10 per cent until the middle of the First World War, and by then Britain had become a first-class market for Cuban exports, taking nearly 25 per cent of the total in 1918.[102] This was mainly because of British dependence on sugar imports at a time when it was cut off from its traditional sources of beet sugar in continental Europe. The British colonies, squeezed out of the US sugar market by Cuba, also benefitted from these peculiar wartime conditions, with big increases in both prices and volumes.[103]

When war was declared by the UK on 4 August 1914, it was expected to last only a few months. As it became clear that this would not be the case, the British view of the world started to change. The UK, dependent on food imports from nonempire sources, had become very vulnerable to hostilities in Europe. Free trade, questioned by Joseph Chamberlain since the 1890s and under attack from the Conservative Party when they went into opposition in 1905, came to an end with the introduction of the McKenna duties in the 1915 budget.[104] This was justified as a temporary measure to raise revenue by

---

[98] British defence policy from the 1890s onwards had become increasingly focused on the perceived threat to national security from German industrial and naval expansion. British foreign policy had to adjust accordingly. See Kneer (1975), p. 100.

[99] See Kneer (1975), pp. 76–8.

[100] See Kneer (1975), p. 86, and Ibarra (2006), pp. 155–72.

[101] The rice came from British India, but the textiles came from the UK. On the structure of British trade with Cuba before and after the Reciprocity Act, see Ibarra (2006), chap. 3.

[102] For Cuban imports from Britain, see Table C.23. For Cuban exports to the UK, see Table C.16.

[103] On the eve of war, 80% of British sugar was imported, and much of this came from the parts of continental Europe that would be either controlled by enemy states (Germany, Austria-Hungary) or the scene of the fiercest fighting (Belgium and France). Because sugar was seen as an essential commodity in the war, the UK had to act quickly to find alternative sources of supply.

[104] McKenna was the chancellor of the exchequer in Asquith's war cabinet.

taxing luxury manufactured goods that were taking up vital shipping space, so the new tariffs did not directly affect the Caribbean. However, this first major breach in the free trade wall would prove to be permanent because the UK now shifted towards imperial preference.[105]

This started in 1919, when the tariffs that then existed were revised to give a preference to those imports coming from the British colonies and dominions.[106] At the same time, tariffs were introduced, with a reduction for empire suppliers, on many commodities of interest to the Caribbean, including sugar, molasses, cacao, coffee and tobacco.[107] And when it became clear that currency depreciation in continental Europe would not be eliminated swiftly by a return to prewar gold parities, the Safeguarding of Industries Act was passed in 1921, introducing tariffs on a wide range of imports, with 100 per cent preference for the colonies and dominions.

When the Conservative Party returned to power at the end of 1924, following the brief interlude of the first Labour government, they extended imperial preference even further, with a widening of the differential tariff for several commodities of interest to the Caribbean, including refined sugar and tobacco. Meanwhile, the dominions and colonies were moving in the same direction, and thus all trade within the British Empire was becoming caught up in imperial preference. The process advanced further in 1928 when the duty on raw sugar was lowered and the tariff on foreign refined sugar was increased.[108] Exports of raw sugar from the British Caribbean to the UK started to increase sharply.

The Ottawa Conference in 1932 took imperial preference a step further and even included quotas on some products. Only the dominions had been invited to Ottawa, the Caribbean colonies being represented by a British minister, but the UK followed up the conference by widening imperial preference and including new commodities, such as bananas, and deepening it in 1934 when the preference extended to the colonies on sugar was made even bigger than that given to the dominions.[109] Sugar exports from the British Caribbean continued their ascent and with it the share of exports from the British colonies going to the UK (see Figure 8.3), until the ISA in 1937 put a brake on this expansion. The increased share of exports going to the UK was complemented by the large British share of the imports of the British Caribbean colonies, which had been rising steadily since the introduction of imperial preference at the end of the First World War.

British trade policy was now not just guided by imperial preference. It was also blatantly protectionist, with large subsidies, for example, paid to beet sugar

---

[105] Some have seen the taxes introduced or increased at the end of the Boer War (1899–1902) as the first breach in free trade. However, these taxes were very modest and usually took the form of excise duties rather than tariffs.

[106] See Russell (1947), p. 20.

[107] See Russell (1947), p. 21.

[108] See Russell (1947), p. 27.

[109] See Russell (1947), p. 95.

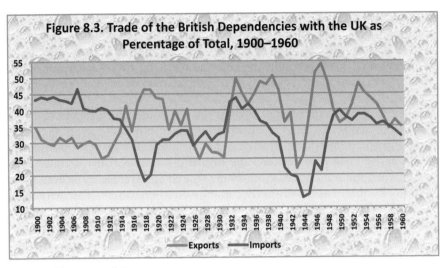

Figure 8.3. Trade of the British Dependencies with the UK as Percentage of Total, 1900–1960

Source: Tables C.16 and C.23.

growers in the UK.[110] And yet, despite this, the Dominican Republic was able to send a much bigger share of its exports to the UK as it found itself shut out of the US market by high tariffs and quotas.[111] This reorientation of Dominican exports had begun after the First World War but gathered pace in the Great Depression. From 1931 until the early 1950s – including the Second World War – Britain was the leading destination for Dominican exports in almost all years and was therefore a more important market for Dominican exports than the United States.[112] The Dominicans, however, received no special favours from the UK and gave none in return, so their imports continued to be sourced mainly from the United States.

The British market was important for some other Caribbean countries also. When the exceptional conditions of the First World War and the postwar boom came to an end, the share of Cuban exports going to the UK had once again fallen below 10 per cent.[113] However, the difficulties of selling sugar and tobacco (especially cigars and cigarettes) in the US market in the interwar period led to a renewed interest in the relatively open British market. In the 1930s, the share of Cuban exports destined for Britain varied between 10 and

[110] See *Sugar Policy: Proposals of His Majesty's Government* (1935).
[111] Dominican sugar paid the full duty in the US market and had been squeezed out by Cuban sugar before the First World War. When sugar import quotas were introduced in 1934 by the US, the Dominican Republic received very little.
[112] The share of Dominican exports going to the UK is given in Table C.16. From 1929 until the Second World War it varied from one-quarter to one-half. In 1943–4, however, it averaged 60 per cent.
[113] See Table C.16.

20 per cent – higher than at any time since independence. And when the oil refineries in the Dutch Antilles came on stream at the end of the 1920s, the UK was the most important market, taking over 40 per cent in the crucial years before the war.[114] As a result, the UK was receiving over 15 per cent of all Caribbean exports in the 1930s – a higher figure than in the first decade of the century.[115]

When it came to supplying imports, the UK could not compete so easily with the United States and the European imperial powers (except, of course, in the British colonies). Tariff discrimination weakened Britain's position in the US and French colonies, and the British position in Cuba declined even further when the preferences given to the United States were made even more generous by the revision of the Reciprocity Act in 1934.[116] The markets in Hispaniola were in theory open, and Britain did increase its share of imports in the 1930s to nearly 10 per cent,[117] but the United States enjoyed all sorts of subtle advantages that were hard to overcome. Still, with nearly 15 per cent of all Caribbean imports in the 1930s, the UK had recovered quickly from its lowly position during and immediately after the First World War and was second only to the United States.[118]

After Franklin D. Roosevelt was elected president in 1932, the United States watched with some concern the rise of imperial preference across the British Empire. It was not the Caribbean colonies that were so much a source of concern as the self-governing dominions, such as Canada, Australia and South Africa. Although the United States had been guiltier than most in adopting the higher tariffs and quotas that crippled international trade after 1929, the Roosevelt administration did its best from 1934 to liberalise trade through reciprocal trade agreements promoted by Secretary of State Cordell Hull. British imperial preference was an obstacle to this endeavour, and the Anglo-American Trade Agreement in 1938 was designed to limit the damage.[119]

The Second World War gave the United States huge leverage over the UK, and the Roosevelt administration pushed for an end to imperial preference.[120] At a crucial meeting in August 1941, the British Prime Minister Winston Churchill had to work hard to include the phrase "with due respect for ... existing obligations" into the Atlantic Charter that inter alia committed both countries to a world free of trade discrimination at the end of the war. The first draft of the Havana Charter in 1947 provided no space for trade discrimination by the UK,[121] but it did exempt the US–Cuba Reciprocity Act

---

[114] See Table C.16.
[115] See Table C.16.
[116] See Thomas (1971), p. 694.
[117] This was more because of Haiti than the Dominican Republic. See Table C.23.
[118] See Table C.22 and C.23.
[119] The Agreement ended imperial preference on some commodities. See Russell (1947), p. 11.
[120] Undersecretary of State Sumner Welles stated in 1943 that 'the whole history of British Empire Preferences is a history of economic aggression.' See Russell (1947), p. 11.
[121] In the final version, however, the British were able to safeguard imperial preference. See Department of State (1948), pp. 45–6, 122.

and the preferences between the United States and the Philippines from the application of the MFN (Most-Favoured Nation) clause. The British may have considered the US position pure hypocrisy, but that was little consolation when their bargaining position was so weak.

In the end, British imperial preference survived the onslaught, and the United States was instead content to use GATT to whittle away the substantive impact of differential tariffs. The British even passed the Commonwealth Sugar Act in 1951, providing a quota for sugar from the British Caribbean colonies and with it much higher prices than those in the world market.[122] This helped to maintain the British share of trade with the British Caribbean despite the erosion of preferences by GATT. Just as important, however, was the impact of the dollar shortage and the lack of currency convertibility.[123] The sterling area, which included almost all the British Caribbean,[124] became something of a fortress in its own right. This was especially true after the sterling devaluation of September 1949, because all British Caribbean colonies were pegged to the pound.[125] Since British trade with the rest of the Caribbean was in relative decline, it was only the tight links with the British colonies that allowed the UK to end the period with 10 per cent of all Caribbean trade.[126]

At the end of the nineteenth century, the Norman Commission had drawn attention to the shocking social conditions in most of the British Caribbean colonies. Seeing no end to the crisis of the sugar industry, it had recommended an extension of small-scale agriculture, export diversification and greater production for the home market. Yet when the Moyne Commission was established in 1938,[127] it found itself not only confronted with a similar situation to that which had existed forty years before, but one that was in some ways even worse as a result of the wave of labour unrest that had spread across the British Caribbean in the last few years.[128]

It was not that no progress had been made. However, the 1902 Brussels Convention, the impact of the First World War on food security in the UK and the impact of imperial preference from 1919 onwards had persuaded British

---

[122] See Burns (1965), p. 707.
[123] The British had been pressured by the US to adopt currency convertibility in 1947, but it was premature and ended in failure. Full currency convertibility did not come until 1979.
[124] At the end of the war, the UK had established the West Indian dollar (pegged to sterling) as the currency in its Caribbean dependencies (except Belize and Jamaica).
[125] On 31 December 1949 the colonial authorities reneged on their commitments and devalued the Belize dollar, which was then tied to sterling for the first time. Thus, the currencies of all British colonies (including Jamaica), being pegged to sterling, were devalued against other core currencies, making imports from those sources more expensive.
[126] The UK had one-third of the trade of British Caribbean dependencies and 10 per cent of the trade of all the Caribbean in 1960. See Tables C.16 and C.23.
[127] This was another Royal West Indian Commission, chaired by Lord Moyne, but its terms of reference – unlike the Norman Commission – were not limited to sugar. See *West India Royal Commission Report* (1945).
[128] This wave of labour unrest had started in St Kitts in 1935 and spread to many other British dependencies. See Bolland (1995). It was not, however, confined to them. See Bryan (2004).

officials that cane sugar exports from the Caribbean still had an important part to play. Thus, the sensible recommendations of the Norman Commission on export diversification and food security had been largely ignored in favour of a return to sugar specialisation. Production and exports of sugar had indeed expanded (at least until the ISA imposed quotas), but costs had been cut, employment had become less permanent and wage rates had not increased. Perhaps the last straw was the closing in the 1930s of the emigration safety valve when employment opportunities outside and inside the Caribbean disappeared (see Chapter 9).

The Moyne Commission, completed in 1940 but not published in full until 1945 for fear that the dismal economic and social picture it presented would be used as enemy propaganda,[129] followed a similar path to the Norman Commission in recommending an extension of small-scale agriculture and food security. However, it went beyond the previous Royal Commission by recommending a system of colonial grants and loans that would become known as Colonial Development and Welfare (CD & W). From 1940 onwards the British Caribbean now had an external source of finance to supplement meagre domestic savings, and the investment rate started to increase.[130] The low-level equilibrium trap, in which much of the Caribbean had found itself since the collapse of sugar prices in 1883–4, was no longer so critical.[131]

The offer of CD & W loans and grants by the UK was very beneficial for the British Caribbean.[132] Less helpful was the desire by the UK to push its Caribbean colonies into a federation as a prelude to self-government on the dominion model. Although there were plenty of precedents, including the formation of the Leeward Islands Federation in 1871, the first major step was taken in 1947 at an imperial conference in Jamaica in which the colonial subjects finally had a voice.[133] Despite major reservations by the islands' representatives, the UK pushed ahead, and the Federation of the British West Indies was established in

---

[129] The recommendations, however, had been published in 1940. See *West India Royal Commission, 1938–1939: Recommendations* (1940).

[130] There had been occasional grants-in-aid for some British colonies in the nineteenth century, and a Colonial Development Fund had been started in the 1930s. However, these new loans and grants were much more substantial. For a list up to 1945–6, see MacPherson (1947). MacPherson was the comptroller for development and welfare in the West Indies and the person most responsible for dispersing the funds voted by the British parliament.

[131] Arthur Lewis, the Nobel-laureate whose pioneering work on development economics had been influenced by his upbringing in the Caribbean, had stated the principal problem of development as the need to raise the investment rate to 10% of GDP when the domestic savings rate was as little as 5%. CD & W was designed in part to achieve this. See Lewis (1954).

[132] CD & W provided real resources. By contrast the Caribbean Commission, established in 1942 by the UK and US, and which France and Holland joined in 1946, provided almost nothing. Its main function seems to have been sharpening the anticolonial views of those West Indians, such as Eric Williams, who served on it. See Ryan (2009), chap. 3. For a more positive view of the Caribbean Commission, see Poole (1951).

[133] See Parry, Sherlock and Maingot (1987), pp. 261–3.

1958.[134] The death knell was provided by the Jamaican referendum on Federation in 1961, after which it fell apart.[135] Independence for each colony was then the only logical step, and this started in 1962.[136]

8.4. THE REST OF THE CORE AND THE CARIBBEAN

With the withdrawal of Denmark and Sweden, the remaining members of the core were the two European colonial powers (France and Holland), the former colonial power (Spain) and Germany. In addition, Canada joined the core by virtue first of its use of imperial preference and later as a consequence of the volume of its foreign trade and the activities of its banks, insurance and mining companies in the Caribbean. Japan in the interwar period came close to being a member of the core as a result of its sales of textiles and other labour-intensive exports in the Caribbean, but it never purchased much from the region in the period studied here.[137] Exports from Cuba to the USSR began in the mid-1950s, but this was not yet on a scale to allow it to be considered a member of the core. The remainder of the core (i.e. in addition to the UK and the United States) therefore consisted of five countries.

The French claim to membership of the core was based not just on its colonies in the region, but also on its position as the leading market for Haitian coffee (the principal export). This had been cemented by the Franco-Haitian trade treaty of 1904 (see Chapter 7), but it was disrupted by the First World War, especially in 1918 when imports from Haiti almost ended. French imports from Haiti were maintained during the US occupation (1915–34), despite the diversification of exports away from coffee.

It was the Second World War that crippled the trade ties between Haiti and France, and the Franco-Haitian Commercial Agreement of 1952 was unable to restore the former colonial power to its previous position. More promising for France was its trade links with the Dominican Republic, which had been strengthened by commercial treaty in 1936[138] and which had made France the third market for Dominican exports by 1939.[139] These trade links, however, withered in the war and were not restored subsequently.

---

[134] See Mordecai (1968), chap. 3.

[135] Without Jamaica, the most populous British colony, the Federation had no future. The British, however, did push ahead with a federal plan for some of the small remaining colonies, out of which eventually emerged the Eastern Caribbean Currency Union (ECCU).

[136] Independence began with Jamaica and Trinidad & Tobago in 1962 and continued until St Kitts & Nevis became independent in 1983. The remaining dependencies (Anguilla, British Virgin Islands, Cayman Islands, Montserrat and the Turks & Caicos Islands) went through various name changes before being finally baptised as British Overseas Territories.

[137] Japan was a low-cost exporter of textiles and clothing – the main import into the Caribbean. As a result, Japanese firms were able to compete despite imperial preference in the Caribbean markets.

[138] See United States, Bureau of Insular Affairs, *Report of the Dominican Customs Receivership* (1936).

[139] Behind the UK and US. See Overseas Economic Surveys (1957), app. 9, p. 31.

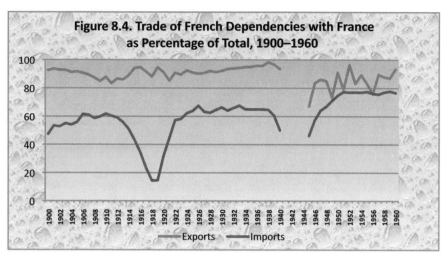

Figure 8.4. Trade of French Dependencies with France as Percentage of Total, 1900–1960

Note: No trade was reported with France between 1941 and 1944.
Source: Tables C.17 and C.24.

Part of the problem in the postwar period was the dollar shortage and the fact that France gave priority to trade within the French currency zone. This, of course, included the three French territories in the Caribbean (French Guiana, Guadeloupe and Martinique). Their dependence on the French market had never wavered, being disrupted only during the Second World War (see Figure 8.4), when trade with Vichy France and German-occupied France came to an end.[140] Indeed, during the First World War rum exports had soared as a result of their use by France, both for medicinal purposes and in the manufacture of explosives.[141] France was also the main supplier of its Caribbean territories, except in the war years, and France even increased its dominant position in the 1950s (see Figure 8.4).

That it was able to do so, unlike in the case of Haiti and the Dominican Republic, was because of several factors. The first was imperial preference, a constant in French commercial policy, which gave tariff privileges to colonial produce in the French market and much lower tariffs – often zero – on colonial imports from France.[142] The second was *départementalisation*, which in 1946 turned the three colonies into French departments. The three French Caribbean

---

[140] Admiral Robert, appointed high commissioner for the French Caribbean colonies in 1939, chose to recognise Vichy France rather than Free France after the German victory. See Robert (1950). In theory, trade could therefore have continued, but the Allies (and the US before it entered the war) did not permit it. No doubt there was some trade (see Roberts, 1942), but none was recorded.

[141] Rum exports then received a further short-lived boost as a result of US Prohibition before the French authorities agreed to clamp down on smuggling.

[142] On French colonial preference before the First World War, see Ashley (1920), pp. 341–2. Tariff preferences in the interwar period were less important because France introduced sugar

territories (no longer colonies) were now entirely inside the tariff wall, and trade with France faced no barriers at all. Indeed, when France became part of the European Economic Community (EEC) in 1958, the Caribbean Départements d'Outre-Mer (DOMs) joined at the same time.

Strictly speaking, commercial ties between the French Caribbean and mainland France no longer constituted foreign trade, but it continued to be treated as such – perhaps because *départementalisation* was initially justified as preparing the former colonies for independence.[143] Just as important were the budgetary implications. As departments, the former colonies received an infusion not only of current spending by the French state but were also eligible – like the British colonies – for capital spending under various headings.

The close ties between France and the Caribbean therefore survived, but the region had long ago lost importance as a result of the acquisition of French colonies in Africa and Asia in the nineteenth century and the expansion of French interests in the Middle East after the First World War.[144] This relative decline of importance of the Caribbean was also true of Holland, whose colonial empire in Asia had grown significantly in the nineteenth century from its base in Java until it occupied the whole of modern-day Indonesia.[145] For Holland, the East Indies would become a source of considerable profit, based in large part on forced labour,[146] compared with the West Indies, which required subsidies in most years.[147]

The Dutch had abandoned mercantilism in 1848 and within a decade had followed the British example in abolishing imperial preference (but not tariffs).[148] From this point onwards exports from the Dutch dependencies to Holland received no special favours. However, the close ties based on the investment of Dutch capital and shipping links ensured that the Netherlands would remain an important export market while imports into the Caribbean dependencies from Holland remained strong. Indeed, these trade ties with Holland increased in the first decade of the twentieth century (see Figure 8.5).

The only other trade partner of significance for the Dutch colonies was the United States, whose importance as a supplier increased sharply in the First World War (Holland was neutral but could not avoid the impact of shipping

and rum quotas for the Caribbean colonies. See Crusol (1980), p. 84, and Smith (2005), pp. 225–7.

[143] See Crusol (2007), pp. 363–5.

[144] These included the League of Nations mandate in Syria, which at that time included Lebanon.

[145] This expansion involved a vicious colonial war in the province of Aceh, till then an independent country. See Kuitenbrouwer (1991), pp. 101–6.

[146] This forced labour system, much admired by King Leopold of Belgium in anticipation of his brutal exploits in the Congo, required the peasants to devote at least 20% of their crops to exports, which were purchased by the Dutch state below world market prices.

[147] Like the British colonies, the Dutch ones in the Caribbean received occasional grants-in-aid. However, the new colonial arrangements put in place by the *Regeerings Reglement* of 1865 led to almost continuous subsidies until the 1930s in the case of the Dutch Antilles, and the 1940s in the case of Suriname.

[148] See Kuitenbrouwer (1991), pp. 37–8.

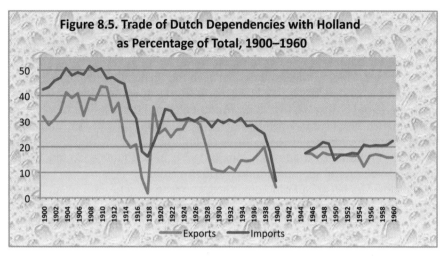

Figure 8.5. Trade of Dutch Dependencies with Holland as Percentage of Total, 1900–1960

Note: No trade was reported with Holland between 1941 and 1944.
Source: Tables C.17 and C.24.

shortages and economic disruption). Yet the situation did not return to normal at the end of the war as a result of the development of mineral exports in the Dutch colonies. In the 1920s, the Dutch Antilles became a major exporter of refined oil and Suriname of bauxite, with US capital playing a key role in both developments. Trade links with Holland declined in importance up to the Second World War, with Germany becoming a market for refined oil from the Dutch Antilles and the United States becoming heavily dependent on bauxite imports from Suriname.[149]

Following the fall of Holland in May 1940, the Dutch government – in exile in London – had the humiliation of watching powerlessly the occupation of Curaçao and Aruba by French, British and US troops in quick succession.[150] The United States also sent troops to Suriname to protect the bauxite mines. Despite this, German U-boats succeeded in sinking twenty-six ships carrying bauxite to the United States.[151] The situation in 1942 was very tense. Yet Queen Wilhelmina chose the final month of that year to make a radio broadcast from London that would lay the basis for a transformation of the relationship between the Dutch Caribbean territories and the Netherlands.

Because of the war in the East Indies, leading to Dutch recognition of Indonesian independence in 1949, the new constitutional arrangement could not be

---

[149] By 1940 about 80% of all US bauxite imports came from Suriname. Because bauxite was used to make aluminium, a key component in aircraft manufacture, the trade relation with Suriname acquired strategic importance.

[150] This was done not only to ensure continued supplies of refined oil for the allies, but also to make sure they did not fall into the hands of Germany. The suspicion remained, however, that some of this oil may have been used to refuel German U-boats.

[151] See Goslinga (1990), p. 703.

implemented until 1954.[152] By that time Holland had joined (in 1948) the customs union formed by Belgium and Luxembourg, but it had no intention of abandoning its Caribbean territories – all that remained of its former overseas empire. The Charter for the Kingdom of the Netherlands gave autonomy in all matters except defence and foreign affairs to each former colony,[153] but what was perhaps more important for the Caribbean territories was the infusion of funds associated with the new arrangements. No longer having to compete with the East Indies in Dutch priorities, the West Indies – as with the other European territories – were able to raise the investment rate through capital spending by the state. This ensured that trade ties with the Netherlands in the 1950s (see Figure 8.5) remained above what one might otherwise have expected.

Spain had finally lost all its Caribbean colonies at the conclusion of the Spanish-American War. Her position in Puerto Rico was rapidly eclipsed by the new colonial power, but she clung tenaciously to a foothold in Cuba. This was not only because of those Spanish investments that survived the war, but also the wave of emigration (from Spain to Cuba) that followed. Despite the advantages given to the United States by the 1903 Reciprocity Act and the loss of Spanish trade privileges, Spain's share of Cuban imports was still close to 10 per cent on the eve of the First World War.[154] Its share of Cuban exports was much smaller, but the Spanish market could not be ignored because it was always an important destination for Cuban cigars (especially in the 1950s) and sometimes for raw sugar.

Spain's position in the Dominican Republic had become very marginal by the end of the nineteenth century, and US financial control from 1905 onwards made it difficult to reverse this. However, Spain clawed its way back with purchases of sugar, cacao and tobacco and was responsible for around 3 per cent of Dominican trade in the early 1930s, when the US market became so difficult to penetrate.[155] Spain then signed a commercial treaty in 1935 with the Dominican Republic, which reduced barriers to trade on both sides.[156] This might have led to an increase in trade, were it not for the Spanish Civil War (1936–9), which put an end to such hopes. Although Spain was neutral in the Second World War, shipping shortages and subsequently the dollar scarcity had reduced Spain's share of trade to less than 1 per cent by 1960.

Spain was a weak European power with a traditionally strong foothold in the Caribbean and net imports of sugar. Germany was the exact opposite and had to rely on the markets of independent countries to gain any foothold in the Caribbean. In this respect it had been very successful and, helped by its resident merchants, had become an important trade partner of both Haiti and the Dominican Republic before the First World War ('independent' Cuba

---

[152] See Griffiths (1980), pp. 264–71.
[153] They had ceased to be referred to as colonies in 1922.
[154] See Table C.24.
[155] See Tables C.17 and C.24.
[156] See *Report of the Dominican Customs Receivership* (1936).

gave many fewer opportunities, and trade in both directions was always very small). Indeed, in 1908 a Haitian-German commercial treaty had been signed giving Haitian exports preferential access and giving German exports the same treatment as France.[157]

The German position was undermined by the US protectorates over Haiti and the Dominican Republic and Germany's enemy status in the First World War. German assets were not confiscated, but transfers by sale were common, and German trade declined. Yet Germany recovered and was responsible for 10 per cent of Dominican imports in the 1930s, vying with Japan for second place after the United States. The inconvertible *aski-mark* used by the Nazi regime to pay for exports, however, was a disincentive, and imports by Germany (principally tobacco, cacao and coffee, but not sugar) never reached the same importance as German exports to the Dominican Republic. Germany was then dislodged from Hispaniola by the Second World War and was unable subsequently to recover its prewar position.

The only country to join the core in this period was Canada. Yet Canada had been a major trade partner for the British Caribbean after the independence of the United States, because Britain used its Navigation Acts to block trade between the United States and its colonies, and Canada (or British North America, as it was known until Federation in 1867) stepped into the breach. Gradually the restrictions on US trade were removed, and Canada was eclipsed as a major trade partner for the British Caribbean (in other parts of the Caribbean, trade with Canada had never been important).

All this changed in 1897, when Canada[158] unilaterally extended to the British Caribbean the preferential tariffs it had agreed with the UK the year before. At the time it was widely assumed that nothing much would come from this act of generosity by Canada, but this changed quickly. First, the Cuba Reciprocity Act pushed sugar from the British West Indies out of the US market, and, second, Canada imposed punitive tariffs on beet sugar imports from Germany.[159] Within ten years Canada had replaced the United States as a market for British Caribbean sugar, and other products followed.

The British were taken by surprise and launched a Royal Commission on Trade Relations between Canada and the West Indies that reported in 1910 on the possibility of strengthening the relationship by extending Canadian preferences in return for British Caribbean preferences for Canadian exports.[160]

---

[157] See Ashley (1920), p. 116n2.
[158] Canada excluded Newfoundland until 1949, when it lost its separate dominion status.
[159] Canada did this in response to the raising of German tariffs, which in turn had been done because Germany was excluded from the preferences extended to the UK by Canada in 1897. Germany's position was based on the 1865 trade treaty with the UK that gave each country MFN treatment. This treaty was part of the reason for British reluctance to move towards imperial preference.
[160] By 1910 Canada had in fact already unilaterally increased its preference for the British Caribbean from 25% to 37.5%. See *Report of the Royal Commission on trade relations between Canada and the West Indies* (1910).

This duly happened, and the links were extended by treaty in 1912, 1920, 1925, 1932 and 1937.[161] The British Empire, however, operated on the assumption that imperial preference granted by one part of the empire to another would always be granted to the UK also. Thus, the UK gained trade preferences in the British Caribbean thanks to the treaties with Canada.

The Royal Commission tackled head-on a question that the theory of international trade policy was unable to resolve: Who receives the preference? The size of the preference was easy to measure because it was the difference between the full and preferential tariff multiplied by the volume of imports at the preferential rate. In the case of sugar imported into Canada from the British Caribbean, this had become substantial by 1909 (the last year for which the Royal Commission had data) and can be estimated at nearly $1 million. This amount was then distributed between the refiner, the importer, the shipper, the financiers, the manufacturers of raw sugar and the grower, with each side claiming they were entitled to all of the preference. The conclusion of the Royal Commission that everyone benefitted was probably correct, even though the commissioners could not say in what proportion.

The trade links between Canada and the British Caribbean were underpinned by imperial preference. Yet Canada emerged as a major player in the rest of the Caribbean, where its interests were represented not only by trade in goods, but also by banks and insurance companies. The Royal Bank of Canada and the Bank of Nova Scotia established branch banking almost everywhere, the first subscribing to the largest number of shares in the National Bank of Cuba when it was established in 1948.[162] By then Canadian insurance companies were writing more premiums in Cuba than US companies and were second only to the Cuban companies themselves.[163] Canadian mining companies were also very active, and not just in the British colonies, with bauxite exports from Suriname being particularly important.

---

[161] See Aspinall (1929), pp. 67–79, and Burns (1965).
[162] See Overseas Economic Surveys (1950), p. 60. On the Bank of Nova Scotia in the Caribbean, see Quigley (1989).
[163] See Overseas Economic Surveys (1954), app. 14, p. 81.

9

Caribbean Foreign Trade

This chapter explores the foreign trade of the Caribbean from 1900 to 1960. Exports of goods remained the major determinant of the performance of the Caribbean economies, providing the foreign exchange for imports, the revenue for government expenditure and the resources to service the public debt. Exports of services, however, in some of the smaller countries replaced commodity exports as the main engine of growth after the Second World War. This drove a wedge between the performance of merchandise exports and total imports in a few cases.

In South America and Mexico this was the period when import substitution came to play an increasingly important role as the republics built up their industrial base behind high tariff walls. This did not happen to anything like the same extent in the Caribbean, but there was some import substitution in agriculture – especially in the Second World War – and a few cases of import substitution in manufacturing on the larger islands (see Chapter 10.1).

The first section of the chapter looks at the commodity structure of exports. The **absolute** volume of sugar exports expanded greatly over the whole period, but there were marked cycles in its evolution. The **relative** importance of sugar, however, rose and then fell – just as it had done in the nineteenth century. Over the whole period, when constant prices are used, about half of all domestic exports came from products other than sugar; it therefore is a mistake to assume that sugar was completely dominant. Commodities remained the most important component of domestic exports, and minerals started to occupy a much more significant role than in the nineteenth century. Manufactured exports (other than those made from sugarcane and tobacco leaf) were also important by the end of the period, but they were heavily concentrated in Puerto Rico.

Section 2 looks at the country structure of domestic exports. Cuba at first increased its relative weight, reaching a peak in the 1920s. This was reversed in the 1930s before Cuba again increased its share during and immediately after the Second World War. There was then a precipitate decline in the Cuban

share in the 1950s. This repeated to some extent the rise and fall of the Cuban economy in the nineteenth century, but Cuba was always the largest (at least as measured by exports). The US dependencies rapidly increased their relative importance, with the increase concentrated in Puerto Rico. The share of the British dependencies fluctuated greatly, and the share of the French declined. The Dutch dependencies steadily gained in importance as a result primarily of the oil refineries on Aruba and Curaçao.

The third section considers the net barter and income terms of trade. Export prices rose steadily after 1900 before accelerating in the First World War and reaching an extraordinary peak in 1920. There was then a descent that reached its floor in 1932. Import prices followed a similar trend until the end of the Second World War, when export prices rose much faster than import prices. Generally, the net barter terms of trade (NBTT) were not unfavourable to the Caribbean for most of this period in contrast to what happened in Latin America. Furthermore, because of the continued emphasis on exports, the income terms of trade improved except in the interwar period.

The final section of the chapter examines the evolution of foreign trade over the whole period, stripping out population change. Exports and imports per head are a reasonable proxy for living standards in the Caribbean in this period, and their rate of change is the best indicator available for the rate of growth of the economy. The contrast between the period before and after the Second World War was very striking for the British and French dependencies, but for Cuba it was the opposite: a phase of rapid growth that ended in the 1920s, followed by long periods of stagnation and relative decline.

9.1. THE COMMODITY STRUCTURE OF EXPORTS

In the period considered here (1900–60), twenty-one commodities provided between 90 and 95 per cent of domestic exports in most years.[1] The importance of these commodities only dropped below 90 per cent in the 1950s as a result primarily of the rise of modern manufacturing in a small number of countries, but the share was still above 80 per cent in 1960.[2] Furthermore, the **ten** leading commodities provided 80 per cent of all domestic exports before the 1950s, and thus – as in the nineteenth century – the main links with the international economy were provided by a small number of products.[3]

Many of these commodities had been exported in the nineteenth century. These included sugar, molasses, rum, tobacco leaf, cigars, cacao, coffee, cotton,

---

[1] See Table C.13. I have treated exports of textiles & clothing as a single commodity.

[2] At constant prices the contribution of individual commodities was at times very different from the contribution at current prices, but for the twenty-one commodities combined it makes little difference.

[3] In addition, there were re-exports. These were always important in a few cases (e.g. Bahamas) and occasionally became of significance for the whole region (as happened in the early years of US Prohibition).

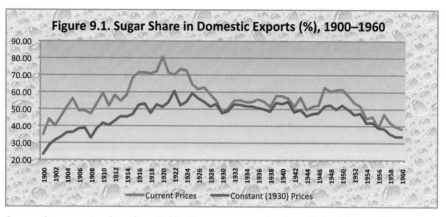

Figure 9.1. Sugar Share in Domestic Exports (%), 1900–1960

Source: Current price share from Table C.13; constant price share derived from Tables C.5 and
C.9.

logwood, mahogany, rubber, spices,[4] bananas, rice, minerals and gold. However, new ones would soon emerge, such as sisal, citrus, petroleum products and
textiles, while bauxite and diamonds would be added to the list of minerals.[5]
All twenty-one products would still be exported in 1960, but the rubber boom
ended with the First World War and the diamond one in the 1920s. Logwood
ceased to be of much importance in the 1930s,[6] gold in the 1940s and cotton
in the 1950s.[7]

Sugar was the most important export throughout the period,[8] but its share
depended on whether current or constant prices are used (see Figure 9.1). At
current prices, the sugar share started at 35 per cent. The share rose steadily
after 1900, driven forward at first by an increase in volume[9] and subsequently
by increases in prices because of the impact of the First World War. Indeed,

---

[4] Loosely defined to include food additives, such as annatto and arrowroot, and cinnamon, nutmeg
    and vanilla.
[5] A small amount of sisal (hemp) had been exported in the nineteenth century from the Bahamas,
    and citrus products had been exported from Dominica and Montserrat. Diamond exports had
    also started in Guyana before the end of the nineteenth century.
[6] Synthetic dyes had been available since the late nineteenth century, but it was the Great
    Depression that undermined the demand for the more expensive natural dye made from log-
    wood.
[7] The cotton industry, based on the sea-island variety, had been reestablished in a number of
    British dependencies in 1903. See Morris (1911), p. 10. It was always expensive but enjoyed
    a brief boom as an alternative to silk to make barrage balloons in the First World War and
    parachutes in the Second World War.
[8] I have included refined with raw sugar here. In practice, refined sugar was only significant as an
    export from Cuba (it was always much less important than raw sugar). Table C.5 separates the
    two products in the Cuban case.
[9] This was mainly from US investments in the sugar industry in Cuba, the Dominican Republic
    and Puerto Rico.

the increase in the sugar price was so great that at one point (1920) sugar accounted for over 80 per cent of all domestic exports. This was the 'dance of the millions', when the sugar price lost all logic as a result of the end of wartime controls and a shortage of supply (particularly of beet sugar).[10] Yet by 1960 the share was down to what it had been in 1900.

At constant (1930) prices, the sugar share was nearly always lower than at current prices.[11] Indeed, sugar was less than one-quarter of domestic exports in 1900 even though it had risen to 40 per cent on the eve of the First World War as a result of US investments in Cuba, the Dominican Republic and Puerto Rico. It reached 60 per cent at its peak in the early 1920s (see Figure 9.1). From that point onwards, sugar's advance was stopped by domestic and international quotas and by tariff barriers, and the volume of sugar exported actually fell in the 1930s. The sugar share therefore declined (at both current and constant prices), but there was a brief resurgence at the end of the Second World War for much the same reasons as at the end of the First World War.[12]

The volume of sugar exports was 1.6 billion lbs in 1900.[13] By the First World War it had reached 7 billion lbs. It then doubled to 14 billion lbs by the mid-1920s, after which it started to fall. It was not until after the Second World War that it recovered the peak achieved in the 1920s. From then onwards the volume of exports rose steadily, reaching 19 billion lbs in 1960. Thus, the volume of sugar exports rose by a factor of 12 over the six decades from 1900 to 1960, but most of this increase was concentrated in the first two decades. From then onwards, the expansion of the industry was curtailed by international trade restrictions.

Under these circumstances it would be surprising if the supply of sugar exports was strongly correlated with the international price. A simple regression of the volume of exports on the unit value of sugar over the whole period does show a positive relationship, but it is barely significant.[14] Indeed, the sugar 'price' becomes increasingly difficult to identify as a result of the segmentation of the sugar market caused by quotas and preferential tariffs.[15]

This is clear from statistical analysis of the sugar price in the different subregions (see Table 9.1).[16] The unit value of exports in Hispaniola (mainly the Dominican Republic) came closest to the free market price because most of the sugar sold did not benefit from preferences. It was highly correlated

---

[10] On the 'dance of the millions' in the Caribbean, especially in Cuba, see Rathbone (2010).

[11] The reason is that the unit value of Caribbean sugar was very low in 1930 for most countries (for other commodities the low point in the price cycle would come later).

[12] The sugar boom was also sustained by the start of the Korean War in 1950.

[13] The volume of sugar exports is obtained from the country data in Table C.5.

[14] The price of sugar is proxied by the unit value of exports (the current value in dollars divided by the volume). The coefficient on prices is not significant, even at the 5% level, and the regression sum of squares is a mere 16%.

[15] In addition, all sugars are aggregated in the sugar 'price' – not just raw and refined, but also muscovado and crystal. All of these in reality were sold at different prices.

[16] I have omitted the Dutch dependencies, because only Suriname exported sugar, and in some years these were zero.

TABLE 9.1. *Correlation Coefficients for Sugar Export Prices, 1900–1960*

	Hispaniola	Cuba	Dependencies:		
			British	French	US
Hispaniola	1				
Cuba	0.957	1			
British Dependencies	0.881	0.899	1		
French Dependencies	0.596	0.697	0.696	1	
US Dependencies	0.873	0.887	0.924	0.668	1

Source: Sugar price derived from Table C.5 by dividing sugar values by volumes for each subregion.

with Cuba, which always had to sell at least part of its sugar outside the US preferential tariff and quota. The correlation was weaker with the British and US dependencies, where imperial preference drove a wedge between the unit value of exports and the world price. Finally, there was only a modest correlation with the sugar price in the French dependencies, because the French market frequently offered a much higher price than could be obtained by anyone else.

The premium received by the French dependencies was especially important after *départementalisation* in 1946, when Martinique and Guadeloupe came completely inside the French tariff wall.[17] In the first decade of the century, however, it was the US dependencies that received the best price for their sugar – their exports entered the US duty-free and were then sold in competition with full-duty sugar. The premium received by US dependencies was always important, and in the 1930s, when US quotas separated domestic from international prices so sharply, it gave Puerto Rico and the Virgin Islands a unit value three times higher than that received by the Dominican Republic and 50 per cent higher than the British dependencies.

The sugar industry clearly thrived on high prices, as the boom at the end of the First World War had shown. Yet it could also survive on low prices for many reasons. First, heavy investments in mechanisation and new technology made it very difficult to respond to falling prices by switching to other crops. Indeed, time and again – especially after 1920 – the sugar industry's response to lower prices was to export a greater volume. Second, heavy investment meant that the variable cost of producing sugar was small in relation to the total cost, so sugar owners were only sure to curtail production when the variable cost was lower than the world price. Third, tariff preferences and quotas ensured that at least some sugar could always be sold at unit values in excess of the world price. Weaning the Caribbean off sugar would prove to be a long and painful affair.

At constant prices the sugar share of domestic exports averaged around 50 per cent (see Figure 9.1). The other 50 per cent was accounted for by twenty

[17] French Guiana did not export sugar in this period.

products. This is too long a list to summarise easily, so we can ignore those whose share of exports was always small.[18] We can then aggregate some of the others and group them into two categories: those that declined in importance and those that increased their share. The first group consisted of (a) molasses and rum, (b) tobacco leaf and cigars, (c) cacao and coffee, and (d) bananas. The second group consisted of (a) petroleum products, (b) non-oil minerals, and (c) textiles and clothing. Let us consider the 'losers' first.

Molasses is generally considered a by-product of sugar. Although it is true that the milling of sugarcane produces molasses, the volume of molasses produced depended on the machinery used. The quality of molasses also determines its end use, because the better grades tended to be used to make rum and the poorer ones were used for cattle feed or industrial alcohol. The foreign market conditions were also very different to those faced by sugar. As a result, the correlation between molasses and sugar exports was not particularly high (0.48 for the volume and 0.4 for the price).[19]

Rum can be made from molasses ('industrial' rum) or directly from sugarcane ('agricultural' rum). As a result, some cane was grown to be made into rum rather than into sugar. This was especially important in the French dependencies, where *rhum agricole* is considered superior to the sort made from molasses.[20] Like refined sugar, rum from the Caribbean suffered from discriminatory tariffs and quotas in the core (these were more severe than those faced by raw sugar). Not surprisingly, the correlation with sugar was low (0.29 for volume and 0.3 for price). There was a brief boom in rum exports during the First World War, the early years of US Prohibition and the Second World War, but the share of exports had fallen sharply by 1960 compared with 1900.

The loss of market share by tobacco products was very marked (see Figure 9.2). In 1900, tobacco leaf had contributed 12.5 per cent and cigars 16.1 per cent to the value of domestic exports at constant prices. In combined terms this was nearly 30 per cent. Yet by 1960 the share of tobacco leaf was 3.6 per cent, and the cigar share was less than 1 per cent. The volume of tobacco leaf exports did at least increase modestly over the six decades. By contrast, the volume of cigar exports actually declined. This was entirely because of the fall in Cuban exports, because the volume of cigar exports from Jamaica and Puerto Rico (the other main exporters) increased.

The main difficulty faced by the Caribbean – yet again – was the tariff and quota system applied by the core. Tariffs were applied to tobacco leaf by most countries in order to protect domestic output. These tariffs, however, were low in comparison to those that applied to manufactured tobacco. Under the revised Reciprocity Act, the United States in 1934 gave Cuba a quota for its

---

[18] Cotton, sisal, rice, logwood, mahogany, rubber, citrus and spices. In the aggregate the share of these eight commodities was around 10%.

[19] Molasses normally accounted for less than 3% of domestic exports. See Table C.13.

[20] So much so that today rum from the French Antilles is protected by the highly valued label Appellation d'Origine Contrôlée (AdOC).

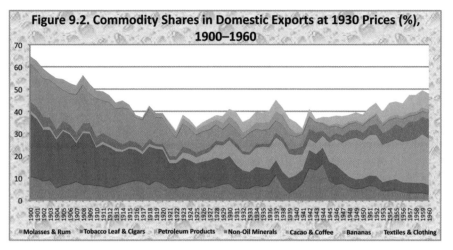

Figure 9.2. Commodity Shares in Domestic Exports at 1930 Prices (%), 1900–1960

Source: Derived from Table C.5.

tobacco leaf, but nothing for other tobacco products.[21] This accelerated the transfer of the Cuban cigar and cigarette industry to other countries.[22] This time, unlike in the nineteenth century, it was not just to the United States, because Puerto Rico was now inside the US tariff wall and Jamaica enjoyed imperial preference.[23]

The other three commodities whose share of domestic exports fell (bananas, cacao and coffee) all faced similar problems. Smallholders were important in these three cases (even bananas), and initially size was not a big disadvantage. Exports competed successfully in the duty-free US market with the same products from other parts of the world. However, smallholders found it increasingly difficult to compete with bananas and coffee from Central and South America and cacao from West Africa. Core preferential tariffs helped the British and French dependencies to increase exports, but the all important US market remained duty-free throughout the period.

The commodity group whose share of domestic exports increased most was petroleum products.[24] Only two countries participated (Trinidad & Tobago and the Dutch Antilles), but the increase was spectacular (see Figure 9.2).[25] The

---

[21] See Chapter 8.2.
[22] See Stubbs (1985), pp. 43–51.
[23] The transfer of part of the Cuban industry to the Dominican Republic, Honduras and Nicaragua would not take place until after the Cuban Revolution.
[24] Including asphalt from Trinidad & Tobago.
[25] The increase would be even more spectacular if the refined oil from the Dutch Antilles was valued gross. However, for reasons explained in the Notes on C. Tables, I have valued these exports net of imports of oil for refining. Exports therefore measure the margin on oil refining in those cases where the crude oil was imported.

United States did apply tariffs to many petroleum products from 1930 onwards, but these did not eliminate the advantages of geographical proximity, and the rest of the core was in any case able to take up the slack. Shipping constraints pushed down the share in the Second World War, but it recovered quickly and represented over 20 per cent by 1960.

Non-oil minerals in 1900 consisted primarily of diamonds, gold and iron ore. The precious metals soon declined in importance, but their place was taken by various other products of the mining industry. These included nickel and chrome, but the most important were bauxite and alumina (the semirefined bauxite product from which aluminium is made). By 1960 the contribution of non-oil minerals (at constant prices) to domestic exports was nearly 10 per cent, and thus altogether minerals (including petroleum products) made up 30 per cent. This was similar to the contribution from sugar (see Figure 9.1) and gave a good indication of the changes under way in the Caribbean by the end of the 1950s.

The final product to be considered here is the export of textiles and clothing, all of which came from Puerto Rico. Even in 1900, a small garment industry existed on the island, and exports went to the United States. The advantages of being inside the tariff wall were at first not enough to stimulate the industry, and exports disappeared in the First World War. However, the industry recovered afterwards and expanded rapidly in the 1920s. When the island became eligible in the 1930s for assistance from various US federal agencies, exports started to increase.[26] A further boost came in the Second World War, when there was a big increase in the federal taxes returned to Puerto Rico.[27] After the war, the Puerto Rican government exempted some new investments from local corporate tax, and industrial exports rose rapidly.[28]

We have noted on frequent occasions the influence of tariffs and quotas on Caribbean exports. Yet nothing has so far been said about the impact of natural disasters, of which the most important to affect the region have been hurricanes, earthquakes and volcanic eruptions.[29] No one who lives in the region or who has visited it can fail to be aware of these events, which are also referred to by almost all writers on the Caribbean. Indeed, one often sees references to the damaging impact of various natural disasters in histories of individual countries.

What was the impact of these disasters on the volume of domestic exports? This is difficult to answer because commodity exports fluctuate for many

---

[26] See Hibben and Picó (1948), pp. 13–27.

[27] See Chapter 10.2.

[28] By 1960, textiles & clothing from Puerto Rico accounted for 7.5% of all Caribbean domestic exports (see Table C.13). Yet this was only half the story, because by then other manufactured exports from the island – including pharmaceutical products and electronic equipment – were just as important.

[29] There have also been tropical storms and droughts.

reasons – not just natural disasters. However, it is worth exploring this question in more depth because of its importance. The appendix to this chapter therefore lists some of the principal natural disasters between 1900 and 1960,[30] the month in which they took place and the change in the volume of domestic exports in the same or subsequent year.[31]

There are forty natural disasters listed, beginning with the volcanic eruptions in Martinique and St Vincent.[32] In three out of four cases, domestic exports fell. In some cases, such as the volcanic eruptions in 1902, we can be fairly certain that the fall in domestic exports was in large part because of the natural disaster. On the other hand, the terrible earthquake in Jamaica in 1907 that destroyed Kingston was followed by only a small decline in domestic exports that might have happened anyway, and domestic exports in Haiti actually rose sharply after the 1909 hurricane.

Hurricanes are assumed to have a very damaging effect, and this seems to be borne out by some of the natural disasters listed here, such as in Belize in 1931 or in Puerto Rico in 1928. However, it depends on the crop. The hurricane season (June to November) occurs after the sugar harvest has ended, and new sugarcane can be grown in three months. Coffee and cacao are normally grown under shade at altitude, where hurricanes tend to do less damage. Bananas are more vulnerable, but new plantings do not take long to reach maturity. The impact of natural disasters on domestic exports therefore tends to be short-term with little long-term effect. This is not much consolation for those who have lost their homes or businesses, yet alone their lives, but it does mean we can separate to some extent the social from the economic impact of natural disasters.

9.2. COUNTRY SHARES IN DOMESTIC EXPORTS

The change in the relative importance of different commodities was bound to have an impact on country shares in domestic exports. We would expect countries specialised in commodities whose share was in decline to perform poorly in comparison with countries specialised in commodities whose share was increasing. This effect will be stronger the more specialised countries are in particular commodities.

Country specialisation in commodities is often expressed in terms of the importance of the first and second product in domestic exports in a single year.[33] When looking at a longer period (1900–60), we can proceed in the same way by summing the values over all years (see Table 9.2). In addition,

---

[30] The hurricanes are those that killed at least twenty-five people. I have excluded those in the war years, because of the peculiar conditions faced by exports at that time.

[31] If the natural disaster was early in the year, I have compared exports with the previous year. If it was later, I have looked at the value of exports in the following year and compared them with the current year.

[32] This is by no means a complete list.

[33] For Latin America in 1913, e.g., see Bulmer-Thomas (2003), p. 58.

TABLE 9.2. *Commodity Concentration by Country, 1900–1960*

Country	First Product	% of Exports	Second Product	% of Exports	Herfindahl Index
Dutch Antilles	Refined Oil	86.9	Straw Hats (a)	2.0	0.75
St Kitts & Nevis	Sugar	83.7	Cotton	9.0	0.71
Antigua	Sugar	83.9	Cotton	8.1	0.71
Turks & Caicos	Salt	73.3	Conches	6.5	0.54
French Guiana	Gold	72.0	Rum	4.0	0.52
Montserrat	Cotton	70.9	Lime Juice	7.9	0.51
Cuba	Sugar	76.2	Tobacco Leaf	7.1	0.49
Trinidad & Tobago	Petroleum Products	67.7	Sugar	13.2	0.49
Barbados	Sugar	64.8	Molasses	25.2	0.48
Haiti	Coffee	63.1	Sisal	10.8	0.42
Grenada	Cacao	54.9	Nutmeg & Mace	34.5	0.38
Suriname	Bauxite	59.7	Sugar	5.8	0.37
Guadeloupe	Sugar	50.2	Bananas	21.5	0.33
Guyana	Sugar	52.6	Bauxite	18.2	0.32
DR (b)	Sugar	51.3	Cacao	14.2	0.30
Martinique	Sugar	38.9	Rum	34.6	0.30
BVI (c)	Live Cattle	50.9	Sugar	0.9	0.26
St Lucia	Sugar	43.7	Bananas	16.0	0.25
Puerto Rico	Sugar	45.6	Textiles & Clothing	16.8	0.24
Belize	Mahogany	41.8	Chicle	15.6	0.22
St Vincent	Arrowroot	39.6	Cotton	16.5	0.21
Cayman Islands	Live Turtles	34.8	Turtle Shells	16.7	0.15
Jamaica	Sugar	25.7	Bananas	23.5	0.14
Dominica	Bananas	28.1	Lime Juice	22.9	0.13
USVI	Sugar	33.4	Rum	11.6	0.13
Bahamas	Sponge	26.0	Lumber	12.5	0.12

Note: (a) This is an estimate because the second product in Table C.5 is all non-oil commodities; (b) Dominican Republic; (c) British Virgin Islands.
Source: Derived from Table C.5.

we can estimate a commodity concentration ratio for each country by using the Herfindahl index.[34] This is also shown in Table 9.2. Sugar was the leading commodity for twelve out of the twenty-six countries. Eleven other countries had as their leading export a commodity whose share of Caribbean domestic

[34] The Herfindahl index is normally used to measure market concentration at the firm level. However, it can easily be adapted to measure commodity concentration. The index has a maximum value of unity, because this is the value when domestic exports are represented by only one commodity.

exports was in decline.[35] Only three countries (Dutch Antilles, Suriname and Trinidad & Tobago) had as their leading export a commodity whose share was increasing.[36]

The countries in Table 9.2 are ranked in terms of the Herfindahl index. We would expect smaller countries to be more specialised,[37] and the first six countries fit this description. However, the seventh country is Cuba, the largest in the Caribbean, but with a very high concentration ratio because of its dependence on sugar (raw and refined). Larger countries should theoretically have more diversified exports, but that was only true of Jamaica in the Caribbean. Paradoxically, the countries with the lowest concentration ratios were in many cases quite small.[38]

The dependence of countries in the Caribbean on one or two products was very high. Comparisons with other regions are misleading, because these nearly always refer to a single year.[39] Over a sixty-year period we would expect sufficient commodity diversification to lower the concentration ratio. Despite this, however, many countries still exhibited a very high dependence on commodities whose long-term future was problematic. The best known example is sugar, but many others fit this description.

The nineteenth century had ended with Cuba still responsible for the largest share of domestic exports, but it had fallen from its peak in 1860–80 (see Chapter 5). It was followed – at some distance – by Guyana, Trinidad, Jamaica, Puerto Rico, Haiti and the Dominican Republic. Indeed, Cuba's share of domestic exports (41 per cent in 1900 at current prices), despite the damage to crops in the war years, was much bigger than the share of all the British dependencies combined.

Cuban exports rose rapidly after 1900 on the back of the sugar boom. Although Cuba was responsible for just over 40 per cent of the volume of sugar exported from the Caribbean at the beginning of the century, it had increased its share to nearly 80 per cent by the 1920s. In that decade, four out of every five tons of sugar shipped from the Caribbean came from Cuba – an astonishing level of specialisation. This could not be sustained in view of the quotas and other restrictions to which Cuban sugar was subject after 1930.

---

[35] The countries were Turks & Caicos (salt), French Guiana (gold), Montserrat (cotton), Haiti (coffee), Grenada (cacao), British Virgin Islands (live cattle), Belize (mahogany), St Vincent (arrowroot), Cayman Islands (live turtles), Dominica (bananas) and the Bahamas (sponges).

[36] The products were refined oil, bauxite and petroleum products, respectively.

[37] The general rule is that smaller countries are more specialised than larger ones in just the same way that a region or province tends to be more specialised than the country in which it is located.

[38] One should not, however, read too much into this. The Bahamas, for example, was constantly seeking new exports as old ones failed rather than producing all at the same time. (Between 1900 and 1960 the Bahamas produced many commodities, but it did not export all of them at the same time.)

[39] Commodity concentration in the countries of the Caribbean in a single year was generally higher than for the period as a whole, because some products stopped being exported and new products were added to the list. This was especially true after 1945.

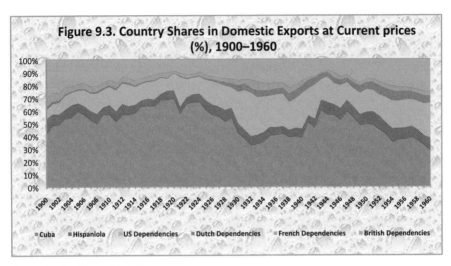

Figure 9.3. Country Shares in Domestic Exports at Current prices (%), 1900–1960

Source: Derived from Table C.6.

However, Cuba was still responsible for 60 to 70 per cent of all sugar exported from the Caribbean in the 1950s.

The Cuban share of Caribbean domestic exports peaked at nearly 70 per cent between 1918 and 1920 (see Figure 9.3). This was partly because of exceptionally high sugar prices, but not entirely because high prices benefitted many other countries. It was also due to increases in volume, because Cuba took advantage of the last years before quantitative restrictions would be applied (first by Cuba and later by others). From then onwards, the Cuban share of Caribbean domestic exports drifted downwards, with a brief reversal of the trend in the period after the Second World War, when sugar prices were high. By the end of the 1950s, the Cuban share was down to 30 per cent – back to what it had been in the 1830s.

Hispaniola experienced only a small decline in its share between 1900 and 1960, but it fell by half in the intervening period before recovering after the Second World War (see Figure 9.3). This apparent stability, however, concealed a big change in the relative importance of Haiti and the Dominican Republic. The domestic exports of the two countries were broadly similar in value until the US occupation of both parts of the island.[40] The Dominican Republic improved its relative performance during the interwar period, but the gap in terms of the value of domestic exports was not yet enormous. It was during the Second World War and subsequently that Haiti was totally eclipsed by its neighbour, with the Dominican Republic being responsible for nearly 85 per cent of the island's exports by 1960.

---

[40] Haiti, however, had a larger population than the Dominican Republic at this time, so exports per head were lower.

The British dependencies, like Hispaniola, saw their share of domestic exports fall after 1900 before increasing again to close the period in 1960 with a slightly smaller share than at the beginning of the century (see Figure 9.3). With sixteen countries involved and with different commodity specialisations, it was inevitable that the British dependencies' share would disguise big variations. As we shall see, this is exactly what happened.

One country (Trinidad & Tobago) saw a huge increase in its relative importance. This rose from one-quarter of British colonial exports in 1900 to one-half in 1960, with the increase concentrated in the period after the Second World War, when exports of petroleum products soared. So great was this change that almost all other British dependencies experienced a **decline** in their share of domestic exports from the British Caribbean.[41] Those countries specialised in sugar – such as Antigua, Barbados, Guyana and St Kitts – all lost out, but so did those specialised in certain other commodities, such as Belize (mahogany), Grenada (cacao) and Dominica (bananas).

Apart from Trinidad & Tobago, only Jamaica experienced an increase in its share of British Caribbean exports – and it was small. The leading exports from Jamaica had been sugar and bananas (see Table 9.2), but Jamaica started to export bauxite and later alumina in the 1950s. Before that Jamaica had not been able to maintain its share of the exports of the British dependencies – yet alone of the Caribbean as a whole. Bauxite, however, was an industry controlled by foreign investors with little employment generation, and thus the impact of the bauxite boom was not as great as many had anticipated.[42]

The French dependencies suffered a sharp decline in their share of Caribbean domestic exports (see Figure 9.3). It fell by more than half from 1900 to 1960. This was partly because of the concentration of the islands (Guadeloupe and Martinique) in sugar, bananas and rum at a time when exports were constrained by French import quotas. A large part of the decline, however, was because of the end of the gold boom in mainland French Guiana.[43] The gold rush led to a neglect of agriculture, and thus the colony had little to fall back on when gold exports declined in the 1920s. Attempts were made to revive gold and to diversify exports, but by 1960 French Guiana was responsible for less than 2 per cent of the domestic exports of the French territories.

The Dutch dependencies (Netherlands Antilles and Suriname) started the century with only a 2 per cent share of Caribbean domestic exports (see Figure 9.3). This fell steadily until it reached a mere 0.4 per cent two decades later. Although Suriname exported sugar, its large estates were uncompetitive, and the Caribbean sugar boom of those years left no mark. The Dutch Antilles experimented with a wide variety of exports, including divi-divi pods, straw

---

[41] These countries also experienced a decline in their share of Caribbean exports as a whole, because the British dependencies' share was smaller in 1960 than 1900.

[42] On the Jamaican bauxite industry, see Girvan (1967).

[43] In 1904 French Guiana, wholly dependent on gold, had been responsible for nearly 30% of all exports from the French Caribbean colonies.

hats, sandals and phosphates, but without much success. The Dutch colonial authorities despaired of their West Indian possessions and focused instead on the East Indies.[44]

In 1915 an Anglo-Dutch oil company (Royal Dutch Shell) decided to make Curaçao the base for processing crude oil from Venezuela.[45] This decision has been widely attributed to concern over political instability if the refinery were built in the South American republic. Yet President Gómez had already been in power over a decade in Venezuela, and the oil company had come very close to locating the refinery there.[46] It seems just as probable that the decision was because of the shallowness of Lake Maracaibo, making it impossible for big ships to enter from the sea, and the desire of Royal Dutch Shell to source crude oil from other countries in addition to Venezuela.[47]

In any event, the opening of a giant refinery on Curaçao and two others built on Aruba transformed the fortunes of the Dutch Antilles. By 1926 the value of their exports had overtaken those from Suriname, and the share of the Dutch dependencies in Caribbean exports would soar, peaking at nearly 8 per cent in the mid-1950s. Much of this was from the Dutch Antilles, but Suriname also experienced an increase in the relative importance of its exports after the discovery of bauxite. The impact of this new product was especially significant during and after the Second World War.

The final subregion to be considered here is the US dependencies (Puerto Rico and the Virgin Islands). Their share of Caribbean domestic exports had jumped to nearly 30 per cent by 1960 (see Figure 9.3). Very little of this was from the Virgin Islands, where sugar exports stagnated despite favourable treatment by the United States.[48] The Virgin Islands even had their own external tariff, much lower than that which applied to Puerto Rico, and were able to keep the revenue.[49] By the end of the Second World War it was clear that the Virgin Islands' comparative advantage would be found in the export of services, but an assembly industry had also taken root after the Second World War, and an oil refinery would be built there in the 1960s.[50]

The increase in share was in fact from Puerto Rico and began with the sugar boom after the island came inside the US tariff wall in 1901. As in Cuba, sugar displaced other exports until the application of quotas in the 1930s brought the boom to an end. Unlike Cuba, however, Puerto Rico was able

---

[44] See Angelino (1931), vol. 2.

[45] See van Soest (1978), p. 225.

[46] See van Soest (1978), p. 226.

[47] Indeed, this is exactly what happened, with crude being imported from Colombia and Mexico as well as Venezuela.

[48] The problem was not tariffs, which did not affect exports to the US, but lack of rainfall. This had always limited sugar production on the Virgin Islands.

[49] The Virgin Islands tariff, of course, applied only to non-US imports; the islands had been allowed to keep their own tariff system in view of the importance of the entrepôt trade.

[50] The Virgin Islands developed a niche market in watch assembly for re-export to the US. See Lewis (1972). On assembly operations more generally, see Hibben and Picó (1948).

to use tax incentives to construct a manufacturing sector based on exports to the mainland. This new activity, the first of its kind in the Caribbean, was highly artificial because the island's ability to compete depended on the continuation of favourable fiscal treatment by federal and local tax authorities. It did, however, shift Puerto Rico permanently away from dependence on primary product exports.

9.3. THE TERMS OF TRADE

Before 1960 the terms of trade loomed large in the life of the Caribbean. As producers of commodities, the region had to live with the uncertainty of volatile prices for the main exports. Where price falls were offset by falls in import prices or by increases in the volume of exports, no great damage was done to the capacity to import (the most crucial element in the standard of living, because so many articles of consumption had to be purchased abroad). If, however, price falls occurred at the same time as rising import prices and/or falling export volumes, the impact could be devastating.

Yet movements in the terms of trade could be favourable. This was often the case in the nineteenth century[51] because import prices – heavily influenced by what happened to the price of textiles – declined in many decades and the volume of exports increased after the mid-century in most countries (and in some cases – such as Cuba – even before). Even the devastating decline in the sugar price after 1883–4 did not necessarily mean a deterioration in the terms of trade. It depended on what happened to the other variables.

The period here (1900–60) is generally considered to be much less benign than the nineteenth century for commodity exporters such as those in the Caribbean. In Latin America, for example, it became an article of faith that the NBTT was subject to secular decline. According to the Prebisch-Singer hypothesis,[52] this was due to several factors. First, commodities (the basis of exports) were subject to income elasticities of less than unity, and thus sales would not grow in line with core incomes unless their relative price fell. Second, manufactured goods (the basis of imports) were income-elastic in the periphery, therefore demand would grow faster than incomes unless their relative price increased. Third, commodity exports were sold in competitive markets in which productivity gains were passed on to consumers in the form of lower prices. Finally, manufacturing in the core was subject to imperfect competition, and strong trade unions ensured that productivity gains were captured by domestic factors of production.[53]

[51] See Chapter 5 and Table A.31.
[52] Raúl Prebisch working in Santiago at the Economic Commission for Latin America and Hans Singer working at the UN in New York developed the hypothesis independently, which is why it carries both their names. See Dosman (2008).
[53] There are many good explanations of the Prebisch-Singer hypothesis. See, e.g., Spraos (1980).

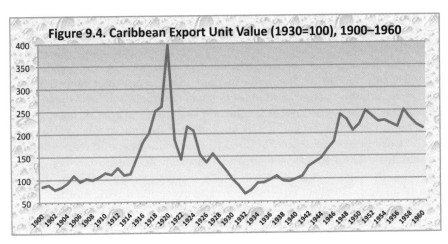

Figure 9.4. Caribbean Export Unit Value (1930=100), 1900–1960

Source: Table C.10.

The empirical evidence for a secular decline in the NBTT even in the case of Latin America has never been overwhelming. Some commodity prices have risen faster than those of manufactures. Oil is a case in point – at least since 1973. The international market for manufactured goods has become increasingly competitive as a result of globalisation and the entry of China, in particular, into world trade. Some commodity exports (e.g. meat) have been subject to high income elasticities of demand in the core. Even if we limit ourselves to the period from 1900 to 1960, we find that five out of seven mainland Latin American countries for which data are available experienced an improvement in the NBTT, and only two suffered a decline.[54]

What happened in the Caribbean is therefore bound to be largely an empirical question that cannot be settled *ex ante* on the basis of theory. It is to this we now turn, starting with export unit values for the region as a whole (see Figure 9.4).[55] The observed trend was not, of course, the same for all subregions (yet alone all countries), but the pattern was in fact quite similar.[56] There was a modest improvement in export prices between 1900 and the beginning of the First World War. There then followed a spectacular increase, which reached its peak in 1920 as a result above all of the rise in the sugar price.[57] Export prices tumbled when the bubble burst, but they did not initially fall to their prewar level.

54 The five countries with an improvement were Argentina, Brazil, Colombia, Mexico and Venezuela. The two with a deterioration were Chile and Peru (derived from export and import unit values for each country in MOxLAD).
55 The methodology for calculating export unit values is given in the Notes on C. Tables.
56 For country and subregional details on export unit values, see Table C.10.
57 This was at a time when sugar accounted for 60–70% of exports (see section 1), so the sugar price was bound to have a major impact on export unit values.

Caribbean export prices started to weaken in 1927 – long before the New York stock market crash in October 1929 – and fell to their lowest level in 1932. The drop from peak to trough was nearly 60 per cent.[58] There was then a modest recovery in prices during the remainder of the decade. The Second World War brought a major increase in the export unit value that was sustained until the 1950s as a result of postwar shortages and the Korean War. The increase in prices was not as spectacular as during and after the First World War, but it lasted longer, and it was not followed by a sharp fall.

The Caribbean experience, captured in Figure 9.4, was different in several respects from Latin America. First, the improvement in export prices during and after the First World War was much greater in the Caribbean than in Latin America. This was largely due to the exceptional nature of the sugar price increase at a time when sugar accounted for such a large proportion of Caribbean exports. Second, the opposite was the case during and after the Second World War, because Latin American export prices improved more than those in the Caribbean. Third, the fall in export unit values after 1930 was much less severe than in Latin America, and prices recovered more quickly.

It is the last difference that reveals a great deal about the evolution of the Caribbean economy. Preferential tariffs have always played a role in the region, but they became much more important in the period considered here. This was because of the establishment of US colonies after 1898, the Cuba-US Reciprocity Act (1903), the Franco-Haitian commercial treaty in 1904, the German-Haitian Treaty of 1908, the return of imperial preference in the British Empire from 1919, the introduction of sugar import quotas by the United States in 1934 and the full incorporation of the French dependencies inside the tariff wall in 1946. As a result only the Dominican Republic was selling its exports at or close to world market prices.[59]

We may take advantage of this to calculate the Caribbean price premium of the leading export (sugar). Figure 9.5 shows the percentage difference between the sugar price for all the Caribbean and the Dominican Republic.[60] The average premium for the whole period is 16 per cent, which works out at an additional $45 million each year as a result of the higher sugar price available to the Caribbean from preferential tariffs and quotas. However, the price premium reached its maximum (over 50 per cent) in the 1930s, and this helps to explain the difference between Caribbean and Latin American performance during and after the Great Depression.

---

[58] The export unit value for the Caribbean (1930=100) was 156.1 in 1927 and 67.5 in 1932 (see Table C.10).

[59] The Dominican Republic was restricted by the US under the terms of the 1907 Dominican-US Convention from signing commercial treaties with third countries. When treaties were signed, therefore, as with France and Spain in the 1930s, they had only a very limited reach.

[60] The unit value of Dominican sugar exports is as close as we can get to the 'free market' price, because most of the crop was sold without the benefit of quotas or preferences. The Caribbean price has been adjusted to exclude the Dominican Republic itself.

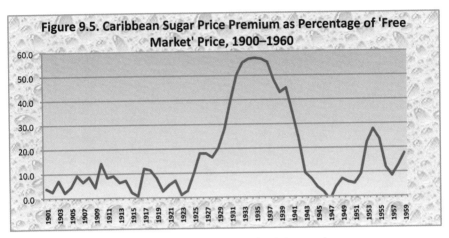

Figure 9.5. Caribbean Sugar Price Premium as Percentage of 'Free Market' Price, 1900–1960

Source: Derived from Table C.5 using a 3-year average (omitting 1920).

The price premium affected most commodities. Bananas, for example, were always free of import duty in the United States. However, if we compare the Latin American with the Caribbean price for bananas,[61] there is a premium for the latter that reached a peak in the years after the Second World War. The premium was due not only to the lower transport costs to the United States, but also to the imperial preference operated by Britain and France. And when France took Guadeloupe and Martinique completely inside the tariff wall in 1946, the prices these major exporters received were two to three times greater than those received by the Dominican Republic and four to five times greater than those paid to Haiti.[62]

If Caribbean export prices evolved differently from those in Latin America, the same could also be said about import prices. The reasons were twofold. First, Caribbean countries imported much of their food supply and could therefore expect to benefit to some extent from falling commodity prices (and suffer if they rose). This was very different from mainland Latin America, where countries were typically self-sufficient in, or net exporters of, foodstuffs. Second, textiles and clothing – whose prices tended to fall in relative and absolute terms because of strong productivity gains – remained a large item in the import bill of all Caribbean countries, but in Latin America it was the first candidate for ISI, and imports had dwindled to insignificance by the Second World War in many cases.

---

[61] I have taken the Latin American price from MOxLAD and rebased the index to 1930. I have calculated the Caribbean price by dividing the value of exports by the volume in Table C.5 before forming an index with 1930=100.

[62] Haiti sold its bananas to the US, so the Franco-Haitian commercial treaty was of no advantage.

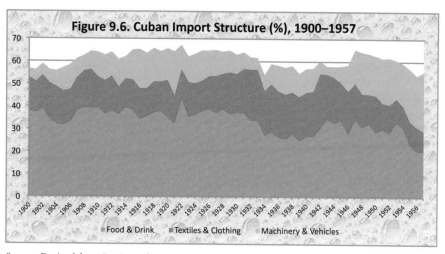

Source: Derived from Instituto de Historia de Cuba (1998).

All this can be illustrated very clearly by the import structure of Cuba (see Figure 9.6). Although the island was larger and more advanced economically than other Caribbean countries, it still depended heavily on imports of food and drink. A revision of the tariff in 1927 designed to encourage import substitution had some impact, but it was not until the 1950s that the share of food and drink dropped below 30 per cent. Textiles and clothing, on the other hand, fluctuated between 15 and 20 per cent until ISI in this sector became important after the Second World War. The third category of imports shown in Figure 9.6 is machinery and vehicles, whose share tended to rise and fall with the general state of the economy. Taken together these three categories accounted for 60 per cent of imports, with the balance consisting of miscellaneous manufactured goods or – in the early years of the century – live animals.[63]

Caribbean import unit values cannot be calculated directly for the whole period,[64] so it is necessary to use weighted averages of core export unit values with the weights varying according to the importance of the United States, the UK and 'mother' in the imports of each Caribbean country.[65] For the Caribbean as a whole, this shows a modest increase in prices before 1914 and a big increase during and after the First World War. However, the spike in prices was not as great as in the case of Caribbean exports. There then followed a fall in prices that was virtually continuous until 1932 – the worst year of the Great

[63] In the first years after the Second War of Independence, live animal imports were important because of the slaughter during hostilities.
[64] There are estimates for some years and some countries. For Jamaica, e.g., see Eisner (1961), pp. 259–60. The results are very similar to those in Table C.25.
[65] The import unit values are given in Table C.25, and the methodological issues are discussed in the Notes on C. Tables.

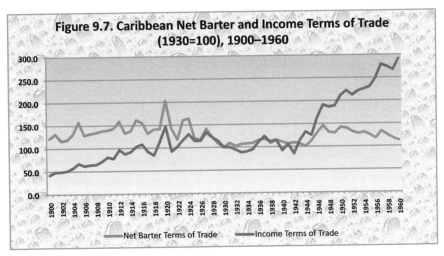

Figure 9.7. Caribbean Net Barter and Income Terms of Trade (1930=100), 1900–1960

Source: Tables C.26 and C.27.

Depression. Thus, Caribbean export **and** import prices were falling together for several years. Finally, there was an increase in prices from the start of the Second World War that marked the permanent arrival of inflation in the core.

We can now put together the export and import unit values for the Caribbean to derive the NBTT – see Figure 9.7. There was no significant change before or even during the First World War. However, as expected, there was a sharp and short-lived improvement at the end of hostilities, despite the increase in import prices. There was then a decline in the NBTT, but this reached a turning point in 1930 because – unlike in Latin America – import prices fell further than export prices in the subsequent years. The NBTT then stabilised and remained largely unchanged (even during the Second World War) until the big improvement in commodity prices at the end of hostilities and during the Korean War. A modest deterioration in the 1950s, as in Latin America, can then be observed, with the region finishing the period with the NBTT at roughly the same level as in the beginning.

The Income Terms of Trade (capacity to import) are also shown in Figure 9.7.[66] Not surprisingly, given the increase in the volume of exports over the period, the Income Terms of Trade (ITT) exhibit a marked improvement, rising sixfold between 1900 and 1960. Only during the interwar period and the early years of the Second World War was there no increase. From 1942 onwards, however, the ITT improved dramatically. The capacity to import increased even further than implied by the graph in Figure 9.7, because imports

---

[66] This is the NBTT adjusted for the change in the volume of exports. It is therefore the value of exports divided by the price of imports and measures the quantity of imports that the value of exports can theoretically purchase. That is why the income terms of trade are often described as measuring the capacity to import.

TABLE 9.3. *Changes in Income Terms of Trade (% per year), 1900–1960*

			Dependencies:				
	Hispaniola	Cuba	British	French	Dutch	US	Caribbean
1900/20	3.3	8.9	−0.1	0.3	−2.1	9.6	6.4
1920/40	−2.0	−5.0	0.1	2.5	11.1	1.6	−2.3
1940/60	7.6	4.2	8.8	4.2	5.6	5.7	5.9
1900/60	2.9	2.5	2.8	2.3	4.7	5.6	3.3

Source: Derived from Table C.27.

after the Second World War were able to outstrip exports for all sorts of reasons (see next section).

The NBTT and ITT in Figure 9.7 refer to the Caribbean as a whole – twenty-six countries during this period – so it is unlikely that all countries had the same experience. In order to understand the variations, I have grouped countries by their constitutional status[67] and estimated the annual percentage change in the ITT for three periods (1900–20; 1920–40; 1940–60) and for the period as a whole. The results are shown in Table 9.3.

Starting with the first period (1900–20), we can see that the US dependencies and Cuba were far and away the best performers. This is when US investment was moving into the former Spanish colonies as a result of their incorporation in whole or in part inside the US tariff wall.[68] The British, French and Dutch dependencies, on the other hand, performed extremely badly as a result both of being squeezed out of the US sugar market by Cuba and of the impact of the First World War on the volume of exports. Hispaniola, where both parts of the island had become US protectorates,[69] was in an intermediate position.

The second period (1920–40) was dismal for Cuba as a result of the constraints imposed on its export sector.[70] The European and US dependencies fared much better than Cuba, helped by preferential tariffs in the case of the British and French territories and the start of the assembly industry in Puerto Rico. The star performers, however, were the Dutch dependencies, as a result of the opening of the oil refineries in the Netherlands Antilles and bauxite exports from Suriname. Once again, Hispaniola – where both countries were under US customs receiverships for the whole time – was in an intermediate position, but its performance was much worse than in the first period.

[67] I have, however, separated Cuba from the other independent countries in view of its size and economic importance.

[68] By contrast, US investment in the Virgin Islands (a US colony only from 1917) was small.

[69] The Dominican Republic came under US customs control in 1905 before being occupied in 1916. Haiti was occupied in 1915, but from 1910 US interests controlled the banking sector.

[70] The biggest problem was the system of quotas applied to sugar first by Cuba, then by the US and finally by the ISA in 1937.

All countries experienced an improvement in their ITT in the third period (1940–60), but Cuba recorded one of the worst performances in relative terms. The other poor relative performance was by the French territories, but this mattered less because the ITT after *départementalisation* were no longer a good proxy for import capacity (see next section). For the first time since emancipation, the British dependencies were now the star performers as a result of government grants and loans, preferential tariffs and mining booms in Trinidad & Tobago and Jamaica. Other countries – Hispaniola, Dutch and US dependencies – were in an intermediate position.

9.4. EXPORTS AND IMPORTS PER HEAD

The capacity to import, as measured by the ITT, is a theoretical construct. It can differ from actual imports for all sorts of reasons. If foreign investors, for example, own the most profitable parts of the economy, then repatriated profits will absorb a large share of foreign exchange earnings, and imports of goods will be smaller than indicated by the ITT. Similarly, if the external debt is large, then interest and amortisation payments may prevent actual imports from growing as fast as the capacity to import implies.

We also need to take account of population change in evaluating import and export growth. As in other parts of the developing world, the decline in the death rate after 1900 was increasing the natural rate of growth of the population.[71] This was offset by outward migration in many Caribbean countries (see next chapter), but the net effect was an increase in the long-run average rate of increase of the population, from 1.5 per cent in the second half of the nineteenth century to nearly 2 per cent in the period considered here (see Figure 9.8). This average rate concealed big differences between the subregions that could be largely explained by net outward migration.[72]

Having established the rate of population increase, we can now calculate exports and imports per head. However, there are many different measures that can be used. Exports and imports can be at current or constant prices; they can refer to merchandise exports and imports; or they can refer to domestic exports and retained imports. All measures have their advantages and disadvantages. Here, however, I have chosen domestic exports (i.e. excluding re-exports) and retained imports – both at constant (1930) prices. This shows the volume of exports and imports per head without the distortions associated with price changes on the one hand and re-exports on the other.

The two series are shown in Figure 9.9. Both series first rise and then fall, returning to their level in 1900 by the middle of the Second World War. There

---

[71] The birth rate in the Caribbean was also falling, but the death rate was falling faster. See Tables C.2 and C.3.

[72] The US, British and French dependencies, with population increases lower than the regional average, experienced net outward migration. Cuba by contrast had net inward migration, but this was concentrated in the period 1900–30.

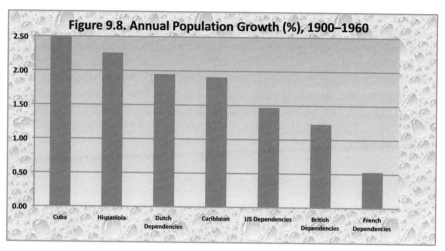

Source: Derived from Table C.1.

was a steady expansion in the first two decades, culminating in the 'dance of the millions' in 1920 when imports per head soared,[73] followed by a decline from the end of the 1920s. It was not until the end of the Second World War that the Caribbean experienced a major improvement in exports and imports per head in real terms. However, when it finally happened, it was spectacular.

There are two periods in Figure 9.9 when imports regularly exceeded exports per head. The first runs up to 1930 and is the result of favourable movements in the terms of trade (see Figure 9.7). Indeed, when exports and imports per head are calculated at current prices, we find that exports were normally higher than imports.[74] This is exactly what we would expect in economies where foreign investors owned a large share of the most profitable activities (e.g. Cuba and Puerto Rico) or where external debt-service payments constituted a large share of foreign exchange earnings (e.g. Haiti and the Dominican Republic). However, the improvement in the NBTT and ITT made it possible for the **volume** of imports to exceed the **volume** of exports per head in many years before the Great Depression.

The second period where imports were greater than exports per head was after the Second World War (see Figure 9.9). This time it makes no difference whether current or constant prices are used, because imports exceeded exports per head in both cases. This is the 'jaws effect', with the gap between the two series growing bigger and bigger and looking like the mouth of the eponymous

[73] Exports per head did not increase to the same extent, but that is because they are here measured at constant prices. It was export prices – not volumes – that soared in the 'dance of the millions'.
[74] This is not shown here, but it can be derived from Tables C.1, C.6 and C.20.

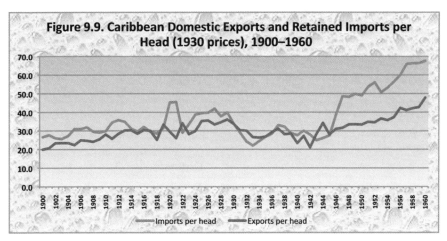

Figure 9.9. Caribbean Domestic Exports and Retained Imports per Head (1930 prices), 1900–1960

Source: Derived from Tables C.1, C.9 and C.21.

shark.[75] The 'jaws effect' was not, however, caused by the improvements in the terms of trade, but by three factors that have played a large part in the evolution of the Caribbean economies in the postwar period.

These three factors are foreign aid, remittances and service exports. All three increased the import capacity of Caribbean countries beyond what could be justified by the export of goods alone. The first refers to the grants and loans made available by foreign governments and international financial institutions to the countries of the Caribbean. The second refers to the money sent back to the Caribbean by those who had migrated outside the region.[76] The third is a reflection of the rise – above all – of the tourist industry. All three factors had been in play before the Second World War, but there was a quantum leap in their importance afterwards.

By the end of the 1950s (see Figure 9.9), commodity exports were only sufficient to purchase about two-thirds of imports (both at constant prices). Some of the smaller countries had already gone much further in this direction. In the Cayman Islands, for example, domestic exports per head in 1960 (at 1930 prices) were a lowly $7.6, but merchandise imports were $147. In the Bahamas the figures were $15.6 and $321 respectively. In French Guiana they were $20.2 and $143. For these countries, and several others, commodity exports were no longer a good guide to the health of the economy.[77]

For this reason, it is necessary to look at the evolution of imports as much as exports per head when examining the performance of the subregions. This

[75] I am grateful to Geoff Bertram for drawing the 'jaws effect' to my attention, based on his research on small-island economies in the Pacific. See Bertram (2004).

[76] Those who migrated within the Caribbean also sent back remittances. This would increase imports per head in the receiving country, but would reduce it in the sending country, so the net effect would be small or zero.

[77] These figures can be derived from Tables C.1, C.9 and C.19.

TABLE 9.4. *Change in Domestic Exports and Retained Imports per Head at 1930 prices (% per year), 1900–1960*

| Exports | Hispaniola | Cuba | Dependencies: | | | | Caribbean |
			British	French	Dutch	US	
1900/20	−0.3	1.3	0.5	1.5	0.3	6.8	2.0
1920/40	−1.2	−3.7	0.3	0.0	10.2	0.4	−1.2
1940/60	2.1	2.2	7.0	0.7	1.8	4.2	3.6
1900/60	0.2	−0.1	2.6	0.7	4.0	3.8	1.5

| Imports | Hispaniola | Cuba | Dependencies: | | | | Caribbean |
			British	French	Dutch	US	
1900/20	3.3	2.1	0.3	−0.5	−2.8	5.3	2.6
1920/40	−5.0	−6.3	0.7	1.1	8.5	2.8	−2.4
1940/60	4.0	3.2	5.9	6.2	3.6	5.9	4.6
1900/60	0.7	−0.4	2.3	2.3	3.0	4.7	1.6

Source: Derived from Tables C.1, C.9 and C.21.

is done in Table 9.4 for the periods used before. For the Caribbean as a whole, as we would expect, imports and exports per head (at constant prices) grew at roughly the same annual rate over the period 1900 to 1960. In the French territories, however, imports grew much faster than exports, but in Cuba the volume of imports per head actually declined.[78]

The gap between import and export growth is even clearer when the shorter periods are considered. In the first period (1900–20), import was much faster than export per head growth in the three independent countries (Cuba, Haiti and the Dominican Republic), and performance was better than in the European dependencies.[79] In the second period (1920–40), when trade was generally in decline, the opposite was true for these three republics, and all the dependencies – helped by imperial preference – fared much better. In the final period (1940–60), when trade everywhere expanded rapidly, import exceeded export per head growth in almost all cases. The exception was the British dependencies, where foreign ownership of petroleum extraction in Trinidad & Tobago led to a growth in imports a little below that of exports.

We can now turn to the performance of individual countries, ranking them at constant (1930) prices in terms of (a) domestic exports per head and (b) retained imports per head at decennial intervals from 1900 to 1960.[80] The top performers by 1960 in terms of exports were the two petroleum exporters (Trinidad & Tobago and the Dutch Antilles). Puerto Rico came next, and

[78] This is partly from the sharp decline in the volume of imports per head in the two years after 1958. Nevertheless, long-run Cuban performance was very unimpressive when population change is taken into account and price increases are stripped out.

[79] The best performer was the US dependencies, where both exports and imports per head increased rapidly.

[80] Derived from Tables C.1, C.9 and C.21.

its privileged position owed a great deal to the fact that it was fully inside the US tariff wall. These three were followed by the main bauxite exporters (Suriname, Guyana and Jamaica), thus five of the top six slots were taken by mineral exporters. All six countries had increased their ranking compared with 1900. The highest placed countries mainly dependent on sugar in 1960 were Guadeloupe, St Kitts & Nevis and Martinique in seventh, eighth and ninth position, respectively.[81]

The top performers by 1960 in terms of retained imports also included the petroleum exporters and Puerto Rico. However, they were now joined by the US Virgin Islands, the Bahamas and the Cayman Islands, where service exports and remittances had become very important, and by French Guiana, where metropolitan transfers made possible very high levels of imports per head. The bauxite exporters did not do so well in terms of imports per head, because of the impact of foreign ownership on profit repatriation.

Six of the bottom seven positions in 1960 in terms of exports per head were taken by small British dependencies. The 'jaws effect' meant that commodity exports had ceased to be of much importance for four of them (Bahamas, British Virgin Islands, Cayman Islands and Montserrat), but they were still significant for the other two (Grenada and St Lucia). The other country was Haiti, which had fallen to the bottom of the rankings by 1930 and has stayed there ever since. By 1960 its domestic exports per head were seventy times smaller than those in Trinidad & Tobago (the highest ranked country).

Cuba had climbed from sixth position in 1900,[82] when war damage still affected the volume of exports, to fourth position in 1920. After 1930 its ranking slipped badly, reaching seventeenth in 1940, eleventh in 1950 and twelfth in 1960. The slide in its ranking was even greater when retained imports per head (at 1930 prices) is used. It had been first until 1920, but was fourteenth in 1940, twelfth in 1950 and twenty-third in 1960, when US trade restrictions were beginning to have a major impact. Whether looking at exports or imports, it is clear that the Cuban economy entered a period of structural decline in the 1920s, from which it could be argued that it has not yet emerged.

The Dominican Republic had overtaken Haiti by 1900 in terms of exports and imports per head. However, its subsequent performance was far from stellar. As late as 1960 it was ranked nineteenth in terms of exports and a dismal twenty-fifth in terms of imports.[83] In view of the fact that the main commodity exports of the Dominican Republic received virtually no preferences before 1960 and that the economy was massively distorted by rent-seeking activities

---

[81] The proximity of these two French territories in many rankings in 1960 is quite remarkable. However, exports per head in Martinique had been much higher than in Guadeloupe at the start of the century. Guadeloupe did not catch up until the 1950s.

[82] Because 1900 is the first year of the period considered here and the last year of the period considered in Chapter 5, we might expect the ranking of the countries to be the same. However, this will only be the case when current prices are used.

[83] This was only one place above Haiti, but Dominican imports per head were nearly three times greater.

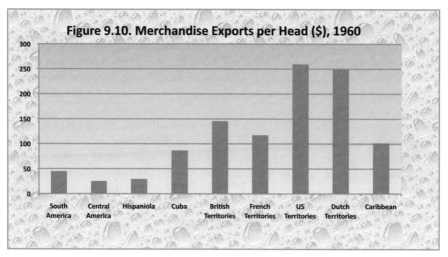

Source: Caribbean data derived from Tables C.1 and C.8; South and Central America from MOxLAD.

during the long presidency of Rafael Trujillo (1930–61), this is not particularly surprising.[84] Thus, the improvement in the standing of the republic was relative to Haiti only. Its improvement relative to the Caribbean would not take place until much later.

The final element of this chapter is a comparison of the Caribbean with other parts of the world at the end of the period. This can best be done at current prices using merchandise exports per head rather than domestic exports.[85] On this basis the Caribbean had an average figure of around $100 with a wide variation from $30 in Hispaniola to around $250 in the US and Dutch dependencies (see Figure 9.10). Cuba by this time was below the regional average, even though it had been above as late as 1958.

The Caribbean figure was more than twice that of South America.[86] Perhaps this might have been anticipated in view of several decades of ISI in the larger Latin American countries. However, the Caribbean figure was roughly four times the figure for Central America (see Figure 9.10), where import substitution had barely begun. It was above Japan and very similar to the United States, but below the British dominions, such as Australia, Canada and New Zealand. It was well above most developing countries, except the city-states

---

[84] In addition, the Dominican Republic's US sugar quota in 1960 had been suspended in reprisal for Trujillo's role in the assassination attempt on President Betancourt in Venezuela.

[85] Secondary sources rarely distinguish between domestic and merchandise exports, so it is safest to assume exports include re-exports.

[86] I have included Mexico in the South American figure.

of Singapore[87] and Hong Kong, and compared favourably even with mineral exporters, such as South Africa.[88]

The Caribbean was therefore highly specialised in international trade at the end of the period, and its position compared favourably with that of many other parts of the world. It had also succeeded in nearly doubling its share of world exports (see Chapter 8.1) at a time when the Latin American share was shrinking rapidly. However, much of this was because of the exceptional performance of foreign trade in the fifteen years after the Second World War. Before the war, the trade performance of the British and French dependencies had been dismal. Hispaniola had also been poor, and it was only the US and Dutch dependencies that had provided any sense of optimism.

Cuba was the enigma. Drawn even further into the US economic sphere by the 1903 Reciprocity Act, Cuba within two decades had taken specialisation in sugar to an extreme level. Yet Cuba controlled none of the policies on which its prosperity as a sugar economy depended. By the mid-1920s Cuba had nowhere to go: unable to take sugar specialisation further, yet seemingly incapable of diversifying its economy away from sugar. Many of the US capitalists who had helped to reshape the Cuban economy now took fright, selling out to Cuban interests and reinvesting elsewhere. Cuba regained control of its sugar industry, but at a time when the sector had lost its dynamism. The respite provided by the Second World War and its aftermath proved to be brief, and Cuba continued its relative decline in the 1950s.

APPENDIX TO CHAPTER 9. A SELECTION OF NATURAL DISASTERS, 1900–1960

| Year | Type | Month | Country | Domestic Exports (a) | |
				Years	% change
1902	Volcano	April	Martinique	1901–2	−26.9
1902	Volcano	May	St Vincent	1901–2	−13.2
1903	Hurricane	August	Jamaica	1903–4	1.8
1903	Hurricane	August	Cayman Is	1903–4	−6.5
1903	Hurricane	August	Martinique	1903–4	−19.3
1906	Hurricane	October	Cuba	1906–7	−7.4
1907	Earthquake	January	Jamaica	1906–7	−3.0
1908	Hurricane	September	DR (b)	1908–9	−2.0
1909	Hurricane	November	Jamaica	1909–10	0.5
1909	Hurricane	November	Haiti	1909–10	80.0

(continued)

[87] The figure for Singapore was nearly $700. See IMF, *International Financial Statistics*.
[88] The figure for South Africa in 1960 was $73. This was before the application of international sanctions.

Appendix to Chapter 9 (continued)

Year	Type	Month	Country	Domestic Exports (a) Years	% change
1909	Hurricane	October	Cuba	1909–10	4.6
1910	Hurricane	October	Cuba	1910–11	−11.0
1912	Hurricane	November	Jamaica	1912–13	−16.4
1919	Hurricane	September	Cuba	1919–20	−19.6
1924	Hurricane	August	Montserrat	1924–5	−29.3
1926	Hurricane	October	Cuba	1926–7	−9.4
1926	Hurricane	July	Bahamas	1926–7	−7.3
1926	Hurricane	July	Puerto Rico	1926–7	−2.4
1926	Hurricane	July	DR (b)	1926–7	−1.2
1928	Hurricane	September	Puerto Rico	1928–9	−13.1
1930	Hurricane	September	DR (b)	1930–1	−8.5
1931	Hurricane	September	Belize	1931–2	−43.5
1932	Hurricane	November	Cuba	1932–3	21.3
1932	Hurricane	September	Puerto Rico	1932–3	−13.1
1933	Hurricane	September	Cuba	1933–4	−1.1
1933	Hurricane	August	Jamaica	1933–4	20.0
1933	Hurricane	July	Trinidad	1933–4	−4.3
1935	Hurricane	October	Haiti	1935–6	51.0
1935	Hurricane	September	Cuba	1935–6	7.9
1945	Hurricane	September	Bahamas	1945–6	−8.5
1950	Hurricane	August	Cuba	1950–1	11.4
1951	Hurricane	August	Jamaica	1951–2	3.6
1952	Hurricane	October	Cuba	1952–3	1.3
1954	Hurricane	November	Haiti	1954–5	−18.8
1954	Hurricane	November	Grenada	1954–5	−0.6
1955	Hurricane	September	Barbados	1955–6	−7.7
1955	Hurricane	September	Belize	1955–6	−9.1
1956	Hurricane	August	Guadeloupe	1956–7	−3.5
1956	Hurricane	August	Puerto Rico	1956–7	7.2
1958	Hurricane	June	Cuba	1958–9	−8.5
1958	Hurricane	June	Haiti	1958–9	−26.7

Note: (a) Percentage change in domestic exports at constant (1930) prices before and after natural disaster; (b) Dominican Republic.

10

The Caribbean Domestic Economy

The previous chapter focused on foreign trade, especially domestic exports. Only part of national income, however, comes from the value added associated with exports. The remainder is derived from the value added from private-sector sales of goods and services to the domestic market and the value added from public services. The Caribbean economies may have been highly specialised in foreign trade, but there was still a branch of agriculture that produced foodstuffs for local consumption, a branch of manufacturing that made goods for the domestic market (sometimes in competition with imports) and a service sector (private and public) that was largely nontraded, although foreign firms played a dominant part in many of its activities.

The first section of the chapter reviews the earliest national income calculations for countries in the region. Except for Cuba, there are no annual estimates before 1940.[1] In the Second World War, calculations were made for several other countries, but it was only at the end of hostilities that time series began to become widely available. By the late 1950s there were estimates for most of the Caribbean countries, which allow not only for the ranking of countries in terms of national income inside and outside the region, but also for a more precise analysis of the degree of export specialisation of the different economies. Finally, household survey and tax data for the 1950s provide some of the first estimates of income inequality in the Caribbean.

The second section examines the structure of the economy as revealed both by the national accounts estimates and by employment surveys. The dominant position of agriculture is confirmed, but its share of GDP and share of employment could be very different. Mining was only important in a few countries, but manufacturing (excluding the processing of raw materials for export) was playing a not insignificant role by the 1950s in all the larger countries and some of the smaller ones. The service sector covered activities in decline, such

---

[1] Eisner (1961) and Moohr (1971) had made point estimates for Jamaica up to 1930 and Guyana up to 1914, respectively, but they did not produce time series.

as domestic servants, and those on the rise, such as public administration and tourism. It would not, however, acquire the dominant position it has today until after 1960.

The third section considers public finance, starting with revenue generation and the heavy reliance in all countries on import duties (export taxes were much less important). Public finances in the independent countries and the dependencies had many features in common, but the former all had standing armies and much greater debt-service problems. Loans, grants, metropolitan transfers and subsidies meant that expenditure was not necessarily limited to the amount collected in taxes. When public expenditure is adjusted for changes in the price level, it is closely correlated with the volume of domestic exports. Both series only start to 'take off' at the end of the Second World War.

Finally, in the fourth section the issue of migration is explored. Most Caribbean countries had surplus labour even before the end of the nineteenth century. Yet the region as a whole still enjoyed net inward migration until the 1920s. Falls in the death rate after 1900 increased the pressure to emigrate, but receiving countries started to impose restrictions on entry from the 1920s onwards. At the same time, the flow of migration to the Caribbean from outside started to dry up. Labour shortages in the United States during the Second World War and in many core countries afterwards made emigration easier. From the 1940s onwards, but not before, there was net outward migration from the Caribbean as a whole.

10.1. NATIONAL INCOME

In the absence of data on national income, there is an understandable tendency in research on the Caribbean to focus on exports, because it is widely (and correctly) assumed that the two are closely correlated in the region.[2] This does need to be demonstrated, however, because it is not true for all regions.[3] National income has been calculated for most Caribbean countries in at least some of the years before 1960. Here we look at these early estimates, the ranking of countries by income per head and the relationship between national income and exports.

As the largest and most important economy in the region, it is appropriate that Cuba should provide the earliest time series on national income. This series starts in 1903 and was subsequently extended to 1958, at which point

---

[2] In this section I use national income interchangeably with GDP, although the two are not the same. The reason is that national accounts calculations for the Caribbean were not at first prepared on a consistent basis. Given the crudeness of the early estimates (whether at factor cost or at market prices), the different methodologies should not concern us unduly.

[3] In Brazil, Russia, US and – until recently – China, for example, the correlation between exports and national income has often been quite weak as a result of the much greater importance of internal demand.

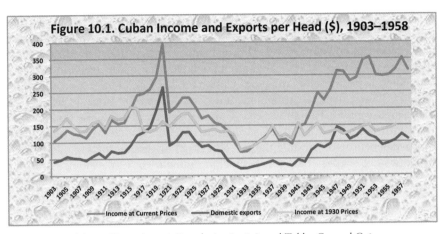

Figure 10.1. Cuban Income and Exports per Head ($), 1903–1958

Source: Derived from Alienes (1950), Brundenius (1984), and Tables C.1 and C.6.

there was a hiatus caused by the Cuban Revolution.[4] The series is shown in per capita terms in Figure 10.1 together with domestic exports per head (both in current dollars).[5] There is a strong overlap between the two series, and the correlation coefficient is an impressive 0.87. This is the first empirical demonstration of the close relationship between exports and national income in the Caribbean.

The share of Cuban exports in national income varied during most of the period between 30 and 50 per cent, but it reached an incredible 67 per cent during the 'dance of the millions'.[6] It was around 40 per cent in the first decade and then climbed steadily, averaging 50 per cent in the 1920s. The Cuban ratio at this point was much higher than in mainland Latin America and was probably one of the highest in the world. As in other countries, the ratio fell in the 1930s as a consequence of the crisis in international trade, but it still exceeded 30 per cent. It rose again in the Second World War but drifted downwards from 1947 onwards as the economy became more diversified and exports stagnated.

---

[4] The series was initially prepared by Julian Alienes at the Central Bank of Cuba. See Alienes (1950). He used (a) public revenues, (b) bank clearings, (c) bank deposits, and (d) exports and spliced these four series from 1903 to an estimate of national income he had made for 1938 based on sales and tax data. See IBRD (1952), p. 1046. The series was then reworked and extended by a number of authors, all of which is conveniently summarised in Brundenius (1984). More recently, however, Cuban authorities have retrospectively estimated GDP from 1950 to 2005 at 1997 prices, including the 'missing years' after 1958. See Vidal and Fundora (2008).

[5] I have taken the population figures from Table C.1 and the export figures from Table C.6.

[6] This was in 1920, as can be seen in Figure 10.1.

The series on national income and exports in Figure 10.1 are in current dollars and so do not take into account price changes.[7] The export series can be expressed in constant prices,[8] but it is much more difficult to do the same for national income. At least two attempts have been made, using in one case US wholesale prices and in the other Cuban food prices.[9] I have used a mixture of the two[10] to calculate national income per head at 1930 prices (see the green line in Figure 10.1). This shows that Cuban income per head rose rapidly after 1903 until 1915. It then entered a long-term decline, punctuated by short-term improvements, before ending the period (1958) at exactly the same level as at the beginning (1903). This was a shocking indictment of development policy in and towards the island.[11]

The decline of Cuban national income per head (at constant prices) after its extreme specialisation in sugar is clear from Figure 10.1. What is not clear is how Cuba compared with other Caribbean countries in terms of national income.[12] The first opportunity to draw comparisons was provided by national income estimates prepared in the Second World War for Puerto Rico and some of the British dependencies.[13] This suggested that by 1942 national income per head (current dollars) was already higher in Puerto Rico than in Cuba, and both were above the five British colonies.[14] The ranking of the latter, starting with the highest, was Guyana, Jamaica, Barbados, Grenada and St Vincent.

Comparisons made during the war years are fraught with difficulties because of the problems associated with foreign trade. Puerto Rican exports, virtually all of which went to the United States, were relatively unaffected (rum sales actually increased). By contrast, Jamaica suffered greatly from the reduction in shipping space for its main exports, the loss of the important German market for rum and the end of banana shipments to the UK. By the 1950s, conditions were much more normal. At the same time, an increasing number of countries

---

[7] The national income data are actually in current pesos. However, the Cuban peso was at par with the US dollar for almost the whole period.

[8] See Table C.9.

[9] Alienes (1950) used US wholesale prices. Brundenius (1984) used a cost-of-living index taken from Zanetti and García (1976).

[10] The Cuban cost of living deflator is superior to the US wholesale price, but there are gaps in the former before 1937. I filled these gaps by reference to US wholesale prices and then respliced the series to 1930 prices.

[11] The conclusion that national income per head was the same in 1903 as in 1958 is not affected by the deflator used, but intervening years often have different figures.

[12] The only comparisons possible before 1940 were with the point estimates for Jamaica and Guyana. Using the data in Eisner (1961), for example, we can calculate that Jamaican income per head (in current US dollars) in 1910 was 43% of the Cuban figure and 70% in 1930.

[13] The Puerto Rican estimates were made for 1940–4. See Creamer and Creamer (1948). The estimates for the British colonies were made for 1942 by Dr. F. Benham, who at the time was Economic Adviser to the Comptroller for Development and Welfare. Benham's estimates and methodology are conveniently summarised in Galletti (1949).

[14] The figures are all given in Baker Fox (1949), p. 239, and refer to 1942 (except for Cuba, which is for 1943). If we use the Cuban figure for 1942 in Figure 10.1, it still shows that Puerto Rico had a higher national income per head.

TABLE 10.1. *National Income and Exports per Head in the Caribbean (current dollars), mid-1950s (a)*

	National Income per Head	Rank	Domestic Exports per Head	Rank	Exports as % of National Income
Dutch Antilles	1,157	1	517	1	44.7
Puerto Rico	455	2	153	3	33.6
Trinidad & Tobago	332	3	216	2	65.0
Cuba	279	4	84	7	30.1
Guyana	262	5	104	5	39.9
Dominican Republic	255	6	43	11	17.0
Suriname	239	7	120	4	50.4
French Guiana	228	8	36	13	15.7
Jamaica	221	9	55	9	25.0
Barbados	209	10	98	6	46.6
Belize	180	11	59	8	32.5
Windward Islands (b)	128	12	38	12	29.5
Leeward Islands (c)	126	13	55	10	43.4
Haiti	83	14	10	14	12.0

Note: (a) The data are all for 1954, except French Guiana and Haiti (1955), Dutch Antilles (1957) and Belize (1946); (b) Dominica, Grenada, St Lucia and St Vincent; (c) Antigua, British Virgin Islands, Montserrat and St Kitts & Nevis.
Source: Domestic exports per head derived from Tables C.1a and C.6; national income for Dutch Antilles from *Statistisch Jaarboek: Nederlandse Antillen* (1965); Suriname from van Schaaijk (1992); Puerto Rico from Carter (2006), vol. 5; Cuba from Figure 10.1; Belize from Carey Jones (1953); other British colonies from O'Loughlin and Best (1960); French Guiana from Blaise (1962); Dominican Republic, Haiti, Barbados and Guyana from CEPAL (2009).

had prepared national income estimates, and the quality was improving all the time. Indeed, for the mid-1950s we have calculations for all except six countries.[15]

These early estimates of national income are shown in Table 10.1.[16] The Dutch Antilles was confirmed as the country with the highest income and exports per head.[17] Puerto Rico came next, maintaining the high ranking it had secured in the 1940s. Cuba was now fourth behind Trinidad & Tobago, where petroleum exports were accelerating. The Dominican Republic was in sixth place, despite low exports per head, because the nonexport economy had been artificially boosted to favour industries controlled by the Trujillo family.[18]

[15] The data for the colonies making up the Windward and Leeward Island Federations, however, are aggregated.
[16] I have used the population figures in Table C.1 in order to derive national income per head.
[17] It had achieved the highest domestic exports per head (at current prices) by 1940.
[18] See Cassá (1982), chap. 8.

The small British colonies in the Windward and Leeward Islands, all dependent on a narrow range of agricultural commodities, scored very poorly in the rankings, as did Barbados – still dependent on sugar after 300 years. Belize, where the main export was forestry, also had a low rank, but this may be affected by the fact that the only national income figures are for 1946. The final position was taken by Haiti, which even in the mid-1950s was in danger of becoming an outlier because its national income per head had fallen so far below all the others.

Table 10.1 also shows domestic exports per head. The correlation with national income (0.96) was very high, but there were some discrepancies. French Guiana had a much lower ranking in terms of exports than income per head as a result of metropolitan transfers consequent to becoming a department of France. Cuba also scored lower on exports than on national income per head, a result of its relatively large domestic market that permitted some industrialisation and greater attention to services. By contrast, national income in Barbados was lower than might be expected from its exports per head. This was because of overspecialisation in sugar to the neglect of the home market.

A comparison of exports and national income per head allows us to calculate the export share (see Table 10.1). The specialisation of the Caribbean in exports is once again confirmed, with the highest ratio (65%) in Trinidad & Tobago and the second highest (50%) in Suriname. The larger countries of the Greater Antilles (Cuba, Puerto Rico, Haiti, Dominican Republic and Jamaica) tended to have lower shares than the others as a result of their bigger domestic markets, but the second lowest share (15.7%) was in French Guiana for the reasons already given.

The data in Table 10.1 confirm the close association between exports and national income per head in the Caribbean: the higher the value of exports per head, the higher, ceteris paribus, would be national income per head. It is no surprise, therefore, that the Dutch Antilles, with its enormous export earnings from refined petroleum, should be ranked first. On the other hand Haiti, where exports had failed to keep pace with population increases since the turn of the century and which therefore had low exports per head, was ranked last.

All this helps to make clear the ranking of countries within the Caribbean in terms of national income. What has yet to be established is the ranking of the Caribbean in relation to the rest of the world. This is done in Table 10.2 where national income per head in the Caribbean and other regions is expressed as a percentage of the world average from 1950 to 1960.[19] The table shows that

---

[19] Maddison has five Caribbean countries in his database (Barbados, Dominican Republic, Jamaica, Trinidad & Tobago and St Lucia), which represent only one-quarter of the population of the region. I have therefore added Cuba, Haiti and Puerto Rico in order to obtain an estimate for the Caribbean that is more broadly based. In the case of Cuba and Haiti, I took the estimates at 1970 prices in MOxLAD and converted these to 1990 prices by comparing the figures for the Dominican Republic at 1970 prices in MOxLAD and 1990 prices in Maddison. For Puerto Rico, I took the figures at 1954 prices in Mitchell (2007) and converted these to 1990 prices by comparing the 1990 national income figure at 1990 and 1954 prices.

TABLE 10.2. *Caribbean National Income Per Head as Percentage of Other Regions, 1950–1960*

	World	Western Europe	Asia	Latin America	North America	Oceania	Africa
1950	111.5	52.8	378.5	89.5	25.3	31.1	260.4
1951	113.2	53.0	380.2	92.3	25.2	33.2	268.3
1952	113.2	52.9	370.8	94.3	25.4	34.3	271.0
1953	101.7	46.9	329.1	86.2	22.9	31.4	247.3
1954	105.4	47.3	338.1	87.7	24.6	31.3	253.2
1955	104.7	46.5	340.7	87.5	24.3	31.7	259.8
1956	109.0	48.0	349.1	92.6	25.8	33.4	273.0
1957	112.4	48.7	359.3	92.9	27.1	35.1	282.4
1958	104.5	45.1	324.3	85.1	26.1	32.2	265.5
1959	105.0	44.9	326.7	88.4	25.5	31.9	265.5
1960	103.1	43.5	320.5	86.8	25.8	32.1	265.6

Source: Derived from Maddison at 1990 prices (available at http://www.conference-board.org/data/economydatabase/) with the Caribbean data adjusted as explained in note 19. Latin America is mainland only (i.e. excluding Cuba, Dominican Republic and Haiti).

Caribbean income per head in 1950 was just above the world average, but only one-quarter of income per head in the rich countries of North America (Canada and the United States), one-third of income per head in Oceania (Australia and New Zealand) and one-half of income per head in Western Europe.

Caribbean income per head was above Asia and Africa. However, it was now below mainland Latin America. This was probably the reverse of the situation in 1900. Thus, in the first half of the century the Caribbean had lost ground to the mainland republics of Latin America, where industrialisation and urbanisation had advanced rapidly. Exports per head may have been much higher in the Caribbean (see Chapter 9), but this only helped to establish rankings **within** the region. Specialisation in foreign trade during a period (1913–48) when foreign trade had been stagnant or falling much of the time had not done the Caribbean any favours.

The Caribbean's relatively lowly position in the world rankings in 1950 helps to explain the dismal picture of the Caribbean often painted in the secondary literature. The Moyne Commission had drawn attention to the dire circumstances facing many of the British dependencies on the eve of the Second World War.[20] Even in Puerto Rico, with one of the highest incomes per head in the Caribbean in the 1940s, it could be said by a sympathetic observer that 'misery and discontent continued to prevail'.[21] A pioneering World Bank report would make much the same comment on Cuba at the beginning of the 1950s.[22]

---

[20] See *West India Royal Commission Report* (1945). Lord Moyne chaired the Commission.
[21] See Baker Fox (1949), p. 39.
[22] See IBRD (1952).

This assessment would not change much in the 1950s. The rise of international trade after a long period of stagnation should have helped the Caribbean to improve its relative position in view of the region's specialisation in exports. However, this was not the case (see Table 10.2). Indeed, the Caribbean finished the decade only marginally above the world average and still behind mainland Latin America. It had also failed to close the gap with the rich countries. Some of the smaller countries, such as Trinidad & Tobago, had done well. However, three of the largest economies (Cuba, Dominican Republic and Haiti) had performed poorly, held back by a combination of political instability and dependence on agricultural commodities facing major obstacles in world markets.

National income figures were not the only reason for the sense of pessimism encircling the Caribbean at mid-century. All commentators had drawn attention to the unequal distribution of income without necessarily being able to measure it. A large pool of agricultural workers, many of them illiterate, received wages that were barely adequate for the crop season and quite inadequate for the rest of the year. At the other end of the social scale, the top income recipients took a very large share of national income, therefore mean income was far above the median. Foreign ownership of the most productive assets also meant that a significant part of the national income accrued to foreigners.[23]

A few studies have been made confirming the degree of income inequality in the 1940s and 1950s. Using the 1953 household survey for Cuba, it has been estimated that the top 5 per cent received 26.5 per cent of income, and the top 10 per cent received nearly 40 per cent. The overall result was a Gini coefficient of 0.55,[24] implying one of the most unequal distributions of incomes in the world at the time.[25] The situation was no better in Puerto Rico, where in 1946–7 the top 11 per cent received over 40 per cent of household income.[26] Finally, in Kingston, Jamaica, in 1954 the 15 per cent richest households were responsible for 50 per cent of household expenditure.[27]

Using the same sources as before, the counterpart of the large share of income taken by the richest was the small share taken by the poorest. In Cuba, where un- and underemployment in the dead season was particularly serious, the bottom 30 per cent are estimated to have received only 4 per cent. In Kingston, Jamaica, 30 per cent of households received 5 per cent. In Puerto Rico 40 per cent of families took around 10 per cent of national income. This was probably an improvement on the situation in 1940, when 86 per cent of Puerto Rican families received only 29 per cent of household income.[28]

[23] If any part of this was remitted abroad, it should theoretically be excluded from national income.

[24] This widely used measure of income inequality can vary from zero (complete equality) to unity (complete inequality). A Gini coefficient in excess of 0.5 is normally regarded as extreme.

[25] See Brundenius (1984), table 5.1, p. 113.

[26] See Perloff (1950), p. 166.

[27] See Cumper (1960), p. 127.

[28] See Dietz (1986), table 4.7, p. 229.

Under these circumstances, it is not surprising that visitors to the region came away with a deeply pessimistic view of social and economic conditions. And yet, as Arthur Lewis always reminded his audiences and Table 10.2 confirms, the Caribbean was not among the poorest regions in the world. Mean income was above the world average, and the distribution of income was probably no worse than in most of mainland Latin America. What had been lacking in the Caribbean was an alternative to dependence on those primary product exports whose relative position in international trade was either in decline or where the Caribbean was uncompetitive without preferences. That would be provided by exports of services, but only the most farsighted were able to see this even as late as the 1950s.

10.2. THE STRUCTURE OF OUTPUT AND EMPLOYMENT

Primary products accounted for almost all exports of goods and provided the bulk of export earnings in the period considered here. Yet there was always a nonexport sector made up of activities such as agriculture for domestic use, manufacturing, construction, commerce, banking, public utilities, public administration and domestic services. We would expect the importance of some of these sectors as a share of both GDP and the Population Economically Active (PEA) to increase with rising incomes per head, the most important being manufacturing and public administration.[29] On the other hand, we would expect others to decline in importance, especially domestic services.

There is no reason to expect the share of a sector in GDP and PEA to be the same. Where the share of employment is larger, the implication is that the sector has below average labour productivity. This was typically the position of agriculture in Latin America, where the low-productivity peasant sector producing for the domestic market was relatively large. Where the share of employment is smaller, the sector has above average labour productivity, and this normally happens where capital requirements per person employed are greater than the average. This is always the case in public utilities and is often the case in manufacturing.[30]

Although there are employment data for the Caribbean for some years before the Second World War, we do not have data on the structure of GDP until national accounts began to be prepared in the 1940s. Indeed, it is not until the early 1950s that we can compare the shares of different sectors in GDP across the region and also compare the share of a sector in GDP and PEA for the same country.[31] The most important sector was agriculture, and the results for

---

[29] This is mainly from the income elasticity effect. Those activities with high income elasticities of demand should increase their share of GDP if income per head is rising.

[30] Not all manufacturing activities are capital-intensive, however, and many of those classified as employed in the manufacturing sector in the Caribbean were artisans working with almost no machinery.

[31] It is possible to do it for a small number of countries in the 1940s, but these early estimates of national accounts are very crude.

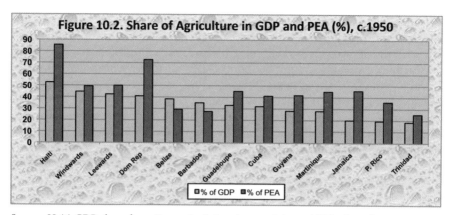

Source: Haiti GDP share from Barros (1984), vol. 2, p. 860, and PEA share from MOxLAD; Dominican Republic GDP share from Perloff (1950), and PEA share from MOxLAD; Guadeloupe and Martinique data from Blérald (1986); Puerto Rico data derived from Dietz (1986); Cuba data from Brundenius (1984); Belize GDP share from Carey Jones (1953), and PEA share from O'Loughlin and Best (1960); other British dependencies data from O'Loughlin and Best (1960).

a sample of countries are given in Figure 10.2, with countries ranked according to the importance of agriculture in GDP.[32]

There is a wide variation in Figure 10.2 in the importance of agriculture in GDP and a close (inverse) relationship with income per head and the relative size of the agricultural sector. The poorer countries (Haiti, the Dominican Republic, the British Windward and Leeward Islands)[33] had a share of between 40 and 50 per cent, but the richer countries (Puerto Rico and Trinidad) had a share of around 20 per cent. Although Caribbean countries were still largely dependent on the export of agricultural commodities, the 'iron law' of development theory – under which the share of agriculture in GDP varies inversely with income per head – could still be applied. Because living standards rose in the 1950s, the share would fall further.[34]

Figure 10.2 also shows the share of agricultural employment in the PEA. The correlation with the share of GDP is not perfect, but the association is clear.[35] In Haiti and the Dominican Republic the share of employment was both very large and greater than the share of agriculture in GDP. This implies below average labour productivity in agriculture and was the consequence of a relatively large peasant sector with low capital requirements and low output

---

[32] In the case of Belize, I have added forestry to agriculture. This is because forestry was the main primary activity – at least in terms of GDP.

[33] The British Windward Islands are Dominica, Grenada, St Lucia and St Vincent. The Leewards are Antigua, British Virgin Islands, Montserrat and St Kitts & Nevis.

[34] Particularly in the French islands, where government posts became much more numerous, and in Puerto Rico, where manufacturing and public administration jobs became very important.

[35] The correlation coefficient is 0.66.

per head. On the other hand, some of the British colonies had a share of employment that was **lower** than the share of GDP. The clearest example is Barbados, where so much of the land was taken by sugar plantations that little was left for small farmers producing for the home market.[36]

The agricultural sector was by far the most important source of employment. Even in Trinidad & Tobago, where exports came mainly from petroleum, no other activity came close. In many countries agriculture accounted for more than 50 per cent of the PEA (see Figure 10.2). These workers, however, were found not just on the plantations producing for export, but also on small farms selling produce to local markets. The census of the British colonies in 1943–6, for example, had identified around 350,000 farms,[37] of which 70 per cent were less than five acres (the proportion was similar elsewhere in the Caribbean).[38]

Some of these small farms did produce commodities for export, but most families concentrated on producing enough for their own needs, with any surplus to be marketed locally. Under these circumstances one might expect the share of foodstuffs in imports to have declined over time, but this did not happen.[39] Small farmers produced 'ground provisions' (fresh fruits, vegetables, corn and beans), but the islands continued to import large quantities of basic grains[40] and processed foodstuffs, such as dairy products. No Caribbean country came close to self-sufficiency, despite the abundance of land in the mainland countries and the larger islands.[41]

By the end of the 1940s it was clear to all but the most blinkered that the agricultural sector alone could not solve the development problems of the Caribbean. The sector was still the largest employer, but employment had not kept pace with population growth. In most of the British colonies, for example, the number employed in agriculture in 1946 was less than in 1891.[42] Seasonal work – especially in sugar – created a problem of underemployment for much of the year; and the lack of capital per worker left those employed with wages that were close to subsistence levels.

Despite this, there was great reluctance on behalf of both officials and private-sector entrepreneurs to accept industrialisation as the way forward. This pessimism stemmed from a variety of reasons, including the small size

---

[36] Mechanisation still had a long way to go, but labour on the sugar plantations still had higher productivity than on small farms because capital intensity was greater.

[37] See O'Loughlin and Best (1960). Nearly 200,000 of these farms were in Jamaica.

[38] In the Dominican Republic in 1950, 55.2% of the 276,848 farms were less than five acres. See Roberts and Callaway (1966), p. 269.

[39] The main exception was during wartime, when countries were cut off from their traditional sources of supply. The most extreme example was the French islands in the Second World War, and the case of Guadeloupe has been studied in depth. See Taitt (2007).

[40] Especially wheat and rice, although Guyana and Suriname, where land was not scarce, did produce enough rice for export.

[41] The Dominican Republic, where land was abundant, produced much of its own requirements for agricultural goods (except wheat and rice), but it still imported many processed foodstuffs.

[42] See Lewis (1950).

of the domestic market, the lack of a skilled labour force, the absence of finance and the assumption that manufacturing would never be internationally competitive even if infant industries were encouraged through higher tariffs.

The last point was crucial. Even Arthur Lewis, who had argued passionately from the late 1930s that the way forward lay with industrialisation,[43] recognised that a domestic market formed by a mass of workers on low wages could never provide a platform to attract foreign capital (as was happening in Puerto Rico – see below in this section). Industrialisation implied manufactured exports, and that in turn required the building of a customs union in the region on the one hand and access to the markets of the developed countries on the other.

Lewis' arguments were never fully accepted. Tariff rates remained low, especially in comparison with mainland Latin America, and continued to be set to maximise revenue. In the dependencies, the protective element was reduced further by imperial preference. Even in the independent countries, where nominal tariff rates were higher, the stimulus to manufacturing was limited. The tariff preferences Cuba gave the United States under the Reciprocity Act applied to many goods that the island might otherwise have produced, while the US Customs Receivership in Haiti and the Dominican Republic emphasised revenue over protection in all tariff decisions.[44]

Yet, in spite of all the obstacles manufacturing faced, the sector had grown in importance by the 1950s. Some activities were virtually nontraded and therefore did not face competition from imports. Others had been established in the war when imports were unavailable. Figure 10.3 shows the share of manufacturing in terms of both GDP and PEA for a sample of countries around 1950, this time ranked in terms of the employment share. Both shares varied between 5 and 20 per cent, and there is a correspondence between the two,[45] but great care must be taken in interpreting the figures for various reasons.

First, in most countries the data include the processing of raw materials for export. This explains the high share in Barbados (see Figure 10.3), where the manufacture of raw and refined sugar accounted for roughly half of the sector's contribution to GDP.[46] Second, the data sometimes include nonfactory workers, and this explains the high share in Puerto Rico, where nearly half of all manufacturing jobs corresponded to home needlework.[47] Third, the

---

[43] Lewis' written submission to the Moyne Commission in 1938 had argued for industrialisation as a solution to the problems of the British colonies. See Tignor (2006), pp. 44–7.

[44] There was also a suspicion that duties under the Customs Receiverships were designed to help those importing from the US. The 1919 tariff law in the Dominican Republic, for example, clearly favoured the import of goods from the US. See Knight (1928), p. 104.

[45] The correlation coefficient is 0.68.

[46] It also explains the relatively high share in the Dominican Republic, where sugar processing accounted for 71% of capital employed in manufacturing as late as 1962. See Roberts and Callaway (1966), p. 305.

[47] There were 115,956 employed in manufacturing in 1948. Of these, 51,871 were in home needlework and 13,308 in sugar mills. See Perloff (1950), p. 55.

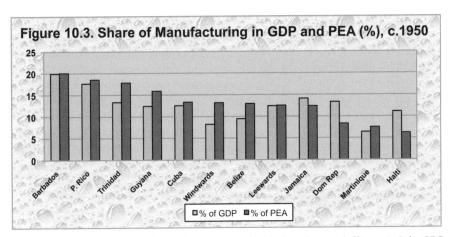

Figure 10.3. Share of Manufacturing in GDP and PEA (%), c.1950

Source: Puerto Rico GDP share from Dietz (1986), and PEA share from Perloff (1950); Cuba GDP share from IBRD (1952), p. 129, and PEA share from MOxLAD; Haiti GDP share from Barros (1984), and PEA share from MOxLAD; Dominican Republic GDP share and PEA share from MOxLAD; Martinique GDP and PEA shares from Blérald (1986); Belize GDP share from Carey Jones (1953); other British dependencies data from O'Loughlin and Best (1960).

manufacturing data in the British colonies included repair work, and water and power supply in some cases. Finally, the industrial sector was so ill defined in the French dependencies that it was not fully disaggregated from the rest of employment until the 1970s.[48]

Cuban industrialisation had advanced furthest despite the fact that the Cuban share of manufacturing in GDP and PEA was below 15 per cent, and that part of this was processing sugarcane, molasses and tobacco for export.[49] By the end of the 1940s, Cuba was manufacturing a broad range of foods and drinks for local consumption, such as canned and powdered milk, peanut oil and beer; intermediate goods, such as cotton and rayon textiles, fibres and yarn, cement and paint; and final consumer goods, such as footwear, paper, matches and soap.[50] This was no doubt only a fraction of what could have been done with more favourable access to finance, less restrictive labour practices and higher tariffs, but it did illustrate that the Cuban market was big enough to support a broad range of industrial activities.

[48] In Martinique 54.6% of the labour force was 'non-declarées' in 1946; the number in Figure 10.3 is the sum of those in industry (1.6%) and artisans (5.9%). See Blérald (1986), p. 255. It was a similar figure in Guadeloupe (see *Annuaire de la Guadeloupe* (1954)).

[49] If it were possible to subtract from the shares in Figure 10.3 the processing of raw materials for export, the Cuban share would almost certainly be the highest except for Puerto Rico. And if home needleworkers are subtracted from the Puerto Rican data, the Cuban share would be much bigger than the Puerto Rican.

[50] See IBRD (1952), p. 130.

It was industrialisation in Puerto Rico rather than Cuba, however, that attracted the most attention. Manufacturing on the island had never been subject to federal taxes, and exports paid no duty on entry to the United States. This had allowed the textiles and clothing industry to flourish, with many of the jobs going to women working at home. Yet this was by and large the limit of industrialisation until the Second World War, when abundant public revenues made possible an unusual experiment in state capitalism.[51] The activities established by the Puerto Rican Development Company were not particularly successful,[52] but they paved the way for 'Operation Bootstrap' in 1948, which gave tax incentives to US companies to invest in the island.

The key incentive was temporary exemption from Puerto Rican corporate income tax, which had been introduced in 1913 and which had a similar rate structure to the mainland.[53] Other tax incentives followed. The number of jobs attributable to these fiscal incentives rose to more than half of all those employed in manufacturing by 1957, but the net impact on job creation was still small because so many jobs in needlework were being destroyed at the same time.[54] It was not until the 1970s that manufacturing would really 'take off' in Puerto Rico.

Arthur Lewis and the architects of Operation Bootstrap had placed their faith in industrialisation in large part as a solution to the problem of un- and underemployment.[55] Yet the first World Bank report on Cuba had begun the chapter on industry by stating: 'The purpose of industry is not to provide employment; it is to convert raw materials into desirable finished products. Employment is a useful by-product.'[56] Unfortunately, the World Bank was closer to the truth, because the employment record of manufacturing in the Caribbean (excluding traditional export processing) was distinctly unimpressive. With job opportunities in primary activities in relative or even absolute decline, this left the service sector to take up the slack.[57]

Services are very heterogeneous, covering work done by the professions, the civil service, hotels and restaurants and domestic servants. The last category had always been important – and the principal source of employment for women in most countries. Yet it was in decline. By the end of the 1940s, for

---

[51] The federal government returned to Puerto Rico the revenue from taxes on Puerto Rican products sold on the mainland. During the war, exports of Puerto Rican rum to the US soared.

[52] The companies produced cement, glass, pulp and paper, clay, and leather and shoes. See Perloff (1950), p. 106.

[53] See Dietz (1986), p. 209.

[54] See Dietz (1986), p. 212.

[55] Lewis had begun his famous article by stating: 'The case for rapid industrialisation in the West Indies rests chiefly on over-population . . . it is, therefore, urgent to create new opportunities for employment off the land'. See Lewis (1950).

[56] See IBRD (1952), p. 127.

[57] There were also jobs in construction, transport, public utilities, finance, real estate and commerce. All except commerce, however, provided very few work opportunities even in the 1950s.

example, only 5 per cent of the labour force were domestic servants in Cuba[58] and Puerto Rico[59] and around 10 per cent in the British colonies.[60] This was partly because of the rise in real wages after 1940 but also the opening up of other opportunities in the service sector. Public-service jobs were increasing – in education, health, policing and public administration – and had become more important than domestic service in most countries by the end of the 1950s.[61]

The jobs that were slow to materialise were in the tourist sector. At the end of the Second World War, 0.3 per cent of the labour force in the British colonies were in 'recreational' services.[62] This low figure could perhaps be blamed on the war, but a few years later Arthur Lewis estimated that only 11,000 jobs in Jamaica could be attributed to tourism, despite the fact that the island was already a major tourist attraction.[63] The figures were a little higher in those countries easily accessible from the United States, such as Cuba and the Bahamas, but the age of mass tourism had not yet arrived. Even at the end of the 1950s, there was a reluctance to recognise the role that the tourism industry would come to play.[64]

The final sector that deserves a mention here is banking. This is not because of the jobs created, which were few, but because of the role that the financial system plays in economic development. The country with the highest financial intermediation was Cuba, where in 1940 seven banks operated with 169 branches.[65] These banks included one Cuban and three US companies, as might be expected. However, the others were all Canadian banks, of which two (Bank of Nova Scotia and Royal Bank of Canada) had a dominant position in the Caribbean, with branches in almost all countries.[66] The main British bank was Barclays,[67] and each French dependency had a state-owned financial institution. The US banks included National City Bank of New York, with major operations in Cuba, the Dominican Republic[68] and Puerto Rico, although its subsidiary in Haiti (Banque Nationale de la République d'Haiti) was taken over by the state in 1935.

---

[58] There were an estimated 74,000 domestic servants in Cuba in 1943. See IBRD (1952), p. 1044. At this time the labour force was 1.521 million (see MOxLAD).

[59] This was the proportion in 1948. It had been 13.1% in 1910. See Perloff (1950), p. 401.

[60] For the British dependencies as a whole it was 11.6% in 1946. However, it was 17.5% in Barbados. See Cumper (1960a).

[61] Especially in the French dependencies. In Martinique, for example, public servants were 11.9% of the labour force by 1961. See Blérald (1986), p. 255.

[62] See Cumper (1960a), p. 160.

[63] This was 2% of the labour force. See Lewis (1950).

[64] The main exception was the US Virgin Islands, where tourist arrivals had risen so rapidly in the 1950s that the governor's *Annual Report* regularly emphasised the sector.

[65] See *West Indies Yearbook*, 1941–2 (1942). This was a far cry, however, from 1920 when there were 334 branches. See IBRD (1951), p. 563.

[66] On the Bank of Nova Scotia (now named Scotiabank) in the Caribbean, see Quigley (1989).

[67] See Monteith (2008). Its name is now First Caribbean Bank.

[68] Its subsidiary in the Dominican Republic was taken over by the state in 1941, becoming the Central Bank in 1947. See Estrella (1971), vol. 2, pp. 74–5.

These banks, many foreign owned, operated on very conservative principles. They preferred to deal with established clients in government or the private sector and therefore did not generally provide long-term finance for new activities. This made diversification of the economy extremely difficult and created a demand for state-owned institutions willing to accept the risks that the private banks abjured.[69] These were slow in coming, but some had been established by the end of the 1940s.[70] Together with official loans from colonial governments, the opportunities for diversification had improved by the 1950s, by which time the World Bank was also providing project finance for the independent countries.

10.3. PUBLIC FINANCE

The national accounts estimates prepared in the 1940s and early 1950s suggested that public administration averaged around 10 per cent of GDP.[71] This is low by modern standards, but it was probably much higher than at the beginning of the twentieth century, when the range of services the state was expected to provide was more limited. As political institutions advanced and as the popular vote was extended in the dependencies, the demand for public services increased. Furthermore, public administration was par excellence an income-elastic good in the Caribbean, so demand increased faster than income.

Public services were mainly paid for by taxation, because financing them through increases in debt was strictly controlled, even in the independent countries, and subsidies to the colonies were generally frowned upon by metropolitan governments. The most important tax in the nineteenth century had been duties on imports – this was the easiest to administer and the hardest to evade. It remained the single most important source of revenue in most countries up to the Second World War, but imported inflation from 1940 onwards undermined the yield, because so much of it was collected as specific rather than ad valorem taxes. From then on, income taxes became more important, with most of the revenue collected coming from companies rather than individuals.

Import duties were designed to raise revenue, but they also provided protection for those domestic products that competed with foreign goods. Indeed, duties were the most important form of protection in the Caribbean, because

---

[69] Henry Wallich in his analysis of the Cuban financial system had said: 'the conclusion may have to be faced that the credit that can safely be given . . . is insufficient . . . for the maintenance of full employment . . . to overcome this divergence between private and social costs, government action will probably be required.' See Wallich (1950), p. 167.

[70] The most famous example was the Banco de Fomento (Development Bank) established in Puerto Rico in 1943. Cuba created an agricultural and development bank in 1950. None were established in the Dominican Republic until after the fall of Trujillo.

[71] Among those countries able to provide a figure, the highest was Puerto Rico (11%) and the lowest was Haiti (7%), with the British dependencies (9.4%) in the middle.

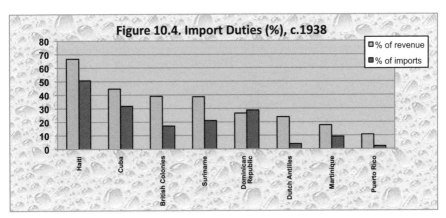

Source: Imports from Table C.20 and revenue from Table C.28. Import duties for Haiti from Banque Nationale de la République d'Haiti (n.d.); for Cuba from IBRD (1952); for the British dependencies from *West India Royal Commission Report* (1945); for Suriname from Hiss (1943); for the Dominican Republic from *Anuario Estadístico Dominicano* (1940); for the Dutch Antilles from *Statistisch Jaarboek: Nederlandse Antillen* (1956); for Martinique from *Budget des Recettes et Dépenses de la Martinique* (1938); and for Puerto Rico, where the figure refers to 1927–8, from Clark (1930).

quotas were comparatively rare and direct subsidies to local producers too expensive. Thus, import duties served a dual purpose, and this is shown for most countries on the eve of the Second World War in Figure 10.4,[72] where countries have been ranked by the share of import duties in public revenue.

The country most dependent on import duties was Haiti, where the proportion was if anything even higher than in the nineteenth century (export duties were now less important). As a consequence, Haiti on the eve of the Second World War had an implicit tariff rate of 50 per cent.[73] The other independent countries (Cuba and the Dominican Republic) had average tariff rates of around 30 per cent, and Cuba was also heavily reliant on the income generated from import duties. However, the Dominican Republic had reduced its dependence on customs duties in order to escape from the clutches of the US Customs Receivership.[74]

[72] In order to simplify the graph, all the British colonies are aggregated, but there was some variation among them. The implied tariff rate was lowest in the British Virgin Islands (10.5%) and highest in Guyana (27.3%), and the share of revenue was highest in the Bahamas (50.9%) and lowest in the British Virgin Islands, where export duties provided a large share of taxation.

[73] This was not as protectionist as it seemed, because the implicit tariff was particularly high in 1938. It had been 30% a decade earlier and would fall to 26% by the end of the 1940s. See Banque Nationale de la République d'Haiti (n.d.), p. 73.

[74] Internal (nontrade) taxes were the responsibility of the Dominican government and could be spent without reference to the US fiscal comptroller. One of the first acts therefore of the Dominican government at the end of the US occupation (1916–24) was to reform the fiscal system and reduce the relative importance of customs duties.

TABLE 10.3. *Public Revenue per Head as Percentage of Caribbean Average, 1900–1960*

			Dependencies:			
	Hispaniola	Cuba	British	French	US	Dutch
1900	53.7	176.9	110.0	93.9	43.2	115.7
1910	46.3	182.2	94.8	71.8	57.4	190.0
1920	36.1	194.9	75.5	45.3	81.1	83.8
1930	39.2	155.1	108.1	147.7	65.3	176.9
1940	33.5	143.5	129.0	99.1	82.6	270.6
1950	61.0	112.9	87.1	73.7	150.1	324.7
1960	41.8	99.4	123.1	60.9	217.3	259.2

Source: Derived from Tables C.1 and C.28.

The British and Dutch dependencies generated a large share of public revenue from import duties, but the implicit tariffs were still modest.[75] However, the other dependencies were in a different position. The French territories[76] imported mainly metropolitan goods on preferential terms and therefore had to generate revenue from indirect taxes other than customs duties. Puerto Rico and the US Virgin Islands imported virtually all their requirements from the mainland at zero tariffs. Furthermore, the duties in Puerto Rico on goods imported from outside the US tariff wall were not collected by the insular government.[77]

Public revenue is correlated with income in the Caribbean. It is not as closely correlated as exports, because the tax base was so varied and tax effort depended on a host of internal and external considerations that differed from country to country. Nevertheless, we would expect to find that countries where exports per head were rising or falling in relation to the Caribbean average would experience a rise or fall in public revenue per head. This is explored in Table 10.3, where public revenue per head in the subregions is expressed as a percentage of the regional average in each decennial year from 1900 to 1960.

Cuba had the highest figure in 1900, despite the disruption caused by the 1895–8 hostilities. Its position would strengthen in the next decades, reaching a peak in 1920 when sugar prices were exceptionally high, but it would then suffer a steady deterioration until in 1960 it had fallen just below the regional average. The Dutch dependencies rose and fell in the first two decades, but the establishment of oil refining in the Dutch Antilles and bauxite extraction in Suriname transformed the tax base from the 1920s onwards. In the period

---

[75] Particularly in the Dutch Antilles, where oil refining reduced non-oil production of import-competing goods to insignificance.

[76] The ratios for Martinique in Figure 10.4 can be taken as representative of the other French colonies.

[77] The import duties were returned to Puerto Rico as part of federal transfers, but they were never large. See Perloff (1950), p. 383. The US Virgin Islands did not apply federal import tariffs, instead operating a flat rate tariff of 6% on non-US imports. It was allowed to keep the revenue.

after the Second World War, public revenue per head was approximately three times the regional average.

In the US dependencies, where the figures are dominated by Puerto Rico, public revenue per head was below the regional average in the first four decades. However, the return to the islands of all taxes on insular produce sold on the mainland transformed the situation after 1940.[78] Furthermore, the islands became eligible for a wider range of federal transfers, which – in other dependencies – might have been treated as subsidies and would therefore have been excluded from revenue. This was indeed the case in the French territories, where *départementalisation* in 1946 reduced the importance of local taxes in financing expenditure.

The British dependencies fluctuated around the regional average, but better economic performance after the Second World War, a widening of the tax base and diversification of revenue sources improved the relative position from 1950 onwards. The establishment of internal self-government was also important in this regard because the pressure to provide additional public services obliged governments to look for new forms of taxation. Revenue diversification also took place in both parts of Hispaniola, but it was much more pronounced in the Dominican Republic than in Haiti. Furthermore, the gap between public revenue per head in Haiti and the Dominican Republic widened as the century advanced.[79]

Revenue was needed to finance expenditure, but the real value of public spending – the quantity of goods and services that could be purchased – depended on the price level. In the dependencies, the price level tended to rise and fall in line with international conditions. Inflation therefore only occurred if it was imported, because the local currency was fixed in relation to the metropolitan one and there was no possibility of printing money. The French territories, where the franc was in circulation, were the most vulnerable because the currency depreciated dramatically against other core currencies during and after the two world wars.[80]

In the independent countries, inflation could have domestic origins, and this had happened in the Dominican Republic and Haiti before the imposition of US fiscal control in 1905 and 1915, respectively. From then on, the two countries followed very orthodox fiscal and monetary policies.[81] Cuba, under the Platt Amendment, was unable to issue debt without US authority, so macroeconomic

---

[78] This was mainly from rum sales, which benefitted from the decline in US whisky production.

[79] Public revenue per head in 1900 had been the same in both countries. By 1930 Haitian revenue per head was around 40% of the Dominican figure and around 20% in 1960. Derived from Tables C.1 and C.28.

[80] The franc had been pegged to the US dollar at 5.18 during the gold standard (see Table C.4). It was repegged in 1927 at 25.5. It appreciated briefly in the 1930s after the US dollar was devalued against gold. It had fallen to 50 by 1945 before collapsing to 490 at the end of the 1950s, when the new franc was introduced. The nominal value of the currency against the dollar, therefore, was roughly 1% of what it had been before the First World War.

[81] The customs receiverships gave the US control over the collection and spending of customs duties at a time when most revenue came from this source.

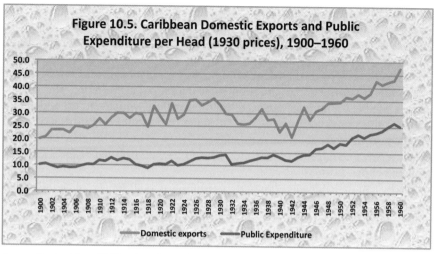

Figure 10.5. Caribbean Domestic Exports and Public Expenditure per Head (1930 prices), 1900–1960

Source: Derived from Tables C.1, C.9 and C.31.

policy was generally prudent.[82] In the late 1930s, however, following the repeal of the Platt Amendment, Cuba briefly experienced inflation of domestic origin as a result of lax fiscal policies. The peso depreciated modestly against the US dollar, but this episode was over by the end of 1940. Thus, the macroeconomic behaviour of the independent countries for most of the period did not differ greatly from the dependencies. Orthodox fiscal and monetary policies were the norm.

It was in 1940 that inflation became embedded in the core and was imported immediately by all Caribbean countries. However, this was not the first episode of inflation – the price level had also risen rapidly during and immediately after the First World War. On the other hand, many years in the interwar period were marked by deflation. Public expenditure therefore needs to be adjusted for changes in the price level in order to measure its impact correctly.[83] In addition, allowance must be made for population growth in order to measure public expenditure per head in real terms.

This is done in Figure 10.5, where the lower line plots public expenditure and the upper line domestic exports per head (both at 1930 prices). There is a close connection between the two,[84] but it is noticeable that expenditure per head barely rose in the first three decades of the century. Instead, we find a level of per capita public expenditure that was virtually unchanged until after the Second World War. Public spending in these early years was little more than

---

[82] In addition, Cuba did not have its own currency until 1914. See Wallich (1950), pp. 31–3.

[83] How this was done is explained in the Notes on C. Tables. The results are generally plausible, but the appreciation of the French franc between 1926 and 1936 inflates the dollar value of public expenditure in the French colonies during those years.

[84] The correlation coefficient is 0.83.

$10 per head.[85] Because health and education accounted for roughly 10 per cent each of public spending, this meant that $1 per year per person was being spent on each of these vital public services.[86] This was far too low to provide anything approximating universal coverage.

Public expenditure per head in real terms rose rapidly after the Second World War (see Figure 10.5). This was mainly due to economic growth, because higher exports per head expanded the tax base and fiscal reform captured a greater share of resources.[87] However, imperial subsidies or transfers became more important in this period. The resulting increase in expenditure made possible improved health and educational services. Coverage was still far from universal, but everywhere a higher proportion of children went to school, and infant mortality rates started to fall. And infrastructure improved through greater spending on public works.

As always, average figures for the Caribbean conceal a wide variation at the country level. Not all cases can be considered here, but some are worthy of special mention.[88] Haiti and the Dominican Republic, for example, had started the century with the same level of per capita state spending. Haitian expenditure then declined despite the imposition of the US Customs Receivership in 1915, while the Dominican level increased and had reached the regional average by the First World War.[89] The gap between the two countries then widened further.[90] Haitian spending never recovered to its level at the start of the century and reached its nadir in 1946, when the value (at 1930 prices) was $1.30. Although Haiti spent roughly the same proportion of its budget on health and education as other countries, the **absolute** amounts were therefore minuscule.

The US dependencies started the century below the regional average. Indeed, Puerto Rico in 1900 had one of the lowest levels of per capita spending anywhere in the Caribbean. Yet they had caught up by the First World War. This was entirely from increased spending in Puerto Rico, because the Virgin Islands were neglected Danish colonies until 1917. The interwar period was difficult for both islands, with the absolute value of public spending per head actually falling in Puerto Rico. The increase in federal transfers during and after the Second World War then transformed the situation. By the mid-1950s, the US Virgin Islands had overtaken the Dutch Antilles to become the country with

[85] To give an idea of the price level, the median annual wage in the British colonies in the interwar period (at 1930 prices) was around $100 (see Macmillan, 1936).

[86] The figures for the British colonies are conveniently summarised in the *West India Royal Commission Report* (1945), app. They were similar in other countries. State spending on health and education was around 1% of the median wage in each case.

[87] Governments became less reliant on customs duties and raised relatively more revenue from income and property taxes.

[88] The interested reader can derive the individual cases from Tables C.1a and C.31.

[89] This has been widely attributed to the Customs Receivership imposed in 1905, but US fiscal control had the opposite effect in Haiti. The main difference was the faster growth of Dominican exports, which had been accelerating since the 1880s.

[90] The Dominican figure was five times greater than the Haitian by the 1950s.

the highest public spending per head in the Caribbean. Puerto Rico was not far behind, in sixth position.

Metropolitan transfers allowed spending in the French territories to outstrip revenue after *départementalisation*. As a result, spending per head doubled in real terms between 1946 and 1960. Yet this was from such a low base that Guadeloupe and Martinique had still not reached the regional average by the end of the period. Indeed, spending per head in these two islands was among the lowest in the Caribbean in the 1950s, and it would not be until much later that they became the beneficiary of vastly increased metropolitan transfers. French Guiana, however, with its tiny population was an immediate beneficiary of the new constitutional arrangements. Spending per head quadrupled after 1946, despite the absence of dynamism in its export sector.

Public finance in the independent countries and the dependencies had many features in common. However, in two respects there were important differences. First, only the independent countries had standing armies, and these absorbed between 15 and 25 per cent of expenditure in most years. This was a burden the dependencies did not have to bear, so they were free to spend additional resources on social and economic development. Second, although most countries had public debts that needed to be serviced, the independent countries had almost nothing to show for it, whereas tight fiscal control in the dependencies ensured not only that the debts were serviced but that they were spent as intended in the first place.[91]

Haiti was the most unfortunate. The three loans of 1875, 1896 and 1910 had brought the government very few additional resources because loan moneys were mainly used to refinance previous debts or were swallowed up in 'commissions'.[92] Under the US Customs Receivership a new loan was issued to the Haitian government in 1922 that replaced all the previous debts,[93] but it had to be serviced through the worst years of the Great Depression, despite the fact that it had not been invested in productive assets. The same happened in the Dominican Republic, where new loans were made from 1908 onwards with the sole intention of replacing previous debts.[94] Haiti and the Dominican Republic, unlike most of the mainland Latin American republics, were then obliged by the customs receiverships to go through the interwar period without defaulting on the public external debt, despite the reduction in their ability to pay.[95]

---

[91] Belize was the worst affected, having to spend 20% of its budget on debt servicing in the 1930s. However, this was because of a loan from the British government, which had at least been used to build a railway that helped to increase exports.

[92] The debt history of Haiti has been explored in great detail. See, e.g., Vincent (1939), Benoit (1954a) and Blancpain (2001).

[93] This was an example of dollar diplomacy, because the loan ensured that in future Haiti's creditors would be US rather than European.

[94] See Knight (1928) and de la Rosa (1969). The latter is a Spanish translation of an outstanding pamphlet originally published in Paris in 1915.

[95] Under the Customs Receiverships, interest on and amortisation of the public debt received precedence over other forms of government expenditure.

Cuba had achieved independence in 1902 with no public external debt, because the nineteenth-century debt owed to Spain had been cancelled.[96] Two large loans had then been contracted with Speyer and Co. in 1904 and 1909, to be followed by ten loans from US banks between 1914 and 1927.[97] Cuba was able to service these debts until the collapse of its export sector in the Great Depression, at which point debt service was suspended on most of the loans contracted during the rule of President Machado (1925–33) on the grounds that they were unconstitutional. The Cuban Supreme Court, however, ruled in 1938 that all the debts had to be serviced. Thus, after some readjustment of the amount owed, Cuba followed Haiti and the Dominican Republic in servicing its public external debt in full.

10.4. MIGRATION

In comparison with today, the population of the Caribbean in 1900 (nearly 7 million) was very small.[98] Yet there was already serious concern about over-population – especially in the British and French insular dependencies.[99] Most of these islands were experiencing net outward migration by the end of the nineteenth century, as we saw in Chapter 3, and this was widely attributed to surplus labour. The theme of overpopulation would become more pronounced after 1900 and was a major theme in all official reports on the British and French islands, in the first World Bank reports on the independent countries and in studies of the US dependencies.

Because the Caribbean today supports a population that is roughly six times what it was in 1900, with a standard of living that is well above the world average, the widely held assumption of overpopulation in the first half of the twentieth century needs to be challenged. Although population density on some of the smaller islands was very high,[100] it could not be argued that there was an absolute shortage of land. Instead, the problem was lack of jobs for those already in the labour market. In particular, the number of agricultural jobs was falling in many countries[101] – despite the growth in population – and new jobs were not being created fast enough in other sectors.

The number of new entrants into the labour force was determined to a large extent by the difference between births and deaths in the previous generation. The Caribbean birth rate was high in 1900. Furthermore, it did not fall in the

---

[96] This had been agreed between the US and Spain at the Treaty of Paris in 1899.

[97] Many of these loans were very dubious. The Speyer loans, for example, forced Cuba to charge reduced rates of profit tax on a whole range of products, and these conditions were still in force long after the loans had been repaid. See IBRD (1952), p. 672.

[98] The precise figure was 6,982,948. See Table C.1.

[99] The mainland dependencies were in a very different position because there was an abundance of land.

[100] The highest in 1900 was in Barbados, with 1,192 per square mile. By contrast, it was less than 4 in Guyana.

[101] In the British colonies, for example, the number of agricultural workers in 1891 was 583,200 and had fallen to 461,900 by the end of the Second World War. See Roberts (1960), p. 34.

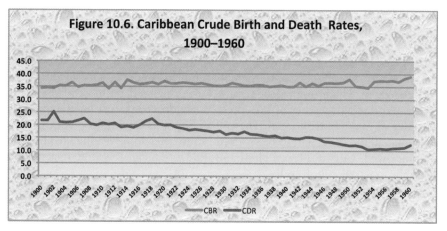

Figure 10.6. Caribbean Crude Birth and Death Rates, 1900–1960

Source: Tables C.2 and C.3.

next sixty years. The Caribbean death rate, on the other hand, experienced a steep decline despite the occasional blip (see Figure 10.6).[102] For the region as a whole, this pushed the natural rate of increase of the population from 1.5 per cent in 1900 to nearly 3 per cent in the 1950s. At the lower rate, the population would double in fifty years, but at the higher rate it would double in twenty-five years (equivalent to an eightfold increase in a century).

There were, of course, subregional and country differences. The greatest variations were in the death rate, which had already fallen below 20 per thousand by 1900 in several countries.[103] It remained stubbornly high in a few cases until the 1920s, but the downward trend in the death rate and the upward trend in the natural rate of increase were then observed everywhere. By 1960 many countries had succeeded in pushing the death rate below 10 per thousand.[104] Only Haiti still had a death rate above 20.

It had been commonplace, when the slave trade was still operating, for deaths to exceed births. Only one country (French Guiana) was still in this position in 1900 and would remain so until the late 1940s. This was usually attributed to unhealthy conditions in the French colony. However, the real reason was the skewed gender balance as a result of the gold prospectors on the one hand and the penal colony on the other. Because these groups were such a large part of the population and were predominantly male, it pushed the birth rate far below what was found in other parts of the Caribbean.

The gold boom ended in the 1920s, and the prospectors left the country or died. By then the penal colony had become internationally notorious, and its closure was finally approved in 1938. The convicts subsequently died or

---

[102] The first was in 1902 as a result of the eruption of Mt. Pelée in Martinique and Mt. Soufrière in St Vincent. The next was the influenza pandemic at the end of the First World War.

[103] These were mainly British colonies. See Table C.3.

[104] The lowest was the Cayman Islands, closely followed by Puerto Rico. See Table C.3.

TABLE 10.4. *Net Annual Migration as Percentage of Population, 1900–1960*

	Hispaniola	Cuba	Dependencies:				Caribbean
			British	French	Dutch	US	
1900–10	0.1	−1.4	0.5	0.1	−0.7	−0.9	−0.3
1911–20	0.3	−1.1	0.7	0.4	0.3	−0.2	−0.1
1921–30	0.1	−0.4	0.0	0.6	−0.4	−0.1	−0.1
1931–40	−0.1	0.3	0.1	0.2	−0.3	0.1	0.1
1941–50	0.0	−0.4	0.1	0.3	−0.4	1.1	0.0
1951–60	0.3	0.4	0.7	0.2	1.1	2.0	0.6

Note: Net migration is outward if positive and inward if negative.
Source: Derived from Tables C.1, C.2 and C.3.

were repatriated (very few stayed), the last ones leaving in 1952. It was only then that French Guiana had a more normal gender balance. This was reflected in the increase in the birth rate, which had become similar to the rest of the Caribbean by the 1950s.

In Figure 9.8 we saw the actual growth of the population in each of the subregions over the whole period. The difference between this and the natural rate of increase is net migration. If net births exceed the increase in population, this means there was net outward migration. If net births were lower, then there was net inward migration. The statistics on population change, births and deaths are not sufficiently robust to estimate net migration precisely for each country in every year,[105] but they can be used to calculate the annual rate in each decade. This is done for all the subregions in Table 10.4.[106]

The last column of Table 10.4 shows net migration for the Caribbean as a whole. It is therefore not affected by intra-Caribbean migration. During the first years of the twentieth century, many workers migrated from the Caribbean to Panama to help in the construction of the canal;[107] others migrated to Costa Rica to work in the banana industry;[108] while there was also a third flow of migration to the United States and a small trickle to Europe and Canada. Yet despite this well-documented outmigration, Table 10.4 shows that in the first three decades there was a small net **inflow** into the Caribbean. How was this possible?

The answer, as so often in Caribbean economic history, was provided mainly by Cuba. The economic boom after the war of independence brought large numbers of migrants from Europe (principally Spain) and smaller numbers

[105] The methodology is outlined in the Notes on C. Tables. The biggest problems are in the Dominican Republic and Haiti, where the first reliable vital statistics date from the 1930s and 1940s, respectively.
[106] The interested reader can calculate it for each country by using the sources listed under Table 10.4.
[107] The main recruiting centre was Barbados. See Richardson (2004).
[108] See Chomsky (1996).

from other parts of the world. In addition, the flow of indentured labour from British India to the Caribbean did not end until 1917, and the Dutch East Indies continued to supply Suriname with labour until the middle of the Second World War.[109] Finally, many West Indians who had worked on the Panama Canal in the first decade had to return home in the second.[110]

The 1920s was a decade of transition. The United States imposed restrictions on immigration in 1924, and this reduced the flow from the Caribbean.[111] At the same time, job opportunities in Central and South America were now becoming scarce. However, this did **not** lead to an increase in net inward migration. Cuba was no longer such an attractive destination, as a result of the difficulties faced by the sugar industry, and migration from British India had come to an end. Yet there was still a small net inward migration in the 1920s into the Caribbean.

From that point onwards, the region as a whole experienced net outward migration. It was small in the 1930s, when restrictions on immigration outside the Caribbean were widespread, but it accelerated in the 1950s. During the Second World War, the United States established in some southern states a temporary work programme for West Indian agricultural workers. When this came to an end after the war, new opportunities opened in Europe. A temporary labour shortage in Britain led to a recruitment drive in the British colonies,[112] and the inhabitants of the French and Dutch dependencies were always free to travel to the metropolis.

At the subregional level, where intra-Caribbean migration must be taken into account, we may observe two very different patterns. The British dependencies as a whole experienced chronic net outward migration. There were, of course, exceptions. Trinidad & Tobago, now fuelled by an oil boom, experienced net inward migration. Guyana did so in the first decade, as did the Bahamas in the 1950s. There was also a small net migration into Jamaica in the 1920s as a result in part of repatriation from Cuba.[113] In general, however, Table 10.4 confirms the lack of job opportunities in the British colonies that had so exercised Arthur Lewis.

The French dependencies as a whole also suffered from net outward migration, but there was migration into French Guiana until the gold boom ended in the 1920s. The islands of Guadeloupe and Martinique faced similar problems to the neighbouring British colonies before the Second World War as a result of the lack of job opportunities created by sugar-dependent economies. Their fortunes only began to change with *départementalisation*. Although many still

---

[109] Migration ended when the Japanese invaded Indonesia.

[110] This was especially true of Barbados. Annual net outward migration in the first decade had been 2.1%, but there was annual net inward migration of 1% in the second decade.

[111] See Richardson (2004) and Palmer (1998), chaps. 3 and 4.

[112] This had begun in 1948 with the famous voyage of HMS *Windrush*, but it would end with immigration restrictions in 1961.

[113] See Knight (1985).

moved to France in search of better work opportunities, there was also a small flow in the opposite direction as the public sector expanded.

In other parts of the Caribbean there was – at least for some of the time – net inward migration. The Dominican Republic was a net recipient in several decades.[114] These workers came from all over the Caribbean, but primarily from Haiti. They worked in the sugar industry for wage rates that were unattractive to Dominicans, and they often entered the country illegally. Job opportunities shrank in the 1930s, and many Haitians became squatters rather than returning home. They were then targeted by Trujillo, who ordered a massacre in 1937.[115] The international community turned a blind eye to this shocking incident, and Trujillo escaped retribution by agreeing to pay compensation to the Haitian government.[116]

There was also net inward migration into the US dependencies in the first decades.[117] In Puerto Rico this was from the sugar boom. When it ended in the 1920s, the exodus to the United States began. It reached a peak in the 1950s,[118] when net outward migration averaged over 2 per cent of the population each year despite the rapid growth of the manufacturing sector. The wage gap between the island and the mainland may have been closing,[119] but the United States imposed no restrictions, and jobs were abundant. The Virgin Islands experienced net outward migration in most decades, despite the early establishment of a tourist industry.

The principal destination for migrants until the 1930s was Cuba. In the thirty years after 1900, the island experienced net inward migration of 700,000,[120] many of whom came from Haiti and Jamaica. Some arrived for seasonal work only, returning to their islands at the end of the sugar harvest, but many stayed.[121] After 1930, however, inward migration slowed to a trickle, and outward migration speeded up. Cuba then experienced net outward migration for the first time in the twentieth century (see Table 10.4). This has been the pattern virtually ever since, although there was inward migration in the 1940s before the exodus began again in the 1950s.

---

[114] Because of the absence of reliable vital statistics before the 1930s, we cannot be absolutely sure, but we do know that the gross inward migration rate was high.

[115] The exact number killed has never been established. Estimates range from 10,000 to 25,000. See Crassweller (1966), pp. 153–6.

[116] The amount agreed was $750,000, with $250,000 to be paid immediately in cash. The balance of $500,000 was reduced to $275,000 in 1939. See Crassweller (1966), pp. 158–9.

[117] The same was true of the Dutch dependencies. The expansion of oil refining in the Dutch Antilles without immigration would have been impossible, and high death rates in Suriname (see Table C.3) made the colony heavily dependent on migration from Java.

[118] Puerto Rican migration to New York was particularly important, as anyone who has seen *West Side Story* will know.

[119] See Dietz (1986), p. 248.

[120] The cumulative figure for the first decade was 265,000; it was 300,000 in the second; and 143,000 in the third.

[121] See Knight (1985) and Pérez de la Riva (1975), vol. 2.

Theories of migration have tended to concentrate on wage differentials to explain the flows between countries. This clearly played a part in the Caribbean. Wage rates in Cuba before 1930, for example, were above those in Haiti or Jamaica, and wage rates in Europe or North America were higher than in all parts of the Caribbean. Yet the overwhelming reason for migration seems to have been the 'push' of job scarcity in the country of origin and the 'pull' of job opportunities in the host. This is borne out by Puerto Rico, where the gap between the minimum wage on the island and the mainland narrowed as the century advanced, while net migration moved in the opposite direction to what might have been expected from consideration of wage differentials alone.

It should never be forgotten also that the Caribbean had always been a region of migration. This had been true before the arrival of Europeans, and it was true afterwards. Inter-island communication was never as difficult, as is sometimes made out, and linguistic barriers have also been exaggerated. In the period considered here some traditional forms of migration ceased, notably inward migration from India and the Dutch East Indies (modern Indonesia), outward migration to Central America and European migration to Cuba. Other migration routes took their place, however, particularly the increased flow to the United States and the start of migration to Canada and Europe. And some migration patterns were unchanged, especially across the border in Hispaniola and into Trinidad & Tobago from other parts of the Caribbean.

By 1960, the population of the Caribbean was three times bigger than in 1900. Yet the earlier claim of 'overpopulation' was being heard less frequently. There was still underemployment, particularly outside the harvest months, and there was even a serious problem of unemployment in a few countries, such as Jamaica.[122] However, jobs were starting to be created with greater frequency outside the agricultural sector. It was widely assumed that these jobs would be found mainly in manufacturing, but this would turn out to be incorrect. It was the service sector – largely ignored and undervalued before 1960 – that would be the key to growth in the final period considered in this book.

---

[122] Jamaica was experiencing high levels of unemployment as early as the 1940s and probably before. See Cumper (1960a).

The Rise, Decline and Fall of the Belizean Economy before Independence

This chapter concludes Part II with a case study of Belize.[1] The country is in many ways unique in the Caribbean and not just because it is located on the mainland of Central America. The settlers who arrived in the seventeenth century may have considered themselves British, but they had to run their own affairs for approximately 200 years before the country became a colony. This makes Belize very different from other imperial dependencies in the Caribbean. In addition, until the second half of the twentieth century, the basis of the economy was forestry rather than agriculture. Finally, in the first decades there were few slaves, so the labour was provided largely by the settlers themselves.

The British government acknowledged Spanish sovereignty over Belize until nearly two decades after the collapse of Spanish authority in Central America and Mexico.[2] The settlement was therefore under constant threat until Spain ceded minimal usufruct rights under the Treaty of Paris in 1763.[3] These rights were extended by Anglo-Spanish treaties in 1783 and 1786,[4] but the territorial

---

[1] During the period considered here, Belize was known by many different names. It was the 'British Settlement in the Bay of Honduras' until the early nineteenth century, when it became known in British sources as the 'Bay of Honduras' or even on occasions 'Honduras'. It became 'British Honduras' in 1862 and 'Belize' in 1973.

[2] Central America declared its independence in 1821, but immediately annexed itself to Mexico. It then separated from Mexico in 1823 (losing Chiapas in the process) and became the United Provinces of Central America. This survived until 1838, after which it broke up into five nation-states. The British government, however, never accepted that the United Provinces or Mexico had inherited Spain's rights over Belize and continued to treat with the former imperial power on all issues involving the settlement. It was only in the 1840s that Britain started to deal with Guatemala, Honduras and Mexico on Belize issues. See Humphreys (1961).

[3] This gave the settlers the right to cut logwood, but the area in which they could do so was not clearly defined. See Naylor (1989), p. 55.

[4] The 1783 treaty clarified the territory in which the settlers could cut logwood (Hondo to Belize rivers), and the 1786 treaty extended the permitted area south to the Sibun River and included the right to cut mahogany for the first time. The western boundary was defined by a north–south line running through the New River lagoon. See Bolland (1988), p. 26.

threat did not disappear. Because Belize was not sovereign British territory, however, the settlers were not subject to the British Navigation Acts and were able to continue trading with the United States after its independence. Furthermore, they were not subject to the import duties and export taxes that the British applied to the trade of their Caribbean colonies.

The first section of this chapter explores the development of the settlement up to the middle of the nineteenth century. During and after the Napoleonic Wars the settlers ignored the boundaries established in the Anglo-Spanish treaties and unilaterally extended the area from which timber could be cut. Logwood (from which a dye was extracted) and later mahogany provided the basis of the economy, and Belize had achieved by 1820 the highest domestic exports per head in the Caribbean. Yet the prosperity of the settlement now no longer rested on forestry alone, because Spain had been unable to prevent the emergence of a clandestine re-export trade with Central America and belatedly gave it legitimacy in 1819.[5] When Spanish authority collapsed in the region in 1821, Belize was exceedingly well placed to take advantage of its new role as an entrepôt centre.

Gradually the British government established its authority over the settlement, which finally became a colony in 1862. Far from ushering in a period of renewed prosperity, colonialism proved to be an uninspiring experience. The second section of this chapter then examines the decline of the economy up to 1900 as a result of the stagnation of mahogany exports, strict fiscal control and the reduction in the entrepôt trade. Official efforts to shift the basis of the economy towards agriculture were thwarted by the structure of private land-holdings, the dismal state of infrastructure and a lack of vision by the imperial government. Sugar and rum exports did begin in the 1860s, but they barely survived the collapse of sugar prices in 1883–4, and banana exports after 1880 could not fully compensate.

There was a brief revival in the fortunes of the colony in the first years of the twentieth century, but this came to an abrupt end in 1914. The third section of the chapter then examines the fall of the economy during an extremely difficult period that culminated with devaluation at the end of the 1940s. These years included the end of logwood exports, the decline of the banana industry through disease and the emergence for the first time of surplus labour. There were riots in Belize on several occasions during this period, and the authorities were forced to take steps that would eventually help the colony to shift away from forestry.

The final section of the chapter examines the diversification of the economy and the rise of nontraditional exports up to independence in 1981. The story begins with the devaluation of the Belize dollar on 31 December 1949, despite the repeated promises of the colonial authorities that it would remain pegged

---

[5] Central America at this time had very few Caribbean ports. This gave Belize an opportunity to import manufactured goods from the UK and re-export them to the region using light vessels that could enter the rivers that flowed into the Caribbean. See Naylor (1988).

to the US dollar (as it had been since 1894). Devaluation did, however, help the country to promote exports other than forest products, and Belize started to become a more diversified economy, although it was not until after independence that the infrastructure improved significantly and the Belizean economy acquired its modern character.

11.1. PROSPERITY WITHOUT SUSTAINABILITY: FROM SETTLEMENT TO COLONY

It is not known exactly when Belize was first settled by the British.[6] It is, however, likely that the first settlers came from different parts of the Caribbean in the first half of the seventeenth century. In the second half, their numbers increased as a result of the logwood trade, which – at £50–£60 per ton – offered phenomenal profits.[7] By 1672 the Jamaican governor could speak with pride of the achievements of the logwood cutters in the Bay of Honduras,[8] and by the first years of the eighteenth century they had established such strong trading links with Boston that a pew was reserved for them in the Great North Church.[9] Ironically, the settlement also benefitted from the successful Spanish efforts to oust British logwood cutters in the Yucatán peninsula because many of those forced out moved to Belize where the logwood trade then concentrated.[10]

   The British government at first imposed an import tax of £5 per ton on logwood. As exports increased, prices fell and the tax became burdensome. Because they were not subject to the British Navigation Acts (Belize was not yet a colony), the settlers could sell their logwood wherever they could find a market. Some logwood was shipped direct to continental Europe.[11] However, the trade with Boston was the most important[12] (and New England traders then exported much of the logwood to consumers outside the UK without paying tax). Nonetheless, prices fell so low after 1750 that mahogany exports provided a welcome alternative and had overtaken logwood in terms of value

---

[6] There are many theories, but no hard evidence. See Winzerling (1946), Dobson (1973) and Naylor (1989).

[7] In the days when Spain had a monopoly on logwood, it was selling at £100 per ton. This encouraged privateers to seize Spanish ships carrying the precious wood. The plunder of Spanish ships gradually declined in the seventeenth century until it was outlawed in 1667 by the Anglo-Spanish treaty of that year. It is widely assumed, therefore, that some of the privateers went into the logwood business themselves, starting in the second half of the seventeenth century.

[8] See Bolland (1977), p. 25.

[9] It is still called the Bay Pew, and the inscription, dated 1727, reads: 'This Pew for the use of the Gentlemen of the Bay of Honduras.' A few years later in 1740 the merchants of Belize donated timber for the steeple.

[10] Spain had at first turned a blind eye to the activities of the logwood cutters on the Yucatán peninsula. However, the Spanish attitude changed after the Treaty of Utrecht in 1713. See McLeish (1926), chap. 3.

[11] See Dobson (1973), pp. 60–1.

[12] See McLeish (1926), p. 29.

by the last quarter of the eighteenth century. Mahogany extraction, however, is much more labour-intensive than logwood, and this explains the increase in the Belizean import of slaves.[13]

Logwood takes only seven to ten years to reach maturity, so there was little danger of the settlers exhausting the supply. Logwood also grows in dense clumps, which makes it relatively easy to extract in large quantities. Mahogany was quite different – it averages one tree per acre in its natural state and takes around 100 years to reach full maturity. There was no attempt at forest management, which was perhaps understandable when property rights were still unclear. However, forest practices remained largely unchanged until well into the twentieth century, and the rise of mahogany exports was inconsistent with any notion of sustainability of the forest resources. Indeed, it is likely that mahogany from 10,000 acres was being cleared every year by the early nineteenth century.[14] At this rate 1 million acres would be cleared before new trees could reach maturity.[15]

The rise of mahogany had a further undesirable consequence. The Baymen, as the settlers were known, had distributed logwood cutting rights among themselves through a system that at first limited each settler to one 'location' based on a river frontage of 2,000 yards and extending halfway back to the next navigable stream or river. This relatively democratic system did not work for mahogany because the trees grow to maturity very sparsely. As a result, mahogany locations were issued on the basis of a river frontage of three miles, and cutters were allowed two locations on each river.[16] The 'principal families' then abused the system by issuing locations in the names of other family members or even servants. It was estimated that about a dozen families held almost all the land in locations by the beginning of the nineteenth century.[17] When locations were turned into freeholds by British officials after 1858, the concentration of private land in a few hands was to prove a major obstacle to economic development.

The unsustainable nature of mahogany cutting in Belize was at first disguised by the unilateral extension of the settlement's boundaries southwards in the

---

[13] The first reference to slaves in Belize is in 1724, when they were said to have only recently arrived, and the total number was only 120 as late as 1745. See Shoman (2011), pp. 28–9. This implies that logwood had been cut for at least fifty years without much use of slaves. The number of slaves then increased rapidly in line with the growth of mahogany exports.

[14] Annual exports averaged 5,000,000 board feet by the 1820s. At approximately 500 feet per tree (see Gibbs (1883), p. 93), this implies annual felling of 10,000 trees.

[15] The land area of Belize today is just over 5 million acres, but mahogany does not grow everywhere, and many of the trees were inaccessible in the nineteenth century. See Hummel (1921) and Romney (1959).

[16] See Bolland (1977), p. 158.

[17] The evacuation of the Mosquito Shore in 1787, as agreed in the Anglo-Spanish treaty the previous year, had swollen the Belize population and threatened the dominant position of the established cutters. They therefore protected their position by ruling that only those with four slaves were entitled to a mahogany work, thereby excluding most of the new arrivals from access to timber. See Bolland (1977), pp. 32–3.

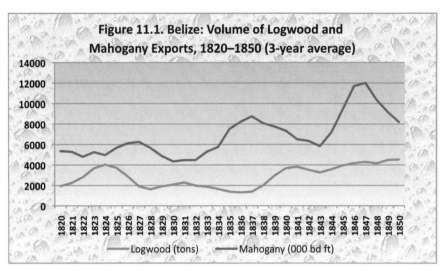

Figure 11.1. Belize: Volume of Logwood and Mahogany Exports, 1820–1850 (3-year average)

Logwood (tons)   Mahogany (000 bd ft)

Source: See Appendix to Chapter 11.

first three decades of the nineteenth century.[18] This was not sanctioned by any treaty, but it gave the settlers access to untouched primary forests, because there were no Spanish and only a small number of Maya in the area.[19] The British superintendents, who resided in the settlement from 1786, connived at this territorial extension. From 1817, however, the superintendent refused to accept new claims to private ownership in view of the uncertain position in international law.[20]

The volume of mahogany exports rose after 1820 (see Figure 11.1), helped by favourable tariff treatment (see below in this section). Before then mahogany had been mainly used in furniture and shipbuilding. However, the use of mahogany in railway carriages provided a great stimulus. The peak of mahogany extraction in Belize was in the 1840s when annual exports occasionally exceeded 10 million feet.[21] The cost of mahogany extraction then increased when the settlers had to go farther inland to secure the trees. Logwood exports also prospered because the rapidly expanding textile industry was still entirely dependent on natural dyes, and Belize was one of the main suppliers to the whole of Europe and North America.

[18] The Spanish had been defeated at the Battle of St George's Caye in 1798, and the settlers then wasted no time in pushing southwards to the Sarstoon River, incorporating an additional area almost as large as that defined by the Anglo-Spanish treaties. However, even this did not satisfy the settlers, because they also extracted some timber from the northern Mosquito Shore where Honduran authority did not yet extend. See Naylor (1989).

[19] We do not know exactly how many, because the first census to include the Maya was not taken until 1861.

[20] See Bolland and Shoman (1977), chap. 2.

[21] This volume of exports would not be surpassed until the 1920s.

Source: For merchandise exports, see Appendix to Chapter 11. Population from Table A.1.

By the 1820s, Belize had by far the highest merchandise exports per head of all Caribbean countries.[22] However, this would prove to be the peak. Not only was there no increase in the value of merchandise exports per head, but they also declined even before the country became a colony (see Figure 11.2). There were three main reasons for this. First, the price of mahogany fell. Second, the population of Belize increased after 1830 through net inward migration, with the new arrivals playing only a small part in the export sector. Third, re-exports declined after 1840.

The price of mahogany, like other commodities, was exceptionally high at the end of the Napoleonic Wars. Prices subsequently dropped, but the fall was no worse than for many other commodities.[23] With the UK the main market, the British import duty on mahogany then became a contro-versial issue – Belizean mahogany should have been charged at the foreign duty rate because the settlement was not a colony. Yet successful lobbying by the exporters and their London agent ensured that Belize was treated **more** favourably than its competitors (including British colonies).[24] Furthermore, in 1832 all mahogany cut in the Bay of Honduras was made subject to this pref-erential duty if cleared through Belize.[25] The abolition of mahogany duties

---

[22] Merchandise exports include re-exports, but even in terms of domestic exports per head Belize was still ranked first in 1820.

[23] Belize did, however, face some special problems as a result of not being a British colony. Belize-built ships were denied a British registry until 1826. See Naylor (1989), p. 257n22. In addition, Belize mahogany was not included as a first-class wood for the construction of vessels of the twelve years' grade by the Lloyd's Committee of British and Foreign Shipping. See Chaloner and Fleming (1851), pp. 81–115, which contains a series of testimonials about the merits of Belizean mahogany from interested parties.

[24] See Dobson (1973), pp. 131–2.

[25] See Naylor (1989), p.256n18. Strictly speaking, some of the mahogany logs shipped from Belize were re-exports because they originated on the Mosquito Shore. However, neither Honduras nor Nicaragua exercised sovereignty over Mosquitia until 1860. It is therefore reasonable to consider the mahogany a domestic export.

by Britain in 1845, however, put Belize on the same footing as everyone else.[26]

The population of Belize was still less than 4,000 at the end of the Napoleonic Wars.[27] It grew slowly at first, in part because some slaves escaped to the neighbouring republics, where slavery had been abolished.[28] After emancipation, however, the population grew rapidly, reaching over 8,000 by 1841.[29] This may have been partly from the return of some former slaves. However, it was also due to the inclusion of the inhabitants of the southern districts, because the British authorities became more confident about their claim to these lands. This area included not only the Maya, but also the Garinagu, who had been expelled from St Vincent by the British in 1797 to Roatán in the Bay Islands.[30] Many had subsequently made their way to Belize and settled in the south.

When Spanish power was at its height, there was little or no re-export trade between Belize and Central America. This began to change during the Napoleonic Wars, when Spain struggled to assert its authority over its mainland colonies. The entrepôt trade then boomed following the independence of Central America, despite the friction caused by the runaway slaves.[31] The re-export trade continued after the dissolution of the United Provinces of Central America in 1838, with Guatemala in particular maintaining ties with Belizean traders. By the late 1840s, however, these republics were starting to explore alternative avenues of import supply, and this process accelerated with the opening of the Panama railroad in 1855. Belize's role as an entrepôt centre for Central America was not destroyed, but it was no longer so important, and the country came to depend more on re-exports to the Yucatán peninsula (including contraband arms sales).[32]

The entrepôt trade at this time was in two parts. First, Belize imported large quantities of British manufactured goods, which were then re-exported to the neighbouring republics. Second, Belize imported commodities from Central America, such as indigo and cochineal, which were then re-exported (mainly to the UK). Both types of re-exports peaked around 1840[33] before starting to decline as the Central American states developed direct shipping links with Europe and the United States. When Central America replaced its traditional

---

[26] Belize was the main supplier to the UK, followed by the Dominican Republic, Cuba and Jamaica. See Naylor (1988), pp. 239–40.

[27] The first census in 1816 gave a figure of 3,824, of which 2,742 were slaves. See *Report of the British Guiana and British Honduras Settlement Commission* (1948), p. 218.

[28] It was abolished by the United Provinces of Central America in 1824 and by Mexico in 1829. See Halperín-Donghi (1985), p. 322.

[29] The annual population data are in Table A.1. The methodology used to derive them is in the Notes on A. Tables.

[30] See González (1988). See also Iyo, Tzalam and Humphreys (2007), pp. 311–2.

[31] See Clegern (1967), p. 8.

[32] The arms were sold to the Santa Cruz Maya during the long *Guerra de las Castas* in Yucatán. See Dumond (1997), pp. 326–7.

[33] Naylor (1988) has a volume series for both kinds of re-exports for many years between 1820 and 1850. These series show clearly that re-exports reached a peak around 1840.

products with coffee after 1850, it would all be shipped direct. However, towards the end of the nineteenth century, Belize companies started to extract products from the forests of the neighbouring countries, and these would be re-exported through Belize.

The entrepôt trade accounted for nearly two-thirds of merchandise exports between 1830 and 1860[34] and had a lasting impact on the currency system of the settlement. Before 1800, Belize had used Jamaican pounds, known as currency, which had a lower value than the pound sterling (and incidentally this causes great confusion in the archival records because both pounds are given by the same symbol, £). The entrepôt trade so flooded the market with coins from Mexico, Central America, Peru, Venezuela and even Chile that the silver dollar became the de facto currency. These silver dollars[35] were then exchanged against the pound sterling at 5 to 1 – a rate very similar to that of the US dollar under the gold standard (4.87 to 1). This arrangement, approved by royal decree in 1838, survived until 1887 when the decline in the silver price of gold forced the authorities to revise the currency regime (see below in the next section).

The exceptional position of Belize in the 1820s meant that the settlement would remain one of the richest Caribbean countries for some decades, despite the problems we have just outlined. Indeed, by 1850 only the Danish Virgin Islands with its vast re-export trade had overtaken Belize in terms of merchandise exports per head.[36] It is true that there was virtually no domestic production in Belize, agriculture having been forbidden by the terms of the Anglo-Spanish treaties, but as a consequence most of the small population was at first engaged in export trades, where labour productivity tended to be highest. The first full-time agriculturalists (apart from the Maya, who had never abandoned farming) were the migrants who came in the nineteenth century.

The settlers were responsible for their own taxation through the Public Assembly that had been in force since the earliest days. Not surprisingly, therefore, public revenue per head (see Figure 11.3) was modest in comparison with the high level of exports per head. In particular, taxes on imports were relatively low because neither of the dominant groups among the settlers (exporters and merchants) had any desire to raise them, and for most of the time imports destined for Central America and Mexico were free of duty.[37] Most public officials were paid by fee rather than by salary, and there was no need for the cumbersome and expensive machinery of colonial rule.

---

[34] See figures for Belize in Table A.10.

[35] They were known collectively as *sol*, which was the name of the Chilean and Peruvian silver dollar. See Bristowe and Wright (1890), pp. 205–10.

[36] The Danish Virgin Islands in 1850 had merchandise exports of $126 per head compared with $114 in Belize. No other countries came close (derived from Tables A.13 and A.1a).

[37] The Public Assembly in the 1820s applied a 5% tax on goods destined for Central America if they did not pass through Belize merchants, but this was later overruled by the superintendent. See Naylor (1989). Central Americans believed the motive for the tax was their refusal to return runaway slaves. See Clegern (1967), p. 8.

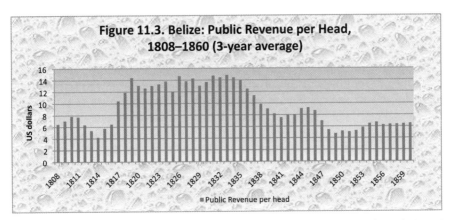

Source: Colonial Department (1836), Martin (1843), Gibbs (1883), Bristowe and Wright (1890) and Burdon (1931), vol. 1. Population from Table A.1.

These arrangements were deeply unsatisfactory for the British superintendents, the first of whom had arrived in the settlement in 1786. The Baymen were not always of the same mind on social and economic policy – the exporters, for example, were strongly opposed to a land tax. Yet they were often united against the British officials sent to the settlement as they fought to preserve their traditional privileges. Indeed, the superintendent had to insist that British laws abolishing the slave trade in 1807 applied to Belize and that slaves should be subject to the same process of registration as in the British colonies.[38]

The end of the slave trade presented the settlers with the same issue as other employers in the Caribbean – how to resolve the chronic shortage of labour. In Belize, however, the problem was exacerbated by the number of runaway slaves. Following the end of the apprenticeship period in 1838, the cutters moved swiftly to a system of advance payments for mahogany and logwood workers (almost all former slaves), which pushed them into debt and tied them to the employer for years. Furthermore, the advance had to be spent in the stores, many of which were owned by the employers, where goods were sold through the 'truck' system.[39]

Pernicious though it was, the advance and truck system survived up to the end of the period of labour scarcity at the beginning of the twentieth century. However, from the point of view of the employers it was much more effective than the alternatives. The settlers had secured a number of *emancipados* from the Anglo-Spanish Court in Havana in 1836, but the results had been little short of disastrous.[40] The settlers were also uncertain about the merits of uncontrolled migration by the Garinagu and by those who came from the

---

[38] Some slaves continued to be legally imported into Belize after 1807 because the trade in slaves among British Caribbean colonies did not end until 1830. See Chapter 3. Some Indians from the Mosquito Shore were also held as slaves, but this was illegal under British law.

[39] See Bolland (1977), pp. 122–3.

[40] See Bolland (1977), p. 121.

neighbouring republics, but in due course they would be reconciled. Tight control of the land market ensured that many had no option but to work for the settlers.

The Baymen for generations had appointed their own magistrates through the Public Assembly, but the superintendent himself succeeded in appointing them directly in 1833.[41] This was followed by the appointment of public officials on salary in the 1840s. The superintendent did not interfere with locations acquired before 1817 between the Sibun and Hondo rivers, and these would be converted to freehold titles after 1858. However, British officials established that all land south of the Sibun River (about half the settlement) should be Crown lands even before Belize became a colony. Thus, the settlement was divided in two parts: a northern half where a small number of 'monied cutters' monopolised the use of the land and a southern half where there was little or no private ownership of land.

In 1854, the superintendent finally succeeded in replacing the boisterous Public Assembly with a tamer Legislative Council with tax-raising powers. The low customs duties favoured by the settlers would be gradually replaced by rates similar to those in the rest of the British Caribbean. The following year, the Laws in Force Act was passed, and British officials then moved quickly to legitimise landholdings in Belize. Although the 1858 Honduras Land Titles Act never received the royal assent, a register of land titles was established anyway, and a revised act was passed in 1859.[42] From this point onwards, owners of freehold titles could buy and sell in much the same way as in other British colonies.

The decision by the British to accelerate the shift to colonial institutions had been preceded by the Clayton-Bulwer Treaty of 1850 with the United States.[43] Although its wording was ambiguous, it would become clear by 1856 that the United States would not oppose British sovereignty over Belize.[44] All that remained were boundary treaties with Guatemala and Mexico. The former signed and ratified a treaty in 1859, but political unrest in the Yucatán peninsula ruled out a treaty with Mexico until 1893. The Anglo-Guatemalan Treaty of 1859 would turn out to be a poisoned chalice, but this would not become clear for some years.[45] The British authorities therefore proceeded to demarcate most of the boundary, and Belize became the colony of British Honduras in 1862.[46]

---

[41] The British Caribbean colonies were obliged to appoint magistrates to oversee the process of emancipation. The superintendent took advantage of this to appoint **all** magistrates in the settlement.

[42] See Bolland (1977), p. 185.

[43] See Naylor (1989), pp. 186–7.

[44] This was made clear by the 1856 Clarendon-Dallas Treaty between the two countries, but the treaty was never ratified because of a technical dispute.

[45] See Shoman (2010), chap. 2.

[46] The boundary was not fully demarcated in the northwest – the exercise had to be abandoned because of opposition from Maya rebels in Mexico.

11.2. COLONIALISM AND ECONOMIC DECLINE

One of the first problems the new colony had to address was the wave of migration from the Yucatán peninsula after 1847. This was a consequence of the *Guerra de las Castas*, which was to last half a century and involved not only a struggle between the Maya Indians, the landowners and the Mexican state, but also major conflicts between the different Maya groups.[47] Without an officially recognised boundary between Belize and Mexico, the conflict spread across the border on many occasions, and thousands of Yucatecans chose to make their home in northern Belize as both economic and political refugees.

There was no official census after 1845 until 1861.[48] However, contemporary estimates suggested the population had jumped to nearly 20,000 by 1857, and the 1861 census confirmed a figure in excess of 25,000. For a country that had recorded a population of less than 4,000 in 1816, this was a huge increase; yet it did not bring an end to the scarcity of labour because most of the new arrivals became squatters on private land and concentrated on subsistence agriculture. Indeed, within a few years of the census, the colony was importing indentured labour from China and India and workers from Barbados (with very disappointing results in all cases).[49]

A large part of the problem was the low natural rate of growth of the population. Although births had exceeded deaths among the slave population just before emancipation, it was only by a small margin.[50] This low birth rate almost certainly continued for many decades, and thus the increase in population was mainly from the inward migration from Mexico and Guatemala.[51] Furthermore, when reliable figures on births and deaths became available from 1886 onwards, they suggested that the natural rate of growth was still close to zero.[52] It was only after 1894 that the births finally exceeded deaths by a significant margin.[53]

Under these circumstances British officials saw no reason to relax the policy of restricting access to land that the Colonial Office – and the private landholders – had exercised even before the establishment of the colony. Crown lands in the south were not at first made available in small parcels at low prices, and

---

[47] See Reed (1964).

[48] See Notes on A. Tables.

[49] Many of the Chinese were so badly treated that they fled across the border and joined the Santa Cruz Maya in Mexico. See Bolland (1977), p. 143.

[50] As elsewhere in the Caribbean, male slaves in Belize outnumbered females before the abolition of the slave trade, and slave deaths at first exceeded births. However, on the eve of emancipation, net births had become positive. See Tables A.3 and A.4.

[51] There was actually a small fall in the population between the 1861 and 1871 census. See Table A.1.

[52] Before 1886, the number of deaths was based on recorded burials and gives an implausibly low figure. On the other hand, the number of births, based on baptisms, was very high. It is only from 1886 onwards that the colony collected accurate figures, and these suggested that annual births and deaths were at first roughly the same.

[53] See Tables A.3 and A.4.

private lands in the north were almost never sold to small farmers. Colonial policy was therefore in line with that preferred by the large landowners, who complained constantly of a shortage of labour, despite the growth of population, and who restricted access to their own land as vigorously as possible. Furthermore, when more enlightened governors[54] explored the possibility of relaxing this land policy, they were firmly overruled by the Colonial Office in London.

Landholdings had been highly concentrated even before the last of the Anglo-Spanish treaties in 1786. However, it would become much more concentrated after the establishment of the colony. By this time (c.1860) it had become normal for exporters in Belize to have associations with merchants in the UK, and in one case this had been formalised in a London-quoted company established under the provisions of the 1856 British legislation permitting limited liability. This enterprise, the British Honduras Company, was formed in 1859, and from the moment of its creation owned well in excess of 1 million acres of freehold land.[55] Its access to capital in London helped it not only to weather the mahogany crisis at the end of the 1860s, but also to buy out many of its competitors. When it became in 1875 the Belize Estate and Produce Company (BEC), it would own more than half of all freehold land in the country.

The BEC, like General Motors in the United States in the twentieth century, considered its interests synonymous with that of the country as a whole, and colonial officials saw no reason to disagree. Its influence on colonial policy included not only land and labour, but also taxation and the exchange rate. It was represented in all the colonial assemblies and could count on direct access to the governor. Furthermore, it was influential in the UK through its shareholders, and at least one of its directors sat in Parliament, and therefore the British government had to take heed of its interests. It is fair to say that BEC played just as crucial (and generally malign) a role in Belize during the first century of colonialism as did the United Fruit Company (UFCO) in Central America in the first decades after its formation in 1899.[56]

What BEC could not do was prevent the crisis in the mahogany industry that was brought about by the decline in demand and the fall in price after the mid-1860s. This was a consequence of the switch to iron in ships and the end of the boom in railway carriage construction in the UK. The company, therefore, switched back to logwood, and other cutters did likewise (see Figure 11.4). By 1870, the value of logwood exports had overtaken that of mahogany, but both were below their levels at the beginning of the century.[57] By 1890, logwood exports were worth twice as much as mahogany exports, and the volume was

---

[54] When Belize became a colony in 1862, it was made a dependency of Jamaica, and thus the senior British official was called lieutenant-governor. It was only in 1884 that Belize ceased to be a dependency of Jamaica, and the senior official became the governor.

[55] This was about one-fifth of the whole colony. See Bolland (1977), pp. 186–7.

[56] Although there have been many excellent monographs on UFCO, there have sadly been none on BEC. Such a book needs to be written.

[57] See figures on Belize in Table A.10.

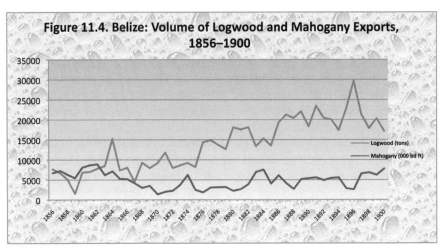

Figure 11.4. Belize: Volume of Logwood and Mahogany Exports, 1856–1900

Source: See Appendix to Chapter 11.

ten times higher than in 1830. However, mahogany enjoyed a revival in the 1890s as a result of increased US demand.[58]

The mahogany crisis in the 1860s had been temporarily disguised in Belize by the boom in re-exports to the Confederacy during the US Civil War.[59] Legal exports soared,[60] but illegal exports probably increased also because part of the trade consisted of munitions. Britain – officially neutral in the Civil War – tried to stop the contraband, but the efforts of colonial officials were not very successful because Belizean merchants had been trading guns to the Maya insurgents in Yucatán for years and were very skilled at concealing the trade.[61]

As the re-export boom ended, officials finally concluded that the colony's long-term salvation depended on the development of agricultural exports alongside timber extraction. It had been clear for years that the rate of extraction of mahogany was beyond what was sustainable in the long run (unless conservation measures – unheard of at that time – were undertaken). Belize, on the other hand, had an abundance of land suitable for agriculture. Yet the Colonial Office was unclear how to proceed, and British officials missed many opportunities to promote the diversification of the economy.

The first missed opportunity had come with the arrival of migrants before the colony was even established. Neither the Garinagu nor the Yucatecans,

---

[58] Because of the high US import duties on semiprocessed products, the mahogany was shipped to the US as trees rather than as squared lumber (as happened in the case of exports to the UK).

[59] By this time, Belizean companies no longer had access to mahogany on the northern Mosquito Shore, because this area had been recognised by the UK as sovereign Honduran territory in 1860. See Naylor (1989).

[60] Merchandise exports, which include re-exports, went from $1.4 million in 1861 to $1.8 million in 1864 despite the fall in the value of mahogany exports during these years.

[61] See Clegern (1967), who makes use of the reports from the US consul in Belize during these years.

yet alone the *emancipados* or returning former slaves, were initially offered Crown lands on favourable terms, and thus a small-scale peasantry could not take root.[62] The minimal development in small-scale agriculture that did take place was a result of squatting, but it never acquired the same scale as in, for example, Guyana, Jamaica, Martinique or Suriname. Furthermore, these squatters were far from Belize City,[63] the only significant urban centre, and therefore no marketable surplus was offered, and the colony continued to depend on imported foodstuffs.

The second missed opportunity came with the arrival of former Confederate soldiers after 1865, but they found the price of both private and Crown land exorbitant, and most of them moved on to other countries or returned to the United States.[64] At least one governor asked permission from London to lower the price of Crown land or even make it available gratuitously, but these overtures had been firmly resisted.[65] The notion of a scarcity of labour had taken such a firm hold that officials were not prepared to take any chances. A handful of Confederates did remain, however, and they helped to develop the sugar industry in the south (see below in this section).

The third missed opportunity was the (lack of) development of infrastructure. Private-sector and colonial elites were convinced there could be no long-term development without a railway connecting Belize with Guatemala. When a US entrepreneur, Walter Regan, came with a serious offer in 1884 and surveyed a route that would have passed through the southwest corner of the colony, there was almost universal enthusiasm. However, the Colonial Office dithered because it wanted to ensure that any railway would meet the terms of the British obligation to Guatemala under the 1859 boundary treaty. The railway to Guatemala was therefore never built.[66]

Colonial officials were reluctant to use public resources to pursue developmental goals. Public revenue per head was higher than in most other British colonies,[67] but the threat from Yucatán meant that in many years much of this was absorbed by military expenditure. Indeed, the danger was so severe in the second half of the 1860s that the Legislative Assembly (responsible for raising taxes) abolished itself in 1870, and Crown colony government was introduced

[62] Crown lands were not offered to the Maya in the south either, but at least their traditional land use was not disrupted.

[63] When the country was known as British Honduras, and even before, the main town was called 'Belize'. It became 'Belize City' when the country's name was changed to Belize in 1973.

[64] See Simmons (2001), pp. 48–53.

[65] The most famous case involved Lieutenant-Governor Austin, who had provisionally awarded a huge grant in the south to Confederate settlers, but he was overruled and forced to return to London by the Colonial Office. See Simmons (2001), pp. 30–1.

[66] On railways, see Clegern (1967), pp. 72–5.

[67] Public revenue per head in Belize varied between $6 and $8 from 1860 to 1900. This was about 20% higher than the comparable figures for all British colonies (the numbers can be derived from Tables A.33 and A.1a).

in April 1871. This backward step had been taken to oblige the British government to absorb more of the cost of colonial defence, because the members of the Assembly had no wish for the land tax they had passed in 1867 to be anything other than temporary.[68]

Public debt under colonialism was first issued in 1863, but it remained at very modest levels and was used primarily to make improvements to Belize City.[69] Frustration with the slow progress in infrastructure development finally persuaded the private sector to finance a tramway a few miles up the Stann Creek valley. This opened in 1892 and helped to promote banana exports (see below in this section). When the shipping line carrying bananas was purchased by UFCO in 1900,[70] the colonial government was lobbied to build a full-scale railway down the whole length of the valley to the nearest seaport. This was built at public expense and opened in 1911, but the arrangement was far too generous to UFCO.[71]

Belize still had no all-weather roads, and the 90-mile journey from Belize City to San Ignacio on the western border took many days by boat. The northern frontier was also inaccessible except by water, and the south remained very isolated. Yet despite the dismal state of infrastructure, the first small steps towards export diversification had been taken by the end of the nineteenth century. This had little to do with colonial policy and initially had nothing to do with the landowners either, but it was very welcome and much needed all the same.

The first significant step was the establishment of a sugar industry by the Yucatecan refugees in the north of the country. Although most refugees engaged in self-sufficient agriculture, a small number experimented with sugar and rum production around the town of Corozal. In 1857, the first small shipment of sugar was made, but this was not repeated until 1862. By then, the British Honduras Company had turned some of its idle lands into sugarcane plantations, and the growth of sugar exports was rapid. The Confederate settlers, especially in the Toledo district, also contributed to the growth of the industry. However, Belize was not destined to become a sugar colony until after the Second World War. The sharp fall in the world price in 1883–4 undermined the industry, and the value of exports declined rapidly (see Figure 11.5).

---

[68] In this they were disappointed because the land tax was made permanent in 1871, albeit at a very low rate.

[69] In fairness, these improvements were much needed. They at first followed the recommendations made by Baron Siccama, but they ended in scandal in the 1880s when Governor Goldsworthy mysteriously awarded the contract to a sworn enemy of his predecessor. See Clegern (1967), pp. 76–8.

[70] This was the Belize Royal Mail and Central America Steamship Company. See Moberg (2003).

[71] UFCO was able to buy Crown land very cheaply, transport its bananas at favourable rates on the public railway, pay no export taxes or import duties and was charged land tax at a lower rate than other growers. In addition, UFCO received a subsidy for carrying the mail to New Orleans. See Moberg (1997), pp. 23–7.

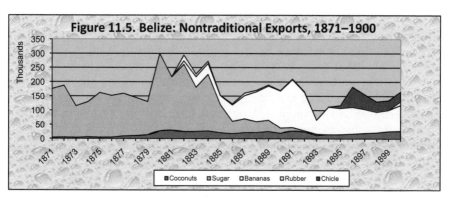

Source: *Statistical tables relating to the Colonial and other Possessions of the United Kingdom* (various years).

The next step was the development of a banana industry centered on the Stann Creek valley. The first regular shipment was made in 1882, and within a few years exports had increased rapidly (see Figure 11.5). The trade was at first in the hands of small-scale farmers, who were able to take advantage of the steamships that were now calling regularly from New Orleans following a decision of Governor Barlee in 1878 to transfer the mail subsidy away from the Jamaica route.[72] A British Honduras syndicate was formed out of several smaller companies, UFCO entered the country after its formation in 1899, and soon after Vaccaro Bros. (later Standard Fruit and Steamship Co.) started calling at Belize to buy bananas.[73] As the century ended, and even before the railway was planned, the prospects for banana exports looked bright.

Colonial officials could take some credit for the next two examples of nontraditional exports. Rubber (*castilloa elastica*) had started to be exported in 1882, but it was at first harvested from the wild. A small botanic garden had been established in the grounds of Government House in 1892, and rubber seedlings were distributed throughout the country.[74] Shortly afterwards, a small export trade in cacao and coffee was started. None of these products amounted to much in volume or value terms, but they did at least show that Belize could produce agricultural exports, and cacao in particular would return to the export list a century later.

Ironically, it was a forest product (chicle) that was to prove the most enduring and successful nontraditional export as the nineteenth century ended. The bleeding of the sapodilla tree produces a latex, which is the basis of chewing gum and was much in demand in the United States. It was harvested from

---

[72] See Clegern (1967), p. 61.
[73] See Moberg (1997), p. 21.
[74] The Botanic Station had been recommended by Daniel Morris, who wrote a book about the colony's resources. See Morris (1883).

June to March and therefore depended on a different labour force to that used in mahogany and logwood extraction. It served the needs of the large estates perfectly, and they started to add chicle to their traditional exports from 1894 onwards (see Figure 11.5).

By no means was all the chicle exported by Belize produced in the country. By the late nineteenth century, the landowners had so exhausted their forest reserves that they were cutting logwood and mahogany across the borders in Guatemala and Mexico.[75] Chicle was soon added to the list, and re-exports once again became of great importance to Belize. The traditional re-export trade to Central America and the Yucatán had not entirely ended – indeed, merchants did a thriving trade supplying the forest workers across the borders – but it had changed character and would remain important for many years.[76]

The rise of nontraditional exports took place as the currency question became especially awkward. The silver dollars (*sol*) circulating in the colony served their purpose well enough until the silver price of gold started to fall after 1873. By 1880, it was no longer possible to maintain the fiction of a fixed rate of exchange against sterling, and the Treasury each year converted *sol* to sterling at a different rate. In 1887, by royal decree, the Guatemalan silver dollar was made the legal tender of the colony, but other silver dollars were still accepted up to small amounts.[77] However, this was only a temporary measure because the silver price continued to fall. Finally, bowing to pressure from different interest groups, the US gold dollar was made legal tender in 1894.

Belize was now effectively on the gold standard, but nominal wage rates had to be reduced in order that exports should remain competitive.[78] The average reduction was 30 per cent, which brought nominal wage rates back approximately to their level in 1892.[79] This caused much grumbling and some rioting (including by the police force in the northern district).[80] From this point onwards, in common with the surrounding republics, Belize enjoyed a period of economic recovery that lasted with only minor interruptions up to the First World War. Exports were becoming more diversified as a result of the growth not only of bananas and chicle but also of coconuts and cedar.

Yet the deep structural flaws remained in place. There was no forest management by either the public or private sector, and thus timber exports were

---

[75] In the 1891 census it was stated that nearly 1,500 Belizean workers and their families (4 per cent of the population) were unenumerated, because they were working in these camps outside the country.

[76] At the end of the nineteenth century, re-exports were equal to one-third of domestic exports. See Tables A.11 and A.12.

[77] See Bristowe and Wright (1890), pp. 205–10.

[78] When the gold dollar was adopted, it was worth roughly twice the value of the silver dollar. See Appendix to Chapter 11.

[79] See *Colonial Report for British Honduras* (1894), p. 6.

[80] One of the causes of the riots was the failure of the colonial authorities to adjust the specific import duties. These had been payable in silver but now had to be paid in gold dollars. Importers therefore raised their prices, and this caused great resentment. See Ashdown (1986a), p. 6.

unsustainable over the long term. Mahogany trees were increasingly difficult to find and expensive to extract (hence the search for cheaper alternatives in Guatemala and Mexico). Chicle was also not being harvested in a sustainable fashion.[81] With the rise of the German chemical industry and the development of aniline dyes in the 1890s, logwood faced a synthetic competitor at the end of the century for the first time. Bananas, as elsewhere in Central America, were at the mercy of diseases for which there were no known cures. And there were still no roads, which seriously impeded efforts to diversify the economy and encourage agricultural exports. Finally, Belize was a small colony in a vast empire, which received neither the best officials nor much attention from London.

Under these circumstances, it is not surprising that the Belize economy by 1900 had lost its privileged position in the Caribbean (it had been ranked first in 1850 in terms of domestic exports per head and second – behind the Danish Virgin Islands – in terms of merchandise exports per head). By 1900 it had fallen to fourth position in terms of merchandise exports per head[82] and sixth position in terms of domestic exports per head.[83] These rankings were by no means disastrous, but more worrying was the **absolute** decline in the Belize position because domestic exports per head in 1900 were roughly half what they had been in 1850, and merchandise exports per head were only one-third of their earlier value.[84] The first half century of colonialism, therefore, had proved to be a great disappointment – especially because the country was now a Crown colony and had lost control of its own affairs.

11.3. THE FALL OF THE BELIZE ECONOMY: 1900–1950

The Belizean economy made some progress in the first years of the twentieth century. The first bank was established in 1903.[85] A new market had been found for mahogany in the United States;[86] chicle had been added to the list of principal exports; bananas were expanding; and the re-export trade was recovering.[87] Agricultural exports only contributed 20 per cent to domestic

---

[81] Chicle can be harvested in a sustainable fashion if the sapodilla tree is not bled too fiercely and if the tree is left untouched for seven years. There is plenty of evidence to suggest this was not the case in Belize. See Hummel (1921).

[82] Behind the Danish Virgin Islands, Trinidad and French Guiana. The figures are derived from Tables A.13 and A.1a.

[83] Behind French Guiana, Trinidad, Turks & Caicos Islands, Guyana and Cuba. The figures are derived from Tables A.11 and A.1a.

[84] The precise figures: domestic exports per head ($45.7 and $26.4); merchandise exports per head ($114.1 and $35.2).

[85] Its name was the Bank of British Honduras. It was purchased by the Royal Bank of Canada in 1912.

[86] The share of domestic exports going to the US jumped from less than 20% in 1900 to nearly 75% just before the First World War. See Table C.15.

[87] The re-export trade now consisted mainly of forest products imported from Guatemala and Mexico and then shipped to the US and Europe.

TABLE 11.1. *Annual Rate of Change of Domestic Exports per Head (1930 prices), 1900–1960*

	Belize	Hispaniola	Cuba	Dependencies: British	French	Dutch	US	Caribbean
1900/20	−0.3	−0.3	1.3	0.5	1.5	0.3	6.8	2.0
1920/40	−0.6	−1.2	−3.7	0.3	0.0	10.2	0.4	−1.2
1940/60	−0.5	2.1	2.2	7.0	0.7	1.8	4.2	3.6
1900/60	−0.5	0.2	−0.1	2.6	0.7	4.0	3.8	1.5

Source: Derived from Table C.9 and C.1a.

exports, and Crown land leased to farmers (large and small) was less than 1 per cent of the colony's surface area,[88] but the authorities could convince themselves that a start had been made in diversifying the economy away from timber. Despite all that had gone wrong since the middle of the nineteenth century, Belize was still in 1910 ranked tenth in terms of domestic exports per head and third in terms of merchandise exports per head. It was also ranked fifth in terms of public revenue per head, the bulk of income still coming from customs duties.[89]

In the next few decades, however, Belize's position would seriously deteriorate, and by 1950 it would be ranked fourteenth in terms of domestic exports per head, placing it in the bottom half of all Caribbean countries. At that time, it was still ranked third in terms of public revenue per head, but this was because of the grants and loans received from the British Treasury after 1931 (see below in this section), not the 'true' revenue raised from local taxation. The four decades after 1910 were therefore critical ones for Belize and mark the years when the economy – still heavily based on forest products exploited in an unsustainable fashion – started to fail. Because the period also coincided with two world wars and the Great Depression, the economies in all other countries were also harmed. Thus, the **relative** decline of the Belize economy needs to be explained along with its **absolute** fall. Furthermore, the relative deterioration continued through the 1950s, but this will be examined in more detail in the next section. As an illustration, the growth of domestic exports per head at constant prices is shown in Table 11.1 for three periods, and it demonstrates clearly how poorly Belize performed not only in relation to the British colonies, but also relative to other subregions. Indeed, over the whole period from 1900 to 1960, domestic exports per head at constant prices fell, and the Belizean performance was worse than all the other subregions shown.

---

[88] Lease of Crown lands to smallholders had begun in the late nineteenth century, but it was on a very small scale.
[89] The land tax usually contributed less than 5% to government income, and an income tax would not be introduced until 1920. See Ashdown (1979), p. 37.

The outbreak of the First World War in August 1914 was, of course, a serious blow for Belize. The mahogany shipped to the United States since the 1890s may have reduced the importance of the British market, but the UK was still a major customer, and continental Europe (including Russia) was also important for logwood. Demand from Europe for timber fell immediately, but mahogany exports to the United States also plummeted because contractors in Mexico, fearful of losing their concessions, had oversupplied the US market following the outbreak of revolution in December 1910. Furthermore, re-exports (mahogany, logwood and chicle) – not just domestic exports – all suffered as a consequence of the Mexican Revolution. Imports, most of which came from the United States,[90] could still be obtained, but the fall in export earnings reduced the Belizean demand.

The slump in demand for exports in the early years of the war reduced the need for labour. In the 1914–15 season, forestry requirements were roughly half what they had been the previous year.[91] For the first time ever the colony experienced surplus labour, a situation made worse by the return of those workers who had migrated to Panama after 1903 to help in the construction of the canal. Belize suffered net migration outwards in every decade after 1900, a complete reverse of what had happened in the nineteenth century.[92] The mahogany industry was rescued, however, by the decision of the British Admiralty to place a large order in 1916. This was used not just in shipbuilding, but also to make propellers for the Royal Air Force.[93]

When the war ended, traditional sources of demand for mahogany returned, and exports rose to previously unheard of levels (see Figure 11.6).[94] Prices, as for other commodities in the Caribbean, fell sharply in 1921, but in Belize they soon recovered. And Belize now had a new and unexpected source of additional income as a result of US Prohibition (1919–33). Re-exports, mainly of whisky imported from Canada, soared to destinations from which they could be smuggled into the United States, and the contraband trade focused on the Mississippi delta.[95] The colonial authorities turned a blind eye until the bilateral treaty between the UK and the United States in 1924 forced the UK to crack down on the trade.

---

[90] The US had been the main source of imports since the adoption of the US dollar as the colony's currency in 1894.

[91] See *Colonial Report for British Honduras* (1915), p. 14.

[92] See Table A.6.

[93] Many Belizeans volunteered to fight, most being sent to Mesopotamia, but it is unlikely that this was the reason for the Admiralty decision.

[94] Before this happened, however, there were serious riots when returning soldiers in 1919 protested at the absence of employment opportunities and the poor social conditions. See Ashdown (1985) and Ashdown (1986).

[95] The contraband trade worked in mysterious ways. Belize imported alcoholic beverages from Canada for re-export to Mexico (and eventually the US), and the Bahamas exported them to Miquelon (a French island in the mouth of the St Lawrence river), from where they were presumably shipped to Canada before going to the US.

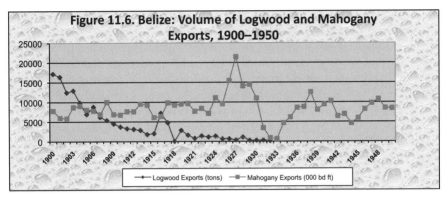

Figure 11.6. Belize: Volume of Logwood and Mahogany Exports, 1900–1950

Source: Table C.5.

While Belize was benefitting from the boom in mahogany exports and the brief revival of the entrepôt trade, its other main commodity exports were facing ever more dismal prospects. The most serious case was logwood, which as late as 1900 was almost equal in value to mahogany. The First World War hit the trade hard (see Figure 11.6), and it never recovered. The textile industry now preferred the cheaper aniline dyes sold by chemical firms, and Belizean logwood exports would fade away in the 1920s after 250 years of continuous exploitation. The trees were, and still are, available in abundance, but the market had changed forever. The last shipments were made in the Great Depression.

Chicle faced a similar problem, but it was nothing near as severe. Even before the First World War, manufacturers of chewing gum had been diluting chicle with cheaper substitutes – mainly from Asia, where they could be obtained at one-third the cost. When peacetime conditions returned, manufacturers had grown accustomed to the cheaper substitutes. In Belize, this included Crown gum, an inferior product that had been mixed with chicle and that had therefore damaged Belize's reputation for a high-quality product. The 1920s were therefore a difficult time for the industry in Belize, and exports fell.[96]

The banana industry faced no competition from cheaper substitutes, and much had been expected from its development, especially after the opening of the Stann Creek railway in 1911. However, Panama disease – so deadly for bananas – soon entered Belize, and exports started to decline from 1917. This was no different from other parts of Central America, but the banana companies in the republics had dealt with the threat by opening new plantations. This option was more difficult in Belize – not because of a shortage of land, but because of the absence of transport and port facilities. Because the multinational companies lost interest in Belize, ships called less frequently and exports became dependent on smallholders with no marketing expertise. The industry

[96] See Table C.5.

enjoyed a significant revival in the late 1930s,[97] but this was then undermined by the spread of Sigatoka disease.

Under these circumstances, the authorities could not postpone any longer the introduction of policies that should have been adopted much earlier. Following a very critical report on the state of the colony's forest resources, a Forestry Department was finally established in 1922, some Crown lands were turned into forest reserves and a public loan was taken out to establish timber on a sustainable basis through conservation on public and private lands (an income tax was finally introduced in 1920 to service this debt). Mahogany was made a priority because the rate of extraction was far in excess of what the colony could sustain, and the aim was to raise the density of mahogany trees from 1 to 40 per acre on conserved land. Finally, the land tax was also increased in the 1920s (first to 1.5 and then to 2.0 cents per acre).[98]

Even before the establishment of the Forest Department, an Agricultural Commission had been set up in 1917. It emphasised the need for improved infrastructure, particularly roads, if there was to be any chance of export diversification. However, its recommendations were ignored on the grounds of cost, and the first steps in road building would not be taken until 1925. Progress was so slow, however, that the road from Belize City to Corozal near the Mexican border was not finished until 1938, and that to San Ignacio close to the western frontier would not be completed until after the Second World War. Not surprisingly, the main advances in agriculture were in coconut and copra exports,[99] where transportation was by sea, not by road, and in citrus production along the Stann Creek valley, where the industry filled the gap left by the banana industry and could make use of the railway.

By the end of the 1920s, Belize was therefore very vulnerable. Despite the efforts at diversification, the colony's prosperity still hinged on forest products, and mahogany was once again the leading commodity – responsible for nearly 70 per cent of domestic exports. Mechanisation, using tractors instead of oxen and short-haul logging railways, began in the 1920s, and this increased the rate of extraction. However, it reduced the need for labour. Furthermore, many firms started to hire labour for six months a year rather than for eleven months as before. Employment peaked in 1924, but mahogany extraction carried on rising until 1927 (see Figure 11.6) at a rate that was not only far too high for Belize, but also saturated the world market.

Some pinned their hopes on marine products as a solution to the problem of export diversification. Belize, after all, has extensive rivers, coasts and offshore islands (cayes). Marine products began to be exported in the 1920s, with a small sponge industry at Turneffe Island, lobster (canned and fresh) on Ambergris Caye and turtle shell throughout the coastal district, but the contribution of

[97] This occurred on lands to the south of the Stann Creek valley, which had not been tainted by Panama disease. The volume figures are given in Table C.5.
[98] The rate was much higher on land close to the Stann Creek railway.
[99] Copra is the dried meat of the coconut, used to make products such as oils and soap.

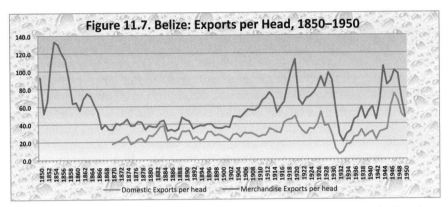

Figure 11.7. Belize: Exports per Head, 1850–1950

Source: 1900–50 from Tables C.1, C.6 and C.8. Earlier years derived from *Statistical tables relating to the Colonial and other Possessions of the United Kingdom* (various years) and Table A.1.

these products to domestic exports was still very small when world trade started to shrink at the end of the decade. Marine exports then disappeared, to reemerge only after the Second World War.

With the start of the Great Depression, and shortly afterwards (in 1931) a devastating hurricane, the Belize economy went into a tailspin. The main problem for Belize was the global collapse in the demand for mahogany after 1929. Exports from Belize fell in one year from 14 to 11 million feet before collapsing to 3.3 million feet in 1931 (see Figure 11.6). Two years later they had fallen to 636,000 feet, their lowest level since the eighteenth century. The fall in demand for chicle was not so precipitate, but by now the logwood had gone, cedar collapsed in line with mahogany,[100] and bananas were of negligible importance. Domestic exports per head fell to $5.8 in 1932 (the worst year) compared with $34.6 on the eve of the First World War and $48.8 in the boom year of 1920 (see Figure 11.7).[101]

Belize faced an additional problem in the Great Depression, which most other Caribbean countries were able to avoid. Imperial preference since 1919 had helped the UK to retain a significant share of the Belize market,[102] but the colony's currency was tied to the US dollar. When, therefore, Great Britain abandoned the gold standard in 1931 and devalued its currency, the Belize dollar was immediately **revalued** against the pound sterling. This helps to explain the astonishing collapse in the volume of Belizean exports after 1930. The decision by the United States to abandon the link with gold in 1933, thereby

[100] Ever since the mahogany trade began, a small export of cedar had accompanied it because the cedar trees tended to be found in the wild alongside the mahogany.
[101] The fall in merchandise exports per head in the Great Depression was also very severe because the re-export trade collapsed (see Figure 11.7).
[102] The UK share of exports and imports from 1900 are in Tables C.16 and C.23 respectively.

devaluing the US dollar against sterling and other European currencies, then helped Belize to recover from the depression.[103]

The 1931 hurricane caused a significant loss of life and damage to property.[104] A loan was hastily agreed with the British Treasury to provide mortgages for those who had lost homes and businesses, but the impact of the depression on public revenue was so severe that the colonial government was forced to accept a loan-in-aid from the British Treasury in the fiscal year 1932–3.[105] Although modest in size, this was the first time the colony had been unable to balance its budget without Treasury assistance, and it brought with it fiscal control from London. Embarrassing though this was, it had a silver lining. The British officials now in charge of public finances were shocked by the poor state of infrastructure.[106] From 1932 onwards, therefore, Belize received a stream of Colonial Development Funds and loans-in-aid that continued after the Second World War. These were spent in large part to give the colony the rudiments of an all-weather road system, but the roads were barely passable in the wet season. As a result of control by the British Treasury and the system of loans and grants, total revenue was much higher than 'true' revenue (see Table 11.2), and public revenue per head performed better than expected after 1931.

Treasury control also helped to improve fiscal effort. Import duties had been steadily raised in the 1920s (to a maximum of 20 per cent) as a consequence of the introduction of imperial preference (yields would otherwise have fallen). They were raised again after the hurricane to a maximum of 25 per cent, and customs duties then continued to provide the bulk of public revenue until 1946, when a new income tax law was forced through a reluctant Assembly by the use of the governor's reserve powers. Revenue from income tax then jumped by 50 per cent in one year (see Table 11.2). The land tax was increased in the 1930s, but the large landowners (including BEC) refused to pay the increase, and the Colonial Office then lowered it to its previous rate. It continued to yield less than 5 per cent of government income (see Table 11.2).

Belize had entered the Second World War still heavily dependent on forest products, but without the benefit of logwood. When demand for mahogany fell sharply after 1941 (see Figure 11.6), the colony became increasingly dependent on chicle. This commodity, the raw material for chewing gum, was close to being a necessity for the United States, and demand fell less precipitately than for mahogany.[107] Banana and coconut exports, on the other hand, were reduced almost to nothing because shipping space was used for other purposes, and citrus virtually disappeared from the export list. No new products emerged

---

[103] It could not prevent serious riots in 1934, however, as a consequence of high levels of unemployment. See Bolland (1988), pp. 167–76.

[104] It was the first hurricane to hit Belize City for eighty years, there was no early-warning system and the public was completely unprepared.

[105] Most revenue came from customs duties, which fell in line with foreign trade after 1929.

[106] See Burns (1949), pp. 128–32. See also Pim (1934).

[107] See Table C.5.

TABLE 11.2. *Belize: Public Revenue, 1932–1948 (c)*

Year (a)	Total Revenue (b)	'True' Revenue	Customs Duties	Land Tax	Income Tax
1932	893.7	764.1	425.9	30.2	25.2
1933	1056.2	685.1	376.2	27.4	10.5
1934	797.7	680.6	353.5	18.1	8.7
1935	1192.7	825.2	405.0	30.8	26.5
1936	1597.5	992.1	451.0	32.0	21.8
1937	1550.8	1188.5	528.7	38.9	24.4
1938	1740.6	1258.1	563.3	42.4	33.9
1941	1577.0	1230.0			
1942	1645.0	1269.0			
1943	1878.0	1428.0			
1944	2510.6	1675.0			132.8
1945	2505.9	1924.2	884.0	37.5	186.4
1946	2634.8	2203.8	920.4	40.2	260.5
1947	2941.0	2506.0	1227.0	39.7	346.8
1948	3209.0	2580.0	999.6	39.4	414.1

Note: (a) 1931–3 are fiscal years ending on March 31; 1935 onwards are calendar years. Colonial figures for 1934 are for 9 months only (adjusted upwards here for 12 months); (b) includes loans and grants from Imperial Treasury; (c) in thousand US dollars.
Source: Colonial Report for British Honduras (various years) and Carey Jones (1953).

during the war, but in 1947 a small trade in pine lumber began, with exports going mainly to Jamaica.[108]

Belize therefore found itself in a difficult position when the war ended, a position not helped by increasing friction with Guatemala.[109] The infrastructure was slowly improving, and the 1946 census showed that nearly 30 per cent of the labour force was now in agriculture, demonstrating the potential for diversification away from forestry.[110] However, private land was still tightly controlled by a tiny number of landowners, principally BEC, and the first national income estimates confirmed the modest position that Belize now held among even the British Caribbean colonies.[111] The colonial authorities seemed at a loss how to proceed, and yet they were unwilling to encourage

[108] The colonial authorities had great expectations of pine exports when they signed in 1904 a contract giving a US citizen (Buckner Chipley) the right to extract as much pine as he could find on Crown land for twenty-five years. The contract, however, was sold and resold on numerous occasions, with almost no pine being exported.

[109] Guatemala had unilaterally abrogated the 1859 treaty in 1939 and later closed the border. The situation became so tense in 1948 that the UK despatched a gunboat, and war was considered a real possibility. The closure of the border had a very negative impact on the re-export trade.

[110] The census figures are reported in Carey Jones (1953).

[111] The first reliable estimate was made for 1946. See Carey Jones (1953). An unreliable (much lower) estimate had been made for 1945.

local participation in any shape or form. It was not until after devaluation (see next section) that the political situation would start to change and the economic diversification of the Belizean economy could accelerate.

11.4. DEVALUATION, DIVERSIFICATION AND DEVELOPMENT

When sterling was devalued in September 1949, the Belize currency – alone in the British Empire – remained tied to the US dollar. It therefore appreciated against the British pound, making imports from the UK cheaper and exports more expensive.[112] Exports and imports to the United States, the main trading partner, were unaffected – except, of course, for the substitution effects induced by the change in relative prices between the sterling and dollar areas.

Despite repeated assurances to the contrary, the British authorities changed their mind, and the Belize dollar was devalued on the last day of the year (it was pegged to the pound at 4 to 1). This event is usually analysed through the prism of politics because it was the trigger for the birth of the nationalist movement and gave rise to the People's United Party (PUP), which would steer the country to independence in September 1981.[113] However, devaluation also had major **economic** consequences – in addition to the rise in the cost of living – that have not received the attention they deserve.

The British authorities justified devaluation in three ways, none of which stands up to serious analysis.[114] First was the slump in demand for forest products in the United States in 1949, but this was because of overstocking in previous months and would have soon been reversed. Second was the reduction in competitiveness of nontraditional products sold in the UK, such as pine and citrus, but these were still a very small share of domestic exports. Third was the lack of confidence in the Belize dollar, which was 'exhibited in many different ways'. This was code for speculation by the private sector against the currency and therefore the worst possible argument for devaluation.

The real reason for devaluation was almost certainly the conclusions of the Evans Report published in September 1948.[115] This was an attempt by the colonial authorities to take a holistic approach to the British Caribbean as part of their efforts to build a Federation of the West Indies, which assumed that outmigration from the islands needed to accelerate and could be absorbed by land settlement schemes in Belize and Guyana. This had been a common theme of colonial studies for some years, but the Evans Report went further by

---

[112] Because sterling went from $4.03 to $2.80, the appreciation of the Belize dollar against the pound was roughly 30%.

[113] See Shoman (1973).

[114] The three justifications are explained in Carey Jones (1953), app. A, with quotes from the Financial Secretary's Report for 1949.

[115] The Evans Report had been published in September 1948 and presented to Parliament by the colonial secretary. See *Report of the British Guiana and British Honduras Settlement Commission* (1948).

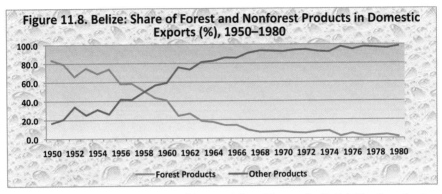

Figure 11.8. Belize: Share of Forest and Nonforest Products in Domestic Exports (%), 1950–1980

Source: Derived by the author from Table C.5, *Colonial Report for British Honduras* (various years) and UNYITS.

concluding that only large-scale settlement schemes would work and that these would require massive public-sector investment in infrastructure.

These ideas were enthusiastically accepted by the postwar Labour government in the UK, and the Colonial Office was ready to increase substantially grants-in-aid to Belize, drawing up projects that would meet the ambitions of the Evans Report.[116] Sterling devaluation, however, and the peg of the Belize currency to the US dollar effectively reduced the value of such grants by one-third. The only way, therefore, to avoid this was to devalue the Belize dollar.[117]

Ironically, the increase in grants-in-aid never fully materialised because the population of Belize was strongly opposed to large-scale immigration from the rest of the British Caribbean and to Federation itself.[118] However, devaluation made nontraditional exports to markets outside the sterling area much more competitive and maintained competitiveness inside the sterling area. By the end of the 1950s (see Figure 11.8), forestry was responsible for less than 50 per cent of domestic exports, and this ratio continued to fall thereafter.

The shift away from forestry, a crucial moment in the history of Belize, was above all a result of the rise of agricultural exports. Efforts were concentrated at first on citrus, bananas and cacao, but Belize also received a generous quota from the UK in 1951 under the Commonwealth Sugar Agreement (CSA). This was finally filled in 1961, and the industry continued to expand as a result of increased quotas under the CSA, a small quota provided by the United

---

[116] The recommendations of the Evans Report were included in the 1949 Development Plan covering the years 1950–4. See Bennett (2008), chap. 4.

[117] This is also suggested by Carey Jones (1953), p. 141.

[118] When the Federation was finally established in 1958, Belize would remain outside it. See Mordecai (1968), p. 147.

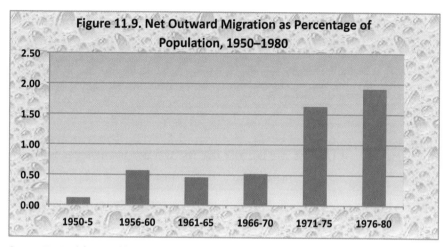

Figure 11.9. Net Outward Migration as Percentage of Population, 1950–1980

Source: Derived from Tables C.1, C.2, C.3, D.1, D.2 and D.3.

States following the suspension of US trade with Cuba and sales in the world market. By 1970, sugar had reached 50 per cent of domestic exports, and this proportion would soar to 80 per cent a few years later, when world sugar prices temporarily quadrupled.

The decline of forestry was at first only relative, and the colonial administration continued to give the industry priority in its development efforts. However, it never recovered from Hurricane Hattie in October 1961, and exports thereafter steadily declined in both volume and value. The advent of internal self-government in 1964[119] also provided an opportunity to apply a tax and land policy that no longer favoured the large forestry companies, especially BEC, and by the time of independence, Belize had finally emerged from the shadow of its origins as a timber-exporting enclave in the seventeenth century.[120]

These structural changes in the Belizean economy, however long overdue, did not mean that the economy had resolved its outstanding problems. The rise of agricultural exports was not fast enough to compensate fully for the decline in forestry, and unemployment remained a serious problem. Net migration had been outwards since 1900, but it accelerated after 1950 (see Figure 11.9). The 1970s witnessed exceptionally heavy outward migration, with most of those leaving heading to the United States.

[119] A universal adult franchise had been adopted in 1954, and internal self-government came on 1 January 1964. See Grant (1976).

[120] The BEC had never fully paid even those taxes for which it had been responsible and had therefore accumulated large arrears. In response to the new policies, it either sold land or gave it to the government in lieu of tax. As a result it had ceased to be a major force in Belize by the time of independence.

Under internal self-government, nationalist politicians were responsible for economic policy. Belize joined the newly formed Caribbean Community (CARICOM) in 1973,[121] but this had very little impact because such a small part of the country's exports went to the other member states (trade links with Central America were even less important). Following the collapse of the Bretton Woods system of fixed currencies, the government took advantage of the fluctuation of the pound sterling to peg the Belize currency once again to the US dollar (this time at 2 to 1).[122] This led to an increase in the share of trade with the United States and a decline in the importance of the UK, and thus in the year before independence the former colonial power was responsible for only 30 per cent of merchandise exports and 15 per cent of imports.

By the 1970s, the Belizean economy had begun to resemble other Caribbean countries. Domestic exports were mainly agricultural, with a small contribution from fishing and garment assembly. The agricultural exports depended heavily on preferential treatment in either the US or UK markets. However, British entry into the European Economic Community (EEC) in 1973 meant that Belize's preferences were now determined under the EEC's Lomé Convention, applicable to all former and current European colonies rather than determined bilaterally between Belize and the UK.[123]

Belize's small population – it had still only reached 100,000 by the mid-1960s – meant that balancing the budget was a constant struggle. Resources for capital expenditure on infrastructure almost invariably had to come from official development assistance. In practice, given Belize's colonial status, this meant from the UK, whose own economic circumstances were far from favourable in the three decades before independence. The poor state of infrastructure made it difficult to diversify the economy beyond the shift from forestry to agricultural exports, and Belize failed to make any headway in developing exports of services.[124]

The result was an unimpressive macroeconomic performance in the last decades of colonialism. At the beginning of the 1950s, domestic exports per head (at constant prices) were roughly the same as the average for the whole Caribbean. From then onwards, the ratio would fall (see Figure 11.10), with

---

[121] This was also the year in which the name of the country was officially changed from British Honduras to Belize, but it remained a colony.

[122] Following devaluation at the end of 1949, the Belize dollar was valued at 1.43 to the US dollar and 4.0 to the British pound. Following the collapse of the fixed exchange rate system in 1971, the pound drifted down against the US dollar, leading to a decline in the value of the Belize dollar against the US dollar (see Table D.4). When the rate reached 2 to 1 in 1976, the Belize government reestablished the peg with the US dollar.

[123] The first Lomé Convention was in 1975 and replaced the Yaoundé Convention, which had applied only to former French colonies. The group of countries that benefitted from the Lomé Convention were known as the ACP (Africa-Caribbean-Pacific) countries. See Hewitt and Stevens (1981).

[124] A modern tourist industry would not start until the 1980s. This was partly because of the reluctance of the Belizean premier, George Price, to promote the industry before independence. See Smith (2011), pp. 246–7.

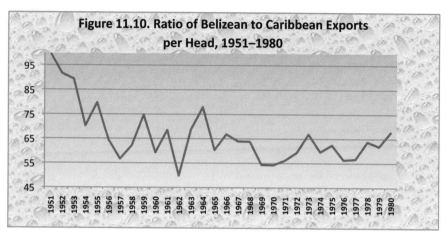

Figure 11.10. Ratio of Belizean to Caribbean Exports per Head, 1951–1980

Note: 1951=100.
Source: Derived from Tables C.1, C.9, D.1 and D.10.

only a brief respite when high sugar prices temporarily raised it.[125] The ratio of Belizean to Caribbean GDP per head, available from 1960, tells a similar story.[126] It was only in the last years before independence, when a serious effort was finally made by the colonial authorities to improve infrastructure, that the gap between Belize and the rest of the Caribbean in terms of GDP per head began to narrow.

Belize had enjoyed the highest exports per head in the Caribbean in the first half of the nineteenth century. Even when it became a British colony in 1862, it was still among the richest countries in the region. Thus, the decline of the economy in the subsequent century was a severe blow. The 'forestocracy' (especially BEC), who resisted diversification and at the same time evaded the tax on land, must bear much of the blame. So should the imperial authorities, who failed to confront the vested interests in the colony and refused before the 1930s to take a long-term approach to the development of infrastructure. Independence for Belize may not have been a panacea, but it was a huge advance on the mean-spirited and short-sighted approach to development that had characterised colonialism.

---

[125] The ratio in Figure 11.10 is a hybrid. From 1951, when the two were almost exactly the same, it measures the ratio of Belizean to Caribbean domestic exports per head at constant (1930) prices. From 1960 onwards it measures the ratio of total (merchandise and service) exports at constant (2000) prices.

[126] The comparison can be derived from Tables D.1 and D.19. In 1960, Belize GDP per head (at 2000 prices) was roughly 50% of the Caribbean average, and it stayed at this level until just before independence.

APPENDIX TO CHAPTER 11. BELIZE'S NINETEENTH-CENTURY EXPORTS

The export data for Belize before 1900 present special problems. This appendix outlines the methodology for resolving the main issues. These are the volume of timber exports (the main domestic exports throughout the century); the price of timber exports; the value of re-exports; and the conversion of currencies used in Belize to US dollars.

LOGWOOD AND MAHOGANY VOLUMES

The years 1800–5 are in Bolland (1977) or Gibbs (1883). For 1819–36 there are figures in Bolland (1977) and Martin (1843). Bolland (1977) also has the 1837 figure for mahogany. For 1837–45 and 1847–51 for logwood, I used British imports from Belize in Naylor (1988) and assumed these represented 94 per cent of Belize logwood exports (this is the ratio in 1846). I took 1846 from Bolland (1977). For 1838–44 and 1847–51 for mahogany, I used British imports from Belize in Naylor (1988) and assumed these represented 75 per cent of Belize mahogany exports (this is the ratio in 1845). Because Naylor's data for mahogany are in tons, I converted to feet at the rate of 340 feet per ton (this is the mid-point of the ratio given in Chaloner and Fleming (1851), p. 65, for Belize mahogany). I took 1845–6 from Bolland (1977). There is a complete series from 1856 to 1868 for both logwood and mahogany in Bolland (1977), and this can be extended to 1900 using *Statistical tables relating to the Colonial and other Possessions of the United Kingdom* (various years) and *Blue Books*.

Colonial sources only distinguish between domestic exports and re-exports from 1871 onwards, but re-exports of logwood and mahogany before 1870 were not important as long as timber originating on the Mosquito Shore and shipped through Belize is treated as domestic (see below in this appendix). The decennial data for 1830–90 are three-year averages, but I have used 1824 for 1820 because this is the first year for which we have the value of exports. I have not been able to find any figures for 1806–18 and 1852–55.

Some of the logwood and mahogany exports shipped from Belize before 1860 came from the Mosquito Shore. This was likely to have been small most of the time because of distance and cost. In addition, mahogany from the Shore incurred higher tariffs than mahogany from Belize in the British market until 1832. From then until 1845 mahogany from anywhere in the Bay of Honduras received the same preferential treatment, with a lower tariff than applied to British colonies provided it was shipped through Belize. This is one of the reasons for the high level of mahogany exports from Belize in the mid-1840s. From 1845 there were no tariffs, and the Republic of Honduras became increasingly hostile to Belize settlers cutting timber on the northern coast of the Mosquito Shore. We will never know how much of the timber exports came from outside Belize before 1860, so it all has to be considered a domestic

export (it was cut by Belize companies that usually paid no royalties, used Belize labour and shipped through Belize).

LOGWOOD AND MAHOGANY PRICES

There is a great scarcity of data on timber prices for Belize before 1870, so I have concentrated only on the decennial years because this is the minimum requirement. As a check on logwood prices, I have used the information in Tooke (1857), quoted in Naylor (1988), p. 286n40, which gives the *cif* price inclusive of duty. By deducting the duty and making allowance for freight, it is possible to estimate the *fob* price and compare with those used below.

1820. A price for mahogany can be derived from Gibbs (1883), which I have assumed is valid for 1824. It is also given in Naylor (1988), p. 286n40. The logwood price is taken from Martinique and is similar to the one derived from Tooke (see above in this appendix).

1830. The price of logwood is again based on Martinique, and mahogany is assumed to be the same as the Dominican Republic (part of Haiti in that year).

1840. The mahogany price is derived from Gibbs (1883). It is also given in Naylor (1988), p.286n40. The logwood price is from Martinique.

1850. The mahogany price is derived from Société Anglo-Française de Honduras (1857). This source includes in the French import price from Belize both the duty and freight charges on Belize mahogany, from which the *fob* price can be obtained. The logwood price is from Martinique.

1860. The logwood price is the three-year average for Jamaica in *Statistical tables relating to the Colonial and other Possessions of the United Kingdom* (various years). I assumed the mahogany price was the same as in 1850.

DOMESTIC EXPORTS, RE-EXPORTS
AND MERCHANDISE EXPORTS

Before 1870, only merchandise exports are recorded in official sources. Domestic exports are therefore based on the sum of the two principal exports (logwood and mahogany), with a small adjustment upwards for minor exports, such as cedar. From 1870 onwards, the value of domestic exports and the value of merchandise exports is given in *Statistical tables relating to the Colonial and other Possessions of the United Kingdom* (various years).

Merchandise exports are given from 1824 to 1836 in Martin (1843). Gibbs (1883) has 1840–1 and 1845–6. There is a continuous series from 1850 onwards in *Statistical tables relating to the Colonial and other Possessions of the United Kingdom* (various years), but there is a gap in 1878–9, when only the value of domestic exports is given. I have therefore estimated the figures, assuming re-exports had the same value in those two years as in 1877.

Re-exports are the difference between merchandise and domestic exports, and they peaked in 1840. Before 1870 they have to be estimated as a residual. However, Gibbs (1883) gives figures for 1824 and 1840 that are similar to the residual, and Naylor (1988), pp. 199–202 and 213–21, has data from 1821 onwards on the volume of Belize re-exports to Britain of goods not produced in the settlement (e.g. indigo and cochineal) and the export to Belize from Britain of manufactured goods, most of which were re-exported to the neighbouring countries. These two series both suggest that Belize re-exports did indeed peak around 1840, as suggested above in this appendix. Naylor (1988), pp. 213–21, also gives official values for Belize exports to the UK, but these cannot be used because they are likely to be very different from declared values.

THE CURRENCY QUESTION

Where the data are in Jamaican pounds, they have been converted to pounds sterling at the prevailing exchange rate. Where they are in silver dollars (*sol*) before 1880, they have been converted to sterling by dividing by 5.0 (the rate fixed in 1838 by the British Crown) and then converted to US dollars. From 1880 to 1894, where they are still in silver dollars, they have been converted to sterling at the Treasury rate as given annually in *Statistical tables relating to the Colonial and other Possessions of the United Kingdom* (various years) and then converted to US dollars by multiplying by 4.87. The Treasury rates were:

1880	5.93
1881	5.93
1882	5.93
1883	6.08
1884	6.08
1885	6.32
1886	6.86
1887	7.18
1888	7.60
1889	7.16
1890	6.49
1891	6.84
1892	7.62
1893	8.75
1894	9.72

The currency was placed at parity to the gold dollar on 1 October 1894, and thus the figures from 1895 onwards are given in US dollars.

PART III

THE CARIBBEAN IN THE AGE OF GLOBALISATION

From 1960 to the Present

The Core and the Caribbean

The period from 1960 to the present has coincided with some of the most important changes in the Caribbean since the Napoleonic Wars. It embraces the Cuban Revolution, the decolonisation of many countries, the creation of a framework for regional integration and the switch from merchandise to service exports. In this period the Caribbean has also had to adjust to globalisation, to the new international division of labour pioneered by multinational companies (MNCs) and to the erosion of preferences for its traditional commodities in the markets of the core countries.

The adjustment process has not been easy for the Caribbean, and it is still far from complete. Yet the economies of many countries have performed well – much better than their image externally might suggest – and average incomes and the standard of living of citizens have been raised to previously unheard-of levels. A few countries have struggled economically and have been tempted as a consequence into unwise policies that brought high levels of inflation and indebtedness. Only one country – Haiti – went backwards, with average income per head lower than in 1960 (even before taking into account the devastating earthquake in 2010).[1]

It is not just the Caribbean, however, that has adapted. The core's relationship with the Caribbean itself has also changed in response to the rise of globalisation, the end of colonial rule in many countries and – in the case of the European members of the core – the emergence of the European Union (EU). The transformation of the EU into a single market meant that France, Holland and the UK essentially disappeared as core countries – to be replaced by the EU itself. And new members of the core emerged – first the Soviet Union through its special relationship with Cuba until 1990 – and, second, China as a leading trade partner for the region.

---

[1] In January 2010 Haiti suffered its strongest earthquake for nearly 200 years, when tens of thousands lost their lives.

This chapter deals in the first section with those changes in the world economy after 1960 that were of particular importance for the Caribbean. The second section explores the relationship between the United States – still the most important member of the core – and the Caribbean over the same period. The next section of the chapter looks at the relationship of the EU and its key member states with the Caribbean. The final section examines the relationship of the rest of the core – Canada, China and the Soviet Union – with the Caribbean, while paying attention to those noncore countries, especially Venezuela, whose regional policies were of increasing importance.

12.1. THE WORLD ECONOMY

By the end of the 1950s, it was becoming clear that the world economy was embarked on a long period of expansion that had in fact begun a decade earlier. The framework had been set at the Bretton Woods conference in 1944, when agreement was reached on the establishment of the IMF and the International Bank for Reconstruction and Development (IBRD – usually known as the World Bank). The IMF oversaw the (re)establishment of a system of fixed exchange rates. This was no longer based on the gold standard, but on a looser gold exchange standard in which the US dollar was pegged to gold at a fixed price ($35 per troy ounce), and only central banks could buy at this price.[2] This framework would last until 1971, when the global imbalances provoked by US deficits, the export of dollars to the rest of the world and the artificial price of gold overwhelmed the system of fixed exchange rates so carefully constructed in the late 1940s.[3]

The system of fixed exchange rates was perhaps the necessary condition for postwar expansion, but it needed a further stimulus. This came after the formation of GATT in 1947. Although intended only as a temporary arrangement, GATT survived for nearly fifty years.[4] Through a series of multilateral trade negotiations, the last being the Uruguay Round, GATT contributed to the dismantling of trade barriers erected between the two world wars.[5] In consequence, the rate of growth of world trade was faster than that of world production in virtually every year after 1948, and therefore almost all countries experienced an increase in their trade openness (the ratio of exports and imports to GDP).

The increase in world trade – in terms of both volume and value – at first seemed irreversible. It had accelerated with the rapid growth of manufactured

---

[2] Central banks were allowed to turn their foreign exchange reserves into gold held by the US at this price.

[3] See Argy (1981), pp. 60–7.

[4] The intention had been to establish an International Trade Organization (ITO) at Bretton Woods, but this was delayed until the Havana conference of 1947–8. Agreement was reached, but it was never ratified, and so the world was left with GATT, which began with only twenty-three members. See Scammell (1980), pp. 43–5.

[5] See Winters (1990).

trade among core countries in response to the lowering of tariff and nontariff barriers among GATT members. Yet it was soon clear that this was no mere recovery of trade patterns disrupted by war and depression between 1914 and 1945. It was qualitatively and quantitatively different, involving a new type of international transaction (exports and imports of the same product group between pairs of countries – intra-industry trade) and a new actor (MNCs).[6] All regions had experienced direct foreign investment (DFI) before the Second World War, but the MNCs took it to a new level and represented a new challenge for host countries.[7]

When the first energy crisis struck in 1973–4 and world oil prices quadrupled, it looked as if a quarter century of global trade expansion was set to end. Yet the crisis proved to be no more than a temporary setback. The collapse of the Bretton Woods system had unleashed an explosion in the global money supply, and prices of many commodities – not just oil – rose sharply. Indeed, many commodity producers tried to replicate the success of the oil cartel (OPEC) in pushing up prices,[8] and commodity price agreements were established – some even before the 1970s – with varying degrees of success. Those of interest to the Caribbean included bananas, bauxite, cacao, coffee and sugar.[9]

World merchandise imports, which had been a paltry $57.3 billion in 1948,[10] reached $2.1 trillion in 1980, $3.6 trillion in 1990 and $6.65 trillion in 2000.[11] Not all of this increase was in volume, especially in the 1970s, but much of it was, and for the exporters an increase in price was still welcome. On completion of the Uruguay Round in 1994, the World Trade Organization (WTO) replaced GATT, membership expanded dramatically and almost all merchandise trade became subject to international rules. Imports of goods then doubled again before a correction took place in response to the global financial crisis that began at the end of 2007.

For a region, such as the Caribbean, specialised in exports this should have been very welcome. Generally, this was the case. However, Caribbean merchandise exports were – with the single exception of Puerto Rico – concentrated in primary products, and the rate of growth of world merchandise trade was much faster in manufactured goods. This encouraged the countries of

---

[6] There was a close relationship between these two because so much intra-industry trade was carried out between subsidiaries of the same MNC. See Scherer (1992).

[7] Scholars will (rightly) insist that there were MNCs long before the Second World War, but what happened afterwards was quantitatively and qualitatively different. See Wilkins and Schröter (1998).

[8] The Organization of Oil Exporting Countries (OPEC) had been founded in 1960, but it was not until 1973 that it succeeded in operating as a cartel by reducing the volume exported and raising prices.

[9] The sugar, coffee and cacao agreements involved consumers and producers, thus preventing the latter from operating as cartels. The banana and bauxite agreements suffered from the lack of participation of some of the key exporters. See Rangarajan (1978).

[10] See United Nations (2009).

[11] See UNCTAD, *Handbook of Trade Statistics* (various years).

the Caribbean to promote industrialisation in the hope both that they could replicate the Puerto Rican experience and that they could participate in the extraordinary growth of manufactured exports.

In this they were helped by the efforts of the United Nations Conference on Trade and Development (UNCTAD) to create a global trading system that gave unilateral preferences to exports of manufactured goods from developing countries.[12] This pressure had led to the Generalized System of Preferences (GSP) in 1971, under which core countries had agreed to import a range of products from the periphery at low or zero tariffs. Unfortunately, the potential benefits of the GSP system were undermined by the application of tariff-quotas, and therefore each exporting country was limited in what it could sell on preferential terms.

A few developing countries were so internationally competitive in certain manufactured products – especially textiles and clothing – that they were able to win market share even without the benefit of the GSP.[13] Caribbean countries were not at first among them, however, and the success that some – especially Puerto Rico – achieved in the export of manufactured goods had less to do with the GSP and more to do with the special schemes operated by different members of the core. These schemes helped a few countries to achieve impressive rates of growth of manufactured exports.[14]

In doing so, they invariably depended on investment by MNCs, who looked to outsource some of the activities previously conducted in the core countries. The Caribbean became part of a complex commodity chain in which goods might be imported from country A to be processed in the Caribbean before being exported to country B – all within the product flow of a single company.[15] Much of this flow of goods was determined by the fiscal arrangements in the core countries, over which the Caribbean had no control. When the arrangements changed, Caribbean participation in the global commodity chain normally changed with it.[16]

The growth of manufactured trade may have outpaced trade in primary products, but the demand for the agricultural and mineral commodities of interest to the Caribbean grew at a rate that was satisfactory by historical standards. This was only partly due to the impact of the income elasticity of demand as average income per head rose in the core countries. After all, there were clearly limits to the volume of bananas, sugar and rum – to name only three traditional exports – that could be consumed by each citizen of the core countries. It was also because of the preferences the Caribbean enjoyed in the core markets and the discrimination this implied against imports from third countries.

---

[12] UNCTAD had been created in 1964, with Raúl Prebisch as its first secretary-general. See Dosman (2008).

[13] These countries were mainly in East and Southeast Asia.

[14] See Chapter 14.

[15] See Gereffi and Korzeniewicz (1994).

[16] See Chapter 14.2.

In the period from the Napoleonic Wars onwards, Caribbean countries had seen preferences extended in some years and eroded in others. The commercial policy of the core, although not irrational, was certainly capricious. Only the French colonies – now Départements d'Outre-Mer (DOMs) – had consistently enjoyed protection against competition from third countries, and even in their case the level of protection had varied widely from one period to the next. Thus, no Caribbean country could count on protection remaining forever. And by the beginning of the twenty-first century it was clear that the remaining preferences for many countries were going to be eroded or possibly disappear completely.

The reasons for this are complex but had much to do with a change of approach by some core countries together with a greater assertiveness by those developing countries discriminated against by traditional preferences. The creation of the WTO in 1995 was the catalyst of the new order in international trade, because discriminatory trade arrangements – including core preferences for select countries – required a waiver by all members (GATT had done the same, but fewer countries were members). If this waiver should not be granted or extended, as would happen in the case of EU arrangements for ex-colonies,[17] the preferential arrangements had to change.

Because a complex set of preferences had been developed for the Caribbean in the twentieth century, it was inevitable that the region would be affected by the new reality. For some it seemed to herald catastrophe, but the reality was more complex. Since the late 1940s, it was not only merchandise trade that had been growing rapidly, but also trade in services. Activities that had been regarded by international trade theory as 'nontradeable', or at least nontraded, entered international trade with no difficulty. And some, such as travel and tourism, which had always been recognised as tradeable, enjoyed a spectacular boom.

As a result, international service imports soared. We do not know their value with any accuracy before 1980, but by then they already accounted for 17.4 per cent of the combined value of total world imports (i.e. goods plus services).[18] From then onwards world service imports rose rapidly (see Figure 12.1), with developed countries, especially the EU, accounting for much of the trade. By 1990, services had reached almost 20 per cent of total world imports, but the commodity price boom at the beginning of the new century reduced the share a little.

Some of the increase in world service imports, such as construction, was not of great interest to the Caribbean. However, most of it was because it consisted of activities in which the Caribbean countries faced no special barriers to entry and enjoyed certain advantages. These activities included travel, transport, communications, insurance, financial services, other business services, cultural and recreational services and government services. The rise in trade in these

---

[17] See Chapter 12.3.
[18] Derived from UNCTAD, *Handbook of Trade Statistics*.

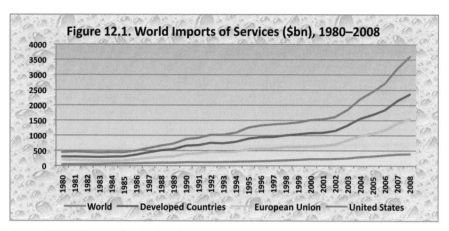

Source: UNCTAD, *Handbook of Trade Statistics* (various years).

services would create exceptional opportunities for the Caribbean, and all countries took advantage of it to a greater or lesser extent.

The most important of these global service imports for the Caribbean was travel. Now known as tourism (the word was not commonly used until after the Second World War), it represented a unique opportunity for the Caribbean that has changed the character of many countries beyond recognition – not always for the better. Tourism – under different names – had started in the Caribbean in the nineteenth century, but it had little impact because of the small numbers of arrivals.[19] This started to change with the growth of air travel between the two world wars and accelerated after the Second World War with the development of the jet engine, the expansion of airports and the rise of average incomes in rich countries. And in the 1960s, US citizens – many without passports – were encouraged by President Johnson (1963–9) to vacation in those parts of the Caribbean where passports were not required and where there was often no need to convert US dollars into foreign currency.[20]

Cuba had been the pioneer of Caribbean tourism, attracting US citizens for short and long stays, so the US trade and travel embargo in 1961 provided the rest of the region with an opportunity to increase US market share.[21] This was only one of many changes that the Caribbean tourism industry has undergone since its establishment. Perhaps the most significant – and troubling from the point of view of the Caribbean – has been the rise of the cruise ship industry, leading the Caribbean to distinguish between those visitors who stay overnight

[19] For a study of the origins of the tourism industry in Jamaica, see Taylor (1993).
[20] The Vietnam War led to large current account deficits in the US. Vacationing in the dollar area, including the Caribbean, was therefore portrayed as 'patriotic' by the Johnson administration.
[21] Cuba had attracted around 400,000 visitors each year before the Revolution, nearly all from the US. This may not sound like a large number today, but it was in the 1950s.

and those who do not. The latter are now more numerous in many countries, but their contribution to the domestic economy is usually minimal.

The second most important service activity for the Caribbean has involved the financial sector (including insurance). This had its origin in the Dutch Antilles during the Second World War, when Dutch companies were unable to carry on normal business as a result of the German occupation of Holland.[22] Following the end of hostilities, MNCs around the world – especially those with headquarters in Europe and North America – began to take advantage of low or zero direct tax rates in the Caribbean to establish subsidiaries. By the 1960s, the potential for the Caribbean was obvious, and legislation was changed in a number of countries to create offshore financial centres. In turn this attracted the attention of organised crime syndicates looking for money-laundering facilities and of high-net-worth individuals interested in tax avoidance and evasion.

These 'tax havens', as they are often described,[23] eventually came under intense pressure from rich countries to change their behaviour for two reasons. First was the loss of tax receipts by governments in rich countries, and second was the need for greater transparency in the fight against international terrorists and organised crime. The campaign against tax havens was orchestrated through a number of institutions in which the core countries were strongly represented. The first was the Organisation for Economic Cooperation and Development (OECD),[24] and the second was the Financial Action Task Force (FATF).[25] All Caribbean countries adapted their rules in the face of this pressure in the first decade of the twenty-first century.[26]

The outlook for tax havens in the Caribbean has been clouded by these developments, but the dependence of the region on the export of services is unlikely to change. The reason is that the Caribbean has become skilled at identifying service activities in which it can specialise and which are growing in importance in the world economy. And tourism has become increasingly specialised, with countries learning how to cater to the fickle needs of visitors from other parts of the world. Most of these are from rich countries, but not all, and the market for service exports by the Caribbean is truly global.

This is a welcome development for a region that has traditionally depended on demand from a small number of countries. However, it is very difficult to know how diversified Caribbean trade – especially exports – has now become. The reason is that no country has complete statistics on the country destination

---

[22] See Langer (2010).
[23] A country could be a tax haven either because it had no direct taxes on income and wealth or because it permitted offshore activities that were not subject to tax. See Shaxson (2010).
[24] The OECD had been established in 1961 to represent the interests of western industrialised countries. It was not, however, until the 1990s that it began seriously to address the question of tax havens.
[25] The FATF was established in 1989 by the G-7, the organisation representing the richest western countries that became the G-8 with the inclusion of Russia after the end of the Cold War.
[26] See Chapter 13.2.

of its service exports by **value**. This did not matter when merchandise exports dominated total trade, but that is no longer the case. This is a challenge that will have to be addressed, because the country destination of merchandise exports may no longer be representative of exports as a whole.

Globalisation – at least in its most recent incarnation – had begun in earnest in the 1980s with the relaxation of balance of payments controls in the rich countries. This led to a surge not only in international capital flows, but also in international trade, output and incomes. It did not, however, lead at first to any narrowing of the gap between rich and poor states, with the exception of a few countries – of which the most important was China. This led to renewed attention to the issue of income distribution **between** countries and resulted – among other things – in a scheme for debt relief that became known as HIPC.[27]

Many countries in the Caribbean were highly indebted, but only two (Haiti and Guyana) were poor enough to qualify for debt relief under HIPC. More relevant for the Caribbean as a whole, therefore, were the Millennium Development Goals (MDGs) adopted by the UN in 2000 and designed to improve conditions in poor and middle-income countries by 2015.[28] By 2010, the Caribbean had made good progress towards achieving the goals, but the MDGs did not give sufficient weight to the problems of violence and drug abuse from which so much of the Caribbean is now suffering.

12.2. THE UNITED STATES AND THE CARIBBEAN

Before the overthrow of Batista in Cuba at the end of 1958, the United States had no particular reason to think that its interests in the Caribbean would be under threat. The United States could count on the cooperation of those European powers with responsibilities in the region, as had been demonstrated when the British government suspended the constitution in Guyana.[29] The only independent countries – other than Cuba – were the Dominican Republic and Haiti, where presidents knew that they ignored US interests at their peril.[30] The efforts by the Trinidadian premier, Eric Williams, to establish the capital of the Federation of the British West Indies at Chaguaramas may have contributed to anti-Americanism in the Caribbean,[31] but it was very mild compared with

---

[27] HIPC stood for Debt Relief Under the Heavily Indebted Poor Countries Initiative and was administered by the IMF and World Bank.

[28] Progress towards meeting the eight MDGs is measured by a series of indicators updated regularly by the UN. See Sharma (2004).

[29] Guyana had achieved internal self-government in 1953 under the premiership of Cheddi Jagan, whose left-wing sympathies brought him to the attention of the Eisenhower administration. Because the country was still a colony, the British governor was able to intervene and suspend the constitution on the most dubious of pretexts in the same year. See Smith (1962), pp. 175–7.

[30] Trujillo had finally learnt this lesson in 1960 when the Dominican Republic's sugar quota was suspended.

[31] The Federation had been established in 1958, and Trinidad & Tobago, still a British colony, had been chosen as the site of the capital. The US occupied a military base at Chaguaramas, which was leased from Britain under the wartime agreement between Roosevelt and Churchill. See Parker (2008).

the reception given to Vice President Nixon during his tour of Latin America in 1958.[32]

Perhaps as a consequence of this relatively relaxed attitude to the Caribbean, the United States had not paid much attention to the development of policies with which to influence countries in the region. The Eisenhower administration, it is true, had responded to the vice president's disastrous tour with a decision to establish an Inter-American Development Bank (IDB), but this would not be operational until 1961.[33] His successor, President Kennedy, would promote the Alliance for Progress. This was an ambitious plan to link US aid to domestic reforms in Latin America, but most of the Caribbean was not eligible.[34] The most important instrument at the disposal of the United States therefore was the sugar import quota, which gave beneficiary countries a higher price than they could expect in the world market.[35] In a futile effort to change the radical course of Fidel Castro's government, the Eisenhower administration therefore suspended the Cuban sugar quota in July 1960.[36]

Punishing Cuba meant that the United States now had the means to reward others by buying more of their sugar. However, the candidates that the United States wanted to reward were drawn from all over the world, and the Caribbean was not the highest priority. The US territories already had unlimited market access, the non-US dependencies had made their own arrangements for sugar with core countries in Europe and – apart from Cuba – there were only two independent countries. Haiti under President Duvalier (1957–71) was at first regarded with suspicion until 'Papa Doc' played the Communist card with great skill and won the US administration to his side.[37] The Dominican Republic was a more obvious candidate for support, especially following the assassination of President Trujillo in 1961,[38] but the subsequent political instability meant that the United States was unsure of what position to take until after it had intervened militarily in 1965 (see below in this section).

The result was that the rest of the Caribbean did not benefit as greatly as it might have hoped from the reallocation of the Cuban sugar import quota. Other countries gained market share also – mainly in tropical Latin America, but some in Africa, Asia and the Pacific. Indeed, by the end of the 1960s (see Figure 12.2) only 20 per cent of US sugar imports – excluding those from US territories – were coming from the Caribbean. Nearly all of this was from the

---

[32] See Connell-Smith (1966), pp. 166–7.

[33] See Inter-American Development Bank (1971).

[34] See Perloff (1969).

[35] The Jones-Costigan Act of 1934 had introduced sugar import quotas. They had been suspended in the Second World War and reintroduced subsequently. Cuba had always received the largest proportion. See Heston (1987), chap. 10.

[36] See Chapter 16.1.

[37] Haiti was not a major sugar exporter, but the volume and value of its sugar exports increased tenfold between 1959 and 1960. See Table C.5.

[38] Despite US wariness of Trujillo in his last days, the volume and value of Dominican sugar exports jumped by nearly 50% between 1959 and 1960. See Table C.5. This was before the suspension of the sugar quota in 1960 could take effect.

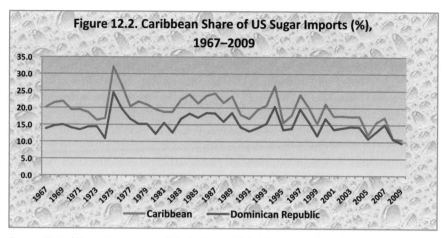

Source: United States Department of Agriculture, *Global Agricultural Trade Statistics* (Web site).

Dominican Republic (see Figure 12.2), with a much smaller share from Haiti. Other producers in the Caribbean were still exporting sugar, mainly to Europe, but Belize did acquire a small quota for the first time in the US market after the suspension of the Cuban quota.

At the beginning of the 1970s, global sugar consumption outstripped production and prices surged, reaching a peak of 57 cents per lb in November 1974. The Caribbean was a principal beneficiary, and its share of US imports rose above 30 per cent (see Figure 12.2). The US administration therefore saw no reason to renew the Sugar Act, and it expired the following month. Prices then drifted lower and domestic price support programs together with import quotas were reestablished in 1977. The quotas contributed to the decline in the Caribbean's share of US sugar imports, which had fallen to a paltry 10 per cent by the end of the first decade of the twenty-first century (see Figure 12.2).

Even this did not tell the full story of the difficulties facing Caribbean sugar exporters in the US market. Higher domestic US prices for sugar after 1977 coupled with subsidies for corn increased the incentives for US food manufacturers to replace sugar made from beet and cane with high-fructose corn syrup (HFCS) made from domestically grown maize. The per capita consumption of HFCS rose rapidly, and that of sugar (cane and beet) fell sharply. When the main soft drink companies switched from sugar to HFCS in 1984, it accelerated this process. As a result, the contribution of Caribbean sugar to total sweetener consumption in the United States fell precipitately.[39]

After the suspension of the Cuban sugar quota, the relationship between the United States and the government of Fidel Castro rapidly deteriorated.

[39] See López (1989).

Remaining US assets were nationalised, and Cuba moved closer to the Soviet Union. This was followed by a US trade embargo and the rupture of diplomatic relations in the last days of the Eisenhower administration. The United States, now led by President Kennedy, then failed to overthrow Castro through proxies at the Bay of Pigs in April 1961. Soon afterwards Castro declared that he was a Marxist-Leninist and that Cuba was socialist. The stage was then set for the Cuban Missile Crisis in October 1962, when the world came as close as it has ever done to nuclear war.[40]

The resolution of the crisis was swift and in some ways unexpected. The Soviet Union withdrew its missiles before they had been armed with nuclear warheads, and President Kennedy – subject to certain conditions – agreed in return that the United States would not invade Cuba.[41] The island had therefore been 'contained', in the language of the Cold War. In theory, therefore, the United States could become more relaxed about the Communist state on its doorstep, but this would not happen until Jimmy Carter (1977–81) was elected president. Until then, successive US administrations regarded Cuba with the deepest suspicions, used a range of instruments to destabilise its government and overreacted to any left-leaning tendencies by neighbouring countries.

One such overreaction was in Guyana where Cheddi Jagan had returned to power as premier in 1961 following elections in August. The Guyanese government still had responsibility only for internal affairs, but the United States was determined that Jagan would not lead the country to independence. The British were therefore persuaded to change the electoral rules so that Jagan could not win.[42] Following the next election in 1964, he was replaced by Forbes Burnham, who led the country to independence in 1966 and presided over the destruction of the economy in the next two decades.

The other major challenge to the US administration was in Hispaniola. Castro's rise to power overlapped with the early years of the Duvalier dictatorship in Haiti and the end of Rafael Trujillo in the Dominican Republic. Both Duvalier and Trujillo bore a striking political resemblance to Batista, the dictator whose misrule had contributed to the Cuban Revolution. Removing both was therefore seen as essential in the view of many in the US administration.

Trujillo's assassination in 1961 was a considerable relief to the Kennedy administration,[43] but it was also an opportunity for the left-leaning forces in the country. Juan Bosch duly assumed the presidency following elections in

---

[40] See White (1996).

[41] The conditions included UN verification of the Soviet withdrawal. Because Castro did not permit this, it was unclear whether the agreement not to invade was binding on the US. See Karol (1971), pp. 272–3.

[42] A system of proportional representation was introduced that was very different from the 'Westminster model' used in other British territories. In ethnically divided Guyana, this ensured that Jagan's People's Progressive Party (PPP) could not win a majority of seats. See Reno (1964).

[43] There was no direct US involvement in the assassination, but the Kennedy administration had made contact with high-level conspirators in the months before.

December 1962.[44] His reformist policies soon led to his overthrow by the military, however, who were in turn deposed by a popular revolt in April 1965 intent on restoring Bosch to power. This was too much for President Johnson, who ordered the US military to intervene. Their departure paved the way for the election as president of the anti-Communist Joaquín Balaguer, who had been close to Trujillo and would dominate the country politically for another twenty-five years.[45]

Military intervention was not used in Haiti, but it was some time before the United States would make its peace with François Duvalier. Indeed, President Kennedy used various methods to destabilise his government until Haiti's support was needed to isolate Cuba at the Organization of American States (OAS) in 1962.[46] A temporary rapprochement with the United States was reached, and Duvalier continued ruthlessly to crush the left – and all other opponents. When Duvalier declared himself president for life in 1963, relations deteriorated again, but this was also short-lived.[47] Foreign aid to the country was restored, and Haiti even became the main supplier of baseballs to the United States from assembly plants located there.[48] The transition in 1971 from 'Papa Doc' to his son, 'Baby Doc', was relatively seamless, and the Duvalier dictatorship would continue with US support for another fifteen years.

There were no further threats to US strategic interests in the Caribbean until the socialist experiments of Forbes Burnham and Michael Manley in the 1970s in Guyana and Jamaica, respectively. Jamaica had won its independence in 1962.[49] The island's bauxite companies, most of which were US-owned, formed a key target because the tax they paid was very modest. Manley's bold strategy to increase taxes paid – a bauxite levy based on the price of finished aluminium ingots – raised revenue substantially despite the companies' efforts to shift production to other parts of the world.[50] However, Manley's other measures – including the nationalisation of most sugar estates – were less successful, and US administrations used their influence to impose tough conditions on external funding.[51] The resulting economic chaos led to the downfall of the Manley administration and the election of the anti-Communist Edward Seaga in 1980.[52]

---

44 Bosch was the candidate of the Partido Revolucionario Dominicano (PRD), whose programme was broadly representative of the democratic left in Latin America. See Ameringer (1974).
45 Balaguer had even been Trujillo's puppet president in the months before his death.
46 See Connell-Smith (1966), pp. 177–8.
47 See Nicholls (1979), pp. 220–1.
48 See Fass (1988), pp. 37–45.
49 The Federation of the British West Indies had crumbled following a negative vote in the Jamaican referendum in 1961. Jamaica was the first British Caribbean colony to achieve independence. Guyana did so in 1966, becoming a republic in 1970.
50 See Lipton (1979).
51 See Looney (1987).
52 Seaga was the candidate of the Jamaican Labour Party (JLP), which – despite its name – was much closer to business than its rivals.

By this time, the United States faced a much more serious challenge to its interests in Central America, where the Sandinistas had overthrown an anti-Communist dictator and taken power in Nicaragua.[53] Guerrilla movements were threatening to do the same in El Salvador and Guatemala. Furthermore, the leftist New Jewel Movement – led by Maurice Bishop – had overthrown the government in Grenada in 1979 and was taking the country out of the US sphere of influence.[54] And Suriname, independent since 1975, had embarked on a socialist experiment following the military coup in 1980, which threatened US interests – especially in the strategically important bauxite industry.[55]

To the Republicans now in power – and many Democrats also – this seemed to demonstrate the bankruptcy of the approach taken by President Carter, which was based on a respect for human rights and the use of foreign aid. Yet the instruments of US 'soft' power of relevance to the Caribbean were limited at this time.[56] The sugar import quota had lost its effectiveness, the Alliance for Progress had been abandoned and the United States did not yet believe in bilateral preferential trade agreements (PTAs). True, the US administration had adopted the Generalized System of Preferences (GSP) in 1974, but this was global in scope, with very limited regional impact because the non-US territories in the Caribbean had such little manufacturing capacity.[57]

Following the trade embargo against Cuba, the share of Caribbean merchandise exports going to the United States had declined sharply (see Figure 12.3). Cuba had been the most important economy in the region. Its exports were the largest, and most went to the United States. Furthermore, a large part of the remaining merchandise exports came from the US territories. The share of exports (excluding the US territories) destined for the United States had fallen to 25 per cent by the mid-1960s (see Figure 12.3). This was the lowest for more than a century.[58] By the time President Reagan came to power in January 1981, it was abundantly clear that the United States needed to develop new instruments of soft power if it was to retain its influence in the region and contain the challenge from the left.

The first response was the Caribbean Basin Economic Recovery Act (CBERA), which went into force in 1984 and embraced all eligible countries of the region (in the Caribbean Cuba was excluded, as were, initially, Guyana and Suriname). Temporary at first, it was made permanent in 1990[59] and became known simply as the Caribbean Basin Initiative (CBI). It was similar to the European Community's Lomé Convention (see next section) in that it

---

[53] See Bulmer-Thomas (1990).
[54] See Searle (1983).
[55] See van Dyck (2001).
[56] 'Soft power' is the phrase invented by Joseph Nye to describe the way in which powerful countries can secure the support of others without the use of force. See Nye (2008).
[57] The US version of the GSP finally went into force in 1976.
[58] This had been the figure in 1850. See Table A.20.
[59] This was the Caribbean Basin Economic Recovery Expansion Act.

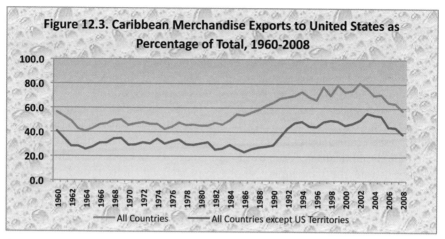

Source: See Appendix to Chapter 12.

proposed nonreciprocal duty-free entry by the United States on a broad range of products, but it had many more political conditions attached and was much more geopolitical in intent. When announced in 1982 by President Reagan (1981–9), it was greeted with great fanfare and attracted broad support from those countries named as beneficiaries. By the time it had been passed by Congress, however, the list of excluded products had expanded significantly as a result of lobbying by US domestic interests.

The biggest disappointment from the point of view of the Caribbean was the exclusion of textiles and clothing, because these were the industries with which modern manufacturing typically started in developing countries and which was advancing rapidly in the region. Its exclusion, together with other 'sensitive' products,[60] was one of the reasons why the share of exports going to the United States (excluding those from the US territories) did **not** rise – indeed, it actually fell, and reached its lowest point in 1986 (see Figure 12.3).[61]

The changes in the CBI made in 1990 helped promote nontraditional exports from the Caribbean, and the share going to the United States started to rise (see Figure 12.3). In addition, a scheme had been developed under which profits made by US firms and retained in Puerto Rico could be loaned at preferential rates to stimulate nontraditional exports in CBI countries.[62] By this time, however, the United States had been converted to the idea of PTAs, and the agreement with Canada, reached in 1989, was expanded to include

---

[60] These included footwear, canned tuna, petroleum products, certain watches and watch parts, certain handbags, luggage, flat goods, work gloves and leather wearing apparel.

[61] When Puerto Rico and the Virgin Islands are included, the share did rise. However, this had nothing to do with the CBI because these territories already had duty-free access for all products.

[62] See Dietz (2003), pp. 158–9.

Mexico.[63] This was the North American Free Trade Agreement (NAFTA), which went into force on 1 January 1994 and gave Mexican companies duty-free access to the markets of its partners for almost all products, including textiles and clothing. Many Caribbean firms could no longer compete, and the demand for 'NAFTA-parity' became very vocal.

The result was a compromise under which US legislation was changed in 2000 to permit duty-free access for textiles and clothing under certain circumstances.[64] These included the use of inputs imported largely from the United States in order to protect the textile industry in certain key states. Finally, a special arrangement was made for Haiti in 2006 – the Hemispheric Opportunity through Partnership Encouragement (HOPE) Act – to allow duty-free access for garments manufactured in the Caribbean's poorest country. The preferential quota for Haiti was further extended in 2008 (it was known as HOPE II).

These amendments to the CBI – perhaps surprisingly – did not have the expected effect, and the share of Caribbean exports going to the United States started to fall again (see Figure 12.3). There were several reasons for this. The first was the boom in commodity prices, which increased the value of primary product exports sold outside the US market. This was especially important in the case of Trinidad & Tobago, whose energy exports rose as never before. The second was the end in 2005 of the Multifibre Arrangement (MFA), under which the United States had been able to set quotas on imports of textiles and clothing from all countries in the world.[65] The benefits under the 2000 version of the CBI had helped Caribbean exporters to withstand competition from China and other parts of Asia, but these now came to an end.

The final reason was the extension by the United States of trade arrangements to countries outside the Caribbean with which the region competed. This included a scheme for Andean countries,[66] but the most damaging from the point of view of the Caribbean was the Central America Free Trade Agreement (CAFTA) signed in 2004. This was because the Central American countries produced a wide range of goods that competed with those from the Caribbean in the US market. The Dominican Republic (DR) lobbied hard for inclusion, and the scheme was modified to allow this, being implemented as CAFTA-DR. Other Caribbean CBI countries were not so fortunate, and many suffered a loss of US market share in sensitive products as a result. Some Caribbean leaders therefore suggested that the United States should sign a PTA with the whole region, but by the time Barack Obama took office in 2009, US congressional interest in such arrangements had ended.

[63] See Weintraub (1994).
[64] The new law was called the Caribbean Basin Trade Partnership Act.
[65] The MFA had been established in 1973 to protect the textile and clothing industries in rich countries from import competition by poor countries. See Teunissen and Blokker (1985).
[66] The Andean Trade Preference Act had been passed in 1991 and was extended in 2002 as the Andean Trade Promotion and Drug Eradication Act. Subsequently, the US signed a PTA with Peru (it already had one with Chile).

None of these trade arrangements between the Caribbean and the United States included services. Yet the United States was a major importer of services from the Caribbean as a result of geographical proximity and the vast size of its market (see Figure 12.1). We cannot be sure what proportion of Caribbean service exports went to the United States, but we can be confident that it was very high in travel, because most countries provide the origin of overnight tourists (although not usually of cruise ship visitors). US tourism to the Caribbean has risen over the long term, but it has been highly volatile as a result of changing domestic conditions in the United States. The US share of other service exports such as finance was also probably high, but here we can only guess because of the secrecy surrounding many of the activities.

In addition to demand for goods and services, there were many other areas in which the United States has had a major impact on the economic life of the Caribbean. The two most important are US drug consumption and US migration policy. The first has led to virtually all Caribbean countries becoming transhipment points for the drug trade. In the case of marijuana, a few have also become exporters in their own right. The income and profits associated with the drug trade have had a powerful effect on the economies and societies of many countries.[67] Just as important, however, has been the violence associated with US-driven efforts to curtail the trade, which have frequently compromised the sovereignty of Caribbean countries.[68]

Migration to the United States – both legal and illegal – has been important throughout the period. US policy since 1960 has privileged migration from Cuba,[69] but it has not been limited to that island, and migration from the US territories has remained unrestricted. Coupled with illegal migration, the numbers of those in the United States from the Caribbean is very large, but it is dominated by those from the Greater Antilles. The flow of remittances sent by migrants back to their families is substantial, although the volume has been very sensitive to the cycles in the US economy.[70] The drug trade and migration overlap in some cases, because the United States often deports gang members – many of whom continue to engage in drug trafficking in one form or another.

Throughout the period, the United States remained the main source of imports for the Caribbean despite the initial loss of the Cuban market. In 1980, the United States was responsible for one-third of all imports, and this had risen to nearly 50 per cent by the early 1990s (see Figure 12.4). Furthermore, US rules were changed at the end of the Clinton administration (1993–2001) to permit exports of food and medicine to Cuba.[71] US firms quickly took

---

[67] See Maingot (1988) and Griffith (2004).

[68] In May 2010, for example, US pressure to extradite a notorious Jamaican 'don' produced a major confrontation between his supporters and the island's security forces.

[69] Even after it was modified by President Clinton to the so-called wet-foot, dry-foot policy, where Cubans would be turned back if apprehended at sea, it was still the case that migrants from the island were treated much more favourably than any others.

[70] See Palmer (2009).

[71] The goods had to be paid for in cash.

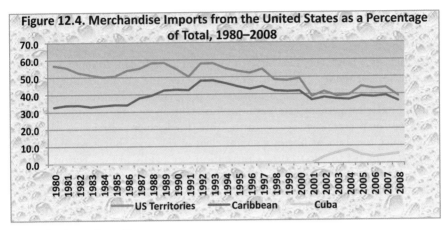

Figure 12.4. Merchandise Imports from the United States as a Percentage of Total, 1980–2008

Source: See Appendix to Chapter 12.

advantage of this and were soon supplying roughly 5 per cent of the Cuban market (see Figure 12.4).[72] Yet, despite this, the US share of Caribbean imports as a whole fell significantly after 1993 (see Figure 12.4). This was, as we shall now see, because of the increased presence of other members of the core.

12.3. EUROPE AND THE CARIBBEAN

The EEC was launched by six countries on 1 January 1958. Nearly fifty years later it had become a European Union (EU) of twenty-seven members and the world's largest importer. By then most members had replaced their domestic currencies with the euro, which competed with the US dollar for global supremacy.[73] The European 'project', as it was often called, was bound to have major implications for the Caribbean, even without taking into account historical ties between the two regions, and this turned out to be correct.

Two of the founding members of the EEC – France and Holland – had territorial responsibilities in the Caribbean. For France the Treaty of Rome presented no special problems, because the Caribbean countries in question were all DOMs and therefore joined the EEC on 1 January 1958 along with the rest of France. Furthermore, migration between these countries – French Guiana, Guadeloupe and Martinique – and mainland France had always been free and would remain so. If the formal status of the DOMs as part of France could not always be maintained (some exports were subject to certain

---

[72] This made the US the fifth most important supplier to Cuba despite the official rhetoric in favour of the trade embargo.

[73] The euro was adopted in 1999 by twelve member states. When Estonia was admitted to the eurozone in January 2011, the number of participants reached seventeen.

restrictions and trade was still treated as 'foreign' until 1995), there was no denying that the DOMs were in a unique position in the Caribbean in relation to Europe.[74]

France did, however, have a large number of African colonies – soon to become independent – and the EEC, as a customs union, could only permit a special arrangement if it applied to all members. Following a five-year transitional arrangement, the Yaoundé Convention was signed in 1963, and it provided for preferential access to the EEC for former colonies in Africa. Its significance for the Caribbean was not clear at the time, but it would become the prototype for the first Lomé Convention (see below in this section).

Membership of the EEC created a different set of issues for the Netherlands. The 1954 constitutional arrangement had made the Dutch Antilles and Suriname partners of Holland in the Kingdom of the Netherlands, but this did not imply future membership of the EEC nor indeed of the customs union Holland had formed with Belgium and Luxembourg in 1948 (it did, however, provide for unrestricted migration to the Netherlands). A new arrangement therefore had to be established, which was only important for Suriname, because the Dutch Antilles was now a service- and oil-based economy that was not much affected by the Common External Tariff (CET) of the EEC.[75] By 1963, Holland had secured associate status for Suriname, which meant that it had roughly the same access to the EEC as was enjoyed by member countries of the Yaoundé Convention.

The constitutional arrangements proved unsatisfactory for Suriname, which proceeded to independence in 1975. This meant loss of associate status, but Suriname gained access to the European market in a similar fashion to what it had previously enjoyed (see below in this section). The Dutch Antilles remained in the Kingdom of the Netherlands, but Aruba objected to control from Curaçao and acquired equal status with the rest of the Dutch Antilles in 1986. This process of decolonisation was taken to its logical conclusion in October 2010 when Sint Maarten and Curaçao themselves chose the same path, and Bonaire, Saba and St Eustatius became special municipalities of Holland (and therefore effectively part of the EU).[76]

The UK had not participated in the discussions leading to the Treaty of Rome and had instead formed EFTA (European Free Trade Area).[77] It gradually

---

[74] This did not mean that all DOM citizens were content with the arrangements, but dissatisfaction often focused on the degree of autonomy within each DOM itself. St Barthélemy and St Martin broke away from Guadeloupe in 2007, each becoming a Collectivité d'Outre-Mer (COM). This preserved their status as part of France, but freed them from control by Guadeloupe.

[75] Most of the refined oil went to the US, but that part which went to the EEC faced no tariff barriers anyway.

[76] The Dutch special municipalities, like other overseas countries and territories of the EU, are not required to apply the EU's Common External Tariff. However, in almost all other respects they are part of the EU by virtue of their status within the Netherlands.

[77] The UK under EFTA could have whatever commercial policy it wanted with third countries, so its formation was not a threat to the Caribbean.

dawned on the UK, however, that a strategic error had been committed by not joining the EEC at birth. Intraregional trade was growing very rapidly in the rival organisation as tariffs disappeared and institutions were taking shape that would be much more difficult to change later. The most important of these for the Caribbean was the Common Agricultural Policy (CAP), which gave European farmers much higher prices than those that prevailed in the world market. Because net imports were replaced by net exports of commodities such as sugar, the surpluses were dumped on the world market with deleterious effects on prices – European producers were protected by the subsidies provided from the EEC budget.

Despite its concerns about the CAP[78] and the need to pool sovereignty with other European states, Britain applied for membership of the EEC in 1963.[79] By then the British colonies in the Caribbean had begun the process of decolonisation, and unrestricted migration to the UK had ended in 1961.[80] It was not until 1 January 1973, however, that Britain became a member of what would later be known as the European Community (EC).[81] Inevitably, this had profound implications for all the British colonies and ex-colonies in the Caribbean because the EC's CET was not compatible with the preferential access they had previously enjoyed in the British market for their main commodity exports. Finding a new framework for access was therefore a priority for all concerned.

The solution was found in the first Lomé Convention, signed in 1975. This gave duty-free access to the EC on a broad range of products for a large number of European ex-colonies (because these countries were mainly located in Africa, the Caribbean and the Pacific, they became known as the ACP countries). For these goods access to all EC member states was not subject to quotas. However, this was not possible for certain products (especially sugar, rum, rice and bananas) of special importance to the Caribbean, which were each made subject to separate protocols.

The sugar protocol was essentially an updated version of Britain's Commonwealth Sugar Agreement (CSA), which had been in force since 1951. ACP countries, including most of those in the Caribbean,[82] now received a duty-free quota in the EC, which normally ensured them higher prices than those in the

<hr>

78 British farmers had come to rely on government subsidies paid directly, which left domestic prices in line with world prices.
79 Its application was vetoed by the French president (General de Gaulle), in part because he did not believe that British overseas responsibilities were consistent with membership.
80 This was as a result of the first Commonwealth Immigrants Act, which was followed by others that became increasingly restrictive.
81 The change of name from EEC to EC (a grouping of all the European Communities) took place in 1993 following the Treaty on European Union (EU). The concept of EC was abolished after the Treaty of Lisbon in 2009, leaving only the EU.
82 The first group of ACP countries in the Caribbean were the British and Dutch ex-colonies. Their numbers increased when other British colonies became independent (the last was St Kitts & Nevis in 1983), and all benefitted from the sugar quota. Eventually, all independent Caribbean countries joined the ACP, but Cuba, the Dominican Republic and Haiti (all of whom joined in the 1990s) were excluded from the sugar protocol.

world market. Strictly speaking, the sugar protocol was not part of the Lomé
Convention – it was negotiated separately. The rum protocol was similar to
the one for sugar, except that it was included in the Convention itself.

The banana protocol was different, because there was no single community-
wide policy. Under these arrangements, market access and prices varied from
country to country. ACP bananas, for example, were sold at high prices in
those EC states (e.g. Britain) where non-ACP bananas were subject to tariffs
and/or quotas, and they earned much lower prices in those states where all
imports were either duty-free (Germany) or subject to a 20 per cent tariff
(e.g. Holland). Furthermore, bananas exported from the French Caribbean
territories were guaranteed a two-thirds share of the French market but of no
other state. The banana trade therefore ran against all the principles on which
the EC had been founded, because the product could not move freely between
countries.

These arrangements, despite the discrimination they implied against non-
ACP countries (including those in the Caribbean), continued for many years.
No formal objections were raised at GATT, and EC states saw them as a
small price to pay for meeting their obligations to former colonies. The Lomé
Convention, including the separate protocols, was regularly renewed[83] and
included not only substantial packages of foreign aid but also funds for sta-
bilizing commodity prices.[84] The framework provided by the Lomé Convention was also one of the reasons why the Caribbean (excluding US territories)
continued to depend heavily on the European market despite the 'pull' of the
United States. In return, the EC remained a major source for Caribbean imports
(see Figure 12.5).

On 1 January 1993, soon after the entry into force of Lomé IV, the European
Union – as it was now named – launched the Single European Market (SEM).
This was a consequence of an agreement signed in 1986, and the member states
had spent the intervening years introducing domestic legislation to ensure that
the aspiration of a single market would become a reality. However, the changes
in the arrangements with the ACP countries that this implied did not receive the
attention they deserved. In particular, no decision was reached on the banana
protocol until the last moment (December 1992).

The solution – a tariff quota for non-ACP bananas and a higher tariff
for imports in excess of the quota coupled with a duty-free quota for ACP
bananas[85] – was to be the start of one of the longest-running international
trade disputes ever. Even before the WTO came into existence, the legality
of the EU banana regime had been challenged by Latin American exporters,
and these protests would be joined by the United States in 1995. Time and

[83] In 1980, 1985 and 1990.
[84] Lomé I had included a program (STABEX) for stabilising agricultural commodity prices. Lomé
II would do the same for minerals (SYSMIN).
[85] The Dominican Republic was designated by the EU as a 'nontraditional' exporter of bananas
in order to avoid giving it a large initial quota.

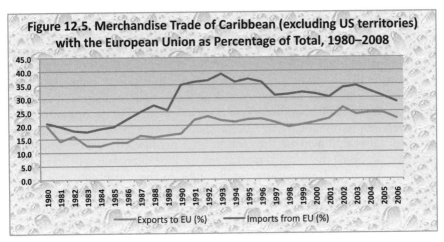

Figure 12.5. Merchandise Trade of Caribbean (excluding US territories) with the European Union as Percentage of Total, 1980–2008

Source: See Appendix to Chapter 12.

again the regime, even when modified, was judged illegal by WTO panels until in 2010 the case was dropped when the EU agreed to a much lower level of discrimination against banana imports from non-ACP countries.[86] This meant, however, much lower levels of preference for Caribbean banana exporters, and it was widely assumed that the industry would decline as a consequence.

The banana dispute was the clearest demonstration that the arrangements between the EU and the ACP countries were unlikely to prevail in the face of a judicial challenge.[87] In any case, the EU had come to the view that one agreement with such a heterogeneous group was unworkable. The Lomé Convention was therefore replaced in 2000 with the Cotonou Convention signed by all ACP states except Cuba.[88] This maintained temporarily the nonreciprocal trade concessions of Lomé IV, while committing ACP countries to reach a series of Economic Partnership Agreements (EPAs) with the EU that would involve reciprocal WTO-compatible trade concessions and which would differ by region.[89] One of these regions was the Caribbean, which included all the independent countries except Cuba and which was named the Caribbean Forum (CARIFORUM).

It is fair to say that the Caribbean states had not anticipated these developments and were not prepared for the consequences. Yet the EPA between

---

[86] This involved a modest tariff on 'dollar' banana imports and no other restrictions.
[87] As early as 1996 the EU had abandoned quotas for ACP rum and moved to full liberalisation without preferences.
[88] Cuba took exception to the clauses referring to democracy and human rights, because it feared these could be used to justify intervention in the country's internal affairs.
[89] Extending the nonreciprocal trade preferences required a WTO waiver. This was granted in 2001, but only until 31 December 2007.

CARIFORUM and the EU was the first to be signed (in 2008).[90] Trade was to be almost completely liberalised on a reciprocal basis, but the Caribbean was given a longer period of transition. Sugar and rice quotas were to be maintained for a brief period, but with a less favourable impact as a result of the planned reduction in EU domestic prices. These were bitter pills for the Caribbean states to swallow. They were sweetened by the promise of increased development cooperation and liberalisation of trade in services. For the optimists – and there were not many in CARIFORUM when the agreement went into force – it was the latter that held out the greatest hope because it raised the possibility of greater access to the vast EU market for Caribbean providers of services.[91]

Given the lack of enthusiasm for the EPA in the Caribbean, it is worth asking why it was signed by the region's leaders. The simple reason is that they had no choice. The absence of an agreement would have ended preferential access to the European market, and the EU was disinclined to forge a new framework that would be compatible with WTO rules. The interest of the EU in the Caribbean had declined sharply since British entry for all sorts of reasons. First, those states that joined after the UK – except Spain and Sweden – had no historical links with the region and very little trade.[92] Second, the development cooperation effort of the EU was becoming increasingly focused on the poorest countries in the world.[93] Third, like other rich countries, EU members were becoming mesmerised by the rise of Asia. Finally, the EU was – perhaps unfairly – disappointed with the pace of regional integration in the Caribbean.

12.4. THE REST OF THE CORE AND THE CARIBBEAN

Before 1960 the only member of the core outside the United States and Europe was Canada, and even it was a marginal member. This would change with the Cuban Revolution, because the US trade and investment embargo would set in motion a series of events that brought other countries to the region as core members. Furthermore, the Cuban economy in 1960 was still the largest in the Caribbean, and its foreign trade almost the most important. A large share of the Cuban market alone would therefore ensure any state of a significant presence in the Caribbean.

---

[90] The agreement was initialled on 16 December 2007 – two weeks before the expiry of the waiver given by the WTO. Haiti, the fifteenth and final country, signed in 2009.

[91] For different assessments of the EPA, see Bernal (2008), Arthur (2008), Nurse (2008) and Girvan (2008). For a simulation of its expected impact, see Rapley et al. (2010).

[92] Denmark, which did have historical ties, had joined at the same time as the UK in 1973.

[93] Shortly after the Cotonou Agreement came into force, the EU had offered the poorest (Least Developed) countries a generous trade concession for Duty-Free Quota-Free (DFQF) access that did not require a WTO waiver. Known as Everything But Arms (EBA), it was another reason why the CARIFORUM countries were under pressure to sign the EPA in 2008 because none of them except Haiti would have benefitted from EBA. Instead, their exports of goods would have entered the European market under the EU's revised GSP scheme – a much less generous scheme than EBA.

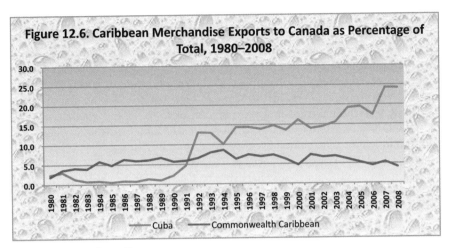

Figure 12.6. Caribbean Merchandise Exports to Canada as Percentage of Total, 1980–2008

Source: See Appendix to Chapter 12.

Canada did not follow the US example and continued to trade with Cuba. Cuban imports increased rapidly and soon reached 20 per cent of those paid for in hard currency.[94] Furthermore, Cuba's need to diversify its exports would lead to Canadian investment in key sectors, such as mining, and thus exports to Canada also rose rapidly – especially after 1990 (see Figure 12.6). Canadian tourists flocked to Cuba when the industry was revived in the mid-1980s. US efforts to curtail Canadian investment were unsuccessful, and economic relations between Canada and Cuba steadily expanded despite the occasional setback.

By virtue of its relation with Cuba alone, Canada would have earned its place as a member of the core. However, imperial preference since the end of the nineteenth century had increased significantly Canada's share of British Caribbean trade, and mining and banking investments had given the dominion a strong presence throughout the whole region. The decision, therefore, by the Reagan administration in 1983 to launch the Caribbean Basin Initiative (CBI) was a potential threat to Canadian interests because it carried with it the risk of trade diversion. Canada responded in 1986 with the Caribbean-Canada Trade Agreement (CARIBCAN), which offered duty-free access for Commonwealth Caribbean exporters.[95] This helped to raise temporarily the share of their exports going to Canada (see Figure 12.6).

Russia had never been a member of the core for the Caribbean, and the same was true at first of the USSR after 1917. However, Cuban overtures in

---

94 Most imports before 1990, however, were from the Soviet bloc and not paid for in dollars.
95 Unfortunately, this carried with it a similar list of exceptions as did the CBI – especially textiles and clothing – so that the favourable impact was diminished and 'NAFTA-parity' was never granted. In due course it was expected that CARIBCAN would be replaced with a reciprocal trade agreement similar to the EU-CARIFORUM EPA. Negotiations for this were still under way as this book went to press.

the middle of the Cold War were too good an opportunity to miss, and the Soviet Union was soon deeply involved in the Cuban economy. This will be examined in more detail elsewhere,[96] but the broad outlines can be sketched here very quickly. The USSR provided a guaranteed market for the main Cuban exports, especially sugar, and supplied in return a mixture of goods (including fuel and weapons), services, investments and foreign aid. Within a short time, the USSR was the main trading partner of Cuba, the island was included in COMECON[97] and Cuba was even more closely linked to the Soviet Union than it had been to the United States before 1960.

Such a high level of dependence carried risks, and the collapse of the Soviet Union after 1990 brought great hardship to Cuba, GDP per head declining by over one-third. Yet the Russian Federation – the successor state of the USSR – did not sever all ties with Cuba and, indeed, would start to strengthen them again at the end of the century (albeit without the high level of preferences that had been in place before). Russia remained a major market for Cuban goods and services, and in return Russia remained an important supplier of military hardware and technology. Yet Russia's relationship with Cuba was not the same as that of the USSR, and the Russian Federation – successor to the USSR – cannot be considered a member of the core.

During the 1960s the Soviet Union's links with the Caribbean had been largely restricted to Cuba. However, this would change in the 1970s when some of the newly independent countries – especially Guyana, Jamaica and Suriname – started to diversify their trade and investment partners. The economic links with these countries were never very strong, however, and neither side was interested in replicating the bilateral relationship between the Soviet Union and Cuba. Grenada under the government of the New Jewel Movement (1979–83) was different, because the Soviet Union was pushed by the leadership to take on the same role as in Cuba, but the US intervention in 1983 cut short any such prospects.

China had given moral support to the Cuban Revolution from the beginning, but it was not at first able to offer much more. Before 1980, China was virtually a closed economy with little need for imports and limited export capacity. Furthermore, Mao Tse-tung had denounced the USSR in 1959, and Cuba could not afford to antagonise the Soviet Union by aligning itself too closely with China. The economic relations of China with the rest of the Caribbean were minimal. In addition, many countries that recognised Taiwan were in the Caribbean, and Taiwan provided generous assistance that made them reluctant to switch allegiance.[98]

---

[96] See Chapter 16.

[97] The Council for Mutual Economic Assistance (COMECON) had been founded in 1949 by the socialist countries. It ended in 1991 following the collapse of the USSR.

[98] Some Caribbean countries subsequently established diplomatic relations with the People's Republic of China, but it was still the case in 2011 that six of the twenty-three countries recognising Taiwan were in the Caribbean.

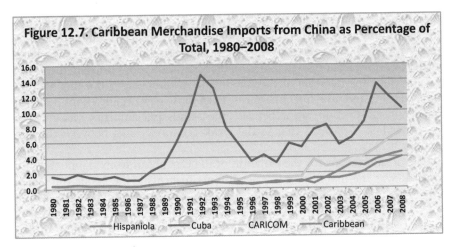

Figure 12.7. Caribbean Merchandise Imports from China as Percentage of Total, 1980–2008

Source: See Appendix to Chapter 12.

China's relationship with the Caribbean slowly began to change after the introduction of economic reform at the end of the 1970s. In 1980, China provided only 0.4 per cent of all Caribbean imports (see Figure 12.7). Nearly thirty years later, however, this ratio had increased tenfold, with every expectation that it would continue to rise. The share of imports coming from China rose sharply in almost all regions, with CARICOM[99] going from virtually zero in 1980 to nearly 10 per cent (only in the markets of the US territories did China fail to make much headway). And Chinese foreign assistance and investment persuaded some states to switch allegiance from Taiwan to the People's Republic.[100]

While the Soviet Union existed, Cuba had not purchased much of its imports from China. This changed dramatically after 1990. Cuban imports started to fall, but the share coming from China rose sharply (see Figure 12.7). As more normal conditions returned in Cuba, the Chinese share of imports declined. However, China remained a major trading partner, and much of the imports were financed by official credits on easy terms. By the end of the period, the Chinese share was once again above 10 per cent, making it Cuba's most important supplier. Chinese tourists were also coming to Cuba in increasing numbers as a result of the designation of the island as an approved destination for group travel.[101]

The United States, the EU, Canada and China constituted the core in relation to the Caribbean as the twentieth century approached its end. Despite

---

[99] The Caribbean Community (CARICOM) is described in detail in Chapter 14.3.
[100] Two states (Belize and St Lucia), however, subsequently switched back to recognising Taiwan.
[101] Chinese visitors may only take organised tours to countries with 'Approved Destination Status'. The number of such countries exceeded 100 by 2011.

geographical proximity, no Latin American state was a member of this group. The separation of the two regions through colonial ties had been reinforced by trade patterns that favoured trade with the metropolitan countries. The independent Caribbean states had joined all the institutions established in the Americas to reflect the interests of their mainland neighbours,[102] but this had not changed trade and investment patterns. Even those new organisations designed to promote closer cooperation between the islands and countries with a Caribbean coastline could not change the weak economic links between the two groups.[103]

One of the reasons for the isolation of the Caribbean from mainland Latin America was the inability of the neighbours to provide the goods the region needed to import. There was, however, one exception – and that was oil. Indeed, Venezuela – and to a lesser extent Colombia and Mexico – had been the source of crude oil for the giant refineries established in the Dutch Antilles in the 1920s. And Venezuelan crude was also used by other refineries in the Caribbean as they came on stream.

The supply of oil to the Caribbean was at first a purely commercial transaction. When the Central American crisis erupted at the end of the 1970s, however, Mexico and Venezuela joined forces to supply energy on concessional terms to the small countries of the Caribbean Basin. This agreement, known as the San José Accord, was reached in 1980 at a time when oil prices were exceptionally high. When prices subsequently declined after 1985, the agreement was less beneficial to importing states. Nonetheless, it generated a great deal of goodwill and demonstrated the value of oil diplomacy to all the participants.

This lesson was not lost on Venezuela, which launched a new preferential arrangement for oil importers – Petrocaribe – in 2005.[104] This has to be seen in the context of the growing tension between Venezuela and the United States, whose relationship had deteriorated sharply after a failed military coup against President Chávez (1999–).[105] The scheme was aimed at independent Caribbean states dependent on oil imports, and all except Barbados eventually joined.[106] Because oil prices were high and climbing, the scheme was immensely popular

---

[102] These included the Economic Commission for Latin America (ECLA), whose name was even changed in 1973 to Economic Commission for Latin America and the Caribbean (ECLAC) to reflect the new reality, the Inter-American Development Bank (IDB) and the Organization of American States (OAS).

[103] These new institutions included the Caribbean Development Bank (CDB), established in 1970, and the Association of Caribbean States (ACS), founded in 1994.

[104] Petrocaribe required eligible countries to pay only part of the cost of energy in cash with the balance financed by debt on concessional terms. The ratio between cash and debt depended on the level of energy prices.

[105] The failed coup in April 2002 was not the work of the US, but it is widely thought that the US was aware of what was happening and did not warn the Venezuelan authorities.

[106] Haiti was not eligible until 2006, because Venezuela did not recognise the previous government. Trinidad & Tobago was not included because it is an oil exporter itself. Barbados declined because of concerns about Venezuelan conditionality.

and was extended to Central America.[107] Petrocaribe started to transform the economic relations between the Caribbean and Venezuela, with the scheme being popular even in those countries that were strong supporters of the United States.

Before the announcement of Petrocaribe, Venezuela had joined forces with Cuba to create ALBA – the Bolivarian Alternative for the Peoples of Our America. Designed to counter the US preference for a Free Trade Area of the Americas (FTAA),[108] ALBA appeared at first to be no more than a bilateral agreement between the two countries in the hemisphere with the greatest differences with the United States. When Bolivia and Nicaragua joined soon afterwards – both countries with a difficult relationship with the United States – it was easy to reach the same conclusion. However, the entry into ALBA of a series of small Caribbean countries – Antigua, Dominica and St Vincent – demonstrated that the organisation had a broader appeal.[109] In particular, Venezuela provided through ALBA foreign assistance that was subject to very few conditions.

Oil had succeeded in changing the relationship between Venezuela and the Caribbean, but it was difficult to say how permanent this would be in view of the fluctuations in energy prices and the polarisation of Venezuelan domestic politics.[110] Perhaps more enduring would be the changing relationship between the Caribbean and Brazil, the largest Latin American state and the one with potentially the most to offer. Brazil, whose maritime borders touch the Caribbean and which shares a land border with three Caribbean countries,[111] had traditionally ignored the region. However, a combination of the promotion of Brazilian exports and the country's search for a permanent seat on the UN Security Council projected Brazil into the Caribbean in a much more visible way in the twenty-first century.[112]

It was too early to conclude from this that Brazil – or, indeed, Venezuela – had joined the core in relation to the Caribbean. Trade, investment, aid, debt and migration ties were still not strong enough. However, it demonstrated that the Caribbean has always had to face a fluctuating core. The European powers had been replaced by the EU, and the Soviet Union had come and gone. Canada had joined the core at the start of the twentieth century, and China 100 years

[107] Nicaragua had been a beneficiary since the start.

[108] This had been promoted by President Clinton at the Summit of the Americas in 1994, but it could not overcome domestic (US) opposition and the lack of support from several South American states.

[109] So much so that the name was changed in 2009 to Bolivarian **Alliance** for the Peoples of Our America.

[110] Such was the level of polarisation in the first decade of the twenty-first century that no Caribbean country could be certain what part of the new relationship would survive if President Chávez lost power.

[111] French Guiana, Suriname and Guyana. Establishing where this boundary ran had been a vexed issue for Brazil, but even when it was solved there had been at first little formal contact.

[112] Brazil led the United Nations Stabilization Mission in Haiti (MINUSTAH) following its establishment in 2004.

later. Only the United States had remained a member of the core throughout the years since the Napoleonic Wars, and even its participation had varied significantly from one period to the next.

APPENDIX TO CHAPTER 12. CARIBBEAN MERCHANDISE TRADE WITH THE UNITED STATES, THE EUROPEAN UNION, CANADA AND CHINA

Before 1960, the Statistical Appendix in this book includes tables on each country's merchandise trade with the United States, the UK and 'mother' country. This approach is not feasible from 1960 onwards for a variety of reasons. First, the 'mother' country has lost much of its significance. Second, it is very difficult to compile each country's exports to and imports from Europe as a result of the growth in EU membership. Third, the data on the destination of merchandise trade for some countries after 1960 is not provided on a consistent annual basis.

For all these reasons a different approach is used here that starts with the trade of the core countries – United States, the EU, Canada and China – with the Caribbean in order to approximate the merchandise exports and imports of the region. This is by no means ideal, but it is important to understand the changes in the destination of merchandise trade after 1960, even if it is impossible to say much about the destination of service trade. Indeed, the only useable statistics on service trade refer to the number of tourists from different destinations visiting the Caribbean.

I. United States

A. *Caribbean Exports to the United States, 1960–1980 (%)*
The main source is the printed version of IMF, *Direction of Trade Statistics* (hereafter DOTS), which gives US imports from most Caribbean countries starting in 1962. The data are *fob* until 1969 and *cif* from 1970. The following adjustments have then been made:

1. US imports (*cif*) from 1970 have been converted to Caribbean exports (*fob*) by assuming a difference of 10%.
2. For the Dutch Antilles, I have assumed that all exports to the US are refined oil and have therefore taken 10% of the gross value in order to be consistent with the methodology of the Statistical Appendix.
3. For Bahamas, I have assumed 50% of merchandise exports (see Notes on D. Tables) went to the US.
4. For Puerto Rico and USVI, I have assumed 70% and 90% of merchandise exports (see Notes on D. Tables) went to the US, respectively.
5. The data for French Guiana are not reliable before 1975. I therefore assumed that 60% of merchandise exports (see Notes on D. Tables) went to the US in these years.

The data for 1960 come from Table C.17. There are no data for 1961, so it has been filled by interpolation. US imports (*fob*) have then been divided by Caribbean merchandise exports in Table D.6 to give the ratio of Caribbean merchandise exports going to the US from 1960 to 1980.

B. Caribbean Exports to the United States, 1980–2008 (%)

The main source is DOTS (Web site version), which gives US imports (*cif*) from most Caribbean countries. The following adjustments have then been made:

1. US imports (*cif*) have been converted to Caribbean exports (*fob*) by assuming a difference of 10%.
2. There are no disaggregated data for the British Overseas Territories, so I have used United Nations, *Yearbook of International Trade Statistics* (hereafter UNYITS) for each country for those years when available and filled the gaps by estimation.
3. For those countries with oil refining not based on domestic crude, I have used the data in DOTS to derive the percentage of exports that went to the US and applied this percentage to each country's (net) petroleum exports (see Table D.5 and Notes on D. Tables).
4. Because there are no data in DOTS for Puerto Rico (it is included in the US), I have used US and Puerto Rican official sources. In the case of the USVI (also included in US in DOTS), I have used USVI, Bureau of Economic Research, *Annual Economic Indicators* for the share of **net** exports going to the US.
5. In those cases (St Kitts & Nevis, Haiti) where the methodology above implies that the ratio of merchandise exports going to the US exceeds 100%, I have used the data in DOTS to derive the percentage of exports that went to the US and applied this percentage to each country's exports in Table D.6.
6. US imports from the French territories are not reported after 1996. I have therefore assumed the same ratio for the missing years as in 1996.

US imports (*fob*) have then been divided by Caribbean merchandise exports in Table D.6 to give the ratio of Caribbean merchandise exports going to the US from 1980 to 2008.

C. Caribbean Imports from the United States, 1980–2008 (%)

The main source is DOTS (Web site version), which gives US exports (*fob*) to most Caribbean countries. The following adjustments have then been made:

1. US exports (*fob*) have been converted to Caribbean imports (*cif*) by assuming a difference of 10%.
2. The data for the British Overseas Territories are assumed to be the same as US exports to 'Western Hemisphere *n.e.s.*'. In 1980–4 this gives a ratio above 100%, which has been rounded down to 100%.

3. Because there are no data in DOTS for Puerto Rico, I have used US and Puerto Rican official sources. In the case of the USVI, I have used USVI, Bureau of Economic Research, *Annual Economic Indicators* for the share of net imports coming from the US.
4. In those very few cases where the ratio was above 100%, I estimated it based on the nearest year.
5. US exports to the French territories are not reported after 1996. I have therefore assumed the same ratio for the missing years as in 1996.

US exports (*cif*) have then been divided by Caribbean merchandise imports in Table D.11 to give the ratio of Caribbean merchandise imports coming from the US between 1980 and 2008.

II. European Union

A. *Caribbean Imports from the EU, 1980–2008 (%)*
The main source is DOTS (printed version), which gives EU/EEC exports to most Caribbean countries (because the EEC had nine members in 1980 and the EU had twenty-seven by 2008, this means that the numbers are not strictly comparable over time; however, the nine members in 1980 accounted for the vast bulk of EU trade even in 2008). Before 2000, DOTS gives both Caribbean imports from EU (*cif*) and EU exports (*fob*) to Caribbean. From 2000 onwards, only the latter is reported. The following adjustments have then been made:

1. From 2000 onwards, European exports (*fob*) have been converted to Caribbean imports (*cif*) by assuming a difference of 10%.
2. The data for the British Overseas Territories have been estimated as the difference between merchandise imports and merchandise imports from the US (this assumes no imports from other countries; this is clearly an exaggeration, but other imports – including from China – were very small).
3. The data for US territories (Puerto Rico and USVI) have been estimated as the difference between total imports and imports from the US (this assumes no imports from other countries; this is clearly an exaggeration but other imports, including from China before 2006, are very small).
4. The data for the French DOMs after 1996 have been derived assuming the EU ratio of total imports is the same as in 1996.

EEC/EU exports (*cif*) have then been divided by Caribbean merchandise imports in Table D.11 to give the ratio of Caribbean merchandise imports from the EEC/EU between 1980 and 2008.

B. *Caribbean Exports to the EU, 1980–2008 (%)*
The main source is DOTS (printed version), which gives Caribbean exports to EEC/EU countries (because the EEC had nine members in 1980 and the EU had twenty-seven by 2008, this means that the numbers are not strictly comparable

over time; however, the nine members in 1980 accounted for the vast bulk of EU trade even in 2008). Before 2000, DOTS gives both Caribbean exports to the EU (*fob*) and EU imports (*cif*) from Caribbean. From 2000 onwards, only the latter is reported. The following adjustments have then been made:

1. From 2000 onwards, EEC/EU imports (*cif*) have been converted to Caribbean exports (*fob*) by assuming a difference of 10%.
2. The data for the British Overseas Territories have been estimated as the difference between merchandise exports and merchandise exports to the US (this assumes no exports to other countries).
3. The data for US territories (Puerto Rico and the USVI) have been estimated as the difference between merchandise exports and merchandise exports to the US (this assumes no exports to other countries).
4. The data for the French DOMs after 1996 have been derived assuming the EU share of total exports is the same as in 1996.
5. The data for Dutch Antilles from 1980 to 1986 have been estimated assuming that 20% of net exports went to the EU.

EEC/EU imports (*fob*) have then been divided by Caribbean merchandise exports in Table D.6 to give the ratio of Caribbean merchandise exports going to EEC/EU from 1980 to 2008.

III. Canada

A. Caribbean Exports to Canada, 1980–2008 (%)
The source is DOTS (Web site version), which gives Canadian imports (*cif*) from Cuba and the Commonwealth Caribbean. These were converted from Canadian imports (*cif*) to Caribbean exports (*fob*) by assuming a difference of 10%. Canadian imports (*fob*) have then been divided by (a) Cuban and (b) Commonwealth Caribbean merchandise exports in Table D.6 to give the ratio of merchandise exports going to Canada from 1980 to 2008.

B. Caribbean Imports from Canada, 1980–2008 (%)
Merchandise imports from Canada have not been estimated, because the ratio was small for almost all countries.

IV. China

A. Caribbean Imports from China, 1980–2008 (%)
The main source is DOTS (Web site version), which gives Chinese exports (*fob*) to most Caribbean countries. The following adjustments have then been made:

1. Chinese exports (*fob*) have been converted to Caribbean imports (*cif*) by assuming a difference of 10%.
2. The data for the British Overseas Territories are assumed to be the same as Chinese exports to 'Western Hemisphere *n.e.s.*' (except 1984–90,

which have been assumed to be 0.1% of British Overseas Territories' merchandise imports).

3. I have used US Census Bureau 2008 figures for merchandise imports from China by both Puerto Rico and USVI. I have then assumed a nominal value of $100 in 1980 and interpolated the intervening years. In 2008 imports from China were 1.3% of merchandise imports in the case of Puerto Rico and 0.1% in the case of the USVI.

Chinese exports (*cif*) have then been divided by Caribbean merchandise imports in Table D.11 to give the ratio of Caribbean merchandise imports from China between 1980 and 2008.

B. Caribbean Exports to China, 1980–2008 (%)
Merchandise exports from the Caribbean to China were still small at the end of the period, with the exception of Cuba. They have therefore not been estimated here.

13

Structural Change in the Caribbean

In the period since 1960 the Caribbean has undergone a series of structural changes that constitute a major break with the past. A visitor coming to the region at the end of the 1950s, after an absence of fifty years, might have been surprised by how little had changed in the intervening period. Another fifty years later, the region would be almost unrecognisable to anyone returning. Whether looking at the economy, the environment, politics or society, the changes have been profound and permanent. For better or worse, and there has been plenty of both, the Caribbean today is very different from the region in 1960.

This chapter focuses on four of the most significant changes in the economy during this period. The first has been the shift within merchandise exports away from agricultural products towards minerals and manufacturing. The days when the Caribbean could be dismissed as dependent on a handful of agricultural exports, such as sugar and bananas, have ended. This transition has not been painless (and is still not complete in a few small countries), but it has taken place with great rapidity.

The second change – even more important than the first – has been the rise of service exports to the point where they account for the majority of export earnings in all but a handful of countries. Indeed, there is no other region of the world that is now so dependent on them, because services constitute such a large part of foreign exchange earnings and exports are a very high share of national income. Tourism has been the main driver of this change, but it has also involved financial, business and government services.

The third change involves the responsibilities of government and the manner in which these public functions are financed. At the end of the 1950s it was still the case that a very high proportion of government revenue came from taxes on trade, that governments – wherever possible – stayed out of production and that public administration constituted a low share of GDP. All this changed after 1960. This was partly because of the end of colonialism in many countries, but also because of the increasing demands placed upon governments by their

electorates throughout the region. And in Cuba, of course, the role of the state was completely transformed.

The fourth change has been the shift to a much higher rate of urbanisation. The agricultural share of employment has collapsed, and most jobs are now in manufacturing or services based in cities. At the same time the total population has been rising, with a growing proportion in urban areas. This shift has been made possible by rapid internal migration from rural to urban areas, with the population concentrated in each country in a handful of cities. Just four cities in the Caribbean – Havana (Cuba), San Juan (Puerto Rico), Santo Domingo (Dominican Republic) and Port-au-Prince (Haiti) – now contain one in five of all people living in the Caribbean.

These four structural shifts took place at a time when the political landscape was altering – in particular, the independence of many more countries. After Jamaica and Trinidad & Tobago in 1962, Guyana and Barbados achieved independence in 1966; Antigua, Bahamas, Dominica, Grenada, St Lucia, St Vincent and Suriname in the 1970s; Belize and St Kitts & Nevis in the 1980s. This requires a change in the subregions used for statistical analysis, with CARICOM (excluding Haiti and Montserrat) becoming a new unit.[1] The labels 'British territories' and 'Dutch territories' therefore refer to those colonies that did not become independent.[2] The other subregions – Hispaniola, Cuba, French and US territories – remain as before.[3]

13.1. MERCHANDISE EXPORTS

At the beginning of the period considered here (1960), merchandise exports constituted the bulk of export earnings. In that same year Cuba was still the most important exporter in the Caribbean (see Figure 13.1), despite the suspension of the US sugar quota in the middle of the year. Indeed, Cuban exports (nearly 30 per cent of the total for the Caribbean) were the same as those from all the future CARICOM states combined and slightly ahead of those from the US territories (Puerto Rico and the Virgin Islands). All this would change in the next decades.

The US trade embargo imposed in 1961 had only a small impact on Cuba's share of Caribbean merchandise exports, because the Soviet Union and its allies quickly provided an alternative market for the main products. Indeed,

---

[1] Haiti joined CARICOM in 2002 but remained outside the Single Market and Economy. Montserrat is a member of CARICOM but is also a British Overseas Territory and therefore not an independent country. The other members of CARICOM – and the ones included here – are the former British colonies together with the former Dutch colony of Suriname.

[2] The British ones are Anguilla (separated from St Kitts & Nevis since 1970), British Virgin Islands, Cayman Islands, Montserrat and Turks & Caicos Islands. The Dutch ones are Netherlands Antilles and Aruba (separated from the rest of the Netherlands Antilles since 1986). The breakup of the Netherlands Antilles in October 2010 came too late to affect the writing of this book.

[3] I use the term 'territory' for the period since 1960 because it is the most neutral word to describe the different constitutional status of British, Dutch, French and US countries in the Caribbean.

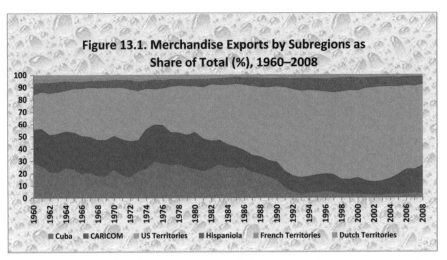

Figure 13.1. Merchandise Exports by Subregions as Share of Total (%), 1960–2008

Note: British Territories have been omitted because their share of merchandise exports was always less than 0.1%.

Source: Derived from Table D.6.

the spectacular increase in the 1970s in the price received by Cuba for its sugar (the main export) helped to push the island's share above what it had been in 1960. Yet this would prove to be the high point. From 1983 onwards, there was a steady decline in the contribution of Cuba to the region's merchandise exports (see Figure 13.1), and this trend accelerated after the dissolution of the Soviet Union in 1991. A decade later, the Cuban share was little more than 2 per cent.

The share of the CARICOM states also fell, but it was not as spectacular as in the case of Cuba. This decline was largely because of the economic difficulties faced by three of CARICOM's most important members (Guyana, Jamaica and Suriname) soon after each country had achieved independence. The CARICOM share had fallen to 10 per cent by the beginning of the new century, but it then underwent something of a renaissance (see Figure 13.1). This was almost entirely due to the energy sector in Trinidad & Tobago, which expanded rapidly on the back of new investments in the petroleum industry together with high oil and gas prices.

The clear winners from the subregional shifts in the contribution to merchandise exports were the US territories.[4] Their share had reached 50 per cent by the mid-1980s and would peak at 75 per cent fifteen years later (see Figure 13.1). By the start of the new millennium, therefore, three out of four dollars exported by the Caribbean were coming from two countries. This was mainly because of Puerto Rico, but it had nothing to do with the agricultural commodities (sugar, coffee and tobacco) for which the island had been famous in

---

[4] The French and Dutch territories suffered a fall in their share of merchandise exports.

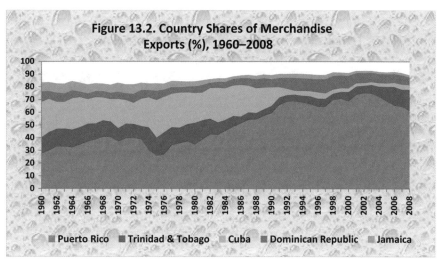

Source: Derived from Table D.6.

the past. Instead, it was a result of the industrialisation programme that had started long before 1960 but had eventually gathered momentum in the 1970s. It began to lose dynamism in the 1990s, however, and it will be considered in detail in the next chapter.

Caribbean merchandise exports were dominated by a handful of countries. This had always been true, but this time it was a different set of countries. Between them, Puerto Rico, Cuba, Dominican Republic, Jamaica and Trinidad & Tobago were responsible for around 90 per cent. In first place now was Puerto Rico, whose share had risen from under 30 per cent in 1960 to 75 per cent at its peak in 2002 (see Figure 13.2). This was as dominant a position as Cuba had enjoyed at the height of the sugar boom after the First World War. No other country could rival Puerto Rico's dominance of merchandise exports, but Cuba held its own until the mid-1970s when manufactured exports from the smaller island accelerated.

The Dominican Republic at first lost ground, the low point reached in 1982 when it had only 4 per cent of Caribbean merchandise exports (see Figure 13.2). However, the promotion of manufactured exports reversed the decline, and the share rose sharply in the next two decades before declining again as a result of increased competition in the US market from countries outside the Caribbean. Trinidad & Tobago also lost ground after the 1970s, and its share had fallen below 5 per cent by 1998, but there was a spectacular recovery based on energy exports in the last few years of the period. Jamaica, on the other hand, experienced an almost constant erosion in its share of Caribbean merchandise exports, ending the period with less than 2 per cent – a far cry from the position 200 years earlier when it was the largest exporter from the region.

It was still the case in 1960 that merchandise exports were dominated by a small number of primary products. Sugar was the most important, with

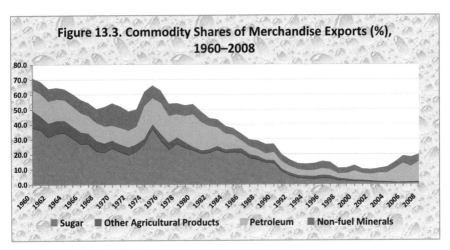

Figure 13.3. Commodity Shares of Merchandise Exports (%), 1960–2008

Source: Derived from Table D.5.

nearly 40 per cent of the total. Second – with nearly 15 per cent – was petroleum.[5] Third was nonfuel minerals (principally bauxite), with nearly 7.5 per cent. Another seven commodities (bananas, molasses, tobacco leaf, coffee, cacao, rice and citrus) added 12 per cent. These ten commodities therefore represented over 70 per cent of merchandise exports. It was not dissimilar to the position in the whole period since 1820.

All this would now change because manufacturing came to assume much greater importance in merchandise exports. The most spectacular decline was in the case of sugar. Its share at first held up well and even recovered to nearly 40 per cent in the mid-1970s when world sugar prices were at their peak (see Figure 13.3). There then followed a collapse that has no precedent in Caribbean economic history. Sugar's contribution would fall below 10 per cent by 1991 and below 1 per cent by 2003. The one product that had done more than any other to define the Caribbean had ceased to be of any major significance for the region as a whole – and there was no likelihood of it returning to importance.

Other agricultural exports fared little better, their share declining from 12 per cent at the beginning of the period to 0.5 per cent at the end. All the main products suffered a drop in their share of merchandise exports. Tobacco leaf went from nearly 4 per cent in 1960 to 0.01 per cent fifty years later. Molasses, coffee, cacao, citrus and rice suffered a similar fate. Bananas went from 2.6 per cent to 0.3 per cent, and thus sugar and bananas combined – about which so much has been said and written in recent years – accounted together for no more than 1 per cent of merchandise exports by the end of the period.[6]

---

[5] Exports have been calculated 'net' in the case of oil refining using imported crude and 'gross' where the crude was domestically sourced. See Notes on D. Tables.

[6] Despite this, bananas still accounted at the end of the period for a high proportion of merchandise exports in a small number of countries (especially Dominica, Grenada, St Lucia and St Vincent). These were all located in the Windward Islands. The highest proportion was in Dominica.

Even minerals were not wholly exempt from this structural shift away from primary products towards manufacturing. The petroleum share at first increased, reaching a peak of 22 per cent in the second half of the 1970s. This was in part because of the opening of oil refineries based on imported crude in Jamaica and Martinique (1965), Antigua (1967), US Virgin Islands (1968) and the Bahamas (1969). However, the increase in refining capacity in Mexico, Venezuela and the United States displaced some exports from the Caribbean, and the share had fallen below 3 per cent by the late 1990s, with several refineries having closed by then.[7] It was only the energy boom in Trinidad & Tobago at the very end of the period that reversed the decline in share, bringing it back to what it had been at the beginning. By that time, Barbados, Belize and Suriname had joined the club of oil exporters based on domestic crude.[8]

Nonfuel minerals at first performed well, and the share of merchandise exports had doubled to 15 per cent in 1970. This was caused by increased exports by established countries and additional exports from Haiti (bauxite), the Dominican Republic (ferronickel) and Cuba (nickel). Later on, gold exports would be revived in French Guiana, Guyana, Suriname and (temporarily) in the Dominican Republic. However, the conflict between governments and foreign companies in three of the main bauxite/alumina producing countries – Guyana, Jamaica and Suriname – led to a sharp fall in the importance of nonfuel mineral exports, and Haiti and the Dominican Republic ceased to export bauxite/alumina after 1982. The share of nonfuel minerals in merchandise exports had fallen below 4 per cent by the end of the period.

The decline in the importance of minerals (fuel and nonfuel) was only relative.[9] In the case of the main agricultural exports, however, the decline was also absolute. In the fifty years after 1960, the volume of exports of sugar, molasses, cotton, coffee, cacao, citrus, rice and tobacco leaf all fell precipitately.[10] In many countries, factors of production – land, labour and capital – were abandoning export agriculture for alternative activities. Some of these were inside the agricultural sector, with production now geared to the home market. As often as not, the resources left the agricultural sector altogether, labour in particular migrating to urban areas or even leaving the country.

The clearest example of these changes was provided by sugar exports. Cuba – the most important Caribbean producer – had tried to diversify away from sugar at the start of the Revolution, but it soon reversed this position because no other commodity could take its place. By the end of the 1960s, Cuba was even hoping to achieve production of 10 million metric tons (MT). This was never

---

[7] Most affected were the Dutch territories. The Aruban refinery closed in 1985 and would not be reopened until 1991. The refinery on Curaçao was only kept open after it had been sold for $1 by Shell to the Venezuelan state-owned PDVSA.

[8] Suriname began to export oil in 1987, Barbados in 2002 and Belize in 2006. Cuba, although a net oil importer, was also an exporter in some years.

[9] The volume of exports increased in most cases.

[10] The volume of banana exports also fell when the beginning and end of the period are compared, but the decline was much less dramatic than in the case of the other agricultural exports.

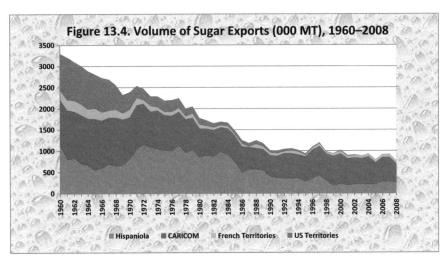

Figure 13.4. Volume of Sugar Exports (000 MT), 1960–2008

Legend: Hispaniola — CARICOM — French Territories — US Territories

Note: Cuba is not shown but is included in the sugar total in Table D.5.
Source: Derived from Table D.5.

achieved, but exports exceeded 7 million MT in several years after the price surge in the mid-1970s. From 1990 onwards, however, the volume of exports drifted downwards because Cuba was forced to place almost all its sugar on the world market at nonpreferential prices. By 2005, the volume of exports had fallen below 1 million MT – lower than the level, for example, in Guatemala – and was far below the level of a century earlier at the start of independence.

Other subregions fared no better. The partial redistribution of Cuba's US sugar quota to the two countries of Hispaniola boosted exports initially, but the Dominican Republic's sugar exports started falling sharply in the 1980s, and Haitian exports ceased altogether in the early 1990s. By the end of the period, exports from Hispaniola were a small fraction of what they had been fifty years earlier (see Figure 13.4). Both countries struggled to export sugar because the US reduced its imports and world market prices remained depressed after their brief spike in the 1970s. Membership of CARIFORUM held out the promise of access to the European market under the EPA, but it was not expected to reverse the downward trend.

The member states of CARICOM fared no better (see Figure 13.4). Antigua, a sugar exporter since the seventeenth century, ceased exports altogether in 1971 (St Vincent had done so in 1963). St Kitts & Nevis, the UK's first Caribbean colony,[11] had virtually ceased to export sugar by 2007. Barbados saw its exports fall to a quarter of their level in 1960, Trinidad & Tobago to 20 per cent, and in Jamaica they fell by two-thirds. Suriname made its last shipment of sugar in 1980. In Guyana, exports at first fell sharply, but they

---

[11] Strictly speaking, it was St Kitts that was the first colony, because Nevis was settled later and was not joined with St Kitts until 1882.

did recover in the last two decades. Only in Belize, a latecomer to the sugar industry, did exports expand from their 1960 level.[12]

It was the same story in the French and US territories (see Figure 13.4), despite their privileged access to the European and US markets, respectively. Exports declined from Guadeloupe, but at least they continued throughout the period. In Martinique, exports ceased altogether in the 1980s, sugar being henceforth used mainly to make rum.[13] Preferential prices in the French market could not fully compensate the two countries for high labour costs because wages moved closer to European levels. In the Virgin Islands, where sugar had struggled to remain competitive throughout the US colonial period, the last exports were made in 1966. Puerto Rican sugar exports continued, but even in this case they had ceased by 2003.

Sugar – and other agricultural exports – were caught in a classic pincer movement. On the one hand, unit costs of production were high because of smaller farms and higher wage rates than in the main competitors outside the Caribbean. On the other hand, the preferential prices and privileged market access, on which the region had come to depend, were under constant attack. Ultimately, there was no escape and no way backwards.

The demise of the sugar industry came as something of a shock to the Caribbean – and yet it was also a liberation. The misery of short-term employment and the long dead season would come to an end. Land previously monopolised by sugar was now available for other uses. The plantations had finally lost their grip, and the owners could not influence economic policy in their own interests. No longer could it be argued, as employers had done for decades, that Caribbean labour did not need to be educated, because now unskilled jobs in the sugar industry were fast disappearing. Governments needed to take into account a broader spread of interests. The decline of sugar was therefore an historic opportunity, but whether that opportunity would be seized depended on what took the place of sugar and the other agricultural exports in decline.

13.2. SERVICE EXPORTS

In the years immediately after the Second World War, international trade was dominated by goods, and services were widely treated as 'nontraded'. Such trade as existed was mainly in finance, shipping and insurance, and a handful of industrialised countries monopolised international exports in these activities. As average incomes started to rise and air travel became more common, tourism was added to the list of services entering international trade. The comparative advantage of the Caribbean, however, was still thought to lie in the export of primary commodities, with alternative thinking focused on the possibility of manufactured rather than service exports.

---

[12] Belize had stopped sugar exports in 1922. They only started again in 1951.

[13] This is the famous *rhum agricole*, which is made directly from fermented cane juice rather than from molasses.

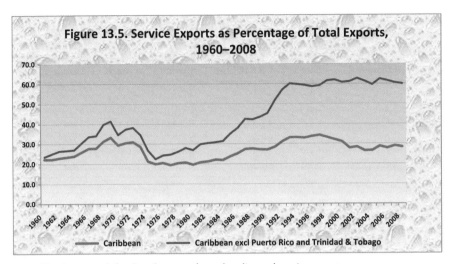

Figure 13.5. Service Exports as Percentage of Total Exports, 1960–2008

Legend: Caribbean — Caribbean excl Puerto Rico and Trinidad & Tobago

Note: Total exports defined as the sum of merchandise and service exports.
Source: Derived from Tables D.7 and D.8.

Despite this, some countries in the Caribbean had in fact been engaged in service exports for many years. Foreigners had been visiting parts of the Caribbean for vacations since the late nineteenth century, and the numbers had increased substantially by the 1950s. Cuba was the market leader with an estimated 400,000 visitors a year before the Revolution, but the Bahamas, Barbados, Jamaica, Puerto Rico and the US Virgin Islands were also important destinations. Some of the smaller countries had even started to exploit their potential as tax havens. The Bahamas, following the example of Bermuda, had been the pioneer in the 1930s, but the Dutch Antilles had gone further in the 1940s, and the smallest British colonies took the first steps in the 1950s towards their specialisation in exports of both financial services and tourism.

These developments were obscured in part by the lack of data on service exports. Yet, as Figure 13.5 shows, service exports in 1960 already accounted for more than 20 per cent of merchandise and service exports. Within a decade, this ratio had risen to one-third, but the rise in commodity prices in the first half of the 1970s then reduced the relative importance of services back to what it had been in 1960. As recently as 1975, it was still not clear that service exports would come to play such a dominant part in the Caribbean.

From 1975 onwards, service exports experienced a qualitative leap in their importance to the Caribbean. This is not immediately apparent when looking at the bottom line in Figure 13.5. However, the two largest Caribbean exporters today are Puerto Rico and Trinidad & Tobago. The first is specialised in manufactured and the second in petroleum exports. When these two are excluded, we can see from the top line in Figure 13.5 that in the rest of the Caribbean (twenty-six countries) service exports have come to represent around 60 per cent of total exports. This makes the Caribbean (excluding Puerto Rico and

TABLE 13.1. *Services as Share of Total Exports by Subregions (%), 1960–2008*

	Hispaniola	Cuba	CARICOM	Territories:			
				British	French	Dutch	US
1960	9.3	4.0	28.8	87.3	29.8	53.0	25.9
1970	13.8	4.0	36.9	96.0	52.6	53.0	32.0
1980	21.2	4.9	23.3	95.2	60.1	59.4	15.7
1990	32.6	9.3	46.0	97.8	69.0	75.2	14.7
2000	35.3	65.0	47.1	98.0	81.6	69.6	13.4
2008	41.5	72.1	29.2	97.8	69.6	79.4	11.2

Source: Derived from Tables D.7 and D.8.

Trinidad & Tobago) the only region in the world where exports come mainly from services.

The degree of specialisation in service exports varied from country to country, but the trend was very clear. In the British territories, where commodity exports had failed to show any dynamism since the nineteenth century, services were seen as the only viable option. Even in 1960, services in these small islands were much more important than commodity exports. Within a decade, the share of services in total exports exceeded 90 per cent, and it has stayed there ever since (see Table 13.1). The ex-British colonies did not specialise in services to the same extent, but the CARICOM[14] share had reached nearly 50 per cent by 2000 (see Table 13.1).[15]

The French territories (French Guiana, Guadeloupe and Martinique) had always enjoyed preferential access to France for their merchandise exports, and this continued after the EEC was created. However, the high cost of producing commodities encouraged a switch to service exports, which dominated export earnings from the 1970s onwards (see Table 13.1). It was a similar story in the Dutch territories (the Netherlands Antilles and Aruba), where the decline in the importance of oil refining in the mid-1980s forced the authorities to pay much more attention to service exports.

In Hispaniola, where service exports were concentrated in the Dominican Republic, the share of services in total exports rose from 10 to 40 per cent over the period considered here (see Table 13.1). This was a big change, and yet the most striking transformation was in the neighbouring island of Cuba, where service exports had at first declined after the Revolution (this was mainly caused by the travel ban on US citizens after 1960, because these had provided the vast majority of visitors up to that date). Indeed, although accurate figures are hard to come by, it is doubtful if service exports accounted for more than 5 per cent of total exports until the mid-1980s. From that point onwards, when

---

[14] Including Suriname.
[15] Subsequently, the share declined as energy exports from Trinidad & Tobago soared.

figures are reliable, service exports rose rapidly in importance and had reached two-thirds of the total by the end of the century (see Table 13.1).

The most important service export for the Caribbean as a whole has been tourism, with visitors coming mainly from rich countries during the northern hemisphere winter (these months have the additional advantage of not coinciding with the hurricane season). As the industry took off in the Caribbean, almost all visitors at first stayed overnight and became known as 'tourist (stopover) arrivals'. The Caribbean has been able to attract tourists from all over the world, but nearly 60 per cent come from North America and 25 per cent from Europe.[16] By 2008, the total number of tourists was 17.5 million.[17]

Interest in the Caribbean as a vacation destination was largely determined by the income and price elasticity of demand. The income elasticity, over which the Caribbean had no control, was greater than unity because foreign holidays are the quintessential income-elastic good. As average income tended to rise, this was good news for the Caribbean. However, the price elasticity was also high because many Caribbean destinations competed with each other by offering similar holidays differentiated only by price. This made it difficult for the Caribbean to increase its global market share, which has remained just below 4 per cent for many years.[18]

The Caribbean has also faced a challenge from the growth of the cruise ship industry, where passengers visit without staying overnight (as a result, they contribute much less to the local economy). Gradually, the number of cruise passenger visitors increased relative to the tourists until the numbers of each in 2008 were roughly equal.[19] Not all countries became cruise destinations (Cuba, in particular, has been largely excluded because so many ships start or finish in Miami),[20] but most did so and have had to adapt to the demands of the industry. This is dominated by a small number of foreign companies, which have used their bargaining power to great effect.

Taking tourists and cruise passenger visitors together, the Caribbean received just over 34 million at the end of the period – equivalent to three visitors for every four citizens of the region. The subregion with the largest participation in this flow of visitors was CARICOM, with nearly 40 per cent (see Figure 13.6). However, the country with the largest number of visitors was the Dominican Republic, closely followed by the Bahamas, the difference being

---

[16] In 2008, the breakdown of tourists by origin was US (46.5%), Canada (12.4%), Europe (24.2%) and other (16.9%). See the Web site of Caribbean Tourism Organization (CTO). The Cuban figure classifies tourist arrivals from the US as 'other'. These are Cuban-Americans travelling legally as well as those breaking US law. I have assumed the figure to be 100,000 in 2008 and adjusted the 'other' figure accordingly.

[17] See CTO Web site.

[18] Based on worldwide figures of 880 million in 2009. See the UN World Tourism Organization (UNWTO) Web site.

[19] Approximately 18 million tourists and 16 million cruise ship visitors in 2008. See the CTO Web site.

[20] A few cruise ships started to call at Cuba from 2010, but they could not start or finish at Miami.

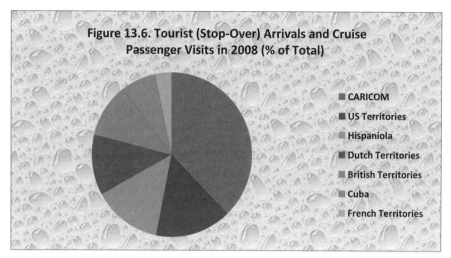

Figure 13.6. Tourist (Stop-Over) Arrivals and Cruise Passenger Visits in 2008 (% of Total)

- CARICOM
- US Territories
- Hispaniola
- Dutch Territories
- British Territories
- Cuba
- French Territories

Source: CTO and UNWTO Web sites.

that most visitors to the larger country were tourists but those to the smaller one came mainly for the day.[21] Cuba received nearly 7 per cent (see Figure 13.6), but its share of tourists was almost twice as large.[22] The tiny British territories received over 10 per cent of all visitors, but three out of four came on cruise ships.

Tourism remains by far the most important service export from the Caribbean. The second most important – a long way behind – is the export of financial services. This is a catchall phrase involving activities as diverse as offshore banking, trusts, international business companies (IBC), captive insurance, mutual funds, hedge funds and stock exchanges. Most of these activities are 'offshore', but some are on 'onshore'. However, virtually everything is concerned with lowering tax liability, so the countries offering these services are usually referred to as 'tax havens'.

Tax havens depend on low or zero tax rates on the activities of interest. They also depend on good (tele)communications with the rest of the world and a legal and regulatory framework that provides guarantees to private property and protection against expropriation. A stable exchange rate, currency convertibility and no capital controls are also necessary conditions for tax havens. Not surprisingly, therefore, not all countries of the Caribbean have been able to market themselves as tax havens, and the most important have been found among the British, Dutch and US territories.

---

[21] The Dominican Republic received in 2008 4.4 million visitors, of which 90% were tourists, and the Bahamas received 4.3 million, of which two-thirds were cruise ship visitors. See the CTO Web site.

[22] This is because Cuba had no cruise ship visitors in 2008.

Before 1960, the most important provider was the Netherlands Antilles, where the authorities took advantage of the tax treaty between Holland and the United States to promote the country as a tax haven.[23] US dividends and interest were taxed much less heavily than in the United States itself, and companies formed in the Netherlands Antilles could be used to avoid death duties, taxes on gifts and real estate gains in the United States. At first, these facilities were used mainly by US citizens, who were able in this way to avoid the interest rate equalisation tax imposed in 1963,[24] but in the 1960s and 1970s other foreigners started to make use of the Netherlands Antilles to invest in US real estate and securities.[25]

Part of the reason for this was the growth of the eurodollar market.[26] Fuelled by spending on the Vietnam War, Europe (especially London) became home to a large supply of foreign currencies – principally dollars – whose owners wished to reduce their tax liabilities. This provided the incentive for other countries in the Caribbean to become tax havens. The Bahamas, where offshore banking had begun early, and the US territories appeared the best placed. However, the Bahamas was following a path to independence, which made it less attractive to potential investors, and the US territories were subject to regulation by the Internal Revenue Service (IRS). The Cayman Islands, on the other hand, had opted to remain a British colony when Jamaica became independent,[27] and in 1966 it put in place the regulatory framework to market itself with great success as a tax haven.[28]

Within a few years, the euromarket had been swollen both by the supply of 'petrodollars' on the back of the quadrupling of oil prices in 1973–4 and by an explosion in funds from the illegal trade in narcotics. Both changes were responsible for the rapid growth of tax havens in the Caribbean.[29] Other countries joined the list, including all the remaining British territories (Anguilla, British Virgin Islands, Montserrat and Turks & Caicos Islands). And when Aruba split from the rest of the Netherlands Antilles in 1986, it followed the same path. A handful of former British colonies (Antigua, Barbados, Belize, Grenada, St Kitts & Nevis and St Vincent) also tried to participate in the rise of financial service exports, but their status as independent countries made it more difficult for them to compete successfully.

[23] The 1948 tax treaty between Holland and the US was extended to the Netherlands Antilles in 1955. See van Soest (1978). It was subsequently repealed, but by then the Netherlands Antilles was well established as a tax haven.
[24] See Shaxson (2010).
[25] See US Department of Treasury (1984).
[26] 'Eurodollar' is shorthand for any currency other than the official one in question. Thus, a Swiss franc deposit in Singapore is considered a eurodollar account.
[27] The Cayman Islands was a dependency of Jamaica until 1962, when Jamaica became independent. Shortly afterwards, the Cayman Islands established the Cayman Island dollar separate from the Jamaican dollar.
[28] See Roberts (1995).
[29] See Marshall (2007).

The rapid growth of financial service exports from tax havens soon came to the attention of those countries whose taxes were being evaded. The US Treasury published a report in 1984,[30] and this was followed in 1990 by one commissioned by the British government.[31] Within a few years the OECD had begun its campaign against 'harmful tax competition', which culminated in the establishment of the Global Forum in 2000. Two years later, the model agreement on exchange of information for tax purposes was laid out, and now all tax havens in the Caribbean are expected to sign a series of tax information exchange agreements (TIEAs) or face inclusion in a blacklist of jurisdictions.[32]

All Caribbean tax havens have complied and have also met the requirements of the EU's Saving Directive for sharing information.[33] They have also been the subject of scrutiny by the Financial Action Task Force (FATF), an intergovernmental body established in 1990 by the G-7, whose first reviews put a number of Caribbean tax havens on a blacklist.[34] All countries were subseqently cleared. There is therefore no reason to believe tax havens in the Caribbean will cease to function, but they cannot expect the rapid growth observed in the past, and some may even go into decline.[35]

Fortunately for the Caribbean, the potential for exporting other services is still substantial. The region's location, widespread use of the English language and good communications with North America and Europe (if not within the Caribbean itself) have helped to promote a wide range of services that are already important for some countries. In addition to travel and finance, there has been growth in telecommunications, data processing, software design, online gambling and shipping registries. Barbados has been particularly successful in diversifying its service exports, and French Guiana has benefitted greatly from the space station used to launch EU and Russian satellites into orbit. And tourism is no longer – if it ever was – homogeneous, with Cuba marketing medical tourism, Dominican Republic promoting itself as a conference centre and several islands holding annual music festivals.

The growth of services means that conventional measures of exports based on merchandise goods have lost their relevance for the Caribbean. Instead it is necessary to work with the notion of **total** exports defined as the sum of goods and services.[36] The export ratio is then total exports divided by GDP. This is

---

[30] See US Department of Treasury (1984).

[31] See Gallagher (1990).

[32] They must sign a minimum of twelve TIEAs. See Shaxson (2010).

[33] This was agreed in 2003. It aims to counter cross-border tax evasion by collecting and exchanging information about foreign resident individuals receiving savings income outside their resident state.

[34] These included Bahamas, Cayman Islands and Dominica. Other Caribbean countries were named, but were said to be 'cooperating'.

[35] The GDP growth of the British territories, all tax havens in one form or another, slowed down dramatically after 2000. See Chapter 15.1.

[36] Before 1960 it is not possible to record service exports, but merchandise exports can be separated into domestic exports and re-exports. From 1960 it is possible to identify service exports, but merchandise exports cannot easily be disaggregated into domestic exports and re-exports.

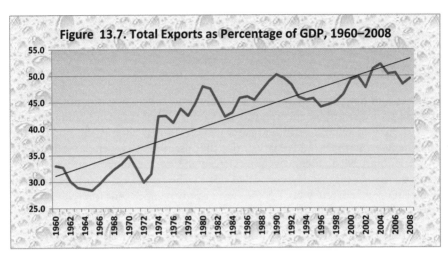

Figure 13.7. Total Exports as Percentage of GDP, 1960–2008

Source: Derived from Tables D.8 and D.18.

a measure of openness in the Caribbean, and it cannot be shown before 1960 because of the absence of GDP data. For the period since 1960, however, it can be measured, and it is shown in Figure 13.7, where the rise in the export ratio from around 30 to 50 per cent is very clear.

A ratio of 50 per cent is high by any standards and is probably as high as the Caribbean has ever experienced.[37] Furthermore, this is only an average, with some of the subregions (notably the British, Dutch and US territories) experiencing much higher ratios because they took export specialisation to extreme levels (in the case of the US Virgin Islands, for example, the ratio reached an extraordinary 250 per cent by the end of the period). These countries reaped the benefits of specialisation in the form of high average incomes, but all were vulnerable to external shocks – and some (notably Montserrat) to natural disasters.[38]

There were also countries with low export ratios. Haiti had begun the period with a ratio above 15 per cent, but it ended with one below 10 per cent, even before the disastrous earthquake in January 2010. Cuba at first experienced an increase, with the ratio peaking in the mid-1980s, but it then declined despite the rise in tourism as a result of the loss of preferential markets. Generally, a decline in the ratio implies a fall in average income per head. The biggest declines, however, were in Guadeloupe and Martinique, where income per head was rising. In these islands, exports became less important because public transfers and state employment became much more significant. Indeed, by the

---

[37] In her work on Jamaica, Eisner estimated the export ratio as 43.5% in 1832, falling to 19.8% in 1930. See Eisner (1961), p. 237.

[38] Montserrat experienced a major volcanic eruption in 1995 that led to the evacuation of much of the island's population.

end of the period, the export ratio in these two countries was around 7 per cent compared with 40 per cent in 1960.[39]

13.3. THE PUBLIC SECTOR

At the end of the 1950s there were still only three independent countries. Even in these nations, public spending as a share of GDP was very small, with a narrow view of what constituted state responsibilities. It was the same in the dependencies, with the added constraint that fiscal deficits were largely limited to what could be financed by grants from the core countries and where an active exchange rate policy was ruled out by the use of core currencies or by the existence of currency boards that gave up to 100 per cent foreign exchange backing to the domestic money supply.[40]

All this changed after 1960, when thirteen countries gained independence and the twelve remaining dependencies acquired greater autonomy. Governments redrew the boundaries between private and public spending, and pressure from below increased the areas of public responsibility far beyond what had been considered appropriate in the 1950s. Public spending as a share of GDP therefore increased sharply, and this necessitated fiscal reform. Tax collection, however, tended to lag behind spending commitments, and deficits became common. These could now be financed not only by grants, but also by loans from international or domestic sources. With the previous straitjackets removed, fiscal and monetary discipline slackened. A few countries even abandoned fixed exchange rate regimes with serious consequences for inflation.

Public spending had been rising in the 1950s, but as late as 1960 it was still only 15 per cent of GDP for the Caribbean as a whole (see Figure 13.8). Nor was there much variation among the subregions, only the tiny British territories having a high ratio (this was caused mainly by grants-in-aid from the British government designed to improve the infrastructure).[41] The lowest ratio was in Cuba, where the public sector had not yet taken over activities previously handled by private entrepreneurs. The situation in the Caribbean was therefore similar to what could be found in mainland Latin America among countries with similar standards of living.[42]

By the end of the century, public spending as a share of GDP had doubled in the Caribbean (see Figure 13.8). This was from much higher expenditure on education, health, housing, social security and infrastructure. These increases were much needed and reflected rising average incomes, urbanisation and electoral priorities. However, the public spending share also rose as a

---

[39] Needless to say, imports were much bigger than exports, with the gap being filled by state transfers. See Daniel (2001).
[40] Even the three independent states had eschewed an active exchange rate policy, having tied their currencies to the US dollar for decades.
[41] See Prest (1960).
[42] See CEPAL (2009).

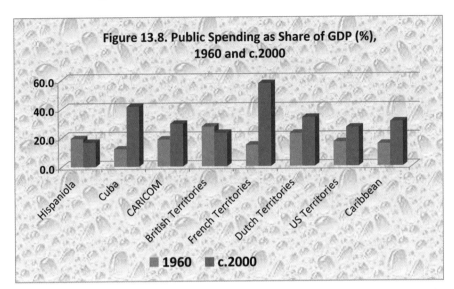

Figure 13.8. Public Spending as Share of GDP (%), 1960 and c.2000

Note: Spending in the French territories is calculated as the sum of revenue plus state transfers ('solde des opérations courantes et en capital de l'Etat') and social security deficits ('solde des opérations courantes et en capital de la Sécurité Sociale'). For Cuba I have assumed in 2000 that all capital expenditure was undertaken by the public sector. For Puerto Rico, the ratio in c.2000 is based on the sum of public spending and federal grants; for USVI, spending is the sum of net revenue, rum excise duties returned and direct federal expenditures.

Source: Public spending in 1960 is from Table C.29. GDP data in 1960 and 2000 are from Table D.18. The spending data for c.2000 (average of 1998–2003) are derived from World Bank (2005) and *World Development Indicators* (WDI) for Hispaniola and CARICOM; from the Caribbean Development Bank Web site for British Territories; from the INSEE Web site for French territories; from CEPAL (2009) for Cuba; from Junta de Planificación de Puerto Rico Web site, and United States Virgin Islands (Bureau of Economic Research) Web site for US territories; from Aruba (Central Bureau of Statistics) and Dutch Antilles (Central Bureau of Statistics) Web sites for Dutch territories. All figures, including those for the Caribbean, are weighted averages.

result of increases in defence and public safety. This reflected the deterioration in public security during the period and the rise in homicide rates. Finally, public spending also rose because of the increase in the cost of debt servicing.

The biggest increase was in the French territories where the welfare system was essentially the same as in mainland France, but average income was lower and unemployment higher.[43] Indeed, public spending reached almost 60 per cent of GDP – higher even than in Cuba – by the start of the new century (see Figure 13.8), and there was essentially no difference in this respect between the three DOMs.[44] This high share was only possible because of the constitutional arrangement reached in 1946, but it took several decades to manifest itself. The increase in real wages under *départementalisation* had rendered most exports (goods **and** services) uncompetitive outside mainland France and generated

---

[43] Tax rates were similar, but lower average income meant the tax yield was smaller.
[44] The figures were 58.1% in French Guiana, 58.2% in Martinique and 56.7% in Guadeloupe.

such high levels of unemployment that social discontent erupted at regular intervals, despite the high standard of living.[45]

The only subregion to experience a significant **decline** in the share of public spending in GDP was the British territories. This was not from a lack of spending on education, health, social security or infrastructure. Instead, it was a reflection of the rapid rise in average income, which meant that they were no longer eligible for foreign aid (Montserrat, however, was an exception following the volcanic eruption in 1995).[46] It was their position in 1960, therefore, that had been unusual, with levels of public spending that could not be explained by their low income per head at that time.[47] And, with very low levels of public indebtedness, these small countries did not have to spend much on debt servicing either.

The two countries of Hispaniola also experienced a small decline in the proportion of GDP devoted to public spending (see Figure 13.8), but for different reasons. In the Dominican Republic during the last years of Trujillo, public spending had been relatively high as a result of the dictator's concern with security.[48] Following the US invasion in 1965, defence spending declined in importance. Consequently, by the early 1970s, the share of public administration in GDP had fallen below 10 per cent.[49] Since then, public spending has risen sharply as a share of GDP, but it still remains low by Caribbean standards.[50]

In Haiti, the ratio of public spending to GDP was very low in 1960. This was partly because of average income[51] but also the nature of the Duvalierist state. This led to the concealment of much state spending through off-budget accounts in order to fund the dreaded secret police[52] and provide for the illicit enrichment of the dictator's family.[53] The fall in the ratio over the next four decades (it averaged only 10 per cent in 1998–2003) therefore requires an explanation, only part of which can be provided by the decline in GDP per head over the intervening years.

---

[45] There were serious riots in 2009 in Guadeloupe and Martinique. It did not, however, stop the inhabitants of both islands from voting in favour of the status quo a year later – a classic case of 'better the devil you know'.

[46] Public spending in Montserrat actually rose above 100 per cent of GDP after the volcanic eruption because there was no other source of expenditure and savings were negative.

[47] Low levels of income per head, ceteris paribus, are expected to lead to low levels of spending as a share of GDP.

[48] See Wiarda (1969), pp. 37–8.

[49] See CEPAL (1978). This metric includes defence spending, but it excludes capital expenditure.

[50] In the quinquennium 1998–2003 it had reached 18% compared with a Caribbean average of 29.8%.

[51] The public spending share tends to rise with average income for all sorts of reasons, which is why it is so much higher in rich than in poor countries.

[52] Known colloquially as the *Tonton Macoutes*, its official name from 1970 was Milice de Volontaires de la Sécurité Nationale.

[53] See Fass (1988), chap. 1.

Spending in the Haitian state has always been heavily constrained by what funding is available. Tax revenue is limited by low income, so resources have been supplemented wherever possible by foreign aid and public debt. Donors and international financial institutions were relatively generous during the early years of the Duvalier regime,[54] but they have suspended disbursements on numerous occasions since then.[55] Thus, the Haitian government has been unable to mimic the public spending pattern of the rest of the Caribbean since 1960. And public expenditure is not only low in terms of GDP, but also on a per capita basis.[56]

These exceptions apart, the rise in public spending as a share of GDP marked a structural change in the Caribbean. It led, for example, to a big improvement in average years of schooling, public health programs and social security coverage.[57] Of course, it had to be financed, and this meant an increase in taxation. Given the traditional dependence on trade taxes, however, this in turn implied fiscal reform. Thus, the shift in the pattern of public spending had major implications for tax systems in the Caribbean.

In the 1950s, import duties were the most important source of revenue in virtually all countries. In the British colonies, for example, they averaged between one-third and two-thirds.[58] Only in the French and US territories were they of little consequence, because almost all imports came from the 'mother' country on a duty-free basis. Yet import duties alone could not carry the burden of increased public expenditure. Two shifts therefore took place. The first involved an increase in other forms of indirect taxation (notably sales and production taxes), and the second led to a rise in the importance of direct (especially income) taxes.

Throughout the Caribbean, with the exception of Cuba, where public spending was largely financed through state ownership of the means of production, this produced a sea change in the tax system. In many countries, indirect taxes were being generated mainly from taxes other than import duties as early as 1980.[59] This trend continued to the point where tariff revenue generated an average of only 15 per cent of government income two decades later in CARICOM and Hispaniola[60] – and even less elsewhere. In its place came production and sales taxes, including a Value-Added Tax (VAT) in some cases, and the tax havens relied heavily on fees and licences.[61]

---

[54] See Fass (1988), p. 16.
[55] Especially after the military intervention in 1991.
[56] This is expected to change as a result of high levels of humanitarian assistance and reconstruction funds following the earthquake in January 2010, but much of this funding has been channelled through NGOs.
[57] See World Bank (2005).
[58] See Prest (1960).
[59] See Hope (1986), p. 147.
[60] See World Bank (2005), p. 32.
[61] For the case of the Cayman Islands, see Roberts (1995).

The bulk of revenue still tended to come from indirect sources, but direct taxes were everywhere increasingly important. The US territories, for example, were generating over 70 per cent of total revenue from income and corporation tax by the beginning of the new century,[62] and Trinidad & Tobago was not far behind.[63] In Jamaica, despite its poor economic performance, almost half of all taxes came from direct sources at this time. The Netherlands Antilles may have marketed itself as a tax haven, but the tax on offshore profits was responsible for nearly 40 per cent of government revenue at the time of the split with Aruba.[64]

These were impressive changes, but they were insufficient to finance the increase in public spending. There were several reasons for this. Fiscal reform included tax incentives designed to promote an increase in investment – especially from abroad. This led to a 'race to the bottom', with countries competing to offer the most attractive package of incentives until foreign investors came to expect it as the norm. These packages often included exemption from import duties, which in any case were falling as a result of tariff reductions and free trade agreements.

Taxation was only one route by which public spending could be financed. The others were foreign aid and public borrowing. As the donor countries came to focus on the poorest countries in the world, the supply of foreign aid to the Caribbean dried up.[65] However, for the independent countries a host of lenders were now available to be tapped. The main sources were the World Bank, the IMF, numerous UN agencies, the Inter-American Development Bank (IDB), the EU and bilateral agencies, the Caribbean Development Bank (CDB), the Export-Import Bank and other US agencies and private financial institutions. A few of these – such as the CDB – could also be accessed by some of the dependencies.[66]

A small number of countries – in addition to Cuba – experimented with public ownership of the means of production.[67] This involved an initial increase in public spending, but it rarely produced the rise in state income that had been anticipated. The biggest problem was nationalisation of underperforming assets, such as sugar factories, rice mills and mines, where profitability was undercut by low world prices. This route was taken by Guyana and Jamaica in the 1970s together with Grenada and Suriname in the 1980s.[68] It would

---

[62] See Alm (2006) for Puerto Rico.

[63] See World Bank (various years), *World Development Indicators* (WDI).

[64] See Wawoe (2000), table 2. This tax alone generated over half of all government revenue in Curaçao.

[65] Only two countries in the Caribbean (Haiti always and Guyana sometimes) qualified as 'poor' according to the new criteria.

[66] The British territories, for example, are all members of the CDB.

[67] There had always been some production units in public ownership in the Caribbean – especially in the former Spanish and French colonies (including Haiti).

[68] See Thomas (1988), chap. 11.

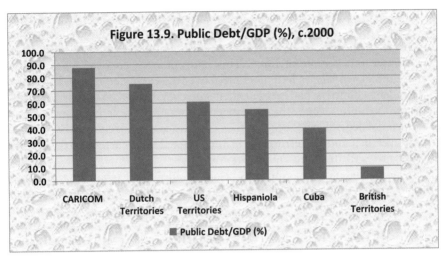

Source: GDP data from Table D.18. Public debt data from same sources as for Figure 13.8 for British, Dutch and US territories; CARICOM and Hispaniola from World Bank (2005); Puerto Rico from Junta de Planificación Web site; Cuba from Pérez (2004).

later be reversed, but not before serious damage had been done to the public finances.

For all these reasons the public sector deficit showed a secular tendency to increase in the decades after 1960. At first, this was manageable, with the gap between spending and taxation being met either by foreign aid or loans on soft terms. The cost of debt service was therefore low. Gradually, however, the debt-to-GDP ratio increased until by the end of the century it had reached very high levels in most subregions. As Caribbean countries became less eligible for foreign aid, the response was not fiscal restraint but increased borrowing – often on commercial terms. Only the French and British territories, where the ability to contract public debt was strictly controlled, escaped this trend.[69]

The subregion with the most serious debt problem was CARICOM (see Figure 13.9).[70] Among its members were several where public-debt-to-GDP ratios exceeded 100 per cent in a number of years. The worst case was Guyana, where the ratio exceeded 200 per cent by the end of the 1990s. Because GDP per head was so low, however, Guyana (together with Haiti) qualified for debt relief under the HIPC initiative, and the ratio came down swiftly after 2004.[71] Others were not so fortunate. Antigua, Belize, Dominica, Grenada, Jamaica and St Kitts & Nevis struggled to cope with debt-servicing payments that came to absorb a large share of total spending.

[69] The 'public debt' of the DOMs is part of the French national debt rather than of the countries themselves.
[70] The Dutch Antilles also had a high ratio, but most of this debt by 2000 was domestic. See Wawoe (2000).
[71] HIPC had been launched in 1996 by official donors.

Public debt is both domestic and foreign. Most of the debt referred to in Figure 13.9, however, was external and therefore had to be serviced in foreign currencies.[72] The cost of debt servicing was thus heavily affected by the type of exchange rate regime in force. This had not been an issue before 1960, because the dependencies had no control over the exchange rate and the three independent countries had pegged their currency to the US dollar for many decades. Even after 1960, the exchange rate was not an active instrument of policy for the dependencies because they either used the currency of the 'mother' country (French and US territories) or they pegged their currency to one of the core countries (British and Dutch territories).

The newly independent countries began by adopting exchange rate regimes inherited from the colonial period. This also meant pegging to one of the core currencies. In the case of those pegged to the pound sterling, however, this caused serious difficulties after the collapse of the Bretton Woods system. These countries therefore switched to a dollar peg in the mid-1970s. The independent countries of the eastern Caribbean (Antigua, Dominica, Grenada, St Kitts & Nevis, St Lucia and St Vincent), together with two British territories (Anguilla and Montserrat), went further and established in 1976 a common currency.[73] At this point all countries in the Caribbean – independent and territories – had adopted fixed exchange rate regimes, with only one exception.[74]

Fixed rates had the disadvantage that countries were vulnerable to imported inflation. However, they were a sensible policy response for small open economies, such as all those in the Caribbean, because the impact of nominal currency devaluation was likely to be an increase in domestic inflation of roughly the same magnitude. Unfortunately, the structural imbalances in a few countries were so great that fixed rates had to be abandoned. This happened to Jamaica and Trinidad & Tobago in the 1970s, the Dominican Republic and Guyana in the 1980s and Haiti and Suriname in the 1990s.[75]

Once the currency started to depreciate in these six countries, inflation accelerated.[76] This in turn required a further nominal devaluation, creating a vicious circle that was very hard to break. The extreme case was Suriname, where the currency went from 1.79 Surinamese guilders per US dollar in 1991 to 2,601 per US dollar in 2003.[77] At that point, however, a successful

---

[72] In the case of Cuba, the public debt in Figure 13.9 is foreign currency only and excludes the debt owed to ex-socialist countries. See Pérez (2004).

[73] This was the Eastern Caribbean dollar, which would in due course be regulated by the Eastern Caribbean Central Bank (ECCB).

[74] The exception was Cuba, where the peso appreciated against the dollar in the 1970s (see Table D.4), but the exchange rate was largely fictitious owing to the absence of trade and capital flows with the US.

[75] Cuba introduced a parallel exchange rate in 1993. However, the nonmarket nature of much of the Cuban economy prevented changes in the parallel exchange rate from spilling over into measured inflation.

[76] See Table D.4.

[77] Inflation peaked at 368% in 1994 (see Table D.20).

stabilisation programme was carried out, and the currency was once again pegged (changing its name to the Surinamese dollar). The other four countries were not able to peg their currencies again, but the rate of nominal devaluation was brought under control by the start of the new century.[78]

13.4. URBANISATION

At the end of the 1950s, there was only one city in the Caribbean with more than a million people. This was Havana, which was the administrative, financial, manufacturing and cultural capital of Cuba. Elsewhere, cities were small, with the second largest – San Juan in Puerto Rico – around one-third the size of Havana. And outside the Greater Antilles, cities of more than 50,000 were still uncommon. Cities were small not just in absolute terms. With employment in agriculture providing the bulk of jobs, the population was overwhelmingly rural, and therefore cities and towns accounted for only a small share of the total. Urban areas represented more than half the population only in Cuba and the small Dutch territories.

This all changed in the decades after 1960, and the driving force was the decline in the importance of agricultural employment. By 2005, agriculture was responsible for a negligible share of jobs in the British, Dutch, French and US territories (see Figure 13.10). In CARICOM and Cuba it had fallen below 15 per cent and was expected to fall further with the continued decline of traditional exports.

Under these circumstances, it is perhaps surprising that agriculture still accounted for more than 20 per cent of employment in the Caribbean as a whole in 2005 (see Figure 13.10). This relatively high share, however, was because of Haiti, where more than half the workforce was still in agriculture at this time. When Haiti with its large population is excluded, the Caribbean share falls to little more than 10 per cent (see Figure 13.10). This was very different from the 1950s, when nearly half the labour force was employed in agriculture.[79]

Economists have long been aware of the tendency of the share of employment in agriculture to decline as income per head rises.[80] In that respect, there was nothing exceptional about the Caribbean. However, the fall in agricultural employment was more rapid than might be expected from the rise in average income alone. Indeed, it was so rapid that – with the exception of Haiti – the **absolute** numbers of those employed in agriculture were also falling after 1980.[81]

---

[78] Following a banking crisis in the Dominican Republic in 2003, there was a brief increase in annual inflation. However, the rate had fallen back to single digits by 2005. See Table D.20.

[79] For the British colonies, see Cumper (1960a).

[80] This is mainly because of Engel's law, under which food consumption increases less rapidly than income.

[81] From over 2 million in 1980 to under 1.6 million in 2008. Including Haiti, the numbers are 3.67 million and 3.85 million respectively. See WDI.

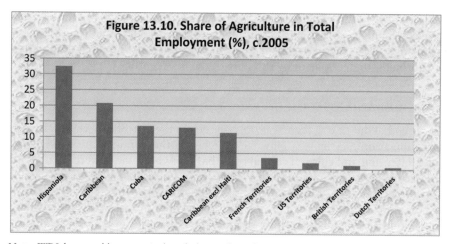

Note: WDI has a table on agricultural share of employment as well as tables on agricultural employment and total labour force. The latter are more complete and appear more reliable. I have used them to derive the share of agriculture in total employment in the case of inconsistencies.

Source: WDI for most countries; INSEE Web site for French territories; national statistics office for British Territories.

The decline of agricultural employment was matched by a rise in other activities. Mining jobs expanded in some countries, but the extraction of minerals is a capital-intensive task, and its contribution to total employment has been relatively small. Fishing and forestry have also been minor employers. Most of the new jobs were in towns and cities, leading to a massive migration from rural to urban areas. And because so many of the new activities were based in the largest city, it also led to migration from smaller ones.

The new jobs were in public administration (see section 3 above), manufacturing (see next chapter) and services. The latter included financial institutions, telecommunications, construction and transport. These were important sectors of the economy that underpinned the shift to service exports. The main sources of employment, however, were in commerce and recreational and personal services. And it was in these sectors that so much 'informal' employment was found.[82] The informal nature of the labour market echoed what was happening in mainland Latin America, where slums were expanding inside the larger cities. It was an inevitable consequence of a labour market in which supply was outstripping demand, and thus will be examined in more detail in Chapter 15.3.

The result of all this was an urban population that increased rapidly and whose share of the total population was also rising (see Table 13.2). The extreme cases were the French and US territories, but the British and Dutch were not far behind. The most spectacular case was Hispaniola, where urbanisation went from just over 20 per cent to nearly 60 per cent in half a century

[82] See World Bank (2005).

TABLE 13.2. *Rate of Urbanisation by Subregions (%), 1960–2010*

	Hispaniola	Cuba	CARICOM	Territories: British	French	Dutch	US	Caribbean
1960	22.4	58.4	31.2	48.1	41.3	64.6	44.7	39.3
1970	29.9	60.3	34.2	51.3	61.4	69.2	58.6	44.8
1980	36.2	68.1	37.6	59.2	78.8	73.3	67.3	51.1
1990	42.0	73.4	39.4	69.1	94.5	76.8	72.6	55.6
2000	49.1	75.6	41.7	79.4	94.0	75.7	94.5	61.0
2010	58.0	75.7	43.7	83.2	93.6	76.5	98.2	65.2

Note: The data on Guadeloupe in UN World Urbanization Prospects suggest that the country was almost 100% urban by 1960. This is incorrect, so I have estimated Guadeloupe from Martinique data.
Source: WDI for most countries; others from Web site of UN World Urbanization Prospects. All figures are weighted averages.

(see Table 13.2). The rise in the Dominican Republic, where average income was rising, was perhaps less noteworthy than the increase in Haiti, where average income **fell** over this period.

Cuba had begun the period with a high rate of urbanisation (see Table 13.2), but internal migration has been controlled since the Revolution. This has not prevented Havana from increasing in size, but it is no longer the largest city in the Caribbean. It was overtaken by San Juan at the beginning of the twenty-first century, and there are now four cities with more than 2 million people. These four – Havana, San Juan, Santo Domingo and Port-au-Prince – had a combined population of nearly 9 million in 2008 out of a Caribbean population of 43 million. So one in five people in the region now live in just four cities.

The fastest growing large city in the Caribbean has been Port-au-Prince – at least up to the devastating earthquake in January 2010, when an estimated 230,000 people died. When François Duvalier became president in 1957, Port-au-Prince had a little over 200,000 inhabitants. The growth of this city is often attributed to the political control exercised by the Duvalier family, necessitating the concentration of all public activities in the capital. Yet state spending never accounted for more than 10 per cent of GDP in Haiti. It is much more likely, therefore, that the growth of Port-au-Prince also reflected the economic crisis of agriculture, deforestation of the countryside and the rise of manufacturing. Furthermore, aid disbursement was massively concentrated in the capital, where Nongovernmental Organisations (NGOs) also tended to be based.[83] Thus it was not only the Duvaliers that were responsible for the premature growth of the capital city.

---

[83] See Fass (1988), pp. 14–26.

14

Import Substitution, Manufacturing Export Promotion and Regional Integration in the Caribbean

It had been apparent long before 1960 that traditional agricultural exports on their own could not sustain the long-run economic development of the Caribbean. The debates inside and outside the region had therefore focused on what should take their place. British and French colonies had tended to favour nontraditional agricultural exports, with some concessions to food security through import substitution in foodstuffs. Dutch dependencies from the 1920s onwards had put their faith in oil refining and non-oil minerals. From the 1940s, the scope for manufactured exports from the US dependencies had been widely accepted if the fiscal regime could be made sufficiently attractive.

It had therefore been left at first to the three independent countries – Cuba, the Dominican Republic and Haiti – to make the case for import-substituting industrialization (ISI). These countries were more familiar with what had been happening in mainland Latin America since the Great Depression and were prepared to implement part of the inward-looking development strategy, but not at the expense of export agriculture. Their experience had shown that ISI did have a role in the Caribbean, even if the cost in terms of economic efficiency was high.

These lessons were not lost on those involved in the anticolonial struggles, and import substitution became a rallying cry for many intellectuals in the British, French and Dutch dependencies. Their most prominent spokesperson was Sir Arthur Lewis, who developed not only a theory of development based on manufacturing but also mapped out the policy instruments that could achieve industrialisation without the economic inefficiencies to which ISI was sometimes subject. And Lewis was also aware of the scope for import-substituting agriculture (ISAg) as a result of the Caribbean's dependence on imported foodstuffs.

Unfortunately, the industrial development that subsequently took place in the Caribbean did not follow the recommendations of Sir Arthur Lewis. Instead, a model was followed that had many of the characteristics of ISI in mainland Latin America where anti-export bias undermined the scope for manufactured

exports.[1] As a result, Caribbean leaders became more interested in the Puerto Rican model, where 'industrialisation by invitation' appeared to offer other countries in the region the chance to promote manufactured exports. This led to an explosion of Export Processing Zones (EPZs) that emphasised assembly operations using cheap labour and a few examples of capital-intensive manufactured exports based on advanced technology.

Latin America, following the recommendations of Raúl Prebisch, had promoted regional integration after 1960 to provide an opportunity for ISI firms to start exporting to partners while being protected from third countries. The Caribbean duly did the same, but the integration experiment (CARICOM) was mainly limited to the former British colonies.[2] CARICOM, however, went further than anything attempted in Latin America and had the added distinction of containing within it the Eastern Caribbean Currency Union (ECCU) – the first monetary union in the Americas and one of the first in the world.[3]

14.1. IMPORT SUBSTITUTION

The Caribbean had been shaped by centuries of European imperialism to produce goods for export. It had done so with varying degrees of success depending on the country and the time period. The first serious doubts about the viability of the Caribbean model had emerged in the last two decades of the nineteenth century, when international prices for sugar and coffee fell sharply. However, the strengthening of the system of imperial preference in the first half of the twentieth century discouraged efforts to shift resources away from traditional agricultural exports towards other activities. And because colonial and – in the case of the independent countries – neocolonial officials had such a strong grip on the instruments of economic policy, it was difficult to carry out any experiments in resource reallocation.

Mainland Latin America had not been so constrained. Indeed, ISI had begun before the First World War and had gathered pace in the interwar period. By the 1950s, most of the mainland Latin American states had adopted an explicit policy designed to promote manufacturing in the domestic market. This policy relied heavily on tariffs now designed for purposes of protection rather than revenue. However, it also made use of nontariff barriers (NTBs), such as quotas and licences, multiple exchange rates and tax incentives to encourage both domestic and foreign investment.

There had been an echo of the mainland Latin American experience in the Caribbean before the Second World War, but it was essentially limited to the independent countries. In all three cases, however, industrial policy was constrained in various ways. First, customs duties were such a large part

---

[1] On ISI in mainland Latin America, see Bulmer-Thomas (2003), chaps. 7–9.
[2] The other participants in CARICOM were Montserrat, Suriname and Haiti.
[3] Some might say that the US was the first monetary union in the Americas, but it was not a union of sovereign countries.

of public revenue that tariffs could not be designed purely for purposes of protection, and the actual rates that could be applied were constrained by treaties with the United States. Second, multiple exchange rates were ruled out by the use either of the US dollar (Dominican Republic) or a fixed nominal rate (Cuba and Haiti). Third, the aggressive use of NTBs was ruled out by their membership in GATT.[4]

Yet, despite these constraints, the independent countries had established a modern manufacturing industry by 1960. Cuba had gone the furthest, following the revision of the tariff law in 1927,[5] but Haiti had pushed industrialisation from 1949 onwards,[6] and the Dominican Republic had adopted its first industrial promotion law in 1950.[7] There was little theory involved in these developments, and the motives were very different. Cuba desperately needed to diversify away from sugar after the 'dance of the millions'; Haitian governments created public and private monopolies to provide new revenue streams;[8] and Trujillo used industrial policy mainly as a vehicle for personal and family enrichment. Nevertheless, all three cases showed that there was room for industrial policy in the colonial Caribbean, despite the scepticism of most imperial officials.

Sir Arthur Lewis had argued the case for industrialisation as early as 1938 with his submission to the West India Royal Commission.[9] His subsequent thinking was influenced both by ISI in the three independent countries and by industrial exports from Puerto Rico. This led to a series of publications that – it is fair to say – had far more influence on the rising class of nationalist politicians than the colonial officials still responsible for many economic policy decisions. In these works Lewis emphasised the need for industry to complement agricultural diversification, to create a new class of industrialists and to promote labour-intensive activities that could compete in regional and domestic markets.[10]

By stressing the need for exports to the rest of the region, Lewis was demonstrating his sensitivity to the familiar argument that the domestic market was too small to justify more than the most minimal pattern of industrialisation. However, the size of the market is not just a function of population. It also reflects average income and imports per head. In this respect the Caribbean was more equipped to handle industrialisation than perhaps even Lewis realised. From 1960 onwards the value of total imports per head at constant prices rose rapidly (see Figure 14.1) in CARICOM and in the Caribbean as a whole.

---

[4] Cuba was a founding member of GATT, and the other two independent countries joined in 1950.
[5] See Chapter 10.
[6] See Overseas Economic Surveys (1956).
[7] See Overseas Economic Surveys (1957).
[8] See Fass (1988), chap. 1.
[9] See Tignor (2006), pp. 44–5.
[10] See Lewis (1950).

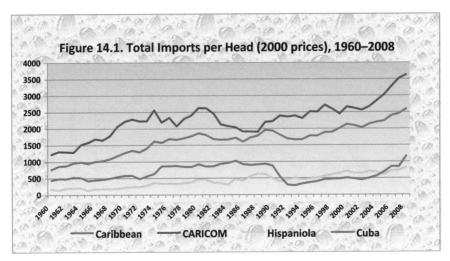

Figure 14.1. Total Imports per Head (2000 prices), 1960–2008

Legend: Caribbean — CARICOM — Hispaniola — Cuba

Source: Derived from Tables D.1a and D.13.

Furthermore, in the dependent territories the values were even higher.[11] It was only in Cuba and Hispaniola that the numbers were relatively low in 1960, and they would remain so throughout the period.[12]

These numbers do need to be put into some sort of context. By the end of the twentieth century, imports per head of goods and services in the Caribbean were higher than in all other regions of the world except the high income OECD and non-OECD countries (see Figure 14.2).[13] Although the Caribbean had total imports per head in 2000 of $2,133, the comparable figure for South Asia was $75, for sub-Saharan Africa, $159, for East Asia and the Pacific, $315, for the Middle East and North Africa, $413, and for Latin America, $872. Thus, an 'average' Caribbean country with 1 million people had the same level of imports as an 'average' South Asian country, with nearly 30 million, or an 'average' sub-Saharan African country, with nearly 15 million. The high level of total imports per head in the Caribbean meant that market size was not as big an impediment to import substitution as had usually been thought.

The instruments to promote ISI in the Caribbean were similar to those in other developing regions, such as mainland Latin America. These included tax incentives, fiscal holidays and import licences. Yet there were some important differences. First, the tariff on competing imports could not be used so aggressively because of the dependence of public revenue on customs duties

---

[11] The values are not shown in Figure 14.1, but by the end of the period they were twice the Caribbean average in the French territories, four times in the US territories, six times in the Dutch territories and eight times in the British territories. See Tables D.1a and D.13.

[12] The value of imports per head at constant prices did rise steeply in Cuba, but it then collapsed precipitately after the mid-1980s. See Figure 14.1.

[13] Even their high figures were exceeded by the British, Dutch and US Caribbean territories.

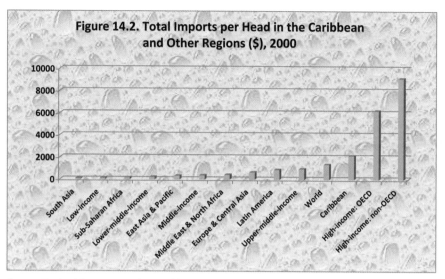

Figure 14.2. Total Imports per Head in the Caribbean and Other Regions ($), 2000

Source: Derived from WDI. The Caribbean value is from Figure 14.1.

in the independent countries and the absence of tariffs on many goods in the case of the territories.[14] Second, multiple exchange rates were not an option for most countries. Third, the small size of the market meant that incentives to produce intermediate and capital goods were less relevant. However, quotas could be used extensively and, for those countries that had opted for, or experimented with, state controls on the economy, there was the option of import prohibition.

Cuba was the most industrialised country in the Caribbean before 1960, and industry would receive preferential treatment after the Revolution. This was partly for ideological reasons because the Cuban intellectuals (including Che Guevara) at first identified export agriculture with neocolonial dependence and saw industrialisation as the way forward.[15] It was also because of the extreme shortage of foreign exchange, which made ISI very attractive from an economic point of view. The priority given to industry did change, but it was always high, and manufacturing usually commanded special attention from the Cuban leadership.[16]

By 1968, industry was 100 per cent state-owned.[17] Imports of most consumer goods were prohibited, and domestic production was limited only by what could be manufactured with available skills and machinery. Cuba also

[14] This effectively ruled out ISI in the French and US territories. What happened in Puerto Rico (and to a lesser extent the US Virgin Islands) was export promotion rather than ISI, and it will be considered in the next section.
[15] There were, however, serious disputes within the Revolution in the early 1960s about the role of heavy industry in the development of socialism. See Chapter 16.1.
[16] See Chapter 16.
[17] Even in 1961 it had been 85%. See Mesa-Lago (2000), p. 347.

extended the industrialisation program into the manufacture of many intermediate goods – cement and fertilizers, in particular. As a result of these efforts,
30 per cent of the labour force was engaged in industry by the time the Soviet
Union collapsed,[18] and the industrial share of GDP was only a little lower.[19]
These were very high figures by the standards of the Caribbean, but they were
unsustainable. As Cuba moved towards a more market-orientated economic
system, the importance of industry declined, and its share of total employment
had fallen below 20 per cent by 2005.[20]

The two countries of Hispaniola had begun their industrialisation programs
much later than Cuba, and they were not nearly so advanced in 1960. However, ISI had become a priority in both countries and would be taken furthest
in the Dominican Republic. The 1950 industrial promotion law was replaced
in 1968, heavily influenced by those industrialists who had gone into business
since the assassination of Trujillo. This Industrial Incentives Law provided very
high tariff rates on final goods[21] coupled with exemptions on intermediate and
capital goods. This led to an Effective Rate of Protection (ERP) that rivaled
those in mainland Latin America.[22] This alone probably would have ensured
rapid growth of manufacturing for the domestic market. However, the Dominican Republic also provided generous tax incentives for periods between eight
and twenty years. In addition, and very unusually for the Caribbean, it operated a dual exchange rate system. This had been first introduced in 1967, and
many consumer goods imports could only be purchased at the parallel rate.
In 1970, the premium was still only 10 per cent, so the implied protection for
manufacturers of consumer goods was still small. However, it rose steadily
thereafter and stood at 60 per cent by 1983, after which the currency was
devalued and unified.

ISI in Haiti was held back in many ways. First, the low average income and
modest levels of imports per head rendered the domestic market unattractive
without major fiscal incentives. Second, tariff rates were never very high because
of the need to maximise public revenue, and they would fall over time as a result
of exemptions on imported inputs and pressure from foreign donors.[23] Indeed,
by 2007 the weighted average tariff rate on manufactured goods in Haiti was
a mere 2 per cent.[24] Haiti did make extensive use of import quotas, but these

---

[18] In 1991, when the series in World Bank, *World Development Indicators* (hereinafter WDI)
begins, the figure was 29.3%.

[19] See Mesa-Lago (2000), p. 360. 'Industry', however, is defined in this table to include mining,
electricity, gas, water and manufacturing.

[20] See (WDI).

[21] These were so high that in 1970 the Dominican Republic had the second highest ratio (32.1%)
of customs duties to imports in Latin America. The average for all countries was 13.5%. See
Robischek and Sanson (1972), p. 308–9.

[22] See Vedovato (1986), p. 117. The ERP measures the percentage change in value added as a
result of the tariff system.

[23] In an extraordinary mea culpa, Bill Clinton admitted to the Senate Foreign Relations Committee
in March 2010 that one of his greatest regrets while US president was forcing Haiti to lower its
tariff on milled rice.

[24] See WDI. It rose in 2008 to 5.6%, but this was still one of the lowest in the Caribbean.

were designed to generate economic rents for favoured families under the rule of the Duvaliers rather than incentives for ISI.[25] As a result, only 8 per cent of the labour force was employed by industry in 1980,[26] and this included those working in the assembly industry geared to exports (see next section).[27]

ISI in the rest of the Caribbean focused mainly on the former British colonies.[28] The main policy instrument was provided by fiscal incentives, especially tax holidays, but all countries did restrict imports of designated goods in various ways. Guyana, following its rebirth as a 'Co-operative Republic', went furthest and nationalised the import trade.[29] It also took over drug and alcohol manufacture along with foundries and shipyards operated by foreign companies.[30] Barbados, despite its small size, pursued industrialisation aggressively, and 25 per cent of the growth in the manufacturing sector between 1954 and 1980 is estimated to have come from ISI.[31]

The results were mixed. By 1970, when manufactured exports were still in their infancy,[32] the share of manufacturing in total employment averaged 14 per cent (see Table 14.1), but it was much lower in the so-called Less Developed Countries (LDCs).[33] This was not negligible. However, the share of manufacturing in CARICOM GDP was smaller than the share of employment, and this was true of most countries (see Table 14.1). Thus, manufacturing labour productivity was generally less than the national average – the opposite of what had been expected and of what was the case in mainland Latin America. And the share of domestic manufacturing in total supply was still less than 30 per cent (see Table 14.1), even after two to three decades of ISI.

ISI in the Caribbean had shown that manufacturing had a role to play in the transformation of the economies. Yet it suffered from many of the weaknesses of its counterparts in mainland Latin America. High unit costs made it difficult to export goods once they had found a profitable local market. Tax holidays, including tariff exemptions on imported inputs, tended to become permanent rather than temporary, as originally intended. Above all, manufacturing was very import-intensive, making its progress vulnerable to balance of

---

[25] See Fass (1988), pp. 26–32.

[26] See WDI. It had risen to nearly 11% twenty years later.

[27] There is a list of volumes produced in the main ISI industries between 1970 and 1984 in Fass (1988), table 1.7, p. 35. It includes flour, cooking oil, cement, soap, detergents, cotton textiles, cigarettes, soft drinks, beer, shoes and matches.

[28] There was ISI in Puerto Rico, but it was dwarfed by export promotion and will therefore be considered in the next section. There was very little ISI in the Dutch territories, and in Suriname industrial employment was mainly in mining. In the French territories, there was so little ISI that the 1974 census in Martinique had no category for manufacturing employment, and in Guadeloupe it was less than 10% of the total labour force. See Blérald (1986), pp. 255, 257.

[29] The name of the country was changed in 1970 to the Co-operative Republic of Guyana.

[30] See Thomas (1988), pp. 251–5.

[31] See Worrell and Bourne (1989), p. 34.

[32] The figures in Table 14.1 exclude sugar.

[33] The LDCs were at first all CARICOM countries, except Barbados, Guyana, Jamaica and Trinidad & Tobago. These four were known as More Developed Countries (MDCs).

TABLE 14.1. *CARICOM Manufacturing, c.1970 (a)*

	Share of GDP (%)	Share of Employment (%)	Share of Total Supply (%) (b)
Antigua	10.2	9.7	17.7
Barbados	10.8	14.7	18.9
Belize	15.6	14.6	33.4
Dominica	8.1	7.6	13.8
Grenada	3.0	8.1	6.1
Guyana	12.2	15.0	22.9
Jamaica	13.6	14.5	30.2
Montserrat	1.7	5.4	3.7
St Kitts	2.7	10.5	5.7
St Lucia	3.8	8.3	8.1
St Vincent	3.8	7.6	9.0
Trinidad & Tobago	11.8	13.5	35.8
LDC Average (c)	8.2	9.6	16.9
MDC Average (c)	12.6	14.4	29.8
CARICOM Average	12.3	13.7	28.6

Note: (a) CARICOM was known as CARIFTA in 1970; (b) Total Supply=Domestic Production + Manufactured Imports; (c) for definition of LDC and MDC, see note 33.
Source: Chernick (1978), table SA10.2, p. 488.

payments crises and foreign exchange shortages.[34] It was to address some of these weaknesses that the countries of the Caribbean turned their attention to export promotion (see next section).

Import substitution is normally associated with the manufacturing sector. However, the Caribbean since Columbus has been an importer of foodstuffs in order to release resources for specialisation in export agriculture. The result has been a high dependence on imported agricultural and agro-industrial products in many countries. Replacing these with domestic production therefore constitutes ISAg, which is particularly attractive for those governments concerned with food security and/or with saving foreign exchange.

While export agriculture remained the top priority, there had been little opportunity for ISAg. The exceptions had been periods of war – especially the Second World War – when shortages of shipping had blocked exports and made imports scarce. Yet the wartime experience also showed what could be done to produce more food locally.[35] As export agriculture declined in importance – releasing land, labour and capital – the opportunities for ISAg should have been considerable. In general, however, this did not happen, and the reasons are not hard to find.

[34] This proved very damaging in Jamaica in the 1970s. See Thomas (1988), chapter 11.1.
[35] For a case study of Guadeloupe, see Taitt (2007).

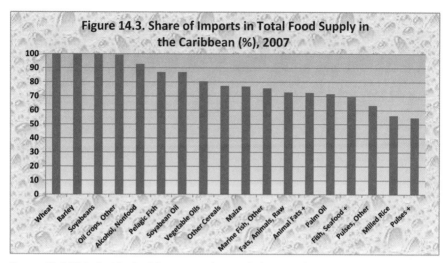

Figure 14.3. Share of Imports in Total Food Supply in the Caribbean (%), 2007

Source: FAO Web site (the Caribbean region here excludes US and French territories).

First, domestic use agriculture (DUA) tends to be the preserve of small-scale farmers in the Caribbean, and the decline in the importance of export agriculture did not necessarily help them. Without land redistributions or subsidised credit, the switch from large- to small-scale agriculture could not take place. Second, the rising service sector (especially tourism) had a voracious appetite for imported foodstuffs that was allegedly justified by the taste preferences of visitors. Third, food aid – especially in Haiti – damaged the prospects for ISAg because local farmers can never compete with subsidised imports. Finally, tariffs on agricultural imports were kept low for fear of adding to inflationary pressures.[36]

As a consequence of these obstacles, imports of foodstuffs remained important and represented around 20 per cent of the import bill for the Caribbean as a whole.[37] Even in Cuba, where some of the obstacles to ISAg should have been much less salient, food imports were a very high proportion of total supply, and considerable quantities were imported from the United States after 2000, when US restrictions were lifted. For the Caribbean as a whole, there were many products where imports represented more than 50 per cent of total supply (see Figure 14.3). Even if some of these products, such as wheat, are not suitable for growing in the tropics, the same could not be said for others, such as maize and rice.

ISAg was therefore a disappointment. The smaller countries could claim a shortage of suitable land, but this was not true of the Greater Antilles, the three Guyanas or Belize. Economics could explain part of this disappointing performance, but not all of it. The inflexible tastes of the millions of visitors

---

[36] They also tended to be lower than for manufactured goods. See WDI.
[37] See WDI.

to the Caribbean were partly to blame, along with the lack of a peasant tradition and the ever-present threat from natural disasters. The biggest obstacle, however, was the preference in the Caribbean for export specialisation rather than import competition. And the promotion of manufactured exports was a key part of this prevailing culture.

14.2. MANUFACTURING EXPORT PROMOTION

Even if we leave aside the processing of primary products, such as sugarcane and bauxite, the export of manufactured products began in the Caribbean long before 1960. The earliest examples had been cigars from Cuba, the Dominican Republic and Jamaica. There had also been straw hats and sandals from the Netherlands Antilles starting in the nineteenth century. The importance of manufactured exports then took a qualitative and quantitative leap with the establishment of oil refining in Curaçao and Aruba in the 1920s, using imported crude, and later in Trinidad & Tobago, using domestic and imported crude. After the Second World War, oil refining facilities would be established in many other countries.

These developments in manufactured exports, however, were not those that especially interested the new generation of Caribbean leaders that came of age in the 1950s. Instead, it was the expansion of manufactured exports from Puerto Rico that fascinated them and that was thought to carry important lessons for other countries in the region. The explosion of manufactured exports from the island in the postwar period coincided with the conviction among many nationalist politicians and public intellectuals in the Caribbean that industrialisation represented the way forward. Industrialisation in Puerto Rico did not begin after the Second World War. On the contrary, as we have seen in earlier chapters, the export of textiles and clothing was of some importance even before the **First** World War. There would then be a hiatus until the momentum was restored in the 1930s based on a broader range of products. The Second World War gave a big boost to industry because it both provided the funds[38] and reduced the competition from imports.

Up to this point, US companies operating in Puerto Rico benefitted only from section 931 of the Internal Revenue Code. This meant they could qualify as 'possessions corporations' and could exclude their Puerto Rican income from their US corporate tax bill, provided they did not repatriate their profits to the United States.[39] However, they were subject to island taxation, including the Puerto Rican corporate income tax, which had come into effect in 1913 (the same year as in the United States). Because the corporate tax rate was similar to that in the United States, it was therefore not tax considerations that

---

[38] Revenue from rum sales in the US soared, and these were returned to the island.
[39] See Dietz (1986), p. 209. A 'possessions corporation' was one that (a) obtained at least 80% of its gross income from sources within a US territory, and (b) derived 50% or more of its gross income from a trade business within a US possession.

primarily attracted US companies to Puerto Rico. It was much more related to differential wage rates and unrestricted access to the mainland.

It was in 1948 that the fiscal incentives open to companies in Puerto Rico changed dramatically with a series of laws that became known as Operation Bootstrap.[40] These exempted qualifying firms not only from property, excise and municipal taxes and licence fees, but also from corporate income taxes for a limited number of years. Two years later, the Administración de Fomento Económico was established, and under its common name of 'Fomento' it would target US companies in particular in the hope of attracting them to Puerto Rico. In the next decade an estimated 9,000 observers came to the island to see for themselves the results of this 'industrialisation by invitation', including many from other parts of the Caribbean.

Operation Bootstrap may have attracted huge interest, but it suffered from a number of weaknesses. First, the stricter application of US minimum wage laws to the island in the 1950s meant that wage rates started to catch up with those on the mainland, making labour-intensive manufacturing less attractive.[41] Second, firms in other countries were gaining easier access to the US market, either as a result of US tariff reductions or special bilateral arrangements.[42] Third, it had been hoped that qualifying firms would reinvest their tax-free profits in productive assets on the island, but many took advantage of the loophole under which the profits could be remitted back to the United States without tax if it was done at the end of the exemption period.[43] Finally, as the deadline for the exemption period approached, the Puerto Rican government felt obliged to provide 'temporary' tax relief in order to continue to attract new entrants.

As the wage rate and location advantage of Puerto Rico declined, the authorities pressed the US administration to increase the fiscal attraction. The result was section 936 of the 1976 Federal Tax Reform Act, which allowed US companies in 'possession' countries such as Puerto Rico to remit their profits **at any time** without paying federal corporate income tax. In return, qualifying companies had to pay a small 'tollgate' tax to the Puerto Rican government on any dividends paid to the parent.[44] And in 1978, the island government replaced complete exemption from local taxes with partial exemption based on a sliding scale.[45]

---

[40] Its name in Spanish was *Operación Manos a la Obra*, which is not quite the same as 'Operation Bootstrap' and was perhaps a more accurate reflection of what happened.

[41] See Dietz (1986), p. 248.

[42] Mexico in particular benefitted from this – long before the country joined NAFTA.

[43] The profits in the meantime had been invested tax-free in Puerto Rican bonds or sent to other US possessions, such as the Virgin Islands. At the end of the exemption period, the company was then liquidated.

[44] The tollgate tax was a maximum of 10%. However, it could easily be reduced by investing in local financial instruments. See Dietz (1986), pp. 301–2.

[45] The scale (90%–50%) depended on the number of years since the original investment and location of the factory.

The tax incentives provided by section 936 had the desired effect of increasing manufactured exports from Puerto Rico, but at a huge fiscal cost and with only a modest impact on employment. Labour-intensive factories producing such goods as textiles and clothing began to be replaced with capital-intensive industries. Among these were chemicals (especially pharmaceuticals), electrical equipment and instruments. In order to minimise their tollgate tax burden, these firms invested heavily in local financial instruments, which by 1983 had reached $5.9 billion – equivalent to 37 per cent of all bank deposits.[46] Indeed, the scale of these financial investments was so large that incentives were provided in the Caribbean Basin Initiative (CBI) for their tax-free reinvestment in productive assets in eligible countries.[47]

US administrations had for decades borne the fiscal burden of the arrangements for Puerto Rico without much political controversy. However, the costs of section 936 were enormous. Through transfer pricing, US firms were under-invoicing imports and overinvoicing exports to generate massive profits in Puerto Rico that were free of tax. It was estimated that each job created in the pharmaceutical industry, for example, cost $70,000 in lost tax revenue, compared with an average salary of $26,471.[48] Such generosity was unsustainable, and in 1996 it was announced by the Clinton administration that section 936 would be phased out by 2005.

The end of section 936 led to a substantial decline in manufacturing employment in Puerto Rico. However, the fiscal incentives did not end entirely. US firms could now register as 'controlled foreign corporations' and receive the same benefits as other US firms operating abroad. This allowed firms to retain the difference between their US tax liabilities and the taxes they paid to the Puerto Rican government until the profits are repatriated.[49] And for one group of companies – pharmaceuticals – this was sufficient to encourage them to continue their island operations.[50]

The Puerto Rican experiment in the promotion of manufactured exports had not evolved as anticipated. Instead of expanding employment, backward linkages and fiscal benefits for the island government, industrialisation in the new century employed fewer workers, purchased very little from the local economy, provided only modest tax revenue and was mainly US-owned. The companies that remained were overwhelmingly in the chemical industry, where they manufactured prescription drugs for the citizens of rich countries. No less than 70 per cent of manufactured exports came from the chemical industry in 2002, but its share of employment was less than one-quarter.[51]

---

[46] See Dietz (1986), p. 303.

[47] See Chapter 12.2.

[48] See Dietz (2001), p. 259.

[49] See Lawrence and Lara (2006), pp. 513–14.

[50] The reason why the new arrangements were attractive to pharmaceuticals is that the industry is very intensive in R&D. In effect, the R&D costs were written off against tax in the US or elsewhere, allowing the companies to make high profits largely free of tax in Puerto Rico.

[51] See Lawrence and Lara (2006), p. 519.

The Puerto Rican experiment in industrial export promotion is no longer held up as a model. However, in its early days it was widely admired, even if it tended to be seen through rose-tinted lenses. Thus, the powerful impact of fiscal incentives on employment and exports was emphasised without paying due consideration to either the fiscal cost or the need for unrestricted access to the US market. Arthur Lewis had tried to guard against these problems in his seminal article, but he himself was guilty of overstating the case, and the enthusiasm for the Puerto Rican model could not be dampened.[52]

Almost all the other countries of the Caribbean adopted fiscal packages designed to encourage investment, especially by foreign companies, in assembly operations that could replicate the success of Puerto Rico under Operation Bootstrap. This was the easy part. Unlike the US territories, however, the rest of the Caribbean did not have unrestricted access to the US market at zero tariffs for their manufactured exports. Thus, progress in export promotion depended in large part on changes by the core (especially the United States) in import policy.

Ironically, the first breakthrough for the Caribbean came with the new restrictions on imports of textiles and clothing imposed by the EEC and United States in 1962 that were designed to protect their domestic industries.[53] By providing quotas for foreign countries, this system, which became the Multi-fibre Arrangement (MFA) in 1974, gave a few Caribbean countries their first chance to export manufactured goods. Indeed, when the MFA was phased out over a decade starting in 1995,[54] it caused major difficulties for those countries in the Caribbean that had made most use of the quota system because they now had to compete with the lowest cost producers around the world.

The second advance was provided by the US Offshore Assembly Tariff Provisions of 1965, which allowed US firms to export manufactured goods on concessional terms to the United States under certain circumstances. This was followed by UNCTAD's Generalized System of Preferences in 1971,[55] by the EC's Lomé Convention in 1975, by the US Caribbean Basin Initiative in 1983 and by Canada's CARIBCAN in 1986. Meanwhile, the French territories had special access to the EC.[56] Thus, by the end of the 1980s a range of measures were in place to improve the access for manufactured exports to the markets of the core countries.[57]

---

[52] In response to concerns about the competitiveness of industry in the Caribbean, Lewis wrote: 'The answer ... seems to be provided ... by Puerto Rico, which, although it pays wages twice as high as the British islands, and has the same sort of psychological and climatic attitudes towards work, has found it possible to compete with the U.S.A. in a wide range of industries, without tariff protection.' See Lewis (1950).

[53] See Grilli (1993), p. 24.

[54] The Uruguay Round had brought the MFA to an end, but the developed countries were able to delay the end of all import quotas for textiles and clothing until 2005.

[55] It was implemented by most core countries in 1972, but not by the US until 1976.

[56] The British and Dutch territories had EU associated status, which gave them similar market access.

[57] For more details, see Chapter 12.

Several Caribbean countries, as we shall see, took full advantage of these opportunities. However, almost as soon as this happened, the Caribbean's privileged access started to be eroded by other core commercial policies. Tariff rates for third countries came down sharply at the end of the Uruguay Round. The United States and Canada extended their free trade agreement to include Mexico – a major competitor of the Caribbean – by forming NAFTA. Other core countries started to sign Preferential Trade Agreements (PTAs) with the Caribbean's competitors. The PTA between the United States and Central America was signed in 2004, and only the Dominican Republic in the Caribbean was able to enter.[58] The United States did make special arrangements for Haiti starting in 2006,[59] and the EU-CARIFORUM Economic Partnership Agreement (EPA) was initialled in 2008, but the EU continued to sign PTAs with other countries that undermined to some extent the benefits of the EPA for the Caribbean.[60]

One of the first countries outside the US territories to take seriously the promotion of manufactured exports was Haiti. Tax incentives had been adopted and expanded in 1949, 1955 and 1959, and by 1972 manufactured goods were 21 per cent of merchandise exports, half of which were assembled from imported components.[61] This, however, was just the beginning. By the time Jean-Claude Duvalier was driven from office in 1986, two-thirds of Haiti's exports of goods were manufactured. At first textiles and clothing were the most important, but they were eventually overtaken by electrical and electronic goods.[62] Yet Haitian-manufactured exports were very sensitive to market access conditions, and UN-sponsored sanctions in 1991–4 took a heavy toll (see Figure 14.4).[63]

Haiti had one of the highest ratios of manufactured-to-goods exports in the Caribbean after 1980. It had started to promote manufactured exports at an early stage when agro-industrial exports faced grave difficulties. However, the volume of manufactured exports was always very small. By contrast, the Dominican Republic came to manufactured export promotion relatively late, the first of its Export Processing Zones (EPZs) opening in 1969 at La Romana. Yet by 1992 there were twenty-three zones in operation with 362 plants, and they accounted for two-thirds of all manufacturing employment.[64]

The assembly firms (*maquiladoras*) in the *zonas francas* of the Dominican Republic have been among the most dynamic in the world, helping to ensure that the share of manufactures in goods exports has been very high (see Figure 14.4). The value of their exports rose from $850 million in 1990 to

---

[58] Hence its name (CAFTA-DR). See Chapter 12.

[59] See Chapter 12.

[60] The US administration would have done so also (notably with Colombia and Panama), but congressional opposition made this impossible until 2011.

[61] See Fass (1988), table 1.8, p. 40.

[62] Sporting goods, especially baseballs, were also very important.

[63] These sanctions were imposed following the overthrow of President Aristide in 1991 and would remain in place until he was restored in 1994.

[64] See Willmore (1996), p. 3. In addition, there were in 1992 another twenty-four establishments with 'special free zone' status.

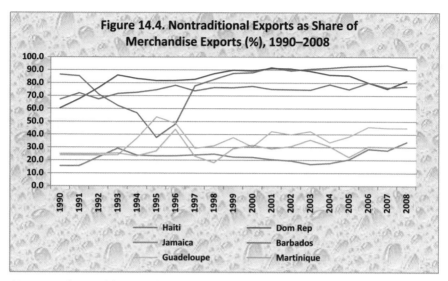

Figure 14.4. Nontraditional Exports as Share of Merchandise Exports (%), 1990–2008

Note: Data for Guadeloupe and Martinique in 1990–2 are estimates. Data for the Dominican Republic include nontraditional exports and assembled goods. Haitian data include handicraft exports.

Source: Derived from CEPAL (2010), UNYITS and INSEE Web site.

$4,771 million in 2000.[65] However, they subsequently declined modestly in value as a result of the phasing out of the MFA quotas in the US market and the competition from Mexico as NAFTA came into force. The proposed PTA between the United States and Central America was then seen as such a potential threat that the Dominican Republic used all its diplomatic skills to ensure it was admitted on the same terms, and CAFTA-DR came into force for the country in 2007.

The other country where manufactured exports have become a very high proportion of goods exports is Barbados (see Figure 14.4). At first this was centered on textiles and clothing, but this declined in importance after 1977, and electrical components, chemicals, machinery and other assembled goods took their place.[66] The manufacturing sector, however, only accounted for 8 per cent of the labour force in 2000, because the assembled exports tended to be very capital-intensive. In any case, the bulk of exports – unlike the cases of Haiti and the Dominican Republic – came from services rather than goods.

The three other countries shown in Figure 14.4 – Jamaica, Guadeloupe and Martinique – never had such a high proportion of goods exports coming from manufactures. Nevertheless, the proportion has not been negligible. Jamaica followed the traditional path by opening a 'free zone' in Kingston in 1976, but it was not until 1982 that investors showed much interest. Unusually, however,

---

[65] By contrast, Haitian-manufactured exports never exceeded $500 million.
[66] See Howard (2006), chap. 6.

Jamaica subsequently allowed some firms to operate exclusively as export processing companies outside the free zones. At first, manufactured exports were dominated by textiles and clothing, but these declined in importance after 1995 for much the same reasons as in the Dominican Republic.

Guadeloupe and Martinique never promoted manufactured exports in the traditional sense. However, their privileged market access to mainland France – and indeed to each other and to the other DOMs – meant that they did not have to worry about core import policy. At the same time, both countries qualified for so many grants and subsidised loans from the EU that private investment in manufactured exports has been very profitable for some firms. For both countries, most of these exports have been capital rather than intermediate or consumer goods. These cannot be said to represent an advanced stage of industrialisation, because they are overwhelmingly assembled from imported components. Yet overall manufactured exports have reached between 30 and 45 per cent of goods exports, a proportion that is much higher than in most countries with similar size populations in the Caribbean.

Trinidad & Tobago, rich in energy resources, came late to the promotion of manufactured exports. Assembly exports in export processing zones did not hold the same attraction as elsewhere in the Caribbean, and the first prime minister (Eric Williams) had always argued that the newly independent country needed to find a 'third way' between Cuba and Puerto Rico.[67] It was not until the mid-1970s, however, following the quadrupling of energy prices, that Trinidad & Tobago put forward serious plans to use its energy resources to promote manufactured exports.[68]

This was the Point Lisas industrial complex, which involved heavy public investment in infrastructure, joint ventures with private-sector firms (many of them foreign) and the promotion of manufactured exports linked to natural gas and iron ore, in particular.[69] Almost as soon as the public investments in infrastructure were begun, however, Trinidad's energy boom faded, and the economy suffered a period of economic decline after 1982. Yet the state persisted, and by the 1990s, when the economy started to recover, the initiative was paying off. Technology- and capital-intensive manufactured exports became significant (see Figure 14.5) and reached 20 to 25 per cent of all goods sold abroad.[70]

The promotion of manufactured exports in the Caribbean had relied heavily on direct foreign investment. This was much less of an option for Cuba, even after the legal barriers to foreign investment were swept away starting in the

[67] See Ryan (2009), chap. 24.
[68] Until then Trinidad & Tobago had relied on such staples as textiles and clothing, but exports of these items never reached even 1% of goods exports and never employed more than 300 people. See Willmore (1996), p. 6.
[69] See Best (2010).
[70] The diversification of the economy made possible by these exports was a cornerstone of the government's *Vision 2020*, an ambitious strategic plan designed to turn Trinidad & Tobago into a developed country by 2020. See Trinidad & Tobago, *Vision 2020* (2007).

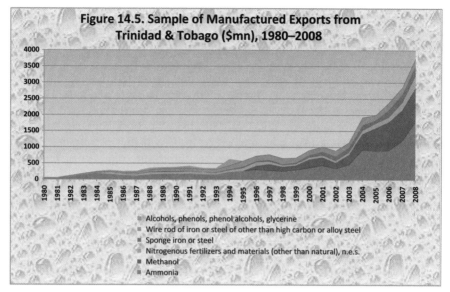

Figure 14.5. Sample of Manufactured Exports from Trinidad & Tobago ($mn), 1980–2008

- Alcohols, phenols, phenol alcohols, glycerine
- Wire rod of iron or steel of other than high carbon or alloy steel
- Sponge iron or steel
- Nitrogenous fertilizers and materials (other than natural), n.e.s.
- Methanol
- Ammonia

Source: Derived from CEPAL (2010).

mid-1980s,[71] as a result of the high cost of labour for foreign companies.[72] Yet Cuba was very interested in export diversification, which became a necessity after the terminal decline of the sugar industry at the end of the 1990s. Cuba therefore embarked on a strategy sometimes called 'export substitution'.[73]

The cornerstone of this strategy in Cuba has been the health sector. Although the country is well known for its export of medical services to other countries and medical tourism in Cuba,[74] it has also developed an important niche in biotechnology exports (see Figure 14.6). These make use of Cuba's undoubted expertise in life sciences, its pool of skilled labour and highly qualified health professionals and its alliances with foreign companies.[75] By 2005 these goods represented around 10 per cent of merchandise exports.

[71] See Pérez (2004).
[72] There were some exceptions, but in general the state has paid workers in foreign firms in national pesos, and the firm paid the government in foreign currency at the official exchange rate. This made wage rates for foreign firms much higher than in most Caribbean countries.
[73] See Monreal (2002), chap. 1.
[74] There are Cuban doctors in many countries of Africa and Latin America, the largest number being in Venezuela, and visitors have come from all over the world for medical treatment in Cuba.
[75] These alliances, crucial for exports to developed countries, have been limited by the difficulty for Cuba of finding partners that will not be penalised under US law. See Baker (2003), pp. 36–7.

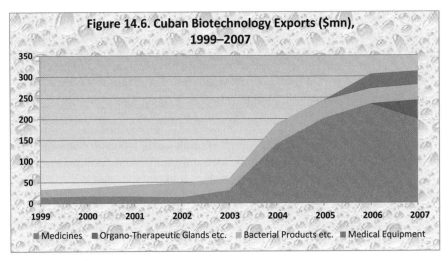

Figure 14.6. Cuban Biotechnology Exports ($mn), 1999–2007

Source: Derived from CEPAL (2010).

14.3. REGIONAL INTEGRATION

When the Federation of the West Indies collapsed in 1962, it seemed that the dream of Caribbean integration – at least for the ten British colonies involved – had ended. However, this was not so, and within three years the first alternative scheme had been promoted.[76] This time, the project focused on economic rather than political integration, and it would lead in 1968 to the Caribbean Free Trade Association (CARIFTA).[77] This scheme was in due course found lacking in ambition by its members, many of whom had recently become independent, and in 1973 the Treaty of Chaguaramas was signed leading to the Caribbean Community (CARICOM).[78] All former British colonies would eventually join CARICOM together with Montserrat. Subsequently, membership would be expanded to include Suriname (1995) and Haiti (2002).

The Treaty of Chaguaramas was a major achievement. It established various goals for CARICOM, including a common market in goods and services, economic and foreign policy coordination, the achievement of a greater measure of economic independence for the members and functional cooperation.[79] In addition to removing barriers to trade among members and the establishment of a

---

[76] This involved a proposal for a free trade area by Antigua, Barbados and Guyana. See El-Agraa and Nicholls (1997), p. 279.

[77] There was huge interest in integration at this time – in part because of the launch of schemes in Latin America. One of these, the Central American Common Market (CACM), was of particular interest because it involved a proposal to establish 'integration industries'. These were industries where one firm would receive preferential treatment in order to achieve regional import substitution. See Brewster and Thomas (1967).

[78] See Hall (1988).

[79] See Payne (1985).

Common External Tariff (CET), the treaty recognised that the smaller countries (at that time all except Barbados, Guyana, Jamaica and Trinidad) should receive special and differential treatment and be known as Less Developed Countries (LDCs).[80] This meant, for example, they would have longer to implement trade liberalisation and would have greater safeguards against import surges.[81]

What the treaty did **not** do was establish any supranational mechanisms for ensuring that the goals were met. In recognition of this, the members drew up the Grand Anse Declaration in 1989, established the West India Commission the following year[82] and announced in 1992 the commitment to the CARICOM Single Market and Economy (CSME), including a monetary union.[83] In terms of deepening, this was such a major step that it led in fact to a two-stage integration process.[84] It was complemented by the establishment of a Regional Negotiating Machinery (RNM) to coordinate the CARICOM position in international negotiations and was crowned with the Revised Treaty of Chaguaramas in 2002. Subsequently, a Caribbean Court of Justice was established that would be the first truly supranational organisation.[85]

CARICOM has always been subject to centripetal and centrifugal forces. The former derive from the shared historical and cultural experience of the ex-British colonies[86] and the sense that small countries have no alternative to integration if they are to cope with the demands of a globalised world. The latter are legion, and have to do with nationalist and ideological rivalries, external pressures and the fact that most trade in goods and services is inevitably with countries outside the Caribbean. Unsurprisingly, therefore, CARICOM has often fallen short of its aspirations. Yet its achievements have also been considerable and should not be underestimated.

One of CARICOM's achievements was the liberalisation of almost all trade in goods among member states and the establishment of a CET at a level that gave a modest level of protection against imports of consumer goods from third countries. This allowed intraregional exports to increase rapidly after CARIFTA was launched in 1968, and their share of merchandise exports rose fairly steadily until 2000 (see Figure 14.7), when it reached a peak of nearly 20 per cent. Since then, however, the share has fallen back to the level of thirty

---

[80] The others were More Developed Countries (MDCs); later Suriname was added to the MDCs and Haiti to the LDCs.

[81] See INTAL-IDB (2005), pp. 11–12.

[82] It reported in 1992. See West Indian Commission (1992).

[83] The CSME had already been outlined in the Grand Anse Declaration in 1989. For the text, see West Indian Commission (1992), pp. 525–8.

[84] The Bahamas remained a member of CARICOM, but it did not join the CSME (Haiti is in the same position, but in theory committed to joining the CSME).

[85] It was established in Trinidad & Tobago in 2005, but not all countries were members at the time.

[86] These centripetal forces predate CARICOM and had led, for example, to the formation of the West Indies Cricket Federation in 1926 and the University of the West Indies in 1948.

Figure 14.7. CARICOM Intraregional Exports as Percentage of Merchandise Exports, 1960–2008

Note: Where intraregional exports were given in Eastern Caribbean dollars, they have been converted to US dollars using the exchange rate for Organisation of Eastern Caribbean States (OECS) countries in Table D.4. Because it only joined CARICOM in 1995, merchandise exports exclude Suriname in earlier years (the Bahamas and Haiti, although members since 2005, are not included in CARICOM Secretariat trade data). Intraregional exports in 2005–8 are incomplete in the CARICOM Secretariat database, so intraregional imports (approximately the same value) have been used for these years.

Source: CARICOM intraregional exports for 1960–89 from El-Agraa and Nicholls (1997), p. 283; for 1990–2000, from CARICOM (2002); for 2001–8, from the CARICOM Secretariat Web site. Merchandise exports from Table D.6.

years earlier.[87] This is an illustration of the centrifugal forces at work, because it has been a consequence both of the promotion of extraregional merchandise exports and the decline in the CET.[88]

CARICOM, as CARIFTA before it, was supposed not just to promote regional import substitution but also to encourage extraregional exports through a process of learning by doing (ECLAC/CEPAL in the 1990s would make this notion fashionable through the idea of 'open regionalism').[89] It is therefore theoretically possible that the decline in the importance of intraregional exports after 2000 is a measure of success. Unfortunately, this interpretation is incorrect because intraregional exports are dominated by Trinidad & Tobago (see Figure 14.8), which has traditionally provided energy and petrochemical products to its CARICOM partners.[90] All other countries, and there

---

[87] As a share of **total** exports (goods and services), this implies an even greater decline because extraregional service exports are now much more important.

[88] The mean weighted tariff on manufactured goods fell between 1996 and 2008 by at least 50% in all CARICOM countries. See WDI.

[89] See Devlin and Estevadeordal (2001).

[90] Trinidadian dominance has increased over time since its share of intraregional exports was 'only' 52% in 1990. See CARICOM (2002).

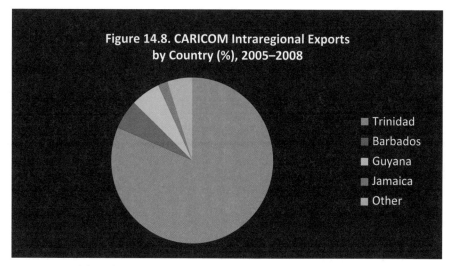

Figure 14.8. CARICOM Intraregional Exports by Country (%), 2005–2008

Source: Derived from database in CARICOM Web site.

are fourteen of them, accounted for less than 20 per cent of intraregional exports in 2005–8 (see Figure 14.8).

Although Trinidad & Tobago has always dominated CARICOM's exports, it has not imported much from its regional partners. This has left it with a large surplus on intraregional trade – so much so that in many years all other countries have had deficits. This was one of the reasons why the members established in the 1970s the CARICOM Multilateral Clearing Facility (CMCF), but it collapsed in 1983 in the wake of severe balance of payments difficulties by some of the members (especially Guyana).[91] Bilateral trade balances have therefore usually had to be settled in hard currency. This can impose strains because the main importers of intraregional goods (see Figure 14.9) have little in common with the main exporters (see Figure 14.8).

The biggest strain on CARICOM has been the region's dependence on extraregional exports (goods and services) for its members' growth and development. In the 1970s, member states had to adapt their trade policy and practice to the Lomé Convention. A decade later they did the same for the Caribbean Basin Initiative and the agreement with Canada (CARIBCAN), while coming under pressure from the international financial institutions to reform their tariff, fiscal and labour market policies. In the 1990s, a huge amount of effort was devoted to the prospect of a Free Trade Area of the Americas (FTAA), which – if it had been established – would effectively have made CARICOM redundant. After 2000, the priority became negotiating the Economic Partnership Agreement (EPA),[92] which in time will give the EU duty-free access to CARICOM

[91] See El-Agraa and Nicholls (1997), p. 288.
[92] The EPA was negotiated with CARIFORUM, which includes the Dominican Republic and CARICOM states. For a preliminary assessment of its likely impact, see Rapley et al. (2010).

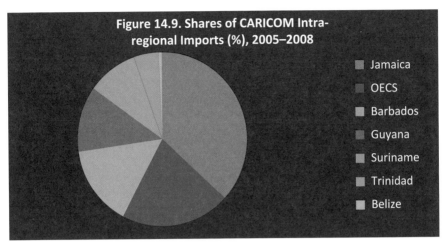

Figure 14.9. Shares of CARICOM Intra-regional Imports (%), 2005–2008

- Jamaica
- OECS
- Barbados
- Guyana
- Suriname
- Trinidad
- Belize

Note: OECS is the Organisation of Eastern Caribbean States.
Source: CARICOM Secretariat database.

and will therefore undermine the protection for regional firms provided by the CET.

Perhaps the biggest threat of all, however, has been the position of Trinidad & Tobago. For a long time a staunch supporter of regional integration, providing financial assistance to its partners in many ways,[93] Trinidad & Tobago has been concerned about Venezuela's establishment of Petrocaribe and ALBA[94] with the participation of many CARICOM states. Because the country imports little from CARICOM and its ambitions go far beyond the region, it is perhaps not surprising that Trinidad & Tobago has often shown its frustration at the pace of change in CARICOM and has pressed for alternative approaches to integration.[95]

Although the original membership of CARICOM embraced only a small proportion of the Caribbean population, it did succeed in establishing itself as the only viable integration scheme in the region. Indeed, the decision of other countries – Haiti and Suriname – to apply for membership is a testament to this. It has been able to negotiate highly favourable PTAs with other countries, including Colombia, Costa Rica, the Dominican Republic and Venezuela.[96] And whatever the shortcomings of the EPA, it must surely be the case that the agreement would have been even less favourable to the Caribbean if CARICOM

---

[93] Through, for example, subsidised finance for energy imports and technical assistance to non-Trinidadian CARICOM firms. See INTAL-IDB (2005).

[94] See Chapter 12.

[95] Trinidad & Tobago, for example, announced in 2008 it was seeking a political union with Grenada, St Lucia and St Vincent.

[96] Those with Colombia and Venezuela have been largely asymmetric, and therefore CARICOM has not had to reciprocate the benefits provided by its partner.

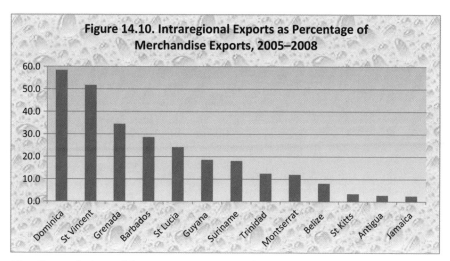

Note: Because Suriname did not report its intraregional exports in 2005–8, I have used Surinamese intraregional imports and divided by its merchandise imports in Table D.11. Antigua only reported in two of the four years (2005–6), and I have therefore estimated the missing two years.

Source: Intraregional exports from database on the CARICOM Web site, and merchandise exports from Table D.6.

did not exist. The Caribbean without CARICOM would be more, not less, vulnerable to outside forces than it currently is.

Indeed, the greatest strength of CARICOM does not lie in its formal apparatus to promote intraregional trade liberalisation, but in the functional cooperation that can be found at so many different levels and that is not even limited to CARICOM members. The Caribbean Development Bank, for example, was founded in 1970 with membership drawn from inside and outside CARICOM (or CARIFTA as it then was). The Caribbean Examinations Council (CXC) sets exams and common standards across the schools system. There are regional organisations for public health, environmental disasters, food security, transport, sport and so on.

For one group of countries, however, CARICOM does provide real benefits through economic integration. These are the tiny states of the eastern Caribbean, which came together in 1981 to form the Organisation of Eastern Caribbean States (OECS)[97] with their own central bank and currency union.[98] For many of these countries – especially Dominica, Grenada, St Lucia and St Vincent – a very high proportion of their merchandise exports consists of goods

[97] The OECS has seven full members, all of which are in CARICOM (Antigua, Dominica, Grenada, Montserrat, St Kitts & Nevis, St Lucia and St Vincent) and two associate members (Anguilla and the British Virgin Islands) that are not.
[98] The Eastern Caribbean Central Bank (ECCB) was established in 1983. The currency union can be said to be much older because it is an outgrowth of the colonial system when all countries were in the sterling area.

sold to their partners in CARICOM (see Figure 14.10). Barbados, although not a member of the OECS, is in a similar position. For firms in these countries making tradeable goods, the regional market is of great importance, even if service exports outside the region are now much greater in terms of their value.

With fifteen CARICOM members, two of whom (Bahamas and Haiti) are not part of the CSME, there are still thirteen countries outside the organisation. Furthermore, these include two of the countries with the largest populations (Cuba and the Dominican Republic). This is a weakness in Caribbean integration that has long been recognised. One attempt to correct it was the creation in 1994 of the Association of Caribbean States (ACS), embracing all the independent countries of the Caribbean and its littoral (Central America, Mexico, Colombia and Venezuela). The ACS, however, has no power to act on its own, and the organisation excludes the dependent territories other than as associate members.[99]

Caribbean integration is therefore a work in progress, and it may take many decades before a regional architecture is in place that can reflect the interests of all countries. In the meantime, CARICOM remains an expression of what can be achieved by small states acting together. At times centrifugal forces have threatened to overwhelm the organisation, and yet it has survived. The main reason is the strong sense of identity enjoyed by citizens of the Caribbean regardless of their nationality. Culture and identity are important in all successful examples of regional integration – in Asia, Europe and Latin America – and the Caribbean is no exception.

---

[99] The French territories are represented by France. The Dutch territories and the Turks & Caicos Islands are also associate members. The US territories are not represented at all.

15

Caribbean Economic Performance

The period since 1960 captures very clearly the dilemmas that have faced the Caribbean since the Napoleonic Wars. The trade-offs between production, distribution and sovereignty remain as acute as ever. Meanwhile the problem of surplus labour has acquired a new dimension with the rise of open (as opposed to disguised) unemployment in so many countries. Finally, an old concern – the environment – has acquired new significance as a result of the renewed focus on sustainability.

The first section deals with production, the conventional metric for which is GDP. By any standards the Caribbean has scored high on this measure. The rates of growth may not have been spectacular, but they have exceeded population growth in all but one country (Haiti), even when GDP is expressed in constant prices. The absolute value of GDP per head now exhibits a variation among countries that is perhaps surprising for such a small region. However, the average GDP per head of the Caribbean exceeds that of all other regions or groupings except the high income countries. It would be premature to say that the problem of production has been 'solved', but the Caribbean has shown since 1960 that it is capable of achieving rates of growth that ensure a high regional level of GDP per head.

Averages can conceal a great deal, and nowhere is this more true than in the Caribbean. In addition to the variance **between** countries, there is the variance **within** them. This comes principally from two sources. First, there is a difference between GDP and Gross National Income (GNI), the latter representing the factor income of residents from home and abroad and excluding the income of nonresidents. For some countries, notably Puerto Rico, this difference is enormous, with much of the GDP accruing to foreigners. Second, there is the size distribution of income between the different deciles of the population. This dimension of inequality, much studied in the case of mainland Latin America, has become increasingly important in the Caribbean and is the subject of the second section.

The third section is concerned with employment issues. If population growth was simply the difference between births and deaths, then the population of the Caribbean would have grown much faster than it actually has. However, in most countries – if not quite all – there has been net outward migration leading to a rate of growth of population that can be considered low by the standards of developing countries. Yet the avenues for outward migration have become increasingly restricted, and the rate of outward migration has fallen decade by decade since 1960. This is one reason – but by no means the only reason – for the seemingly inexorable rise in rates of open unemployment in many countries.

The environment, the subject of the final section, has always been of concern to the Caribbean – partly because of the frequency of natural disasters and also because of the (mis)use of land through deforestation, soil and coastal erosion, intensive farming and water contamination. The decline of export agriculture since 1960 should have eased some of these problems, but the rise in population and the heavy demands of the tourist industry have in many cases exacerbated them. The fragile nature of the Caribbean ecosystem may be better understood today than in the past, but the threats to that system are as great – if not greater – than ever.

15.1. PRODUCTION

The global economy since 1960 has been marked by a rise in foreign trade at a rate faster than output, leading to an increase in trade openness (exports plus imports divided by GDP) in almost all countries. For some countries, notably the larger countries of mainland Latin America, this has involved a painful process of adjustment because the economies had previously been focused on inward-looking development.[1] The Caribbean, however, has always been export-oriented, so the increase in the relative importance of trade – especially when services are included – should have favoured the region.

This is exactly what has happened. When production is measured by GDP at constant (2000) prices, we may observe an impressive increase in the different subregions (see Figure 15.1). The most spectacular performance has been in the tiny British territories,[2] where GDP rose at an annual rate of 9.3 per cent in the half century after 1960, but all subregions have done well when the beginning and end of the period are compared.[3] Even the sharp fall in GDP in Cuba between 1989 and 1993 has been largely reversed.[4] And for the Caribbean as a whole the annual rate of growth of GDP over the whole period

[1] See Bulmer-Thomas (2006).
[2] These five countries, today known as British Overseas Territories, are Anguilla, British Virgin Islands, Cayman Islands, Montserrat and Turks & Caicos Islands.
[3] These growth rates are derived from Table D.19.
[4] In these years GDP fell by more than one-third. See Chapter 16.3.

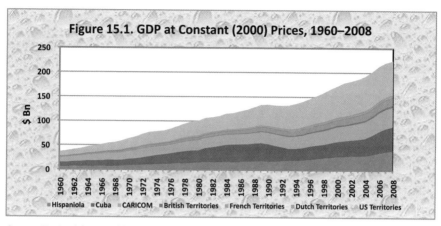

Source: Derived from Table D.19.

has been nearly 4 per cent, with no subregion exhibiting a rate of less than 3 per cent.

Because growth rates have not all been the same, the shares of the different subregions have altered. At the beginning of the period in 1960, Cuba, CARI-COM and the US territories each had roughly 25 per cent of the Caribbean's total GDP. The share of Cuba and CARICOM then declined, but that of the US territories rose rapidly – largely as a result of the industrialisation programme in Puerto Rico. The Cuban share recovered in the 1970s and 1980s – mainly at the expense of CARICOM – and Cuba once again had become the largest component of the Caribbean by the mid-1980s (a position it would retain until the early 1990s). The share of the US territories, however, continued to climb until the peak was reached in 2001. Since then there has been a serious decline as a result of the difficulties faced by Puerto Rico.[5]

The impact of GDP growth on living standards depends in part on the rate at which the population is expanding. This is shown in Table 15.1, where the annual growth rate in each decade since 1960 is given. In virtually every subregion there has been a steady decline in the annual growth rate. Indeed, in Cuba the population has for all intents and purposes ceased to grow, and it is not much different in the US territories and CARICOM. In some of the small British, French and Dutch territories, the growth in population – as we shall see below in section 3 – is mainly because of net inward migration. It is only in Hispaniola that we find rapid population growth as a result of births exceeding deaths, and even there it has declined over time. Finally, for the Caribbean as a whole annual growth is now below 1 per cent, and thus it

---

[5] All these figures derived from Table D.19.

TABLE 15.1. *Annual Rate of Growth of Population by Subregions (%),* 1960–2008

				Territories:				
	Hispaniola	Cuba	CARICOM	British	French	Dutch	US	Caribbean
1960–1970	2.58	2.01	1.61	2.94	1.66	1.62	1.52	2.06
1970–1980	2.25	1.21	0.99	2.28	0.39	0.83	1.74	1.58
1980–1990	2.17	0.77	0.92	2.99	1.76	0.8	0.98	1.38
1990–2000	1.86	0.48	0.81	2.72	1.25	0.67	0.75	1.16
2000–2008	1.59	0.13	0.63	4.06	1.23	1.23	0.44	0.93
1960–2008	2.11	0.95	1.01	2.95	1.26	1.02	1.11	1.44

Source: Derived from Table D.1a.

may take 100 years or more for the population to double from its current level.[6]

These numbers imply that annual Caribbean GDP per head at constant prices since 1960 has risen at nearly 2.5 per cent.[7] This is a respectable, if unspectacular, figure. It does not come close to the rate of growth of the so-called Asian Tigers, but it compares favourably with mainland Latin America and other parts of the developing world. However, at the country level it conceals a very high variance from nearly 8 per cent in the case of the British Virgin Islands to −1.3 per cent in the case of Haiti (see Figure 15.2). The median growth rate, however, is closer to 3 per cent, the mean being dragged down by a small number of underperformers with relatively large populations.[8]

One striking feature of Figure 15.2 is the large number of nonindependent countries in the top ten. There are in fact seven, and the three independent countries (St Kitts & Nevis, Grenada and Antigua) only became sovereign states long after 1960.[9] This inevitably invites the question of whether there is a trade-off between growth of production and formal political sovereignty. The answer – with all the usual caveats – has to be in the affirmative, but not for the reasons that might be widely assumed. Thus, the first four countries in Figure 15.2 are all tiny British colonies that have succeeded in exporting services – especially financial – in large part **because** much of the Caribbean has become independent. In other words, it is very difficult to imagine that these four countries would have performed so well if **every** country was a colony.[10] Similarly, the presence of both US territories and a French one in the top ten

---

[6] It is possible that the population will never double if rates continue to fall.

[7] The exact figure, derived from Tables D.1a and D.19, is 2.38%.

[8] With twenty-eight countries, the median is the average of the fourteenth and fifteenth countries. These were Montserrat and the Dominican Republic with growth rates of 3.05% and 2.96%, respectively.

[9] In 1983, 1974 and 1981, respectively.

[10] When nearly every country **was** a colony, the growth performance of these four countries was very unsatisfactory.

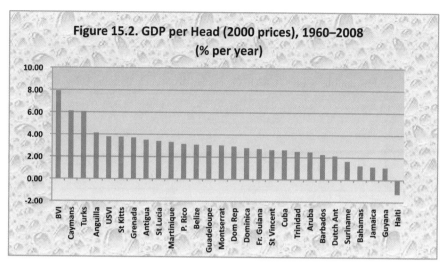

Figure 15.2. GDP per Head (2000 prices), 1960–2008 (% per year)

Note: For Anguilla, the period is 1970–2008, and for Aruba 1986–2008.
Source: Derived from Tables D.1a and D.19.

is because of special fiscal and tariff arrangements that could never have been extended to the whole of the Caribbean.[11]

Some of the countries in the tail of the distribution in Figure 15.2 have been a cause of special concern. Haiti is the best known case, with GDP per head since 1960 actually falling. Because it was already very low in 1960, this is deeply troubling and means that there has been no 'convergence' in the Haitian case.[12] The country's poor performance has been analysed extensively and reflects the systemic crisis that has afflicted the country since the 1890s (see Chapter 7), although most scholars focus mainly on the years since 1950.[13] The second worst performance has been in Guyana, where the self-inflicted wounds under Forbes Burnham took a heavy toll on the growth of an economy that was one of the most successful in the nineteenth century.[14] Much the same could be said of Suriname, where an irresponsible military coup in 1980 led to a long period of economic instability and underperformance.[15]

One of the most troubling cases in Figure 15.2 is that of Jamaica. This is not because the island has been any stranger to underperformance (it had

[11] Dependent status, on the other hand, is not a sufficient condition for successful GDP per head growth. The Dutch territories (Aruba and the Netherlands Antilles) are in the bottom ten, while French Guiana, Guadeloupe and Montserrat are in the middle.
[12] Convergence refers to the assumption that countries will grow faster/slower if the level of GDP per head is below/above the average for the group. See Barro and Sala-i-Martin (1995).
[13] See, among others, Moral (1961), Lundahl (1979), Dupuy (1989) and Fass (1988).
[14] See Modeste (1976) and Thomas (1988).
[15] See van Dijck (2001). The leader of the 1982 coup, Colonel Desiré Bouterse, became president again in 2010.

declined in absolute terms for roughly fifty years in the nineteenth century), but because Jamaica had grown rapidly in the decade before independence in 1962. This growth in fact continued until 1972, the year in which Michael Manley became prime minister. Manley's heroic efforts to change the terms of Jamaica's engagement with the global economy ultimately proved unsuccessful because his government's policies were undermined by a hostile external environment (political and economic), internal resistance by the Jamaican bourgeoisie and administrative failures. This episode has been extensively analysed,[16] but it does not explain why Jamaican GDP per head growth has **continued** to lag behind the rest of the Caribbean. Indeed, GDP per head at constant prices has still not recovered the peak it reached in 1972, suggesting that Jamaica – like Haiti – faces a systemic crisis that goes beyond mere errors in economic policy.[17]

The only other major underperformer has been the Bahamas (see Figure 15.2). This is a problem of a different order to that of the other laggards, because the Bahamas actually has a high level of GDP per head. The problem has really been twofold. First, the Bahamas – already enjoying a high income level in 1960 thanks to its early switch into service exports[18] – lost market share to new entrants in the tourism and financial service markets. Second, the Bahamas suffered a severe fall in GDP per head in the mid-1970s when drug-related corruption and the uncertainties associated with political independence led some foreign and local investors to take flight.[19] However, from the low point in 1975 the growth of GDP per head has been respectable and has compared favourably with the rest of the Caribbean.

A comparison of long-run growth rates of GDP per head since 1960 for the different subregions is also illuminating. For the Caribbean as a whole there was a fall in the growth rate until a very modest improvement after 2000 (see Table 15.2). However, this is less alarming than might at first appear. It was largely because of the special problems of a small number of countries – especially Haiti, Jamaica and Puerto Rico – that have been analysed elsewhere. This is troubling for the countries concerned, but it does not mean that the Caribbean has lost its ability to increase production. Indeed, the growth rate in Hispaniola (mainly because of the Dominican Republic), in CARICOM (in large part because of Trinidad & Tobago) and in Cuba was high after 2000.

The rapid growth of the British territories since 1960 – at least until the 1990s – has been based on the export of services, among which finance has figured prominently. The decline in the growth rate since 1990 of one of these

[16] See Looney (1987), Davies (1984) and Jefferson (1999).

[17] This crisis now includes institutionalised crime and violence as a result of the interconnection of domestic politics with criminal gangs.

[18] It was the first to move into financial services and among the first to exploit the opportunities in tourism.

[19] Independence in 1973 coincided with the decision by the Colombian cartels to route cocaine smuggling to the US through the Bahamas. See Ramsaran (1984), McCoy and Block (1992) and Maingot (1988).

TABLE 15.2. *Annual Rate of Growth of GDP per Head (2000 prices) by Subregions (%), 1960–2008*

	Hispaniola	Cuba	CARICOM	Territories: British	French	Dutch	US	Caribbean
1960–1970	0.78	1.85	4.07	9.75	6.45	0.24	6.71	3.63
1970–1980	3.83	5.23	1.48	12.13	1.86	7.46	2.57	3.01
1980–1990	−0.54	3.04	0.13	5.60	2.91	1.35	2.56	1.54
1990–2000	2.73	−1.90	1.70	3.75	1.66	1.89	3.11	1.33
2000–2008	3.03	5.93	3.16	−0.03	2.53	−0.10	0.59	2.42
1960–2008	1.91	2.66	2.05	6.42	3.09	2.23	3.20	2.38

Source: Derived from Tables D.1a and D.19.

countries – Montserrat – was primarily caused by the volcanic eruption in 1995. However, in the case of the other four (Anguilla, British Virgin Islands, Cayman Islands and Turks & Caicos Islands) the negative growth rate since 2000 (see Table 15.2) was partly from the sustained and increasingly aggressive campaign against 'tax havens' by the governments of the rich countries and the international financial institutions.[20] It is unlikely that this will lead to the end of offshore activities (too many multinational companies depend on them), but it is improbable that they will provide the economic dynamism in the future that they provided in the past. Reinventing these small economies on the basis of other service exports is the big challenge they currently face.

In much of the period since the Napoleonic Wars, economic growth and decline has been associated with – indeed, caused by – movements in the net barter terms of trade (NBTT). This was caused by the impact of commodity price changes on economies that were very open to foreign trade and where exports were dominated by primary products. Since 1960, however, the importance of commodity exports has steadily declined, but the share of exports in GDP has risen. The reason for this has been the rise of manufactured and service exports. Thus, the NBTT for most countries no longer depends primarily on movements in commodity prices.

Measuring the NBTT of economies whose exports are dominated by services is very difficult.[21] Using the information available, however, we may note the apparent stability of the NBTT in much of the period since 1960 for the Caribbean as a whole (see Figure 15.3). After declining by nearly 20 per cent in the first decade (in line with what was happening in mainland Latin America), the NBTT then improved sharply as a result of the commodity price boom of the mid-1970s when sugar prices in particular quadrupled. Yet this would be

[20] See Chapter 13.2.
[21] The methodological problems are discussed in the Notes on D. Tables.

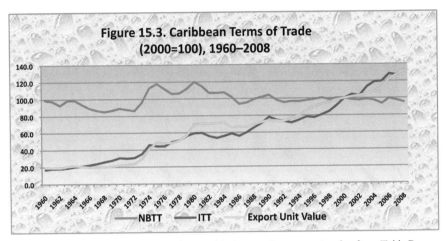

Figure 15.3. Caribbean Terms of Trade (2000=100), 1960–2008

Source: NBTT from Table D.16, ITT from Table D.17 and export unit value from Table D.9.

the last time that commodity price movements had much impact, and the NBTT finished the period where it had started in 1960. In other words, the weight of services in total exports cancelled out much of the impact of commodity price changes on merchandise exports after 2000.

This does not mean that the unit value/price of exports did not rise. Indeed, it did – as Figure 15.3 makes clear. However, import unit values rose at a similar rate over the period as a whole, leaving the NBTT unchanged. Thus, the income terms of trade (ITT), the NBTT multiplied by the volume of exports, becomes a proxy for the increase in exports at constant prices. This rose nearly eightfold over the whole period (see Figure 15.3), confirming what we already know about the strong performance of total exports since 1960.

This suggests that there has been a structural break in long-run economic performance of the Caribbean since 1960. Export growth has always been the main determinant of GDP growth, and this has been confirmed by all statistical analysis of the region.[22] However, it is the **volume** of exports that is now the key determinant of real GDP growth, with price changes relegated to secondary importance in all but a few cases.[23] This is clearly true for those countries – the majority – dependent on service exports, but it is also true for those, such as Puerto Rico, where exports are dominated by manufactured goods. Of the exceptions, the most important is Trinidad & Tobago, where the price of energy (oil and gas) remains a key determinant of real economic performance.[24]

---

[22] See Nicholls, S. (2001). The World Bank (2005), chap. 1, uses a slightly different methodological approach, but it does not fundamentally diverge from this conclusion.

[23] Prior (2010), for example, finds a strong correlation between visitor arrivals and growth rates since 1980.

[24] The NBTT of Trinidad & Tobago increased threefold from 1960 to 2008. See Table D.16.

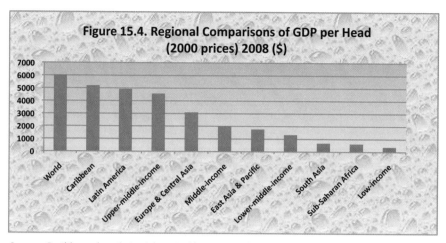

Source: Caribbean data derived from Tables D.1a and D.19. All other data derived from WDI.

The Caribbean since 1960 has increased GDP per head at a rate that almost certainly compares favourably with previous periods of economic expansion.[25] However, this does not necessarily mean it has performed well in relation to other regions. Yet the evidence strongly suggests that it **has** achieved increases in GDP per head since 1960 that have been high by world standards. And if we concentrate on the **level** of GDP per head at the end of the period considered here (2008), there can be little argument. As Figure 15.4 shows, the GDP per head of the Caribbean is above that of all other developing country categories. It is marginally above that of mainland Latin America and above the average for upper-middle-income countries. In Figure 15.4 it is only below the world average, which is skewed upwards by the high-income countries (OECD and non-OECD).

This is a salutary reminder that, although the Caribbean continues to face a series of monumental challenges, increasing GDP per head is not the principal problem. The export-oriented nature of the economies, the dominance of services, the presence of natural resources facing favourable price movements in recent years, the openness to foreign investment and the generous fiscal incentives have all combined to produce steady increases in GDP per head. The region does, of course, have some countries that have lagged behind (with nearly thirty it would be very surprising if this were not the case). Yet only one (Haiti) is regularly classified by the World Bank as low-income,[26] and many are high-income, with GDP per head at 2000 prices in excess of $10,000.[27]

[25] We cannot be certain, because we lack GDP data for most countries before 1960.
[26] Guyana has been classified as low-income in some years (its GDP per head has fluctuated around the benchmark).
[27] Exactly half of the countries in 2008 were in this position.

15.2. DISTRIBUTION BETWEEN AND WITHIN COUNTRIES

At the end of the Napoleonic Wars, there was already a significant gap between the richest and poorest countries in the Caribbean. It might have been expected that over nearly 200 years, there would have been a process of convergence as a result of higher returns to capital in the poorer countries. This does not appear to have happened. On the contrary, when measured by GDP per head the gap between the richest and poorest was a factor of nearly 100 at the start of the new millennium.[28] This must surely be greater than the gap in 1820, which – when measured by domestic exports per head – was a factor of 'only' 62.[29] Indeed, the gap has grown substantially even when the comparison is made with 1960, because at that time the GDP per head of the richest (Dutch Antilles) was a 'mere' twenty-nine times that of the poorest (Haiti).[30]

These comparisons are made in US dollars converting GDP from national currencies at the official exchange rate. It has long been recognised that official exchange rates can distort comparisons where income per head is very different, the main reason being the very different prices for nontraded goods and services when expressed in a common currency.[31] Because the gap in average income is so great in the Caribbean, it is appropriate to recalculate GDP per head by converting official to Purchasing Power Parity (PPP) exchange rates.[32] This is not a simple matter because the conversion rates have not been published for many countries, but it can be done.[33]

The PPP conversion rates are expected to raise the GDP per head of the poorest countries relative to the richest and narrow the differentials.[34] This is exactly what happens with the difference in GDP per head of the richest and the poorest, narrowing to a factor of 40 (see Figure 15.5). Haiti, for example, now has a GDP per head in 2000 of $1,065 rather than $449 when official exchange rates are used. Yet the gap is still enormous and much bigger than might be expected from such a small geographical region. In the Caribbean, it would appear, geography is not destiny.[35]

---

[28] GDP per head in the Cayman Islands in 2000 was $42,811 and in Haiti $449 (derived from Tables D.1a and D.19).
[29] Derived from Tables A.1a and A.11. The gap narrows to 22 if Belize is excluded.
[30] Derived from Tables D.1a and D.19.
[31] See MacDonald (2007).
[32] These rates are obtained by valuing a common basket of goods and services in different countries at national currencies. When divided by the cost in the US, the result is the Purchasing Power Parity (PPP) exchange rate against the US dollar. See Officer (1982).
[33] The biggest problem is that very few countries in the Caribbean, if any, are included among the benchmark countries for PPP purposes. The PPP for the missing countries then has to be estimated by regression analysis. This is done by the World Bank for WDI-reporting countries, and I have also done it for the countries not included in WDI.
[34] The rankings of countries is very similar regardless of the exchange rate used, with a correlation coefficient of 0.99, but this is partly because of the estimation of PPP rates themselves by regression analysis.
[35] This flawed idea has once again become fashionable. See, e.g., Gallup, Sachs and Mellinger (1998).

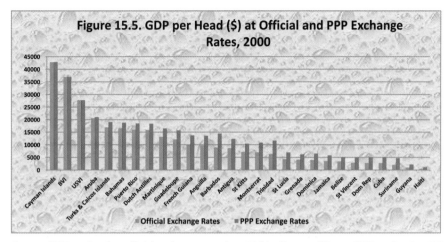

Source: GDP per head at official exchange rates from Tables D.1a and D.18. GDP per head at PPP exchange rates is from WDI, except for the nonindependent countries, the Bahamas and Cuba. The PPP conversion rate for these countries has been derived by applying the results of a simple regression of PPP conversion rates against GDP per head at official exchange rates for the other countries, except for the British Virgin Islands, Cayman Islands and US Virgin Islands, where the PPP is assumed to be the same as the official exchange rate.

It is not difficult to explain the differential in GDP per head in the Caribbean. All countries of the region have a relatively high degree of openness to foreign trade, and there is a broad consensus that variations in export specialisation explain most of the income differentials.[36] In addition, the nonindependent countries have certain special advantages because of privileged market access and transfers from the metropolis. If these advantages are captured using dummy variables,[37] it is possible to show that most of the variation in GDP per head comes from (a) the degree of export dependence, (b) the types of exports in which the country is specialised, and (c) the dummy variables.[38] Other variables – such as the role of education, the rule of law and the quality of institutions – are not so important.[39]

We find therefore that the richest countries in the Caribbean (see Figure 15.5) are not only very trade dependent, but are also specialised in service

[36] See the references in notes 22 and 23.

[37] This is a rather lazy technique used in econometrics to capture differences between countries without trying to explain why they are different. Despite this, however, it can occasionally be a powerful statistical tool.

[38] A multiple regression run by the author with GDP per head in 2008 as the dependent variable and (a) the share of total exports in GDP, (b) the share of services in total exports, (c) dummy variables for (i) British territories, (ii) French territories, (iii) Dutch territories, and (iv) US territories as independent variables 'explains' 60% of the variation in GDP per head, with each coefficient having the expected sign.

[39] See Nicholls, S. (2001).

exports. Furthermore, all but one of the ten richest countries are nonindependent countries – the exception (the Bahamas) being highly specialised in service exports. By contrast, the bottom ten countries are all independent and are specialised either in natural resources (e.g. Suriname) or in manufactured goods (e.g. Haiti). Thus, in the Caribbean at least there is no correlation between income per head and the degree of specialisation in manufactured exports, and continuing specialisation in natural resources appears to be a distinct disadvantage. Even the energy-rich Trinidad & Tobago fails to appear in the top ten countries despite its specialisation in oil and gas exports.

The explanations for the variation in GDP per head do not identify the causal mechanism at work. However, all countries in the region – even Cuba now – are open to direct foreign investment (DFI). Indeed, most countries have always relied on DFI to supplement low levels of domestic savings and promote higher levels of investment than would otherwise be possible. Thus, part of the GDP does not accrue to nationals, and it is therefore necessary to take account of the share of GDP that is received by nonresidents. This, when expressed in net terms, is known as the GNI, and it measures the gross income of residents after adding to GDP their factor income from abroad (but not remittances) and deducting the income of nonresidents.[40]

In most OECD countries the gap between GDP and GNI is very minor. This is also the case in Cuba, where nonresident income is still minimal and many foreign investors have struggled to make profits since DFI was permitted in the mid-1980s.[41] However, the gap is large in almost all other Caribbean countries.[42] It is especially high in the US territories. In Puerto Rico, GNI is only two-thirds of GDP as a result of the high proportion of gross trading profits accruing to nonresident companies. Furthermore, the trend in the gap between GNI and GDP in both Puerto Rico and the Caribbean appears to have been growing since 1970 (see Figure 15.6), although there was a modest improvement after 2004.

The growing gap since 1970 between GNI and GDP in the Caribbean reflects among other things the increase in DFI, but the gap could well be much bigger than implied by Figure 15.6. The reason is that in most Caribbean countries there are many wealthy residents who have dual nationality and who have found ways of accruing income outside the country without it being classified as nonresident by the authorities. This problem is particularly acute in the area of real estate. In addition, the authorities tend to focus only on the large foreign investors in calculating GNI, while making no adjustment for the many expatriate individuals whose factor income strictly speaking should be excluded.

It follows that GNI for the Caribbean could well be as much as 20 per cent below GDP when these adjustments are taken into account (even without any

---

[40] GNI is the expression now used for what used to be Gross National Product (GNP).
[41] On DFI in Cuba, see Pérez (2004).
[42] The gap in the Caribbean between GNI and GDP is typically around 5–10%.

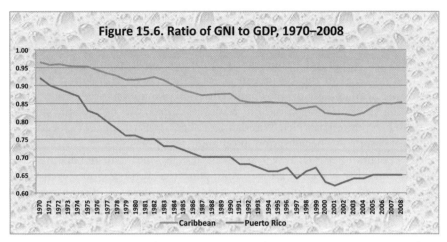

Source: United Nations National Accounts (UNNA) Web site using current price GDP and GNI data in US dollars. The Caribbean is the sum of all Caribbean countries in the UNNA database (only the French territories and the US Virgin Islands are excluded).

adjustments it was 15 per cent lower in 2008 – see Figure 15.6). Yet average income per head in the Caribbean is still relatively high by world standards. If the average income of residents today is around $4,000 rather than $5,000 (see Figure 15.4), this amounts to more than $10 per day, and the figure would be even higher if PPP exchange rates were used. Because the international benchmark of halving extreme poverty in the first Millennium Development Goal (MDG) is set at $1.25 per day (PPP), there should be little or no room for the kind of poverty levels that blight other parts of the developing world. With the exception of Haiti, where indigence is widespread as a result of low average income, this is generally the case in the Caribbean.[43]

The international benchmarks, including the poverty line used by the World Bank of $2 per day (PPP), set the bar too low. Given the price levels in the Caribbean, it is virtually impossible to survive on less than $2 per day. Most Caribbean countries recognise this and instead use a poverty line based on national criteria, which is much higher than the ones used in international comparisons by the World Bank.[44] In the Dominican Republic, for example, where both are published, nearly half the population is classified as poor on the national criteria, but the World Bank figure is a little over 10 per

---

[43] Extreme poverty in Haiti, before the earthquake in 2010, was estimated at 54.7% of the population, using the MDG figure of $1.25 per day (PPP). See UN MDG Indicators Web site.

[44] CARICOM states have tried to establish homogeneous regional benchmarks to measure progress towards the MDG. These are not reported here because they are not in practice widely used.

cent.[45] Similarly, in Guyana over one-third of the population is classified as poor on national criteria, but it is 50 per cent less using the international benchmark.[46]

Using **national** criteria, poverty is widespread in the Caribbean. In Table 15.3 countries have been ranked by the proportion of the population classified as poor. Most countries are in the range from 10 to 50 per cent.[47] The data are not strictly comparable because the poverty line is drawn differently in each country.[48] However, countries with relatively high average incomes, such as the French territories or some of the British Overseas Territories should not have such high levels of poverty. Even in some of the independent countries, such as Belize, Dominica and Suriname, poverty is higher than might be expected on the basis of average income alone. Table 15.3 also provides data on the poverty gap, which measures the gap between the average income of the poor and the poverty line itself.[49]

Because poverty is serious even in many countries with high average income, the working hypothesis is that income is very unequally distributed in these cases. That is exactly what turns out to be the case. Using the Gini coefficient,[50] the degree of income inequality is generally very high in the Caribbean (see Table 15.3). The worst case is Haiti, but others with high Gini coefficients are Puerto Rico and Suriname.[51] In these countries the distribution of income is as unequal as anywhere in the world and compares (unfavourably) with the most unequal countries of mainland Latin America.[52] Furthermore, there is no evidence that income distribution has improved. On the contrary, it has stayed the same or even deteriorated in those countries with frequent estimates.[53] That is certainly the case in Cuba, where income distribution was one of the most equal in the world until the mid-1980s, but it is now only average by the standards of the Caribbean.[54]

---

[45] See WDI.

[46] See WDI.

[47] Only Haiti is above 50%, and this is based on the World Bank benchmark of $2 per day (PPP).

[48] In calculating national poverty lines, the cost of a minimum bundle of food is first estimated and then an adjustment is made for minimum nonfood expenditure. This means that national poverty lines can vary greatly, because the cost of food and the importance given to nonfood expenditure are different in each country.

[49] See Bulmer-Thomas (1996), chap. 1.

[50] This is one of the most common measures of inequality, and it varies from zero (complete equality) to unity (complete inequality).

[51] The Gini coefficient in Table 15.3 for Suriname refers to 1999. However, there is a higher figure (0.549) for 2004 in Sno (2008).

[52] The highest Gini coefficients in mainland Latin America in 2007–8 were 57.2 in Bolivia, 55.0 in Brazil, 51.6 in Mexico and 50.5 in Peru. See WDI.

[53] The Gini coefficient was 47.8 in the Dominican Republic in 1986 compared with 48.4 in 2007. In Jamaica it went from 43.2 in 1988 to 45.5 in 2004. See WDI.

[54] The Gini was estimated at 24.0 in 1986, but had fallen to 38.0 fifteen years later (Espina Prieto, 2004).

TABLE 15.3. *Income Distribution and Poverty, c.2005*

Country	Year	Population % Poor (a)	Poverty Gap (b)	Share of Bottom 20% (c)	Share of Top 20%	Gini Coefficient (d)
Haiti	2001	72.2	41.8	2.5	63.0	59.5
DR	2007	48.5	16.8	4.4	53.8	48.3
Belize	2009	43.0	10.8	5.8	48.8	42.0
Dominica	2002	39.0	10.2	5.4	44.6	35.0
Grenada	2008	37.7	10.1	7.3	45.7	37.0
Guyana	1998	36.9	16.2	4.3	50.1	43.2
St Vincent	2008	30.0				
St Lucia	2005	28.8	9.0	5.1	39.3	42.0
Suriname	1999	27.2	11.7	3.1	57.4	52.8
Fr. Guiana	2006	26.5	9.8	7.1	42.9	30.7
Turks &. Caicos Is.	1999	26.0	5.7			37.0
Anguilla	2002	23.0	6.9	6.5	39.7	31.0
BVI	2002	22.0	4.1	6.1	46.6	23.0
St Kitts	2007	21.8	6.4	6.3	47.7	39.7
Martinique	2006	19.8	5.7	6.9	40.6	30.8
Antigua	2005	18.3	6.6	4.5	55.3	47.6
Guadeloupe	2006	17.8	5.3	7.3	38.2	28.8
Trinidad	2005	16.7	4.6	5.5		39.0
Jamaica	2005	16.0		4.6	51.2	38.0
Barbados	1996	14.0	2.3			41.0
Puerto Rico	1999	11.0		2.6	50.4	57.4
Bahamas	2001	9.3				46.0
Cayman Is.	2007	1.9		5.8		39.9
Aruba	2000			4.8	45.6	40.0
Cuba	See Sources			5.4	36.6	38.0

Note: (a) 'Population % poor' is the headcount index of poverty based on the national poverty line, except for Haiti and Suriname where it is $2 per day (PPP); countries are ranked in terms of this index (there are, however, no data for Aruba and Cuba); (b) 'poverty gap' measures the gap between the average income of the poor and the poverty line; (c) 'share of bottom/top 20%' is based on either income or expenditure with household data adjusted to individual data wherever possible.

Source: World Bank databases (WDI and MDG); Caribbean Development Bank (Poverty Assessment Reports); INSEE (2009) for French territories with Gini coefficients estimated by author from quintile data; Howard (2006) for Barbados; CEPAL (2004) for Puerto Rico; Aruba Central Bureau of Statistics for Aruba (Web site); St Vincent from latest national Poverty Assessment Reports on the Caribbean Development Bank Web site; data for Cuba from Espina Prieto (2004). There are no useable data for Montserrat, USVI and Netherlands Antilles.

As a further check on the degree of inequality in the Caribbean, we can use one of the indicators for the first MDG. This is the share of income received by the bottom quintile and is shown in Table 15.3.[55] There are a few countries

[55] Some countries use share of expenditure rather than income.

(Haiti, Puerto Rico and Suriname) where this is low even by the standards of mainland Latin America.[56] Where it is not low, it tends to reflect some of the special conditions of the Caribbean, such as public transfers (as happens in the French territories),[57] remittances from abroad, which will be considered in the next section, and food subsidies in those countries where the share of the bottom quintile is measured using expenditure rather than income.

Where income is unequally distributed and the bottom quintile receives a relatively high share, the inevitable conclusion is that the top quintile is likely to have benefitted disproportionately. This turns out to be the case (see Table 15.3). In the Dominican Republic, for example, the most recent figure for the share of the top quintile is above 50 per cent.[58] It is a similar story in Guyana and Suriname, but data refer only to the late 1990s. In Jamaica the share has exceeded 50 per cent since the start of the millennium.[59] In the French territories, Anguilla, Aruba, Cuba and St Lucia, however, the share of the top quintile is much more modest, suggesting that there is nothing inevitable about high income inequality in the Caribbean.

The extent of poverty and the unequal distribution of income in many countries of the Caribbean is an illustration of the flaws in the dominant economic model. It may be capable of increasing production – as measured by GDP – at a satisfactory rate, but it has failed to distribute income in an equitable fashion in most countries. And, just as there has been a trade-off between production and sovereignty in some countries, there has been a trade-off between production and distribution in others. The French territories, for example, have performed comparatively well in terms of income distribution,[60] but not so successfully in terms of production. The same could be said of Cuba. Only the British Virgin Islands has increased GDP rapidly, with a low Gini coefficient and modest poverty levels, but it is not an independent country.[61]

Poverty and the distribution of income have not received as much attention in the Caribbean as in mainland Latin America.[62] We are therefore less knowledgeable about the causes. Clearly, there are some factors in common. The tax system, for example, is not designed to redistribute income, and most adults do not in any case pay income tax. There are serious educational and skill deficits, which lead to great inequality in the distribution of wage income.

---

[56] The share of the bottom quintile in mainland Latin America in 2007–8 was 2.7 in Bolivia, 3.0 in Brazil, 3.6 in Peru and 3.8 in Mexico. See WDI.

[57] Most of the income of the bottom **three** quintiles consists of public transfers in the French territories, and in the case of the **lowest** quintile these transfers account for nearly all income. See INSEE (2009).

[58] It was above 55% in most years after 1990.

[59] See WDI.

[60] The share of the top quintile in 2006 was around 40% in all three countries (see INSEE (2009)); the share of the bottom quintile and the Gini coefficient are given in Table 15.3.

[61] The poverty rate in the BVI appears high at 22.0 (see Table 15.3), but this is because of the unusual national poverty line in which food accounts for only 27% of minimum income. There is no indigence in the BVI.

[62] For Latin America, see Székely and Montes (2006).

There are monopolistic and oligopolistic forces at work in the product market, which generate returns on capital that contain an element of economic rent.

Yet there are also elements that are peculiar to the Caribbean. The region suffers from high rates of open unemployment – especially among the poorly educated young – that are reflected in the low incomes earned by those in the bottom deciles. These can be offset to some extent by transfers of one sort or another, as in the French territories, but most governments lack the resources to do this and have no control over the destination of remittances. This is not a new problem, but it has grown worse in recent decades because the region has switched to a service-based economy in which the wage rate has adjusted to the supply and demand for international services rather than – as before – to the world market for primary products and where the 'reservation' wage rate has risen for various reasons. These issues are examined in the next section.

15.3. THE LABOUR MARKET, MIGRATION AND REMITTANCES

The Caribbean is no stranger to surplus labour. It began to appear at the end of slavery in a small number of countries and became widespread in the last two decades of the nineteenth century.[63] Throughout the twentieth century most countries suffered from surplus labour, and the problem has **not** disappeared as the growth rate of the population has declined. Only a handful of countries have avoided this fate in recent decades, and they are all very small. Surplus labour is a constant reminder that the Caribbean economic model may have delivered a relatively high level of GDP per head, but it has failed to provide adequate levels of employment for the region's citizens.

Surplus labour at first manifested itself in net outward migration.[64] In Barbados and the Cayman Islands, for example, ex-slaves were leaving for other countries as soon as the apprenticeship period was over. Gradually, however, surplus labour began to show up in other ways. The most important were the 'dead' months for seasonal workers, the growth of an informal sector[65] and disguised unemployment in the formal sector. These are still important, but a new manifestation of surplus labour – open unemployment – has become particularly acute in many countries.

The low demand for labour outside the harvest season was especially serious in the sugar industry. With the introduction of the *central* and mechanisation in many parts of the industry, employers needed a large labour force for only a few months a year. It was not generally in their interest that workers should have a second job because this could interfere with the supply of labour during the harvest. Cuba before the Revolution was very badly hit by this phenomenon,

---

[63] See Chapter 3.

[64] Defined as the difference between net births and population change in a given period.

[65] There is no universally accepted definition of the informal sector in the Caribbean, but it is normally associated with unregistered self-employment and/or small-scale establishments (usually outside the tax net). See World Bank (2005), p. 121.

but other countries suffered too. With the absolute decline of the sugar industry, this problem has diminished. However, the seasonal demand for labour is still a serious issue as a result of the needs of the tourist industry, where labour is not required at the same rate throughout the year.[66]

The informal sector has evolved in the Caribbean along similar lines to its development in mainland Latin America, where it has become very significant.[67] Indeed, in three countries – Dominican Republic, Guyana and Jamaica – informal-sector employment is estimated to be around 40 per cent of total employment.[68] It is probably even higher in Haiti, but there are no reliable figures.[69] Informality is found in almost all sectors of the economy, as a detailed study of Jamaica makes clear,[70] but it is not as widespread as in mainland Latin America and – with the exception of the three countries mentioned – affects a smaller share of the labour force. In Barbados, for example, a small society where social policies are designed to keep working-age people in the formal sector or in full-time education, informality only affects around 10 per cent of the labour force.[71]

Disguised unemployment was once assumed to be limited to agriculture.[72] It is still important in a few countries, especially Haiti, where almost certainly a large part of the labour force could be withdrawn from the sector without a loss of output. As the importance of agriculture has declined, however, disguised unemployment has tended to show up elsewhere. One of its most important manifestations has been in the public sector, because governments increased payrolls in response to political and social pressures. The most extreme example of this has been Cuba, where perhaps one-quarter of the labour force could be withdrawn from the state sector without much – if any – loss in output.[73] Inflated public-sector payrolls are also very important in the French territories[74] and in some of the smaller islands, such as Antigua and Barbados, where the competition between political parties is especially acute.[75]

---

[66] More than half of tourist arrivals normally occur between December and May. The months of September and October are especially quiet. See CTO Web site (monthly arrivals).

[67] See Stallings and Peres (2000), chap. 5, and ILO, Key Indicators of the Labour Market (Web site).

[68] See World Bank (2005), table 6.1.

[69] Even before the earthquake in January 2010, the formal sector was estimated to account for only a small part of total employment.

[70] See Witter (2005).

[71] See World Bank (2005), table 6.1.

[72] Arthur Lewis' model of a dual economy focused in particular on disguised unemployment in agriculture. See Lewis (1954).

[73] In August 2009, President Raúl Castro gave a speech referring to the possibility that 1 million public-sector workers – 20% of the labour force (95% of whom are employed by the state) – might be surplus to requirements. In September 2010, it was announced that 500,000 of these would lose their jobs in the next few months.

[74] The informal sector is much less important in the French territories than in the rest of the Caribbean, and thus the state has been under even greater pressure to deliver public-sector jobs. See Daniel (2001).

[75] See World Bank (2005), fig. 6.2.

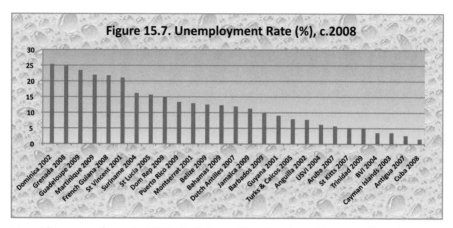

Figure 15.7. Unemployment Rate (%), c.2008

Note: There are no figures for Haiti; the Suriname figure is estimated by author from the number of unemployed, assuming a labour force of 90,000.

Source: For independent countries WDI, ECLAC (2010), CARICOM Secretariat, Caribbean Development Bank (CDB), ILO, Key Indicators of the Labour Market (Web site), and national statistics offices; for French territories, INSEE; for British territories, CDB; for US territories, Portal de la Junta de Planificación de Puerto Rico and Virgin Islands, Bureau of Economic Research; for Dutch territories, CBS-Aruba and ILO, Caribbean database.

With all these manifestations of surplus labour, it is not surprising that some of the poor are found among the employed. These are the 'working poor', and they constitute many of those in poverty in every country.[76] Indeed, in Haiti almost all the poor are in this category because unemployment is not a realistic option.[77] Since 1960, however, an increasing proportion of the poor are to be found among the openly unemployed. This phenomenon, virtually unknown in the region a century ago and still comparatively rare in mainland Latin America, is now common in almost all Caribbean countries (see Figure 15.7).

National definitions of the unemployed vary, but there are sufficient commonalities to make comparisons legitimate.[78] There are no less than six countries, including all three French territories, where the rate of (open) unemployment exceeds 20 per cent. There are an additional ten where it exceeds 10 per cent. And among the remaining eleven countries (there are no figures for Haiti), there are two – Cuba and Guyana – with a major problem of disguised unemployment. It is only in some of the smallest countries – the Cayman Islands,

[76] The proportion varies from country to country. See the Poverty Assessment Reports on the Web site of the CDB.

[77] There are no unemployment figures for Haiti, but the number is likely to be very low.

[78] The ILO defines 'unemployed' as all persons above a specified age who during the reference period were: (a) without work; (b) currently available for work; and (c) seeking work. For many years Jamaica used a definition that was significantly different from the rest of the Caribbean, but it has now followed other countries, and the unemployment rate has fallen as a consequence. See World Bank (2005), annex 6.1, and ECLAC (2010).

British Virgin Islands and Antigua – that open unemployment is not a serious issue.

Unemployment is therefore widespread in the Caribbean. Not surprisingly, a great deal of attention has been paid to the problem. The unemployed, it would seem, are more likely to be young (fifteen to twenty-four), female, from large families and poorly educated.[79] In recognition of this, governments have gone to great lengths to tackle the problem through various schemes. At first, the easiest solution was to expand public-sector payrolls, but the fiscal difficulties in many countries in and after the 1990s made this impossible. Now much more emphasis is placed on education, training and apprenticeships. As a result, coupled with faster growth, the rate of unemployment actually declined in a few countries – especially in Trinidad & Tobago.[80] Yet it is still too high, and the fact that labour force growth will eventually fall – in line with past population growth – is small consolation.[81]

High rates of unemployment occur when workers prefer to seek jobs rather than take work that pays less than their 'reservation' wage. One reason for this is that job seeking is time-consuming, and the only chance of well-paid work is to have the hours needed to devote to the search. This phenomenon was often associated with public-sector jobs, which typically pay a premium over equivalent jobs in the private sector and provide more job security. This is less prevalent today, because public-sector jobs have declined in so many countries. This has not ended the notion of a reservation wage, however, which is underpinned by a combination of social security payments, private transfers and the probability of finding work through outward migration.

Migration, as we have repeatedly seen, has been a hugely important part of the Caribbean story, and it has continued to be so in the period since 1960. The most intense period of net outward migration was in the 1960s, when the Cuban exodus accelerated.[82] However, the rate of net outward migration from other parts of the Caribbean was even faster than from Cuba, with the rate exceeding 1 per cent of the population annually in CARICOM and the British territories and not much lower in the French and US territories (see Table 15.4).[83]

These rates of net outward migration could not be sustained, and the rate for the Caribbean declined in every decade after the 1960s (see Table 15.4). This has partly been caused by the fall in the natural rate of growth of the population, because the region's birth rate has been dropping continuously

---

[79] PROBIT regression results on unemployment by country can be found in World Bank (2005), annex table 6.7.

[80] It fell from 12.2% in 2000 to 5.3% in 2009. See ECLAC (2010), table 1.2.17.

[81] There is always a lag between the fall in the rate of growth of the population and the fall in the rate of growth of the labour force, even if the participation rate is unchanged.

[82] Cubans had been emigrating before. See Chapter 10.

[83] The high rate in the US territories in the 1960s was because of Puerto Rico, where the annual rate in the 1960s was 0.83%. By contrast, there was net inward migration in the USVI.

TABLE 15.4. *Net Outward Migration per Year as Percentage of Population, 1961–2008*

				Territories:				
	Hispaniola	Cuba	CARICOM	British	French	Dutch	US	Caribbean
1961–1970	0.26	0.56	1.16	0.72	0.89	0.34	0.70	0.59
1971–1980	0.36	0.34	1.23	−0.72	1.17	0.67	0.07	0.49
1981–1990	0.43	0.28	1.00	−1.65	−0.38	0.60	0.33	0.45
1991–2000	0.37	0.23	0.68	−1.46	0.07	0.41	0.18	0.35
2001–2008	0.30	0.31	0.45	−2.90	−0.09	−0.59	0.13	0.29

Source: Derived from Tables D.1, D.2 and D.3.

since 1962.[84] It has also been because of the increasing restrictions placed by the core on inward migration from the Caribbean.[85] Only citizens of the US, French and Dutch territories now enjoy unrestricted access to the 'mother' country, and Cubans are no longer as welcome in the United States as they were during the Cold War.[86] The core increasingly targets those immigrants it wants rather than the other way round, and therefore migrants to North America and Europe tend to be richer and better educated, leading to a serious drain of financial and human capital from the Caribbean.[87]

In some subregions there has been net **inward** migration. This happened in the British territories in every decade since 1960, with the new arrivals coming mainly from the rest of the Caribbean.[88] A large part of the current population of the Turks & Caicos Islands, for example, has come from Haiti, and the same is true of the Bahamas.[89] It has also been true of the French territories in some decades, with these countries experiencing very high rates of unemployment and net inward migration at the same time.[90] And the Dutch territories, after a long period of net outward migration, enjoyed net inward migration after 2000 in response to improved economic conditions. There has also been net inward migration into some of the smaller countries since 2000, including Antigua, Bahamas, Barbados, St Kitts & Nevis and St Lucia.

[84] The CBR peaked at 39.4 in 1962. It had fallen to 18.7 by 2008. See Table D.2.

[85] See Thomas-Hope (2002), Byron and Condon (2008) and Palmer (2009).

[86] The Clinton administration in 1995 adopted the 'wet-foot, dry-foot' policy under which Cubans would only receive refugee status if they first reached dry land in the mainland US. Those found at sea would be returned.

[87] See World Bank (2005), chap. 6.

[88] In addition, some migrants came from rich countries in response to the opportunities offered by the expanding service sectors, especially finance.

[89] Haitians constitute around one-quarter of the population in the Bahamas and nearly half in the Turks & Caicos Islands.

[90] Especially French Guiana, which has had net inward migration in every decade since 1960. There was also net inward migration into Guadeloupe in the 1980s.

Overall, however, the Caribbean has continued to lose population through migration, and the numbers are striking. If there had been no (net) outward migration after 1960, the population fifty years later would have been 53 million – nearly 10 million higher than it actually was.[91] Nor should we forget those that left before 1960. It is therefore not surprising that the Puerto Rican population outside Puerto Rico (4 million) is estimated to be as large as that on the island[92] and that the US Census in 2000 estimated another 3 million from the Caribbean among the total immigrant population (the 2010 Census is expected to show a much higher figure).[93] In addition, there are at least 1.5 million of Caribbean origin in the UK,[94] nearly half a million in France[95] and perhaps a similar figure in each of Holland, Spain and Canada.[96]

The sheer number of migrants outside the Caribbean has led to a significant flow of remittances back to the region (the estimated value of these flows should be regarded as the minimum, because part of it is undocumented). These flows have risen as official development assistance has declined. When expressed as a percentage of GDP, they exceed 20 per cent in some countries. The highest ratio is found in Guyana (see Figure 15.8), closely followed by Haiti. For nearly half the countries of the Caribbean, it exceeds 5 per cent of GDP. Cuba, however, is not among those countries, because remittances from the United States (the principal source) were restricted under the Bush administration (2001–9), and the Cuban government taxed receipts in dollars until 2011.[97]

The flow of remittances has helped to alleviate poverty in the Caribbean, because at least some of it reaches the bottom deciles.[98] It has boosted investment, encouraged start-up businesses by small entrepreneurs and allowed some children to continue in education. It has also helped the poor to avoid dependence on a cash-strapped state that has not always been very successful at reaching those most in need. Yet it is also a severe reminder that the Caribbean economic model has failed to provide the jobs that the region's citizens have the right to expect. And as more resources are poured into education, the perverse result is obtained whereby the better educated migrate outside the region and the worst educated are unable to find jobs that meet their reservation wage.[99] Breaking this vicious cycle is one of the main challenges the region now faces.

---

[91] Because there has been some inward migration, especially to Trinidad & Tobago, the gross outward migration must have been even higher.
[92] See Duany (2002).
[93] See World Bank (2005), chap. 6.
[94] See Byron and Condon (2008).
[95] See Crusol (2007).
[96] Canadian figure from World Bank (2005). Most of those in Holland are from Suriname (see van Dijck 2001). Spain has always attracted a large number of Cubans.
[97] The Cuban government delegalised the US dollar in 2004, and at the same time imposed a tax on the exchange of US dollars for Cuban currency. See Notes on D. Tables.
[98] See Nurse (2004).
[99] See Nicholls, S. (2001).

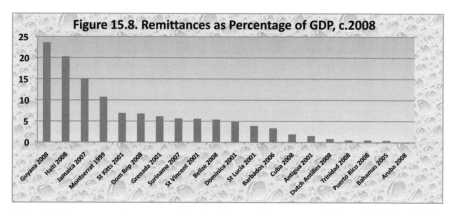

Note: Remittances are those reported in the balance of payments and then divided by GDP in Table D.18. For some countries (e.g. Puerto Rico), remittances are given as **net** private transfers and are therefore underestimates; I have not reported the data for those countries (e.g. Anguilla) where net private transfers are outward rather than inward; for Cuba, I have assumed remittances of $1.2 billion in 2008 (for earlier estimates, see Togores and García (2004), p. 252).

Source: For independent countries (except Cuba) and Dutch territories: WDI, CEPAL (2010) and Caribbean Development Bank (CDB); for Cuba, see note; for British territories, CDB; for US territories, Portal de la Junta de Planificación de Puerto Rico. There are no reliable data for USVI and French territories.

15.4. THE ENVIRONMENT AND SUSTAINABLE DEVELOPMENT

Long before the arrivals of humans in the Caribbean,[100] its environment had been transformed on a regular basis by natural disasters. These included tsunamis, hurricanes, earthquakes, volcanic eruptions and drought. Since the arrival of the Europeans in 1492, the impact of these natural disasters has been part of recorded history, and their devastation has continued right up to the present era.[101] The earthquake in Haiti in January 2010, which killed tens of thousands of people and displaced over a million, was a particularly brutal illustration of the power of nature in the Caribbean, but there have been many others, and they have often had major implications for society. Hurricane Hattie in Belize in 1961, for example, led to the relocation of the capital inland to Belmopan; the 1995 volcanic eruption in Montserrat nearly led to the complete evacuation of the island; and persistent drought in the Virgin Islands (US and British) was largely responsible for the demise of the sugar industry and the early rise of service exports.

---

[100] The first humans are estimated to have reached the Caribbean around 6,000 years ago. See Higman (2011).

[101] See Watts (1987).

Human action has also had a major impact on the environment of the Caribbean. The population of the Caribbean at the time of the arrival of Columbus was already large, but it would fall rapidly following the destructive actions of the Europeans and would not recover its level of 1492 for at least 400 years.[102] During the period of Taino civilisation, many species of fauna were rendered extinct, contributing to the low biodiversity of the region.[103] Yet the system of agriculture practised by the indigenous population, based on *conucos*, ensured that much of the forest cover was preserved and permitted a great floral diversity.[104] Indeed, many plant species in the Caribbean islands are endemic, with endemism reaching an impressive 50 per cent in Cuba.[105]

The arrival of the European plantation changed the relationship between man and the Caribbean environment in a very destructive way.[106] Forests were cleared to make way for export crops, vegetation was stripped from hills and mountains for the same reason, many fauna were hunted to extinction and the number of floral species shrank significantly. The biodiversity of the islands, never very high outside the Greater Antilles, fell to insignificant levels. Even in the larger islands (except Cuba) and the mainland countries, biodiversity has dropped to dismal levels. A recently constructed Biodiversity Potential Index (see Figure 15.9) shows not only that the index has a very low value in the Caribbean, but that it has continued to fall in most countries since it was first developed.[107]

The spread of plantation agriculture under European imperialism was associated from the very beginning with deforestation. Small islands, such as Barbados, had become almost completely denuded by the end of the seventeenth century. The destruction of the virgin forests of Haiti was very advanced even before independence in 1804.[108] When peasant agriculture gained a foothold in some countries after the end of slavery, it continued this destructive process, because forests were now needed for fuel and for the land they occupied.[109] Improvements in transport, especially the railways in Cuba, led to an acceleration in deforestation, because more lands could now be cleared profitably to make way for sugar. Finally, as the rate of increase of the population accelerated after the mid-nineteenth century, with much higher levels of population density than had prevailed before, the pressure to chop down the forests became even greater.

[102] A conservative estimate of the population in 1492 would suggest around 3 million in Hispaniola and as much again elsewhere. See Watts (1987), Wilson (1997) and Higman (2011). Much higher estimates are found in Borah and Cook (1971).

[103] The Taino culture flourished in the Greater Antilles and the Bahamas for nearly 2,000 years before Columbus. See Wilson (1997).

[104] The *conuco* was an artificial mound and was the basis of the shifting cultivation used by the indigenous population to provide a plentiful supply of food.

[105] See Watts (1987) and Higman (2011).

[106] See Watts (1987).

[107] It has a maximum value of 100 (assumed to be found only in Brazil).

[108] See Lundahl (1979), pp. 195–6, quoting Moreau de Saint-Mery.

[109] The timber was used to make charcoal.

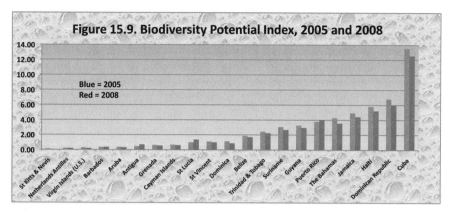

Figure 15.9. Biodiversity Potential Index, 2005 and 2008

Note: The Global Environmental Facility (GEF) Benefits Index for biodiversity is a composite index of relative biodiversity potential for each country based on the species represented in each country, their threat status and the diversity of habitat types in each country. The index has been normalised so that values run from zero (no biodiversity potential) to 100 (maximum biodiversity potential).

Source: Dev Pandey et al. (2006). Data updated to 2008 (available on World Bank Web site).

Under these circumstances, it would not be surprising to find that the forests had virtually disappeared. That has happened in a few countries, but in general the proportion of land area covered by forest today is not negligible (see Figure 15.10). Indeed, for the Caribbean as a whole the figure is two-thirds.[110] This is because of the importance of the large mainland countries of South America (French Guiana, Guyana and Suriname), where the high proportions are caused primarily by low population densities. Yet half the countries of the Caribbean have managed to retain over 40 per cent of the land in forests and only in four is it less than 10 per cent (see Figure 15.10).

There are many reasons for this, but one of the most important has been the decline of agriculture – especially sugar – and the rise of services. The latter, as we shall see, bring their own environmental problems. However, the collapse of plantation agriculture in most countries has at least eased the pressure on the forests. Indeed, the proportion of the land area that is forested has **increased** in some countries in recent years. In Cuba, for example, where the sugar industry has gone into decline, it has risen by one-third since 1990.[111] It is mainly in Belize, where the pressure on the forests is exacerbated by illegal logging, peasant farming and the continuation of plantation agriculture, that deforestation continues at a rapid rate.[112]

Another consequence of the (absolute) decline of plantation agriculture has been the fall in the consumption of fertilizers. This peaked at the end of the

---

[110] This may be generous, because governments have a tendency to submit overoptimistic estimates of forest cover.
[111] See UN MDG Indicators Web site.
[112] See Cherrington et al. (2010).

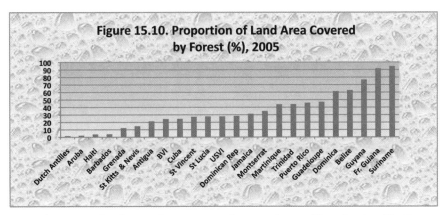

Figure 15.10. Proportion of Land Area Covered by Forest (%), 2005

Note: The UN MDG Indicators for some countries are estimates. Those for Anguilla, Cayman Islands and Turks & Caicos Islands in particular should be treated with caution. I have replaced the UN MDG figure for Belize with a more accurate number.

Source: UN MDG Indicators Web site, except for Belize, which is from Cherrington et al. (2010) and where data refer to 2010.

1980s (see Figure 15.11), and its decline in the 1990s was very marked.[113] There has been an especially strong fall in Cuba, because the island's consumption constitutes such a large part of that of the Caribbean as a whole, and is caused by the absolute decline of the sugar industry and by foreign exchange shortages for imports. However, the decline in consumption has been observed in many other countries also, such as Barbados (peak demand in 1981), Dominica (1991), Jamaica (1989) and Suriname (1986).[114]

The switch to services has been marked by the increasing importance of the tourist industry. With its emphasis on beaches, the tourist industry has put exceptional demands on the coastlines of Caribbean countries. Mangroves have been destroyed, coastal vegetation cleared and beaches have eroded as a consequence. Coral reefs have been damaged by human action.[115] The tourist industry also generates a very high demand for water, and some countries, such as Barbados, have exceeded safe levels of freshwater consumption.[116] Financial services, by contrast, make very low environmental demands on the countries where they are located, and some kinds of tourism are clearly much less destructive of the environment than others.[117]

Caribbean governments and the people to whom they are accountable are very conscious of these new pressures on the environment. As elsewhere in the

[113] See Thomas-Hope (2001).
[114] See WDI.
[115] There has also been severe damage from temperature changes and bleaching.
[116] Annual freshwater withdrawals as a percentage of internal resources reached 112% in 2007. See WDI.
[117] Ecotourism ought to be among these and generally is, but some activities carrying the 'eco' label put huge strains on the environment.

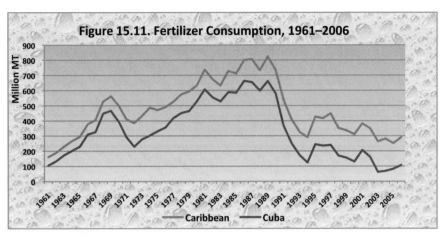

Figure 15.11. Fertilizer Consumption, 1961–2006

Note: The Caribbean is the sum of all countries reporting fertilizer consumption to the World Bank. There are no data for the British, Dutch and French territories, Puerto Rico, Antigua and Grenada. Where there were gaps in the series for reporting countries, I have estimated the values.
Source: WDI.

region, there has been an increase in the proportion of land and sea in protected areas, but it has usually started in the Caribbean from a very low base. Thus, the average (unweighted) for all Caribbean countries went from 3 per cent in 1990 to 5 per cent twenty years later.[118] However, only Belize and the Dominican Republic have a ratio above 20 per cent, and in both countries there are grave doubts over the ability of the state to provide adequate protection for such a large area.[119]

The switch from agriculture to services has not affected all countries equally, so it is no surprise that the 'carbon footprint' of the Caribbean differs by subregion (see Figure 15.12). The lowest has been in the British territories, where the specialisation in financial services has produced a level of carbon dioxide (CO_2) emissions per million dollars of GDP[120] that is roughly one-seventh of that in the Dutch territories and CARICOM (the latter is skewed upwards by the inclusion of energy-intensive Trinidad & Tobago together with the mining sectors in Guyana, Jamaica and Suriname). The French territories also have a low carbon footprint, which has fallen significantly since 1990 in line with the decline of the agricultural sector. The biggest fall, however, has been in Cuba where, since the peak in 1994, the decline of sugar and the rise of services led to a fall of 50 per cent in CO_2 emissions per million dollars of GDP in the next twelve years.[121]

[118] See UN MDG Indicators Web site.
[119] There has, for example, been a great deal of illegal logging, small-scale farming and Xate extraction in the Belize protected areas.
[120] At constant (2000) prices.
[121] The volume of emissions in Cuba has also fallen from the peak in 1990, but for the Caribbean as a whole they rose by one-third between 1990 and 2006. See WDI.

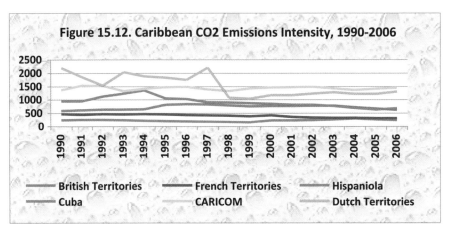

Figure 15.12. Caribbean CO2 Emissions Intensity, 1990-2006

Note: Figure 15.12 measures CO_2 emissions in metric tons per million US dollars of GDP at constant (2000) prices. The line for the British territories is based on BVI, Cayman Islands and Montserrat only, because data for Anguilla and Turks & Caicos Islands are incomplete.

Source: UN MDG Indicators Web site for emissions per head in metric tons (there are no data for US territories); GDP per head from Tables D.1a and D.19.

The Caribbean, with the exception of Haiti, does not suffer from the kind of extreme environmental degradation found in many other parts of the world. It does not generally experience the long-term droughts that ravage some countries in sub-Saharan Africa or the urban pollution that blights megacities in mainland Latin America and Asia. Yet its ecosystem is extremely fragile, and global warming could cripple what is left of the magnificent coral reefs found throughout the region. The Caribbean also faces the risk of a loss of territory in the future to rising sea levels, with grave implications for the tourist industry. The current global focus on the need for sustainable development is a timely reminder of the dependence of the Caribbean on a natural environment that offers unparalleled beauty, but which can never be taken for granted.

16

The Cuban Economy since the Revolution

There are several reasons for ending this book with a chapter on Cuba. First, the Cuban economy has been sui generis since the defeat of Batista at the end of 1958 and has not followed many of the trends found elsewhere in the Caribbean. Second, the performance of the Cuban economy in this period has often been misunderstood as a result of its different accounting systems and because of the extent of state control over prices and the allocation of resources. Third, the economy suffered a collapse after the fall of the Berlin Wall in 1989 that is almost without parallel in the history of the Caribbean. Yet, despite this, Cuba remains – as it always has been in the last 200 years – one of the two largest and most important economies in the region. What happens in Cuba is therefore of great importance for the region as a whole.

The first section of the chapter is devoted to the transition from capitalism to socialism in the years 1959 to 1963. These five years constitute a short period in terms of time, but this was the moment when the foundations of the new Cuba were laid. The tension between the island's government and the United States led to a rapid deterioration in the bilateral relationship and the emergence of the Soviet Union as a new strategic partner, together with China and Eastern Europe in lesser roles. The establishment of socialism was fraught with difficulties, and macroeconomic performance was poor, but Cuba was still able to make substantial progress on the social programs for which it is justly famous. At the same time, the transition introduced a number of structural problems, which have still not been overcome today.

The second section covers the quarter century from 1964 to 1989. This is usually broken down by scholars of Cuba into different periods, and it is true that there were sharp swings in performance and policy. Yet this was a period dominated by state planning in which the price mechanism played only a minor role and in which Cuba could count on solid support from its Communist allies in other parts of the world. The Cuban economy performed relatively well in these years – especially in the first half of the 1980s when mainland Latin America and part of the Caribbean was struggling with the aftermath of the

1982 debt crisis. This was also the period when Cuba returned to sugar as the key sector of the economy, despite the failure to achieve the target of 10 million tons in 1970.

Section 3 considers the fall of the Berlin Wall, the collapse of the Soviet Union and the end of the special trading arrangements, all of which caused the economy to go into a tailspin. Even those scholars who cast doubt on the reliability of Cuban statistics have no trouble in accepting the official version that GDP per head fell by nearly 40 per cent from peak to trough. As the economy started to decline, Fidel Castro launched the 'Special Period' – a moment of exceptional austerity designed to prevent the complete collapse of the socialist system on the island. A modest recovery in the second half of the 1990s was not enough to reverse all the decline, but the years after the millennium brought an improvement in economic performance in which Venezuelan and Chinese assistance would prove to be very helpful.

The final section of the chapter, which concludes the book, looks at the Cuban economy in relation to the rest of the Caribbean over the last two centuries. No country has experienced greater swings in its relative performance, and this has been a consequence of the island's extreme vulnerability – even by Caribbean standards – to external shocks. This vulnerability has been because of the importance of exports in GDP, the reliance on one or two commodities within exports and changes in the policy of the main trading partner. Cuba, even after fifty years of socialism, had not fully overcome these vulnerabilities, but the definitive decline of sugar after 2000 as the mainstay of the economy had created the best opportunity for a very long time.

16.1. FROM CAPITALISM TO SOCIALISM: 1959–1963

Batista seized power in 1952, in defiance of the 1940 constitution that he himself had introduced, but Cuba continued to receive economic, financial and military assistance from the United States. The Cuban economy performed poorly during his final tenure as a result primarily of the difficulties faced by sugar in world markets. The US sugar quota was reduced, prices drifted downwards and Batista's government even sold 500,000 tons to the Soviet Union in one year. In an effort to reduce costs, the length of the harvest was cut,[1] and unemployment in the sugar industry – already severe – became catastrophic.[2] The decline of the sugar industry led to difficulties for all those rural and urban activities dependent on it, Batista launched a wave of repression against any manifestations of discontent, and the stage was set for the collapse of a regime that was eventually abandoned even by the United States.[3]

---

[1] See Roca (1976), p. 34.
[2] See Rodríguez and Carriazo (1987), pp. 12–13.
[3] The Eisenhower administration suspended military supplies to Batista in March 1958. See Welch (1985), p. 30.

Fidel Castro was the undisputed leader of the Revolution, but he did not become prime minister until 13 February 1959 and would not engineer the appointment of a loyal supporter to the presidency until July.[4] The first six months were dedicated to policies that were radical but not exceptional by Latin American standards.[5] These included a reduction in rents by 50 per cent, the intervention of public utilities to reduce tariffs and the adoption of the first agrarian reform law.[6] This was aimed at giving title to the smallest farmers and breaking up the largest farms, many of them foreign-owned, and distributing the land to those that previously worked it – in cooperatives or state farms rather than small parcels.[7] Compensation was offered, but in the form of bonds rather than cash,[8] and many large landowners escaped altogether because the maximum size permitted was set generously.[9]

The Eisenhower administration (1953–61) was the first to recognise the new government,[10] but it proceeded cautiously. It did not offer to renew military supplies nor did it offer financial assistance. The United States was surprised, however, that Castro did not ask for foreign aid on his first trip to Washington, DC, in April, and Vice President Nixon formed the view that Castro was unreliable from the US perspective.[11] This perspective hardened in the second half of the year when the 26th of July Movement[12] split into reformists and radicals. Castro sided with the latter and brought known Communists into his government, despite his previous distrust of their party.[13] Crucially, however, the sugar quota was not changed, and the United States contented itself with precautionary measures that included establishing contacts with anti-Castro

---

[4] The first president of Cuba after Batista fled was Manuel Urrutia, but he was replaced by Osvaldo Dorticós on July 18. See Karol (1971), pp. 572–3.

[5] Several of these measures had in fact been adopted in Cuba during the short-lived administration of President Grau San Martín (1933–4). See Pérez (1990).

[6] See Boorstein (1968), pp. 22–25.

[7] See Ghai, Kay and Peek (1988), pp. 8–11.

[8] The 1940 Constitution stated that compensation should be paid in cash, but no one expected this in view of the looting of the treasury by Batista when he fled. See Welch (1985), pp. 36–7.

[9] Not only was the maximum set at 30 *caballerías* (403 ha), but there were also exemptions up to 100 *caballerías* (1,342 ha) for the most efficient. See Huberman and Sweezy (1960), pp. 110–2.

[10] It did so on January 6, the day after President Urrutia was installed in Havana. See Welch (1985), p. 29.

[11] Castro was not on an official visit because he had accepted an invitation from the American Society of Newspaper Editors. Nevertheless, he did meet Nixon, who recorded his impressions of the meeting. See Welch (1985), pp. 34–5.

[12] This was the name given to the movement formed by Castro in Mexico in 1955 and named after the date of the storming of the Moncada barracks in 1953. At the time Fidel Castro was a member of the Orthodox Party. See Szulc (1986), pp. 147–51.

[13] The Partido Socialista Popular (PSP) was the name of the Communist Party in Cuba, and it did not support the 26th of July Movement until just before the fall of Batista. In particular, it failed to heed Castro's call for a general strike in March 1958, and without PSP support the strike was bound to fail. Relations between Castro and the PSP were therefore tense at first. See Sweig (2002), pp. 154–5.

groups and preparing the Organization of American States (OAS) for a possible rupture in the relationship with Cuba.[14]

The deterioration of the bilateral relationship accelerated rapidly in the following year. This began with the visit of the Soviet deputy prime minister, Anastas Mikoyan, to Havana, which led to a trade agreement, including an offer to buy 425,000 tons of sugar in 1960 and supply a limited amount of crude oil.[15] When the Eisenhower administration ordered US refineries on the island not to process the Soviet crude, they were all 'intervened', and immediately supplies were switched from Venezuela to the Soviet Union.[16] This was too much for President Eisenhower, who suspended the remainder of the Cuban sugar quota for 1960 on July 6.[17] Castro responded by nationalising those US companies that had not already been taken over.[18] In turn, Eisenhower imposed in October a trade embargo on Cuba, except for essential foods and medical supplies, and broke diplomatic relations in January 1961, just before handing over office to President Kennedy.

Any hopes that the new US president might be able to improve the bilateral relationship were ended when Kennedy immediately announced the continued suspension of the Cuban sugar quota and the maintenance of the trade embargo.[19] He also gave covert approval for the Bay of Pigs invasion by anti-Castro groups that took place in April 1961. It was a resounding failure, and Castro was left in a stronger position than before. The United States was forced to resort to multilateral measures that included the expulsion of Cuba from the OAS in January 1962 and pressure on other countries not to trade with the island.[20] It was only the discovery of Soviet missiles on the island that allowed Kennedy to recover the initiative and force the Soviet Union to withdraw them in October 1962 after promising not to invade Cuba.

---

[14] See Connell-Smith (1966), pp. 246–50.

[15] Mikoyan was en route to Mexico to open a trade fair, but he agreed to include Havana in his tour of the region at Cuba's request. The offer of crude oil by the Soviet Union was to pay for the import of sugar rather than precipitate a rupture between Cuba and the US, which did not suit the geopolitical purposes of the USSR at that point. See Karol (1971), pp. 188–9.

[16] Not all the refineries were US-owned, but they were all intervened anyway. This included the Anglo-Dutch Shell Company.

[17] At the time Cuba had already shipped 2,300,000 tons of its US import quota of 3,120,000 tons, leaving a balance of 820,000 tons, which it was then able to sell to the Soviet Union and its allies at a comparable price. See Welch (1985), p. 50. Nonetheless, in view of the dependence of the Cuban economy on sugar, this was an extremely aggressive act by the Eisenhower administration, and it gave Castro little incentive to act with restraint towards US interests in Cuba.

[18] It had already taken over some sugar mills, a textile factory, construction firms and the telephone company under an 'ill-gotten gains' law. See Boorstein (1968), p. 54.

[19] Because the sugar quota was set at zero at the beginning of the year, it was much more significant than the suspension by Eisenhower the previous July. Cuba now had no choice but to find alternative markets for all its sugar exports previously sold to the US.

[20] The OAS vote was 14 to 1 – just enough to force Cuba's expulsion – with Argentina, Bolivia, Brazil, Chile, Ecuador and Mexico abstaining. See Welch (1985), p. 97.

TABLE 16.1. *Cuban Trade with the United States and the USSR as Percentage of Merchandise Trade, 1959–1963*

	Exports		Imports	
	to US	to USSR	from US	from USSR
1959	69.9	2.0	68.2	0.001
1960	53.2	16.7	48.6	12.6
1961	5.6	48.6	2.0	37.4
1962	1.3	42.6	1.9	54.2
1963	0.02	30.1	4.6	53.2

Source: Tables C.15, C.22; Mesa-Lago (2000), p. 374; Carter (2006), vol. 5; and IMF, DOTS.

Although the Soviet Union had purchased Cuban sugar in the 1950s, this was a purely commercial transaction on both sides. The Cuban Revolution was not seen as heralding a radical new role for the USSR in the Caribbean, because it coincided with Khrushchev's pursuit of 'peaceful co-existence' with the United States. In any case, there was no certainty that the Revolution would survive in the face of US hostility. Trade in 1959 remained minimal (see Table 16.1), despite a tour of Eastern Europe by Ernesto Guevara,[21] and Cuba bought a mere $10,000 from the Soviet Union in that year.

The Soviet attitude to Cuba started to change early in 1960, and this was reflected in the trade pattern (see Table 16.1). Cuban exports to the Soviet Union – mainly sugar, but also minerals – rose sharply and so did imports from the USSR. The United States, however, remained the most important trade partner by far, despite the suspension of the sugar quota in July and the trade embargo in October. It was not until 1961 that trade with the United States collapsed and the Soviet Union became the main market for exports and source of imports. Furthermore, over 70 per cent of Cuban trade in that year was with socialist economies. These included the rest of COMECON[22] along with China, Albania, North Korea and Yugoslavia.[23]

The architects of the Revolution had no doubt that they wanted to diversify the Cuban economy, reduce its dependence on exports (especially sugar) and accelerate import substitution. The agrarian reform was therefore not only intended to break up the largest estates, but also to provide the opportunity to grow the products that Cuba had previously imported. The nationalisation of foreign-owned assets in industry, coupled with the

[21] Ernesto 'Che' Guevara was an Argentine who met Castro in Mexico in 1955. A Marxist from an early age, he was the first director of the Industrialization Department of the Instituto Nacional de Reforma Agraria (INRA) before becoming president of the National Bank in November 1959 and later minister of industry.
[22] The Council of Mutual Economic Assistance (COMECON) was the regional integration scheme that embraced the USSR and its Eastern European allies. Cuba joined in 1972.
[23] See Mesa-Lago (1981), p. 93.

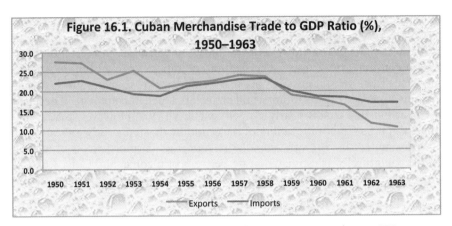

Source: Merchandise exports and imports from Tables C.6, C.18, D.6 and D.11. GDP at current prices from 1960 in Table D.18; for years before 1960, see Notes to D. Tables.

introduction of a planned economy,[24] was designed to replace many of the manufactured imports previously obtained from abroad.

Provided the reduction in export dependence was matched by an increase in import substitution, there was no reason for the economy to become unbalanced. However, this was not what happened. The share of exports in GDP fell rapidly after 1958 (see Figure 16.1), despite the fact that GDP itself was falling in most years (see below in this section). The import ratio also declined, but at nothing like the same rate, because it proved impossible to bring on stream the new industries outlined in the first plan. Thus, the large trade surplus of the 1950s had become a structural trade deficit by 1963 and required foreign finance to bridge the gap. This was an uncomfortable position for Cuba in view of the difficulties of obtaining credit from western sources.

Income distribution in Cuba before the Revolution – between rural and urban areas and between deciles – was very unequal, and its improvement became another target of the new government. This was the justification for many of the earliest measures, such as the reduction in rents and public utility prices. Land reform, however, had the greatest redistributive consequences because the workers previously employed for only a few months were now given permanent jobs.[25] A second agrarian reform in 1963, lowering the maximum size of landholding to 67 hectares (ha), took this a stage further.[26] New jobs were also being created in education, health and other public services as the state pushed ahead with its ambitious social goals, including the elimination of

[24] The planning framework was set by the Central Planning Board (JUCEPLAN), first established in March 1960.
[25] See Rodríguez and Carriazo (1987), pp. 61–9.
[26] See Ghai, Kay and Peek (1988), pp. 14–15.

illiteracy.[27] There was also a host of new jobs created as a result of the increase in defence and security expenditure.

All these changes coincided with continued outward migration, yet the population continued to grow.[28] The qualitative impact of migration was more important than the quantitative because of the exit of so many professionals with much-needed capital (human and financial). Open unemployment declined in Cuba, but it was still nearly 10 per cent in 1963.[29] However, purchasing power ran far ahead of the ability of the economy to supply the goods and services demanded. By 1962 the cumulative monetary surplus (excess of income over expenditure) was estimated at 90 per cent of income, and Cuba was suffering from a severe monetary overhang.[30] The Cuban government therefore faced a clear choice between inflation and rationing.

The decision to introduce rationing in 1962[31] may have protected those on lower incomes from a rise in the price of basic goods and services, but it had serious long-term consequences. The peasantry, whether in small-scale plots or cooperatives, was obliged to sell produce to the state at fixed prices without being able to buy much in return. The incentives to increase production were therefore undermined, farm labour productivity fell and Cuba continued to remain dependent on imported foodstuffs. Urban workers, their jobs now much more secure than before, also had little incentive to increase productivity, because the goods available through the ration book declined rather than increased.[32]

Under these circumstances, it was not surprising that GDP per head, already falling before the Revolution, continued to fall (see Figure 16.2). The decline was not dramatic, and there was even an increase in 1962. Furthermore, income distribution improved sharply.[33] However, the model was not sustainable, and the Cuban leadership was forced to engage in a serious debate about future policy in order to ensure that the economy did not shrink any further. The key ingredient in this debate was the role of exports, and Castro returned from a visit to the Soviet Union in 1963 to announce that sugar would once again play a pivotal role in the Cuban economy.

By the end of 1963, the Cuban government had gained control of the 'commanding heights' of the economy. One-quarter of retail trade was still in the hands of the private sector, but these were small stores. Nearly one-third of

---

[27] This included the famous adult literacy campaign in which volunteers toured the country teaching those who could not read (mainly peasants). It would become the model for other such experiments in Latin America.

[28] Net outward migration averaged 65,000 in 1960–2, yet the population still increased by more than 100,000 each year. See Mesa-Lago (2000), p. 388.

[29] See Mesa-Lago (2000), p. 385.

[30] See Rodríguez and Carriazo (1987), pp. 76–8.

[31] See Mesa-Lago (1981), pp. 157–60.

[32] The amount available in different years is shown in Mesa-Lago (2000), p. 387. See also Brundenius (1984), p. 118.

[33] See Brundenius (1984), pp. 180–1, and Mesa-Lago (2000), p. 385.

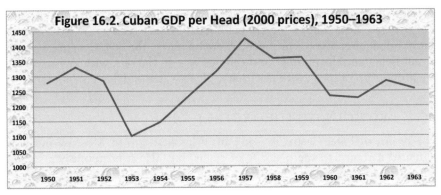

Figure 16.2. Cuban GDP per Head (2000 prices), 1950–1963

Source: Population from Tables C.1 and D.1; GDP at constant (2000) dollars from 1960 in Table D.19. The series from 1950 to 1960 splices the data on GDP at constant (1997) prices in Vidal and Fundora (2008) to Table D.19.

agricultural land was outside the state sector, but the farmers were obliged to sell most of their produce to the government at fixed prices.[34] Almost everything else – mining, manufacturing, construction, transport, communications, whole-sale trade and services – were in state hands. Crucially, for an economy as dependent on foreign trade as Cuba, all exports, imports and banking transactions were controlled by the state.

The Cuban economy had therefore made the transition from capitalism to socialism in a very short period. Most workers were now employed by the state and wages were regulated.[35] Private profits were negligible and private investment even more so. Thus, the rate of investment now depended on capital formation by the state. This, however, was very disappointing even by the less than exacting standards of the prerevolutionary Cuban economy. Gross fixed capital formation, estimated at less than 18 per cent of GDP in the 1950s,[36] had fallen to 13 per cent in 1962–3,[37] and the reasons would become very familiar: a shortage of foreign exchange for imports of capital goods and a high level of current spending by the state on social services and defence that left little room for investment.

Yet there had been solid achievements in these five years despite the hostile external environment, the US trade embargo, the outward migration of those with key skills, the inevitable chaos associated with the transition from the free market to state planning and acts of sabotage by enemies of the Revolution. The income of the lower deciles had increased and unemployment had fallen without the inflationary pressures that normally accompany massive exercises

[34] This was a result of the *acopio* system, under which farmers had to sell part of their crops to the state.
[35] See Rodríguez and Carriazo (1987), pp. 61–76.
[36] See Mesa-Lago (2000), p. 355.
[37] Mesa-Lago (2000), p. 355, for investment, and GDP from Table D.18.

in redistribution. Economic activity, whether measured by GDP or – as the Cubans were now doing – by Global Social Product (GSP),[38] may have been flat or falling, but school enrolments were booming, the literacy campaign was in full swing and the number of dwellings was on the rise, with an increase in the proportion of those with electricity, piped water and flush toilets.[39]

16.2. GROWTH WITH EQUITY: 1964–1989

The return of Fidel Castro in 1963 from his first trip to Moscow not only signalled a return to the primacy of sugar, but also a postponement of the push for heavy industry. The Soviet Union promised over the next few years to buy increasing quantities of Cuban sugar at a fixed price, and Cuba needed to reallocate resources to the sugar industry to make this possible. Helped by an increase in world sugar prices and a much improved harvest,[40] the value of exports soared in 1964.[41] As a result, the economy grew rapidly from its low level in 1963, helped by a strong performance from nickel and sugar exports and impressive growth in the construction and livestock sectors.[42]

The much improved economic performance in 1964, welcome though it was to the Cuban leadership, did not mean that the underlying structural problems had been overcome. What followed was a twenty-five year upswing (1964–89) that can be broken down into three distinct phases (see Figure 16.3). The first was a period of stagnation that lasted until 1970. There were then fifteen years of exceptionally rapid growth punctuated only by a brief recession in 1980. This was followed by another period of stagnation in the second half of the 1980s, but by this time GDP per head was much higher than during the first decade of the Revolution.

The stagnation between 1964 and 1970 had many causes. At the beginning the OAS had imposed a trade embargo against Cuba[43] that left the island even more dependent on the Communist countries. The agreements Cuba made with the latter were crucial, but they were not (yet) exceptionally generous. Furthermore, geopolitical disputes led Cuba to be punished from time to time.

---

[38] GSP measures the gross value of goods and material services, but it excludes nonmaterial services, and GDP measures the net value of all goods and services. See Zimbalist and Brundenius (1989).

[39] See Brundenius (1984) and Mesa-Lago (2000).

[40] The agreement with the Soviet Union did not stop Cuba from selling sugar in the free market. Cuba therefore often switched exports between markets depending on which offered the highest price.

[41] Merchandise exports jumped by 31.3% between 1963 and 1964. See Table D.6.

[42] Just how fast the economy grew in this one year is difficult to estimate with accuracy. GDP at constant prices (see Table D.19) grew by 15%, but GSP at constant prices (see Mesa-Lago, 2000, p. 348) grew at 7.3%. This implies that nonmaterial services (excluded from GSP) grew very fast and, indeed, they are estimated to have grown by 23.4% (see Zimbalist and Brundenius, 1989, p. 40).

[43] Among the Latin American countries, only Mexico refused to implement it. Mexico (and Canada) also maintained diplomatic relations with Cuba.

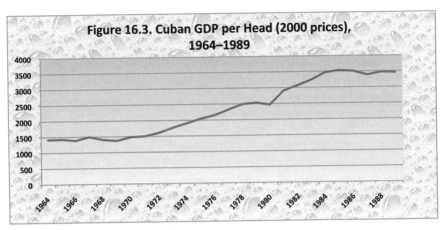

Figure 16.3. Cuban GDP per Head (2000 prices), 1964–1989

Source: Derived from Tables D.1 and D.19.

The Chinese cut rice exports to Cuba in 1966, and the Soviet Union slowed down the supply of oil in 1967.[44] Furthermore, the average price paid for Cuban sugar was slightly below that received by most other countries in the Caribbean (see below in this section).

The period also began with an energetic debate between those, led by Guevara, favouring moral incentives and those, led by Carlos Rafael Rodríguez, who believed that material incentives could not be avoided.[45] This led to a decision by Fidel Castro to allow part (mainly agriculture) to be run under one system (material incentives) and the rest of the economy (including industry) to be an experiment in building Guevara's 'new man'.[46] The operation of the two systems side by side caused considerable confusion, and the budgetary system of accounting favoured by the Guevarists led to a great deal of inefficiency.[47]

A small private sector had survived the first waves of nationalisation, and the shortages of many goods and services allowed a number of businesses to make substantial profits. This led to the Revolutionary Offensive launched by Fidel Castro in March 1968.[48] It eliminated many of the remaining privately owned farms in agriculture, curtailed private-sector operations in retailing and

---

[44] The Sino-Soviet dispute in the 1960s made it difficult for Cuba to please both. The Chinese were displeased by Cuban participation in an international conference in Moscow, and the USSR took exception to Cuban attacks on their policy of peaceful co-existence with the US. See Karol (1971).

[45] See Bernardo (1971). Carlos Rafael Rodríguez was a veteran Communist who had joined Batista's cabinet in 1942. He had been sent by the PSP to meet Castro in the Sierra Maestra in 1958 and was one of the first Communists to be invited by Castro to take part in his government.

[46] Guevara's 'new man' was a heresy in terms of socialist orthodoxy, but the ideas could be traced to the writings of Mao Tse-tung. See Guevara (1967).

[47] Budgetary accounting was different from the self-financing favoured by Rodríguez. It imposed less discipline on managers and made it more difficult to control theft and corruption in the workplace. See Mesa-Lago (2000).

[48] See Brundenius (1984), pp. 54–7.

shut down many of the self-employed businesses in services.[49] Henceforth, almost the only legitimate supplier of goods and services was the state, and shortages became even more apparent. Many visitors to the island at this time commented on the long queues for even the simplest articles of consumption.[50] Labour productivity suffered both from the time wasted and from the lack of incentives to increase earnings.

On his return from a second visit to Moscow,[51] Fidel Castro made explicit what had only been hinted at before: Cuba was going to specialise in sugar to the point where it could produce 10 million tons by 1970. The justification was the growing market in the Soviet Union and other Communist countries, whose governments would now be expected to curtail their own – relatively expensive – production of sugar beet. However, to meet this highly ambitious target, the whole Cuban economy had to be subordinated to the needs of the sugar sector.[52] Land previously used for other crops was planted with sugarcane, scarce foreign exchange was used to repair or replace milling equipment, transport was diverted to the needs of the sugar industry and labour was switched from other activities to prepare for the 10-million-ton *zafra*.[53]

The 1970 *zafra* produced 8.5 million tons of sugar.[54] This was a record for Cuba and in many ways an astonishing achievement. However, the opportunity cost was enormous. By now Cuba had virtually eliminated unemployment,[55] despite the slow growth of the economy, because labour productivity was stagnant or falling and so many citizens had moved into education or the armed forces.[56] Thus, the sugarcane had to be harvested by many volunteers with no experience or by workers taking time off from their other jobs. Cuba's allies, especially the Soviet Union, were not impressed and called for greater rationality in the allocation of economic resources.

This duly happened, and Cuba (re)established conventional Soviet planning methods based on material incentives and, starting in 1976, detailed five-year plans.[57] This would no doubt have led to an improvement in economic performance. However, the new orthodoxy also coincided with a rise in world sugar prices that reached their peak in 1975. Because the price quadrupled, Cuba's Communist allies had to adjust the prices they offered for the island's

---

[49] The state nationalised 55,600 small private businesses and restricted sales by small farmers to any outlets other than those controlled by the government.
[50] My own diary, written during a two-month visit in 1968, stated of Havana: 'the queues for restaurants and refreshments were vast, yet the crowds seemed happy to wait patiently.'
[51] This was in 1964. See Karol (1971).
[52] The shift in resources required was massive. See Roca (1976).
[53] This is the Cuban name for the sugar harvest.
[54] The harvest was actually spread over two years because it started in October 1969 and did not end until May 1970. This was longer than normal. See Roca (1976), p. 12.
[55] See Rodríguez and Carriazo (1987), p. 62.
[56] See Mesa-Lago (2000), pp. 202–4.
[57] The plans produced before 1976 by JUCEPLAN were either indicative or sectoral and did not strictly conform to the standard plans used in the Soviet Union.

sugar. This assured Cuba an exceptional price for its sugar in whatever market it sold, and the volume available was now much greater as a result of the efforts made to achieve a 10 million ton *zafra*. Furthermore, the price of nickel and other primary product exports also increased sharply. Thus, the value of exports soared, and the Cuban economy grew rapidly.[58]

The world price of sugar, still far and away the main export,[59] declined rapidly after 1975. If Cuba had been a typical Caribbean country, it would have suffered as a consequence. However, new arrangements with the Soviet Union under the five-year plan allowed Cuba to continue to receive the high price for sugar (and nickel) and to pay a below-market price for oil imports. Furthermore, the Soviet Union agreed that any oil imports saved by Cuba through energy-saving measures would be sold and transferred to the island as hard currency.[60] In addition, the Soviet Union continued to provide loans on concessionary terms.

These arrangements, far more generous than those that prevailed in the first fifteen years of the Revolution, allowed the Cuban economy to grow very rapidly after 1970. GDP per head (at 2000 US dollars) reached a peak of $3,535 in 1985. This implied an annual rate of growth since 1969 of over 6 per cent. This compared very favourably with the performance in the 1960s, with the rest of the Caribbean in the same years and with the rest of the world. Furthermore, the period included the first half of the 1980s when almost all Latin American and many Caribbean countries experienced a sharp fall in GDP per head as a result of the 1982 debt crisis.

The most generous part of the Soviet package was the price paid for sugar. This implied a large subsidy to the Cuban economy, but the size of the subsidy has been controversial. Many scholars have calculated it by reference to the free market price of sugar. However, the latter is not an appropriate metric because only a small part of world sugar trade passes through it. Furthermore, in most years (1973–5 were exceptional) it has been an artificially low price because surpluses have been dumped on it by large exporters, such as the EU.

Most exporters of sugar made from cane sell their surpluses under long-term quota arrangements with importing countries. The most important have been the US, Canadian and EU sugar quotas, allowing exporters to benefit from high domestic prices in importing countries. Thus, the relevant price for comparison is the average price received by other Caribbean countries. We can group these as (a) Hispaniola, (b) CARICOM, (c) US territories, and (d) all Caribbean countries (excluding Cuba). The results are shown in Table 16.2, which shows the annualised premium paid for Cuban sugar as a percentage of GDP.

[58] The value of merchandise exports in 1975 was nearly six times greater than in 1969. See Table D.6.
[59] Sugar's share of merchandise exports varied between 75% and 90% throughout this period.
[60] They would appear in the Cuban balance of payments as re-exports, but the oil never entered Cuba.

TABLE 16.2. *Annual Sugar Subsidy Received by Cuba as Percentage of GDP,*
1964–1989

| Year | Cuban Subsidy Relative to Sugar Price Received by: | | | Caribbean (excl Cuba) |
	Hispaniola	CARICOM	US Territories	
1964–72	−1.3	−0.15	−0.9	−0.8
1973–89	10.0	7.5	6.9	8.6
1964–89	8.2	6.3	5.6	7.1

Source: Derived from Tables D.5 and D.18. The numbers are calculated as the difference between the sum of the value of Cuban sugar exports in the years stated and the value obtained by multiplying the volume of Cuban sugar exports by the unit value for sugar for each subregion divided by the sum of current GDP for the same years.

The first point to notice about Table 16.2 is that the premium received by Cuba up to 1972 was actually negative. In other words, Cuba was paid an average price slightly lower than that received by the other subregions. The Soviet Union and the other Communist countries may have paid a price higher than the free market, but it was not as high as the price paid by the EU, the United States or Canada under special arrangements. After the new arrangements with the Soviet Union came into force, however, the subsidy was substantial and amounted to between 7 and 10 per cent of GDP on an annual basis. When the other subsidies are taken into account (see above in this section), it is not unreasonable to suggest that Cuba was receiving a foreign aid package equivalent to at least 10 per cent of GDP per year.[61]

Under these circumstances, it is not surprising that Cuban GDP grew rapidly. Indeed, in the second five-year plan (1981–5) actual GSP growth was faster than planned growth.[62] Furthermore, population growth was steadily declining, and thus GDP per head grew almost as fast.[63] There was no major diversification of the economy, but there were many small changes. The tourist industry recovered from its nadir in the 1960s, the fishing industry expanded, the foundations were laid for biotechnology exports and a 1982 law permitted joint ventures with foreign companies in certain areas.[64] There was even a relaxation of the straitjacket in which the private sector operated, with farmers' markets being reestablished and greater opportunities for self-employment.

---

[61] Cuban officials point out that the Soviet subsidy has to be set against the annual cost to the economy from the trade embargo. The latter is hard to quantify, but it has undoubtedly been substantial.

[62] Planned GSP growth was 5.0% per year, and actual GSP growth was 7.3% per year. See Mesa-Lago (2000), p. 365.

[63] The CBR halved in the twenty-five years after 1960, and annual population growth averaged only 1% in the 1980s.

[64] See Mesa-Lago (2000), pp. 243–4.

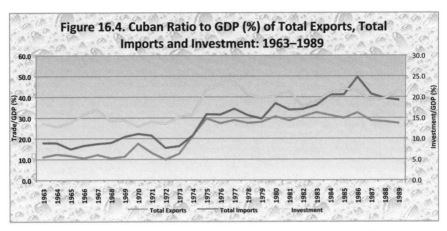

Source: Trade/GDP ratios derived from Tables D.8, D.13 and D.18; investment from Mesa-Lago (2000), p. 355, and converted to dollars using Table D.4.

The fast growth of the Cuban economy after 1970 allowed the government to make substantial progress towards achieving its social ambitions.[65] Secondary school enrolment jumped from 25 per cent of the age group to 85 per cent in 1985.[66] Tertiary went from 5 to 21 per cent over the same period. Most urban houses and about one-third of rural dwellings were joined to the main water supply by 1985. By 1975, the number of doctors per 10,000 inhabitants had surpassed its prerevolutionary level and would then double in the next ten years. Mortality rates, general and infant, declined sharply, and life expectancy reached the standards of the richest countries. And the rate of net outward migration dropped below 10,000 per year after 1972, with the exception of 1979–81.[67]

Despite this economic and social progress, the Cuban Revolution failed to overcome fully the three structural weaknesses that had emerged before 1964: trade deficits, low rates of investment and the monetary overhang. The increase in the average sugar price had pushed up the ratio of exports to GDP after 1972, but it did not eliminate the trade gap, except in the exceptional year of 1975 (see Figure 16.4). This trade deficit had to be financed, and not all of it could be covered by soft currency loans from the Communist countries. Thus, Cuba had built up a hard currency debt that may not have been as burdensome as in the rest of Latin America, but it still had to be serviced at a heavy cost in terms of

---

[65] It also allowed it to fulfill some of its international ambitions, with Cuban troops playing a leading role in several African conflicts – especially in Angola. See Gleijeses (2002).

[66] These and subsequent numbers are taken from Mesa-Lago (2000).

[67] This was caused by the Mariel boatlift, when all restrictions were lifted, and nearly 150,000 left in one year (1980).

TABLE 16.3. *Revenue, Expenditure and the Monetary Surplus in Cuba,*
1965–1989

Year	Revenue/GDP (%)	Expenditure/GDP (%)	Monetary Surplus/Income (%)
1965	41.5	41.5	72.9
1970	na	na	83.1
1975	71.8 (a)	71.8 (a)	36.6
1980	70.4	70.3	30.9
1985	57.9	57.9	30.0
1989	59.3	65.9	35.2

Note: (a) = 1978.
Source: Derived from Mesa-Lago (2000); Tables D.4 and D.18.

foreign exchange.[68] Similarly, the investment/GDP ratio may have risen from its low rate in the 1960s, but it rarely exceeded 20 per cent, despite the low level of private consumption as a share of GDP.

The low level of **private** consumption was a consequence of the high rate of **public** consumption. Public revenue and expenditure constituted just over 40 per cent of GDP in 1965, but these ratios had risen to 70 per cent by 1980, after which they declined modestly (see Table 16.3). By this time, the monetary overhang (the monetary surplus expressed as a percentage of income) had fallen, but it had not disappeared (see Table 16.3). This overhang fuelled the black market and allowed the small private sector to make profits much greater than the numbers involved might have implied.

These were some of the reasons for the Rectification Process launched by Fidel Castro in 1986.[69] This involved a return to many of the policies of the late 1960s, including – once again – a major clampdown on the small private sector. Cuban officials explained it in terms of the need to tackle corruption, crime and waste in the public sector, growing inequality in income distribution and the need to revive the revolutionary spirit. Others pointed to the need to tackle the growing trade deficit and the tendency for public expenditure to outstrip revenue (as happened in 1989 – see Table 16.3).

Whatever its causes, the Rectification Process coincided with renewed stagnation of the Cuban economy. The Soviet Union itself was going through a painful process of adjustment and could not maintain the previous level of support for Cuba. The average price received by Cuba for its sugar declined after 1986. The foreign exchange earned from energy savings fell, and Cuba defaulted on its hard currency debt, leading to a rapid increase in its nominal value as unpaid interest accumulated. These external difficulties were then compounded

---

[68] The hard currency debt had reached $4.985 billion by 1986, at which point it went into default. About half of it was owed to official bilateral creditors and most of the remainder to private financial institutions. See Mesa-Lago (2000), p. 380, and Morris (2008).

[69] See Eckstein (1994).

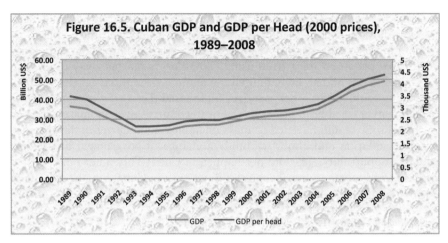

Figure 16.5. Cuban GDP and GDP per Head (2000 prices), 1989–2008

Source: Tables D.1 and D.19.

by the Rectification Process itself, which may have promoted income equality but undermined growth. The only bright spots were the growth of biotechnology exports and an increase in foreign visitors. In time, Cuba would no doubt have overcome its economic difficulties. However, no one had anticipated the possibility that the Soviet Union might collapse.

16.3. THE SPECIAL PERIOD AND ITS AFTERMATH

Mikhail Gorbachev[70] came to power in 1985 and attempted to tackle the economic problems of the Soviet Union the following year with the policies that became known as *perestroika*. Cuba began to feel the shock of these economic reforms almost immediately, but it was not until the collapse of the Berlin Wall on 9 November 1989 that the full implications would become clear. In January 1990 the members of COMECON (including Cuba) agreed that henceforth trade between member states would be conducted at market prices and paid for with hard currency.[71] At the same time soft loans on concessionary terms disappeared. All that remained was the military assistance – and it would soon vanish.

The impact on Cuba was dramatic. GDP at constant prices fell drastically after 1989 (see Figure 16.5) and did not stop falling until 1993. In this short period, GDP per head (also at constant prices) fell by 36.6 per cent – one of the biggest declines ever recorded in Latin America or the Caribbean. Thus, Cuba suffered five years of economic stagnation in the second half of the 1980s followed by five years of collapse.[72] The US Congress, wishing to accelerate

[70] Gorbachev was the sixth and last secretary-general of the Communist Party of the Soviet Union.

[71] In addition, preferential rates for shipping disappeared, placing an additional burden on the Cuban economy. See Banco Nacional de Cuba (1995), p. 2.

[72] At constant prices, GDP per head peaked in 1985. See Tables D.1 and D.19.

the long-anticipated demise of the Castro regime, then chose this moment to pass into law the Cuban Democracy Act,[73] which tightened the embargo on Cuba, imposed sanctions on foreign subsidiaries of US companies that traded with Cuba, penalised ships from using Cuban ports on their way to or from the United States and severely limited the amount of remittances that Cuban-Americans could send to their relatives on the island.

In any other Caribbean or Latin American country, an economic collapse of this magnitude would have led to mass unemployment, currency devaluation, imported inflation and almost certainly a change of government at the next available opportunity. This did not happen in Cuba. This is not only because the electoral route to political change did not exist in Cuba, but also because it was not a market economy. Thus, the collapse took a very different form. The crisis years were designated the Special Period in Time of Peace by Fidel Castro, drastic – even radical – measures were taken by the government, and the regime survived despite a stream of books and articles predicting the imminent end of Communism on the island.

The crisis at first took a familiar form. The sale of commodity exports at world prices pushed the value of merchandise exports down from $5.35 billion in 1989 to a low of $1.0 billion in 1993.[74] Total imports, valued at $8.1 billion in 1989,[75] then fell even more sharply because there were no more soft loans to finance a balance of payments deficit, and loans from western creditors were unavailable because the hard currency debt had been in default since 1986. The absence of imported spare parts and raw materials crippled the ability of manufacturing to maintain production, and output fell in all sectors.[76] Government revenue, heavily dependent on the circulation tax applied to the products of state-owned enterprises, declined.

In a capitalist country this would have required a drastic cut in public expenditure. Yet this did not happen in Cuba. Instead, the state maintained the level of overall public spending (see Table 16.4). The unemployment rate, which had been creeping up in the 1980s, then remained virtually unchanged.[77] Inevitably, there was a big increase in the public-sector deficit (see Table 16.4), but this did not bring inflation,[78] because the state controlled the price of almost all goods and services. Instead, there was a huge increase in the monetary overhang, which was reflected in the rise of the liquidity to GDP ratio and the

[73] Passed into law in 1992, it is usually known as the Torricelli Act after its congressional sponsor. See Barberia (2004), p. 393.

[74] See Table D.6.

[75] See Table D.8.

[76] Carmelo Mesa-Lago has for many years compiled physical indicators for the Cuban economy. Between 1989 and 1994 not a single one of his principal products increased. See Mesa-Lago (2000), pp. 358–9.

[77] It had reached 7.9% in 1989 as a result of a big increase in the female participation rate during the 1980s (see Monreal (2002), p. 148). Five years later the unemployment rate was 6.7%. See Monreal (2002), p. 147.

[78] At least as normally defined, but there was a big increase in prices in the uncontrolled markets.

TABLE 16.4. *The Crisis Years in Cuba: 1989–1994*

Year	mn pesos Expenditure	mn pesos Deficit	mn pesos Liquidity	Liquidity % of GDP	Unofficial Exchange Rate	Investment GDP Ratio
1989	13,904.2	−1,403.4	4,162.0	19.7	5.0	21.4
1990	15,481.6	−1,958.1	4,986.0	23.1	7.0	20.4
1991	14,713.8	−3,764.8	6,563.0	36.8	20.0	19.5
1992	15,048.3	−4,869.0	8,361.1	51.2	35.0	13.9
1993	14,566.5	−5,050.6	11,044.2	66.7	78.0	11.4
1994	14,178.3	−1,421.4	9,943.8	47.2	95.0	8.0

Source: Banco Nacional de Cuba (1995) for state expenditure and deficit; Marquetti (1998) for liquidity (money in circulation plus bank deposits); unofficial exchange rate from Barberia (2004); and investment ratio from Figure 16.4 for 1989 and CEPAL (2010) for other years.

collapse of the extra-official exchange rate (see Table 16.4).[79] The investment ratio also fell sharply (see Table 16.4) because the state was only able to maintain or increase **current** spending, and **capital** spending, more heavily dependent on imports, collapsed.

The Special Period demanded special measures, and these were not long in being adopted. The desperate need for foreign exchange led to a revision of the foreign investment law and a more welcoming attitude to new proposals.[80] State farms were converted into cooperatives and renamed Unidades Básicas de Producción Cooperativa (UBPC). Farmers' and artisan markets, closed since 1986, were reestablished. Prices of goods and services controlled by the state were adjusted upwards. Small businesses and self-employment were permitted in a much wider field of activities. Finally, the US dollar was legalised in 1993, and the black market exchange rate became a parallel rate.[81] When the following year the government introduced the Cuban convertible peso (CUC) at parity with the US dollar, Cuba had three legal currencies circulating side by side.[82]

With one exception, these measures proved to be timely and in different degrees important. The number of joint ventures with foreign companies soared,[83] and the country began to develop a first-class tourist infrastructure and expertise in mining.[84] Uncontrolled markets and upward price adjustments in controlled ones helped to soak up liquidity, which fell sharply between

[79] This market was illegal until 1993, but there is no shortage of data on the black market exchange rate before then.
[80] See Pérez (2002) and (2004).
[81] These measures were criticised by some Cuban economists as not going far enough. See Carranza, Gutierrez and Valdes (1995) and (1996).
[82] At least until 2006, when the US dollar was declared illegal. On the monetary and exchange rate system in Cuba in these years, see Ritter (2004).
[83] See Pérez (2004).
[84] On tourism, see Brundenius (2002), pp. 383–6. On mining, where the Canadian company Sheritt became a key investor, see Pérez (2004).

1993 and 1994, and reduced the fiscal deficit (see Table 16.4). The parallel market exchange rate peaked at 120–130 in July 1994.[85] There was a big increase (from a very low base) in those registered as self-employed. The one reform that did not work as planned was the UBPCs.[86] They failed to bring about the much needed reversal of agricultural decline – their ability to do so was crippled by the shortage of foreign exchange and continuing controls on what products they could grow and where they could sell them.

These reforms helped the economy to recover from its low point in 1993. The recovery, however, was desperately slow, and neither GDP nor GDP per head (at constant prices) exceeded its 1989 level until 2005 (this meant that the Cuban economy had lost **two** decades because GDP per head had actually peaked in 1985). This was only partly because of the further tightening of the US embargo in 1996, which was aimed in particular at discouraging foreign investment in Cuba.[87] It also had much to do with the long-standing inefficiencies in the Cuban economy and the continued shortage of foreign exchange. As a consequence, although there was plenty of scope for import substitution (in both agriculture and industry), this did not contribute much to economic growth after 1993 because firms very often could not gain access to foreign exchange for spare parts and raw materials[88] (the one exception was energy, because oil and gas production climbed steadily from their low levels in 1989 and made Cuba less dependent on imports).[89]

The recovery was in fact export-led. This had virtually nothing to do with sugar, which suffered under the weight of low world prices and antiquated mills. Indeed, following the closure of many mills in 2002,[90] sugar exports ceased to be of much importance, with the volume dropping to its level before the Second War of Independence.[91] Instead, export growth was caused by an increase in earnings from mining, other goods and – above all – services (see Figure 16.6). Mining benefitted both from an increase in output (especially nickel and cobalt, where Canadian companies became strategic partners of the

---

[85] See Marquetti (1998), which also shows the rates quoted in different parts of the country.

[86] Ironically, this was the one reform on which the Cuban authorities appeared to have pinned much of their hopes.

[87] This was the Cuban Liberty and Democratic Solidarity Act, otherwise known as the Helms-Burton law. For the first time it introduced penalties for trafficking in property allegedly taken from US citizens.

[88] This is not the view of Marquetti and García (2002), who have a table (p. 88) showing the contribution of import substitution to the growth of industrial production between 1989 and 1999. However, the decline of the internal market was so large that it almost cancelled out the import substitution effect.

[89] Oil production jumped from 500,000 MT in 1989 to a peak of 3,691,000 in 2003. Gas jumped from 17.3 mn cubic meters in 1995 to a peak of 1218 mn in 2007. See CEPAL (2010) and ONE (2010).

[90] More than fifty mills were closed (roughly one-half of the total). See Pollitt (2004).

[91] The lowest point was 2005, when the volume exported fell to 687,500 tons. This was almost down to the level in 1890.

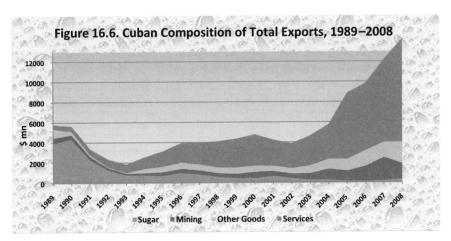

Figure 16.6. Cuban Composition of Total Exports, 1989–2008

Source: Derived from Tables D.5, D.6 and D.7.

Cuban state) and also from much higher world prices. Other goods included biotechnology exports (described in Chapter 14).

Merchandise exports never recovered their value in 1989. Thus, the growth of total exports, as Figure 16.6 shows, came to depend on services, which were more important than goods by 1997.[92] Cuba joined the growing ranks of Caribbean countries, where exports were dominated by services rather than merchandise, despite the fact that cruise visitors were almost ruled out by the US trade embargo. The number of tourists, a mere 270,000 in 1989, had exceeded 1 million by 1997 and 2 million by 2004.[93] In that year they generated more than $2 billion in gross earnings and dominated earnings from services. In the twenty years after the collapse of the Soviet Union, Cuba had become one of the most important destinations for tourists in the Caribbean, with large numbers of visitors from Canada, Europe and Latin America along with a rapidly increasing number from China.[94]

Until 2004, service exports were dominated by tourism. The following year, however, the contribution of tourist earnings to service exports dropped to one-third. This was a consequence of the bilateral agreements with Venezuela, the first of which had been signed in October 2000.[95] The cornerstone of the Cuban-Venezuelan accords was the supply of crude oil to Cuban refineries in return for the provision of medical and educational services in Venezuela

[92] See Tables D.6 and D.7.
[93] See Mesa-Lago (2000) and CEPAL (2010).
[94] China designated Cuba an approved destination for group travel, and the numbers of tourists grew rapidly after 2000.
[95] These bilateral agreements need to be distinguished from both Petrocaribe and ALBA (see Chapter 12), in both of which Cuba participated.

by Cuban professionals,[96] but there were many other elements.[97] Thus, Cuba imported Venezuelan oil – nearly 100,000 barrels per day at its peak – and paid for it through professional services.[98]

Critics of Cuba – and there have always been many – argued that Venezuela had simply replaced the Soviet Union as the provider of subsidies without which the island economy would have collapsed. Yet the size of the subsidy clearly depended on the price of oil. At $25 a barrel, there was arguably **no** subsidy because Venezuela received a valuable service for which it was paying effectively a market price.[99] As the price of oil rose, there **was** a subsidy that could be roughly valued at $2 billion when crude oil reached $80 per barrel.[100] With a GDP of around $60 billion at current prices in 2008,[101] this would represent a subsidy of just over 3 per cent – far lower than the Soviet subsidy for sugar alone (see Table 16.2).[102]

Venezuelan support was not limited to the supply of crude oil, and Cuba also received generous assistance from China.[103] At the same time, Cuba did not pay much in debt servicing, because loans from the Soviet Union had effectively been written off, hard currency debt was in default and much of the rest was on very soft terms.[104] Furthermore, remittances to the island from those living abroad also rose rapidly.[105] Most of this was from Cuban-Americans in the United States, despite the restrictions imposed during the presidency of

[96] The Cubans continued to receive their salary in pesos on the island (deposited to their bank accounts), and their expenses in Venezuela were covered by the Venezuelan government. Any savings could be converted into goods or hard currency and repatriated to the island free of tax. In addition, returning professionals were given priority if they wanted to buy consumer durables such as cars (information derived by the author from interviews in both Cuba and Venezuela).

[97] Venezuela financed the refurbishment of an oil refinery, guaranteed a regular supply of tourists to the island, provided soft loans and for a time sent tens of thousands of Venezuelans to Cuba for medical operations. See Sánchez (2007).

[98] Cuba also exported professional services to many other countries, but none on the same scale as to Venezuela.

[99] At $25 per barrel, it would cost Cuba around $900 million to replace Venezuelan crude oil with other imports. Assuming the average cost (salaries, overheads and training) of a health or educational professional in Venezuela to be $3,000 per month, it would have cost Venezuela the same to replace the 25,000 Cubans working in the country.

[100] The cost of replacing Venezuelan crude would rise to $2.9 billion at $80 per barrel (average price between 2005 and 2010), but the cost of replacing Cuban professionals remained the same.

[101] GDP in 2008 was $62.7 billion in current dollars. See Table D.18.

[102] In addition, there was a cost to Cuba in the form of medical and educational services foregone as a result of the temporary absence of so many professionals.

[103] Much of this was in the form of soft loans to buy Chinese products. That is why imports from China increased so rapidly after 2000 (see Chapter 12).

[104] In 2003, the external debt was valued at $11.3 billion (see CEPAL 2010). The following year it dropped to $5.8 billion as a result of a decision by the Cuban authorities to record only the debt that was being currently serviced. This then rose to $9.9 billion in 2008 (equivalent to 15.8% of GDP). On debt issues more generally, see Morris (2008).

[105] See Barberia (2004).

George W. Bush (2001–9).[106] Thus, it was not surprising that the growth rate of the Cuban economy started to accelerate after 2003 (see Figure 16.1).[107]

The Cuban economy has therefore not only recovered since 1993, but has also grown, with GDP per head at constant (2000) prices reaching a respectable $4,355 in 2008.[108] However, this time it was not growth with equity. The authorities still controlled wage and pension rates for most of the population, but they had lost control of a large part of household income through the impact of remittances, tips paid in hard currency and the earnings of those in self-employment or small businesses. Furthermore, many Cubans had become highly skilled at stealing from their workplace and selling goods in the black market,[109] and the state itself oversaw an expansion in incentive payments to key workers in the form of convertible rather than national pesos.[110]

The result was not only an increase in inequality, but also in poverty. Inequality increased not so much because of the variance in wages paid in pesos, which remained very low.[111] It had much more to do with access to hard currency (including convertible pesos). Official estimates suggested that about half of Cuban households received such payments, but the rest did not.[112] As a result, the Gini coefficient was estimated to have jumped from 0.24 in the mid-1980s to 0.38 fifteen years later.[113] Those in receipt of hard currency could either use it directly to purchase goods and services not available at subsidised prices or sell it in the parallel market for national currency.

Those without access to hard currency had to survive on their income in national pesos. As the state reduced the amount of goods and services available at subsidised prices, it also increased the minimum wage, and average salaries in national pesos duly rose.[114] As the proportion of income spent at subsidised prices fell,[115] those families without access to hard currency struggled to make

---

[106] These were lifted in 2009 by President Obama.

[107] There is a break in the series in 2005 as a result of the decision by the Cuban statistical authorities to value some public services at market value rather than cost (government income and expenditure increased by one-third in that year – see CEPAL 2010). This means that some of the growth in 2005 (perhaps half) is artificial, but this does not affect growth rates in subsequent years because the same methodology has continued to be applied. See ONE (2010).

[108] Derived from Tables D.1 and D.19.

[109] This is a very sensitive subject, but the estimates of theft from state-owned enterprises have been extraordinarily high.

[110] Before the dollar was outlawed in 2006, some of these payments were made in US dollars. Subsequently, they were all made in convertible pesos or in kind.

[111] The range of average monthly salaries in 2009 in state-owned and mixed entities went from 418 in public services to 537 in mining. See ONE (2010), table 7.4.

[112] See, e.g., Añé Aguiloche (2000), p. 519.

[113] See Espina Prieto (2004).

[114] From 284 pesos per month in 2004 to 429 in 2009. See ONE (2010), table 7.4.

[115] This proportion is difficult to measure accurately, but it had probably dropped to one-third for the average household soon after 2000. For details of the ration book in different years, which excludes subsidised services, see Togores and García (2004), p. 269.

ends meet in the uncontrolled markets.[116] Indeed, urban poverty – virtually eliminated by 1989 – had risen to between 15 and 20 per cent of the urban population by the early 2000s.[117] Nobody starved in Cuba, but conditions became very harsh for some of its citizens, and frustration was widespread.[118] The state had also maintained employment beyond what was needed in order to avoid an increase in open unemployment – therefore, perhaps 1 million workers were surplus to requirements and suffering from low morale.[119]

The Cuban economy therefore survived the Special Period, and some of its citizens even prospered. Yet the revolutionary spirit, so apparent to visitors even in the 1980s, had died somewhere along the road, and the island's citizens became increasingly effective in venting their frustrations against the system.[120] The new government of President Raúl Castro (2008–) clearly recognised this and was prepared to make a number of concessions, both to the liberalisation of markets and to personal freedom.[121] Yet it looked to many like too little, too late, and political reform was not included on the agenda at all. By the time the first decade of the new millennium ended, there was no danger of imminent collapse, but the sense of a revolution having run its course was very strong.

16.4. THE CUBAN ECONOMY SINCE THE NAPOLEONIC WARS

Cuba is not the biggest country in the Caribbean, but it is by far the largest island.[122] In the period covered by this book, it has always had the largest population. It is not surprising, therefore, that the Cuban economy has been among the most important in the region since the end of the Napoleonic Wars. This might puzzle anyone familiar only with Cuba in the middle of the eighteenth

---

[116] It is, however, economically illiterate to calculate – as so many Cubanologists do – the average income of Cubans in dollars as the monthly salary in pesos divided by the parallel exchange rate. The standard of living of the average Cuban measured in dollars depended on the dollar value of the subsidised goods and services together with the dollar value of goods and services purchased in the uncontrolled markets. The former, which includes rent, was still worth a great deal even after all the changes introduced by the authorities.

[117] This is based on nonfulfillment of basic needs rather than the proportion falling below the poverty line. See Espina Prieto (2004).

[118] It is often forgotten that university enrolment plummeted in the 1990s during the Special Period and the number of 'inactive' increased sharply, and thus a whole cohort of the labour force was underskilled in relation to their older and younger peers. See Monreal (2002), p. 150.

[119] This was the estimate of Raúl Castro shortly after he became president in 2008 and explains the decision in August 2010 to shift 500,000 workers (10% of the labour force) out of state employment.

[120] This took many forms, including public demonstrations, blogs on the Internet and hunger strikes in prison.

[121] One of Raúl Castro's first acts was to give Cubans access to tourist hotels and the freedom to purchase mobile telephones and personal computers.

[122] The land area of Guyana is nearly 20 million ha, Suriname 15.6 million and Cuba nearly 11 million. French Guiana has 9.1 million and the largest island after Cuba (the Dominican Republic) has only 4.8 million.

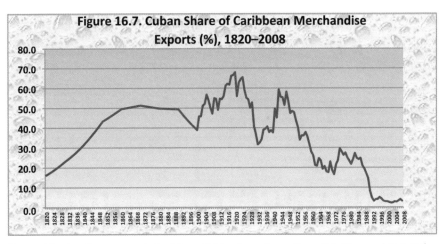

Figure 16.7. Cuban Share of Caribbean Merchandise Exports (%), 1820–2008

Source: Merchandise exports derived from Tables A.1a, A.13, C.1a, C.8, D.1a and D.6. Before 1900 interdecennial data have been filled by interpolation.

century, when it was a backward Spanish colony with a small population and without a major export sector. However, the Cuban economy was transformed in the fifty years after the British occupation of Havana in 1762 as a result of the arrival of French planters and their slaves from Haiti, the end of the state tobacco monopoly and – crucially – the right granted in 1818 to trade with any country in the world.[123]

Before 1960, in the absence of national income statistics for all countries, the best gauge of the importance of the Cuban economy is provided by the ratio of the island's merchandise exports to those of the Caribbean as a whole. This is shown in Figure 16.7, where the Cuban share in 1820 was a relatively modest 16 per cent and the value of the country's exports was still less than that of Jamaica. By 1860, however, the Cuban share had reached 50 per cent and would stay close to that level until 1890, after which there was a steep decline. This was quickly reversed after the Second War of Independence, and the Cuban share then rose to its highest level in 1920, when it represented just over two-thirds of all Caribbean merchandise exports. From then onwards there was a downward slide punctuated only by a brief respite before, during and just after the Second World War. By the time of the Revolution the share was down to one-third – the same as in the 1840s.

After the Cuban Revolution, the share of merchandise exports continued to fall but then recovered and fluctuated between 20 and 30 per cent until the mid-1980s. There was then a collapse because Soviet support came to an end and the share had fallen below 3 per cent by the end of the century. Using total exports (including services) as the measure of relative Cuban performance makes only a small difference. However, the Cuban economy was by then no longer so

[123] On these economic reforms, see Santamaría and García (2004).

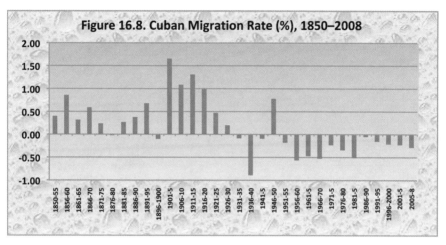

Source: Table A.6 up to 1900 and derived from Tables C.1, C.2, C.3, D.1, D.2 and D.3 thereafter.

dependent on exports as a result of the much greater importance of (nontraded) public services and import-competing activities geared to the domestic market. As a result, it remained one of the two most important economies in the region when measured by GDP at current or constant prices.[124]

Cuba may have had the largest population of any Caribbean country in the last 200 years, but the share has fluctuated. It began at one-quarter in 1810, but then reached one-third fifty years later. By the end of the Spanish-American War (1898) it was down below one-quarter again before jumping back to around one-third in 1930. It then stayed at roughly that level until 1970, after which it started a slow descent as a result of a fall in the birth rate (the death rate was already very low) that was faster than in the Caribbean as a whole. By 2008, the Cuban share of Caribbean population was once again down to one-quarter.[125] This trend will probably continue for a while, but the share is unlikely to fall below 20 per cent because the rest of the Caribbean can be expected in due course to experience the same fall in the birth rate as in Cuba.

These trends in the Cuban share of Caribbean population have been determined not only by birth and death rates, but also by net migration (see Figure 16.8). We cannot measure this with great accuracy before 1850, when much of it consisted of the illegal traffic in slaves, but it was certainly inwards.[126] This net inward migration continued until the second half of the 1890s, despite the

---

[124] See Tables D.18 and D.19. The other large economy since 1960 has been Puerto Rico, which overtook Cuba in 1986 at current prices (it was already marginally ahead of Cuba in 1960 at constant (2000) prices).

[125] All these ratios have been derived from Tables A.1, C.1 and D.1.

[126] The gross annual inward migration (including illegal slave traffic) can be estimated (see Chapter 3), but there are no complete annual figures on births and deaths, so the net migration rate cannot be calculated in these years.

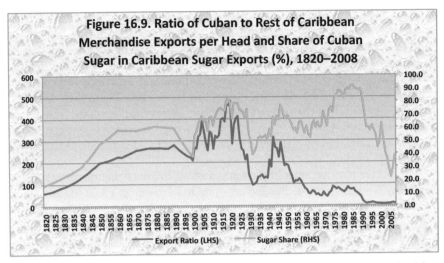

Figure 16.9. Ratio of Cuban to Rest of Caribbean Merchandise Exports per Head and Share of Cuban Sugar in Caribbean Sugar Exports (%), 1820–2008

Source: Sugar share derived from Tables A.10, C.5 and D.5. Merchandise exports per head from Tables A.1a, A.13, C.1, C.8, D.1 and D.8. Before 1900 interdecennial data have been filled by interpolation.

fact that the Cuban share of Caribbean population (see above in this section) was falling after 1870. The reason for this was the very high death rate in Cuba (the birth rate was more normal), which necessitated a high rate of net inward migration to prevent the population stagnating or even declining.

The period after the Second War of Independence was marked by exceptionally high rates of net inward migration (see Figure 16.8), which included Spanish subjects (from the mainland and the Canary Islands) and migrants from other Caribbean islands (especially Jamaica and Haiti). This came to an abrupt halt at the end of the 1920s, after which Cuba experienced net outward migration in every quinquennium except 1946–50, when postwar prosperity was temporarily underpinned by high sugar prices. Net outward migration since the Revolution has fluctuated, but it has normally been less than 0.5 per cent per year (see Figure 16.8).

The evidence so far suggests marked cycles in the evolution of the Cuban economy. To establish the nature of these cycles more precisely, it is necessary to compare Cuban performance with the rest of the Caribbean in the same way as was done for Haiti in Chapter 7. This requires using exports per head, but this time comparing Cuba with the **rest** of the Caribbean (i.e. excluding Cuba), because the island was such a large part of the total Caribbean economy. The result is shown in Figure 16.9, which gives the ratio of Cuban to the rest of the Caribbean merchandise exports per head from 1820 to 2008 at current prices. Figure 16.9 also shows the contribution of Cuban sugar to total Caribbean sugar exports in the same period.

The Cuban-to-Caribbean ratio of exports per head was around 50 per cent in 1820 (see Figure 16.9). It reached equality in the 1830s, was twice the

value of the rest of the Caribbean by mid-century and then reached a peak around 1870, where it stayed until the precipitate decline in the late 1890s associated with the destruction of life and property during the Second War of Independence. Within a few years, however, the Cuban ratio had exceeded the previous peak and would average between three and four times the average of the rest of the Caribbean until the end of the 1920s. There then followed an horrendous decline that was only temporarily reversed from the mid-1930s to the late-1940s. Cuban exports per head were back to the average of the rest of the Caribbean by the end of the 1950s and ended the period at about one-fifth the value of the rest of the region.

The relative performance of the Cuban economy over the long run is made very clear by Figure 16.9, but exports per head became a less useful metric after the Revolution. What is also clear from Figure 16.9 is that periods of over- or underperformance are only weakly correlated with the share of Cuba in Caribbean sugar exports. This rose steadily after 1820 to reach over 50 per cent by 1870. It then stayed high – with a brief decline in the 1890s – before jumping above 70 per cent in the First World War and even reaching 80 per cent in a few years after the end of hostilities. The share then fell until the introduction of US sugar quotas in 1934, after which Cuba continued its extraordinary specialisation in sugar. Furthermore, this did not end with the Revolution because the Cuban share peaked at over 90 per cent in the 1980s. It was only after the collapse of the Soviet Union that the Cuban share declined and had fallen to one-quarter in the first years of the new millennium.

So far we have measured long-run Cuban performance in relative terms, thereby avoiding the problem of changing prices, because these are roughly similar for all countries (at least in dollar terms). In order to gauge Cuban performance in absolute terms, it is necessary to work with constant prices (GDP per head after 1960 and exports per head before). In the interests of greater precision, an annual series of exports per head at constant (1860) prices was constructed from 1810 to 1900 and spliced to the series at 1930 prices for 1900–60. This series, covering 150 years, is shown in Figure 16.10.

Domestic exports per head at constant prices started to expand rapidly after the decision by the Spanish authorities to permit free trade in 1818. There then followed a forty-year period of almost uninterrupted growth driven on the supply-side by the slave trade, the construction of railways and the establishment of banks, and the demand-side was boosted by the end of imperial preference in the UK and rapid consumption growth in the United States. This period of expansion was interrupted by the US Civil War, the expansion of beet sugar in Europe and tariff discrimination against tobacco products everywhere.[127] However, the 1890 McKinley tariff and the subsequent Foster-Canovas Treaty between Spain and the United States promised a glorious future

---

[127] It was not, however, much interrupted by the First War of Independence because the fighting was concentrated in the eastern half of the island, and export activity was mainly in the western half.

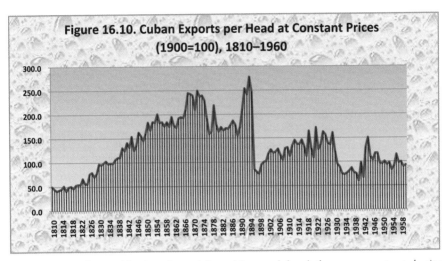

Figure 16.10. Cuban Exports per Head at Constant Prices (1900=100), 1810–1960

Source: Derived from Tables A.1, C.1 and C.9, with annual data before 1900 constructed using the same eight commodities and same methodology as in Table A.10. In those cases where the volume of commodity exports is only available in three-year or five-year averages, gaps have been filled by interpolation. The years 1810–20 have been filled using the same sources as for later years. See Notes on A. Tables.

for Cuban exports, and the volume soared to previously unheard-of levels (see Figure 16.10). The replacement of the McKinley by the Wilson tariff in 1894 followed by the Second War of Independence then pushed domestic exports per head in 1898 down to their level in 1830.[128]

The twentieth century began with a strong upswing driven by massive capital inflows and the 1903 reciprocal trade treaty between Cuba and the United States. However, the upswing was neither as long nor as powerful as that experienced before 1870, and thus the previous peaks were not achieved. By the mid-1920s, when the last new sugar mills were built, Cuba had become trapped by its dual dependence on sugar exports and the US market.[129] The downswing started before the Great Depression and would continue down to the Revolution, broken only by a brief surge in exports per head during and immediately after the Second World War. By the end of the 1950s, domestic exports per head at constant prices were down to their level of the late 1820s.

This did not mean that income per head had fallen at the same rate. The economy had become much more diversified – especially after 1930 – because import-competing activities and services became more important.[130]

---

[128] It should also be remembered that Cuban exports were much bigger than imports in the last few decades of the nineteenth century because the country had to service a fictitious debt owed to Spain.

[129] See Pollitt (1997).

[130] See Pérez-López (1987) and Santamaría (2000).

TABLE 16.5. *Income per Head in Current Dollars: Latin America (1956) and Caribbean (1960)*

Latin America, 1956		Caribbean, 1960	
Venezuela	1,143.4	Dutch Antilles	2,046.6
Chile	659.5	Bahamas	1,548.7
Uruguay	600.7	US Virgin Islands	960.3
Argentina	581.2	Puerto Rico	716.7
Colombia	525.4	Trinidad & Tobago	635.8
Costa Rica	444.4	Turks & Caicos Islands	511.1
Panama	404.2	Cuba	480.1
Latin America	365.9	Caribbean	396.3
Mexico	309.5	Caribbean excluding Haiti	466.9
Cuba	307.9		

Note: The gap between the value of Cuban income in 1956 and 1960 is not only because of changes in prices, the real economy and population, but also the fact that 1956 refers to GNP and 1960 to GDP.

Source: All Latin American countries in 1956 except Cuba are GDP per head and are from CEPAL (2009); Cuban income is GNP per head and is from Santamaría (2000) based on Alienes (1950), IBRD (1952), Banco Nacional de Cuba (1957) and CEPAL (1958). Population from Table C.1. All Caribbean countries in 1960 from Table D.1 and D.18.

Nevertheless, the Cuban economy was in serious difficulties by the mid-1950s and had gone backwards in many ways. As Table 16.5 shows, Cuban income per head was now below the Latin American average and was ranked only ninth among the twenty republics.[131] Even among the Caribbean countries, the Cuban ranking was in decline. By 1960, it had been overtaken by six countries (see Table 16.5) and was only 20 per cent above a regional average, which was in any case pulled down by Haiti.[132]

Why, therefore, is there still a myth of a Cuban golden age in the 1950s ruined only by Fidel Castro? It has, of course, been perpetuated by the exile community for obvious reasons, but it has also been defended by serious scholars.[133] Part of the reason is that Cuba had developed by the 1920s a sophisticated physical and social infrastructure that did not disappear with economic decline, and the postwar boom had permitted Cubans to import consumer durables.[134] It is also because of the allure of Havana, one of the

[131] The countries with income per head below Cuba can be found in CEPAL (2009).

[132] It may seem unfair to single out Haiti in this way, but it was the most populous country after Cuba in 1960.

[133] See Santamaría (2000). Wallich (1950), writing before the Revolution, went one step better, stating (p. 3): 'it seems safe to say that among all tropical countries Cuba has the highest per capita national income.'

[134] This helps to explain the high ranking of Cuba on a number of key indicators as late as the 1950s.

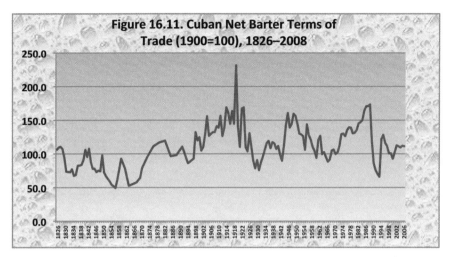

Figure 16.11. Cuban Net Barter Terms of Trade (1900=100), 1826–2008

Source: 1900 onwards derived from Tables C.26 and D.16; before 1900, I have used an annual export price index based on exports at constant prices in Figure 16.10; exports at current prices constructed from same sources as for Table A.10 and an import price index based on same sources as for Table A.30.

great cities of the world that continued to sparkle even in the 1950s.[135] Perhaps the most important reason, however, is the extreme income inequality in Cuba that allowed the top decile – including many middle-class professionals – to enjoy a standard of living that was high by international standards, the memories of which were carried away by exiles.

If Cuban prosperity in the 1950s is a myth, so is the notion that the economic cycles have been caused primarily by movements in the net barter terms of trade. The NBTT dropped sharply after the 1820s (see Figure 16.11), at a time when the Cuban economy was expanding rapidly.[136] The reason was new investments that cut costs and raised labour productivity. Subsequent movements in the NBTT bear more relation to the cycles in the real economy, but the changes are not enough to explain the extreme volatility suffered by Cuba, and the NBTT ended the period at a level very similar to what it had been nearly 200 years before.

From 1960 onwards it is possible to chart Cuban economic performance using GDP per head at constant prices and other measures. This is shown in Figure 16.12, where Cuba was already below the average of the rest of the Caribbean at the beginning of the period.[137] It was also below the average using

---

[135] See Pérez-Stable (1993), p. 30. Similarly, Rathbone (2010) captures this sense of prosperity in Havana in the 1950s in his biography of the sugar magnate Julio Lobo.

[136] See also Salvucci and Salvucci (2000).

[137] The reader will have noted that Cuba was **above** the average when current prices are used (see Table 16.5). The fact that Cuba is **below** the average using constant prices is because of the choice of 2000 as the reference year, because dollar prices are estimated to have risen faster in the rest of the Caribbean than in Cuba over the years 1960 to 2000.

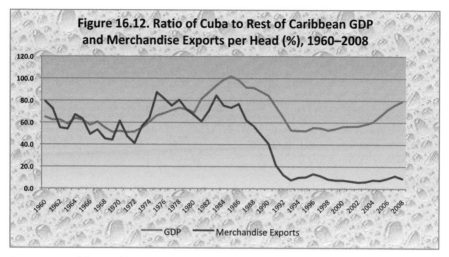

Source: Derived from Tables D.1, D.19 and D.6.

another useful measure (merchandise exports per head – see Figure 16.12). Thus, Cuba was underperforming by almost any yardstick at the end of the 1950s, and this could not be explained away by what happened in the first months of the Revolution.

The relative underperformance of the Cuban economy continued in the 1960s, but it was less marked when GDP per head is used as the appropriate measure. From then onwards, however, GDP per head started to catch up with the rest of the Caribbean and by the mid-1980s had done so – helped by a debt crisis that left Cuba untouched while damaging economic performance in the rest of the Caribbean. There was then a decline in the relative performance of GDP per head that brought it back to the level of the late 1960s. Finally, after 2003 the Cuban economy managed to recover some of its losses and finished the period with GDP per head equivalent to 80 per cent of the average of the rest of the Caribbean, with a much lower proportion in the case of merchandise exports per head.[138]

The long-run performance of the Cuban economy illustrates so much that is characteristic of the Caribbean as a whole. Export specialisation, especially in a small number of commodities, brings opportunities that can be enhanced or undermined by the commercial policies of core countries. It also magnifies the chances of external shocks that can be benign or malign. Cuba, inspired it would seem by Toulouse-Lautrec, took everything to extreme levels.[139] It specialised in sugar to excess and neglected the domestic market; it became too

[138] Despite this, exports – at least in constant prices – were an important determinant of GDP per head throughout the period. See Vidal and Fundora (2008).

[139] His motto had been 'everything in excess' in contrast to the famous ancient Greek proverb ('everything in moderation').

dependent on the United States, whose commercial policies were never designed with Cuba in mind; it then became too dependent on Soviet subsidies and is now perhaps too reliant on Venezuelan ones. Yet it was the richest country in the Caribbean for much of the period and may even become so again – especially now that its long-run economic performance no longer depends on sugar.

Statistical Appendix

This Statistical Appendix is available in electronic form at http://www
.cambridge.org/9780521145602. Throughout the Statistical Appendix values
are expressed in US dollars ($) unless otherwise specified.

A. NINETEENTH CENTURY

D. 1960–2008

Notes on A Tables

The A. Tables start in the early nineteenth century and end (except for data on slavery) in 1900. If they appear in black, they are taken from primary or secondary sources. The data in red are estimates (normally obtained by interpolation for the years between the data in black). The data in blue are either incomplete or are small 'trace' elements (see below). The data in green refer to the slave population (except for Table A.2, where all data refer to slaves). This colour-coding is used the first time an entry is used, but not if the information is repeated subsequently (in which case it appears in black). The subregional data in the table, being aggregates of country data, are therefore all given in black.

Many countries changed names during the nineteenth and twentieth centuries. To avoid confusion, I have used only the name by which countries have come to be known in English in recent decades. 'Guyana' therefore refers to the country known after 1831 as British Guiana (before that, it consisted of two colonies: Demerara & Essequibo and Berbice). I have used the name 'Belize' to describe the country that was first called the British Settlement in the Bay of Honduras, then British Honduras (in 1862) and finally (in 1973) Belize. I have used the name 'British Virgin Islands' (often abbreviated to BVI), but the colony was sometimes referred to by the name of its main island only (Tortola). The other Virgin Islands (St Croix, St John and St Thomas) are called 'Danish Virgin Islands' (often abbreviated to DVI).[1]

The Dominican Republic was called Santo Domingo until 1821; during its brief independence from 1821 to 1822 it was known as El Estado Independiente del Haití Español; it reverted to Santo Domingo after the end of the Haitian occupation in 1844 and only adopted the name República Dominicana

---

[1] The Danish authorities preferred to call them 'Danish West Indies', but because they later became the 'US Virgin Islands', I call them 'Danish Virgin Islands' in the A. Tables.

(Dominican Republic) after the end of the Spanish annexation in 1865. 'Suriname' was also called Dutch Guiana before independence in 1975, and the name 'Dutch Antilles' or 'Netherlands Antilles' only emerged after 1845, when the six islands ceased to be administered from Paramaribo. Where countries are an amalgam of islands (e.g. Antigua & Barbuda), I have listed the first island only. However, an exception is made for those countries that formed a union during the period covered by this book, that is, Turks & Caicos Islands, St Kitts & Nevis and Trinidad & Tobago, in order to avoid confusion.

At the end of the country columns in most tables, there are subregional groupings. These are based on the constitutional status of countries during most of the nineteenth century. Haiti and the Dominican Republic, independent for most of the nineteenth century, are referred to as 'Hispaniola' – the English version of the name first used by Columbus for the whole island. Haiti (independent in 1804) and the Dominican Republic (independent in 1844) therefore represent the sovereign Caribbean, despite the fact that the eastern part of the island was under Haitian control from 1822 to 1844 and under Spanish control from 1861 to 1865 (it should also be noted that the Dominican Republic was under Spanish control from 1809 to 1821). 'Spanish colonies' consist of Cuba and Puerto Rico, despite the fact that they ceased to be ruled by Spain in 1898.

Some of the 'British Colonies' were not officially British in 1810, but they were occupied by British forces. St Lucia became British by treaty in 1815 and Guyana in 1816. None of the other British colonies changed their colonial status in the nineteenth century, but for some the administrative arrangements were altered. Anguilla was a dependency of St Kitts, and the Cayman Islands of Jamaica. However, there is sufficient demographic data to treat them as separate colonies in some tables. The Turks & Caicos Islands were part of the Bahamas until 1848, but I have been able to separate them for the whole period. Nevis became part of a federation with St Kitts in 1882, and Tobago was federated with Trinidad in 1889 (the two countries then formed the union of Trinidad & Tobago in 1899), but I have kept them separate throughout. The British colonies of Antigua, British Virgin Islands, Dominica, Montserrat, St Kitts (including Anguilla) and Nevis were administered as a single Leewards Islands Federation from 1871, but I have kept each separate. Belize was not officially a colony until 1862 (but it was administered from London as if it were a colony some years before that).

The 'French Colonies' are French Guiana, Guadeloupe and Martinique, all of which were occupied by the British or its allies in 1810. Guadeloupe was transferred by the UK to Sweden in 1813, but it was transferred back to France the following year (Britain then paid an indemnity to Sweden in compensation). Guadeloupe includes its dependencies (e.g. St Martin). The Scandinavian colonies are the Danish Virgin Islands and Swedish St Barthélemy.

The 'Dutch Colonies' (all occupied by the British in 1810) are Suriname and the Dutch Antilles. The latter consisted of six islands: three in the Dutch

Windwards (St Eustatius, Saba and Sint Maarten)[2] and three off the coast of Venezuela (Aruba, Bonaire and Curaçao).[3] Sint Maarten (Dutch) and St Martin (French) are parts of the same island. The administrative arrangements for the Dutch Antilles changed several times in the nineteenth century.

'Scandinavian Colonies' consist of St Barthélemy and the Danish Virgin Islands (DVI), but St Barthélemy became a dependency of Guadeloupe in 1878. Except for population it is impossible to separate St Barthélemy from Guadeloupe after this date, so 'Scandinavian colonies' in the last part of the nineteenth century normally refers to DVI only. The Danish Virgin Islands comprised the islands of St Thomas, St John and St Croix – all occupied by Britain in 1810 and returned to Denmark in 1815. Their status did not change in the rest of the century, despite lengthy negotiations with the United States on the terms of a sale.

TABLES A.1–A.9

Tables A.1–A.9 contain data on population, slavery, migration, school enrolment and wage rates in the nineteenth century. The titles are as follows:

Table A.1. Population
Table A.1.a Population (adjusted for per capita calculations)
Table A.2. Slave Population
Table A.3. Crude Birth Rates
Table A.4. Crude Death Rates
Table A.5. Slave Imports
Table A.6. Net Migration (excluding slave imports) as Percentage of
    Population
Table A.7. School Enrolment
Table A.8. Predial Wage Rates (1870=100)
Table A.9. Trade Wage Rates (1870=100)

SOURCES FOR TABLES A.1–A.9

TABLE A.1. POPULATION

When there are no data for the first (1810) or last (1900) year in each column, the interpolation has been carried out using data before 1810 (for the first year) and after 1900 (for the last year). The sources for these earlier or later years are listed below along with the sources for the other figures.

---

[2] The Dutch always referred to these three islands as being in the Windwards, but the British and others placed them in the Leewards. This is because of the circular route taken by Dutch ships during the age of sail.
[3] These three islands, often referred to as the ABC islands, for the Dutch were in the Leewards because of the circular shipping route referred to in note 2.

Estimation by interpolation is valid in most cases. However, health epidemics were particularly serious at certain times in the nineteenth century. Where we know the numbers who died, an adjustment has been made to the interpolation to take account of the death toll in specific years. Further details are provided below for the different countries where this was done.

The maroon and Amerindian population has been included in the figures as far as possible. In most cases, the numbers are so small that it does not make a big difference. However, in the case of Suriname it does. The enumerated population in Suriname in the nineteenth century excludes the maroons and Amerindians, so an additional column has been added in Table A.1, where an estimate is made for them. The two columns are then included in the subregional total for the Dutch colonies.

Hispaniola

Haiti

No reliable census was taken for Haiti in the period between 1810 and 1900. The first Haitian census was taken in 1804 (the year of independence) and gives an estimate of 380,000 (see Victor (1944), p. 28). This census is generally thought to be reasonably accurate. The second census was taken in 1824 and gives a figure of 873,867 for the Haitian part of the island (see Mackenzie (1830), p. 110–2). All are agreed that this figure is vastly inflated, but many secondary sources still use it even today (see, e.g., Engerman and Higman (1997), p. 51). Mackenzie (appointed British consul in Haiti in 1826) gained access to an unpublished population figure, also derived from the census, which gives a much lower number and which was used by the Haitian government for tax purposes. This figure is probably too low, because it implies Haitian population actually fell between 1804 and 1824. Many secondary sources have widely inconsistent numbers, but Tippenhauer (1893) estimates both Haitian and Dominican population up to 1890 (it is also quoted in Marte (1984), p. 279). This is the basis for the figures in black in Table A.1 up to 1860. However, I have allowed for some acceleration in the growth of population between 1860 and 1890 compared with Tippenhauer's figures.

For 1900 there is an estimate (1,250,000) derived from records provided by the Catholic Church. The original estimates can be found in Victor (1944). This is too low because it implies very fast growth in the first two decades of the twentieth century. Much higher numbers can be found for 1900 in other secondary sources (e.g. Sánchez-Albornoz (1986)), but these are all based on a figure produced a decade later by the Haitian government without the use of a census. We do know, however, that the population was calculated at 2 million in 1922 during the US occupation.

To estimate the population in 1900, I have therefore worked backwards from 1922. I have assumed a CBR of 45.0 and a CDR of 25.0 in this period, but I have made some allowance for net emigration (0.5% per year) because we know that Haitians were emigrating after 1900 to Cuba (see Pérez de la Riva

(1975), vol. 2, p. 48) and the Dominican Republic in significant numbers. This gives a population figure of 1,434,257 in 1900, which implies annual growth between 1900 and 1922 (after outward migration) of 1.5 per cent.

Dominican Republic

The population figures for the Dominican Republic are also contentious. Both Moya Pons (1974) and Hoetink (1982) describe in detail the different censuses and estimates that were taken in the nineteenth century. The main dispute is over the estimate for 1863 based on Catholic Church records that was dismissed by a US Commission of Inquiry as being inflated. However, the estimate for 1871 produced by that same Commission of Inquiry looks far too low. I have therefore relied on the same source (Tippenhauer (1893)) as for Haiti (also quoted in Marte (1984), p. 279), and this is the basis for the figures in black up to 1890. The figures are consistent with evidence from other sources (see, e.g., Billini (1885), pp. 40–1). The figure in black for 1900 is taken from Franco (1999) and is consistent with the data provided by Moya Pons (1975). However, many secondary sources (see, e.g., Barón Castro (1945) and Wilkie (1974)) have much higher figures, which are almost certainly wrong in the light of the unofficial Dominican census taken in 1908.

Spanish Colonies

Cuba

Several censuses were held in Cuba in the nineteenth century, and a good summary can be found in Santamaría and García (2004), pp. 74, 256, which is the basis for the figures in black in Table A.1 for 1827, 1846, 1862, 1877, 1887 and 1899. I have followed this source in ignoring the 1841 census (if the 1841 census were to be accepted, it would mean a sharp fall in the slave population between 1841 and 1846, and this is not credible).[4] There is an excellent discussion of the whole matter in Kiple (1970), chap. 5.

The 1817 census is also problematic. There is an excellent discussion of all the issues in Instituto de Investigaciones Estadísticas (1988), pp. 130–44, which sets out the different estimates for the same year and the reasons why they vary. I have opted for the estimate made by Alexander Humboldt, which starts from the census figure (c.552,000) but adds nearly 80,000 to allow for military personnel stationed on the island, transients and slaves trafficked in 1817. The figure for 1810 is not from a census; it was prepared by Valle Hernández and includes a figure for the slave population (212,000) that is widely used. See Instituto de Investigaciones Estadísticas (1988), p. 132.

Cuba suffered from a very severe attack of cholera in 1833, in which an estimated 30,000 died. There was another attack of cholera in 1853 when

---

4 The other possibility is that the 1846 census is unreliable and that the drop in the slave population is caused by an effort by the Spanish authorities to conceal the extent of the illegal traffic in slaves. Plausible though this might seem, it is not the view of most scholars of Cuba.

another 20,000 are estimated to have died. See Marrero (1983), vol. 9, pp. 173–4. Both of these epidemics have been taken into account in the interpolations. The annual increase in population is adjusted upwards between the census data (in black) to take account of the high death toll in 1833 and 1853. Cuba is also known to have suffered between 1870 and 1899 another 21,448 deaths from yellow fever and 12,722 from smallpox. See Bureau of the Census (US) (1909). This represents an average of 1,178 deaths per year at a time when the population was rising at around 6,000 per year. I have not adjusted the population figures because it is not known in which years between 1870 and 1899 the epidemics were most serious.

The 1899 figure in black is from the census held under US occupation. The next census was held in 1907, and an estimate is made of the population in 1900 based on the increase between 1899 and 1907. See Bureau of the Census (US) (1909).

Puerto Rico

Perhaps because the number of slaves was much lower, the enumeration of the population in Puerto Rico seems to have been less problematic. I have used Lavallé, Naranjo and Santamaría (2002) for 1811, 1820, 1824, 1827, 1829, 1832, 1840, 1854, 1860, 1867, 1880, 1883 and 1890. The same source also has a figure for 1807, which is the base year for calculating 1810. I have used Coll y Toste (1899) for other years except 1899. In that year a census was held under US occupation. The figure for 1900 is taken from Carter (2006), vol. 5, which has a consistent series for the whole twentieth century. The interested reader should also see Jimeno Agius (1885).

There was a major cholera epidemic in 1855–6, in which an estimated 30,000 died. See Figueroa (2005), p. 74. This falls inside the two census years of 1854 and 1860, so I have adjusted the interpolated figures to take account of this epidemic.

British Colonies

The figures in black after 1850 all come from UK government official sources found in *Parliamentary Papers* (PP). See the various issues of (a) *Statistical Abstract for the several Colonial and other Possessions of the United Kingdom* and (b) *Statistical tables relating to Colonial and other Possessions of the United Kingdom*. The few exceptions to this are listed below. Before 1850, the figures come in the main from the *Blue Books* for the various colonies. However, in the period up to the mid-1830s much of this information has been conveniently collected in Martin (1834) and Martin (1843).

There was a major outbreak of cholera in many of the British colonies in the 1850s. Because we have figures on births and deaths for the intercensal years (1851–61), I have revised the population figures for net births. Assuming the figures are accurate, the resulting population figure for 1861 should be the same as the census in the absence of net migration. Because there was some

net migration, the figures for 1852–60 have therefore been adjusted upwards or downwards by the ratio of the estimated 1861 population to the census population.

For Anguilla and the Cayman Islands, the data have been supplemented with estimates found in Higman (1984) and Engerman and Higman (1997). For the Bahamas and Turks & Caicos Islands before 1850, the population estimates have been separated by reference to the disaggregated figures in the primary sources for each island. For Guyana, the figures published in the decennial census after 1831 (there was no census in 1901) do not always agree with those published in PP. The difference appears to be because of the treatment of the Amerindian population. I have always used the higher figure in order to include the Amerindian population as far as possible.

The population figures for Belize before 1861 (when the Maya and Garinagu populations in the south were first included) require special attention. The first census after 1810 was taken in 1816, and all major secondary sources (e.g. Dobson (1973), *Report of the British Guiana and British Honduras Settlement Commission* (1948), Shoman (2011) and Bolland (1977)) give the same figure (it excludes the indigenous population). There is a figure for 1806 in Dobson (taken from colonial records), which is then used as a starting point to interpolate the figures from 1810 to 1815 (there is a much higher figure for 1806 in *Report of the British Guiana and British Honduras Settlement Commission* (1948), but this figure is derived from Belize's London agent, who may have had an interest in exaggerating the number).

The next reliable figure is 1823, and this is given by all main secondary sources. Bolland (1977) and *Report of the British Guiana and British Honduras Settlement Commission* (1948) then have wildly different figures for 1826 (even after deducting from the latter the number of troops stationed in Belize), but no number is given by Dobson (1973). I have therefore next used Dobson's figure for 1829, but it is higher than *Report of the British Guiana and British Honduras Settlement Commission* (1948) or Bolland (1977), because the primary source is given as colonial records. There are then very unreliable – and implausibly low – figures for 1831, 1832 and 1835 in various secondary sources. Because Dobson states explicitly that her 1831 figure excludes the free coloured population, I have ignored all these figures and moved to 1841, which Dobson provides with the source given as *Parliamentary Papers*. Dobson also gives a figure from the *Blue Book* for 1845.

The next reliable figure is the census in 1861. However, the superintendent of Belize wrote to the governor of Jamaica in 1858 giving an estimate of the population in 1857, and I have also used this. See Burdon (1934), vol. 2. From 1861 onwards there are decennial census data. Thus, the figures in black are 1816, 1823, 1829, 1841, 1845, 1857 and the census data from 1861 onwards. Gaps have been filled by interpolation.

Using this methodology, the population is estimated to have grown continuously from 1810 to 1861 rather than to have experienced a sharp fall in the 1830s as is usually assumed. Although we know that the slave population

declined through escape and manumission before emancipation (see Chapter 11), the Belize economy experienced a boom after 1820 as a result of the growth of the entrepôt trade and domestic exports, so a large decline in the total population is not plausible. In any case, it is stated in *Report of the British Guiana and British Honduras Settlement Commission* (1948), p. 217, that the early estimates often underreported the free coloured population.

French Colonies

For French Guiana, the figures come mainly from Mam-Lam-Fouck (1987) and Mam-Lam-Fouck (1999), but Moreau de Jonnès (1842) is another excellent source for the early years. The only exception is 1837, which comes from Société d'Etudes pour la Colonisation de la Guyane (1844). These numbers are supposed to include the maroons and Amerindians, but at first they exclude the penal population (later the convicts were added, and the penal population reached about 7,000 at its peak – a high proportion of the total). The population estimates for Martinique come from Moreau de Jonnès (1842), Blérald (1986) and Tomich (1990) and from various issues of the *Annuaire de la Martinique*. The estimates for Guadeloupe come from Moreau de Jonnès (1842), Blérald (1986), Bangou (1987) and Buffon (1979) and from various issues of the *Annuaire de la Guadeloupe*. Note that the figures for Guadeloupe and the French colonies in Table A.1, but not A.1a, exclude St Barthélemy, even after 1878.

Dutch Colonies

Dutch Antilles

There are population figures for the six islands of the Dutch Antilles for some years in Goslinga (1990) and Hiss (1943) and for Curaçao only in Hartog (1968). There are also figures for each island in *Almanak voor de Nederland-sche West-Indische Bezittingen*, which was published in various years between 1856 and 1860. However, the best source is Benjamins and Snelleman (1917),[5] because this encyclopedia gives the population figures for each island in every census year. The years are not always the same, so I interpolated the population of each island in the missing years and then summed the total for the six islands.

Suriname

The figures for Suriname are in two columns. The first column refers to the enumerated population. There are figures in van Lier (1991), Buschkens (1974), Panday (1959) and Goslinga (1990) for different years. It is difficult to reconcile

---

[5] See entries under each island (the figures for Curaçao in 1854–62 erroneously include other islands).

these numbers, so I used Benjamins and Snelleman (1917), p. 665, which gives the population at different intervals, and interpolated the gaps.

The enumerated population of Suriname excludes the maroons and Amerindians, so the second column makes an estimate of this population. There are scattered figures in Goslinga (1990) and a more systematic attempt to measure the numbers in Price (1976) and de Groot (1985).

Scandinavian Colonies

Danish Virgin Islands

The figures in black are census data and are all taken either from Westergaard (1917), Hornby and Justesen (1976), Brøndsted (1953), vol. 2, or *Statistisk Aarbog for Danmark* (published annually with a section on the Danish Virgin Islands from 1900). The first source has a population figure for the three islands in 1797, which is the base year for calculating the figures before 1815. There are also some data on population in Knox (1852). The 1900 figure is interpolated backwards from the census figure in 1901 (given in Westergaard (1917) and all other quoted sources).

St Barthélemy

There is only one Swedish colony (St Barthélemy) because I have ignored the brief period (1813–4) when Guadeloupe was also Swedish. The figures for St Barthélemy up to 1872 are taken from Hyrenius (1977). There is a figure for 1878 (the year the island was transferred back to France) in Bourdin (1978), p. 343. The population was estimated to be 2,654 in 1889 and 2,549 in 1921 (see *Annuaire de la Guadeloupe*) and 2,519 in 1931 (see Platt et al. (1941), p. 63), so I have estimated the population in 1900 at 2,600.

The numbers for St Barthélemy after 1878 in Table A.1 have been deducted from the figures found for Guadeloupe in the sources listed above (see French Colonies). When added together, therefore, the figures after 1878 give the estimated population for Guadeloupe and all its dependencies (see Table A.1.a).

TABLE A.1a. POPULATION (ADJUSTED FOR PER CAPITA CALCULATIONS)

The data in the nineteenth century from Table A.10 onwards are based on decennial data. Table A.1 has therefore been adjusted to facilitate per capita calculations. Because the data from Table A.10 onwards include Anguilla with St Kitts, Cayman Islands with Jamaica and St Barthélemy with Guadeloupe from 1880, Table A.1a adjusts the population data in Table A.1 in the same way. In addition, the two columns for Suriname have been added together. It is then possible to obtain per capita values in the nineteenth century for all countries and subregions using Table A.1a. As explained at the beginning of this note, the entries in Table A.1a are all in black because they have appeared before in Table A.1.

TABLE A.2. SLAVE POPULATION

Hispaniola

Slavery was abolished in Haiti (or St-Domingue as it was then called) in 1793. The following year, slavery was abolished in all French colonies. Although Napoleon restored slavery in the French colonies in 1802, this French law had no effect in St-Domingue. With the declaration of Haitian independence in 1804, slavery was legally ended in the western part of Hispaniola.

In the Dominican Republic (Santo Domingo), unlike in St-Domingue, slavery had ceased to be of much importance by the end of the eighteenth century. On the eve of the French Revolution, there were an estimated 12,000 slaves in a population of 125,000. During the first Haitian occupation of Santo Domingo by Dessalines (1804–5), slavery was abolished. Although there may have been some slaves before Santo Domingo declared independence in 1821, there is not much evidence for it. In any case, slavery was finally abolished during the second Haitian occupation (1822–44). It was not revived even under the Spanish annexation (1861–5).

We may therefore assume that there were no slaves in either country in the relevant years, so the columns in Table A.2 are blank.

Spanish Colonies

Cuba

There are figures in each year of the census (see note to Table A.1). However, for the data before the 1862 census, I have chosen to use Kiple (1970), table 2, pp. 156–8, because it provides a yearly estimate from 1810. This series starts with the slave numbers in the population estimate for 1810 (see Table A.1 above). The series then takes into account the change in the slave population as a result of the slave trade, the difference between slave births and deaths and manumissions. The numbers are also very close to the census figures before 1862, except for 1817 where I have used the figures from Humboldt (see Table A.1 above). For 1862 and 1877, I have used Santamaría and García (2004).

Slavery was legally abolished in 1880 and replaced by the *patronato* system. It is common to find estimates of Cuban slaves up to the end of the *patronato* system in 1886. However, this would be inconsistent with the slave series for the other countries in Table A.2. I have therefore stopped the series for Cuba in 1880, just as the series for the British colonies stops in 1834, for the Swedish colonies in 1847, for the Danish and French colonies in 1848 and for the Dutch colonies in 1863, despite the fact that they many of them had 'apprenticeship' systems after that date. The interested reader will find the *patronato* numbers for Cuba after 1880 in Scott (1985), p. 194.

Puerto Rico

The main sources are Curtin (1969), p.34; Lavallé, Naranjo and Santamaría (2002); Coll y Toste (1899); Jimeno Agius (1885); and Curet (1980). The

interested reader should also consult Morales Carrión (1974); Díaz Soler (1974); and Dorsey (2003).

British Colonies

All the data are taken from Higman (1984), with the following adjustments:

Antigua & Barbuda. The two islands have been aggregated.

Guyana. Demerara & Essequibo and Berbice have been aggregated.

Turks & Caicos Islands. This has been separated from the Bahamas by assuming that the slave population was 15% of the total.

Grenada. The slave population was falling after 1810. However, the estimated slave population before 1820 has been reduced from that given in Higman (1984), because it is greater than total population in 1810 in Table A.1. The adjustment is very minor (I have assumed 1819= 1820+100; 1818=1819+100; etc.).

French Colonies

Slavery was finally abolished in 1848,[6] but the sources only provide data up to 1847. I therefore estimated 1848 assuming the same decline in the number of slaves as between 1846 and 1847.

French Guiana. All the data come from Mam-Lam-Fouck (1987).

Guadeloupe. The years 1815–38 are from Moreau de Jonnès (1842). This is also the source for 1788 from which 1810 is derived by interpolation. The source for 1847 is Blérald (1986).

Martinique. The data for 1832–47 are from Tomich (1990). The other years (1816, 1826 and 1831) are from Curtin (1969), p. 78. Curtin also gives a figure for 1807, from which 1810 can be interpolated.

Dutch Colonies

Dutch Antilles

For 1816, the data for Curaçao come from Hartog (1968); the data for other islands are from Goslinga (1990). The data for 1790, from which 1810 is derived by interpolation, is from Goslinga (1990). For 1863, the data are all from Goslinga (1990). For other years, I assumed Curaçao was 60 per cent of the total; the data on Curaçao for these years are from either Hartog (1968) or Goslinga (1990). There are also figures for 1854 and 1856–8 in *Almanak voor de Nederlandsche West-Indische Bezittingen* (1856; 1858–60).

Suriname

For the years up to 1831, I have used Benjamins and Snelleman (1917). For 1848–62, there is a series in Panday (1959), p. 170. The figure for 1863 comes

---

[6] It had been abolished in 1794, but Napoleon restored it in 1802.

from Goslinga (1990). Gaps have been filled by interpolation. The column for the maroon and Amerindian population is empty because none were slaves.

Scandinavian Colonies

All the data for St Barthélemy come from Hyrenius (1977). All the data for the Danish Virgin Islands come from Westergaard (1917). There are also figures on the slave population before 1848 in Dookhan (1974).

TABLES A.3. AND A.4. CRUDE BIRTH RATES AND CRUDE DEATH RATES

The quality and quantity of information on births and deaths leaves a lot to be desired. In addition, being flows rather than stocks, annual births and deaths fluctuate sharply from year to year. In the case of deaths, the variations are sometimes extreme as a result of occasional epidemics (e.g. cholera in the 1850s). As a result, interpolation of missing entries is not always appropriate. I have, however, been able to construct numbers for all British colonies in 1820, 1830, 1840, 1845 and all years from 1850 to 1900. For other countries, the numbers are less complete.

Table A.3 gives the Crude Birth Rate (CBR), which is the number of births per 1,000 population. Table A.4 gives the Crude Death Rate (CDR), which is the number of deaths per 1,000 population. Tables A.3 and A.4 are generally derived by dividing births and deaths by the relevant population numbers in Tables A.1 and A.2. In a few cases, however, I have entered estimated values for the CBR and CDR directly.

As before, the data are colour-coded. The numbers in black are taken from official sources. The numbers in red are estimated. The numbers in blue mean that the primary source is incomplete. A number in green means that the Crude Birth Rate (CBR) and Crude Death Rate (CDR) have been obtained by dividing slave births/deaths by slave population in Table A.2.

There is no consistency in the treatment of infant mortality. During slavery, a child was often only registered if it survived the first few days, weeks or even months. Higman (1984) has made an adjustment for slave births and deaths during the registration period (1817–34), and the difference is significant. Following emancipation, there were some colonies where stillbirths were recorded in some years, but there is no clear pattern. Although this does affect birth and death rates, it should not affect the estimates of the net increase in population.

The registration of births and deaths has been used wherever possible. Where these are not available, I have used baptisms as a proxy for births and burials as a proxy for deaths. In these cases, there is probably some underreporting. The colonial secretary in St Vincent, for example, reported on the figures for 1859 and 1861 that 'this is not a complete return, as many deaths occur which are not reported and some baptisms escape registration' (*Parliamentary Papers* (1863), cd3219, p. 204). In these cases, I have not adjusted the figures because

there is normally no reason to believe that the degree of underreporting is different for births and deaths.

Hispaniola

Haiti

There are virtually no data for Haiti. The only information in the tables is derived from the number of births and deaths in Cap Haitien between 1821 and 1826. See Mackenzie (1830). From this, the CBR and CDR for Cap Haitien can be worked out, and this has then been applied to the whole country for those years (in blue because the numbers are based on incomplete data). I have estimated the CBR and CDR for 1900 as 45 and 25, respectively.

Dominican Republic

The data for 1838 and 1839 come from Marte (1984). The primary source quoted by Marte gives births and deaths in the south of the country for 1838 and for the north in 1839. From this, I have constructed the CBR and CDR and applied this to the whole country for the two years. Marte (1984) also gives the number of births and deaths in 1883.

The CBR and CDR for 1900 are estimated from the data for 1906. These can be found in *Dominican Republic* (1907).

Spanish Colonies

Cuba

Vital statistics for Cuba in the nineteenth century are very deficient. For 1827, Marrero (1983), vol. 9, gives the CBR for the free population (white and nonwhite), and I have made an assumption about the slave CBR based on later years. For 1841, 1846 and 1862, I have used births given in the census in those years.[7] For 1900, I have used the figure in the 1907 census (see Bureau of the Census (1909)), but adjusted it upwards assuming a similar degree of underreporting of births as in 1906 (the census found that births in 1905 were 10,000 fewer than the number recorded as one year old in 1906). I have then interpolated the CBR for 1835, 1855, 1877, 1887 and 1895. I have not used the CBR from 1889 to 1900 in Schroeder (1982) because the numbers are too low to be credible.

For deaths, I have relied on the figures given for Havana only throughout the nineteenth century (they are therefore in blue). These are given as decennial averages from 1830 onwards in the Bureau of the Census (1909), but annual figures for the 1870s can be found in Porter (1899), p.165, and there is also a figure for 1900 itself. Because this is a consistent series, albeit for only one part of the country, it is likely to be more reliable than other methods of

[7] Although the 1841 census is unreliable on the population and number of slaves, I saw no reason not to use it for births and deaths.

constructing CDRs. The CDRs for Havana have then been used to calculate deaths in Cuba in the corresponding years. The results are reasonable for 1841 and 1846 (when we have census information on deaths). However, the 1862 census records 33,034 deaths, implying a CDR in that year of only 23.4. This is much lower than that for Havana in the 1860s, and I have not used it, but the difference could possibly be explained by various epidemics that affected Havana – but not the rest of Cuba – in that decade.

Most of this information on vital statistics is conveniently summarised in *Anuario Estadístico de Cuba 1914* (1915), where it is also disaggregated by ethnicity.

Puerto Rico

There are figures for births and deaths in 1814, 1818 and 1828 (average of 1823–32) in Jimeno Agius (1885). There is also a figure for deaths in 1867, but not births. Curet (1980), p. 217, gives the CBR and CDR for the slave population in Ponce only in 1864, and I have used this as an estimate for the slave CBR and CDR for the whole island in that year. There is then a series from 1888 to 1898 in the 1899 census. See Sanger, Gannett and Willcox (1900). The 1900 figures are estimates based on the nearest census years (1899 and 1910).

British Colonies

For 1820 and 1830, I have used Higman (1984) with minor adjustments (see below). These data refer to slave births and deaths only. I have used Higman's adjusted data rather than registered births and deaths. This makes an allowance for underreporting (particularly of infant deaths). Higman gives the CBR and CDR for a grouping of years. I have used the mid-point to derive 1820 and 1830, unless it is the end or beginning year. In that case, I have taken an average. These CBRs and CDRs have then been multiplied by the slave population (see Table A.2) to give slave births.

For 1840 onwards, I have used colonial sources (*Blue Books* before 1850 and *Parliamentary Papers* afterwards). *Blue Book* numbers are usually based on baptisms (proxy for births) and burials (proxy for deaths) and may therefore underestimate births and deaths. In addition, some parishes within colonies failed to report in some years, making the data incomplete.

Anguilla

The slave CBR in 1820 is not reported in Higman (1984). I have assumed a value of 40. In the case of the CDR in 1820, I have assumed it was the same as in 1830. From 1840 onwards, Anguillan births and deaths were assumed to be 10 per cent of St Kitts (excluding Nevis), except for deaths in 1854 when there was a cholera epidemic in St Kitts. From 1882 onwards, when the Federation of St Kitts, Nevis and Anguilla was formed, this is equivalent to 6 per cent of the Federation.

Antigua

For 1820 and 1830, I have aggregated the data for Antigua and Barbuda in Higman (1984).

The Bahamas

For most of the years before 1850, the data on the Bahamas include the Turks & Caicos Islands. I have assumed the CBR and CDR for Turks & Caicos in 1820 and 1830 to be the same as for the Bahamas and applied this to the slave population in Table A.2. (the Bahamas numbers have then been adjusted to exclude Turks & Caicos). The births and deaths in Turks & Caicos in 1840 and 1845 have been interpolated based on the numbers from 1850. I have adjusted the Bahamas births and deaths in those years, because the *Blue Book* says that the numbers are incomplete. I have assumed the 1850 figure for the Bahamas to be the same as 1851. From 1851 onwards, the figures on births and deaths are fairly complete for both colonies.

Barbados

Baptisms and burials are reported for almost the entire period, rather than births and deaths. There are no data for 1850 to 1855, so these years have been interpolated by reference to the figures in 1845 and 1856. There is a big drop in deaths after emancipation. This could be because of underreporting following the end of the registration period. However, Barbados is a small island where church records of burials were reasonably complete. The colonial secretary, for example, regularly reported that over 50 per cent of deaths were of children under nine years old, suggesting that child deaths at least were recorded.

Belize

There are no data in Higman (1984) for 1820 and 1830, so I have assumed a CBR of 35 and a CDR of 30 in both years. The figures for 1840 are in fact for 1836 (see Martin (1843)). There is also a figure in Martin for total births in 1832, which is consistent with the estimate of slave births in 1830 (slaves were roughly half the population in that year). Baptisms and burials are reported from 1845 onwards, but there is a gap between 1871 (1869 in the case of burials) to 1885. This has been filled by interpolation, and the figures are therefore in red.

British Virgin Islands

There are only a few gaps in the primary sources, and these have been filled by interpolation.

Cayman Islands

After emancipation, I have assumed a CBR of 20.0 and a CDR of 10.0 in all years because there are no data in the primary or secondary sources.

Dominica

There are figures for 1840 (births only), 1845, 1850 and 1860 onwards, but not for 1851 to 1859. These years have been filled by interpolation using the average of 1859–61 as the end year.

Grenada

There are no data for 1840. There are baptisms and burials for 1845, but they are so low I have ignored them. I have therefore adjusted slave births and deaths in 1830 for the nonslave population and used this as the basis to interpolate 1840 and 1845 from the 1850 data. There are almost complete figures from 1851, and I have assumed 1850 to be the same as 1851.

Guyana

The data for Demerara & Essequibo and Berbice in Higman (1984) have been aggregated to give the figures for 1820 and 1830. There are estimates of births and deaths in the *Blue Book* for 1843, but nothing after that until 1882, except for an estimate in 1857. There are, however, decennial figures on net migration, so I have proceeded as follows:

> *Deaths.* I have assumed a CDR of 35 based on the data from 1882 onwards. This has then been applied to the missing years, except for 1857, for which we have an observation (it implies a CDR of 39, and it is stated in the official records that 1857 was a year of cholera).
> *Births.* I have calculated births in each of the missing years as the difference between the annual change in population, net migration and deaths. This implies a CBR that varies from year to year.

Jamaica

There are no data after emancipation until 1879. I have therefore adjusted the slave figures in 1830 to derive total births (using the ratio of slave to total population). I have then completed the gaps through interpolation up to 1879 (with the final year an average of 1879–81). This gives a CBR that is similar to the estimates in Eisner (1961), pp. 133–40. For deaths it is necessary to take into account the epidemics that swept the island between 1850 and 1854. I have therefore assumed that the CDR fell to 30 in 1840 and 26 in 1845 and stayed at that level until the 1870s (see Eisner (1961)). I have then added to this an additional 35,000 deaths between 1850 and 1854 as follows: 1850 (5,000), 1851 (20,000), 1852 (5,000), 1853 (0) and 1854 (5,000). This is consistent with what we know about the number of deaths from cholera and yellow fever in those years.

Montserrat

Interpolation from 1840 to 1850 has served for 1845. The figures from 1888 include stillbirths.

Nevis

There are figures for Nevis in most years. Interpolation from 1840 and 1850 fills in for 1845. For Nevis after 1882, see St Kitts.

St Kitts

The primary sources give figures for St Kitts only up to 1882. From then onwards, the numbers include Nevis and Anguilla because they refer to the Federation of St Kitts, Nevis and Anguilla. Based on the data in 1882, I have assumed Nevis in the case of births to be 30 per cent of the Federation total and St Kitts to be 64 per cent. The balance is accounted for by Anguilla. In the case of deaths, the figures are 25 per cent for Nevis, 68 per cent for St Kitts and the balance accounted for by Anguilla. For St Kitts, the years 1850–4 have been estimated. The number of deaths in 1855 was very high because of the cholera epidemic in that year.

St Lucia

From 1882, births are said to include stillbirths (there is no way of telling if they are included in earlier years).

St Vincent

I have adjusted the figures in 1830 to make an allowance for nonslave births and deaths. This is then the base for interpolation of 1840 and 1845, using 1850 as the end year. From 1850 the data are fairly complete, but the numbers for 1853 and 1854 given in the primary source are the same (I have not made any adjustment). Births from 1879 onwards are said to exclude stillbirths.

Tobago

The figure for 1845 has been interpolated from 1840 and 1850. From 1850 onwards, the figures are mostly complete. Tobago was federated with Trinidad in 1889, and this became the unified colony of Trinidad & Tobago a decade later. However, the data are reported separately until 1899. Births and deaths in 1899–1900 were assumed to be 7.5 per cent of Trinidad & Tobago, based on figures for earlier years. The Trinidad figures have then been adjusted. For Tobago, births from 1882 are reported to include stillbirths. There is a superb two-volume study on Tobago in this period by Craig-James (2008).

Trinidad

For 1899–1900, see Tobago. Total births in 1830 have been estimated from slave births using the ratio of slaves to total population. This is then the basis for interpolation of figures in 1840 and 1845. The figures are reasonably complete from 1850 onwards except for 1855–8. These years have been filled by interpolation.

Turks & Caicos Islands

See the Bahamas above.

French Colonies

French Guiana

Mam-Lam-Fouck (1982), p. 147, is the source for 1824. This is also the source for slave births and deaths in 1845. I have adjusted this to allow for nonslave births and deaths. See also Mam-Lam-Fouck (1987), p. 31.

For 1831–8, the source is Moreau de Jonnès (1842). For 1849 onwards, the source is Mam-Lam-Fouck (1987), p. 178. The 1900 figures for CBR and CDR are taken from Tables C.2 and C.3.

Guadeloupe

The figures for 1831 to 1838 are from Moreau de Jonnès (1842). From 1839 to 1900, I have used the annual average figures in *Annuaire Statistique de la Guadeloupe* (1954). This is an historical series giving births and deaths in the whole period up to 1953, from which the CBR and CDR can be derived.

Martinique

Moreau de Jonnès (1842) is the source for births and deaths between 1834 and 1838. Slave births and deaths between 1839 and 1847 are from Tomich (1990). The years 1863–5 come from *Annuaire de la Martinique*. The CBR and CDR for 1900 are taken from Tables C.2 and C.3.

Dutch Colonies

Dutch Antilles

For Curaçao, there are data on slave births and deaths for 1845 to 1850 in Dorsey (2003), p. 199. These are given in blue because they refer to only one island. For Aruba, there are data on slave births and deaths for some years, and I have also used these up to 1853. See Hartog (1961), p. 220. These are in green. For 1854 and 1856–8, there are full data (slave and nonslave) for all six islands in *Almanak voor de Nederlandsche West-Indische Bezittingen* (1856; 1858–60). The CBR and CDR in 1900 are taken from Tables C.2 and C.3.

Suriname

For 1839–41, nonslave births and deaths are from van Lier (1971), pp. 98–9, and slave births and deaths from Goslinga (1990). I have added them together to derive total births and deaths. For 1848, slave data are from van Lier (1971), p. 170, and all births and deaths from 1849 to 1862 can be found in the same source. For 1863–7, the source is Goslinga (1990) and for 1868–72 it is van Lier (1971), p. 188. For 1873–4, the source is Goslinga (1990). Finally, for 1860s–1900s CBR and CDR for each decade can be found in van Lier (1971), p. 293. I used these to interpolate the gaps and to calculate births and deaths. There is also a very detailed table on births and deaths in the colony for 1855 in Focke (1855), p. 140.

Scandinavian Colonies

Danish Virgin Islands

For the Danish Virgin Islands, Johansen (1981) has a very thorough study of slave births and deaths up to emancipation in 1848. His figures suggest a slave CBR of 40 and a CDR of 50 in the 1840s. The annual *Statistisk Aarbog for Danmark* gives births and deaths from 1896 (both include stillbirths). For earlier years there are incomplete data on births in Hornby and Justesen (1976), but not enough to estimate the CBR and CDR.

St Barthélemy

Hyrenius (1977) gives a figure for births only in St Barthélemy in 1845. After his adjustments, this comes out as a CBR of 40. Because Hyrenius estimates that births exceeded deaths by 0.3 per cent, this gives a CDR of 37 for the same year.

TABLE A.5. SLAVE IMPORTS

The trade in slaves was abolished by Denmark from 1 January 1803, by the United States and the UK from 1808, by Sweden from 1814, by France and Holland from 1818 and by Spain from 1820. However, an illegal trade continued in some cases until much later. Table A.5 contains data on slave imports from 1815. During most of this time, the slave trade was illegal in all countries.

When the trade was illegal, there were no official figures. However, the net trade in slaves is the difference between the change in the slave population, net slave births and manumissions. It is therefore possible to make estimates for the illegal trade in slaves even when there are no figures for slave trafficking itself. The resulting figures are the net inflow of slaves, and most of these slaves would have come from Africa, with a smaller number from other parts of the Caribbean or the southern United States. For a few countries, the methodology suggests outward migration of slaves, but the figures are not presented here. In these cases, the slaves would have been sold elsewhere (usually to the Spanish colonies).

Spanish Colonies

Cuba and Puerto Rico were responsible for most of the traffic in slaves in the period after 1815. The trade was legal up to the first Anglo-Spanish treaty in 1817, which committed Spain to end it by 1820. This treaty had little impact, and the second Anglo-Spanish treaty in 1835 was equally ineffective. The Spanish Penal Law in 1845 was more important, but the trade did not seriously decline until after the US Civil War when US slave traders to Cuba were finally subject to severe penalties.

Cuba

I have used the annual series in Pérez de la Riva (1979). Eltis (1987) has a similar series but it stops in 1867. Both are comparable with the series in Kiple (1970), table 2, which stops in 1860. There are estimates in Curtin (1969), but research since then means that these figures need to be updated. The Eltis series stops in 1867 on the grounds that there were no more slave imports. However, Pérez de la Riva (1979) claims to have found evidence of slave imports until 1873, and these figures have also been used by Santamaría and García (2004).

Puerto Rico

There is an estimate in Curtin (1969), but I have used my own estimate. This uses a similar methodology but different assumptions on slave vital statistics. Curtin assumed that slave deaths exceeded slave births by so much that the slave population would decrease by 2 per cent per year without the slave trade (as he assumed for Cuba). This may have been correct for Cuba, but it seems too pessimistic for Puerto Rico in view of what we now know about its vital statistics. I have therefore started with the change in the slave population (see Table A.2) and assumed that the slave population would have declined by 1.5 per cent in 1815–19, by 1 per cent in 1820–9, by 0.5 per cent in 1830–9 and 0 per cent in the 1840s (when the slave trade to Puerto Rico appears to have ceased). I have also assumed that manumissions were – like the slave population – 10 per cent of the Cuban figure (estimated by Kiple (1970)). Eltis (1987) includes Puerto Rico in his estimates of the nineteenth-century slave trade, but the figures are aggregated with other American regions.[8] Although slave purchases stopped in 1846, Kiple (1970) has estimates of slave sales (1,000 per year) to Cuba for 1846–55.

British Colonies

The illegal trade after 1808 was almost certainly very small, and I have therefore made no allowance for it. There was, however, a legal trade in slaves between different British Caribbean colonies until 1830. See Eltis (1972). It consisted mainly of imports by Guyana and Trinidad, which had a severe labour shortage from the moment they became British colonies. I have annualised the figures for Guyana, Trinidad and the other British colonies given in Eltis (1972) for the periods 1815–25 and 1825–30.

---

[8] Eltis (1987), p. 134n66, explains that the Puerto Rican slave import figure is assumed to be 10% of the Cuban figure over the years 1811–45 and, although not shown, has been distributed across each year according to the distribution of imports into the sugar-growing municipality of Ponce as given in Scarano (1984), pp. 136–7. This seems too crude a basis on which to proceed. Eltis et al. (1999) also has a magnificent database giving details on ships bringing slaves to Puerto Rico and other countries in the Caribbean, but it does not give a complete picture of the illegal slave trade.

French Colonies

France had committed itself in 1814 to end the traffic in slaves within five years, and this was confirmed in the Anglo-French treaty of 1818. The trade continued without interruption, however, until 1831 when a new Anglo-French treaty introduced an equipment clause that allowed the British navy to search French ships suspected of carrying slaves.

I have used Eltis (1987) for all three French colonies. There are also estimates in Curtin (1969). The Eltis series stop in 1831, but it is possible that the trade continued in a small way until emancipation in 1848.

Dutch Colonies

The Anglo-Dutch Court in Suriname, which sat until 1845, dealt with only one ship carrying illegal slaves. However, it is widely assumed that many shipments escaped the attention of the Court. I have therefore relied on the estimate of 1,000 imported slaves each year from the end of the Napoleonic Wars to 1826 in Emmer (1998), p. 122. For the Dutch Antilles, by contrast, there appears to have been outward migration from the beginning. See Dorsey (2003). This would have been centered on Curaçao, which had always been an entrepôt for the slave trade. See van Soest (1978).

Scandinavian Colonies

There were some sales of slaves to other islands after the end of the legal trade (see Dorsey (2003)), but these are likely to have been so small that they can be ignored for quantitative purposes.

TABLE A.6. NET INWARD MIGRATION (EXCLUDING SLAVE IMPORTS) AS PERCENTAGE OF POPULATION

The figures in Table A.6 are quinquennial averages. In all cases the data refer to inflows less outflows, and the figures are therefore net. A positive entry implies net inward migration, and a negative entry implies net outward migration. The data in Table A.6 are given relative to the equivalent population. Thus, the data for 1851–5 have been divided by the sum of the population for 1851–5 and expressed as a percentage. All countries experienced some net migration over the period, but in several cases it was either insignificant or we have no data.

Hispaniola

Haiti
There was a serious attempt by President Boyer to attract free blacks at the beginning of the 1820s, and around 6,000 are known to have arrived in 1824.

At the time, Haiti and the Dominican Republic were one country, and many of the migrants settled in Samaná Bay in what is now the Dominican Republic (see Stephens (1974)). Other attempts were made by Haiti to attract migrants, especially in the 1860s, but these were not very successful. See Redpath (1861). Some migrants did come from the French Antilles after emancipation in 1848, and there were at least 3,000 immigrants from the British colonies in Haiti by the 1890s. I have not, however, included any estimates for Haiti in Table A.6 because there are no data on net migration.

Dominican Republic

A number of Cuban families settled in the Dominican Republic during the first Cuban War of Independence. By the end of the century, the growth of the sugar industry was beginning to attract migrants from elsewhere in the Caribbean, but the numbers were still small. See Lluberes Navarro (1978). I have not included any estimates for the Dominican Republic in Table A.6 for the same reason as for Haiti, but we do know that some migrants were coming in the 1890s, attracted by the expansion of the sugar industry.

Spanish Colonies

Cuba

Chinese migration of indentured labourers began in 1848, but the inflow was not significant until 1853. See Turner (1974). It stopped in 1874 following the visit of Chinese inspectors to Cuba (they wrote a damning report on the treatment of the Chinese – see Cuba Commission Report (1993)). The number that left China between 1848 and 1874 was 141,391; 16,576 died on the voyage and 124,813 entered Cuba.

Migration from the Yucatán also started in 1848, but by the time of the census in 1862 there were only 763 in the whole of Cuba, so the net annual migration must have been low. Yucatán migration began again in 1871, but it never reached the scale of Chinese immigration.

Long before the end of the slave trade, a major effort was made to attract white immigrants to Cuba. Some came during the Napoleonic Wars, particularly from Haiti. However, the publication of the *Real Cédula de Gracias* in 1817 provided new incentives for immigrants, and there is no doubt that some took advantage of this, but not enough to increase the white population above what might have been expected anyway through net births. Between the censuses of 1846 and 1862 there was a large net migration of Spaniards (*peninsulares*) and Canary Islanders. I have estimated net migration for each group as the difference between the observed increase and what would have happened if the two groups had grown from 1846 at 3 per cent per year (the white population as a whole grew at 3.7 per cent in this period).

Following the end of the slave trade, immigration from Spain became very important. The net flows are included in the table, starting in 1882. During the Second War of Independence, the net migration turned negative. However,

the gross flow was enormous even in the 1890s. Altogether, it is estimated that 524,658 Spaniards came to Cuba between 1882 and 1899; of these 427,185 returned to Spain, leaving a net inward migration of 97,437. See Santamaría and García (2004). The sugar boom in the last decades of the century also attracted a number of migrants from the rest of the Caribbean after 1880. See Knight (1985).

All these migration flows have been put together in Table A.6 for Cuba, which therefore includes net white migration between 1846 and 1862 (from Spain and the Canary Islands); Chinese gross migration between 1848 and 1874; Caribbean gross migration after 1880; and Spanish net migration from 1882 to 1899.

For 1900, the US Census estimated a net inward migration of 23,000, but this has not been entered in the table because it refers to a single year.

Puerto Rico
It is clear from the decennial figures for population (see Table A.1a) that there must have been substantial net migration into Puerto Rico in the 1820s. A study on migrants from the rest of the Caribbean before 1850 (Chinea (2005)) shows that Caribbean migration was not significant in numerical terms. That suggests that the net migration was primarily from Spain and had much to do with the *Real Cédula de Gracias* promulgated in 1815 (two years before Cuba). Because we have CBRs and CDRs for Puerto Rican population in the period before 1830 (see Tables A.3 and A.4), it is possible to calculate net migration in the 1820s.

From 1830, the growth of the white population (see Figueroa (2005), table 2.1, p. 48) was consistent with what we know about net births. However, there was a surge in the nonslave black and mulatto population in the 1850s. This surge coincided with the end of the slave trade. It cannot be explained by manumission or by the difference between CBRs and CDRs. I have therefore assumed that the natural growth of this group was 2 per cent, and thus the remainder is net migration. Presumably, most of this came from the rest of the Caribbean, but some may also have come from the United States or even the northern states of South America.

The final Puerto Rican net migration taken into account in the table is in the 1890s. This time there was a net outmigration because the black and mulatto population declined quite sharply. Again, I have assumed a 2 per cent natural growth and estimated outmigration as the residual. It is likely that most of these migrants went to the United States.

British Colonies

Net annual migration is the difference between the change in population and net births. This means that for the British colonies from 1850 onwards it can be derived for each year from Tables A.1, A.3 and A.4. These numbers then capture all net migration, assuming that the population and vital statistics are

accurate. I have also included estimates of migration before 1850 for some countries using secondary sources.

Migration was particularly important for Guyana and Trinidad throughout the period after 1830 and of some importance elsewhere. In these years, migrants came from Europe (mainly Madeira), Africa (mainly freed slaves), India, China and from other British colonies in the Caribbean. European immigration from countries other than Portugal began in the 1830s, but this was a failure and amounted to only a few thousand. Immigration from Madeira began in earnest in the 1840s and was important in Guyana (30,000 had arrived by 1882), but much less so elsewhere. African migration began in 1840. Between 1841 and 1867, 36,000 Africans migrated to the Caribbean, and almost all went to either Guyana (12,810), Trinidad (8,000) or Jamaica (11,000). See Moore (1987), pp. 42–7.

Indian indentured labour was authorised in 1845 to Guyana (one ship privately contracted had arrived as early as 1838), Jamaica and Trinidad, but it was quickly stopped and not resumed until 1851. See Roberts (1966), Look Lai (1993) and Laurence (1994). Later that decade it was authorised to Grenada, St Lucia, St Vincent and St Kitts. Chinese immigration to the British Caribbean began in 1852 and lasted until 1879, but it was not very important. Migration from one British colony to another, however, was important, and census data (giving the birthplace of migrants) suggest that it started as early as the 1840s.

Official sources indicate that the migrants to Guyana and Trinidad, in particular, came from a wide variety of countries. The decennial Guyana census, for example, shows that Portuguese (i.e. Madeirans) had reached the country by 1841, when they were 2.6 per cent of the population. By 1891 there were 12,166 'Portuguese' in the country (4.4% of the total) of which 5,378 had been born in Madeira. In the 1851 census there were 4,925 people whose birthplace was Barbados, and another 4,353 had come from other British colonies. In Trinidad, Venezuelans dominated the 'other' category, which represented 2 per cent of the population in 1871.

Belize received some Indian migration following the Indian mutiny in 1857. However, the most important source of migration to Belize was from Mexico during the Caste Wars in the Yucatán. There was also some migration of Amerindians from Guatemala. Belize, in common with some other countries, received a small number of *emancipados* from Cuba. These were Africans who had been taken illegally from Africa, but whose ships had been apprehended by British or Spanish warships. The net migration after 1850 is captured in Table A.6 in the usual way, but I have also estimated the inward migration from 1836 to 1850 because it was proportionately very large.

Looking at the decennial population figures in Table A.1a, it is clear that there must have been net migration into the Bahamas in the second half of the 1830s, because the figures are too large to be explained by net births alone. However, this was followed by a decade of outward migration. The migration flows from 1836 to 1850 have therefore been included. On the growth of the Bahamian population, see Johnson (1996).

French Colonies

French Guiana
After slavery, the first migrants came in 1851 from Madeira, but this did not continue. Between 1854 and 1859, there was a small inflow of Africans. Indian migration (from both French and British India) began in 1856 but ended in 1877. There was a very small migration from China and Vietnam ('Annamites'). See Mam-Lam-Fouck (2002). The forced migration of French prisoners to the penal colony (*la bagne*) after 1851 has not been taken into account.

Guadeloupe
Indian inward migration began in 1854 and continued until 1889. It was significant in net terms and even more so in gross terms. See Blérald (1986).

Martinique
Indian migration was important and started in the 1850s. See Tinker (1993), p. 96.

Dutch Colonies

Dutch Antilles
The sale of slaves to other islands has already been considered (see Note to Table A.5). Other net migration does not appear to have been very important.

Suriname
The 'apprenticeship' period ended in 1873, and that is the year in which migration from British India began. Migration from Java (a Dutch colony) began in 1888. The figures are given net in both cases. See Hoefte (1998).

Scandinavian Colonies

I have estimated net migration in the Danish Virgin Islands on the assumption that the natural growth of the population was -1 per cent each year, because deaths exceeded births (see Tables A.3 and A.4). This suggests there was net inward migration into the Danish Virgin Islands between 1850 and 1870 and again after 1880.[9] In the case of St Barthélemy, I assumed the natural growth of the population was 1 per cent per year after 1850 and estimated net migration accordingly. On this assumption, net migration was outward most of the time before the transfer to France.

---

[9] In 1863 the Danish Virgin Islands imported 321 indentured Indians following lengthy negotiations with the British government. This was one of the reasons for the (gross) inward migration during the period 1860–70 of 4,068. See Sircar (1971).

TABLE A.7. SCHOOL ENROLMENT

School enrolment covers primary and secondary schools, but even at the end of the nineteenth century secondary enrolment was a very small part of the total. Where a variety of figures are given in the primary sources, I have excluded evening enrolment and Sunday school attendance. For some British colonies in the last decades of the century, there are figures on both enrolment and average attendance. I have given the enrolment figures, but it should be noted that average attendance varied from 40 to 70 per cent.[10]

The numbers for the British colonies come from *Parliamentary Papers* from 1850 onwards. There are no separate data for Anguilla and the Cayman Islands. After federation in 1882, I calculated that Nevis was 20 per cent of the total for St Kitts & Nevis based on the figures for 1879–81. In the case of Tobago, I assumed it was 10 per cent of the figure for Trinidad & Tobago in 1900 based on the figures in 1888–90. The figure for 1832 is from *Parliamentary Papers* (cd. 53). For 1840, I have used Martin (1843) and the *Blue Books* for the different colonies.

For Haiti the figures come from Rotberg (1971), p. 101, and are based on Logan (1930); in the case of the Dominican Republic, the figures come from Marte (1984). For Cuba the source for 1817, 1836 and 1861 is Knight (1970), pp. 295–300. For other years it is Bureau of the Census (1909). For Puerto Rico, it is Jimeno Agius (1885), pp. 17–18. For French Guiana, it is Farraudière (1987), pp. 77, 153. For Guadeloupe, it is Bangou (1987), vol. 2, p. 58. For Dutch Antilles, it is Benjamins and Snelleman (1917), p. 525. For Suriname, it is van Lier (1971) and Goslinga (1990). The Danish Virgin Islands figure is from Brøndsted (1953), vol. 2, p. 474. I have not been able to find data for Martinique and St Barthélemy.

To understand the trends in the nineteenth century, I have filled in the decennial years wherever possible (because there are insufficient records for 1830, I have used 1832 for the first decade). To provide a consistent record, I have interpolated any missing figures for the British colonies for the years 1832, 1840, 1850, 1860, 1870, 1880 and 1890 using the nearest available numbers. For Haiti, I have used 1876 for 1880; for the Dominican Republic, I have used 1883 for 1880; for Cuba, I have used 1836 for 1832, 1860 for 1861, 1882 for 1880, 1888 for 1890 and 1899 for 1900. In 1900, school enrolment in Cuba is given as 172,000 – twice the level in 1899 – but this is misleading in terms of the nineteenth-century trends. For Puerto Rico, 1857 is used for 1860, 1866 for 1870, and 1883 for 1880. For Guadeloupe, 1888 is used for 1890. For the Danish Virgin Islands 1886 is used for 1890. The Suriname data are given for every five years starting in 1870.

TABLES A.8 AND A.9. PREDIAL AND SKILLED
WAGE RATES (1870=100)

Wage rates for estate workers are given in Table A.8 for a sample of eight British colonies (the labour is described as 'predial', which means it is essentially

---

[10] See Bacchus (1994).

unskilled agricultural labour). The data are taken from *Parliamentary Papers* for the period from 1850 to 1900. Before 1850, I have used Rivière (1972) and *Blue Books* for the individual colonies. The data are usually given per day or per task. Where shown per week, they have been converted to the daily rate. I have chosen 1870 as the base year, so 1870=100.

The data are sometimes reported as a spread of rates (from minimum to maximum). The range can reflect many things, including the amount the workers paid in rent for estate cottages (see Bolland (2001), pp. 591–7), the extent of provision grounds and the skill level of the tasks involved. Because it is impossible to disentangle all these elements, I have taken the median value in all cases where a spread is given. Any gaps have been estimated by interpolation and are therefore shown in red.

Nominal wage rates for skilled workers ('trade' wage rates) are given in Table A.9 for the same sample of British colonies. The data are taken from *Parliamentary Papers* for the period from 1850 to 1900 and from the *Blue Books* for the individual colonies for earlier years. As before, 1870 is chosen as the base year, median values have been used where a spread of wage rates are shown and any gaps have been filled by interpolation and are shown in red.

TABLES A.10–A.22

Tables A.10–A.22 contain decennial data from 1820 to 1900 on exports. The tables are as follows:

Table A.10. Export Data by Country
Table A.11. Domestic Exports
Table A.12. Re-exports
Table A.13. Merchandise Exports
Table A.14. Domestic Exports (1860 prices)
Table A.15. Unit Value of Exports (1860=100)
Table A.16. Export Volume Index (1860=100)
Table A.17. Value of Commodity Exports (current and 1860 prices)
Table A.18. Structure of Domestic Exports (current and 1860 prices)
Table A.19. Prices of Principal Export Products
Table A.20. Exports to the United States (%)
Table A.21. Exports to the UK (%)
Table A.22. Exports to the 'Mother' Country (%)

The sources used to construct these tables are given by country below. First, however, some general principles are laid out. These principles also apply to the remaining A. Tables (A.23–A.38) and in many cases to the B., C. and D. Tables. They are therefore not repeated.

Data are colour-coded as follows: data from primary or secondary sources in black; estimated data in red; small 'trace' elements (see description of Table A.10) in blue.

Export data have been constructed at decennial intervals starting in 1820. Decennial data are three-year averages unless stated otherwise. Thus, 1820 is the average of 1819–21, 1830 is the average of 1829–31, and so on. The exception is 1900, where a single year is used in order to be consistent with the export tables covering the twentieth century that start in 1900 (see Table C.5 onwards). The use of decennial data based on three-year averages is designed to reveal long-term trends. It does not capture intradecennial fluctuations, such as those caused by the US Civil War in the 1860s or the impact of the Second Cuban War of Independence in the 1890s.

Wherever possible, a distinction is made between domestic exports (Table A.11) and merchandise exports (Table A.13). The difference is explained by re-exports (see Table A.12). Re-exporting is a service activity, which contributes both to total economic activity and to the balance of payments. Assuming that the markup between imports and re-exports was 10 per cent, we can – where appropriate – incorporate the service element of re-exports into domestic exports. This is done occasionally in some of the chapters in Part I using the data in Tables A.11 and A.12.

I have used volume and value data on the principal exports for every country in each decennial year, from which unit values or prices can be derived (see Table A.10). The volume data are extremely useful, because – when multiplied by price – they can be used as a check on the value of domestic exports from primary or secondary sources and to provide the basis for the export series at constant prices from which the unit value of exports is derived. The volume and value data for each commodity for each country can then be summed to give commodity exports for the whole Caribbean at constant and current prices (see Table A.17).

In order to make the volume data comparable, they have been converted into common units. In the case of dry measures of weight, I have almost always used the British ('short') pound (2,240 lbs=1 ton) and converted other measures accordingly. The main exceptions are mahogany (measured by board feet), bananas (measured by bunches), salt (measured by bushels), cattle (measured by units) and gold (measured by troy ounces). In the case of liquid measures, I have used the imperial gallon (4.5 litres=1 gallon).

In the primary and secondary sources volume is often given in units that are no longer in use. There are several Web sites that help to identify the modern equivalents of these old measures. See also Clarence-Smith (2000), app. 4. In the British colonial records, for example, there are numerous measures of volume that need to be adjusted. I have converted liquids measured in casks at 1,022 per gallon, puncheons at 70 per gallon (up to 1890 but at 100 per gallon from 1900 onwards because the colonial conversion rate changed), hogsheads at 52.5 per gallon and barrels at 31.5 per gallon. These were the conversion rates for Jamaica, and they are assumed to apply to other countries. In the case of dry measures, especially important for sugar, the conversion rate varied by country for hogsheads, tierces, barrels and bags. For the British colonies, I have used the conversion rates given in *Parliamentary Papers* (cd. 7904, p. 40), and

I have applied the rates for Jamaica in those cases where the conversion is not given.

The volume data are converted to values using prices. These prices are usually the unit values for the country concerned (they do not appear in Table A.10, but can be derived by dividing values by volumes in that table). I then used these prices to build up a master list for each commodity from which prices can be 'borrowed' in those cases where there are no price data (see Table A.10 below).

The dominant global currency in the nineteenth century was the pound sterling, but for the twentieth and twenty-first centuries (at least so far) it has been the US dollar. I have therefore converted all values and prices to US dollars in order to have consistent data for the whole period dealt with in this book. This requires the use of exchange rates. For the conversion rate of the US dollar to the main currencies used in the Caribbean colonies, I have used Schneider, Schwarzer and Zellfelder (1991). This invaluable three-volume source lists the annual rate of exchange of the US dollar to various European currencies (but not Caribbean currencies – see below).

In theory, it is necessary to know among the core countries the rate of exchange of the US dollar to the currencies of the UK, France, Spain, Holland, Denmark and Sweden. In practice, because data for the Scandinavian colonies are nearly always given in US dollars or their equivalents (e.g. Danish West Indian dollars)[11] and the Spanish colonies did not adopt the Spanish *peseta* (see below), it is only necessary to know the rate of exchange of the dollar to the pound sterling, the French franc and the Dutch guilder.[12]

The following table lists the decennial values based on three-year averages (except 1900, which is a single year). It will be seen that the rate of exchange was very stable, so I have chosen to ignore minor fluctuations, and I have rounded the values for simplicity. Thus, the US dollar is converted to the pound sterling at 4.80 (i.e. £1=$4.80) in 1820 and 1830 and 4.87 thereafter. The US dollar is converted to the French franc at 5.0 (i.e. 5 Fr=$1) throughout the period and to the Dutch guilder at 2.5. The Dutch Antilles and Surinamese guilders were initially quoted at different rates, but the data I have used have all been converted from Dutch guilders. Because I have used decennial data, it is possible to ignore the depreciation of the US dollar during the US Civil War.

[11] The Danish West Indian dollar had a value very similar to the US dollar (the difference was never more than 5%). It declined in importance after 1898 when the Bank of St Thomas (responsible for note issues) collapsed. In 1904, a new bank was founded and given a thirty-year monopoly on currency issues. The new currency was the Danish West Indian franc (equivalent to 0.2 Danish West Indian dollars and therefore roughly equal to the French franc). This currency in turn was withdrawn in 1934 when the monopoly ended, by which time the US dollar had become the main currency.
[12] The Dutch colonies, especially the Dutch Antilles, did have some special currency problems from time to time, and these are referred to in the notes below.

Exchange Rate of US Dollar to Core European Currencies
(three-year average except 1900) and the Gold/Silver Ratio

Year	Pound Sterling*	French Franc	Dutch Guilder	Gold/Silver Ratio**
1820	4.76	5.43	2.57	100
1830	4.80	5.24	2.51	100
1840	4.87	5.22	2.49	100
1850	4.87	5.21	2.50	100
1860	4.87	5.18	2.42	100
1870	4.87	5.18	2.45	100
1880	4.87	5.18	2.51	86.2
1890	4.87	5.18	2.50	74.9
1900	4.87	5.18	2.49	47.2

* By convention, the US dollar is quoted to the pound sterling as the number of US dollars that can be exchanged for one pound sterling. For all other currencies, it is the other way round (i.e. foreign units per US dollar). The exchange rate shown for sterling is the par value.

** This is the ratio in 1820 (=100) based on 10 oz fine gold having a value of £38.90 and 10 oz fine silver having a value of £25.19. The decline in the index after 1870 means that the value of silver was falling in relation to gold.

The table also shows the gold/silver ratio and the depreciation of silver in terms of gold after 1870. This created a problem for those countries whose monetary system was partly based on silver currencies during the nineteenth century. These included Haiti, the Dominican Republic, Cuba, Puerto Rico, Guyana and Belize.

The independent countries (Haiti and the Dominican Republic), not being European colonies, had their own currencies. The rate of exchange of the Haitian gourde and the Dominican peso to the US dollar depreciated severely for much of the nineteenth century. However, precisely because both were weak currencies subject to frequent devaluations, exports are almost always recorded in hard currencies (usually US dollars or Spanish *pesos fuertes*, French francs or pounds sterling), and therefore the derivation of US dollar values for the countries of Hispaniola is possible. Indeed, the US dollar was legal tender in the Dominican Republic by 1900.

The Haitian exchange rate is discussed in detail in the Notes on B. Tables, where Table B.1 shows the gourde's annual value. Like the gourde, the Dominican peso was very unstable. The *peso fuerte*, the old Spanish unit of account, circulated before independence in 1844 and was effectively at par with the US dollar. However, in 1844 at the time of independence a national peso was created with a nominal value of 40 per Spanish doubloon (roughly 16 per US dollar). Paper issues immediately after independence reduced its value by 1855 to 1,000 to the doubloon. See Marte (1984), p. 160. Thereafter it fell even more precipitately until it had become worthless by the time of the Spanish annexation in 1861. Because this unit of account was so depreciated, the medium of

exchange was usually gold and silver coins (*moneda fuerte*) with an equivalent value in dollars. The Spanish government during annexation (1861–5) reestablished a hard currency (*peso fuerte*) valued at roughly $1. All Dominican note issues after the end of the Spanish annexation were fraught with problems, and they were made illegal in 1896. However, because trade taxes, which accounted for the bulk of public revenue, were payable in hard currency, it is relatively easy to estimate public revenue and use this as a check on trade figures.

The Spanish colonies did not use the *peseta* introduced by Spain at the end of the 1860s (it later exchanged under the gold standard at 6.16 per US dollar, and I have used this value for Spanish trade with the Caribbean colonies when they are quoted in *pesetas*). Instead, they used the *peso fuerte*. Until the fall in the gold value of silver, this was close enough in value to the US dollar to make no difference. The depreciation of silver before 1880 is not big enough to be a matter of concern, so values in *pesos fuertes* can still be used in that year. Furthermore, by 1900 the United States was the occupying power, and the US dollar was in use. The only decennial year that is problematic is therefore 1890. The trade figures are usually quoted in gold, so I have decided not to alter the values in pesos, but any figures quoted in silver pesos will be overvalued. The extent of this overvaluation is hard to judge. Based on Dietz (1986) and Porter (1899), it could be around 25 per cent.

The British colonies distinguished at first between 'pounds currency' and 'pounds sterling', both using the same symbol (£). I have always used the latter, because the conversion to US dollars is much easier. In the case of Belize (British Honduras) and Guyana (British Guiana), a colonial dollar was adopted towards the end of the nineteenth century that fluctuated in value before being pegged (the annual rate of exchange is given in *Parliamentary Papers*). The Belizean dollar was eventually pegged to the US dollar (and can therefore be converted from sterling at 4.87), and the Guyanese dollar was pegged at 4.80 to sterling (making the Guyanese dollar worth $1.01458).

The Belizean dollar had an unusual history. Before its introduction, Belize trade with Central America was very important. Coins from the Central American republics were therefore used together with Mexican silver dollars and Peruvian and Chilean *soles*. The silver dollar (known in Belize as *sol* regardless of its origin) was then the de facto currency, being converted to pounds sterling at the fixed rate of 5.0. However, the fall in the silver price after 1870 forced the colonial authorities to take some action, and their first response (in 1887) was to make the Guatemalan silver peso legal tender. See Bristowe and Wright (1890). This, however, did not resolve the problem because the Guatemalan peso continued to depreciate. The US dollar (based on gold) was therefore made legal tender in 1894. From 1879 to 1894, therefore, the exchange rate of *sol* in Belize varied as a result of the depreciation of silver against gold. See Chapter 11.

The constant price series use 1860 (average of 1859–61) as the base year. This is exactly half way between the start (1820) and end (1900) of the period and also avoids most of the price distortions caused by the US Civil War.

The current and constant price series for 1860 are therefore the same. This means that unit values (prices) can be constructed that have 1860 as their base (1860=100).

No data series on exports for the nineteenth-century Caribbean will ever be completely accurate. The biggest problem is likely to have been caused by smuggling because traders sought to avoid trade taxes. This was less of a problem for exports than imports, but it nonetheless must still be taken into consideration (it was probably most serious in the case of Cuban cigars, because they were so heavily taxed in the US). Comparisons of the value of export 'x' to country 'y' with the value of the commodity 'x' imported by country 'y' invariably show up a difference that cannot be explained by the normal discrepancy between *fob* and *cif* prices. Other sources of error are the use of 'official' prices to value commodities that do not reflect market prices and the counting of re-exports as domestic exports.[13]

It is important not to exaggerate these problems. The most reliable figures we have are likely to be the volumes of the principal exports (see Table A.10), and these provide the building blocks for many of the tables. The ability to compare prices from other countries for the same commodity reduces the risk of major errors in pricing, and the value of domestic exports must always be at least as great as the sum of the value of the principal exports. These checks and balances reduce the chances of major errors in the tables.

DESCRIPTION OF TABLES

TABLE A.10. EXPORT DATA BY COUNTRY

Table A.10 contains the commodity export data for each country. The principal commodities are given (a) by volume, (b) by value, and (c) at 1860 prices. Where a commodity had ceased to be exported by 1860 or where it started after 1860, I have added a small 'trace' element ($100) for that year, and it is shown in Table A.10 in blue (the volume is derived by dividing the value by a price taken from the master list). These trace elements are needed to ensure that all principal commodities contribute to the different indices constructed from Table A.10. The sum of the values of the principal commodities at current and constant prices are also shown and are labelled 'subtotal'. They usually represent above 90 per cent of the value of domestic exports (also shown).

Prices are not shown in Table A.10, but they can be derived by dividing values by volumes. The sugar price for Barbados in each year, for example, is simply the value divided by the volume of sugar exports in that year. Where the value and volume are three-year averages, the price or unit value is therefore also a three-year average. These commodity prices are *fob* and even for the same year they vary from country to country. The master list of prices for each commodity for each year uses an average of these prices that can be used to fill

---

[13] For a discussion of these problems in relation to Latin America, see Platt (1971).

in the gaps for any country when the price is not known. This is what is meant by the use of the 'master list' in the country descriptions below.

There are no export data for either Anguilla or the Cayman Islands, because their exports are subsumed in St Kitts and Jamaica, respectively. When constructing per capita measures, therefore, the population data for Anguilla must first be added to St Kitts, and that for the Cayman Islands must be added to Jamaica. Similarly, there are no export data for St Barthélemy after 1870, because its exports are included in Guadeloupe from 1880 onwards. The population data for St Barthélemy for 1880, 1890 and 1900 in Table A.1 must therefore be added to that for Guadeloupe before constructing per capita measures. All these adjustments are done in Table A.1a.

TABLE A.11. DOMESTIC EXPORTS

This table contains domestic exports at current prices (also shown in the final column of Table A.10 for each country). Usually, the numbers are derived from primary or secondary sources (see country descriptions below). Where there are no data or where the data are not credible, I have used instead the sum of the value of principal commodities in Table A.10 and made a small adjustment for minor exports where appropriate.

TABLE A.12. RE-EXPORTS

This table contains re-exports for those countries where figures were available. In some countries no figures are provided, but it is clear from a comparison of the sum of the principal exports and the value of merchandise exports that re-exports must have taken place. In that case, I have included an estimate of re-exports, and these figures are shown in red. Re-exports were particularly important for the Danish Virgin Islands, the Dutch Antilles, St Barthélemy (1820 and 1830 only) and Belize. All countries had some re-exports, but it has not been possible to estimate them in every case.

TABLE A.13. MERCHANDISE EXPORTS

This table contains merchandise exports. It is the sum of domestic exports in Table A.11 and re-exports in Table A.12.

TABLE A.14. DOMESTIC EXPORTS (1860 PRICES)

This table contains domestic exports at constant (1860) prices. To obtain these figures, I first constructed an index of the volume of exports (1860=100) based on the sum of the principal commodities at constant (1860) prices in Table A.10. This index was then applied to the value of domestic exports in the year 1860 in Table A.11 to give the value of domestic exports at constant (1860) prices. The values in Tables A.11 and A.14 for 1860 are therefore the same.

TABLE A.15. UNIT VALUE OF EXPORTS (1860=100)

Table A.15 contains the unit value of exports (1860=100) for each country. This is obtained by dividing the sum of the value of principal commodities in Table A.10 at current prices by the sum of the value of principal commodities at 1860 prices in the same table. The subregional indices (e.g. French colonies) are obtained in the same way by first aggregating the subtotals for the relevant countries and then dividing the current values by the constant price values. The index for the whole Caribbean was also constructed in this way.

TABLE A.16. EXPORT VOLUME INDEX (1860=100)

Table A.16 contains the export volume index (1860=100). This is derived for each country from Table A.10 using the sum of the principal commodities at constant (1860) prices. For the subregions and the Caribbean as a whole, it is obtained in the same way by first summing the subtotals for the relevant countries.

TABLE A.17. VALUE OF COMMODITY EXPORTS (CURRENT AND 1860 PRICES)

Table A.17 contains the values of the principal Caribbean commodity exports at current and constant (1860) prices. These values are all derived from Table A.10.

TABLE A.18. STRUCTURE OF EXPORTS (CURRENT AND 1860 PRICES)

Table A.18 contains the commodity export structure at current and constant (1860) prices. It is obtained by dividing the commodity values in Table A.17 by the value of Caribbean domestic exports at (a) current (in Table A.11) and (b) constant (in Table A.14) prices.

TABLE A.19. PRICES OF PRINCIPAL EXPORT PRODUCTS

Table A.19 contains the prices of the principal Caribbean commodity exports (sugar, molasses, rum, cacao, coffee, cotton, tobacco, cigars, logwood, mahogany, bananas, rice, spices, coconuts, salt, sponge and gold). This is obtained by dividing the value of exports of each commodity for all the countries in Table A.10 by the volume of exports for the same countries. The results are expressed as US cents per unit of volume.

TABLE A.20. EXPORTS TO THE UNITED STATES (%)

Table A.20 shows the proportion of domestic exports (%) going to the United States.

TABLE A.21. EXPORTS TO THE UK (%)

Table A.21 shows the proportion of domestic exports (%) going to the UK.

TABLE A.22. EXPORTS TO THE 'MOTHER' COUNTRY (%)

Table A.22 shows the proportion of domestic exports (%) going to the 'mother' country. The 'mother' is the colonial power. In the case of the independent countries, it is the former colonial power (France for Haiti and Spain for the Dominican Republic). For Cuba and Puerto Rico in 1900, Spain is still treated as the 'mother'. For St Barthélemy, the 'mother' is Sweden until the transfer to France.

SOURCES FOR TABLES A.10–A.22

Hispaniola

Haiti
Haiti has a separate Statistical Appendix (Tables B.1–B.10), from which the Haitian entries in Tables A.10–A.22 have been derived. The details on Haiti are contained in the Notes on B. Tables and are therefore omitted here to avoid repetition.

Dominican Republic
The Dominican Republic was a Spanish colony in 1820, under Haitian occupation in 1830 and 1840 and annexed by Spain from 1861 to 1865. In the 1890s, political tensions reached boiling point, culminating in control of the customs house by the United States in 1905. Not surprisingly, therefore, there is a paucity of consistent data on exports for the nineteenth century. Yet it is possible to put together a series beginning in 1820. Marte (1984) is a particularly useful compendium of primary sources, and Gómez (1979) has data for the period after 1870 that are difficult to find anywhere else. There are also data in Franco (1999), Rodríguez and Vélez (1980), Moya Pons (1976) and Cassá (1987), 2 vols. In addition, Clarence-Smith (2000) has figures on cacao exports, Baud (1995) on tobacco exports and Deerr (1949) on sugar exports.

The main exports were mahogany and tobacco (all years), sugar (starting in 1860), cacao (1820 and again from 1860), coffee (from 1860) and hides (1820–60 and again in 1900), cigars (1820–60) and bananas (1900 only). Mahogany and tobacco accounted for almost all exports by value until the rise of sugar after 1860. Minor exports (not shown in Table A.10) include *lignum vitae* and beeswax.

1820. Volumes of the principal exports (in 1822) are taken from Marte (1984). Prices (for 1820) are as follows: mahogany (as for Haiti); tobacco (from the master list); cacao (from Martinique); hides (from the detailed

trade data for the Dominican Republic in 1847–8 in Marte (1984)). The value of exports is based on the sum of the value of the principal exports with an allowance for minor exports. The export share for the UK is derived from Marte (1984) and is based on exports in 1825 from the ports of Santo Domingo and Puerto Plata. Other export shares are estimated.

1830. There are no data for 1829–31, so I have used the data for 1835 in Marte (1984), separating Haiti and the Dominican Republic. The prices, however, are for 1830. Mahogany and tobacco prices are from the master list, and the price of hides is the same as in 1820. The value of exports is based on the sum of the value of the principal products with an allowance for minor exports. Export shares are as for 1820 (see 1820 above).

1840. The volumes are in Marte (1984), separating Haiti and the Dominican Republic, and prices for mahogany and tobacco are from the master list. The price of hides is assumed to be the same as in 1820 and 1830. The value of exports is based on the sum of the value of the principal products with an allowance for minor exports. The UK export share is derived from Marte (1984) and refers to 1836. The other export shares are estimates.

1850. This is the first year in the tables in which the Dominican Republic is independent, and the figures are an average of 1850 and 1851. There are complete trade data for 1847–8 and data on the volumes of mahogany and tobacco for the relevant years (see Marte (1984)). Prices for both are taken from the master list. There is a figure for merchandise exports in Marte (1984) for 1850–1. This is much higher than the sum of the value of the principal exports, even after allowing for minor exports, and must include re-exports. Because no allowance is made for re-exports in any other year, I have estimated the value of exports from the sum of the principal exports. This is much more consistent with the value of exports in the fiscal year 1847–8, when mahogany and tobacco represented 93 per cent of domestic exports (see Marte (1984), p. 84). Export shares are derived from Marte (1984) and are based on ship nationality.

1860. The volume of tobacco is given in Marte (1984), and the price is from the master list. The volume of mahogany is estimated by interpolation from the 1850 and 1870 data, and the price is from the master list. All other exports in 1860 (sugar, cacao, coffee and hides) are trace elements, with a nominal value of $100 each. Export shares for the United States and the UK are based on Marte (1984) and refer to 1856. The export share for the 'mother' country, i.e. Spain, is an estimate.

1870. The volume of sugar, cacao, coffee and tobacco exports are in Gómez (1979), p. 35, and prices are taken from the master list. The volume of mahogany (1869 and 1870 only) is in Franco (1999), and the price is also taken from the master list. The value of exports based on the principal exports is close to the value of exports for 1869 in Marte (1984) and for 1872 in Gómez (1979). Export shares are estimates.

1880. The volume figures for sugar, coffee, cacao and tobacco are from Gómez (1979), p. 63, for 1880–2. Prices are taken from the master list.

The volume of mahogany is from Franco (1999) and is an average of 1880 and 1882 only. The price is from the master list. The value of exports for 1880–2 is in Gómez (1979), p. 63. Export shares are estimates. Franco (1999) gives the US export share in 1882 as 90 per cent, but this is too high.

1890. The volume figures for sugar and tobacco are from Gómez (1979), p. 63, and refer to 1892. Note, however, that Baud (1995), table 2, p. 220, has three separate figures for tobacco exports at the beginning of the 1890s. In the case of cacao, the figure is the average of 1889–91 in Clarence-Smith (2000), app. 2. Prices are from the master list. Mahogany volume is for 1888 and is from Gómez (1979), p. 61. The price is from the master list. Gómez (1979) has exports by value for 1890 (average of 1889–91). The export share for the United States is derived from Consular Reports in Department of State, *Commercial Relations of the United States with Foreign Countries* (various years),[14] but others are estimates.

1900. The volume of sugar exports is from Deerr (1949), p. 123. The volume of cacao exports is from Clarence-Smith (2000), app. 2. The volume of coffee is from Clarence-Smith (2000) and Clarence-Smith and Topik (2003), app. The volume of banana exports is in Lloyd Jones (1931), p. 139. Prices for these four products are from the master list. There is an export volume for tobacco for 1900 in Baud (1995), p. 220, and therein two graphs suggesting that the price in 1900 was similar to that in 1905. See also Mutto (1974) for the 1905 price. The volumes and prices of mahogany and hides are taken from *Dominican Republic* (1907) and refer to 1905. The value of exports is based on the sum of the principal exports. The export share for the United States is from *Commercial Relations of the United States with Foreign Countries* (1901), for the UK from Léger (1907) and for Spain it is estimated.

Spanish Colonies

Cuba

Cuba remained a Spanish colony until 1898 when it was occupied by the United States at the end of the Spanish-American War (it became independent in 1902). As the largest and most important economy in the Caribbean, it is well served by several excellent economic histories that contain a mass of statistical information. These include the three-volume work on the sugar industry by Moreno Fraginals (1978), the fifteen-volume work up to the First War of Independence in 1868 by Marrero (1974–1992), *Cuba: A Handbook of Historical Statistics* by Schroeder (1982), the study on Spanish trade with Cuba by Maluquer (1974), the Cuban Economic Research Project (CERP, 1965), Instituto de Historia de Cuba (1998), the two-volume *Anuario de Estudios*

---

[14] This will normally be referred to from now on as US Consular Reports.

Cubanos by Pérez de la Riva (1975), and the book by Santamaría and García (2004).

At the same time, reconciling all this information into a consistent series for exports is not a simple matter. First, there is no reliable *fob* export price for sugar, the most important commodity throughout the period. Second, tobacco exports include not just leaf tobacco – a relatively homogeneous commodity with internationally recognised prices – but also manufactured tobacco products (cigars, cigarettes, snuff and plug), for which quantities, prices and values are hard to find. Other countries, such as the Dominican Republic and Puerto Rico, exported tobacco manufactures, but only in Cuba was the amount truly significant. Indeed, in 1900 tobacco of all sorts represented over half the value of exports.

Cuba does have official figures on the value of exports in each of the decennial years except 1820. These were published in the *Balanzas de Comercio Exterior* and can be found in CERP (1965) as annual data up to 1860, as triennial data (gross) in Goizueta-Mimó (1987) and as quinquennial data (annual average) in Santamaría and García (2004). Most of these figures are useable, but the value of exports for 1850 and 1860 is too low in relation to the subtotal of exports, and so I estimated the value in those years. The alternative would have been to lower the sugar price for those years, assuming that the quantities are accurate, but this would have implied a sugar price that is not credible. It is therefore more likely that the *Balanzas de Comercio Exterior* use official values that are too low in those years (a common problem in nineteenth-century Latin America).

I began by estimating the value of sugar exports. Volumes can be found in the sources listed below. For 1820, I used the *fob* export price for Martinique because it is almost the only Caribbean country for which it can be derived in that year (there are many *cif* prices, but they are less useful because of transport costs). I then used the Brazilian *fob* export price up to 1870. Because both countries were slave states that sold most of their sugar in the free market, this is plausible. For 1880 and 1890, I used the US import price because the US market was by then the crucial determinant of the Cuban price. The Brazilian price is derived from IBGE (1987) and the US price from Carter (2006), vol. 3. The 1900 volume and value of sugar are taken from Table C.5.

I then proceeded as follows: the volume of leaf tobacco is given in Santamaría and García (2004) at quinquennial intervals up to 1895–9. This was used for all years except 1900, when the figures are taken from Table C.5. Prices for Cuban leaf tobacco could not be taken from the rest of the Caribbean, because it commanded a huge premium owing to its high quality. I have therefore used Stubbs (1985), Jacobstein (1907) and Marrero (1984), vol. 11, to estimate prices and derive values. I have used the series in Santamaría and García (2004) on the volume of Cuban cigar exports and have derived prices from the same sources used for tobacco leaf. The 1900 figures are from Table C.5. Other tobacco exports, such as cigarettes and snuff, have been treated as minor exports.

Tobacco leaf and cigar exports were by far the most important tobacco exports from Cuba. Their combined value in 1900, for example, was $23 million. As a check on my estimated values of Cuban tobacco exports, I have used the series on the value of tobacco exports to the United States in volume 3 of Moreno Fraginals (1978). This suggests that total tobacco exports to the United States varied between one-third and one-half of the total, which is consistent with what we know about imports of Cuban tobacco into other countries.

Having estimated sugar and tobacco exports, I then calculated the value of all other leading agricultural exports (molasses, rum, coffee, bananas) using prices for the rest of the Caribbean. I have also included a series for copper in those years when it was exported using the information on volumes and values in Santamaría and García (2004). There was also a long list of minor exports, including honey, beeswax, timber, hides, cacao, fruits and cotton. Exports to the 'mother' country are to Spain.

1820. The volumes of sugar, molasses and rum for all years are in Moreno Fraginals (1978), vol. 3, so this will not be repeated (the figures for 1900 are from Table C.5 to ensure consistency). As usual, the figures are three-year averages except 1900. The volumes of coffee and tobacco leaf are in Santamaría and García (2004), and the data are five-year averages. Prices in all cases in 1820 are taken from Martinique. This is done even for tobacco leaf in 1820 because the Martinique price was very high. The value of exports is then based on the sum of the value of the principal exports. Re-exports have been ignored. Export shares are from Marrero (1985), vol. 12, p. 78, and refer to 1814.

1830. The volume of coffee, tobacco leaf, cigars and copper are taken from Santamaría and García (2004), where they are given as five-year averages for 1815–19, 1820–24, etc. Because these quinquennia cover my decennial years, I have therefore taken a ten-year average. Thus, 1820 is an average of 1815–24 and so on. All prices (except sugar, tobacco and cigars – see 1820 above – and copper) are taken from the master list. The price of copper is estimated based on later values. The value of exports (three-year average) is from CERP (1965). It can also be found in Fernández (2002). Export shares are from Marrero (1985), vol. 12, and are an average of 1826 and 1835.

1840. As for 1830. The price of copper is in Santamaría and García (2004). The coffee price is based on the US wholesale price. Export shares for the United States and Spain are from Marrero (1985), vol. 12, and are an average of 1836 and 1845. The UK export share is an estimate.

1850. As for 1840. Banana exports appear for the first time with the quantity estimated from Santamaría and García (2004). The US export share is from Marrero (1985), vol. 12, and is an average of 1846 and 1855. The export share for Spain is derived from Maluquer (1974). The UK export

share is estimated. Domestic exports are estimated based on the subtotal of exports.

1860. As above, except that the copper price is now an estimate based on 1850. The volume of rum is an average of 1859 and 1860 only. Export shares are from Marrero (1985), vol. 12, and refer to 1859. Domestic exports are estimated based on the subtotal of exports.

1870. As above, except that the volume of rum refers only to 1872 and the value of exports is from Goizueta (1987). The US export share is derived from Moreno Fraginals (1978), the Spanish share is derived from Maluquer (1974) and the UK share is an estimate.

1880. As above. Rum exports are estimated by interpolation. The volume of copper is an average of 1875–9. The volume of coffee is from Goizueta (1987). Export shares are from Santamaría and García (2004) and refer to 1877.

1890. The volume of coffee is from Goizueta (1987). The value of exports (average of 1888–93) is from Goizueta (1987). Export shares are from Santamaría and García (2004).

1900. The data are all taken from Table C.5 so as to be consistent with the tables for 1900 to 1960. The value of exports is from Instituto de Historia de Cuba (1998). The value of sugar is also in the same source. The volume of rum is an estimate. The volume of coffee (Goizueta (1987)) is an average of 1895–7. The volume of bananas is from Lloyd Jones (1931), p. 139. The sources for the volume and value of tobacco leaf and cigars have been given above. The export shares for the UK and the United States are from Pérez (1975) and the Spanish share is from Mitchell (2007).

Puerto Rico

There are several excellent studies on Puerto Rico from which a consistent series for exports can be constructed. The first of these, and still very valuable, is Jimeno Agius (1885); I have also made extensive use of Coll y Toste (1899), Bergad (1983), Lavallé, Naranjo and Santamaría (2002), Dietz (1986), Maluquer (1974), Scarano (1984) and US consular despatches for some years (in *Despachos de los cónsules norteamericanos en Puerto Rico* (1982)) and various issues of the *Boletín Histórico de Puerto Rico*.

The principal exports were sugar, coffee and tobacco (all years); molasses (most years), and cigars (1900 only). Rum, cotton, cattle and honey were minor exports and do not appear in Table A.10. Because Puerto Rico was a Spanish colony until annexation by the United States in 1898, the 'mother' country is Spain.

1820. The volumes of sugar, tobacco and coffee (1820 only) are from Jimeno Agius (1885). The price of sugar is from Martinique and the price of tobacco is from the master list, but the price of coffee is an estimate. The value of exports is from Jimeno Agius (1885), and re-exports are assumed to be negligible. Export shares are estimates.

1830. As for 1820, but volumes and the value of exports are now five-year averages, and molasses (three-year average) comes from Scarano (1984). Sugar, coffee and molasses prices are from Martinique, and the tobacco price is from the master list. The gap between the sum of principal exports and domestic exports is assumed to be explained by minor exports (not re-exports). Export shares are estimates.

1840. As above, but this time I have included the volume and value of minor exports based on US consular reports. Export shares are from consular reports in *Despachos de los cónsules norteamericanos en Puerto Rico* (1982).

1850. As above. The molasses figure comes from Scarano (1984) and is an average of 1849–50. Export shares are from consular reports in *Despachos de los cónsules norteamericanos en Puerto Rico* (1982).

1860. As above. The volumes of the minor exports (molasses, rum, cotton, hides and cattle) refer to 1859 only. The value of exports is also for 1859 only. The US export shares is from Dietz (1986), p. 120, and the others are from consular reports in *Despachos de los cónsules norteamericanos en Puerto Rico* (1982) and refer to 1859.

1870. As above. The value of exports is for 1870 only. The US export share is from Dietz (1986), the Spanish export share is derived from Maluquer (1974) and the UK share is estimated.

1880. Jimeno Agius (1885) has the volume and value of cattle and honey exports (1881 only) along with sugar, coffee and tobacco (five-year average). The value of exports is an average of 1879–83. Export shares for the United States and the UK are in Jimeno Agius (1885), and for Spain it is derived from UK, *Statistical Abstract for the Principal and Other Foreign Countries*.

1890. The volume and value of sugar and coffee exports are derived from Bergad (1983). The volume of tobacco exports is an estimate. There is no value of exports, so it has been estimated based on the sum of the value of the principal exports. The US export share is from Dietz (1986), p. 120, the UK export share is from Hill (1898), p. 162, and the Spanish share is derived from Maluquer (1974).

1900. The source for all volumes and values is Clark (1930). The year is fiscal 1900–1, which began on July 1. Minor exports are fruits (canned and fresh), textiles, and manufactures from straw hats and palm leaf. They also include cigars, which were 12 million in volume and $306,000 in value. According to Clark, 'miscellaneous exports' are mainly re-exports consisting of goods first imported from the United States. Export shares are from Clark (1930).

British Colonies

For the purposes of administrative convenience, the British authorities had reduced the number of their Caribbean colonies to eleven by 1900 through the

absorption of Anguilla by St Kitts in the 1820s, the inclusion of the Cayman Islands in Jamaica in 1863, the fusion of St Kitts and Nevis in 1882, the federation of Trinidad and Tobago in 1889 and the formation of the Leeward Islands Presidency in 1871 that incorporated St Kitts-Nevis-Anguilla, Antigua, Montserrat, British Virgin Islands and Dominica. This is, however, an unnecessarily high degree of aggregation for the purposes of economic history.

There are virtually no separate trade data for Anguilla and the Cayman Islands in the nineteenth century, so I have merged them with St Kitts and Jamaica, respectively. No great harm is done by this, because Anguilla was estimated to have had exports of around $6,000 in 1845 (see Petty (1991)) and the Cayman Islands as late as 1906 only had exports of $30,000 (see Craton (2003)). However, I have kept Nevis separate from St Kitts throughout the nineteenth century and have done the same for the other colonies within the Leeward Islands Presidency. I have also separated Trinidad from Tobago in 1900 (the only year when the data are aggregated). The result is separate data for seventeen British colonies in Table A.10 onwards.

Because the data sources and methodology applied to these seventeen colonies are very similar, it is not necessary to provide a separate note on each country. Instead, the general principles are listed under each year together with any exceptions.

1820. The nearest year for which a value of exports can be found is usually 1822. This number can be found in *Parliamentary Papers* and is conveniently summarised in Martin (1834) and Martin (1843) together with export shares for each colony. Volumes of the principal exports are also found in Martin, but not prices. These are taken from the master list. The sum of the value of the principal exports is used to estimate the value of domestic exports, taking into account any minor exports, and the difference between this figure and the merchandise value of exports is assumed to be re-exports.

The main exception is Jamaica, for which the **value** of merchandise exports is not given in primary sources until later. Jamaica does, however, have figures for the **volume** of principal exports. I have therefore estimated the value of Jamaican exports from the sum of the value of its leading exports (prices are from the master list). The Bahamas have been separated from Turks & Caicos by assuming that each was responsible for 50 per cent of salt exports and that salt was the only principal export from the Turks & Caicos (the same is done in 1830 and 1840).

The starting date for the British Virgin Islands is 1824, and the volume of sugar is taken from Deerr (1949). For Dominica, sugar volumes (average of 1819–21) are taken from Deerr (1949), and other exports are from Martin (1843) for 1828. The data for Demerara and Essequibo are aggregated with Berbice to make Guyana, but this did not happen officially until 1831.

There is an appendix to Chapter 11 devoted to the sources used in deriving the export data for Belize. This is therefore not repeated here.

1830. *Parliamentary Papers* (cd 53, 1835) contains a consistent series for 1832 for all the colonies except Belize covering the volume and unit price of the principal exports and the merchandise value of exports. This same source can be used to estimate the value of domestic exports and therefore re-exports. It also gives export shares.

1840. As for 1830, but using *Parliamentary Papers* (cd 303a, 1845), which contains a consistent series for 1841.

1850. This is the average of 1850 and 1851, with all volumes, prices and values to be found in *Parliamentary Papers* (cd 2127, 1856). There are no prices for Antigua, so I have used the master list. The Turks & Caicos Islands are disaggregated from the Bahamas from 1852, so the data refer to 1852 only.

1860. This is the average of 1859–61. See *Parliamentary Papers* (cd 3219, 1863).

1870. This is the average of 1869–71. See *Parliamentary Papers* (cd 1038, 1874) and *Parliamentary Papers* (cd 2029, 1878).

1880. This is the average of 1879–81. See *Parliamentary Papers* (cd 4519, 1884–5). From this year on, data on bullion and specie are included in exports. I have excluded them except in the case of those countries that actually mined and exported gold.

1890. This is the average of 1889–91. See *Parliamentary Papers* (cd 7527, 1894) and *Parliamentary Papers* (cd 8606, 1897). In the case of the Leeward Islands, I used the sugar volumes in Deerr (1949) and applied these proportions to the volume for the Leeward Islands Presidency as a whole. Other products for the Leeward Islands were separated using the 1880 proportions. The same was done for St Kitts and Nevis.

1900. See *Parliamentary Papers* (cd 1324, 1902). In the case of the Leeward Islands, I used the *Blue Book* for 1900, which provides detailed trade data for each of the colonies. The separation of St Kitts and Nevis was done as for 1890. US Consular Reports also helped in separating the different components of the Leeward Islands. In estimating lime juice exports from Dominica, I have used Trouillot (1988) and *Parliamentary Papers* for this and earlier years.

The Belize (British Honduran) dollar in 1900 was valued at par with the US dollar, so the conversion rate to sterling is 4.87. The British Guiana dollar was used for all Guyanese values, and these are converted to US dollars at 1.01458.

By 1900, the data for Trinidad and Tobago have been aggregated to form the colony Trinidad & Tobago. I have disaggregated the data using the proportions in 1890.

French Colonies

The French Antilles (Guadeloupe and Martinique) are well served in terms of primary sources thanks to the *Annuaire de la Martinique* and the *Annuaire de la Guadeloupe*. These publications contain export data by volume that start

in 1818 and go through the whole century up to the date of publication. The *Annuaire de la Martinique* also has export data by value so that unit values or prices can be derived. These prices can be used for Guadeloupe because the export market and structure for these two islands was so similar. By contrast, the *Annuaire de la Guyane Française* (for French Guiana) contains very little information on foreign trade. However, exports, imports and trade shares (for all three colonies) can be found in Ministère des Colonies, *Statistiques coloniales, etc. Renseignments généraux sur le commerce des colonies françaises et la navigation* (various years) and Ministère des Colonies, *Statistiques coloniales, etc. Statistiques du commerce des colonies françaises* (various years).[15]

The secondary literature on the French colonies is quite extensive, and I have made considerable use of it (see references below).

French Guiana

One of the most neglected countries in the Caribbean (at least by economic historians), French Guiana in fact has a wealth of information for the nineteenth century. Much of this has been collected in various books by Serge Mam-Lam-Fouck. Indeed, without his numerous contributions, it would have been very difficult to put together a consistent series on French Guiana. Bassières (1900) is also a useful source on commodity exports for the nineteenth century, and Pétot (1986) is invaluable for gold (the leading export after 1860). The French colonial sources included a wealth of information on French Guiana, and the annual reports of the Ministère des Colonies contain data on exports and imports back to 1845. I have assumed some re-exports between 1830 and 1870.

The principal exports were sugar (1820–80), cotton, cacao, cloves (*girofles*) and coffee. Annatto (*roucou*), an ingredient used widely as a natural dye, was also a principal export, but its importance declined sharply after 1880. All these products, however, were eclipsed by gold, which began to be exported from the late 1850s, and to a much smaller extent by phosphate (late 1880s onwards).

> 1820. The volumes of sugar and cotton are taken from Mam-Lam-Fouck (1999), chap. 2. Other volumes are estimated based on later years. The prices are from Martinique, except annatto and cloves, which are estimated. The value of exports is then based on the principal exports. Re-exports are assumed to be zero. Export shares are estimates.
>
> 1830. All volumes and the value of exports are from Mam-Lam-Fouck (1999), chap. 2. Prices are from Martinique except annatto and cloves, which are estimates. Minor exports include the cayenne pepper for which French Guiana is famous. The French export share is from Mam-Lam-Fouck (1999). Others are estimates.

---

[15] Both publications are referred to hereafter as Ministère des Colonies.

1840. As above. There is a list of minor exports (for 1836) in Société d'Etudes pour la Colonisation de la Guyane (1844). See also Bassières (1900). The French export share is from Mam-Lam-Fouck (1987), p. 46. Others are estimates.

1850. As above. Annatto and cotton volumes are for 1850 only, and cacao, coffee and cloves are for 1848 only. The cotton price is based on the US wholesale price. The value of exports and the French trade shares are from Ministère des Colonies. Other trade shares are estimates.

1860. The volume of sugar and annatto is an average of 1859 and 1860 only. The volume of gold exports is from Pétot (1986) and has been converted from kilograms to troy ounces (at the rate of 31.1035 grammes per troy ounce); the price is from Guyana. Trace elements in blue ($100) are added for cotton, cloves and phosphate. The value of exports and the French trade shares are from Ministère des Colonies. Other trade shares are estimates.

1870. The volumes of sugar and annatto are for 1869 only. The volume of gold is derived as before, and the price is from the master list. The value of exports and the French trade shares are from Ministère des Colonies, but refer to 1869 **only** to avoid the disruption caused by the Franco-Prussian War. Other trade shares are estimates.

1880. The volume of sugar is for 1879 only and the volume of annatto for 1880 only. The volume of gold is derived as before, and the price is from the master list. The value of exports is derived from Mam-Lam-Fouck (1999), p. 261, because exports are massively undervalued in Ministère des Colonies between 1872 and 1883. By this time, gold was around 90 per cent of domestic exports. Export shares are from US Consular Reports.

1890. Gold by now was over 95 per cent of domestic exports, with figures from Mam-Lam-Fouck (2002), p. 101. Cacao and coffee are from Bassières (1900), and phosphate volume is from *Annuaire de la Guyane Française*. The price of phosphates has been derived to be consistent with the merchandise value of exports. The US export share is from US Consular Reports, the French share is from *Annuaire de l'économie politique* (1892) and the UK share is assumed to be zero.

1900. Gold volume is from Pétot (1986), and other volumes are from Bassières (1900) and *Annuaire de la Guyane Française*. The French and US export shares are from US Consular Reports. The UK share is assumed to be zero.

Guadeloupe

Guadeloupe was at one time so important as a European colony that in the negotiations leading to the Treaty of Paris in 1763, Great Britain gave serious thought to acquiring it from France in exchange for British territory in Canada. Following the British occupation during the Napoleonic Wars, its commercial and strategic importance had diminished to the point where Sweden was

granted control in 1813. At the Treaty of Paris the following year, however, the UK agreed to restore French sovereignty and paid Sweden an indemnity. The 'mother' country is therefore France.

Guadeloupe is not as well served as Martinique (see below), but there are good secondary sources on the French Antilles that have some data on Guadeloupe. These include Buffon (1979), Blérald (1986), Bangou (1987), Chauleau (1973), Schnakenbourg (1980, 1980a), Achéen (1973) and Crusol (2007). There is also a series of excellent articles in *Bulletin de la Société d'histoire de la Guadeloupe*. A most useful source is *Annuaire de la Guadeloupe* (1904), because it contains the volume of all the principal exports from 1818 to 1900. I used this for the volumes of all principal exports and then applied the prices from Martinique to obtain values.

The principal exports were sugar, molasses, rum, cacao, coffee and cotton; logwood and annatto were also exported from 1850; the minor exports were tobacco, cassia (cinnamon) and pineapples (starting in the 1880s).

1820. The value of domestic exports is estimated from the sum of the value of the principal exports. There is a value for merchandise exports in Mitchell (2007), the series starting in 1821. Re-exports are assumed to be the difference between merchandise exports and domestic exports. The French export share is from Buffon (1979) and refers to 1825. Other export shares are estimates.

1830. Merchandise exports are from Mitchell (2007). The sum of the value of leading exports is well below the merchandise value of exports, so again re-exports are assumed to have taken place. The French export share is from Buffon (1979). Others are estimates.

1840 and 1850. As for 1830.

1860. Merchandise exports are from Mitchell (2007). The French export share is from *Annuaire de la Guadeloupe*. Other export shares are estimates.

1870. The value of exports is from Mitchell (2007), and the French export share is from Ministère des Colonies. Other export shares are estimates.

1880. Merchandise exports are from Mitchell (2007). The French export share is from Ministère des Colonies. The US and UK export shares are from US Consular Reports.

1890. Merchandise exports are from Mitchell (2007). The French export share is from Ministère des Colonies. The US share is from US Consular Reports, and the UK share is estimated.

1900. The value of exports is in Mitchell (2007). The French and US export shares are from US Consular Reports. The UK share is assumed to be zero.

Martinique

Many of the studies listed for Guadeloupe above are also relevant for Martinique. The work of Chauleau (1973) is particularly useful because it reproduces

the detailed export data for Martinique from the *Annuaire de la Martinique* covering the years 1818 to 1883. The *Annuaire de la Martinique* (1936) also has export data for the whole period up to 1900. In addition, there is the fine study of Tomich (1990), and Mitchell (2007) has exports and imports from 1821.

The principal exports were sugar, molasses, rum, coffee, cotton, cacao and logwood. However, cotton ceased to be exported after 1870. Minor exports include cassia (*casse*), which is a kind of cinnamon, and annatto.

1820. Chauleau (1973) was used for volumes, prices and values. The value of domestic exports is derived from the sum of the principal exports, leaving a large residual, which is assumed to be re-exports. Export shares are from Sainte-Croix (1822).

1830. As above. Cassia, the minor export, has a value of $3,000. Export shares are estimated. Re-exports have been calculated as the difference between merchandise exports and domestic exports in this and subsequent years.

1840 and 1850. As above. Export shares are estimated.

1860. As above. The French export share is from *Annuaire de la Martinique*. The other shares are estimated.

1870. As above. Annatto now appears as a minor export alongside cassia. The French export share is from *Annuaire de la Martinique*. Other export shares are estimates.

1880. As above. Annatto has now virtually disappeared from the export list. The French export share is from the UK, *Statistical Abstract for the Principal and Other Foreign Countries*. Other shares are estimated.

1890. *Annuaire de la Martinique* (1936) for all volumes and values. The French export share is from *Annuaire de l'économie politique* (1892), the US export share from US Consular Reports, and the UK share is estimated.

1900. *Annuaire de la Martinique* (1936) for all volumes and values. The US export share is from US Consular Reports. Others are estimated.

Dutch Colonies

Dutch Antilles
The six islands that constituted the Dutch Antilles in the nineteenth century consist of two groups of three: the ABC islands off the coast of Venezuela (Aruba, Bonaire and Curaçao) and the Dutch Windward Islands (Saba, St Eustatius and Sint Maarten). Apart from their status as Dutch colonies and their dependence on the entrepôt trade for much of their colonial history, they never had much in common. Sadly, this applies also to their statistics, which are scarce and sometimes difficult to reconcile.

Because some of the islands had 'free ports' for much of the period (especially Curaçao), re-exports from the Dutch Antilles were more important than domestic exports. However, Curaçao was always in the shadow of St Thomas

as a free port, because it was not until 1826 that the colonial authorities finally eliminated most export and import duties, and Venezuela – a major market – imposed punitive duties on imports from the island from 1882. Because exports from Curaçao (the main island) were not subject to duties for much of this period, they were not always recorded. Merchandise exports are therefore assumed to be the same as merchandise imports. Re-exports are estimated as the difference between merchandise imports and domestic exports.

The main source for the Dutch Antilles is Goslinga (1990). Johannes Hartog produced a series of interesting books on the individual islands, but they contain very little data. The *Almanak voor de Nederlandsche West-Indische Bezittingen* also has very little data on the islands. Fortunately, Benjamins and Snelleman (1917) has some excellent articles, as does Hoetink (1969). Van Soest (1978) is a useful source, but the data refer mainly to Curaçao only.

The domestic export list changed frequently. Beginning with sugar, cotton and salt, they later included phosphates, gold and divi-divi (a pod whose dye was used in the tanning of leather). Soon after the middle of the century, 'Panama' hats – straw hats woven on the island – became briefly the main export from Curaçao. Curiously, the orange peel that gives its name to the Curaçao liqueur was never important by value as an export. I have treated salt, sugar, phosphates and straw hats as the principal exports and all others as minor. The volume data on major exports are in Goslinga (1990) for each of the six islands, and values have been derived using prices in the master list where there are none in Goslinga (1990). There was a boom in cotton exports in the 1860s as a consequence of the US Civil War, but this was very brief and had ended by 1870.

Because I have had to work backwards from 1900, the notes on the series begins in the final year.

1900. The value of domestic exports for both Curaçao and the Curaçao dependencies (all other islands) is given in Goslinga (1990), p. 571, for 1905. I have rounded this down for 1900. This is similar to the figure in US Consular Reports. The US export share is taken from US Consular Reports. Other shares are estimates.

1890. The value of domestic exports for the Curaçao dependencies, but not Curaçao, is given in Goslinga (1990), app., so I have estimated Curaçao and therefore the total assuming the same proportions as in 1905. The US export share is taken from US Consular Reports. Other shares are estimates.

1880. As for 1890. The figure for the Curaçao dependencies is for 1886. Export shares for the UK and Holland were derived from Goslinga (1990), but the US share is an estimate.

1870. I have used an index derived from government revenue to estimate domestic exports back from 1880 to 1870. Export shares for the UK and Holland were derived from Goslinga (1990), and the US share is from US Consular Reports.

1860. As for 1870. Export shares were taken from Goslinga (1990).

1850. As for 1860. The government revenue figure is for 1855, so I have revised down the estimated value of exports assuming some growth between 1850 and 1855. Export shares are based on ship tonnage in Goslinga (1990) and are assumed to be the same as import shares.

1820–40. Domestic exports are based on the value of the principal exports (sugar and salt). Re-exports are, as before, estimated as the difference between merchandise imports and domestic exports. Both domestic exports and re-exports are estimated to have declined between 1820 and 1830, and this is consistent with the fall in the tonnage of ships visiting Curaçao (the main island). Export shares are based on ship tonnage in Goslinga (1990) and are assumed to be the same as import shares.

Suriname

At the end of the Napoleonic Wars, the colony of Suriname was the jewel in the Dutch empire. Indeed, for a number of years all Dutch possessions in the Caribbean were administered from Paramaribo, the capital of Suriname. Later in the century, Suriname was eclipsed by the Dutch East Indies, which attracted the bulk of Dutch colonial investment. Nevertheless, there is a wealth of data for nineteenth-century Suriname from which a consistent export series can be constructed.

There are several excellent studies of colonial Suriname, many of which cover at least part if not all of the nineteenth century. These include Goslinga (1990), Panday (1959), van Lier (1971), Emmer (1998) and Lammens (1982). I have also used various issues of the *Surinaamsche Almanak* and the *Almanak voor de Nederlandsche West-Indische Bezittingen*, which includes the Dutch Antilles and Suriname.

The principal exports were sugar, molasses, coffee and cacao (all years); cotton (up to 1880); rum (from 1840); gold (from 1880); and balata (from 1890). This is such a comprehensive list that minor exports can be assumed to have been very minor indeed.

1820. Volumes of principal exports are in Panday (1959) and Lammens (1982). Prices are from Martinique. The value of exports is based on the sum of the value of the principal exports, and re-exports are assumed to be negligible. Export shares are estimated.

1830. As above. The volume of molasses exports is estimated based on the change in the volume of sugar. Export shares are estimated.

1840. As above, but the volumes, including molasses, refer to 1840 only. Export shares are estimated.

1850. There is a value for exports for this and subsequent years in Benjamins and Snelleman (1917), p. 348. I have used this series except for 1880, when the number is too low in relation to the value of the principal exports. The volumes are for 1850 only, and the volume of molasses is an estimate. Prices are taken from the master list. Export shares for

Holland and the United States are from Goslinga (1990). The UK share is estimated.

1860. The volumes are from Panday (1959) and various issues of the *Surin-aamsche Almanak*, which also provides prices for sugar, cotton, coffee and cacao and values for rum and molasses. Export shares for Holland and the United States are from Goslinga (1990). The UK share is estimated.

1870. Volumes and the value of exports are in Emmer (1998). The sugar price is a residual to ensure that the sum of leading exports does not exceed the value of exports. Export shares for Holland and the United States are from Goslinga (1990). The UK share is estimated.

1880. Volume data for sugar are in Deerr (1949), cacao in Clarence-Smith (2000) and coffee in Clarence-Smith and Topik (2003). There are also volume data in *Surinaamsche Almanak* (1893) for cotton (and other products) with data for 1880 only. The volume of gold is from Benjamins and Snelleman (1917), p. 317. The volumes of molasses and rum are estimates. Prices are from the master list. The value of exports is from the *Surinaamsche Almanak*, and the sugar price is a residual as in 1870. Export shares for Holland and the United States are from Benjamins and Snelleman (1917), p. 348. The UK share is estimated.

1890. As for 1880. *Surinaamsche Almanak* (1893) has volume data on the main products for 1890 and 1891, and gold is from Benjamins and Snelleman (1917), p. 317. Export shares for Holland and the United States are from Goslinga (1990). The UK share is estimated.

1900. The figures are taken from the first year of the C. Tables.

Scandinavian Colonies

Danish Virgin Islands

The three Danish colonies of St Thomas, St John and St Croix made up the Danish Virgin Islands in the nineteenth century. Sugar production was concentrated on St Croix and, together with rum, dominated domestic exports. The minor exports included molasses and cotton. St Thomas, by contrast, was a centre of the entrepôt trade, so I have included an estimate of re-exports in each year. These are the difference between domestic and merchandise exports, and I have assumed merchandise exports to be the same as merchandise imports in each year. The value of domestic exports is derived from sugar and rum exports only, but there was a brief revival of the cotton industry during the US Civil War.

The secondary sources in English include Westergaard (1917), which deals with the period of company rule up to 1754 but has a supplementary chapter covering the nineteenth century; Dookhan (1974); Gøbel (1994); and Knox (1852), but this latter stops in mid-century. There is also a superb guide to sources for the Danish Virgin Islands by Gøbel (2002). The secondary sources in Danish include the magnificent Brøndsted (1953), vol. 2, which was expanded later into an eight-volume edition, three of which are relevant to this

book – see Vibaek (1967), Skrubbeltrang (1967) and Norregaard (1967); other
helpful sources are Toft (1982);[16] Hornby and Justesen (1976); and the annual
Statistisk Aarbog for Danmark, which had a special section on the Danish West
Indies starting in 1900. Denmark measured sugar exports in the Danish lb (2
Danish lbs=1 kg), so I have converted volumes to short lbs.

1820. The volume of sugar is from Deerr (1949); the figure for St Croix
is for 1820 only, and those for St John and St Thomas are averages
of 1821-6. There are also volume figures in Brøndsted (1953), vol. 2,
p. 342. The price is assumed to be the same as for Suriname up to 1840.
The volume of rum is based on 1840 and assumes exports moved in line
with sugar, with prices assumed to be the same as for Suriname up to
1860. The value of sugar and rum exports is grossed up by 5 per cent
to make an allowance for minor exports, such as molasses and cotton.
The Danish export share is from Brøndsted (1953), vol. 2, p. 342, and is
based on the volume of sugar exports only. The other export shares are
estimated.

1830. As for 1820, except that the volume of sugar for St John and St
Thomas is estimated by interpolation. The Danish export share is from
Brøndsted (1953), vol. 2, p. 342, and is based on the volume of sugar
exports only. The other export shares are estimated.

1840. Sugar volumes for St John and St Thomas are averages of 1838–40.
The volume of rum (average of 1843–51) is from Hornby and Justesen
(1976), p. 286, which also has figures for the rest of the century at roughly
decennial intervals. There are also figures at five-year intervals in Toft
(1982), p. 167, from 1875. The Danish export share is from Brøndsted
(1953), vol. 2, p. 342, and is based on the volume of sugar exports only.
The other export shares are estimated.

1850. The volume of sugar is for St Croix only, because sugar was no longer
exported from the other two islands. The volume figure is an average of
1850–5, and the price is from Toft (1982), p. 168. The Danish export
share is from the UK, *Statistical Abstract for the Principal and Other
Foreign Countries*. Other export shares are estimates.

1860. The volume of sugar is an average of 1855–60 and 1860–70. All
figures from Deerr (1949), and the price (for 1862) is from Toft (1982),
p. 168. The volume figure in Dookhan (1974) for 1857–9 is similar.
Export shares are estimated.

1870. The volume of sugar is from Dookhan (1974) and is an average of
1872–7. The prices of sugar and rum for 1870, 1880 and 1890 are from
Toft (1982), p. 168. Export shares are estimates.

1880. The volume of sugar is from Dookhan (1974) and is an average of
1875 and 1885. The US export shares is derived from *Statistical Abstract
of the United States*, and other shares are estimates.

---

[16] An abbreviated version of this article can be found in Jensen (1983).

1890. The volume and value of sugar is from US Consular Reports, as are domestic exports. There are also annual figures for St Croix exports (assumed to be the same as domestic exports) from 1884 in Toft (1982), p. 173. The US export share is from US Consular Reports, and others are estimates.

1900. There are figures on the volume and value of sugar and rum exports and domestic exports (average of 1898–1902) in *Statistisk Aarbog for Danmark* (1911), p. 194. Because this is the only source giving values for the principal exports, I have used it despite the fact that it is an average of five years rather than for 1900 only. As before, merchandise imports and exports are assumed to be the same, and re-exports are then the difference between domestic exports and merchandise imports. The Danish export share is derived from Danish imports from the Danish Virgin Islands (adjusted to *cif* by adding 10%) in *Statistik Aarbog for Danmark* and domestic exports. The US share of domestic exports is based on sugar only (it represented 95%) and is from Toft (1982), p. 174. The UK share is derived in the same way from the UK, *Statistical Abstract for the Principal and Other Foreign Countries*.

St Barthélemy

The colony of St Barthélemy belonged to Sweden until it was returned to France in 1878 and became a dependency of Guadeloupe. It is therefore only necessary to estimate exports for the period 1820 to 1870. However, this is not a simple matter because the secondary sources even in Swedish contain only a small amount of data, and there is also very little in the primary sources in the Swedish National Archives. There is a monograph by Bourdin (1978), but it has virtually no data on exports. The best sources are Statistiska Centralbyrån (1863–5), which gives detailed figures for 1856–62, Högström (1888), which gives the main exports for some other years, and Brändström (1976).

The principal exports were cotton and pineapples, and the minor exports were straw hats, salt and fish. Domestic exports were never large. However, St Barthélemy had prospered before and during the Napoleonic Wars from the entrepôt trade (including the slave trade), and thus re-exports were at first important. These stopped after 1830, and merchandise exports then became very modest indeed.

The 'mother' country was Sweden for the whole period (1820–70). From 1880, St Barthélemy is included in Guadeloupe, whose 'mother' was France.

1820 and 1830. Merchandise exports are assumed to be equal to merchandise imports, which have been calculated from import duties for 1819–21 and 1829–31, respectively. See Statistiska Centralbyrån (1863–5). Most exports are assumed to be re-exports. Half of domestic exports are assumed to be cotton, and the other half pineapples, thus ignoring minor exports, with volumes derived from prices in the master list

(I have used the Bahamas for pineapples). Export shares are estimated based on 1840.

1840. Merchandise exports estimated as for 1830, but re-exports are now assumed to be zero because the value of exports has fallen so sharply. Export shares are based on ship departures in the Swedish National Archives (Bunt XIV, F035-3-32852).

1850. The volume and value of pineapples (for 1855) is from Högström (1888), which also gives the value of exports (in 1855). Export shares are assumed to be the same as 1840. The value of cotton is the residual, and the volume is derived from prices in the master list.

1860. The value of exports, the volume of pineapples and cotton and export shares (based on ships cleared) are all in Statistiska Centralbyrån (1863–5). The value of cotton and pineapples has been derived from prices in the master list.

1870. The volume of cotton exports is in Brändström (1976), and the volume of pineapples (for 1871) is in Högström (1888). The value of exports is assumed equal to imports, which is estimated from customs duties. The cotton price is from the master list, and pineapples are assumed to be the residual. Export shares are based on ship departures in Swedish National Archives (Bunt XX, F035-3-32872).

TABLES A.23–A.32

Tables A.23–A.32 contain decennial data from 1820 to 1900 on imports and the terms of trade as follows:

Table A.23. Merchandise Imports
Table A.24. Merchandise Imports (1860 prices)
Table A.25. Retained Imports
Table A.26. Retained Imports (1860 prices)
Table A.27. Imports from the United States (%)
Table A.28. Imports from the UK (%)
Table A.29. Imports from the 'Mother' Country (%)
Table A.30. Import Price Index (1860=100)
Table A.31. Net Barter Terms of Trade (1860=100)
Table A.32. Income Terms of Trade (1860=100)

Import data have been constructed at decennial intervals starting in 1820. Decennial data are three-year averages unless stated otherwise. The exception is 1900, which is given as a single year in order to be consistent with the tables covering the twentieth century that start in 1900.

In most cases, it is impossible to distinguish in the primary and secondary sources between merchandise imports and retained imports for domestic consumption. Table A.23 therefore refers to merchandise imports. A crude method of obtaining retained imports is then to deduct re-exports (less 10% for the assumed markup) from merchandise imports. This is done in Table A.25 using

the data in Table A.12 and A.23. Tables A.24 and A.26 then convert merchandise and retained imports to constant (1860) prices using the import price index in Table A.30 (see below).

The next three tables (A.27–A.29) show the share of imports from the United States, the UK and the 'mother' country, respectively. In the case of the British colonies, the 'mother' country is of course the UK. In the case of Haiti and the Dominican Republic, the 'mother' is France and Spain, respectively, but Haiti was not a colony for any part of the period and the Dominican Republic for only a few years. The trade ties between Haiti and France actually strengthened as the century advanced, but those between the Dominican Republic and Spain withered to insignificance.

The 'source' of imports is always problematic – even today – so too much reliance should not be placed on the figures. Imports from the imperial countries sometimes include imports from other colonies of the same imperial power. Some countries, for example, put the UK as the source for their rice imports, but almost certainly they came from British India. Imports from France into the French colonies may have come from other French colonies as well as from France itself. Imports from Spain into the Spanish colonies almost certainly include some imports from Cuba (in the case of Puerto Rico) and vice versa.[17] These problems are well known to economic historians and need not detain us further. The broad trends, particularly the rise in importance of imports from the United States, are clear enough from the tables.

Table A.30 gives the import price index for each country and subregion and for the Caribbean as a whole. These import price indices cannot be constructed directly because there are not enough homogeneous products for the whole period with volumes and prices given in consistent form. Instead, I have used the price indices for the core countries (wholesale by preference, retail otherwise)[18] and weighted these price indices by the share of imports from the United States, the UK and the 'mother' country (the weights are scaled up to equal unity). The reason for this is that the United States, the UK and the 'mother' countries accounted for between 70 and 90 per cent of imports for all countries throughout the period, and domestic price movements were highly correlated with price movements in the core.[19]

The next table (A.31) measures the Net Barter Terms of Trade (1860=100). This is the unit value of exports in Table A.15 divided by the price of imports in Table A.30. The final table in this section is Table A.32, which measures the

[17] See Maluquer (1974).

[18] The indices are found in the relevant volumes of Mitchell. Gaps (e.g. Holland before 1880) have been filled in using the average for all other core countries.

[19] Santamaría and García (2004), p.344, find that the correlation coefficient for Cuban and US prices from 1872 to 1897 was 0.96 and for the UK 0.89. It was much lower for Spain (0.05), but most Cuban imports came from the US and the UK at this time. Similarly for Jamaica, Eisner (1961), p. 259, writes: 'as most of the imports came from North America and the United Kingdom, the price index reflects fully changes in the price levels of those countries'.

Income Terms of Trade (ITT). This is the Net Barter Terms of Trade (Table A.31) adjusted for the volume of exports (Table A.16).

SOURCES FOR TABLES A.23–A.32

Hispaniola

Haiti
As with exports, there is a separate Statistical Appendix for Haiti, so the sources for the Haitian data are all given in the Notes on B. Tables.

Dominican Republic
1820–40. The fact that the Dominican Republic was nominally a Spanish colony in 1820 and occupied by Haiti in 1830 and 1840 makes it difficult to construct import figures before 1850. I have therefore assumed that imports in 1820, 1830 and 1840 were the same as exports. The import shares are estimates based on 1850 figures.

1850. The import figure refers to 1850 and is taken from Marte (1984). The import shares are also taken from Marte (1984) and are based on ship tonnage.

1860. The import figure refers to 1856 and is taken from Marte (1984). The import shares refer to 1856 and are also taken from Marte (1984).

1870. The import figure (average of 1869–71) is taken from Marte (1984). The import shares are estimated.

1880. The import figure is an average of 1880–1 and is taken from Marte (1984). The import shares refer to 1883.

1890. The import figure is from Gómez (1979). The US import share is from US Consular Reports, and the UK and Spanish import shares refer to 1888 and are derived from Franco (1999), p. 119.

1900. There are no published figures on imports for 1900. However, we do have US exports to the Dominican Republic in that year in US sources (see *Statistical Abstract of the United States*). I have therefore grossed up the US figure using the US share of imports in US Consular Reports for other years. The UK and Spanish import shares are from *Dominican Republic* (1907) and refer to 1905.

Spanish Colonies

Cuba
1820. There are no figures on imports for 1820, so instead I have used those for 1814 and import shares for the same year. All the information is in Marrero (1985), vol. 12.

1830. The import figure is from CERP (1965). There is also an average of 1825–34 in Lavallé, Naranjo and Santamaría (2002). The import share figures are an average of the same years and are taken from Marrero

(1985), vol. 12. There are some figures on trade shares for this and other years in Salvucci and Salvucci (2000).

1840. The import figure is from CERP (1965). There is also an average of 1835 and 1844 in Lavallé, Naranjo and Santamaría (2002). The import shares for the United States and Spain are an average of 1836–45 and are taken from Marrero (1985), vol. 12. The UK import share is an estimate.

1850. The import figure is from CERP (1965). There is also an average of 1845–54 in Lavallé, Naranjo and Santamaría (2002). The import shares are an average of 1846–55 and are taken from Marrero (1985), vol. 12. The UK import share is an estimate.

1860. The import figure is from CERP (1965). All the import shares refer to 1859 and are taken from Marrero (1985), vol. 12.

1870. The import figure is an estimate. The Spanish import share is derived from Maluquer (1974), and the UK and US import shares are estimates.

1880. The import figure is an average of 1875–84 and is taken from Lavallé, Naranjo and Santamaría (2002). The import shares refer to 1877 and are taken from Santamaría and García (2004).

1890. The import figure is an average of 1885–94 and is taken from Lavallé, Naranjo and Santamaría (2002). The import shares refer to 1891 and are taken from Santamaría and García (2004).

1900. The import figure is from the Instituto de Historia de Cuba (1998). The import shares are all in Mitchell (2007).

Puerto Rico

1820. The import figure is an average of 1821–3 and is taken from Jimeno Agius (1885). The import shares are estimates based on 1840 figures.

1830. The import figure is an average of 1829–31 and is taken from Jimeno Agius (1885). The import shares are estimates based on 1840 figures.

1840. The import figure is an average of 1838–40 and is taken from Jimeno Agius (1885). The import shares are taken from *Despachos de los cónsules norteamericanos en Puerto Rico* (1982).

1850. The import figure refers to 1853 and is taken from *Despachos de los cónsules norteamericanos en Puerto Rico* (1982). The US import share refers to 1848 and is taken from Dietz (1986), p. 120, the Spanish import share is derived from Maluquer (1974), and the UK import share is an estimate.

1860. The import figure refers to 1859 and is taken from *Despachos de los cónsules norteamericanos en Puerto Rico* (1982). The US import share refers to 1860 and is taken from Dietz (1986), p. 120. The Spanish share is derived from Maluquer (1974), and the UK share is from *Despachos de los cónsules norteamericanos en Puerto Rico* (1982).

1870. The import figure refers to 1870 only and is from Coll y Toste (1899). The US import share refers to 1870 and is taken from Dietz (1986). The Spanish share is derived from Maluquer (1974), and the UK share is estimated.

1880. The import figure is an average of 1879–81 and is taken from Jimeno Agius (1885). The import shares are an average of 1879–84 and are taken from Jimeno Agius (1885).

1890. The import figure is an average of 1885 and 1895. The US import share refers to 1890 and is taken from Dietz (1986), p. 120. The UK import share refers to 1895 and is taken from Hill (1898), p. 162. The Spanish import share refers to 1895 and is taken from Maluquer (1974).

1900. All the figures are from Clark (1930) and refer to the fiscal year 1900–1, which started on July 1.

British Colonies

The import data and import shares are from *Parliamentary Papers*. From 1850 to 1900, there are annual data for all colonies. For 1840, I have used the *Blue Books* for individual colonies (for Belize I have also used Gibbs (1883), pp. 94, 101). For 1830, I have used the data (mainly for 1832) in *Parliamentary Papers*, but for Belize I have used an average of 1829–31 in Martin (1843). For 1820, or the nearest year, I have used Martin (1834), Martin (1843), *Blue Books*, and *Parliamentary Papers*. For 1860 for Belize, I have used 1861 only because the three-year average implies an implausibly low figure for retained imports.

French Colonies

French Guiana

1820. The import figure is an estimate based on exports. The import shares are estimates based on later figures.

1830. The import figure refers to 1831 and is taken from Mam-Lam-Fouck (1999), p. 165. The import shares are estimates based on later figures.

1840. The import figure is an average of 1839–41 and is taken from Mam-Lam-Fouck (1999), p. 165. The import shares are estimates based on later figures.

1850. The import figures and the French import share are taken from Ministère des Colonies. Other trade shares are estimates.

1860. The import figures and the French import share are taken from Ministère des Colonies. Other trade shares are estimates.

1870. The import figures and the French import share are taken from Ministère des Colonies. Other trade shares are estimates.

1880. The import figures and the French import share are taken from Ministère des Colonies. The import share for the United States is taken from US Consular Reports, and the UK figure is assumed to be zero.

1890. The import figures and the French import share are taken from Ministère des Colonies. The import share for the United States is taken from US Consular Reports, and the UK figure is assumed to be zero.

1900. The import figures and the French import share are taken from Ministère des Colonies. The import share for the United States is taken from US Consular Reports, and the UK figure is assumed to be zero.

Guadeloupe

1820. The import figure refers to 1821 and is taken from Mitchell (2007). The import share for France is for 1825 and is taken from Buffon (1979). The other shares are estimates.

1830. The import figure is the average of 1829–31 and comes from Mitchell (2007). The import share for France is for 1830 and is taken from Buffon (1979). The other shares are estimates.

1840. The import figure is a three-year average and is from Mitchell (2007). The import share for France is for 1841 and is taken from Buffon (1979). The other shares are estimates.

1850. The import figure is a three-year average and is from Mitchell (2007). The import share for France is for 1850 and is taken from Buffon (1979). The other shares are estimates.

1860. The import figure is a three-year average and is from Mitchell (2007). The import share is from *Annuaire de la Guadeloupe*, and the other shares are estimates.

1870. The import figure is a three-year average and is from Mitchell (2007). The French import share is from UK, *Statistical Abstract for the Principal and Other Foreign Countries*, and the others are estimates.

1880. The import figure is a three-year average and is from Mitchell (2003). The French import share is from Blérald (1986), and the US and UK import shares are from US Consular Reports.

1890. The import figure is a three-year average and is from Mitchell (2007). The French import share is from *Annuaire de l'économie politique* (1892). The US import share is derived from US Consular Reports. The UK share is an estimate.

1900. The import figure is from Ministère des Colonies. The French and US import shares are from US Consular Reports. The UK share is an estimate.

Martinique

1820. The import figure is an average of 1819–21 and is taken from Tomich (1990). The import shares are taken from an early French report on Martinique (see Sainte-Croix (1822)).

1830 **and** 1840. The import figures are taken from Tomich (1990). The import shares are estimated.

1850. The import figure is from Chauleau (1973). The import shares are estimated.

1860. The import figure is from Chauleau (1973). The French import share is from *Annuaire de la Martinique*. The other import shares are estimates.

1870. The import figure is from Chauleau (1973). The French import share is from UK, *Statistical Abstract for the Principal and Other Foreign Countries*. The other import shares are estimates.

1880. The import figure is from Chauleau (1973). The French import share is from Blérald (1986). The other import shares are estimated.

1890. Imports are from Mitchell (2007). The import share is from *Annuaire de l'économie politique* (1892). The US share is from US Consular Reports (assuming it is similar to the share for Guadeloupe). The UK share is estimated.

1900. The import figure is from UK, *Statistical Abstract for the Principal and Other Foreign Countries*. The import shares for France and the United States are from US Consular Reports. The UK share is estimated.

Dutch Colonies

Dutch Antilles

Great care has to be taken to construct the import series. Sometimes the data are given for individual islands only rather than the six islands together, and the entrepôt trade was also important throughout the period. As with exports, it is necessary to work backwards starting at 1900.

1900. Merchandise imports are taken from Tables C.18 and C.20. The import shares are from Tables C.22–C.24.

1890. The import figure refers to 1892 and is derived from Goslinga (1990), app., which gives all islands except Curaçao, together with US Consular Reports (Curaçao only). The US import share is from US Consular Reports, and the other shares are derived from ship arrivals in Goslinga (1990), pp. 338–43.

1880. The merchandise import figure is for 1884 and is from Goslinga (1990), p. 345. The import shares are derived from ship arrivals in Goslinga (1990), pp. 338–43.

1870. The merchandise import figure is estimated based on the growth in the number of ships, ship tonnage and the proceeds of the patent-tax on imports. See Goslinga (1990), p. 345. The import shares are derived from ship arrivals in Goslinga (1990), pp. 338–43.

1860. The merchandise import figure is for 1856 and is derived from Goslinga (1990), p. 345. The import shares are based on ship arrivals in Goslinga (1990), pp. 338–43.

1850. The merchandise import figure is from Goslinga (1990), p. 345. Import shares are based on ship arrivals in Goslinga (1990), pp. 338–43, and refer to 1855.

1840. The merchandise import figure is an average of 1839 and 1841 and is based on the 1 per cent patent-tax on imports in Goslinga (1990), p. 100. Import shares for the US are based on ship tonnage in Goslinga (1990), pp. 92–7. The UK and Dutch shares are estimated.

1830. The merchandise import figure is an average of 1829 and 1831 and is based on the 1 per cent patent-tax on imports in Goslinga (1990), p. 100. Import shares for the United States are based on ship tonnage in Goslinga (1990), pp. 92. The UK and Dutch shares are estimated.

1820. The merchandise import figure is estimated on the assumption that imports fell between 1820 and 1830 (based on ship tonnage arriving and departing and the proceeds of the patent-tax on imports). Import shares for the United States are based on ship tonnage in Goslinga (1990), pp. 92–7. The UK and Dutch shares are estimated.

Suriname

1820–40. The import figures are estimated on the assumption that imports moved in line with exports before 1850. The import shares are estimated based on later figures.

1850. The import figure for this and subsequent years is from Benjamins and Snelleman (1917), p. 348. There is also a similar figure in Panday (1959). The Dutch import share is from Goslinga (1990), and the US import share is from Benjamins and Snelleman (1917), p. 348 (both based on ship tonnage). The UK share is estimated.

1860. The US and Dutch import shares are from Goslinga (1990). The UK share is estimated.

1870. The US and Dutch import shares are from Goslinga (1990). The UK import share is estimated.

1880. The import shares for Holland and the United States are from Benjamins and Snelleman (1917), p. 348. The UK share is estimated.

1890. The US and Dutch import shares are from Goslinga (1990). The UK share is estimated.

1900. The figures are all from the first year of the C. Tables.

Scandinavian Colonies

Danish Virgin Islands

In relative terms, there was probably no country as dependent on imports for subsequent re-exporting as the Danish Virgin Islands. This entrepôt trade passed mainly through the island of St Thomas. This trade was well established even before the Napoleonic Wars, following the famous royal decree of 1764,[20] and expanded rapidly thereafter, until the replacement of sail by steam led to a reduction after 1870. However, St Thomas did succeed in reinventing itself as a coaling station (for US ships in particular) until shortly after the Spanish-American War, when the US navy had other alternatives.

As with the Dutch Antilles, it is easier to explain the procedure used by starting at 1900 and working backwards.

[20] See Hall (1985), p. 15.

1900. Merchandise imports are from *Statistisk Aarbog for Danmark*, and I have used an average of 1898–1902 to be consistent with exports (see Tables A.10, etc., above). The Danish import share is based on Danish exports to Danish Virgin Islands (converted to *cif* by adding 10%) in *Statistisk Aarbog for Danmark* and merchandise imports. The UK share is from UK, *Statistical Abstract for the Principal and Other Foreign Countries* (the UK share is based on St Thomas only and is lower than the share of ships sailing under the British flag arriving in St Thomas in Gøbel (1994)). The US share is derived from merchandise imports and US exports to Danish Virgin Islands in the annual *Statistical Abstract of the United States* (adjusted to *cif* values by adding 10%).

1890. The import figure and import shares are from US Consular Reports. There are also annual figures on merchandise imports (St Croix only) from 1884 in Toft (1982), p. 173. Import shares, based on ship tonnage, are in Dookhan (1974).

1880. The import figure is based on US exports to the Danish Virgin Islands in *Statistical Abstract of the United States*, assuming the United States had the same share as in 1870 and 1890, and Gøbel (1994), which has a figure for St Thomas only in each decade from 1850 onwards. The UK share is from US Consular Reports. The Danish source is an estimate.

1870. The import figure is from Gøbel (1994). The US import share is derived from Pletcher (1998). Other import shares are estimated.

1860. The import figure is from Gøbel (1994). Import shares are estimated.

1850. The import figure is from Knox (1852). The Danish import share is from UK, *Statistical Abstract for the Principal and Other Foreign Countries*. Other shares are estimates.

1820, 1830 and 1840. Imports are estimates based on the change in tonnage and ship arrivals in Gøbel (1994), p. 162. Import shares are based on ship tonnage entering St Thomas. See Knox (1852), Gøbel (1994) and Brøndsted (1953), vol.2, p. 333.

St Barthélemy

It is only necessary to estimate the series up to 1870, because the Swedish colony was transferred back to France in 1878 and became a dependency of Guadeloupe. Merchandise imports, which I have assumed to be the same as merchandise exports, have been derived in each year where there are no export data from customs duties (see Tables A.33–A.38 below) on the assumption that the latter represented 20 per cent of the value of imports. These years are 1820, 1830, 1840 and 1870.

1820 and 1830. Import shares are assumed to be the same as in 1840.

1840. Import shares are based on ship arrivals in Swedish National Archives (Bunt XIV, Fo35-3-32852).

1850. Import shares are assumed to be the same as 1840.

1860. Import shares (based on ship arrivals) are all in Statistiska Centralbyrån (1863–5).

1870. Import shares are based on ship arrivals in Swedish National Archives
(Bunt XX, F035-3-32872).

TABLES A.33–A.38

Tables A.33–A.38 contain decennial data from 1820 to 1900 on public revenue
and expenditure as follows:

Table A.33. Public Revenue
Table A.34. Public Revenue (1860 prices)
Table A.35. Trade Taxes, 1850–1900
Table A.36. Tariff Rates (%), 1850–1900
Table A.37. Public Expenditure
Table A.38. Public Expenditure (1860 prices)

This note covers the tables dealing principally with public finance. Detailed
information for each country is given below. Here some general principles are
laid out.

Data have been constructed at decennial intervals starting in 1820, but
Tables A.35 and A.36 start in 1850. Decennial data are three-year averages
unless stated otherwise. The exception is 1900, which is given as a single year
in order to be consistent with the tables covering the twentieth century that
start in 1900.

Public revenue (Table A.33) excludes subsidies from the metropolitan countries (these were important for some British colonies by 1900, for St Barthélemy
between the 1830s and the transfer to France in 1878, for French Guiana before
1890, for both the Dutch colonies in almost all years and for the Danish Virgin
Islands in many years).

It is not possible to calculate the annual change in prices for most Caribbean
countries with any accuracy in the nineteenth century. However, we can use
the import price index (Table A.30) as a proxy for domestic price changes given
the importance of imports in all items of final expenditure. Public revenue at
1860 prices (Table A.34) is therefore public revenue adjusted for the change in
import prices.

The most important source of public revenue was taxes on foreign trade
(customs duties). These are shown in Table A.35 starting in 1850 (before 1850,
trade taxes were less important because so much trade was with the 'mother'
country at relatively low rates of tax). Of the taxes on trade, import duties
were normally much more important than export taxes. When customs duties
are divided by the current value of imports, we therefore obtain a rough proxy
for the average tariff rate (Table A.36).[21] However, in the case of Haiti and the
Dominican Republic, I have deducted export taxes from customs duties before

---

[21] This should be considered an upper limit because some trade taxes were collected on exports.

dividing by imports in Table A.36.[22] I have used the value of merchandise imports (Table A.23) rather than the value of retained imports to calculate this implicit tariff rate, because imports for re-export were usually taxed along with imports for retained consumption.

Public expenditure is shown in Table A.37. No attempt is made to distinguish between current and capital expenditure, but the latter was usually very small. The figures include transfers to the metropolis, but these were only important for the Spanish colonies and St Barthélemy in 1820 and 1830. Public expenditure at 1860 prices (Table A.38) is calculated as for public revenue (see above).

Unlike trade data, public finance data are normally expressed in domestic currencies or at least in the currency of the metropolitan power. Thus, the reader should refer to the treatment of exchange rates above. The main difficulties in converting currencies to US dollars arise between 1880 and 1890 when the gold price of silver fell, leading to depreciation of national currencies in certain countries. This problem was much less serious in 1900 because the US dollar was by then in use in three of the most affected countries (Cuba, Dominican Republic and Puerto Rico).

SOURCES FOR TABLES A.33–A.38

Hispaniola

Haiti
There is a separate Statistical Appendix for Haiti, so the sources for the Haitian data are all given in the Notes on B. Tables.

Dominican Republic
1820. Revenue and expenditure are based on 1817, when the country was still a Spanish colony. See Rodríguez y Velez (1980).

1830. The revenue and expenditure figures are assumed to be 14 per cent of Haiti. This number is based on 1840 (see below).

1840. Marte (1984), p. 108, gives revenue and expenditure for the whole island by ports. I have assumed that the revenue and expenditure for the Dominican Republic came entirely from Santo Domingo and Puerto Plata.

1850. I have calculated public revenue and customs duties from the budget data for 1849 given in Marte (1984), p. 160, on the assumption that income from *moneda nacional* can be converted to *moneda fuerte* at an exchange rate of 10.0 (this figure is also given in the same source). I have also assumed that trade taxes accounted for 80 per cent of the total (70% import duties and 10% export duties).

---

[22] Export duties were important in both cases, so the failure to deduct them from customs duties leads to a serious overestimate of the implied tariff rate.

1860. The trade taxes are taken from Franco (1999) and are assumed to represent 80 per cent of total revenue (as in 1850). Expenditure is based on revenue.

1870. The revenue data are all taken from Cassá (1987) and refer to 1870. They can also be found in Hazard (1873). The expenditure figure is from Franco (1999) and refers to 1872.

1880. The revenue and expenditure figures are based on the division of taxes given in Gómez (1979) for 1880 and are estimates. There is a higher figure for revenue and a lower figure for expenditure in Billini (1885), but these figures are not credible.

1890. The trade tax figures are for 1887 and are taken from Marte (1984). Using Cassá (1987), it is assumed that trade taxes are 97 per cent of the total. Expenditure is based on revenue.

1900. The revenue and customs duties figures are from Gómez (1979) and refer to 1896. The division of taxes is based on 1890 ratios. Expenditure is based on revenue.

Spanish Colonies

Cuba

1820. The revenue figure is an average of 1819–21 and is derived from Schroeder (1982). Total trade taxes are taken from Marrero (1985), vol. 12, and are an average of 1817–21. Public expenditure is taken from Santamaría and García (2004), who estimates that transfers to Spain were still small (less than 1%).

1830. As for 1820, except that trade taxes are assumed to be 50 per cent of the total (as in 1820). Santamaría and García (2004) provide data on transfers to Spain, from which we can estimate that they represented around 8.5 per cent of public expenditure. Marrero (1985), vol. 12, puts military expenditure at 63.7 per cent of total expenditure in 1828–32.

1840. As for 1830. Transfers to Spain between 1835 and 1844 were 32.3 per cent of public expenditure based on the 1840 figure. See Santamaría and García (2004).

1850. As for 1840, except that expenditure is an estimate based on revenue. For this year, and for some others until 1880, there are also revenue and expenditure figures in Roldán de Montaud (1990), p. 152. Transfers to Spain are now estimated at 17.2 per cent of public expenditure and military spending at 51.4 per cent (based on 1848–9 figures).

1860. As for 1850. Transfers now estimated at 13.2 per cent of public expenditure (see Santamaría and García (2004)) and the military at 53.4 per cent (see Marrero (1985), vol. 12). The figures on revenue and expenditure in Roldán de Montaud (1990), p. 152, are about 20 per cent higher than those for revenue in Schroeder (1982) that I have used. I have not been able to find out why there is such a big difference.

1870. As for 1860, but the revenue figure is an average of 1868–9. Marrero (1985), vol. 12, estimates that military spending in 1866–7 was 41.1 per cent of the total. Marrero (1985), vol. 12, also has import and export duties for 1866–7. Santamaría and García (2004) estimate a drop in transfers but a rise in external debt service because Cuba was forced to take on part of the Spanish debt stock. The circumstances surrounding this debt are discussed in detail in Roldán de Montaud (1990).

1880. Revenue figure from Schroeder (1982) for 1880–1. Trade taxes are from Santamaría and García (2004) for 1880, representing 58 per cent of the total. Expenditure is from Schroeder (1982) for 1880–1. Military spending is now estimated at 30 per cent of the total.

1890. Trade taxes are from Santamaría and García (2004) for 1885–93. Revenue and expenditure are from Schroeder (1982) for 1890–1. The silver peso had depreciated against the US dollar by around 25 per cent at this time, but I have not made any adjustment for this because some of the revenue was collected in gold currency. Transfers to Spain and external debt service are estimated by Santamaría and García (2004) at 47.2 per cent.

1900. Revenue and expenditure are from the US military occupation figures. See CERP (1965). They are in US dollars. There is also a revenue figure for 1900 in Schroeder (1982). This is much lower than the figure for 1898–9. However, the latter figure was the last to be drawn up by the Spanish authorities using the peso, and the former was the first prepared under the US occupation using the dollar. Even allowing for the fact that the years are not the same, the difference can be explained both by the exchange rate (the silver peso was estimated to be worth only 60 US cents in 1900) and by a reduction in tariffs.

In the 1898–9 budget, Porter (1899) estimates that education accounted for 0.9 per cent of public spending and trade taxes for 56 per cent of total revenue. I have used this ratio to calculate the trade taxes for 1900.

Puerto Rico

1820–40. Revenue and expenditure figures are based on growth of imports up to 1850. Transfers to Spain are estimated at around 20 to 25 per cent of public expenditure based on figures in Lavallé, Naranjo and Santamaría (2002).

1850–70. Trade taxes are from Sonesson (1990). Revenue and expenditure are from Coll y Toste (1899).

1880. Trade taxes are estimated to be 60 per cent of total revenue – otherwise as for 1870.

1890. Trade taxes are for 1893 in *Annuaire de l'économie politique* (1892). Otherwise as for 1880.

1900. Budgeted revenue and expenditure for 1899–1900 are in Coll y Toste (1899) in pesos. The Puerto Rican peso had lost value by this time, so

the numbers in Coll y Toste need to be adjusted downwards. According to Dietz (1986), the Puerto Rican peso was worth 75 per cent of the US dollar in the 1890s. Under the Foraker Act in 1900, however, the Puerto Rican peso was required to be converted at 60 per cent. See Clark (1930). I have therefore converted pesos to dollars in 1900 at this rate.

Clark (1930), p. 157, gives trade taxes (import duties only) in 1897–8 as 43 per cent of total revenue. I have used this ratio to calculate the trade taxes for 1900.

British Colonies

There is no need to list each colony separately because the same procedures were used. The sources are *Parliamentary Papers* and the exceptions are all listed below.

1820. The source is either Martin (1843) or *Blue Books*. The starting year is not always the same, and some numbers are estimated. For Antigua, the year is 1821, and expenditure is estimated based on revenue. Bahamas is 1827 and is assumed to be 77 per cent of the combined figures for Bahamas and Turks & Caicos Islands (same ratio in 1830, 1840 and 1850). For Turks & Caicos Islands it is 23 per cent. Barbados start year is average of 1821–3. British Virgin Islands is an estimate based on import growth. Dominica start year is 1821. Grenada is 1822. Guyana is 1821, and I have estimated revenue and expenditure for Berbice and added it to Demerara & Essequibo. Jamaican figures are estimates based on import growth. For Montserrat, Nevis, St Kitts and St Lucia, the start year is 1821. For St Vincent it is 1827 and for Tobago 1828. Trinidad is 1827 and so is Turks & Caicos Islands (see Bahamas above). Belize is an average of 1819–21, with Jamaican currency converted first to pounds sterling and then to US dollars.

1830. Average of 1829–31, except in the following cases: British Virgin Islands (1827–8); Dominica (1833–4); Jamaica (1831–2); Montserrat (1834); Nevis (1830–1). The source is either Martin (1843) or *Blue Books*. The source for Belize is Colonial Department (1836).

1840. Average of 1839–40, except in the following cases: Barbados (1841–2); Guyana, Jamaica and Montserrat (1840); St Vincent (1840–1); and Tobago (1840). The source is *Blue Books*. The source for Belize is Gibbs (1883) and Burdon (1936), vol. 3.

1850. Average of 1850–1. Antigua, British Virgin Islands, Montserrat and Trinidad customs duties are estimated. Grenada trade taxes are for 1845, and Tobago trade taxes are for 1850 only.

1860–80. Three-year averages in all cases.

1890. Average of 1889–91. Nevis is assumed to be 21 per cent of St Kitts/Nevis figures (also in 1900). St Kitts is assumed to be 79 per cent.

1900. Tobago is assumed to be 1.5 per cent of Trinidad & Tobago total, except that import duties have been adjusted to give same average tariff as for Trinidad. Trinidad is assumed to be 98.5 per cent of total.

French Colonies

Some figures can be found in the relevant *Annuaire* for each country. In addition, colonial authorities in each country published the budget in most years after 1860, from which the figures can be derived (these are available digitally from the French Bibliothèque Nationale). These figures do not refer to actual revenue and expenditure, but it is unlikely that the outturn could have differed much from the budget because of the fiscal discipline applied by the metropolitan power. Trade taxes were not nearly as important as sources of revenue as in other countries and, as a result, implied tariff rates are low.

French Guiana

1820–50. All figures are estimates based on the growth of imports and work backwards from 1860 (the first year in which we can state the budget with confidence). Trade taxes in missing years are assumed to be 30 per cent of total revenue (this ratio is based on the figure in later years).

1860. The figures refer to the budget for 1862 and come from Duval (1864). I have excluded the subsidy from the state from revenue, which was almost as large as local receipts.

1870. The figures are from the official *Annuaire de la Guyane Française*. The metropolitan subsidy is excluded from revenue, which explains why expenditure is bigger.

1880. The figures are from *Annuaire de la Guyane Française*. I have not included the tax on gold exports in customs duties. The French subsidy is now very small.

1890. The figures are from *Annuaire de la Guyane Française*. There was no metropolitan subsidy.

1900. The figures are taken from *Annuaire de la Guyane Française*. There was no metropolitan subsidy.

Guadeloupe

1820–50. All figures are estimates based on the growth of imports and work backwards from 1860 (the first year in which we can state the budget with confidence). Trade taxes in missing years are assumed to be 30 per cent of total revenue (this ratio is based on the figure in later years).

1860. The figures refer to the budget for 1862 and come from Duval (1864). There are similar figures in *Annuaire de la Guadeloupe* for 1863.

1870–90. The revenue and expenditure figures are from the relevant issues of the *Annuaire de la Guadeloupe*, but the 1870 figure is for 1871. Trade taxes are assumed to be one-third of revenue.

1900. All figures are for 1900 in the historical series found in *Annuaire de la Guadeloupe* (1949). This shows that customs duties were 34.8 per cent of revenue in that year.

Martinique

1820–50. All figures are estimates based on the growth of imports and work backwards from 1860 (the first year in which we can state the budget with confidence). Trade taxes in missing years are assumed to be 30 per cent of total revenue (this ratio is based on the figure in later years).

1860. The figures refer to the budget for 1862 and come from Duval (1864).

1870. The figures are for 1870 and come from *Budget des Recettes et des Dépenses pour la Martinique*. The customs duty figure is very low.

1880. The figures are for 1880 and come from *Budget des Recettes et des Dépenses pour la Martinique*. The trade tax figure excludes export taxes.

1890. The figures are for 1890 and come from *Budget des Recettes et des Dépenses pour la Martinique*. The trade tax figure excludes export taxes.

1900. The figures are from the first year of the C. Tables.

Dutch Colonies

Dutch Antilles

The six islands of the Dutch Antilles were governed from Paramaribo until 1845 as part of the unified Dutch West India Possessions. This subordination to Suriname was in recognition of their decline in importance since before the Napoleonic Wars. Their previous prosperity had been based on free trade, and Adam Smith in *The Wealth of Nations* (1776) had remarked: 'Curaçao and Eustatia . . . are free ports open to the ships of all nations; and this freedom, in the midst of better colonies whose ports are open to those of one nation only, has been the great cause of the prosperity of those two barren islands.'

The need to avoid budget deficits had led to the islands of the Dutch Antilles reestablishing import and export duties. However, in 1826 Curaçao again became a free port and St Eustatius soon after, with only a small harbour tax being retained. Not surprisingly, the islands then suffered from deficits that had to be covered by subsidies from Holland. These subsidies are reported in Benjamins and Snelleman (1917), pp. 300–1.

The monetary system of Curaçao, the main island, was chaotic up to the late 1820s. Both gold and silver coins had lost their intrinsic value through various forms of fraud. However, the authorities kept the accounts in 'book-pesos', with a fixed value to the Dutch guilder, rather than the 'coin-pesos' that steadily depreciated. This situation was only remedied in 1828 with the monetary reform that included the creation of the Bank van de Nederlandse Antillen – the Caribbean's first bank. See van Soest (1978).

1820. The revenue figure is based on Curaçao and refers to 1822. See van Soest (1978), p. 388n9. It is given in pesos, which I have assumed to be

'book-pesos' (see above). The expenditure figure is an estimate, based on the assumption that there was a deficit.

1830. Revenue and expenditure figures include Aruba and Bonaire along with Curaçao, and the year is 1832. See Goslinga (1990), p. 76.

1840. As for 1830. The year is 1841. See Goslinga (1990), p. 76.

1850. The year is 1855, and the figures include all six islands. Trade taxes (import duties only) for this and subsequent years are from Goslinga (1990), p. 345.

1860. The figures are from Goslinga (1990), p. 317.

1870–1900. The revenue, expenditure and trade tax figures (three-year averages except for 1900, which is a single year, and 1870, which refers to 1872) are from Benjamins and Snelleman (1917), p. 302.

Suriname

1820. The revenue and expenditure figures refer to 1816. See Goslinga (1990).

1830–40. Estimates based on import growth.

1850. The revenue, expenditure and trade tax figures refer to 1852–3. See Goslinga (1990).

1860. Estimates based on import growth.

1870–1900. The revenue, expenditure and trade tax figures (three-year averages except for 1900 which is a single year) are from Benjamins and Snelleman (1917), pp. 297–8. Import duties were 70 per cent of trade taxes in 1900, and I have assumed this ratio held for earlier years.

Scandinavian Colonies

Danish Virgin Islands

1820–1840. Figures are all estimated in line with the growth of imports.

1850. The revenue and expenditure figures are for 1850 and come from Knox (1852). The trade taxes (import duties only) are derived from Hornby and Justesen (1976), p. 327. There are also detailed budget figures for 1854 in Evans (1945), p. 189, giving very similar figures for revenue, expenditure and trade taxes.

1860–70. The revenue and expenditure figures come from Dookhan (1974), table 3, p. 245. The trade taxes (import duties only) are derived from Hornby and Justesen (1976), p. 327.

1880–90. The revenue and expenditure figures (three-year averages) come from Toft (1982), which has annual figures for both St Thomas and St Croix from 1875–6 and the proportion of income represented by indirect taxes (assumed to be the same as trade taxes). Skrubbeltrang (1967), pp. 129–31, also has figures for 1879–80, including trade taxes.

1900. The revenue and expenditure figures are from Toft (1982), which has annual figures for both St Thomas and St Croix and the proportion of

income represented by indirect taxes (assumed to be the same as trade taxes).

St Barthélemy

This colony was the property of the Swedish king until 1845, when it reverted to the Swedish state.[23] Until the early 1830s, it was highly prosperous, and revenue exceeded expenditure. Indeed, the colonial government transferred funds to the king at this time. However, the decline of the entrepôt trade meant that revenue was insufficient to cover expenditure in most years after 1830, and the island received a subsidy from Sweden (payable at first by the king).

1820. The revenue and expenditure figures are an average of 1819–21 and are taken from Statistiska Centralbyrån (1863–5). Customs duties can also be found in the same source. The average transfer to Sweden from St Barthélemy in 1819–21 was 39.6 per cent of public expenditure.

1830. Same source as for 1820, and the figures refer to 1829–31. There was a small subsidy **received** from Sweden (equivalent to 10.4% of revenue) and a much larger transfer **paid** to Sweden (equivalent to 44.1% of public spending).

1840. As before with an average of the years 1839–41. The subsidy from Sweden is now equivalent to 17.2 per cent of revenue, but there is no transfer to Sweden because revenue has fallen drastically with the decline of the entrepôt trade.

1850. The figures refer to 1849–51, and the subsidy from Sweden is now 85.7 per cent of revenue.

1860. The figures refer to 1859–61. The subsidy from Sweden is now 201.7 per cent of revenue.

1870. The revenue figures are from the Swedish National Archives (Bunt XX, F035-3-32872), and the expenditure figure is estimated. Customs duties are from Högström (1988).

---

[23] See Brändström (1976).

Notes on B Tables

From independence in 1804 until the US occupation in 1915, the quantity of official statistics on the Haitian economy is very limited. This is especially true of the demographic data. There have been a number of attempts to estimate foreign trade at different time periods, but none of these is a complete series. There have been even fewer attempts to estimate public revenue and expenditure.

The most comprehensive attempt to measure exports was made by Robert Rotberg, with the assistance of Christopher Clague (see Rotberg (1971)). This was a pioneering attempt and is still of some use. However, the series is not complete, and all volumes have been translated to values using US *cif* or wholesale prices. In addition, no attempt was made to reconcile the resulting estimates of the value of domestic exports with either previously published figures or with the value of imports from Haiti by the main trading partners. Because nearly fifty years have now passed since Rotberg's calculations were first made, it is time for a more comprehensive attempt at quantifying the Haitian economy before the US occupation, and this is what is attempted here.

TABLES B.1–B.10

Tables B.1–B.10 contain annual data from c.1815 until c.1915. It covers population, exports, imports and public finance. The titles are as follows:

Table B.1. Population and the Exchange Rate
Table B.2. Exports of Four Main Products by Volume and Value
Table B.3. Domestic Exports (current and 1860 prices)
Table B.4. Domestic Exports per Head (current and 1860 prices)
Table B.5. Domestic Exports by Main Market (%)
Table B.6. Imports (current and 1860 prices)
Table B.7. Imports by Main Market (%)
Table B.8. Net Barter and Income Terms of Trade (1860=100)

Table B.9. Public Revenue and Import Duties
Table B.10. Public Expenditure by Category (%)

SOURCES FOR TABLES B.1–B.10

TABLE B.1. POPULATION AND THE EXCHANGE RATE

Population

Population data, from 1810 to 1917, are all taken from the annual series in Table A.1 (1810–1900) and Table C.1. (1900–60). The Notes on A. Tables and Notes on C. Tables should therefore be consulted for further details.

The Exchange Rate

The Haitian currency was the gourde, and many statistics were quoted in it. The conversion of the gourde to the US dollar is not a simple matter, but it does need to be carried out. What follows is an explanation of how this was done.

At the time of independence (1804), there were no banks and no paper money. The only currency was gold and silver coins (specie), which can be considered at par with the US dollar. The shortage of coinage was so severe, however, that in the south of the country, President Pétion debased the coinage by minting new coins with the same nominal value but a lower intrinsic value (i.e. lower metallic content). This encouraged counterfeiting, and false coins entered Pétion's republic – primarily from the United States. Pétion also issued paper money in 1813, which was not withdrawn until 1819 (see Turnier (1955), pp. 278–9). The result is that, at the time of Pétion's death in 1818, the gourde had lost two-thirds of its value. By the time President Boyer united the country in 1820, the exchange rate of the gourde to the dollar was therefore estimated to be 3 to 1 (see International Bureau of the American Republics (1893), p. 96).

This is important because many contemporaries were content to maintain the fiction that the gourde and the US dollar were still at par (scholars in the twentieth century made the same mistake – see, e.g., Leyburn (1941), p. 318, and Rotberg (1971), p. 86). Indeed, the figures on revenue and expenditure given by Ardouin (1853–60) for 1819–42 in gourdes (see below) are often reproduced as if they were dollars. This would be acceptable if dollar imports could have been paid for in gourdes at par, but this is hardly likely given the reduction in the metallic content of coins and the depreciation of paper money. It is therefore necessary to calculate the exchange rate annually.

Following the imposition of the French indemnity in 1825, Boyer was forced to ransack the treasury for approximately $1 million to meet the first year's payment. The result was an extreme shortage of specie, and Boyer – reluctantly, one suspects – issued paper money in 1826. This made counterfeiting even

easier, and the republic was the victim of fraud carried out in many cases by foreigners. Nevertheless, public finances were still generally sound, and the currency had only lost another third of its value by the time Boyer was forced from office in 1843. Because the exchange rate was 3 until 1826, this means it had fallen to 4 in 1843 (St. John (1889) estimates it at 2.5 to 1, but he does not take into account the fall in its value before 1826). Assuming a linear depreciation, we can then calculate the exchange rate in each year up to 1843 and use this to convert budget figures for those years into dollars.

The political instability between 1843 and 1847 led to new issues of paper money. By 1849, the exchange rate to the US dollar had fallen sharply from its 1843 level. In the International Bureau of American Republics (1893), the exchange rate is said to have fallen from 4 in 1843 to 14 in 1849, and I have used these figures. Other authors estimate a rate of exchange in 1848–9 of 4.0–4.5 (St. John (1889) says 4.5, Marte (1984) includes a budget for 1848 in which it is 4.0 and Turnier (1955) says it was 4.0), but they are assuming that the rate was much stronger than 4.0 in 1843. Whichever rate is used (I have used 14), there was a very fast rate of devaluation between 1843 and 1849. I have not, however, interpolated the intervening years because I did not have to convert any figures from gourdes during those years. Under President Soulouque (1847–59), issues of paper money continued, and the currency declined, being quoted at 20 in 1859, according to the International Bureau of the American Republics (1893), when Soulouque was forced from office (St. John (1889) says 18 and Turnier (1955) says 17.5).

In 1835, Boyer had decreed that all import duties must be paid in hard currency (equivalent to US dollars). However, export duties, the land tax and other taxes were still paid in gourdes. At the rate of exchange in 1843, the taxes collected in gourdes still had some real value, but by 1849 they had ceased to do so. Lundahl (1979), normally a very reliable source, is therefore wrong when he says that nontrade taxes were still important at this time. That is one reason why Soulouque in 1850 required that the main export duties be paid in kind. The other taxes were still paid in gourdes and therefore had lost their value in real (US dollar) terms. Thus, by the end of the 1840s, the public revenue of Haiti had come to depend almost entirely on customs duties (taxes on imports and exports). In particular, the land tax – payable in gourdes – was no longer of any importance, although it was not abolished until 1870.

President Geffrard in 1860 abolished the payment of export duties in kind, but he replaced it with payment in hard currency. Nevertheless, the currency still weakened and was quoted at 30 when he was forced from office in 1867. From then until the end of the civil war in December 1869, when the currency was quoted at 4,000 (St. John (1889) says 3,000), there was an explosion of paper money issues, and the gourde had become completely worthless. Helped by the measures introduced by President Saget (1870–4), it had recovered to 300 by 1872, and it was then withdrawn altogether. In practice, the main currency in use during the rest of the 1870s was the US dollar, so the exchange rate ceased to be relevant.

The gourde was reintroduced by President Salomon in 1880 at par with the US dollar. By 1888, it was quoted at 1.25 (see Blancpain (2001), p. 194), and we may assume a linear depreciation because we do not have annual data (using figures in St. John (1889), p. 387, it appears to have been 1.2 in 1886). From 1889 until 1917, the exchange rate was very volatile but subject to a long-term decline (see Chatelain (1954), p. 36, who uses data provided by the Banque Nationale de la République d'Haiti; Berloquin-Chassany (2004), p. 305, also has figures from 1889 to 1911, but he does not give the source). From 1918, the de facto rate of exchange was 5.0, but this was only legally established in May 1919 during the US occupation.

The exchange rate of the (old) gourde to the US dollar is given in Table B.1. This covers the period from 1819 to 1872. The exchange rate of the (new) gourde to the US dollar is also given in Table B.1 and covers the period from 1880 to 1915. From 1872 to 1879 there is no exchange rate, because the gourde was not used in foreign trade or the budget.

TABLE B.2. EXPORTS OF FOUR MAIN PRODUCTS BY VOLUME AND VALUE

Table B.2 covers the years 1817 to 1915 for the four main export products (coffee, logwood, cacao and cotton).

Coffee Exports

Before 1842, the figures are from Ardouin (1853–60)[1] and have been conveniently reprinted in Barros (1984), vol. 1, p. 344. They are given in long lbs. These can be converted to short lbs at the rate of 1.083, but I have rounded this up to 1.1. The data for 1818–20 are assumed to refer to the Republic of Haiti only, excluding the Kingdom of Haiti, and those for 1821 are assumed to include both. The figures after 1821 include the eastern part of the island. However, coffee exports from the Dominican Republic were negligible, so the figures can be assumed to refer to the western part of Hispaniola only.

The figures for 1843–49 are from Marte (1984), p. 85.[2] This series starts at 1836 and is consistent with Ardouin (1853–60), so it is safe to assume the unit is long lbs. In his series on the volume of coffee exports, which is similar to the one here, Rotberg (1971), pp. 387–8, has a gap for the years 1843 to 1858, but he does include a figure for 1845, which is the same as the one in Marte (it is also in St. John (1889), p. 364). The Rotberg series is also given in *Bulletin de l'Académie des Sciences Humaines et Sociales d'Haiti* (1983), p. 12.

For 1850 and 1851 there are figures in *Annuaire de l'économie politique et de la statistique* (1852). For the years up to 1858, there are incomplete figures.

---

[1] This important multivolume work is available on the Web site of the French Bibliothèque Nationale.

[2] Marte (1984) does not always give his sources, but in many cases for Haitian coffee it is Tippenhauer (1893), pp. 353–6.

However, Marte (1984) has a table (p. 95) recording the French volume of coffee imports from Haiti between 1850 and 1857 and another table (p. 286) recording exports of coffee from Hispaniola to the UK and Germany starting in 1853 (Marte also includes the US in this table, but Turnier (1955) has a more complete series for these years for coffee imports by the US from Haiti, so I have used Turnier for the US figures). Because the Dominican Republic did not export coffee at this time, we can use these two tables to estimate Haitian exports to the core for the years 1853 to 1857, and I have used the resulting figure grossed up by 30 per cent for coffee exports to other markets. The year 1852 has then been filled by interpolation, and 1858 is from Tippenhauer (1893), p. 354. The figure for 1859 is from St. John (1889), who also gives figures for 1835 and 1842 that are similar to, but not exactly the same as, Ardouin (St. John took his figures from Thomas Madiou's *Histoire d'Haiti*).[3]

The figures for 1860–4 are from Barros (1984), vol. 1, p. 212, and are derived from a special issue of the Haitian journal *Panorama* of December 1978 devoted to Geffrard. There is then a gap in the national record until 1872. However, the table in Marte (1984), p. 286, to which reference has already been made, extends to 1882 and includes France (Le Havre only, but this was by far the most important port for Haitian coffee) from 1860. Coffee imports from Haiti by four core countries (France, Germany, UK and US) can be obtained from this. Turnier (1955) also has the figures for US coffee imports in these years, but there are some gaps (1861–2 to 1863–4, 1868–9 to 1870–1), so I have used Marte (1984) only. Assuming that these four countries represented around 70 per cent of coffee exports, I have added another 30 per cent to estimate the total. This covers the gap from 1865 to 1872. However, Marcelin (1892), vol. 1, p. 32, has a table on the volume of **all** coffee exports in various years that includes 1866 and 1871, so I have used these figures for those years.

As a check on the volume of French coffee imports, we can use the data in Joachim (1972). This shows total French imports from Haiti in each year (I have used the series for 'special' rather than 'general' trade). He also gives the average share of coffee in these imports by decade (1847–56=64%; 1857–66=74%; 1867–76=70.6%); I have then assumed 70 per cent for 1877–82. Joachim (1972) then provides *cif* import prices at Le Havre (the main port for Haitian coffee up to 1859). I have extended this series to 1882 using the US *cif* import price for coffee (see below). It is then possible to estimate the volume of French imports of coffee from Haiti in each year from 1850 to 1882. This can be compared with the volumes given in Marte (1984). Although the figures are not the same in each year, the sum for the whole period is almost exactly the same. This gives us some confidence in using the figures and suggests that a three-year average should iron out most of the problems.

---

[3] This multivolume work was republished many times in the twentieth century. See, e.g., Madiou (1988).

There are four long series, each of which has gaps for the early years (but the gaps are not always the same) and which can be used to complete the series after 1882. The first is Tippenhauer (1893), pp. 354–5, which has figures on the volume of exports (in long lbs) from 1818–26; 1835–40; 1842; 1845; 1853; 1856–64; 1873–86. The second series is from the _Tea and Coffee Trade Journal_ (1935). This series has occasional annual data from 1789 to 1863. Starting in 1879–80, the data span two years. However, the coffee harvest runs normally from October to February, so I have assumed that the year 1879–80 refers to 1880, and so on. The third is Benoit (1954), and the figures are given in 1,000 tonnes (one tonne is 1,000 long lbs). The years before 1843 in this source are from Ardouin (1853–60). There is then a figure for the year 1863 and for 1875 and 1876. There is then a complete series from 1886–7 (assumed to refer to 1887 for reasons explained below). The fourth is Rotberg (1971), which is based on Benoit (1954), but Rotberg does have figures for 1873–4.

This means that there is only one year – 1852 – where we have no data and where the gap has had to be filled by interpolation. This means we can have some confidence in the coffee volume series, which is essential given its importance to the Haitian economy.

To obtain the value of coffee exports, it is necessary to convert volumes by multiplying by prices. Except for a handful of years when consular reports provide the volume and value data from which they can be derived, there are no _fob_ prices for Haitian coffee exports. Instead, I have been able to identify six series covering most of the years required: (a) US import prices _(cif)_ from 1821 onwards based on coffee from all sources (Carter (2006), vol. 5); (b) US import prices _(cif)_ from 1821 based on coffee from Haiti only (Turnier (1955), app.); (c) Brazil export prices _(fob)_ from 1821 onwards (IBGE (1987)); (d) French import prices _(cif)_ at Le Havre from 1821 to 1859 (Joachim (1972)); (e) Martinique export prices _(fob)_ from 1818 onwards (_Annuaire de la Martinique_); and (f) UK import prices _(cif)_ from Jamaica from 1831 onwards (Eisner (1961)). There is a close correlation between the first five price series, but the UK series gives much higher prices in many years (the imports were from Jamaica and included Blue Mountain coffee, which commanded – and still commands – a huge premium).

None of these series is ideal. The first series includes coffee from all sources and is given _cif_ (this is the series used by Rotberg (1971), app. B). The second refers only to Haiti, and a comparison of the unit price between (a) and (b) suggests that Haiti was exporting inferior grades of coffee to the United States. The third series has the advantage of being given _fob_, but the best grades of Haitian coffee were thought to be superior to the Brazilian ones. The fourth series is in principle the best, because most Haitian coffee went to France. However, the series is _cif_ and stops in 1859. The fifth series is based on a very small volume of coffee, but it did go to France and is given _fob_. The sixth is the least suitable because it is both _cif_ and based only on expensive Jamaican coffee. There is no perfect solution, but – after lengthy experimentation – I used the series for French imports from Haiti up to 1859, adjusted to _fob_ prices by

deducting 20 per cent (sail was in use almost all the time so a large deduction for transport costs is justified), and the Brazil series (*fob*) from 1860. All the price data have been converted to short lbs.

There is also the issue of export taxes. The export tax was set in hard currency from 1860 and from 1850 was paid in kind in the form of one sack for each five exported (this means the export tax from 1850–9 should be equivalent to 20% of the *fob* price). I then compiled a series for the export tax from 1850 onwards (before that date the tax was paid in highly depreciated national currency and was not a major burden on exporters). In a few years the export tax per pound was almost as large as the *fob* price, so the authorities must have had great difficulty at times in collecting it.

In most years, Haiti had an export surplus. This made it possible for the merchants in control of foreign trade to pay the customs duties in hard currency to the government, which then used the resources to pay the service of the external debt.

Logwood Exports

The data before 1850 are from the same sources as for coffee (see above). The data from 1850 to 1858 have been estimated and filled by interpolation. The figure for 1859 is from St. John (1889), who also gives a figure for 1842 that is similar to, but not the same as, Ardouin (1853–60). However, his figure for 1835 is much lower and almost certainly wrong. The figures for 1860–4 are from Barros (1984), vol. 1, p. 212. The figures from 1865 to 1871 are estimates and have been filled by interpolation.

From 1872 the figures on US imports are given in Turnier (1955), pp. 343–4. For the first two decades when we have both US logwood imports and total logwood exports (1880s and 1890s), the US share averaged 50 per cent. I have therefore applied this ratio to the US import figures from 1872 to 1877. There are then figures on total exports in some years from 1878 in Turnier (1955), p. 156. These are based on consular reports (1878–83) and the Banque Nationale de la République d'Haiti (n.d.) (1887–8 onwards). For 1885–7 there are also figures in Rotberg (1971), app. B. This means that the estimated figures for the logwood volume series are 1850–8 and 1865–71.

There is then a complete series in Benoit (1954) starting in 1888. I have used this up to 1914–15 (assumed to be 1915). I have not included the figure for 1915–16 because it is enormous (nearly five times greater than the previous year) and would distort the series. It is not that I do not trust the figure (US imports also jumped), but it is clearly a result of postponed sales that were now made possible under the US occupation rather than a reflection of increased annual production. The three-year average for logwood in 1915 is therefore a two-year average based on 1914–15.

Logwood prices are based on three series. The first is the US import price (*cif*) from 1874, which is when Turnier (1955) provides both volumes and values. I have assumed that the *fob* price was 90 per cent of the *cif* price (the distance

was short), and this explains the prices from 1874 to 1915. There are two gaps
in the series (1878 and 1911), and I have filled these by interpolation. There
is then a London *cif* price for Jamaican logwood in Eisner (1961) from 1845.
I have assumed that the *fob* price was 55 per cent of the *cif* price (logwood
was an expensive commodity to transport to Europe because of its value-to-
weight ratio). For the years when this series overlaps with the one derived from
Turnier (1955), there is a good fit when both prices are expressed as *fob*. For
the years before 1845, I have derived unit prices from the Martinique series
on volumes and values in Chauleau (1973) and spliced this to the 1845 price.
Because there are no data for 1817, I have assumed the price was the same as
1818.

Cacao Exports

The data before 1850 are from the same sources as for coffee (see 'coffee
exports' above). The data from 1850 to 1858 have been estimated and filled
by interpolation. The figure for 1859 is from St. John (1889). The figures for
1860–4 are from Barros (1984), vol. 1, p. 212. The figures from 1865 to 1878
are estimates and have been filled by interpolation.

There are figures in consular reports for 1879 and 1883, and Rotberg (1971)
provides figures for 1880, 1885 and 1886. There is then a complete series in
Benoit (1954) starting in 1888. The missing years (1881, 1882, 1884, 1887)
have been interpolated.

Cacao prices are assumed to be the same as Brazilian export prices (derived
from IBGE (1987)) up to 1900. Because these are *fob*, no adjustments have
been made. From 1900, I have used the index of cacao prices in MOxLAD and
spliced it to the figure for 1900. I have assumed the cacao price was unchanged
before 1821.

Cotton Exports

The data before 1850 are from the same sources as for coffee (see 'coffee
exports' above). The data from 1850 to 1858 have been estimated and filled by
interpolation. There are figures for cotton exports in Marcelin (1892), vol. 1,
p. 36, for 1853 and 1858. I have used these and estimated the gaps (1850–2
and 1854–7) by interpolation. The figure for 1859 is from St. John (1889).
The figures for 1860–4 are from Barros (1984), vol. 1, p. 212. They show a
significant rise as a result of the opportunities created by the US Civil War.

We do not have figures for the years immediately after 1864, but we do have
consular figures for 1879 and 1883, and Rotberg (1971) provides figures for
1880, 1885 and 1886. There is then a complete series in Benoit (1954) starting
in 1888. The missing years (1865–78) have been interpolated, and other years
(1881, 1882, 1884, 1887) have been estimated.

Cotton prices are assumed to be the same as US export prices (see Carter
(2006), vol. 5) up to 1900. Because these are *fob*, no adjustments have been

made. From 1900, I have used the index of cotton prices in MOxLAD and spliced it to the figure for 1900.

TABLES B.3–B.5

The most reliable way to compile an annual series from 1817 to 1915 for domestic exports at current prices (first three columns of Table B.3) is through the summation of the values of the main commodities (see Table B.2), with a small percentage added to allow for minor exports. By examining those years where we have details on all commodity exports by volume and estimating their value, it is clear that minor exports averaged around 5 per cent of the total. I have therefore added 5 per cent to the value of the sum of the four main exports to derive an estimate of the value of domestic exports (see Table B.3). This has then been converted to domestic exports per head by dividing by population, and the results are given in the first column of Table B.4.

Domestic exports at constant (1860) prices (see Table B.3) have been obtained in exactly the same way as for all other countries. A volume index was constructed (1860=100) based on the value of the four main exports at 1860 prices (all this information is derived from Table B.2, and the volume index itself is given in Table B.8). This index was then applied to the value of domestic exports in 1860 to give the value of domestic exports at constant (1860) prices. The results, when divided by population, give domestic exports per head at constant (1860) prices. See Table B.4.

The value of domestic exports at current prices in Table B.3 can then be compared with two other series. The first are the estimates of domestic exports for some years provided both by resident consuls and by Haitian sources. Marcelin (1892), vol. 1, p. 66, and Marte (1984) are the best sources before 1890; US Consular Reports provide estimates for other years;[4] Léger (1907) gives the figure for 1904; and the Pan-American Union (PAU) (1952) gives the figure for 1912. Given the methodology described above for my estimates and the fact that the other figures typically refer to fiscal not calendar years, we would not expect a perfect match. I consider it a 'good fit' if the difference is close to 10 per cent, a 'fair fit' if it is around 20 per cent and a 'poor fit' if the difference is more than 20 per cent. The results are in general satisfactory (see Appendix to Notes on B. Tables), because the 'poor fit' usually has a straightforward explanation.

Table B.5 gives the domestic exports by main markets (three-year average) for 1822 to 1914. This is a second check on the reliability of the value of domestic exports in Table B.3 because the sum of exports to the main markets (France, UK and US) should be close to the value of the domestic exports as a whole. Turnier (1955) provides an almost complete series for US imports from

---

[4] These can be found in Department of State, *Commercial Relations of the United States with Foreign Countries*.

Haiti from 1820–1.[5] Joachim (1972) provides a complete series for the *cif* value of French imports from 1828 to 1884. There are patchy data for the UK, and the sources are given in the Notes on A. Tables. There are also data for other years for France and the UK in some secondary sources (e.g. Blancpain (2001) and Firmin (1901)). I have then estimated the remaining gaps by interpolation and expressed the results as a percentage of domestic exports (see Table B.5).

The results are good with one exception. This is the period 1882–4 when French imports appear to exceed the whole value of Haitian exports. It is notoriously difficult even today to match export and import figures, and this is also true for Haiti in the nineteenth century, because the main commodities could be stored and shipped after harvest (coffee, cacao) or felling (timber) and because of smuggling. The years in question (1882–4) were very turbulent in Haiti, and I suspect the most likely explanation is increased smuggling, which is reflected in the French imports but not in my estimate of Haitian exports. I have therefore adjusted downwards the share of exports going to France in those years.

I have assumed no re-exports for Haiti, so merchandise exports are the same as domestic exports.

TABLES B.6–B.7

Table B.6 gives imports at current prices from 1821 to 1915 and at 1860 prices (three-year average) from 1822 to 1914. Table B.7 gives imports by source (three-year average) from 1822 to 1914. There are some official and consular figures for current imports, and I have used the following:

1825. Mackenzie (1830)
1853–8. Marte (1984)
1859. Marcelin (1892)
1861. Marcelin (1892)
1862. Marte (1984)
1863–4. Marte (1984)
1866. Marcelin (1892)
1876–7. Marte (1984)
1878. Marcelin (1892)
1890. Marcelin (1892)
1901. Mitchell (2007)
1904. Léger (1907)
1909–14. Mitchell (2007)

---

[5] I have adjusted this to calendar years from fiscal years and also converted it to *fob* values by deducting 10%; this may not be strictly correct because transport costs fell sharply after the replacement of sail by steam; however, the US Consular Report for 1900 states that freight rates to the US in 1899 jumped by 100% following the reduction of competition!

For those years where I had figures for import duties (see Table B.9 below), I estimated imports from the ad valorem rate. This covered 1837, 1839, 1840, 1841, 1845, 1848 and 1850. For other years I have based the estimates of imports on exports to Haiti by the core as follows:

1821–4. I assumed US share equalled 50 per cent (US exports to Haiti are from Turnier (1955)).

1827–36. I assumed imports are the sum of exports by France, the UK and the United States (their exports are to the whole island, but they are *fob* so these errors may more or less cancel out).

1867–84. I assumed US and French share equalled 80 per cent (US exports to Haiti in Turnier (1955) and French exports in Joachim (1972)), except 1875 when imports are assumed to be almost the same as the sum of US and French exports. This ratio (80%) is similar to that given by Blancpain (2001), p. 32, for 1870, 1881, 1890 and 1905.

1885–9. I assumed US share equalled 60 per cent.

1891–7. These years are based on both US exports in Turnier (1955) and US share of imports in Turnier (1955).

1898. I assumed US share equalled 65 per cent.

1899. I assumed US share equalled 60 per cent.

1900. This year is based on US exports in Turnier (1955) and US share of imports in Blancpain (2001).

1902–3. I assumed US share equalled 70 per cent.

1905–8. I assumed US share equalled 70 per cent. For 1905, Blancpain (2001), p. 32, gives 71 per cent.

1915–16. I assumed US share equalled 90 per cent.

The remaining years (1826, 1838, 1842–4, 1846–7, 1849, 1851–2, 1860 and 1865) have been filled by interpolation. Imports at current prices are then given in the first column of Table B.6. They are also given as three-year averages in the second column. The import price index (see Table B.8) is then applied to this figure to give the three-year average of imports at constant (1860) prices. See final column in Table B.6.

Import shares for the United States, France and the UK (see Table B.7) have been calculated as follows: for the years 1822–43, I have deducted 10 per cent from the values of exports to Haiti from these countries to allow for the share going to the Dominican Republic. I have not, however, changed the values from *fob* to *cif*. US exports to Haiti, the most important source of imports for Haiti for most years, include specie (the value of specie in trade between Haiti and the United States is given for most years in Turnier (1955)), so that the undervaluation of imports using *fob* values is to some extent compensated by including coinage.

The US share is then US exports to Haiti (see Turnier (1955)) divided by Haitian imports (see Table B.6) for all years except 1904. In that year, Léger (1907) gives the breakdown of imports (for 1903–4) for the United States, the UK and France, and I have used his figures. The French share is French

exports to Haiti (see Joachim (1972)) divided by Haitian imports for the years 1825–84. For the years before 1825, I have used the implied shares in Franklin (1828). For the years after, I have used a variety of sources (e.g. Turnier (1955), Blancpain (2001), Léger (1907)) and filled in the gaps by interpolation. For the UK, I have used *Parliamentary Papers* for the years 1825–36. For the earlier years, I have used Franklin (1828). For later years I have used the same sources as for France and interpolated the gaps. Whenever the sum of the three shares was greater than 100, I have adjusted the UK share first because this is the least reliable figure. The results are given in Table B.7.

The three-year averages for the three countries demonstrate that the United States was at first displaced by France following recognition in 1825, but that this was reversed from the 1840s onwards. With the exception of the US Civil War years, there is a secular increase in the dependence of Haiti on imports from the United States after 1840.

TABLE B.8. NET BARTER AND INCOME TERMS OF TRADE (1860=100)

The Net Barter Terms of Trade (NBTT) is calculated as the price of exports divided by the price of imports. All three series are shown in Table B.8 and are expressed as three-year averages from 1822 to 1915 (the last year is a two-year average). The price of exports is obtained by dividing the value of the four main commodity exports at current prices by their value at constant prices (see Table B.2). The import price index (1860=100) uses a weighted average of the wholesale prices of the United States, France and the UK. The prices for the United States are derived from Carter (2006), vol. 5, and the prices for France and the UK are derived from Mitchell (2007). The weights for these prices indices are obtained from Table B.7 (the figures for each year are grossed up so that the sum is unity).

The Income Terms of Trade (ITT) is also expressed as a three-year average (1915 is a two-year average). It is obtained by multiplying the NBTT by the export volume index. The latter is derived from the value of the four main commodities at constant (1860) prices (see Table B.2).

TABLE B.9. PUBLIC REVENUE AND IMPORT DUTIES

Table B.9 contains data on public revenue from 1818 to 1915 and import duties at irregular intervals. The data from Ardouin (1853–60) before 1821 refer to the Republic of Haiti only (not the Kingdom); 1821 is both; 1822–42 includes the eastern part. The numbers are reprinted in Barros (1984), vol. 1. Based on the data in Candler (1842) and Marte (1984), which gives the division of the main taxes between all ports in the whole island for 1837, 1839, 1840 and 1841, we may assume that 90 per cent of public revenue between 1822 and 1842 accrued to Haiti and 10 per cent to the Dominican Republic.

The data in Ardouin (1853–60) are in gourdes. From 1818 to 1835, I have applied the exchange rate in Table B.1. In 1835, however, Boyer decreed that all import duties must be paid in hard currency (effectively dollars). Because Ardouin treats all taxes in the same way, that is, valuing the gourde at par with the dollar, it is necessary to subtract import duties in dollars from revenue in gourdes before applying the exchange rate in Table B.1 to the balance. This requires knowledge of import duties in the years between 1836 and 1842. They are given in Candler (1842) and Marte (1984) for 1837, 1839, 1840 and 1841. I have therefore interpolated the missing years (and then assumed that 90% went to Haiti).

The data after 1842 are taken from a variety of sources. For 1845, we have the import duties in French francs (see *Annuaire de l'économie politique et de la statistique* (1852)). By this time, the dollar value of all other taxes had shrunk because of the depreciation of the currency. I have therefore calculated public revenue by assuming the same ratio of import duties to the total as in later years. For 1848, there is a very detailed budget in Marte (1984), which also converts gourdes to dollars and allows us to calculate the ratio of import duties to total revenue (there are slightly lower figures in St. John (1889), p. 383, but these are the sum of expenditures and do not take account of note issues during the year). St. John (1889), p. 383, has a figure for 1849, but it is too low, and the author says that 'these budgets are not to be trusted, and do not represent the real expenses'. There is sufficient data in Marte (1984) to calculate public revenue for 1850. The few missing years (1843, 1844, 1846, 1847 and 1849) have then been filled by interpolation.

For 1860 and 1861 there are data in Marte (1984) on customs duties and in St. John (1889) for 1860–2. However, by now virtually all revenue in dollar terms came from taxes on trade, so I have rounded up the figures on customs duties to estimate public revenue in those years (for 1862, St. John (1889) estimates minor taxes at 4.6%). There are then figures in St. John (1889) for 1863–4, 1876–7 and 1885–6. For 1879, public revenue is given in the US Consular Report. For 1883, there is a figure in Marcelin (1892), p. 112. It is in *piastres*, which is equivalent to US dollars. For 1886, there is a figure in gourdes in *Bulletin de l'Académie des Sciences Humaines et Sociales d'Haiti* (1983), p. 14, which I have converted to dollars (see Table B.1). The British Library has the Haitian budget for 1888–9 (see Chambre des Comptes (1890)). Rotberg (1971), p. 399, gives the average receipts from customs duties in 1876–9, 1880–5 and 1886–90, and these figures have been rounded up to estimate the gaps in public revenue for the years from 1876 to 1889. Benoit (1954a) gives the division of revenue in 1886–7 between the main taxes, but he does not give the revenue itself.

From 1889–90 (assumed to be 1890) the data are given annually in Banque Nationale de la République d'Haiti (n.d.). The data are in gourdes, but it is clear from the note that the original revenue figures in gourdes have been converted to dollars at the current exchange rate and then reconverted to gourdes at the

fixed rate of 5 established in 1919. Thus, these figures can be divided by five to derive US dollars.

This leaves two gaps: 1851–59 and 1865–75. These gaps are too long to fill by interpolation. However, in all these years public revenue came primarily from customs duties (including the export duty paid in kind in the 1850s). It is then possible to estimate customs duties using exports and imports because export duties were a percentage of volume in the 1850s and specific from 1860 onwards, and import duties were largely ad valorem. The rates for these taxes are given in Benoit (1954a) and International Bureau of the American Republics (1893).

Exports by volume and value were estimated in the manner explained above (see Table B.2 and B.3). For imports we need only values, and these were estimated in a different way (see Table B.6). A few specific tariffs on imports were introduced in 1835, but the yield is not known (it is likely to have been small). Benoit (1954a) states the ad valorem tariff rate, which was raised to 12 per cent in 1819 and 16 per cent in 1827. Starting in 1863, various surcharges were added to import tariffs, and these are also listed in Benoit (1954a).

Using this information, it is then possible to estimate public revenue for the missing years. First, the ad valorem tariff rate was applied to the estimate of the value of imports to give import duties. For export duties, I used only the coffee tax (by far the most important). In the 1850s, when it was a tax in kind, this was assumed to yield 20 per cent of the *fob* value of exports. In later years, I applied the specific tax given in Benoit (1954a) and International Bureau of the American Republics (1893) to the volume of coffee exports. This gives export duties.

Customs duties are the sum of import and export duties and can be rounded up to give public revenue. For those years between 1850 and 1880 when we can compare the results with known public revenue, it suggests my figures are overstated by about 10 per cent (in the 1850s the tax in kind is probably overstated by assuming the state was able to sell at *fob* prices; in practice, it is likely to have received less because it sold the coffee to Haitian merchants, who then exported it at *fob* prices). I therefore multiplied my results by 0.9. This gives public revenue, which I converted to public revenue per head before taking a three-year average (see Table B.9).

TABLE B.10. PUBLIC EXPENDITURE BY CATEGORY (%)

Although there are scattered data on public expenditure, I have not tried to build an annual series. Instead, I have estimated expenditure by type for different years between 1820 and 1914 and then expressed the results as a percentage of public revenue taken from Table B.9. The types of expenditure are (a) external debt service, (b) internal debt service, (c) settlement of claims, (d) armed forces, (e) education, and (f) education.

External Debt Service

I first estimated external debt service for each year as follows:

1820–4. There was no external debt.

1825–7. Haiti agreed in 1825 to pay an indemnity of 150 million French francs (roughly $30 million) in return for recognition. The first instalment of this indemnity (30 million francs) was met mainly with the proceeds of a French loan. This loan had a face value of 30 million francs, but only 24 million francs was disbursed. Strictly speaking, this was the first external debt, because the indemnity was not a loan. However, it is customary to refer to the loan and the indemnity as the double debt. Most of the balance of the loan (6 million francs) was remitted in specie, but there remained a balance (700,000 francs), which was not paid. The dollar value of what was paid in specie (5.3 million francs) was about $1 million, which was more than public revenue for the year. However, it was not paid from the budget, so I have not included anything for 1825.

The interest on the 30 million franc loan was paid in 1826–7, but not by Haiti. It was paid by the French government to the French bankers and was therefore added in theory to what Haiti owed to France. Haiti therefore paid no debt service in these years, and the loan went into default (Rotberg (1971), p. 397, states that interest payments were made, but this is misleading – see Blancpain (2001)).

1838–1883. The indemnity was renegotiated in 1838 and reduced from 150 million to 90 million francs (of which some 30 million francs had been paid leaving 60 million). The terms on which the indemnity (60 mn), the principal (30 mn) and interest (3%) on the loan and the balance from 1825 (700,000 francs) were to be paid, were all set out clearly in an annual schedule, but the rate of exchange would cause difficulties because the debt had to be paid in francs (see Blancpain (2001)). For domestic reasons (political upheaval in Haiti), payments were suspended in 1843–8 and 1867–9 (but two small payments were made in the latter years – see Blancpain (2001)). In theory, this pushed back the final payment from 1868 to 1876. However, for various reasons, the final payment was not made until December 1883 (see Blancpain (2001)). It is thus possible to estimate the cost of external debt service attributable to the double debt in the years from 1838, when Haiti first met debt-service payments from the budget, to 1883.

1874–1915. It is first necessary to estimate the external debt service on new loans only (contracted in 1874, 1875, 1896 and 1910). Apart from the first loan, which was intended to pay off the double debt, each new loan was intended – among other things – to pay off the previous loan. This did not happen primarily because Haiti was cheated of the funds due through excessive commissions. The 1875 loan was particularly scandalous, and the amount repayable was scaled down in the 1880s. Nevertheless, Haiti had to repay far more than it had received (even when interest is excluded). The

loans had different maturities and different interest rates, but the debt stock at various dates is given by many authors (e.g. Firmin (1905), Vincent (1939), Benoit (1954a), Rotberg (1971)). Using this information, I have calculated roughly the interest payable each year. Very little principal was repaid (except between 1889 and 1891).

The service on these new loans was then added to the service of the double debt (see above). Expressed as a percentage of the budget in three-year averages, this is the first column in Table B.10.

Internal Debt Service

From time to time, and with increasing frequency after 1860, the Haitian state issued debt domestically. Some of this was paper money. This was not generally backed by hard currency, but from the 1870s onwards it was on occasions linked to certain customs receipts, and the government sometimes refused to accept its own paper in payment, but at least it was interest-free, so it did not need to be serviced (it was redeemed from time to time using the hypothecated taxes referred to above).

More important for our purposes are the loans made by merchants to the government. These merchants could be foreigners or nationals, but the debt is always considered internal (it was nearly always made in gourdes even if repayment was sometimes required in hard currency). The stock of internal debt is given in different years (see list of sources for the external debt), and a few estimates were made of annual debt-service payments by the same authors. I have used this information to estimate internal debt service, which is given in column 2 of Table B.10 as a percentage of public revenue.

The sum of external and internal debt service is total debt service. However, total debt service as a percentage of the budget is given for a number of years (e.g. Blancpain (2001)), and I have used this to adjust the figures on external and internal debt service. The results are clearly more reliable for the more recent years and from 1890 onwards are probably quite accurate.

External Claims

Claims were made by foreigners against the Haitian state from an early stage. These were based either on property damage, allegations of false arrest or breach of contract and were brought against the government. These claims are dealt with at some length by many authors (e.g. Montague (1940), Léger (1907), Douyon (2004)). That most of them seem to have been either frivolous or inflated was no consolation for the Haitian state, because foreign governments seem to have taken a particular delight in pursuing these claims on behalf of their nationals (in a few cases the negotiations went on for decades). We do not know exactly how much the Haitian government had to pay each year, but Frédéric Marcelin, who was finance minister for a number of years, estimated the total at $2.5 million from 1879 to 1902, and an

earlier estimate by Louis Joseph Janvier suggests $16 million in the fifty years up to 1880. See Joachim (1979), p. 187. I have annualised the estimate by Marcelin, who is a very creditable source, and extended it to 1914. Expressed as a percentage of the budget, this is column 3 in Table B.10. For the years before 1880, I have assumed that 2 per cent of revenue was spent on external claims (the Janvier figure would suggest a much higher figure, but I think that is inflated).

Armed Forces

From Franklin (1828) and Mackenzie (1830) we learn that the armed forces absorbed about 50 per cent of expenditure in 1820. The size of the army fell under Boyer, and the proportion spent on the armed forces must also have fallen to accommodate debt-service payments. The size of the army shrank further under Geffrard (see St. John (1889)), and thus from 1860 to 1900 it averaged between 25 and 30 per cent of the budget according to the figures we have. From 1900 onwards we have more frequent data. This is column 4 of Table B.10.

Public Education

Education was a priority in Christophe's Kingdom of Haiti, but less so in the southern republic ruled by Pétion – but he did found the famous *lycée* that still bears his name. Boyer is not noted for promoting education, but some spending certainly did take place, and I have assumed a figure of 5 per cent until mid-century. Soulouque, despite or perhaps because of being illiterate himself, took public education very seriously and made it compulsory for each family to send at least one child to school. Under Geffrard, a Concordat was reached with the Vatican in 1860, and rural schooling in particular increased. Figures on educational spending in the early 1860s (St. John (1889)) suggest that spending on education had risen to 10 per cent of public revenue, and other sources confirm it for later years. I have kept this figure until the last year (1914), when the chaotic financial conditions made it inevitable that spending on public education must have fallen. These are the figures in column 5 of Table B.10. School enrolment figures are given in Logan (1930), Rotberg (1971) and Lundahl (1979).

Agriculture

This became an item in the official budget from 1860 onwards, because the Haitian government recognised the need for the promotion of agriculture. However, very little of the budget could be devoted to agriculture in view of the demands made by other items of expenditure. The limited information we have has been put together in Table B.10, and I have assumed that there was no expenditure before 1860.

APPENDIX TO NOTES ON B TABLES

Estimates of the Value of Domestic Exports ($), 1821–1912

Year	Table B.3	Other	Source	Fit	Notes
1821	7,512,943	6,856,658	Franklin (1828)	Good	
1822	5,540,306	9,030,397	Franklin (1828)	Poor	Franklin's figures are much too high, as he himself accepts
1825	4,639,382	5,949,488	Marte (1984)	Fair	
1829	3,182,985	727,968	Marcelin (1892)	Poor	Primary source used by Marcelin is unreliable
1835	5,839,882	5,000,000	Marcelin (1892)	Fair	
1836	4,586,331	4,501,993	Marte (1984)	Good	
1853	4,794,165	3,948,128	Marcelin (1892)	Fair	
1855	4,341,447	3,178,384	Marcelin (1892)	Poor	The difference is probably caused by smuggling because of coffee tax
1856	5,139,595	4,715,840	Marcelin (1892)	Good	
1858	6,185,507	6,456,000	Marte (1984)	Good	
1859	5,380,156	5,017,400	Marte (1984)	Good	
1861	5,608,950	6,433,982	Marte (1984)	Fair	
1862	7,210,416	8,800,000	Marte (1984)	Fair	
1863	11,434,158	11,970,460	Marte (1984)	Good	
1864	8,774,819	9,228,650	Marte (1984)	Good	
1865	7,230,216	5,816,370	Marcelin (1892)	Fair	
1866	7,942,743	8,742,161	Marcelin (1892)	Good	
1876	13,877,519	11,000,000	Marcelin (1892)	Fair	
1877	9,151,104	7,971,000	Marcelin (1892)	Fair	
1878	10,037,339	10,600,000	Marcelin (1892)	Good	
1879	7,273,638	6,731,860	US Consular Reports (a)	Good	
1882	7,837,497	7,575,759	US Consular Reports (a)	Good	
1883	5,981,038	7,344,173	US Consular Reports (a)	Fair	
1884	6,181,917	7,400,238	Turnier (1955)	Fair	
1885	9,840,473	6,387,809	St. John (1889)	Poor	St. John's figure is for 1884–5, and this may explain the difference

Year	Table B.3	Other	Source	Fit	Notes
1886	7,403,181	6,120,354	St. John (1889)	Fair	
1887	7,553,564	14,668,383	Marcelin (1892)	Poor	Primary source used by Marcelin is a propaganda book
1890	14,620,221	14,245,779	Price (b)	Good	
1899	4,968,152	12,747,900	US Consular Reports (a)	Poor	The US consul's figure must be in gourdes, but it is said to be US dollars
1904	8,948,546	8,585,687	Léger (1907)	Good	
1912	14,747,073	11,316,000	PAU (1951)	Poor	The PAU figure is for the fiscal year 1912–13

Note: (a) US Consular Reports from Department of State, *Commercial Relations of the United States with Foreign Countries* (various years); (b) 'Price' is Hannibal Price whose estimate is generally considered very accurate and is quoted in Marcelin (1892).

Notes on C Tables

The C. Tables start in 1900 and end in 1960. If the entries appear in black, they are taken from primary or secondary sources. The data in red are estimates (normally obtained by interpolation for the years between the data in black). The data in blue are either incomplete or are small 'trace' elements (see Table C.5 below). This colour-coding is used the first time an entry is used, but not if the information is repeated subsequently (in which case it appears in black). The subregional data in the table are all given in black.

The first year (1900) is normally taken from the A. Tables. This time, however, Trinidad & Tobago are aggregated together and so are St Kitts & Nevis. Similarly, St Barthélemy is included in the figures for Guadeloupe. The Danish Virgin Islands have been renamed US Virgin Islands, but the transfer of sovereignty did not take place until 31 March 1917. All colonies have been renamed 'dependencies' in view of the constitutional changes that took place during the period.

The subregional totals in this period are in some cases different from those in the A. Tables. The Scandinavian colonies no longer appear. In addition to British, French and Dutch dependencies, there are now US dependencies (Puerto Rico and the US Virgin Islands). This means the 'mother' for Puerto Rico and the US Virgin Islands is the United States. Hispaniola (Haiti and the Dominican Republic) remains the same, but Cuba – independent from 1902 – is treated both as a country and as a subregion in view of its importance.

TABLES C.1–C.3

These tables contain the demographic data for the period. All figures on net migration are derived from these tables. The titles are as follows:

Table C.1. Population
Table C.1.a. Population (adjusted for per capita calculations)

Table C.2. Crude Birth Rates
Table C.3. Crude Death Rates

SOURCES FOR TABLES C.1–C.3

TABLES C.1 AND C.1A. POPULATION

Table C.1 gives the population from 1900 to 1960 for twenty-seven countries, including Anguilla. However, in all other tables for the period 1900–60, Anguilla is aggregated with St Kitts & Nevis. Table C.1a, therefore, presents the population data for twenty-six countries, with Anguilla added to St Kitts & Nevis. This is the table that must be used to calculate per capita values.

The years 1950–59 are in many cases taken from CEPAL (2009), and the final year (1960) is from Table D.1 (this is also the first year in the series in World Bank, World Development Indicators (hereafter WDI), and these two are the main sources for the population data from 1960 onwards). However, neither CEPAL (2009) nor WDI include the three French territories (now called Départements d'Outre-Mer) or some of the British colonies (today called British Overseas Territories). These countries are French Guiana, Guadeloupe, Martinique, Anguilla, British Virgin Islands, Montserrat and Turks & Caicos Islands (the Cayman Islands, although a British Overseas Territory, is included in the population tables in WDI).

Hispaniola

Haiti
The population data for much of this period are still not precise. There was a rough estimate soon after the start of the US occupation of 2,000,000, and this is believed to be a reasonably accurate figure for 1922. Wilkie (1974) has a series from 1900 onwards, but his 1900 figure is taken from the *Statesman's Yearbook* and is too low because it implies exceptionally **fast** growth from 1900 to 1922. Wilkie's 1900 figure is also the same as the estimated number of Roman Catholics (see Victor (1944)), but not all Haitians were Catholic, and some protestant denominations were well established by then. Other secondary sources, for example, Angus Maddison's *Historical Statistics* (hereafter Maddison – available at http://www.conference-board.org/data/economydatabase) and Sánchez-Albornoz (1986), have a much higher figure in 1900, but this then implies too **low** a rate of growth between 1900 and 1922.

As explained in the Notes on B. Tables, I have estimated the population between 1900 and 1922, taking into account not only assumed birth and death rates, but also net outward migration. The first modern census was held in 1950, giving a figure of 3,097,000, but this is believed to be an underestimate (see Lundahl (1979), p. 191). A Haitian demographer, Jacques Saint Surin, adjusted the figure upwards to 3,380,000, and this is the figure included in

Wilkie (1974). Subsequent work revised this down to 3,221,000, and this is the figure I have used (see CEPAL (2009)).

Between 1922 and 1930, it is necessary to allow for a small increase in net emigration because this is when the largest numbers of Haitians entered Cuba (see Pérez de la Riva (1975), vol. 2). I have assumed net annual migration outwards of 0.7 per cent. With a CBR of 45 and a CDR of 25, this gives the population in 1930. From then until 1950, I interpolated the figures. I have also assumed that net outward migration ceased in the 1930s because Cuba no longer welcomed Haitians. The massacre of Haitians in the Dominican Republic in 1937 can also be assumed to have stopped emigration to the neighbouring country for a time. For the years 1950–9, I have used CEPAL (2009). The 1960 figure is the same as in the WDI.

Dominican Republic
There was an unofficial estimate made in 1908 of 638,000 (see Moya Pons (1998), p. 21). However, the first official census figure is 1920 (see Dominican Republic (1975)), and I have used this, interpolating the data between 1900 and 1920 (this gives a figure for 1908 of 632,000 – very close to the unofficial figure for that year). The implied annual rate of growth after 1900 is high, but the Dominican Republic was attracting inward migration in these years, so it is plausible.

A census was next taken in 1935, and I have used this figure, interpolating the intervening years (1921–34). The years 1950–9 have been taken from CEPAL (2009), and the years 1936–49 have then been interpolated. The 1960 figure is the same as in WDI.

Wilkie (1974) has a much higher starting point in 1900, but this figure was taken from the *World Almanac and Encyclopedia* for 1901 and is not plausible because it implies very slow growth in the first decades of the century. Even so, it has been reproduced in many secondary sources.

Cuba

There is a series in Wilkie (1974), which has been widely reproduced in the secondary literature. See, for example, Mitchell (2007) and MOxLAD. This series, in turn, comes from CERP (1965) for 1903–43 and ECLA (1966) thereafter. Unfortunately, although consistent with the data for the census years, it contains serious errors because the 1931 figure is repeated in three years (1931–3), and the resulting annual population changes are either implausibly large or small.

There is a different series in Maddison, which begins by using the series compiled by Alienes (1950). This reproduces the census figure for 1943 found in Alienes, but it is a little different between 1928 and 1942. The biggest problem with the Maddison series, however, is the jump in the population between 1949 and 1950, which is not plausible.

Santamaría (2000) has tried to address the problems of the Cuban population estimates in this period by producing his own series. In particular, he draws attention to the underreporting in each census before 1930 as a result of the treatment of nonnationals. This valid criticism should not apply to the 1930 census, but Santamaría still inflates this and also has the same figure for 1931–3.

I therefore proceeded as follows: I used the Alienes series up to the census figure in 1943. From 1950 onwards I used the series in CEPAL (2009), because it is based on primary sources, and interpolated the missing years (1944–9). The 1960 figure in CEPAL (2009) is the same figure as in WDI.

British Dependencies

The British authorities took a census for almost all their colonies in 1901, 1911 and 1921. There were also official estimates of population in 1931. A census was then taken for all countries between 1943 and 1946. CEPAL (2009) starts in 1950. I have therefore used the census data together with the CEPAL series and interpolated the gaps.

Mitchell (2007) has annual data for Barbados, Guyana, Jamaica and Trinidad & Tobago, but these series must be used with great care. The Guyana series in Mitchell does not include the Amerindian population until 1940, but each census before 1946 did make a rough estimate that I have included, and so the interpolated years include the Amerindian population. Also, the early figures for Barbados in Mitchell (2007) are very unreliable, so I have only used this source from 1921. Similarly, the Trinidad & Tobago series in Mitchell (2007) is only reliable from 1931.

In the case of those British dependencies (except the Cayman Islands) not included in CEPAL (2009), I have used census data and interpolated the gaps. For the Cayman Islands, I have used Cayman Islands (1992).

French Dependencies

French Guiana
I have used the data in Mam-Lam-Fouck (1999) up to 1946, interpolating any missing data. From 1952 onwards I have used the figures in INSEE (1990). The gap between 1946 and 1952 has been filled by interpolation. The decision to close the penal colony in 1938 led to a drop in the population, because the number of convicts, included in the total in the twentieth century, gradually fell to zero. The last convicts were released or died in the 1950s.

Guadeloupe
Mitchell (2007) has the census figures at different years but also a note stating that the population is overenumerated in the first decades of the twentieth century. This is borne out by a comparison of the figures from 1946 onwards (assumed to be reliable) with the earlier census figures. I therefore took the

annual series in Mitchell (2007) for the years 1946–8 and then the series in *Annuaire Statistique de la Guadeloupe* for 1949 onwards. Using data on net births (see below under Tables C.2 and C.3), I then estimated the population back to 1931 (assuming no net migration in those years). I then interpolated the population from 1900 to 1930 using the figure for 1900 in Table A.1.

Martinique

Mitchell (2007) has the census figures at different years but also a note stating that the population is overenumerated in the first decades of the twentieth century. This is borne out by a comparison of the figures from 1946 onwards (assumed to be reliable) with the earlier census figures. I therefore took the annual series in Mitchell (2007) for the years 1946–55 and then the series in INSEE (1990) for 1956 onwards. There are births and deaths in INSEE (1990) from 1950, deaths in Mitchell (2007) from 1946 and births and deaths in *Annuaire de la Vie Martiniquaise* (1946) from 1940. I used all this information to calculate the population from 1940 and interpolated the population before that using the figure for 1900 in Table A.1. However, I have included a big fall in population in 1902, when Mt. Pelée erupted and killed all but two of the inhabitants of St Pierre.

Dutch Dependencies

Dutch Antilles

From 1900–12, I used the same method as for Table A.1. There are then census figures at regular intervals in *Statistisch Jaarboek: Nederlandse Antillen* (1956 onwards) and gaps have been filled by interpolation. The figures in *Statistisch Jaarboek* are disaggregated by island. The figure for 1960 in all issues of *Statistisch Jaarboek* is higher than that in WDI. Because the latter is the source both for the Dutch Antilles (excluding Aruba) and Aruba from 1960 onwards, I have used it. I therefore interpolated the data from 1956–9 using the 1955 census figure in *Statistisch Jaarboek* as the start year.

Suriname

The first census to include all the inhabitants was 1921. For earlier years I used Benjamins and Snelleman (1917) for the enumerated population and added an estimate for the maroons and Amerindians. I then filled any gaps by interpolation backwards to 1900 (my estimate for that year also includes all inhabitants). As a check on the estimated population before 1921, I used the religious affiliations in the colony given at five-year intervals in Goslinga (1990), p. 630. These, however, are not census figures, and they exclude the Amerindians and maroons.

From 1950–9, I have used CEPAL (2009), and the 1960 figure is the same as WDI. For the intervening years I have used the change in population in Lamur (1973), table 58, p. 136, and worked backwards to 1921 (this required a small adjustment to the annual change in population in order that the estimated

figure in 1921 should be the same as the census figure). There are figures in Goslinga (1990), app., p. 738, for the population from 1920 to 1942, but these exclude the Amerindians and maroons.

US Dependencies

Puerto Rico
There is a time series from 1900 in Carter (2006), vol. 5, for all years.

US Virgin Islands
The years up to the transfer from Denmark to the United States are derived from the censuses held in 1901, 1911 and 1917. There is a time series from 1940 in Carter (2006), vol. 5. The years from 1918 to 1939 have been taken from Bulmer-Thomas (2001a). There is a small discrepancy between Carter (2006) and WDI for 1960. Because Carter (2006) is likely to be more accurate, I have used it.

TABLES C.2 AND C.3

Table C.2 contains Crude Birth Rates (CBR) and Table C.3 contains Crude Death Rates (CDR). The 1900 figures are all consistent with those in Tables A.3 (CBR) and A.4 (CDR). The 1960 figures are consistent with the CBR and CDR in Tables D.2 and D.3. See Notes on D. Tables for sources.

Hispaniola

Haiti
There are no complete figures for births and deaths. However, it is generally accepted that there was net outward migration in Haiti from 1900 to 1930, so the difference between the CBR and the CDR needs to be greater than the rate of growth of population. The first serious estimate of the CDR is for 1935–44 and was estimated at 25.0 (United Nations (1949)). I assumed that this had not changed since 1900 because by 1960 the CDR had only fallen to 22.0. The same source estimated the CBR at around 45.0, and I have used this figure for the whole period until 1960, when it was estimated at 44.0.

These vital statistics and the population estimates in Table C.1 are consistent with the migration of sugarcane workers to Cuba before 1930, the migration to the Dominican Republic before 1937, when the slaughter of at least 10,000 Haitians occurred, the temporary migration of Haitians to the United States as farm workers during the Second World War and the postwar migrations to both the United States and the Dominican Republic. Nonetheless, the estimates are still very crude.

Implied net outward migration after 1900 using Tables C.1–C.3 will not always be the same as the recorded immigration of Haitians into Cuba (the main destination) before 1930 (see Pérez de la Riva (1975), vol. 2), because the latter

is gross, covers only migration to Cuba and excludes illegal migration. There was also an unknown number of Haitians who migrated to the Dominican Republic. However, it should never be forgotten that Haiti was also **receiving** migrants – notably those who came from the Ottoman Empire before its demise (known in Haiti as 'Syrians') and those who came following the US occupation (excluding the occupation force itself).

Dominican Republic

The 1920 census (see Dominican Republic (1975)) recorded births and deaths, from which I have derived the CBR and CDR. These are very similar to the figures for 1900 taken from Tables A.3 and A.4. The *Anuario Estadístico Dominicano* then has a series from 1936 to 1954. I have estimated by interpolation the years 1955–9. The 1960 figure is from WDI.

Cuba

There are quinquennial estimates in Mitchell (2007) up to 1945–9, which are taken from Collver (1965). In my view, however, both the CBR and CDR in this source are implausibly high. I have therefore used the annual figures from *Anuario Estadístico de Cuba 1914* (1915), Schroeder (1982) and Mitchell (2007) with the exception of the CBR from 1915–46. The reported birth rates for these years in Schroeder and Mitchell are too low in many years, so I have smoothed the series from 1914 to 1947. The CDR series looks realistic, and all sources agree that it was falling rapidly after 1920.

British Dependencies

Mitchell (2007) provides vital statistics for Guyana (all years), Trinidad & Tobago (all years), Jamaica (all years) and Barbados (1910 onwards). All other figures have been obtained from (a) *Statistical Abstract for the several Colonial and other Possessions of the United Kingdom*, (b) *Statistical Abstract for the British Empire*, (c) *Colonial Reports*, and (d) *Blue Books*. However, the CBR and CDR reported in these sources, although using births or deaths in the current year, sometimes use population from the **previous** census. Where the population changed significantly in the intervening years, this distorts the results. In these cases I have used births and deaths and divided by the population in Table C.1 for the current year to derive the CBR and CDR.

The high CDR in some years is because of exceptional circumstances. For example, in 1902 in St Vincent it was caused by a volcanic eruption.

French Dependencies

French Guiana

Vital statistics from 1952 onwards are in INSEE (1990) and also in the relevant issues of *Annuaire de la Guyane Française*. Births and deaths for some earlier

years are in Mam-Lam-Fouck (1999), and I have used these to calculate the CBR and CDR for the relevant years and then interpolated the gaps.

French Guiana was notorious for having a death rate higher than the birth rate in the first half of the twentieth century. Birth rates were biased downwards because the enumerated population included convicts and gold prospectors, both of whom were almost entirely male. Many prospectors emigrated after the gold boom ended, and the penal colony stopped taking new convicts in 1938. The remaining prisoners then died or were repatriated, and the gender balance became more equal in the 1950s.

Guadeloupe and Martinique
The vital statistics after the Second World War are in the *Annuaire* for each country (CBR from 1948 and CDR from 1946). Martinique also published figures on births and deaths between 1940 and 1945 in *Annuaire de la Vie Martiniquaise* (1946), but I have had to estimate the earlier figures (making a special allowance for the high death toll in 1902, when Mt. Pelée erupted). Guadeloupe published births and deaths in 1900–4 and also in each year from 1931 in *Annuaire Statistique de la Guadeloupe* (1954). The years 1905–30 were never reported, but *Annuaire Statistique de la Guadeloupe* (1954) estimates the net births for the whole of this period as 25,000. This is an average of 1,000 per year, and I have adjusted the CBR and CDR to yield that figure.

Dutch Dependencies

Dutch Antilles
Statistisch Jaarboek: Nederlandse Antillen (1956 onwards) has some data for earlier years (starting in 1938). For 1941, there are figures in Hiss (1943), p. 193. For 1900, I have used the figure for 1898 (Curaçao only) in *Oranje en de Zes Caraibische Parelen* (1948), which has figures also for 1908, 1918, 1928, 1938, 1946 and 1947. Remaining gaps have been filled by interpolation.

Suriname
Lamur (1973) has the CBR and CDR from 1923. Van Lier (1971), p. 293, has the CBR and CDR at quinquennial intervals up to 1910. The gaps have been estimated by interpolation.

US Dependencies

Puerto Rico
The figures from 1910 are in Carter (2006), vol. 5. The 1900 figures are from Tables A.3 and A.4. Clark (1930) has the average figures for 1901–4. I have estimated 1905–9.

US Virgin Islands
There are figures on births and deaths (both including stillbirths) up to 1915 in *Statistisk Aarbog for Danmark*. There are figures up to 1919 in US, Department

of Commerce (1920). These exclude stillbirths and are therefore preferable.[1] There is a series on births and deaths from 1924–45 in Proudfoot (1954), p. 396. The *Annual Report of the Governor of the US Virgin Islands* from 1931 onwards contains figures for most years.[2] There are also some data in the *Annual Report of the Governor of the US Virgin Islands* presented to the US Senate by the US Naval Administration in 1925–6. For 1924 to 1930 there are data on deaths in US, Department of Commerce (1931), *Mortality Statistics*. The *Annual Report of the Governor of the US Virgin Islands* also gives the average CDR for the Virgin Islands for the years immediately prior to the transfer of sovereignty. Any gaps have been filled by interpolation.

TABLES C.4–C.32

These tables contain annual data on exchange rates, exports, imports, the terms of trade, public revenue and public expenditure. The tables also contain numerous series at constant prices. I have chosen 1930 as the base year, because it is exactly halfway between the start (1900) and end (1960) of the series. It is more common in economic histories of this period to use the late 1920s as the base period. However, commodity prices peaked in the late 1920s and reached their trough in 1932–3, so 1930 is a more appropriate base year. The titles are as follows:

Table C.4. Exchange Rates
Table C.5. Country Export Data
Table C.6. Domestic Exports
Table C.7. Re-Exports
Table C.8. Merchandise Exports
Table C.9. Domestic Exports (1930 prices)
Table C.10. Unit Value of Exports (1930=100)
Table C.11. Export Volume Index (1930=100)
Table C.12. Value of Commodity Exports
Table C.13. Structure of Domestic Exports (%)
Table C.14. Commodity Prices
Table C.15. Exports to the United States (%)
Table C.16. Exports to the UK (%)
Table C.17. Exports to the 'Mother' Country (%)
Table C.18. Merchandise Imports
Table C.19. Merchandise Imports (1930 prices)
Table C.20. Retained Imports
Table C.21. Retained Imports (1930 prices)
Table C.22. Imports from the United States (%)

[1] Deaths excluding stillbirths start in 1901. All island figures on births are only available from 1907, so I used *Statistisk Aarbog for Danmark* for earlier years.
[2] These *Annual Reports* are all available on the Digital Library of the Caribbean (DLOC) Web site.

TABLE C.4. EXCHANGE RATES

The exchange rates to the US dollar are given in Table C.4. For sterling the rate is given as US dollars per pound, but for the other currencies it is the other way round. The French franc is given in old francs up to 1960, but also in new francs for 1958–60 (when two zeros were taken off). Sources sometimes give values in old francs even after the new franc was introduced. The rates for the US dollar against the pound sterling, the French franc and the Dutch guilder are given in Carter (2006), vol.5, and Schneider, Schwarzer and Zellfelder (1991).

The Dutch guilder had the same value to the US dollar as the Surinamese and Dutch Antilles guilder until 1945. However, only the Dutch guilder was devalued in that year, so both rates are given in the table. The Haitian gourde is given in all years, but it was fixed at 5 to the US dollar in 1919 (before that it fluctuated – see Table B.1 and Chatelain (1954)).

From 1900 until 1947, the US dollar was the only legal currency in the Dominican Republic. The Dominican peso, reintroduced in 1947, was always at par with the US dollar in this period, so its rate is not given in Table C.4. Nor is the Cuban peso, reintroduced in 1914 at par with the US dollar, but in three years (1938–40) its rate against the US dollar fell below par[3] (the US dollar was used in the US occupation from 1898 to 1902 and remained the only currency until 1914). The US dependencies (Puerto Rico and the US Virgin Islands) used the US dollar. Before 1917, the US Virgin Islands used a variety of currencies, including the Danish West Indian dollar (until 1898), which was almost at par with the US dollar, and the Danish West Indian franc (1904–34), which was roughly at par with the French franc.

Most of the British dependencies adopted the British West Indian dollar (BWI$) at 4.80 per pound sterling in 1946. This rate was maintained through the sterling devaluation in 1949, so the BWI$ depreciated against other currencies. I have converted all BWI$ to sterling before converting to US dollars at the exchange rate in Table C.4.

Guyana had its own currency (the British Guiana dollar – BG$) throughout the period that was always fixed at 4.80 to sterling. I have converted Guyanese

values to sterling, where they were not already in pounds, before converting to US dollars at the exchange rate in Table C.4.

Belize had its own currency (the British Honduran dollar – BH$) that was at par to the US dollar until the end of 1949. However, the colonial authorities converted values in Belize dollars to sterling at a rate that was similar to, but not always exactly the same as, the dollar/pound rate in Table C.4. Where the data are given in sterling, they therefore need to be converted back to BH$ (i.e. US dollars) at the rate given for the BH$ in Table C.4 and not at the US dollar/pound rate. This procedure was used from 1900 to 1949.

When sterling was devalued in September 1949, the BH$ was the only colonial currency that did not depreciate against the US dollar. However, this was reversed on 31 December 1949 when the BH$ was fixed at 4.0 per pound sterling, implying a devaluation against the US dollar of 43 per cent. From 1950 onwards, therefore, values in BH$ can be converted to sterling by dividing by four and then converted to US dollars at the exchange rate in Table C.4.

TABLE C.5. COUNTRY EXPORT DATA

Table C.5 gives the volume and value of the principal exports for each country. The data are colour-coded – red indicates an estimated volume or value, and blue is used either for incomplete data or for the 'trace' elements in 1930 ($100 for the value with the volume determined by the average price of the commodity in that year). The 'trace' elements are used when a commodity was not exported in 1930 but was a principal export before or after 1930.

Table C.5 also gives the value of domestic exports in current US dollars. The difference between this and the subtotal of principal exports is the value of minor exports. The minor exports are almost always less than 10 per cent of domestic exports. The detailed sources for Table C.5 are listed by country at the end of this note.

TABLES C.6–C.8. DOMESTIC EXPORTS, RE-EXPORTS AND MERCHANDISE EXPORTS

Table C.6 repeats the value of domestic exports from Table C.5, but this time without colour-coding. Table C.7 gives the value of re-exports, and Table C.8 is the value of merchandise exports (domestic exports plus re-exports with no colour-coding). Merchandise exports do not include exports of services, which were already beginning to be important for some countries by 1960. Because WDI contains merchandise exports (but not domestic exports) for seventeen of the countries from 1960, I have made a small adjustment to the 1960 figure, where there was a difference, to equal the WDI figure and then made re-exports in 1960 the residual between domestic and merchandise exports. The only exception is where the WDI figure is so rounded (e.g. Antigua, Bahamas) that I have kept my original figures because they are more accurate. The result is that the WDI figures can then be grafted onto the figures in Table C.8 to

bring them up to the present. This is done in Table D.6. The detailed sources for Tables C.6–C.8 are listed by country at the end of this note.

TABLE C.9. DOMESTIC EXPORTS (1930 US DOLLARS)

Table C.9 gives domestic exports at constant (1930) prices. This starts by multiplying for each country the volume of the principal exports in Table C.5 by their price in 1930. Because some of the main commodities were not exported in 1930, I have introduced 'trace' elements to give a nominal value of $100 (volume and value in blue) in that year and 'borrowed' a price (from Table C.15 – see below) to give the implied quantity. The subtotal of principal exports at 1930 prices is then the sum of these major commodities.

So far the treatment of domestic exports at constant prices is the same as for the nineteenth century. However, I have made an adjustment in this period (1900–60) for minor exports at constant prices. The value of minor exports at current prices is domestic exports less the subtotal of principal exports (see Table C.5). These have then been deflated by a weighted price index (1930 prices) covering twenty-four commodities derived from Ocampo and Parra (2003) and reported in MOxLAD.[4] These minor exports at 1930 prices are then added to the subtotal of principal exports at 1930 prices to give domestic exports at 1930 prices.

The reader should note that this will give the same result as the methodology used for the nineteenth century, provided that the share of minor exports is constant and the price deflator for the minor exports is the same as for the major exports. However, minor exports varied quite sharply in importance in the period 1900–60, and price changes were also more important. Thus, this refinement to the methodology is worthwhile.

TABLE C.10. UNIT VALUE OF EXPORTS (1930=100)

Table C.10 gives the unit value of domestic exports (1930=100). It is obtained by dividing the value of domestic exports at current prices in Table C.6 by their value at constant (1930) prices in Table C.9.

TABLE C.11. EXPORT VOLUME INDEX (1930=100)

Table C.11 is the export volume index (1930=100). It is derived from the value of domestic exports at constant (1930) prices in Table C.9.

TABLE C.12. VALUE OF COMMODITY EXPORTS

Table C.12 gives the value of the main commodity exports at current prices for the whole Caribbean. It is obtained from Table C.5. The totals for 1900 are

---

[4] There are four series, and I have chosen the nonfuel one (Commodity Price Index III) in which weights vary with the share of each commodity in world trade of that year.

not always the same as those in Table A.17 because the commodities recorded in Table A.10 and Table C.5 are not necessarily the same. This will happen, for example, when a commodity (e.g. molasses) is recorded for a country in Table C.5 but not for the same country in Table A.10. The differences, however, are small, and for the main commodity (sugar) they are zero.

TABLE C.13. STRUCTURE OF DOMESTIC EXPORTS (%)

Table C.13 gives the structure of commodity exports expressed as percentages of domestic exports for the whole Caribbean. It is derived from Tables C.6 and C.12.

TABLE C.14. COMMODITY PRICES

Table C.14 gives prices of the main commodities for the Caribbean as a whole. It is obtained by summing the value of the same commodity exported by each country in Table C.5 and then dividing this value by the equivalent volume (also obtained from Table C.5). The price of sugar, for example, is the value of sugar exported by all countries divided by the volume exported by all countries. The price is therefore the unit value. The prices in 1900 are not necessarily exactly the same as those in Table A.19 (see Table C.12 above). For example, logwood now includes logwood extract exported from Jamaica (because this had a higher price than logwood, the logwood unit value in 1900 in Table C.14 is slightly higher than in Table A.19). Most prices in 1900, however, are the same as in Table A.19.

TABLES C.15–C.17. EXPORTS BY DESTINATION (%)

Tables C.15, C.16 and C.17 give the main markets for exports in percentages. These ratios are based on domestic exports (in general re-exports did not go to the UK, the United States and the 'mother' country in the same proportion as domestic exports). As before, the countries are the United States (Table C.15), the UK (Table C.16) and 'mother' country (Table C.17), where 'mother' is the colonial or former colonial power. The United States is therefore the 'mother' for Puerto Rico and the US Virgin Islands. The 'mother' for Cuba and the Dominican Republic remains Spain. For Haiti, France is the 'mother'. The detailed sources for Tables C.15–C.17 are listed by country at the end of this note.

TABLES C.18–C.21. MERCHANDISE AND RETAINED IMPORTS AT CURRENT AND CONSTANT (1930) PRICES

Table C.18 gives merchandise imports at current prices. Merchandise imports exclude bullion, transhipments and bunker coal. As with Table C.8, there are figures in WDI for seventeen of the countries from 1960 on merchandise

imports, and I have therefore adjusted my figures for that year where necessary, unless the WDI figures are so rounded (e.g. Antigua, Bahamas, St Kitts & Nevis) that my figures are more accurate.

Table C.19 is merchandise imports at constant (1930) prices. This is obtained by dividing imports at current prices by an import price index (see Table C.25 below).

Table C.20 is retained imports. This is obtained by subtracting 90 per cent of re-exports (see Table C.7) from merchandise imports. Table C.21 is retained imports at constant (1930) prices. It is derived from Table C.20 by dividing retained imports by an import price index (see Table C.25 below). The detailed sources for Table C.18–C.21 are listed by country at the end of this note.

TABLES C.22–C.24. IMPORTS BY SOURCE (%)

Tables C.22, C.23 and C.24 give the share of merchandise imports[5] from the United States, the UK and the 'mother' country, respectively. In the case of the British dependencies, the import shares are based on imports, including bullion, up to 1922. However, these ratios can safely be applied to merchandise imports, excluding bullion in Table C.18 because bullion imports were usually small. The detailed sources for Tables C.22–C.24 are listed by country at the end of this note.

TABLE C.25. IMPORT PRICE INDEX (1930=100)

Table C.25 gives the import price index (1930=100). It is derived from the export price indices of the relevant core countries (US, UK and 'mother'). Core countries in this period typically have export unit values for (a) all exports and (b) manufactured exports. I used (a) because all the Caribbean countries imported primary and manufactured goods. For the United States, I used Carter (2006), vol. 5, and spliced the two indices reported before rebasing to 1930=100. For three countries (UK, France and Holland), I used United Nations (2009) and filled the gaps by first using the wholesale prices for each country in Mitchell (2007a) and then adjusting the wholesale prices for exchange rate changes as given in Table C.4. Although Spain is the 'mother' for Cuba and the Dominican Republic, I left it out because its exports to those two countries – except briefly for Cuba in the first few years of the century – were a very small proportion of the total.

The export price indices (1930=100) were then weighted by the share of the United States, the UK and the 'mother' country in each Caribbean country's imports (the weights summing to unity). During part of the Second World War, imports from France and Holland fell to zero, so the weights for the French

---

[5] The shares of merchandise and retained imports will not necessarily be the same, but the differences are likely to be small. The reported figures in Tables C.22–C.24 refer to merchandise imports.

and Dutch colonies in those years are based only on the United States and the UK.

TABLES C.26–C.27. NET BARTER TERMS OF TRADE AND INCOME TERMS OF TRADE (1930=100)

Table C.26 is the Net Barter Terms of Trade (NBTT). It is the export price index (Table C.10) divided by the import price index (Table C.25). The Income Terms of Trade (ITT), that is, the NBTT multiplied by the volume of exports (Table C.11), is given in Table C.27.

TABLES C.28–C.31. PUBLIC REVENUE AND EXPENDITURE AT CURRENT AND CONSTANT (1930) PRICES

Tables C.28 and C.29 give public revenue and expenditure at current prices. The constant price tables (C.30 and C.31) are obtained by deflating current values in Tables C.28 and C.29 with the price index in Table C.32. The detailed sources for Tables C.28–C.29 are listed by country at the end of this note.

TABLE C.32. PRICE INDEX FOR PUBLIC REVENUE AND EXPENDITURE (1930=100)

Table C.32 is the price deflator for public revenue and expenditure. In the absence of consumer or wholesale price indices before the 1930s, some scholars have used either import price deflators or core wholesale prices as a proxy for Caribbean price movements. Alienes (1950), for example, used US wholesale prices to deflate Cuban GDP from 1900. For the nineteenth century, I used import price indices derived from core wholesale or consumer prices (see Tables A.34 and A.38, for example).

For the period from 1900–60, however, these proxies are very unsatisfactory for several reasons. First, annual data rather than decennial data based on three-year averages means that we must pay more attention to short-term trends. Second, the bulk of public expenditure consists of wages and salaries of public employees, and it is inconceivable that these rose and fell with the velocity of core wholesale prices (yet alone the even more volatile import price indices) for much of the period between the First and Second World Wars.

Until 1940, with the possible exception of Cuba (see below), nominal wage rates exhibited very little variation in the Caribbean. In the British dependencies, nominal wage rates did not respond quickly to price changes, and this is likely to have been even more true of the wages of public employees (Eisner (1961), p. 379, gives wage rates of various categories of workers in Jamaica in different years from 1832 to 1932, and the low variance is striking). Thus, an increase (fall) in current revenue is likely to have translated not only into an increase (fall) in real revenue but also real expenditure because it could purchase more (fewer) teachers, soldiers, nurses, clerks, and so on.

We cannot, however, assume that there was **zero** change in the nominal wage rates of public employees. Prices rose rapidly during and immediately after the First World War before falling very sharply in the early 1920s. They then rose again before falling in the 1930s. Despite the absence of an organised labour movement, there must have been some response in terms of the wage rates paid to public employees. And even if 60 to 80 per cent of public expenditure consisted of wages and salaries (see Clark (1930) for the case of Puerto Rico), there was still a part that was spent on goods and services, whose prices clearly did fluctuate.

I have therefore proceeded as follows: with the exception of Cuba (see below), I have used a five-year average of US consumer prices from 1900 to 1938 (1900 is an average of 1898–1902) as a proxy for the price index to be applied to public revenue and expenditure. US consumer prices were not as volatile as wholesale or export prices, and the five-year average also removes some of the more extreme volatility found even in consumer prices. I stopped this series in 1938 because we then have sufficient data for the Caribbean countries to use other proxies.

From the late 1930s, prices and wage rates in the Caribbean started to rise rapidly. I have been able to put together a series for eight countries. The series for Guyana, Jamaica and the Dominican Republic are in Mitchell (2007) and refer to wholesale or consumer prices. Part of the series for Puerto Rico is also in Mitchell (2007), but I have been able to extend the series backwards using *Anuario Estadístico de Puerto Rico: Estadísticas Históricas* (1959). The series for Trinidad & Tobago is from *Statistical Digest* (1961). The price series for the Dutch Antilles was compiled from various editions of the *Statistisch Jaarboek: Nederlandse Antillen* (1956 onwards), with the gaps filled by reference to Trinidad & Tobago. The series for Guadeloupe is based on wage rates (adjusted for exchange rate change) taken from various issues of *Annuaire Statistique de la Guadeloupe*.

For Cuba I was able to build a series for the whole period. This is important because Cuba was not only the largest and most important Caribbean country, but also the only one where wage rates may have started to increase significantly even before the First World War. In the dependencies, metropolitan authorities were able to apply strict wage discipline in the public sector in normal times. Similarly, Haiti and the Dominican Republic were under the control of the US Customs Receivership for most of the period before 1940, and thus wage rates for public sector workers were not very flexible. This was not the case in Cuba, where the neocolonial relationship with the United States could not prevent monetary disorder in the 1930s (see IBRD (1952)) or wage inflation even before the First World War (see Santamaría and García (2004), p. 355).[6]

For Cuba I therefore proceeded as follows: I used the food price index compiled by Santamaría and García (2004) from 1903 to 1927 (for 1900 to

---

[6] The interested reader should note, however, that the nominal and real wage series have been put in the wrong columns.

1903 I used the five-year average of US consumer prices). From 1927 to 1958, I used the GDP deflator derived from dividing the GDP series at nominal and constant prices in Brundenius (1984). This deflator is in fact the consumer price index based for the earlier years on food prices (see Zanetti and García (1976)). For 1959–60, when we have no satisfactory information on wage rates or prices, I estimated the changes.

I then used an average of Guyana, Jamaica and Trinidad & Tobago for the other British dependencies, Guadeloupe for the other French dependencies, the Dominican Republic for Haiti, Puerto Rico for the US Virgin Islands and the Dutch Antilles for Suriname. The results capture very clearly the rapid increase in wages and prices from 1938 onwards – especially during the Second World War. These data, except for Cuba, were then spliced onto the series for US consumer prices for 1900–38.

The remainder of this note is devoted to the individual countries broken down by (a) *Exports and Imports*, (b) *Principal Export Products*, (c) *Trade by Main Market (%)*, and (d) *Public Revenue and Expenditure*.

Hispaniola

Haiti
For 1900–15, see Notes on Tables B.1–B.10.

EXPORTS AND IMPORTS
There is an export and import series in Benoit (1954) up to 1952 (the same figures are also in Banque Nationale de la République d'Haiti (n.d.) up to 1948). The figures are for the fiscal year, but because this ended on September 30, I have made no adjustment, so therefore 1916–17 is assumed to be 1917, and so on. The figures are in gourdes, but these can be converted at the fixed rate of 5 per US dollar (the exchange rate was not finally fixed until 1919, but it had de facto settled at 5 by 1916–17). From 1952 on, it is possible to use the figures in Mitchell (2007). Although these figures start irregularly in 1900 and are said to be in gourdes, they are actually only in gourdes from 1922 (at which point they can be all converted at the fixed exchange rate of 5.0). For 1960, the figure is the same as in IMF, *International Financial Statistics* (hereafter IFS).

Domestic exports in 1916 are estimated from the subtotal of the principal exports, assuming that the latter were 95 per cent of the total. Imports in 1916 are estimated based on the value of domestic exports in that year. Re-exports are assumed to be zero in all years.

PRINCIPAL EXPORT PRODUCTS
In 1916, the first year after Table B.2 ends, there were only four principal exports (coffee, cacao, cotton and logwood). The volumes are all in Benoit (1954), and I have estimated the values by applying prices based on 1915 and 1917 in Haiti and in 1916 in the British dependencies.

For subsequent years, the volume of coffee up to 1952 (fiscal year 1951–2 ending on September 30) is in Benoit (1954). For 1953–6, I have used Institut Haitien de Statistique (1963). From 1957, I have used Food and Agriculture Organization, *Trade Yearbook* (hereafter FAO *Trade Yearbook*) for volumes. There is also a volume series in Mitchell (2007), but the figures are not always the same as in FAO *Trade Yearbook*. The value figures up to 1952 can be obtained from Benoit (1954), because he gives the value as a percentage of domestic exports. From 1953–6, the values are in Institut Haitien de Statistique (1963). From 1957, I have used *United Nations Yearbook of International Trade Statistics* (hereafter UNYITS).

I used the same sources for logwood as for coffee up to 1956. Thereafter the volumes and values are estimated. For cacao I used the same sources as for coffee. However, 1959–60 are estimated. For cotton I used the same sources as for coffee, but 1958 is estimated. For other agricultural products (sisal, bananas, sugar), I used the same sources as for coffee. For mineral products (bauxite only), the volume of production from 1957 is in Mitchell (2007). I have converted this from metric tons (tonnes) to tons and assumed that it was all exported. Values were obtained by assuming the same price as in Suriname.

TRADE BY MAIN MARKET (%)

Table B.5 and B.7 have figures up to 1914 using three-year averages. The years 1915 onwards refer to single years. The exports and imports by main market from 1917 are in Benoit (1954), and I have estimated the shares for 1916. From 1948 onwards, I have used Overseas Economic Surveys (1956) and UNYITS.

PUBLIC REVENUE AND EXPENDITURE

From 1916 to 1948 public revenue is in Banque Nationale de la République d'Haiti (n.d.) and from 1949 to 1953 in Benoit (1954a). From 1954–9, I have used Mitchell (2007). All the figures from 1916 have been converted from gourdes to dollars at 5.0. Although the currency was not pegged by law at this rate until 1919, it was already trading at close to 5.0 in the earlier years. See Table C.4. There is no figure for 1960, so I have estimated it from the change in the contribution of public administration to GDP between 1959 and 1960 given in CEPAL (1978).

Public expenditure up to 1915 is assumed to be the same as revenue. From 1917 to 1948 it is in Banque Nationale de la République d'Haiti (n.d.) and from 1949 to 1953 in Benoit (1954a). I have estimated the 1916 figure. From 1954–9, I have used Mitchell (2007). There is no figure for 1960, so I have estimated it from the change in the contribution of public administration to GDP between 1959 and 1960 given in CEPAL (1978).

Care should be taken when using Mitchell (2007) or MOxLAD for Haitian public revenue and expenditure because many of the figures have been entered incorrectly. I have only used Mitchell (2007) for those years (1954–9) when other sources were not available.

Dominican Republic
EXPORTS AND IMPORTS

From 1905 there is a consistent series in several sources. I have used the figures in the annual reports of the US Customs Receivership, reproduced by Mutto (1974), *Anuario Estadístico Dominicano* and Mitchell (2007). There is a great deal of overlap between these, Wilkie (1974), IFS and MOxLAD. However, from 1950 onwards there are clearly errors of transcription in MOxLAD, with some years put in the wrong order. This is confirmed by the data given in IFS (various years).

The figures for 1900–4 are based on the subtotal of the principal exports. In 1905 and subsequent years, these were nearly 95 per cent of exports, so I have grossed up the missing years assuming minor exports were 5 per cent. Re-exports are taken from Overseas Economic Surveys (1957) and UNYITS.

PRINCIPAL EXPORT PRODUCTS

The principal exports in this period were sugar (raw and refined), molasses, cacao, coffee, maize, meat, bananas, chocolate, tobacco leaf and – starting in 1959 – bauxite. From 1905 most of the volumes and values can be found in the annual reports of the US, *Report of the Dominican Customs Receivership*,[7] the *Anuario Estadístico Dominicano* with data starting in 1933 and Mutto (1974). I have filled gaps from the International Institute of Agriculture, *International Yearbook of Agricultural Statistics* (with data starting in 1909), FAO *Trade Yearbook* (with data starting in 1945), UNYITS and Mitchell (2007). The bauxite figures are from Mitchell (2007), converted from metric tonnes to tons, and assuming all output was exported.

The 1900 figures are taken from the last year of the nineteenth-century database (see Table A.10). The missing years (1901–4) have been filled as follows: the volume and value of sugar from Mitchell (2007) and the volume of cacao from Clarence-Smith (2000). Other gaps have been filled by interpolation or left empty, because in many cases (e.g. roasted coffee, chocolate, maize and meat) it is safe to assume zero exports in these years. Prices have been borrowed from the master list to obtain any missing values.

TRADE BY MAIN MARKET (%)

The data are in US, *Report of the Dominican Customs Receivership* and *Anuario Estadístico Dominicano*. Before 1905, the US figure can be derived from *Statistical Abstract of the United States* and Department of State, *Commercial Relations of the United States with Foreign Countries*. The 1900 figures are taken from Tables A.20–A.22 and A.27–A.29. For 1948–60, I have used Overseas Economic Surveys (1957) and UNYITS.

---

[7] This is a difficult publication to find in print, and I am very grateful to Richard Phillips at the University of Florida for agreeing to make all copies held by the Smathers Library available in digital form through DLOC.

PUBLIC REVENUE AND EXPENDITURE

The 1900 figures are from Tables A.33 and A.37. From 1901–4, the figures are estimated, with revenue and expenditure assumed equal, based on the change in the value of imports. This is done because we know from Gómez (1979) that customs receipts at this time were approximately 100 per cent of revenue, and most customs duties came from imports.

The US Customs Receivership began in 1905, and the receipts for the first year (1 April 1905 to 31 March 1906) are given in Schoenrich (1918). This figure is allocated to 1905 and is in blue because it excludes noncustoms receipts. However, these will have been very small in that year. Expenditure is assumed to be the same as revenue in that year.

From 1906 to 1935, I have used the figures in Mitchell (2007) for both public revenue and expenditure. Although the US Customs Receivership published an annual report, the US authorities were only responsible for customs collection; because noncustoms receipts became increasingly important, this source becomes less useful over time, and it contains nothing on expenditure other than debt service. From 1936 to 1956, I have used *Anuario Estadístico Dominicano*. From 1957 to 1960, I have again used Mitchell (2007).

The Dominican Republic used the US dollar until 1946. In 1947 the peso was (re)introduced, but it was at par with the US dollar, so no exchange rate issues arise.

Cuba
EXPORTS AND IMPORTS

I have used Pérez de la Riva (1975), vol. 1, but the series stops in 1958, because the numbers are less rounded than in other secondary sources. The figures, including 1959–60, can also be found in Mitchell (2007) for 1901 onwards. There is a great deal of overlap between these, Wilkie (1974), IFS and MOxLAD. The figures are also given up to 1939 in Instituto de Historia de Cuba (1998) and can be found in Zanetti and García (1976). The numbers in all cases refer to merchandise exports. The only source for re-exports is *Anuario Estadístico de Cuba 1914* (1915). I have deducted these from merchandise exports to derive domestic exports for 1900–14 and have assumed that re-exports were zero thereafter (they were very small before).

PRINCIPAL EXPORT PRODUCTS

Sugar and tobacco (volume and value) are in Mitchell (2007), with only a few gaps, but there are some errors when comparison is made with the primary sources (tobacco volume exports in 1950 in Mitchell (2007), for example, are five times larger than recorded in other sources). However, these figures cannot be used without adjustment. Sugar volume is raw and refined sugar, but sugar value includes molasses until 1915. Furthermore, tobacco volume and value includes manufactured products (cigars, cigarettes and snuff) along with leaf tobacco.

It is important to separate molasses from sugar and raw from refined sugar. I have therefore proceeded as follows. The volume of refined sugar is given in CERP (1965) for all but four years (1900, 1901, 1959 and 1960). I have assumed a volume of zero in 1900–1, and I have used FAO *Trade Yearbook* for 1959–60. The volume of refined sugar can then be deducted from total sugar volume (in Mitchell) to give raw sugar volume (I used FAO *Trade Yearbook* for 1959–60). For 1959–60, I have used UNYITS for both raw and refined sugar. I have deducted the value of molasses from total sugar as described below.

Before 1946 there are not many figures for the value of molasses and even fewer for the volume. For 1901–2, I have interpolated the value based on 1900 and 1903. From 1904 to 1915, I have used the value of molasses in CERP (1965) on the assumption it was all exported. From 1916 to 1939 (except for 1927), I have used the difference between the figure in Pérez de la Riva (1975), vol. 1, for the value of all sugar exports, which does include molasses, and Mitchell (2007), which does not. For 1927 there is a figure in CERP (1965). From 1946–56, the value of molasses exports are in *Anuario Estadístico de Cuba 1957* (1958). For 1940–5, I have interpolated the data, assuming a value of $1 million in 1940. For 1957–8 there are also figures in CERP (1965), and I estimated values for 1959–60. The value of molasses exports can then be deducted from the series in Pérez de la Riva (1975), vol. 1, to give the value of raw and refined sugar for the earlier years (see above). I have then deducted the value of refined sugar to obtain the value of raw sugar for the same years.

For the volume of molasses exports, we have figures for 1903, 1927 and 1952–8 in CERP (1965) and for 1946–56 in *Anuario Estadístico de Cuba 1957* (1958). However, CERP also gives the unit value of exports and/or output for molasses in most years, and I have filled in the gaps from the price by assuming the same ratio to the price in the British dependencies for the missing years as in the years when both prices are available. This price can then be used to derive the volume of molasses exports for the missing years. I have converted the volume data from US gallons to imperial gallons at the rate of 0.83268 (1 US gallon is 3.78533 litres and 1 imperial gallon is 4.54596 litres).

The volume and value of rum exports for most years is in either Schroeder (1982) or CERP (1965). Many of the missing years coincide with Prohibition in the United States, when (officially recorded) exports would have been low, so I have estimated the missing entries accordingly. For 1904 to 1914, I have used the figures in CERP (1965) on the assumption that they refer to exports not production. I have not included *aguardiente* in rum exports. Where there are values but not volumes, I have used the unit price for the British dependencies to estimate volumes.

The volume of tobacco leaf exports is in Mitchell (2007), but his figures for 1903 and 1950 are much too high. There is a series from 1904 to 1939 in Instituto de Historia de Cuba (1998) whose figures are the same as Mitchell (but less rounded). The original source is given as *Anuario Estadístico de Cuba 1957* (1958). For 1959–60, I have used FAO *Trade Yearbook*. There is a series on the value of tobacco exports in Mitchell (2007), but this refers to **all** tobacco

products exported and not just leaf tobacco, so it is not comparable with his volume series on leaf tobacco.

The volume of cigar exports is from several sources. Instituto de Historia de Cuba (1998) has figures from 1904 to 1939 (1901–3 are estimated). IBRD (1952) then has the figures until 1949. The figures up to 1957 are then in *Anuario Estadístico de Cuba 1957* (1958). I estimated the volume in 1958–60 using the values in Stubbs (1985).

Tobacco leaf and cigar values up to 1914 are in *Anuario Estadístico de Cuba 1914* (1915). From then onwards, it is much more difficult to calculate, but there are some figures in Schroeder (1982), CERP (1965) and Roberts and Hamour (1970). I have started by building a series for the value of cigar exports using *Anuario Estadístico de Cuba 1914* (1915), IBRD (1952), Roberts and Hamour (1970) and Stubbs (1985). For the missing years (1915–34), I have estimated the unit value of cigar exports by using the cigar price for the British dependencies as an index (assuming Cuban prices moved in line with other prices). The value of cigar exports has then been deducted from the total value of tobacco exports in Mitchell (2007) and Pérez de la Riva (1975), vol. 1, to give the implied value of tobacco leaf exports. Because this is a residual, it includes the value of snuff and cigarette exports (these had a combined value of about 5 per cent of all tobacco products in the years for which data exist), so the value of leaf tobacco exports is overstated by a small amount.

Coffee volume for 1932 to 1960 is in Clarence-Smith and Topik (2003), giving the source as FAO (1961). I have filled in gaps back to 1909 from the International Institute of Agriculture, *International Yearbook of Agricultural Statistics*. Production was still important in 1904–5 according to *Anuario Estadístico de Cuba 1914* (1915), so I have assumed a modest decline in exports until then and a rapid one thereafter. There are also figures in CERP (1965) for most of these years. All volumes have been converted to values using average prices for the British dependencies where values are not given.

Cacao volume from 1900 to 1909 is from Clarence-Smith (2000). From then onwards I used the International Institute of Agriculture, *International Yearbook of Agricultural Statistics* and later the FAO *Trade Yearbook*. Volumes have been converted to values using the average of the prices for the British dependencies. This is very similar to the price series for the Dominican Republic, which starts in 1905.

The volume of banana exports in 1900, 1913 and 1929 is from Lloyd Jones (1931), p. 139. Intervening years have been filled by interpolation, but I have assumed a drop in the First World War. The banana series in the International Institute of Agriculture, *International Yearbook of Agricultural Statistics* starts in 1925 and is continued by the FAO *Trade Yearbook* up to 1960. Prices are taken from the average of the British dependencies.

I have also included minerals among the principal exports. Mitchell (2007) has the output (sometimes volume of exports) of the main minerals (chrome, copper, nickel, iron ore, manganese), and there are figures on the volume and value of exports in CERP (1965). Schroeder (1982) and CERP (1965) also have

figures on the volume and value of the sum of mineral exports for many years. All this can be put together to make one series that covers the exports of all the minerals. The only gap is for the volumes between 1928 and 1936, where I have estimated the unit price and then worked out the implied volumes from the values for those years.

TRADE BY MAIN MARKET (%)

Pérez de la Riva (1975), vol. 1, gives the values of exports and imports to the United States and the UK up to 1958. Mitchell (2007) gives the data for Spain ('mother') for all years, and I have used Mitchell for 1959–60 for the UK and the United States. The Spanish import figure for 1960 is estimated.

PUBLIC REVENUE AND EXPENDITURE

For 1900–02, when the country was under US occupation, I have used the figures in CERP (1965) provided by the military authorities for both public revenue and expenditure. For 1903–1914, I have used *Anuario Estadístico de Cuba 1914* (1915) for revenue, because this source distinguishes the budget and actual receipts. In the years up to 1937 and again from 1949 to 1958 the fiscal year began on July 1, and I have allocated everything to the later year, and thus 1902–3 refers to 1903, and so on. Note that Mitchell (2007) does the opposite, that is, he allocates 1902–3 to 1902, and so on. From 1938 to 1949 there were no budgets approved by Congress, and the 1938–9 budget was simply extended annually by presidential decree – see IBRD (1952), p. 653. That is why it is so important for Cuba to use actual rather than budgeted receipts.

For 1915 onwards for public revenue I used Schroeder (1982), who also allocates revenue and expenditure to the later year. However, the switch back to a fiscal year in 1948–9 leads Schroeder to repeat the figure for 1949 and 1950. Fortunately, the 1949 figure is given in IBRD (1952). Schroeder (1982) has figures for revenue in 1959 and 1960, the first two years of the Revolution. These revenue figures are exactly the same as the accumulated monthly revenue for those two years given in CERP (1965), p. 653, so they can safely be used.

For expenditure after 1902, I used *Anuario Estadístico de Cuba 1914* (1915) and Mitchell (2007) until 1911, but both only have budgeted expenditure. From 1912 to 1926 I used Mitchell (2007), whose series refers to budgeted expenditure up to that year (the series in Schroeder (1982) cannot be used because it contains serious errors for these years). From 1927–39, I used CERP (1965), whose series refers to actual expenditure. From 1940, all sources are very similar, and I used Schroeder (1982), but Schroeder repeats 1950 and 1951, so I estimated 1950 by interpolation. The Schroeder expenditure series stops in 1958, and it is safest to estimate expenditure as being equal to revenue in 1959–60 in view of the changes in the role of the state in those years, but there is a similar figure in Mitchell (2007) for expenditure in 1960.

I have treated the Cuban peso and US dollar as equivalent throughout, but the Cuban peso did depreciate modestly between 1938 and 1940.

British Dependencies

The data for the British dependencies, including re-exports, are available from a variety of sources. I first used the *Statistical Abstract for the British Empire* (various years up to 1947). This gives data for 1911–13 and 1922–47 (in a few cases 1945 is the last year). The gaps have then been filled by (a) the *Colonial Reports* for each country, (b) *Statistical tables relating to the Colonial and other Possessions of the United Kingdom*, (c) the *Blue Book* for each colony, (d) the *Handbooks* for the individual colonies, and (e) UNYITS. The last, which started in 1950, includes some of the British colonies even before their independence. A very useful additional source is the *Handbook of the British West Indies, British Guiana and British Honduras* (Aspinall (1929)), because it contains the quantities of all principal commodities for each colony in 1913 and 1920 onwards.

I have separated domestic exports from merchandise exports, the difference being explained by re-exports of merchandise (excluding transhipments) and exports of bullion. Transhipments in Guyana and Trinidad & Tobago were initially included by the colonial authorities in merchandise exports (and imports) but had been dropped by the First World War, so it is more consistent to exclude them altogether. Gold exports from Guyana, but not currency, are included in domestic exports because this was produced locally.

The share of exports by main market is based on domestic exports unless otherwise specified. These shares can usually be applied to merchandise exports also, because re-exports were small for most countries. This was not true for Belize, however, or for the Bahamas in the 1920s (see below under the countries concerned). Imports are merchandise imports excluding the import of currency in gold or silver. Imports by main country source are based on merchandise imports **excluding** bullion. However, before 1924 the import data by country are based on merchandise imports **including** bullion, so the import share for these years has been obtained by dividing by total imports **inclusive** of bullion. Because the import of bullion was always a very small part of imports, this does not cause any major problem.

Where the data were given in sterling in the sources used, they have been converted using the sterling-to-dollar exchange rate in Table C.4. In some cases after 1946, it has been necessary first to convert data in British West Indian dollars (BWI$) to pounds sterling before converting to US dollars. This has been done using the fixed rate of 4.80 BWI$ to the pound.

In general, I have not below reported separately on (a) exports and imports, (b) principal export products, (c) trade by main market (%), and (d) public revenue and expenditure because the sources are similar for each colony. The exception is the first colony (Antigua). This was part of the Leeward Islands Federation, whose members present special problems because the trade data were aggregated in most sources. The following detailed description for Antigua can be applied to the other members of the Federation (British Virgin Islands, Dominica (until 1940), Montserrat, St Kitts & Nevis (including Anguilla)).

Antigua

EXPORTS AND IMPORTS

As one of the Leeward Islands, Antigua is aggregated with the other Presidencies in almost all official publications. The main exception is the *Blue Book* for the Leeward Islands, from which detailed figures can be extracted for each country. The *Blue Book* was published in all years up to 1945 except 1940–4. For the years 1940–2, there are data for the aggregated Leeward Islands in the *Statistical Abstract for the British Empire*, from which the figures for individual countries can be estimated. There are no data for 1943–4, but the Food and Agricultural Organization (FAO (1947)) gives the volume of sugar for the missing years. I have then applied the sugar price from Jamaica for these years. Other gaps have been filled by interpolation assuming that prices were similar to the previous year.

After 1945, the main sources are the *Colonial Reports*. These covered all the Leeward Islands from 1947 to 1954, but no report was published in 1951–2, and there is no data for 1953. For the missing years (1951–3), there are data on sugar exports in the FAO *Trade Yearbook*, and I have applied the sugar price for Jamaica. Other gaps have been filled by interpolation assuming that prices were similar to those in previous or subsequent years. After 1954 a separate colonial report for Antigua was published.

Because the Leeward Islands was a federation, the inter-island trade presents special problems, and some secondary sources have excluded it. However, the figures are given in the *Blue Books*, and I have therefore included exports to the other islands in domestic exports where they were classified as such. Imports from the other islands are included in merchandise imports. Inter-island trade was not large, but it cannot be ignored.

PRINCIPAL EXPORT PRODUCTS

Antigua remained dependent on sugar exports throughout this period, and the figures can be found in the sources listed above. The other principal exports were molasses, rum and cotton, which were exported in most but not all years. In 1940–2 there are aggregated figures for the whole of the Leeward Islands in *Statistical Abstract for the British Empire* (1946), and I have assumed that the volume and value of Antigua's leading exports moved in line with the aggregated figures. I have then filled 1943–4 by interpolation (see above). There are gaps in 1951–3, and, apart from sugar, I have filled these by interpolation also (see above).

TRADE BY MAIN MARKET (%)

The figures are in the *Blue Book* or *Colonial Reports*. The data, however, are not reported for 1946 to 1956. These gaps have been filled by interpolation.

PUBLIC REVENUE AND EXPENDITURE

The figures are given for almost all years in the colonial records. As with the trade figures, I first used the *Statistical Abstract for the British Empire*

(various years up to 1947). The gaps have then been filled by (a) the *Colonial Reports*, (b) *Statistical tables relating to the Colonial and other Possessions of the United Kingdom*, (c) the *Blue Book*, or (d) the *Handbooks*. There are only two years where the figures are estimated. The first is 1919, when the Leeward Islands was switching from a fiscal to calendar year, and the second is 1952 when the colonial record is incomplete. In both years I have estimated by interpolation (average of previous and following year). From 1950 onwards, the public revenue figures include Colonial Development & Welfare funds and Imperial Grants-in-Aid.

Bahamas

The domestic export mix of the Bahamas changed frequently as old commodities dropped out of the list and new commodities entered. The twelve commodities I have used for the Bahamas were sponge, fresh fruit, preserved pineapples, tomatoes, salt, fish, hemp/sisal, lumber, pulpwood, pitprops, turtle shell, and shell and straw-work. Sponge was the most important at the beginning, but pitprops were the most important at the end.

Several of these commodities were not exported in 1930, so it is necessary to estimate a price for that year in order to construct the constant price series. The commodities for which this was done were fresh fruit, preserved pineapples, salt, fish, pulpwood, pitprops, and shell and straw-work. There are no volume estimates for shell and straw-work, so I have assumed a unit price of $1 in 1930 and 1939 (when exports start), $2 in 1950 and $3 in 1960, with the intervening years interpolated.

Re-exports have always been important to the Bahamas (in the nineteenth century, for example, the value of salvage from wrecked ships was officially entered in the trade statistics). Proximity to the United States has always provided the Bahamas with a profitable re-export trade. However, Prohibition in the United States from 1919 to 1933 led at the beginning (1919–23) to a huge increase in re-exports from the Bahamas, which had to be routed through third countries (most went to the French island of Miquelon in the mouth of the St Lawrence river).

The Bahamas was one of the first countries to become dependent on service rather than goods exports. By 1960, domestic exports were only 11 per cent of total exports, and thus commodity exports – never very important – had ceased to play a dynamic role by then.

Only one year (1936) is missing in the public revenue and expenditure series. It has been filled by interpolation.

Barbados

Barbados remained a 'classic' British colony dependent on sugar, molasses and rum throughout the period. The only other commodity export of significance was cotton. Most of the data for Barbados are of good quality, and there are no gaps except for trade shares between 1948 and 1950. These have been filled by interpolation. Revenue and expenditure data are in general from official

colonial sources, but for 1912–23 they are from Aspinall (1929), and for 1936 onwards they are from Mitchell (2007). From 1946 the unit of account is the BWI\$, which I have converted to sterling at 4.80 before converting to US dollars.

Belize

The *Statistical Abstract for the British Empire* gives the main data for 1911–13 and 1922–47. As with all other colonies, the data are given in pounds sterling. These have been converted by the colonial authorities in London from Belize dollars to sterling because Belize used the British Honduran dollar (BH\$), which was at par with the US dollar until 1950. I have converted back to BH\$ (same as US dollars before 1950) using the exchange rate in Table C.4.

The Belize dollar was the only colonial currency not to be devalued against the US dollar at the time of the sterling devaluation in September 1949. However, it was devalued three months later on 31 December 1949, being pegged at 4.0 per pound sterling (equivalent to 1.43 per US dollar).

There are some gaps in the Belize colonial record, when no *Blue Book* was published (1915–16, 1918–21) or when full data were not reported (1959). However, the *Blue Book* for 1922 has all the data needed for 1921. I have used various sources to fill the remaining gaps, including Metzgen and Cain (1925), Pim (1934), *Report of the British Guiana and British Honduras Settlement Commission* (1948), Anderson and Burdon (1963), Ashcraft (1973) and the *Colonial Report for British Honduras* for the relevant year. For 1959 I have also used UNYITS. A further problem is that Belize had an important re-export trade, which included commodities such as chicle and timber, which also constituted its own domestic exports. Great care has to be taken in separating out domestic produce from re-exports, otherwise the export figures are massively distorted. The main import for re-export was chicle, most of which came from Guatemala and went to the United States.

The main commodity export for the period was mahogany. Logwood was important at first, but it ceased to be exported after 1932. Cedar was exported throughout the period, and pine exports started sporadically in the 1920s, but they only became important after the Second World War. Chicle (used to make chewing gum) was exported in every year. Sugar, rum, cacao and rubber were all exported before the First World War, but they ceased to be important afterwards (except sugar, which revived in the 1950s). In the 1920s, lobster and citrus exports began in a small way and would become much more important after the Second World War. Bananas and coconuts were also exported throughout the period. Altogether there are sixteen commodities in the series for Belize.

The revenue and expenditure data in colonial sources are in a mixture of pounds sterling and Belize dollars, depending on which colonial source is used. Belize dollars are the same as US dollars until 1950, so wherever possible I used sources giving data in this currency. In some years from 1914 to 1949,

however, the British Treasury converted Belize dollars to sterling at a slightly different rate to the US dollar/sterling rate (see first and last columns in Table C.4), so care must be taken in these years in converting sterling to US dollars. From 1950, I have converted Belize dollars to pounds sterling at the fixed rate of 4.0 before converting to US dollars. The figure for 1934 in colonial sources is nine months only, so I have estimated the calendar year value by extrapolation.

British Virgin Islands

The British Virgin Islands was a member of the Leeward Islands Federation, so it has been treated in the same way as the other members. A detailed description is given above under Antigua, so it is not repeated here. After 1954, a separate *Colonial Report* was produced for the British Virgin Islands, which I have used for the years 1955–60.

The principal export was cattle, for which we have volumes and values for almost all years. Sugar was also exported in small amounts before the First World War. The minor exports not reported in Table C.5 included charcoal and cotton.

The revenue figures from 1953 include Colonial Development & Welfare funds and Imperial Grants-in-Aid and local receipts.

Cayman Islands

The Cayman Islands was a dependency of Jamaica until the latter's independence in 1962, but separate statistics began to be published at the beginning of the twentieth century. There are no trade figures for 1900–1, so I have interpolated a figure backwards from 1902. This has then been deducted from Jamaica because the latter's trade statistics included the Cayman Islands up to 1901 (and possibly in later years also, but the Cayman Islands' imports and exports were a tiny proportion of the total, so the extent of double counting – if it occurred – is very small). There are many gaps in the trade record before 1922, and the share of exports and imports in some years after 1947 has had to be estimated.

The main commodity exports were live turtles and turtle shell. Minor exports, not shown in the tables, included coconuts. However, the Cayman Islands, even in the nineteenth century, had depended on remittances and earnings from its sailing industry. In addition, the export of services became very important from the end of the Second World War. As a result, domestic exports were a smaller and smaller share of merchandise imports.

There are no public revenue and expenditure figures before 1903, so I have assumed revenue and expenditure moved in line with merchandise exports in 1900–2. Because these figures would have been included in Jamaica, I have also subtracted the Cayman Islands' figures from Jamaica for those years. The figures for 1936–7 are estimated by interpolation because there is a gap for those years in the colonial record. After 1950, the revenue figures include Colonial Development & Welfare funds and Imperial Grants-in-Aid.

Dominica

Dominica was part of the Leeward Islands until 1940. From that date it became part of the Windward Islands. All Windward Islands colonies were separated for statistical purposes, so there are no major problems with the data after 1940. For these years I have used *Statistical Abstract for the British Empire* up to 1947 and the *Colonial Reports* thereafter.

Before 1940 the same principles have been applied to Dominica as in the case of the other Leeward Islands (see Antigua above for details). However, Dominica presents special problems in the early years of the century because the colonial authorities did not distinguish between the different lime products, lumping them all together and giving the value only.

The lime products are green limes, raw lime juice, concentrated lime juice, citrate of lime, essential oil of limes (also called distilled lime oil) and otto of limes (also called ecuelled lime oil). Citrate of lime was first exported in 1906 and is recorded separately. Green limes in volume are first recorded in 1906, raw and concentrated lime juice and lime oil (both kinds) in 1911, but it is safe to assume that exports began earlier. I have filled in the gaps by holding prices constant and ensuring that the sum of the value of lime products is equal to the figure given in the *Colonial Report*.

From 1949, the colonial report for Dominica gives public revenue inclusive of Colonial Development & Welfare funds and Imperial Grants-in-Aid.

Grenada

The main exports from Grenada were cacao, nutmeg, mace and cotton. However, bananas were of some importance by the end of the period. The data are generally good, but trade by country has had to be estimated for 1950–59 (the 1960 figure is actually for 1964 and is taken from O'Loughlin (1968), p. 136). The *Colonial Report* also records that much of the exports of cacao to the UK before the First World War actually went to France.

The volume of cacao exports in early years is given in bags, and I have converted this to pounds at 180 lbs per bag. The 1900 figures for nutmeg and mace assume that 80 per cent of all spices in exports are nutmeg and the rest is mace. I have also assumed that 'other spices' before 1911 is mace.

The public expenditure figures for 1912–13 are from Aspinall (1929). The revenue figures after 1950 include Colonial Development & Welfare funds and Imperial Grants-in-Aid because it is not possible to deduct them.

Guyana

Guyana included transhipments in merchandise imports and exports in the first years of the century. These are not the same as re-exports, so I have excluded them from both imports and exports in all years. Merchandise imports are therefore exclusive of both bullion and transhipments in all years, and merchandise exports are the sum of domestic exports and re-exports only. Gold exports, except currency, are included in domestic exports.

The principal exports were sugar, molasses, rum, gold, diamonds, rice, coffee, cacao, timber, balata and bauxite. The data on volume and value are generally of a good quality, but some issues needed to be resolved. First, the data in the *Colonial Report* after 1955 are given in value only in accordance with the Standard International Trade Classification (SITC) rather than by volume and value of each product. In most cases it is possible to derive the appropriate values for each product, but care must be taken. Second, sugar includes molasses, but Mitchell (2007) gives the figures for sugar only, so the difference is assumed to be molasses. I have also used UNYITS for the last years of the 1950s to establish volumes and values.

Before 1955 the figures on timber exports refer to 'greenheart, round or roughly hewn'. From then on the values include all timber, such as dressed and sawn pine. I have assumed an unchanged price in these years and derived the volume accordingly.

Missing prices have been taken for the same years from other British colonies with comparable products. Thus, I have used the Jamaica price for bauxite to estimate volumes in the small number of years in the 1950s when the Guyanese figures were given in value only.

Public revenue and expenditure figures are from official colonial sources except for 1912–23, which are from Aspinall (1929), and 1936 onwards. The latter are in Mitchell (2007) in Guyanese dollars, which I have converted to sterling before converting to US dollars. Guyana switched from a fiscal to calendar year in 1916, and therefore the 1915 figures in the sources are for nine months only. I have grossed these up to allow for the missing months.

Jamaica

Jamaica's exports were more diversified than the other British Caribbean colonies, so great care needs to be taken to include as many as possible of the major commodities. These therefore include fifteen products: sugar, rum, cacao, coffee, logwood and logwood extract, bananas, coconuts, copra, grapefruit, oranges, cigars, ginger, pimento, bauxite and alumina. Coconuts and copra ceased to be exported after the Second World War, bauxite began to be exported in 1952 and alumina is recorded separately from 1955 in UNYITS.

The Cayman Islands, a dependency of Jamaica, was included in Jamaican trade figures until 1902. Because the Cayman Islands (see above) have been treated as a separate colony throughout the period, the figures for Jamaica have therefore been adjusted in 1900 and 1901. The adjustment is very small and does not involve any of the major commodities because these were not exported by the Cayman Islands.

Public revenue and expenditure figures are from official colonial sources except for 1912–23, which are from Aspinall (1929), and 1936 onwards. The latter are in Mitchell (2007). For 1900–2, I have deducted the Cayman Islands figures to avoid double counting, but it is possible that the Cayman Islands (and Turks & Caicos Islands) were included until much later in Jamaican figures.

Montserrat

Montserrat was a member of the Leeward Islands Federation, so it has been treated in the same way as the other members. A detailed description is given above under Antigua, so it is not repeated here. After 1954, a separate *Colonial Report* was produced for Montserrat, which I have used for the years 1955–60.

The principal exports were sugar (until 1928), cotton and lime juice products. The latter, as in Dominica, consisted of six products: green limes, raw lime juice, concentrated lime juice, citrate of lime, distilled lime oil and ecuelled lime oil. Before 1913 only the gross value of all lime juice products is given, but I have disaggregated this in line with the distribution in 1913 and borrowed prices for each product from Dominica to estimate volumes.

The minor exports include cattle, which was of some importance in 1900 but ceased to be important very soon. This explains why the subtotal of principal exports is only around one-third of domestic exports in 1900, but it quickly rises to a much higher ratio following the start of cotton exports.

The ratio of trade with the UK and the United States for 1946–59 is estimated by interpolation (the 1960 figure is actually for 1964 and is taken from O'Loughlin (1968), p. 136).

As for the other members of the Leeward Islands Presidency, the public revenue and expenditure figures for 1919 and 1952 are estimated by interpolation (see Antigua above). The public revenue series after 1950 include Colonial Development & Welfare funds and Imperial Grants-in-Aid.

St Kitts, Nevis & Anguilla

St Kitts, Nevis & Anguilla is one colony for the whole of the period 1900–60. The 1900 figures are therefore the sum of Nevis and St Kitts (which includes Anguilla except for population data) in the A. Tables. The principal exports were sugar, molasses, rum and cotton.

St Kitts & Nevis, as it is more commonly known, was a member of the Leeward Islands Federation, so it has been treated in the same way as the other members. A detailed description is given above under Antigua, so it is not repeated here. After 1954, a separate *Colonial Report* was produced for St Kitts & Nevis, which I have used for the years 1955–60.

The ratio of trade with the UK and the United States for 1948–59 is estimated by interpolation (the 1960 figure is actually for 1964 and is taken from O'Loughlin (1968), p. 136).

As for the other members of the Leeward Islands Presidency, the public revenue and expenditure figures for 1919 and 1952 are estimated by interpolation (see Antigua above).

St Lucia

Total imports before the mid-1920s are massively distorted by the import of bunker coal, which was then used for refuelling by visiting ships. I have therefore recalculated the figures to exclude bunker coal in these years, using

the information in the *Blue Book*. Imports are still much bigger than exports, but this is no longer because of the impact of bunker coal.

There are no trade data for 1942 to 1944. However, FAO (1947) has figures for some of the main exports by volume, from which estimates of exports and imports can be prepared. There is also a gap in 1959, where I have used FAO figures on the volume of the main export (bananas).

Imports soared in the Second World War as a result of the opening of a US military base on the island under the 'bases for destroyers' agreement.

Public revenue and expenditure shifted to a calendar year basis in 1920. The figures for 1919 are therefore grossed up from the nine months figures for that year in Aspinall (1929). After 1950 the revenue figures include Colonial Development & Welfare funds and Imperial Grants-in-Aid.

St Vincent

The main exports were arrowroot, cacao, cotton (grown on the island of Cariacou), sugar, molasses, copra and bananas. Only arrowroot, however, was of major importance throughout the period. Banana exports began after the Second World War, with volume given in lbs. I have converted these to bunches at the rate of 25.5 lbs/bunch. This is the ratio used in St Lucia.

The data for 1946 are very deficient. I have estimated domestic exports by grossing up the subtotal of principal exports for that year. In general, however, the data for St Vincent are fairly complete and of good quality.

The ratio of trade with the UK and the United States for 1946–53 is estimated by interpolation. The figures from 1954 are taken from St Vincent, *Digest of Statistics* (various years).

After 1950 the revenue figures include Colonial Development & Welfare funds and Imperial Grants-in-Aid.

Trinidad & Tobago

Trinidad & Tobago was a unified country from 1899. In the A. Tables, it was possible to separate them up to the end of the period in 1900. However, this is neither possible nor desirable for the period from 1900 to 1960, so the figures for 1900 are the sum of Trinidad and Tobago in the nineteenth-century tables.

Exports are tricky because the official figures in the early years of the century include transhipments (as distinct from re-exports) and not all exports of petroleum products. For example, the *Statistical Abstract of the British Empire* (1950) stated: 'Figures are exclusive of the following approximate quantities of petroleum oils exported to destinations withheld from publications in the original returns'.

I have excluded transhipments from both exports and imports, because this is the only way to have consistent figures for the whole period (some secondary sources, e.g. Mitchell (2007), do not do this, so it is difficult to use the figures). Re-exports are therefore exclusive of transhipments.

The main exports are sugar, molasses, rum, bitters, cacao, coffee, bananas (converted to bunches at 33 lbs per stem), citrus, asphalt and petroleum

products. The data are generally good, but there are a number of issues that had to be resolved. First, the *Colonial Reports* stopped reporting trade data in the last few years, so gaps have been filled from a variety of sources, including FAO *Trade Yearbook*, Mitchell (2007) and UNYITS. Any remaining gaps have been filled by interpolation.

Second, citrus products include fresh fruit and juice, and the volume data are often not given after 1931. I therefore constructed a price index for all citrus products for Belize for the period from 1931 on the grounds that Belize had a similar mix of oranges, grapefruits and citrus juice. I then applied this index to the unit value in 1931 and estimated the volume of citrus exports accordingly.

Third, petroleum exports began before the First World War and very quickly became the dominant export. The figures, however, refer to all petroleum exports, including crude oil, refined oil and aviation fuel. The unit value is therefore a weighted average of all these subproducts.

Public revenue and expenditure figures are from official colonial sources except for 1912–23, which are from Aspinall (1929), and 1936 onwards. The latter are in Mitchell (2007).

Turks & Caicos Islands

After separation from the Bahamas in 1848, the Turks & Caicos Islands became a dependency of Jamaica. Despite this, there are separate figures for almost all years. The main exports were salt, conch and sponge. Where there are gaps in either volume or value, I have used prices from other countries (e.g. the Bahamas' sponge) to estimate the missing entries.

The official figures cease to provide estimates of re-exports of goods after 1938. However, re-exports were not very important at any time. By contrast, remittances were always important, and exports of services developed rapidly after the Second World War, and thus merchandise imports provide a much better guide to economic activity than domestic exports.

There is no public expenditure figure for 1920, so I have assumed it was the same as revenue. The revenue and expenditure figures for 1936–7 have been interpolated. After 1950 the revenue figures include Colonial Development & Welfare funds and Imperial Grants-in-Aid.

French Dependencies

The French colonies became Départements d'Outre-Mer in 1946 and therefore part of metropolitan France. Their description as 'dependencies' to cover the different constitutional arrangements throughout the period from 1900 to 1960 is therefore not strictly accurate.

In addition to the country sources listed below, there are some very useful French sources giving information for each country as part of the colonial statistics. The best are the annual Ministère des Colonies, *Statistiques coloniales etc. Statistiques du commerce des colonies françaises*, and Ministère des Colonies, *Statistiques coloniales etc. Renseignements généraux sur le commerce*

des colonies françaises et la navigation. The former is the only source I have been able to find that gives trade with countries other than France along with re-exports.

For public revenue and expenditure, we are fortunate that there is an historical series for Guadeloupe in *Annuaire de la Guadeloupe* (1954), which covers all the years up to 1946 (except 1901, for which there are no data). For French Guiana, we are also fortunate that the annual budget has been digitalised by the French Bibliothèque Nationale for most years up to 1931. In the case of Martinique, there is a very useful series for the budget that covers the period up to 1945 in *Annuaire de la Vie Martiniquaise* (1946). The series starts again in *Annuaire de la Martinique* in 1953, this time separating actual revenue and expenditure from the budgeted figures. Wherever possible I have used ordinary revenue, excluding the use of the colonial reserve and exceptional receipts. Expenditure, however, includes extraordinary spending on public works and other such projects.

French Guiana

EXPORTS AND IMPORTS

There is a series on exports and imports from 1900 to 1918 in Mam-Lam-Fouck (1987) in French francs. This can be extended to 1928 using the French sources listed above. From then until after the Second World War there are irregular data that can be found in, or derived from, Mam-Lam-Fouck (various publications), *Annuaire de la Guyane Française*, the *South American Handbook* and Dupont-Gonin (1970). Mam-Lam-Fouck (1987) is particularly useful because he gives for numerous years the percentage share of gold in domestic exports, from which the latter can be derived. He also often gives exports as a percentage of imports.

Re-exports were rarely more than 1 per cent of merchandise exports except for a brief period after the First World War. I have assumed that they came to an end just before the Second World War.

PRINCIPAL EXPORT PRODUCTS

Gold was the leading export throughout the period, but the volume of exports declined after the First World War. There is an annual series on production in Pétot (1986) that goes back to 1857. This is the output declared to the authorities and taxed by them, and the volume of exports, but not given in any source annually, was similar. There was, however, a lively contraband trade in gold, which left the country through Brazil or Suriname and did not enter into the trade statistics.

The production series in gold is in kilograms, and this has been converted to troy ounces at the rate of 31.1035 grammes. Wherever possible, I have used French colonial sources for the volume and value of gold exports. Where there is only volume, I have used the Guyana gold export price to derive values.

Although sugar exports had ceased to be of any importance before the end of the nineteenth century, even before the First World War there were other

exports. These included rum, balata, timber and essence of rosewood. I have been able to put together a volume series on rum using the sources listed above, and I converted this to values using Martinique prices where none were available for French Guiana (there are data on values in the 1930s in the *South American Handbook*). There was a boom in the value of balata, timber and essence of rosewood exports during and immediately after the First World War. This temporarily pushed down the share of gold in domestic exports below 50 per cent. However, gold – although now declining in volume and value – would once again account for over 90 per cent of exports by the 1930s. Even after the Second World War, when timber became much more important, gold was nearly always in excess of 50 per cent.

TRADE BY MAIN MARKET (%)

There are data for the years before 1930 in the French colonial sources listed above. There are also some data in *French Guiana* (1920), for 1917 in *French Yearbook* (1919), for mid-1920s in Meehan (1927) and *Annuaire de la Guyane Française*, and for the 1930s in the *South American Handbook*. Except for the middle years of the Second World War (1942–4), when there was no trade with the metropolis, France was always the most important trade partner.

PUBLIC REVENUE AND EXPENDITURE

The figures for public revenue and expenditure in 1900 are from Tables A.33 and A.37. From 1901 to 1931, I have used the figures in the *Annuaire de la Guyane Française*, with any gaps estimated by interpolation. The figures are budgets, not actual receipts and expenditures. However, *French Guiana* (1920) gives the average for 1900–7 for both actual receipts and expenditures, and they are very similar to the budgeted figures (Caribbean dependencies – unlike independent countries – had little opportunity to avoid budgetary constraints).

For 1932–7, I calculated revenue as a share of foreign trade based on the ratio before 1932 and after 1937. This gives a ratio of around 0.2, which I used to estimate public revenue. Expenditure in these years is assumed to be the same as revenue.

From 1938 until *départementalisation* in 1946 there are figures on revenue and expenditure in *Annuaire Statistique d'Outre-Mer* (1949). The figures are in two parts because the French authorities had created in 1930 a separate administrative unit for the interior called 'Inini'. The sharp spike in 1945 is because of the postponement of devaluation until the following year.

For 1950 and 1951, there are figures on revenue and expenditure in *Annuaire de la Guyane Française*. The gap from 1947 to 1949 has then been estimated by interpolation, the fall in revenue being explained largely by currency depreciation. From 1952 onwards, there are figures on total tax receipts in the national accounts. See Blaise (1962). For expenditure there are figures in 1959 and 1960 in *Annuaire de la Guyane Française*, and I filled the missing years from the contribution of public administration to GDP in the source above.

Following *départementalisation*, the gap between public revenue and expenditure grew bigger and bigger as a result of metropolitan subsidies.

Guadeloupe

EXPORTS AND IMPORTS

The data before 1930 are from the French sources listed above. There is also a series in Mitchell (2007) in French francs. There are data from 1949 onwards in *Annuaire Statistique de la Guadeloupe*. The exchange rate is in Table C.4. In a few years the export figures derived from Mitchell (2007) are not credible because they greatly exceed the subtotal of principal exports. For these years I have used the dollar value of Guadeloupe exports given in League of Nations, *Statistical Yearbook*, and UNYITS. In 1930–1 and 1947–8, I estimated the value of exports based on the subtotal of main exports for those years.

The French colonial sources suggest re-exports were of some importance. I have therefore included them where known and estimated the value in other years. However, I have assumed that re-exports ceased in the Second World War, and I have ignored them afterwards.

PRINCIPAL EXPORT PRODUCTS

The main exports were sugar, molasses, rum, cacao, coffee, logwood, bananas and vanilla. There are very few gaps in the volume series, but no values are given until 1949 in *Annuaire de la Guadeloupe*. There are, however, data on values in the French colonial sources for most years before 1930. In other years, it is necessary to 'borrow' prices, which I have taken either from Martinique or the British colonies.

Sugar volume is in Mitchell (2007) for all years, and the value is also given for 1938 and from 1948 onwards. The volume figures are also given in *Annuaire de la Guadeloupe* up to 1930. *Annuaire Statistique d'Outre-Mer* (1949) covers the crucial years 1938–48, and the 1954 edition of *Annuaire Statistique de la Guadeloupe* also has historical statistics on volumes, and data from 1954 onwards are in later editions of *Annuaire Statistique de la Guadeloupe*. There is only one year where Mitchell's figure is different, and I have used the primary source by preference in that year. However, in 1929 both Mitchell (2007) and *Annuaire Statistique de la Guadeloupe* have an extremely low figure for sugar exports by volume, which is reproduced in International Institute of Agriculture, *International Yearbook of Agricultural Statistics*. This figure does not bear any relation to the output of sugar figure in Mitchell (2007) or in Deerr (1949). I have therefore used Deerr's export volume figure for that year. Generally, I used the unit value of Martinique sugar exports and applied it to the volume series for Guadeloupe where there was no figure for the value.

The volumes of all the other exports were obtained from the same sources as for sugar. Banana exports begin in 1921, and logwood exports end in 1929. Molasses exports end in the 1920s but begin again in 1951. Where there were no values, I used the average unit values from either Martinique or the British colonies.

TRADE BY MAIN MARKET (%)

There are data for the years before 1930 in the French colonial sources listed above. The figures from 1948 onwards are in *Annuaire Statistique de la Guadeloupe*. Overwhelmingly, exports went to France, and most imports came from France. There was no trade with France in 1942–4.

PUBLIC REVENUE AND EXPENDITURE

The figures up to 1947 (1946 for revenue) are from the historical series in *Annuaire de la Guadeloupe* (1954). Later figures are in subsequent issues of the *Annuaire Statistique de la Guadeloupe*. Figures refer to actual revenue and expenditure rather than the budgeted figures, except for 1942–7. The gaps (1901 for revenue and expenditure, 1947–8 for revenue and 1948–9 for expenditure) have been estimated by interpolation.

Martinique

EXPORTS AND IMPORTS

The data are all taken from *Annuaire de la Martinique* or from Mitchell (2007) and are in French francs. In most years the figures are the same, but Mitchell is rounded to the nearest million. However, in the First World War (and in the 1920s for imports) the trade figures are very different. I have used Mitchell (2007) for these years. In 1902, no values are given in *Annuaire de la Martinique*, perhaps as a consequence of the destruction of St Pierre by the eruption of Mt. Pelée in that year. However, there are volumes and values in Ministère des Colonies, *Statistiques coloniales etc. Statistiques du commerce des colonies françaises* (1904) for that year. The exchange rate is in Table C.4. For 1947, probably because of the exchange rate conversion, the export figure derived from Mitchell (2007) is not credible. I have therefore estimated the value in that year based on the subtotal of principal exports.

Re-exports were important before the Second World War and averaged around 10 per cent of merchandise exports. As with the other French colonies, I have assumed that they ended with the Second World War.

PRINCIPAL EXPORT PRODUCTS

Sugar volumes and values are in *Annuaire de la Martinique* up to 1934 and also for 1938 and 1946. Volumes are given in *Annuaire Statistique d'Outre-Mer* (1949) for 1938 to 1948 and volumes and values from 1952 in *Annuaire de la Martinique* (published at irregular intervals but covering all the years up to 1960). The gaps in volumes have been filled from International Institute of Agriculture, *International Yearbook of Agricultural Statistics* or FAO *Trade Yearbook*. There are also figures on volume of exports in Mitchell (2007) for all years, but the value is given for 1960 only. The missing entries for values have been filled by using unit values for sugar from the British colonies, with an adjustment for the premium received by Martinique based on a comparison of those years when both unit values exist or by using Ministère des

Colonies, *Statistiques coloniales etc. Statistiques du commerce des colonies françaises*.

Banana exports are given in metric measures and have been converted to bunches at 50 lbs per bunch (see FAO, *Trade Yearbook 1948* (1949), p. 186). Exports started in the 1920s and accelerated from 1932 following the introduction of a refrigerated shipping line between Martinique and France in 1931. The volumes are given in *Annuaire de la Martinique, Annuaire Statistique d'Outre-Mer* (1949), International Institute of Agriculture, *International Yearbook of Agricultural Statistics* and FAO *Trade Yearbook*. The values are given for 1932–4, 1938, 1946 and from 1952 onwards in *Annuaire de la Martinique*. Gaps have been filled by reference to prices in the British colonies.

Other major exports are molasses, rum, cacao, coffee, logwood and conserved pineapples (molasses and logwood exports stop in 1929). Volumes and values are given in *Annuaire de la Martinique* up to 1934 and in 1938, 1946 and from 1952 onwards. There are also figures for rum production in 1935–7 in *Annuaire de la Martinique*, from which exports can be approximated for those years. Volumes are given in *Annuaire Statistique d'Outre-Mer* (1949) for 1938–48, and other gaps have been filled from International Institute of Agriculture, *International Yearbook of Agricultural Statistics* and FAO *Trade Yearbook*. Any gaps in values have been filled by reference to prices in British colonies.

TRADE BY MAIN MARKET (%)

There are data for the years before 1930 in the French colonial sources listed above. There are also data for trade with France, the UK and the United States in some years in *Annuaire de la Martinique*, the *French Yearbook* and *Commercial Relations of the United States with Foreign Countries* (hereafter US Consular Reports). Exports were overwhelmingly to France and imports mostly from France, but there was no trade with France in 1942–4. Gaps have been filled by interpolation.

PUBLIC REVENUE AND EXPENDITURE

The revenue figures are taken from the budgets for the years up to 1945 using the series in *Annuaire de la Vie Martiniquaise* (1946). There is a gap in 1902 as a result of the eruption of Mt. Pelée and another in 1911. Both have been filled by interpolation. Actual revenues from 1953 are reported in *Annuaire de la Martinique* (later issues are titled *Annuaire Statistique de la Martinique*). The years 1948–52 have been estimated by interpolation.

I have used the budget figures for expenditure up to 1938 and for 1946–7. From 1939 to 1945, I have used *Annuaire Statistique d'Outre-Mer* (1949) because this separates revenue and expenditure. The actual expenditure series from 1953 are reported in *Annuaire de la Martinique* (later issues are titled *Annuaire Statistique de la Martinique*). The years 1948–52 have been estimated by interpolation.

Dutch Dependencies

Dutch Antilles

EXPORTS AND IMPORTS

There are export data in Mitchell (2007) for all six islands from 1905 up to 1954 (except 1912, which I have filled by interpolation). The data from 1955 exclude the three Leeward Islands (Saba, St Eustatius and Sint Maarten). However, their exports by then were minuscule in relation to the others, so their omission is not too serious. The export data before 1905 in Mitchell are for all islands **except** Curaçao. I have taken the 1900 export figures from Tables A.11–A.13. There is a figure for 1904 in US Consular Reports, so the incomplete years are only 1901–3. Goslinga (1990) separates the figures in 1905 between Curaçao and the other islands. I have done the same for 1900 using my figure for merchandise exports and Mitchell's for non-Curaçao exports. The missing years for Curaçao have then been estimated by interpolation and added to the figures in Mitchell for non-Curaçao exports.

There are import data in Mitchell for all islands from 1913. There is no figure for 1912, and the earlier years are for Curaçao only. I grossed up the years before 1912 using the ratio of Curaçao imports to merchandise imports in 1905 in Goslinga (1990). I have interpolated 1912.

The exchange rate is the same as for Suriname (the Dutch Antilles guilder was fixed in 1939 and was not devalued in line with the Dutch guilder after the Second World War – see Table C.4).

The Dutch Antilles was the first country in the Caribbean to establish a modern oil refining industry (based on the import of crude oil from Venezuela, Colombia and – to a much smaller extent – Mexico). This raises special problems because the gross value of exports and imports is enormous from the 1920s onwards. The value of domestic exports per head then becomes by far the highest in the region. To avoid distortions in the regional and subregional totals, I have therefore constructed two series based on gross and net exports. Net exports include all non-oil exports and a margin on oil of 10 per cent. The net exports series is used in all the comparative tables, but both the gross and net series are shown in Table C.5. For imports I have separated oil and non-oil imports. The gross import series includes both, and the net import series is non-oil imports only. The net import series is the one used for merchandise imports in Table C.18.

Non-oil domestic exports at the beginning of the century consisted of products such as straw hats, divi-divi pods, goat skins, aloes and phosphate of lime. I have estimated the value in current dollars and deflated by the price index for minor exports used for other countries to obtain the series of non-oil exports at constant prices.

Before 1917, I have split merchandise exports between domestic exports and re-exports according to the ratio in 1900 (see Tables A.11–A.13). From 1925, I have assumed no re-exports. Domestic exports and re-exports from 1918 to 1925 have been estimated to fit merchandise exports.

PRINCIPAL EXPORT PRODUCTS

Oil exports began in a very small way in 1918, but they started to expand rapidly after 1920 – even before the completion of the Shell refinery in Curaçao in 1926. The volume of crude petroleum and petroleum product exports is in Mitchell (2007) starting in 1926 (I have converted these from metric tonnes to tons). The value of crude petroleum and petroleum product exports is also in Mitchell (2007) from 1929, with a few gaps where I have estimated the price based on the closest year. Previous years can be found in Hiss (1943) and Hartog (1968). Although this latter source gives figures for Curaçao only, it can be safely used before 1930 because only Curaçao had a major oil refinery until a second one was established on Aruba in 1929 by Standard Oil (a smaller one had been built earlier on Aruba by the Eagle Co.).

Both Hiss (1943) and Hartog (1968) have miscellaneous figures on non-oil exports in volume and value. Hartog (1968) refers only to Curaçao, but all phosphate and straw hat exports after 1900 came from Curaçao, so it is still a useful source. Hartog (1968) also gives non-oil exports and imports for Curaçao, showing that non-oil imports (about one-third of which came from Holland) were still important even after the oil refinery was established. There is a wealth of data on non-oil exports in *Oranje en de Zes Caraibische Parelen* (1948), and the *Statistisch Jaarboek: Nederlandse Antillen*, which started in 1956, has data on non-oil exports at irregular intervals from 1938.

TRADE BY MAIN MARKET (%)

The shares refer to **net** exports and imports, but gross and net are the same before 1918. See Hiss (1943) and *Statistisch Jaarboek: Nederlandse Antillen* (1965). Most entries, however, are estimated.

PUBLIC REVENUE AND EXPENDITURE

Public revenue and expenditure for 1900 are from Tables A.33 and A.37. Thereafter I have used *Statistisch Jaarboek: Nederlandse Antillen* (1956 onwards), Hiss (1943), *Oranje en de Zes Caraibische Parelen* (1948), van Soest (1978) and Goslinga (1990). Until decentralisation in 1954, the figure for Curaçao was in fact the figure for all islands, so Hartog (1968) can also be used. Gaps have been filled by interpolation.

Suriname

EXPORTS AND IMPORTS

The series are taken from Mitchell (2007) and are in guilders. The Surinamese guilder was the same as the Dutch guilder until 1945. However, it remained fixed at 1.88 to the US dollar when the Dutch guilder was devalued. The exchange rate of the Surinamese dollar is shown in Table C.4 and was used to convert the data in Mitchell (2007).

PRINCIPAL EXPORT PRODUCTS

The leading exports were sugar, coffee, cacao, rice, balata, bauxite and gold. The volumes and values up to 1939 are all in van Traa (1946). This is the best

source, but there are also figures for some years in Goslinga (1990), Meehan (1927), Panday (1959) and Hiss (1943). There is also a volume series for sugar in Deerr (1949) until 1935 and from International Institute of Agriculture, *International Yearbook of Agricultural Statistics*, and FAO *Trade Yearbook* thereafter. The volume of coffee for part of the period is in Clarence-Smith and Topik (2003).

The gaps after 1939 have been filled from International Institute of Agriculture, *International Yearbook of Agricultural Statistics*, and FAO *Trade Yearbook*. The volume of cacao is in Clarence-Smith (2000) until 1914 and International Institute of Agriculture, *International Yearbook of Agricultural Statistics*, and FAO *Trade Yearbook* thereafter. Rice exports are also in these *Yearbooks*. Balata exports were often reported in the International Institute of Agriculture, *International Yearbook of Agricultural Statistics*, and FAO *Trade Yearbook*, but are also in the annual *South American Handbook* (1924–) in most years. The volume of bauxite is in Mitchell (2007), and I have converted from metric tons to tons. Gold is in Goslinga (1990).

Some of these sources also give values and volumes after 1940. Van Lier (1971), p. 202, has a very useful graph giving the share of the main commodities in domestic exports up to 1945 (but there is an error in 1903, when the shares exceed 100%). I have used this for values between 1940 and 1945 and the sources mentioned above for values from 1946–60. For the 1950s figures, there are several detailed Surinamese publications, including Algemeen Bureau voor de Statistiek Suriname (1959) and *Jaarcijfers voor Suriname* (1963). Any gaps have been filled by borrowing prices from the British colonies for the same products.

TRADE BY MAIN MARKET (%)

Van Traa (1946) has the share of exports and imports with Holland and the United States up to 1939. There are figures up to 1950 at ten-year intervals in Goslinga (1990). See also Hiss (1943).

PUBLIC REVENUE AND EXPENDITURE

Public revenue and expenditure in 1900 are taken from Tables A.33 and A.37. I then used van Traa (1946) until 1940 (this very valuable source also shows from 1915 to 1930 that most of the budget deficit was covered by grants and much less by loans from the Dutch government). Thereafter I have used the series in Mitchell (2007) and converted to dollars using the exchange rate for Suriname in Table C.4. I have assumed that revenue in 1942 was the same as expenditure.

Before 1941 the Dutch government provided a large subsidy to meet the difference between public revenue and expenditure. The details are given up to 1914 in Benjamins and Snelleman (1917) and in van Traa (1946) for 1915–30, which shows how much of the deficit was met by grants and how much by loans. See also Goslinga (1990). This subsidy was included in the revenue figures in subsequent years.

United States Dependencies

Puerto Rico
EXPORTS AND IMPORTS

The figures up to 1956 are taken from *Anuario Estadístico de Puerto Rico: Estadísticas Históricas* (1959). Later years are taken from subsequent issues of *Anuario Estadístico de Puerto Rico*. There is also a series in Carter (2006), vol. 5, where Puerto Rico is included in US 'outlying territories'. However, this series is not always the same as the numbers in *Anuario Estadístico de Puerto Rico: Estadísticas Históricas* (1959) and in some years (e.g. 1921) is clearly incorrect.

The fiscal year ends on June 30, and I have called 1901–2=1902, and so on. However, 1900 is from Table A.13 and is based on fiscal year 1900–1. That leaves 1901, and I have interpolated the figures for this year as an average of 1900–1 and 1901–2. This procedure is followed for the principal exports, imports and trade shares.

There are figures on re-exports in *Anuario Estadístico de Puerto Rico: Estadísticas Históricas* (1959), and there is also a figure for 1900 in Table A.12. I have assumed re-exports were roughly the same between 1900 and 1933.

PRINCIPAL EXPORT PRODUCTS

The main source is *Anuario Estadístico de Puerto Rico: Estadísticas Históricas* (1959), which gives volume and value data for the main commodity exports from 1956 back to 1920–1. There are also volume and value data for the main manufactured exports from 1933–4 along with a series on the value of clothing exports to the United States that starts in 1920–1. Data after 1956 are in subsequent editions of *Anuario Estadístico de Puerto Rico*. The only figures for 1959, however, are for sugar, which comes from Mitchell (2007). The others are interpolated using an average of 1958 and 1960.

For earlier years, I have proceeded as follows. Sugar volume and value up to 1928–9 are in Clark (1930). As with exports and imports, I have used Clark's figures for 1900–1 as referring to 1900, but from then on assumed that the figures refer to the later of the two years. Thus, 1901–2 is 1902 and so on. This leaves 1901, which I have filled by interpolation. For 1930–33, I have used the volume and value for sugar exports to the United States only in *Anuario Estadístico de Puerto Rico: Estadísticas Históricas* (1959), because there are no other figures. However, we know from other years that virtually all sugar went to the United States, where it entered free of duty.

Coffee volume and value before 1921 are from Clark (1930), with 1901 treated in the same way as for sugar. From 1921 onwards, the figures on volume and value are in *Anuario Estadístico de Puerto Rico: Estadísticas Históricas* (1959). I then did the same for tobacco leaf (including scrap), cigars and molasses. In the case of rum, no exports are given before 1935, and I assumed this to be correct (in any case there would have been no legal

exports after 1918 because Puerto Rico went 'dry' even before the mainland United States).

I have also included series for coconuts, fresh pineapples and canned pineapples. In the case of coconuts, Clark (1930) gives the values but not volumes. I estimated the missing volume data by using the Jamaican price and adding a premium of 25 per cent based on a comparison of Jamaican and Puerto Rican prices after 1929. The volume of fresh pineapples in Clark (1930) has been converted to pounds at the rate of 85 per crate based on those years (1927–9) when we have an overlap in crates (Clark) and in pounds (*Anuario Estadístico de Puerto Rico: Estadísticas Históricas* (1959)). I have estimated the years 1900–5 assuming that 50 per cent of 'other fruits' was fresh pineapples and 25 per cent was canned pineapples. For the years before 1930, I have assumed a fixed price per pound of canned pineapple to estimate the volume.

Finally, I have also included a series on textiles and clothing exports because Puerto Rico was the first Caribbean country to export manufactures in a significant way. There are figures on cotton manufactured goods in Clark (1930) from 1900 with a gap from 1912 to 1919. According to Dietz (1986), exports of cotton manufactures were zero in 1915, so I have estimated the values on either side to fill the gaps. From 1921 there is a series on textile and clothing exports to the United States (by far the most important market) in *Anuario Estadístico de Puerto Rico: Estadísticas Históricas* (1959). To convert this series into constant prices, I deflated by an index (1930=100), based on US wholesale and producer textile and apparel prices, that is in Carter (2006), vol. 3.

TRADE BY MAIN MARKET (%)

For 1957 onwards I have used *Anuario Estadístico de Puerto Rico* (1964). This gives the United States only. For earlier years, I have used *Anuario Estadístico de Puerto Rico: Estadísticas Históricas* (1959), which gives US data in all years and UK data from 1934–5.

PUBLIC REVENUE AND EXPENDITURE

Revenue and expenditure for 1900 are from Tables A.33 and A.37. There are figures in Mitchell (2007) for 1906 and a revenue figure in Clark (1930) for 1907. There are figures in Mitchell (2007) from 1910 onwards. Carter (2006), vol. 5, starts in 1940. I have used the latter from 1940, Mitchell (2007) and Clark (1930) for earlier years, and estimated any gaps by interpolation.

The revenue figures exclude import duties – see Clark (1930), p. 157. Most imports entered duty-free from the United States, but Puerto Rico – unlike the US Virgin Islands (see below) – did not keep the revenue from duties on imports from third countries.

US Virgin Islands

EXPORTS AND IMPORTS

For 1900–15, I have used the annual *Statistisk Aarbog for Danmark* for domestic exports (St Croix only) and merchandise imports (all three islands)

and assumed that merchandise exports were the same as merchandise imports in those years. Re-exports are then the difference between merchandise exports and domestic exports.

I have used Hornby and Justesen (1976), p. 294, to derive merchandise imports in 1916 (assumed equal to merchandise exports). Domestic exports in 1916 have been estimated as follows: the figures in *Statistisk Aarbog for Danmark* are for the fiscal year ending on March 31. I placed 1915–16 in 1915, as with earlier years, but there are no figures for 1916–17. I therefore grossed up the subtotal of principal exports assuming their share of domestic exports was the same as in 1915.

There is an official series starting in 1917, the year of the transfer from Denmark to the United States (from 1925 to 1934 the figures refer to trade with the US only, but this was by far the biggest market by that time).[8] Only one year (1949) of exports is missing, and this has been interpolated. The export figures are merchandise exports, but I have assumed that the principal exports continued to represent 90 per cent of domestic exports, with re-exports being the difference. The trend of re-exports was steadily downwards for many years as a result of new shipping routes that reduced the need for entrepôt trade, but re-exports revived after the Second World War as a result of the increase in tourism.

PRINCIPAL EXPORT PRODUCTS

The main export for the first decades was sugar. This was followed by rum until US Prohibition in 1919, after which rum exports rapidly declined (the last year recorded was 1922). Exports of bay rum then expanded (although this product uses rum in its manufacture, its sale was legal because it was not used as a beverage).[9]

The year 1900 is taken from Table A.10. For the years 1901–15, I used *Statistisk Aarbog for Danmark*. This gives the volume of sugar and rum (but not bay rum) in all years and the value also from 1910. However, this source also gives the average value before 1910 for various five-year periods from which prices can be derived. To fill in any gaps before 1917, including bay rum, I have also used Deerr (1949), National Bank of Commerce (1917), Dookhan (1974), International Institute of Agriculture, *International Yearbook of Agricultural Statistics*, de Booy (1918) and Zabriskie (1918). For 1916, I have converted sugar volumes to values using the Cuban rather than Puerto Rican price because the Danish Virgin islands did not yet have duty-free access to the United States (its main market).

There is a series on the volume of sugar exports from 1917 in Carter (2006), vol. 5. For those years where there are no values given in the *Annual Report*

---

[8] The figures are in Carter (2006), vol. 5 ('outlying territories'), but the import figures have been placed in the column for Federated States of Micronesia by mistake (the Puerto Rican import figures have then been placed in the column for the Virgin Islands).

[9] Its method of production is described in detail in Brock, Smith and Tucker (1917), pp. 30–1.

of the Governor of the US Virgin Islands, I have converted this series to values using the Puerto Rican price (both countries had duty-free access to the US market).

The statistics on rum and bay rum after 1917 are found in the *Annual Report of the Governor*. However, they are not complete. Gaps have been filled in various ways, including Paiewonsky and Dookhan (1990). Previously was governor of the US Virgin Islands for many years, but also a businessman, and this source gives useful figures on rum and bay rum exports in different years. There is a series on the volume of rum exports from 1934 in Hibben and Picó (1948), p. 16. Because this is in US gallons, I have converted it to imperial gallons and assumed the price before 1945 moved in line with the rum price for the British colonies. From 1954, the US federal government returned to the Virgin Islands the tax on rum exported to the United States. The figures are in Paiewonsky and Dookhan (1990), p. 495, and can be used to approximate rum exports for some missing years.

The US Virgin Islands after the Second World War became much less dependent on commodity exports, with the three principal products (sugar, rum and bay rum) accounting for a smaller and smaller share of merchandise exports. In addition, the rise of service exports meant that there was a growing gap between merchandise imports and exports.

TRADE BY MAIN MARKET (%)

Imports from the United States for 1900 are from Table A.27. For 1901–16, I have used US exports to the Danish Virgin Islands in *Statistical Abstract of the United States* (converted to *cif* by adding 10%) and divided by merchandise imports (see above). There are figures on the UK share of imports in US Consular Reports in some years and in Zabriskie (1918).

Exports to the United States for 1900 are from Table A.20. For 1901–12 and 1915–16 shares are based on a weighted average of exports of sugar and rum at various intervals in Toft (1982), p. 180. For 1913 and 1914, there are figures in Brock, Smith and Tucker (1917), p. 37, on domestic exports from St Croix shipped to the United States. Exports to the UK are assumed to be zero.

Trade with Denmark has been ignored because the United States is treated as the 'mother' in these tables, but the United States only replaced Denmark as the colonial power in 1917. However, trade with Denmark was very small even before the transfer.

Exports and imports to the United States after 1917 are often given in the *Annual Report of the Governor*. Missing years have been estimated. Exports to the UK are assumed to be zero, and the UK import share is assumed to have declined to insignificance after 1917.

PUBLIC REVENUE AND EXPENDITURE

Public revenue and expenditure for 1900 are from Tables A.33 and A.37. For 1901–15 there are figures in Toft (1982) for both St Thomas and St Croix. For 1916 there are figures in Zabriskie (1918).

The US navy was responsible for administration after the purchase of the islands from Denmark until the transfer to a civilian administration in 1931. In this period there are figures in Dookhan (1974) giving the average for a period of years, and I have taken the mid-point and estimated the gaps by interpolation when no other sources were available.

From 1931 there are figures in some issues of the *Annual Report of the Governor* and, starting in 1940, there is a series with a few gaps in Carter (2006), vol. 5. Where the *Annual Report of the Governor* has different figures from Carter (2006), vol. 5, I have relied on the former. Revenue soared after 1950 as a result of the return to the islands of the federal taxes levied on US Virgin Islands rum on its entry into the mainland states. See Paiewonsky and Dookhan (1990).

Notes on D Tables

The D. Tables start in 1960 and end in 2008. The colour-coding is black or, if the data are estimated, red.

The data for this period for most countries are much more easily accessible than for the years before 1960. I have made extensive use of the Internet version of World Bank, *World Development Indicators* (hereafter WDI); the Internet version of the United Nations Database (hereafter UND); the Internet version of the United Nations National Accounts (hereafter UNNA); the historic series prepared by CEPAL (2009); various issues of ECLAC, *Statistical Abstract for Latin America and the Caribbean* and ECLAC, *Economic Survey of Latin America and the Caribbean*; IMF, *International Financial Statistics* (hereafter IFS); United Nations, *Statistical Yearbook* (hereafter UNSY); and United Nations, *Yearbook of International Trade Statistics* (hereafter UNYITS). For the French Départements d'Outre-Mer (DOMs), I used the Web site of the Institut National de la Statistique et des Etudes Economiques (hereafter INSEE).

Anguilla is treated separately from St Kitts & Nevis from 1970 onwards, after the federation of St Kitts, Nevis & Anguilla came to an end, and Aruba is treated separately from the Dutch Antilles from 1986 onwards after it left the Dutch Antilles and became a unit within the Kingdom of the Netherlands.

Thirteen countries became independent after 1960 and in due course formed the Caribbean Community (CARICOM), and the constitutional position of those that remained dependencies was changed in many cases. This therefore requires a change in the subregions. These are now: Hispaniola (Haiti and the Dominican Republic), Cuba, CARICOM (including the Bahamas and Suriname, but excluding Haiti and Montserrat), British Overseas Territories (Anguilla, British Virgin Islands, Cayman Islands, Montserrat and Turks & Caicos Islands), the French Départements d'Outre-Mer (French Guiana, Guadeloupe and Martinique), Dutch territories (Aruba and Dutch Antilles) and US 'Outlying Territories' (Puerto Rico and the US Virgin Islands). The

nonindependent countries are now listed as British, French, Dutch or US territories in the subregional headings.[1]

I have ignored the recent changes in the constitutional position of St Barthélemy and St Martin, preferring to include them with Guadeloupe. St Barthélemy and St Martin ceased to be dependencies of Guadeloupe in mid-2007; they remained in the EU as part of France, and each became a Collectivité d'Outre-Mer (COM). In 2008, they were excluded from the figures in Guadeloupe for the first time, so I have made adjustments to include them. I have added their population to the figures for Guadeloupe and used the relevant growth rate in 2007–8 to estimate the other variables.

In October 2010, Bonaire, Saba and St Eustatius became Dutch autonomous municipalities; and Sint Maarten and Curaçao acquired autonomy within the Kingdom of the Netherlands – as Aruba had enjoyed since 1986. This does not affect the database because it took place after the final year.

In this part of the database, it is possible to include service exports and imports. 'Total' exports (imports) are therefore the name given to the sum of service and merchandise exports (imports), and merchandise exports continue to be the sum of domestic exports and re-exports. Merchandise imports are, as before, the sum of retained imports and those for re-export.

The database also contains for all years from 1960 estimates of GDP for the countries of the Caribbean. These are given at both current and constant (2000) prices, from which the GDP deflator can be derived. There are also estimates of annual inflation rates. The titles of the D. Tables are:

D.1. Population
D.1a. Population (adjusted for per capita calculations)
D.2. Crude Birth Rates
D.3. Crude Death Rates
D.4. Exchange Rates
D.5. Principal Commodity Export Values
D.6. Merchandise Exports
D.7. Service Exports
D.8. Total Exports
D.9. Total Exports Price Index (2000=100)
D.10. Total Exports at 2000 Prices
D.11. Merchandise Imports
D.12. Service Imports
D.13. Total Imports
D.14. Total Imports Price Index (2000=100)
D.15. Total Imports at 2000 Prices
D.16. Net Barter Terms of Trade (2000=100)

---

[1] Just as 'dependencies' was used in the C. Tables instead of 'colonies' in the A. Tables, so 'territories' is used in the D. Tables in view of the constitutional changes that took place in this period.

D.17. Income Terms of Trade (2000=100)
D.18. Gross Domestic Product
D.19. Gross Domestic Product (2000 prices)
D.20. Annual Inflation Rates (%)

TABLES D.1 AND D.1a. POPULATION

Table D.1 gives the population for all countries from 1960 onwards. Anguilla is given in all years, but it only became separate from St Kitts & Nevis from 1970. The data for St Kitts & Nevis before 1970 therefore exclude Anguilla. Aruba separated from the Dutch Antilles in 1986, but the data for both countries are given in all years. The first year (1960) of Table D.1 is taken from the last year in Table C.1 (with Aruba and Dutch Antilles now treated separately).

There are twenty-eight countries in Table D.1 compared with twenty-seven in Table C.1 because Aruba is treated separately for the first time. Table D.1a then aggregates Anguilla with St Kitts & Nevis up to 1969 and Aruba with Dutch Antilles up to 1985 in order to provide the population data in a form that can be used to calculate per capita values.

The main sources for Table D.1 are WDI, UND and CEPAL (2009). The first source includes the Dutch and US territories, and the second also has information on the British Overseas Territories starting in 1970. The only gaps for the British Overseas Territories are therefore 1961 to 1969, which have been filled from country sources or by interpolation.

None of these sources has data on the French territories. For Guadeloupe and Martinique, I used INSEE (1990) from 1961 to 1982 (a census year) and Mitchell (2007) up to 2004 for Guadeloupe and up to 1990 for Martinique. From 1990, I used INSEE for Martinique, because Mitchell's figures are inconsistent. For French Guiana, I used the census data provided by INSEE, with the intercensal years filled by interpolation, and annual data from 1995. From 2005, I used the INSEE population data in *L'Année Economique et Sociale* for each DOM. This excludes St Barthélemy and St Martin from Guadeloupe in the last year, so I added them back (INSEE has population data for St Barthélemy and St Martin in 2008).

There are a few countries (Belize, Dominica, St Lucia) for which the data in CEPAL (2009) and WDI are slightly different. In these cases, I used CEPAL (2009) because this is the source for 1950–60 in Table C.1.

TABLES D.2 AND D.3. CRUDE BIRTH AND DEATH RATES

The main source is WDI, but this does not have data for all countries, and there are gaps in the series even for those countries in WDI. Gaps in the CBR in the 1960s for ex-British colonies and Montserrat were filled using Chernick (1978), tables S.A.1.6 and S.A.1.7, wherever possible. Otherwise gaps were filled by interpolation. The data for the British Overseas Territories are taken

from the statistics office of each country or from the Web site of the Caribbean Development Bank (CDB).

Where the data for the earlier years are given as the CBR/CDR together with the estimated population, I first calculated the implied births and deaths and then recalculated the CBR/CDR using the population in Table D.1 (this is necessary in view of the later revisions to the population figures). The Cayman Islands government Web site is particularly useful because it makes use of Cayman Islands (1992) to give a complete series on births and deaths from 1960 to 2008. The CBR from 1960 to 1979 and the CDR from 1960 to 1975 for Anguilla are assumed to be the same as St Kitts & Nevis. For the Turks & Caicos Islands in 1970 and 1980–8, there are data in the *Statistical Yearbook* (1989). The sources for the French territories are the same as for population (see above).

TABLE D.4. EXCHANGE RATES

All rates are expressed in local currency units (LCU) per US dollar and are nominal exchange rates. They are taken from WDI, except for the British Overseas Territories (other than Cayman Islands, which is in WDI), the French DOMs, Puerto Rico, Cuba and Suriname (1989–94 only – see below). In most countries there was also a black market rate for the US dollar, and in some countries there was also a legal parallel rate (not shown here). The exchange rates for those countries **not** taken from WDI were as follows:

Cuba

The rate given is the official exchange rate of the Cuban peso to the US dollar. This was unity until 1971, after which the Cuban peso was revalued until it was restored to parity with the US dollar in 1986. See Mesa-Lago (2000). In 1993, the US dollar was made legal tender, and a parallel exchange rate open to all was established in which the Cuban national peso fluctuated against the US dollar (this rate is given annually in ECLAC, *Economic Survey of Latin America and the Caribbean*). The authorities also introduced a new currency at this time, the *peso convertible* or CUC, whose official rate to the US dollar remained at unity until 2004, after which the *peso convertible* was revalued by 8 per cent against the US dollar. The US dollar ceased to be legal tender in 2006, and a tax of 10 per cent was also applied to sales of US dollars, but not other currencies, until 2011. The rate shown in Table D.4 is net of the tax.

Anguilla and Montserrat

Because both countries use the Eastern Caribbean dollar, the exchange rate is the same as for the other members of the Eastern Caribbean Currency Union (ECCU). These other members are Antigua, Dominica, Grenada, St Kitts & Nevis, St Lucia and St Vincent.

British Virgin Islands and Turks & Caicos Islands

The US dollar is the unit of account.

French Guiana, Guadeloupe and Martinique

Because the three countries use the same currency as the rest of France, the exchange rate to the dollar is the same as for France. The French currency was the franc until 1999, when it became the euro. In Table D.4, therefore, I have included the franc/dollar rate until 1998 and the euro/dollar from 1999. INSEE, however, uses the new currency from 1993 in its revised GDP series (see below), but strictly speaking it was the European Currency Unit (ECU) before 1999 rather than the euro. The ECU/dollar rate before 1999 can be found in IFS.

Suriname

The Surinamese guilder was replaced in 2004 by the Surinamese dollar at the rate of 1 per 1,000. WDI quotes the currency rate before 2004 as if the Surinamese dollar was in use, but this is incorrect. I therefore quote the rate of the Surinamese guilder to the US dollar before 2004 and the rate of the Surinamese dollar to the US dollar from 2004. The guilder was pegged to the US dollar (first at 1.89 and then at 1.79). The rate quoted by WDI does not change until 1994, after which there is a dramatic collapse. This is misleading because most trade by then was passing through the parallel market. Indeed, the World Bank itself recognises this in its conversion of current local currency unit GDP to US dollar GDP, because WDI uses an implicit exchange rate after 1988 that is different from the official rate. To complicate matters further, UNNA in its own series on current LCU and US dollar GDP uses a slightly different implicit exchange rate. The three rates are shown below for 1988–95:

Year	WDI Official	WDI Implicit	UNNA Implicit
1988	0.00179	0.00179	0.00180
1989	0.00179	0.00492	0.00440
1990	0.00179	0.00973	0.00630
1991	0.00179	0.01023	0.00690
1992	0.00179	0.01500	0.00900
1993	0.00179	0.03350	0.02270
1994	0.22246	0.13412	0.11980
1995	0.44277	0.44223	0.44350

I used the WDI implicit exchange rate in Table D.4 (converted back to Surinamese guilders at 1,000 to 1), which differs from the official rate between 1989 and 1994.

Puerto Rico

The currency is the US dollar.

TABLE D.5. PRINCIPAL COMMODITY EXPORT VALUES

This table contains exports for ten primary products from 1960 onwards. The ten products constituted 70 per cent of merchandise exports in 1960, the balance consisting almost entirely of manufactured exports (including rum). By 2008, the share of the ten primary products had fallen to 20 per cent. The manufacturing share therefore went from 30 per cent to 80 per cent (before the oil price rise in the first decade of the twenty-first century, it was 90%).

Sugar

The data for 1960 come from Table C.5 (with volumes converted to metric tonnes), and the basic source for 1961 onwards is the Web site of the Food and Agricultural Organization (hereafter FAOSTAT). I have included refined and raw sugar. Not all countries are included in FAOSTAT, so the gaps have been filled as follows:

Guadeloupe and Martinique

For years before 1995, the main source is UNYITS, with gaps filled from INSEE. From 1995 onwards only Guadeloupe exported sugar, and I have used the INSEE Web site for the volume and value of exports.

Puerto Rico and US Virgin Islands

There are data on volume in Carter (2006), vol.5, until 1997, but only Puerto Rico was exporting after 1966. For the value of Puerto Rican exports, I used *Anuario Estadístico de Puerto Rico* (various years). Where no value data were available for either Puerto Rico or US Virgin Islands, I used Barbados prices to convert volumes to values. From 1997, I used the Web site of the Junta de la Planificación de Puerto Rico. Puerto Rico ceased to export after 2002.

Molasses

The data for 1960 come mainly from Table C.5, and the basic source for 1961 onwards is FAOSTAT. However, molasses was not included for some countries in Table C.5 that do appear in FAOSTAT, and some countries are in Table C.5 but not in FAOSTAT. The most important of the former are Belize, Haiti and Jamaica, and the most important of the latter are Puerto Rico, Guadeloupe and Martinique. I have added the volume and value for 1960 for Belize, Haiti and Jamaica from UNYITS. Puerto Rican data are from *Anuario Estadístico de Puerto Rico*, with exports assumed to have ceased in 1970, and I have ignored Guadeloupe because exports stopped soon after 1960 (they had ended already

in Martinique). The FAOSTAT series are in metric tonnes (MT), whereas Table C.5 is in gallons. I therefore estimated the MT equivalent of gallons for 1960 based on a comparison of the average price per gallon in 1960 and the average price per MT in 1961. The value of molasses exports in 1960 in Table D.5 is $23,771,931, whereas the value of molasses exports in 1960 in Table C.5 is $21,987,804. This is mainly because of the exclusion of Jamaican molasses exports from Table C.5.

Bananas

The main source is FAOSTAT, which starts in 1961. Because the data in FAOSTAT are in MT, I converted the volume data in Table C.5 for 1960 from bunches to MT for consistency (based on a comparison of average prices per bunch in 1960 and per MT in 1961). The main Caribbean banana exporting countries not in FAOSTAT are Guadeloupe and Martinique. I used UNYITS up to 1995 and the INSEE Web site thereafter for these two islands.

Tobacco Leaf

The main source is FAOSTAT, which starts in 1961. Data for 1960 are from Table C.5 (converted from lbs to MT). The volume and value for Jamaica in 1960 are estimated because Jamaica's tobacco leaf exports are not included in Table C.5. Puerto Rican data are from *Anuario Estadístico de Puerto Rico* or *Anuario Estadístico de Comercio Exterior de Puerto Rico*. Where no data were available, I used the production series in FAOSTAT, and I assumed that the volume of exports moved in line and estimated the value using international prices. The FAOSTAT series for Puerto Rico is not reported after 1981, so I assumed exports ceased in that year.

Coffee

The main source is FAOSTAT, which starts in 1961. Data for 1960 are from Table C.5 (converted from lbs to MT). Puerto Rico's coffee exports are from *Anuario Estadístico de Puerto Rico* up to 1970. Because they are not given in FAOSTAT, I estimated them after 1970 from production, which is included in FAOSTAT. The assumption was that exports were 5 per cent of production (the ratio in 1970) and that prices moved in line with the rest of the Caribbean. Guadeloupe is also excluded from FAOSTAT, so I used UNYITS for volume and value.

Cacao

The main source is FAOSTAT, which starts in 1961. Data for 1960 are from Table C.5 (converted from lbs to MT). Table C.5 includes exports from

Guadeloupe and Martinique, but these ended soon after 1960, and so I have not included them in Table D.5.

Citrus

The main source is FAOSTAT, which starts in 1961. It includes grapefruit and orange exports of all types, but not limes. I therefore excluded Dominica and Montserrat from the table. Data for 1960 are from Table C.5. I have only included the value because the volumes are so heterogeneous. The value in 1960 in Table C.5 is larger than the value for 1960 in Table D.5 because of the exclusion of Dominica and Montserrat.

Rice

The main source is FAOSTAT, which starts in 1961. Data for 1960 are from Table C.5 (converted from lbs to MT).

Petroleum

The data for 1960 come from Table C.5. The value is net, estimated at 10 per cent of gross exports, if based on imported oil. The value is gross if based mainly on domestic oil. WDI has the fuel share in merchandise exports for many countries, but for not all years. However, fuel exports include petroleum products other than crude and refined oil, so it must be used with care. ECLAC, *Economic Survey of Latin America and the Caribbean*, lists the share of oil in domestic exports for those countries where it was one of the ten leading products. The other sources are listed under the country in Table D.6 below.

Nonfuel Minerals

This includes mainly bauxite, alumina, nickel and gold. The data were obtained as follows:

Hispaniola
HAITI
    Bauxite was exported until 1982 (see UNYITS). From 1961 to 1970 no data are provided, so I interpolated those years.

DOMINICAN REPUBLIC
    Bauxite/alumina exports ceased in 1982 and did not reenter the export statistics until 2008. The data up to 1982 come from UNYITS, and 2008 is from UND. Ferronickel exports began in 1969, and the data come from UNYITS, UND and ECLAC, *Economic Survey of Latin America and the Caribbean*. There is a gap in 1972–4, which I have filled by interpolation. The gold series is from ECLAC, *Economic Survey of Latin America and the Caribbean*.

Cuba

The series begins with all mining exports (nickel, copper, manganese and chromium ore) and is taken from UNYITS up to 1989, with only two gaps (1962 and 1985), which I have filled by interpolation. From 1993 onwards I have used UND, UNYITS, ECLAC, *Economic Survey of Latin America and the Caribbean*, and Cuba's Oficina Nacional de Estadísticas (ONE). There is then a gap from 1990–2 and 1997, which I have filled by interpolation. No values are given for nickel exports after 2005 in the balance of payments, so their value in 2006–8 has been derived by deducting all other entries from merchandise exports and assuming that 'other products n.e.s.' increased by 5 per cent per year. The value of mining exports from 2006–8 is from ONE (2010), table 8.8.

CARICOM

GUYANA

In 1960, manganese started to be exported along with bauxite. I have included both, but manganese was never very important and stopped being exported in 1969. There is a series in UNYITS up to 1981, with only one gap (1980), which I filled by interpolation. There is then a long gap from 1982 to 1989, after which the series in ECLAC, *Economic Survey of Latin America and the Caribbean* begins. I used the production series in ECLAC, *Statistical Abstract for Latin America and the Caribbean*, together with unit prices for bauxite and alumina from Jamaica to fill the gaps. The gold series is from ECLAC, *Economic Survey of Latin America and the Caribbean*.

JAMAICA

Both bauxite and alumina were exported by 1960 (see Table C.5). For 1961–71, I used Chernick (1978), table SA3.15, because UNYITS seriously underestimates the value of exports in these years. From 1972, I used UNYITS, adding SITC 51365 (aluminium oxide, hydroxide) in those years (1975–80) when it is treated separately from SITC 28 (metalliferous ores). It is not possible to use WDI's mining share of merchandise exports because there are many gaps, and even in those years where there are numbers, it often refers only to bauxite and not alumina. There are also data in ECLAC, *Economic Survey of Latin America and the Caribbean*, from 1997 and on the Web site of the Jamaican Statistical Institute from 2005. The gaps in the series (1985–7) have been filled by using bauxite production (see ECLAC, *Economic Survey of Latin America and the Caribbean*) and assuming that bauxite/alumina exports moved in line with production in the missing years.

SURINAME

UNYITS can be used for bauxite/alumina until 1976. There is then a gap until 1987, which I have filled using the value of bauxite and alumina exports in van Schaaijk (1992). This series, which stops in 1990, is given in Surinamese guilders, and I have converted to US dollars at the exchange rate in Table D.4. From then on I have used UND, ECLAC and UNYITS, with the gaps (1991

and 1993–6) estimated from the production series in ECLAC, *Economic Survey of Latin America and the Caribbean* and prices for other countries. The gold series is from UNYITS and ECLAC, *Economic Survey of Latin America and the Caribbean.*

French Territories

FRENCH GUIANA

The volume of gold exports is given in Pétot (1986) and Taubira-Delannon (n.d.) up to 1999. There is also a series in UNYITS for gold starting in 1980 and ending in 1995. Prices have been taken from IFS where there are gaps. After 1999, the data are reported in INSEE for French Guiana on an annual basis.

TABLE D.6. MERCHANDISE EXPORTS

This table records all merchandise exports (i.e. the sum of domestic exports and re-exports). The source for 1960 for all countries is therefore Table C.8. From 1961 onwards it is generally merchandise exports in WDI. This series, in the trade section of WDI, covers more years than exports of goods in the balance of payments section (although these two series should be the same, they are not always).

Merchandise exports include re-exports and are therefore known as general exports (they do not, however, include transhipments). When they exclude re-exports, they are known as special exports. In a few cases, official data refer only to special exports, and in a handful of cases the series changes from one to another over time. Wherever possible, I have ironed out these inconsistencies.

WDI normally includes refined oil in merchandise exports. For those countries with no domestic crude oil production, this massively inflates the export figures. Fortunately, WDI also gives the share of fuel in merchandise exports in some cases. I have therefore adjusted merchandise exports for the relevant countries in the same way as for the Dutch Antilles before 1960. This means that merchandise exports include only the margin on refined oil (assumed to be 10%) when the crude oil was imported. The countries and years where this was done are listed below. I have not adjusted exports if energy exports were mainly based on domestic production of crude oil or gas.

Manufactured exports since 1960 increasingly reflect the assembly of goods under various tax incentive regimes. The valuation of these exports is not entirely consistent across the Caribbean, but I have left the data unadjusted. WDI includes the imported components in merchandise imports, and thus exports reflect gross value. That is why exports from Puerto Rico form such a large part of the total for the Caribbean.

WDI could not be used in all cases because it generally only has data on independent countries. The following notes explain what was done when there were no data in WDI or where the data in WDI needed to be adjusted:

Cuba

I have not adjusted merchandise exports for those years after 1980, when Cuba re-exported part of the oil it imported from the Soviet Union. Although important in some years, there are too many gaps in the series to make adjustments possible. Cuba also started exporting some of the petroleum that it produced in the 1990s, but it was still a net importer.

CARICOM

Antigua

From 1961 to 1984, the figures are taken from IFS because they are less rounded than in WDI. However, an adjustment has been made between 1967 and 1975 in the case of refined oil (from 1976 onwards, refined oil exports were much less important and are not included in WDI exports). The refinery started production in 1966 and made its first exports in 1967 (see O'Loughlin (1968), p. 27). The share of fuel in merchandise exports is given in WDI for 1973–5 and is taken from Chernick (1978) in earlier years. I have then calculated merchandise exports as all nonfuel exports plus 10 per cent of fuel exports.

The Bahamas

In addition to the traditional re-export trade, Bahamas after 1960 established an oil refining and chemical industry based exclusively on imports. There is no consistency in the treatment of oil refining, chemicals and re-exports either over time or across sources, so therefore great care needs to be taken in constructing a series. In the 1990 edition of IFS there are data on merchandise exports and oil exports from 1960 up to 1987. The difference between them is the value of non-oil exports, and this is the same as goods exports in the balance of payments, which starts in 1973. Thus, we can use these data to construct a series for merchandise exports, including 10 per cent of oil exports up to 1987. I then used IMF balance of payments exports for 1988–91, which exclude oil, and added a 10 per cent margin for refined oil exports (SITC 334) using the detailed export statistics in UNYITS. This extends the series to 1991. WDI excludes oil exports from 1992, and I used these figures unadjusted. Refined oil exports continued to be exported, but from now on they were mainly transhipments and should not therefore be included in merchandise exports. These oil transhipments went largely to the United States, and, for the interested reader, US imports from the Bahamas and average import prices can be found on the Web site of the US Energy Information Administration.

Barbados

Crude oil exports began in 2002 (see CEPAL (2010)). Because this was based on domestic crude production, I have not adjusted the figures. Nor have I made any adjustment for the export of other petroleum products throughout the whole period.

Belize
Crude oil exports began in 2006 (see CEPAL (2010)). Because this was based on domestic crude production, I have not adjusted the figures.

Jamaica
Oil exports began in 1964. Because these were based on imports rather than domestic production, I adjusted them as explained above. Gross oil exports from 1972 were calculated from the fuel share of merchandise exports in WDI. Before 1972, I used Chernick (1978), table SA3.3, pp. 302–3. Net oil exports are assumed to be 10 per cent of gross exports.

St Lucia
The country imported and exported refined oil for a brief period in the 1970s, but it was not sufficiently important to justify adjusting the export figures. The ratio of fuel in merchandise exports is given in WDI.

St Kitts & Nevis
There are no data in WDI before 1970, when Anguilla was part of St Kitts & Nevis. However, the 1985 edition of UNYITS has figures (in Eastern Caribbean dollars) that can be used back to 1964. I estimated 1961–3 by interpolation, starting with the 1960 figure taken from Table C.8. It is not clear when St Kitts & Nevis stopped including data for Anguilla, so it is possible there is a small amount of double counting after 1969.

Trinidad & Tobago
Unlike other Caribbean countries specialised in energy exports, the natural resources of the country are largely domestic rather than imported. No adjustment was therefore made to the value of merchandise exports for refined oil exports based on crude oil imports, but this activity did – and does – take place (see CEPAL (2010)).

Suriname
Oil exports are first recorded in 1987, but production began in 1983. Because they are based mainly on domestic production, I have included them gross. The sources for oil exports are UND from 1994 and UNYITS for earlier years (there appears to be an error in UNYITS in 1991 so I estimated the value). For 1999–2002, WDI merchandise exports are less than the sum of the commodity exports, so I used CEPAL (2010) for those years because this gives both commodity and merchandise exports.

British Territories

Anguilla
There are data in UND from 1988 onwards. For earlier years (the Anguilla series starts in 1970) I deducted services in Table D.7 from total exports in Table D.8 (see below) to estimate merchandise exports.

British Virgin Islands

There is a series starting in 1970 in UND and a series in UNYITS for earlier years. The only gap is 1987–94. This has been estimated by interpolation (merchandise exports were unimportant by then). The year 2008 is estimated.

Cayman Islands

Merchandise exports, never very important, were obtained from UNYITS for 1971–80 and from 1982 onwards from Cayman Islands, *Foreign Trade Statistics Report*. The years before 1970 are in Cayman Islands (1992). The gaps (1970 and 1981) have been filled by interpolation.

Montserrat

Merchandise exports were taken from UNYITS and UND. Missing years (1966 and 1969) have been filled by interpolation.

Turks & Caicos Islands

Merchandise exports are in the UND from 1999 onwards. For the earlier period, starting in 1973, the data are reported irregularly in various editions of the relevant issues of the Economist Intelligence Unit, *Quarterly Report for the Bahamas etc.* The gaps from 1961 onwards have then been filled by interpolation, starting with the 1960 figure taken from Table C.8. Merchandise exports were much less important than service exports in this period.

French Territories

French Guiana

The latest INSEE national accounts series goes from 1993 to 2006 and is available from the INSEE Web site (it is given in euros in all years, but before 1999 the unit of account was the ECU; the numbers before 1999 have therefore been converted to US dollars at the ECU/dollar rate[2] and from 1999 using the exchange rate in Table D.4). It covers merchandise exports and services. For 2007–8, I used *L'Année Economique et Sociale de Guyane* (available on INSEE Web site). Before 1993, I have used two sources. The first is UNYITS, which I used back to 1965 (it is not reliable for earlier years). The second is *Annuaire de la Guyane Française*, which I used for 1961–4.

Guadeloupe

The latest series runs from 1993 to 2006 and is available from the INSEE Web site (see French Guiana above for method of conversion into current dollars). It covers merchandise exports and services. For 2007–8, I used *L'Année Economique et Sociale de Guadeloupe* (available on INSEE Web site). From 2008, INSEE excludes St Barthélemy and St Martin from Guadeloupe's statistics. Because I used the 2007–8 growth rate, however, the merchandise export

---

[2] This can be found in IFS.

figure in Table D.6 includes Guadeloupe and the two former dependencies on the assumption that their merchandise export growth was similar to that of Guadeloupe. Before 1993, I have used UNYITS. I have not made any adjustment for refined oil exports because they did not begin until the end of the period and were never as important as in Martinique.

Martinique

The latest series goes from 1993 to 2006 and is available from the INSEE Web site (see French Guiana above for method of conversion into current dollars). It covers merchandise exports and services. For 2007–8, I used *L'Année Economique et Sociale de Martinique* (available on INSEE Web site). Before 1993, I have used UNYITS. Refined oil exports, based on imports, began in 1965, so I have adjusted the value of energy exports, and they are shown net (i.e. 10% of gross exports).

Dutch Territories

Dutch Antilles

WDI has a series on merchandise exports in all years and the ratio of fuel in merchandise exports for most years up to 1995. I used these two series to calculate net exports (i.e. non-oil exports and 10% of oil exports) up to 1985 (the gaps in WDI were filled using the *Statistical Yearbook: Netherlands Antilles* for the relevant years). From 1986 onwards, when the state-owned Venezuelan company PDVSA bought the refinery operations, the Dutch Antilles switched to a different methodology, under which the operations of the oil refining companies are treated as offshore. As a result, the export of goods in the balance of payments refers to non-oil exports only. This series is reported in IFS, and I used it from 1986 onwards. The merchandise exports from 1986 onwards therefore exclude the margin on oil exports (they also exclude Aruba), and all that remained was to calculate 10 per cent of oil exports from 1986 onwards. This was done using the data on oil exports (SITC 33) in UNYITS, the value of exports including oil in WDI and the share of fuel in merchandise exports in WDI. Non-oil merchandise exports are dominated by re-exports sold through the duty-free zones, because non-oil domestic exports are very small (domestic exports, i.e. excluding oil and re-exports, are now reported on the Web site of the Central Bureau of Statistics of the Dutch Antilles).

Aruba

The WDI series begins in 1986, after Aruba separated from the Netherlands Antilles. The oil refinery, built in 1929, had closed in the previous year, and the second refinery had closed even earlier. There was then no oil refining until 1991, when production and exports restarted. I have estimated Aruba net oil exports as a proportion of those from the Netherlands Antilles based on the volume of exports of refined oil given in international petroleum sources. By 2004, after which statistics are easily available, the two countries had roughly

the same volume of refined oil exports. Before 2004, I assumed that the Aruba ratio in 1991 was only 10 per cent and interpolated the ratio for the intervening years (1992–2003).

US Territories

Puerto Rico
Merchandise exports starting in fiscal 1969–70 are in UND. I have allocated the fiscal year to the later of the two calendar years (i.e. 1969–70 = 1970). For the years before 1970, there is a series in Carter (2006), vol.5. Although some merchandise exports consist of refined oil, it was a very small proportion of the total, and I have therefore made no adjustment to the series (US imports of refined oil from Puerto Rico can be found in US Energy Information Administration from 1995 onwards and virtually ceased after 2002).

US Virgin Islands
There is a series starting in 1990 in US Virgin Islands, Bureau of Economic Research, *Annual Economic Indicators* (various years), which separates oil and non-oil merchandise exports. Before 1990, I used the series on merchandise exports in Carter (2006), vol. 5. WDI has fuel as a percentage of exports in a number of years, but it does not have exports themselves. Refined oil exports started in 1968, and I estimated the share of fuel in exports for those years before 1990 not reported by WDI. Net exports were then calculated as non-oil exports plus 10 per cent of oil exports.

TABLE D.7. SERVICE EXPORTS

This table records service exports in current US dollars. The main source is commercial service exports in WDI. However, there are many gaps in WDI because the data rarely go back before the 1970s, even for those countries for which WDI has figures. For those countries in WDI, the normal procedure to estimate the missing entries was to construct an index number based on tourist expenditure or, failing that, tourist arrivals, and to use this to extend the exports of services back to 1960. In those few cases where this was not possible, an index was constructed from total imports, and this was used to extend backwards exports of goods and services before deducting merchandise exports to obtain exports of services as the residual. The data were obtained as follows:

Hispaniola

Haiti
Commercial service exports are first recorded in 1971 in WDI. CEPAL (2009) has a series on service exports in the balance of payments starting in 1950. For those years where the two series overlap, the CEPAL series is higher.

I used the CEPAL series to construct an index and spliced this to the 1971 value in WDI.

Dominican Republic

Commercial service exports are first recorded in 1968 in WDI. CEPAL (2009) has a series on service exports in the balance of payments starting in 1950. For those years where the two series overlap, the CEPAL series is higher. I used the CEPAL series to construct an index and spliced this to the 1968 value in WDI.

Cuba

There are no commercial service exports recorded in WDI. However, CEPAL (2009) has a series on service exports in the balance of payments starting in 1990. This includes exports of professional services (especially to Venezuela) since 2004. In its annual *Economic Survey of Latin America and the Caribbean*, ECLAC from 1978 to 1987 also provided exports of services in a table on Cuba's balance of payments in freely convertible currency. After deducting interest received from service exports, I then linked the two series using figures on visitor expenditure in 1988–9 in UNSY. For the earlier years, I assumed services were the same proportion of exports of goods and services as in 1978. For 2008, I used the growth in exports of goods and services in the national accounts (see CEPAL (2010)) and deducted merchandise exports in Table D.6 to derive service exports.

CARICOM

Antigua

Commercial service exports in WDI begin in 1977. Tourist arrivals from 1960 onwards are in Henry (1985), p. 123. I used this series to estimate service exports before 1977. There are also detailed figures on tourist expenditure in 1964–5 in O'Loughlin (1968). There is much useful information on the growth of service exports in Nicholls, G. (2001).

The Bahamas

Commercial service exports in WDI begin in 1976. The Bahamas, *Quarterly Statistical Digest* has figures on invisible receipts from 1965 onwards. Earlier years are estimated from an index of tourism derived from arrivals in UNSY.

Barbados

Commercial service exports in WDI begin in 1970. However, CEPAL (2009) has a series on service exports in the balance of payments, which I used for the years before 1970. There are also figures on tourist arrivals from 1960 to 1969 in Barbados, *Abstract of Statistics* for 1969, and tourist expenditure for 1969–70 are given in UNSY. The year 2008 is the difference between exports of goods and services in UNNA and merchandise exports in Table D.6.

Belize

Commercial service exports are first recorded in 1984 in WDI, when they represented only 13.1 per cent of exports of goods and services. Tourism was almost completely undeveloped until the 1980s, so there are no reliable figures for the earlier years. I therefore assumed commercial service exports were 10 per cent of exports of goods and services in 1960 and interpolated the ratio from then until 1984.

Dominica

Commercial service exports are first recorded in 1976 in WDI. Tourist arrivals from 1970 are given in World Bank (1980). I then assumed that tourists in 1960 were roughly one-third of those in 1970 and interpolated the tourist arrivals for the missing years. From this an index was constructed that I used to estimate commercial service exports before 1976.

Grenada

Commercial service exports are first recorded in 1977 in WDI. There are some figures on tourist arrivals and receipts in UNSY, but the numbers are incomplete and inconsistent. Service exports were 50 per cent of exports of goods and services in 1977, so I assumed they were 30 per cent in 1960 and interpolated the ratio for the missing years.

Guyana

Commercial service exports are first recorded in 1977 in WDI. However, CEPAL (2009) has a series on service exports in the balance of payments, which I used for the years before 1977. There is a gap in the series for the years 1986–91 in WDI. For these years I used IFS, which has a series in domestic currency for exports of goods and services in the national accounts section. I converted this to US dollars, constructed an index and spliced this to exports of goods and services in 1985. I then deducted merchandise exports (see Table D.6) to derive service exports. The estimates are plausible, except for 1991 (inflation was very severe in that year). For 1991, I therefore assumed services were 20 per cent of exports of goods and services.

Jamaica

Commercial service exports are first recorded in 1976 in WDI. However, CEPAL (2009) has a series on service exports in the balance of payments, which I used for the years before 1976.

St Kitts & Nevis

Commercial service exports are first recorded in 1980 in the most recent editions of WDI, but earlier editions of WDI have exports of goods and services starting in 1977, from which services can be derived as the residual. There are no satisfactory data on tourist arrivals or expenditure for the earlier years, so

I assumed services were 20 per cent of exports of goods and services (the same ratio as in 1977).

St Lucia
Commercial service exports are first recorded in 1976 in WDI. St Lucia, *Annual Statistical Digest* has tourist arrivals by sea and air back to 1964, which I used to construct an index and splice to service exports in 1976. For 1960–3, I assumed that services were 35 per cent of exports of goods and services.

St Vincent
Commercial service exports are first recorded in 1978 in WDI. There is a series on passenger arrivals from 1960 in St Vincent, *Digest of Statistics*, but it stops in 1973. I assumed passenger arrivals rose by 30 per cent between 1973 and 1978 and estimated the intervening years by interpolation. I then constructed an index from these passenger numbers and spliced it to service exports in 1978.

Suriname
Commercial service exports are first recorded in 1977 in WDI. However, CEPAL (2009) has a series on service exports in the balance of payments starting in 1950. For those years where the two series overlap, the CEPAL series is lower. I used it to construct an index and spliced this to the 1977 value in WDI.

Trinidad & Tobago
Commercial service exports are first recorded in 1975 in WDI. However, CEPAL (2009) has a series on service exports in the balance of payments, which I used for the years before 1975. The year 2008 is based on tourism receipts, assuming the same ratio to commercial service exports as in the previous year.

British Territories

Anguilla
Exports of services are in UND from 1988 to 2006. For 2007–8, I used the balance of payments credit entry for services in IFS. From 1970 to 1987, I assumed they were the same proportion of total exports as in 1988.

British Virgin Islands
There is a series on exports of goods and services in UNNA from 1970. I deducted merchandise exports (see Table D.6) from this to derive service exports as the residual. The years 1960–9 have been estimated on the assumption that exports of goods and services moved in line with total imports. I then deducted merchandise exports to estimate service exports in those years.

Cayman Islands

There is a series on exports of goods and services in UNNA from 1970. I deducted merchandise exports from this (see Table D.6) to derive service exports as the residual. The years 1960–9 have been estimated on the assumption that exports of goods and services moved in line with total imports. I then deducted merchandise exports to estimate service exports in those years.

Montserrat

Commercial service exports from 1975 to 1986 are in UND. From 1990 onwards they are in the database of the Secretariat of CARICOM (this includes the impact of the volcanic explosion in 1995). However, it is difficult to use these data consistently. From 1970 to 2008, I therefore derived them as the difference between exports of goods and services in UNNA and merchandise exports (see Table D.6). Before 1970, I interpolated backwards using a guesstimate of their value ($100,000) in 1960.

Turks & Caicos Islands

Service exports from 2000 are in UND. From 1970 to 1999 services are calculated as the difference between merchandise exports in Table D.6 and exports of goods and services in UNNA. Before 1970, I assumed that total exports moved in line with total imports and estimated service exports as the difference between total and merchandise exports.

French Territories

French Guiana

There are data on service exports from 1993 to 2006 in INSEE. These are dominated by the space station, which began operations in 1968. In addition, INSEE makes a 'territorial correction' to allow for nonresident expenditure. Because this is equivalent to visitor expenditure, I adjusted service exports upwards by the territorial correction (it is not very important for French Guiana, but it is for Guadeloupe and Martinique). For 2007–8, INSEE gives exports of goods and services in the national accounts, and I deducted merchandise exports to derive service exports. I estimated service exports in 1968, when the space station started, on the assumption that they were the same proportion of total exports as in 1993, and then interpolated the intervening years. Before 1968 service exports were not important, so I assumed they were only 10 per cent of total exports.

Guadeloupe

There are data on service exports from 1993–2006 in INSEE. By this time services were very important as a share of total exports. For 2007, INSEE gives exports of goods and services in the national accounts, and I deducted merchandise exports to derive service exports. The year 2008 is an estimate (for treatment of St Barthélemy and St Martin in 2008, see Table D.6 above). In the

absence of detailed information on service exports before 1993, I assumed that they were 30 per cent of total exports in 1960 and interpolated the intervening years. As with French Guiana (see above), I added the territorial correction to service exports.

Martinique

There are data on service exports from 1993 to 2006 in INSEE. By this time services were very important as a share of total exports. For 2007, INSEE gives exports of goods and services in the national accounts, and I deducted merchandise exports to derive service exports. The year 2008 is an estimate. In the absence of detailed information on service exports before 1993, I assumed that they were 30 per cent of total exports in 1960 and interpolated the intervening years. As with French Guiana (see above), I added the territorial correction to service exports.

Dutch Territories

Dutch Antilles

Commercial service exports are first recorded in 1968 in WDI. For earlier years I assumed that services were the same proportion of exports of goods and services as in 1968. The year 2008 is an estimate.

Aruba

Commercial service exports from 1986 are in WDI.

US Territories

Puerto Rico

Service exports from 1970 (fiscal 1969–70) are in UND. For earlier years I constructed an index based on visitor arrivals in Carter (2006), vol.5, and spliced this to service exports in 1970.

US Virgin Islands

There are data on visitor expenditures in 1980 and from 1990 onwards in US Virgin Islands, Bureau of Economic Research, *Annual Tourism Indicators*. Before 1990 there are visitor arrival numbers in Carter (2006), vol.5, which I used to construct an index and splice to visitor expenditure in 1980 and 1990. This gave a series for tourism, and I assumed tourism was 80 per cent of service exports in 1960, falling to 50 per cent in 2008.

TABLE D.8. TOTAL EXPORTS

In general, this is the sum of Tables D.6 and D.7. In a few cases, however, exports of goods and services were obtained independently and were then used

to derive service exports by deducting merchandise exports in Table D.6. These cases (all British territories) are as follows:

Anguilla
There is a series in UNNA from 1970 in current US dollars, from which I derived service exports in 1970–87.

British Virgin Islands
There is a series in UNNA from 1970 in current US dollars, from which I derived service exports in 1970–2008.

Cayman Islands
There is a series in UNNA from 1970 in current US dollars, from which I derived service exports in 1970–2008.

Montserrat
There is a series in UNNA from 1970 in current US dollars, from which I derived service exports in 1970–2008.

Turks & Caicos
There is a series in UNNA from 1970 in current US dollars, from which I derived service exports in 1970–99.

TABLE D.9. TOTAL EXPORTS PRICE INDEX (2000=100)

The main sources are WDI, using exports of goods and services at current and constant (2000) prices, and UNNA, using exports of goods and services at current and constant (1990) prices in the national accounts. From these a price index for exports of goods and services (2000=100) can be derived. Because the data in WDI and UNNA are incomplete, various additional steps had to be taken to complete the table. These are explained below, but certain general principles have been applied.

First, there are estimates of exports of goods and services at constant prices in some official sources for years and countries for which there are no WDI and UNNA data. These include ECLAC, IDB and early editions of World Bank, *World Tables*. I have used these wherever possible, adjusting them to 2000 prices, and derived the export price index using total exports at current prices in Table D.8.

Second, where there are no official estimates of exports of goods and services at constant prices, I have separated merchandise from service exports, and constant price estimates have been constructed for both for missing years. The two have then been added together to give exports of goods and services at constant (2000) prices, from which an export price index can again be derived using Table D.8.

Third, merchandise exports have been separated into (a) commodities and (b) other goods. Commodity exports (e.g. sugar) have been estimated at constant (2000) prices for each country using volumes multiplied by 2000 unit values. Petroleum exports (gross or net) have been converted to constant prices using the US Bureau of Labor Statistics series (hereafter BLS-fuel) on processed fuel wholesale prices (data before 1998 in Carter (2006) and later years on BLS Web site). Other goods (the residual) have been converted to constant prices **either** using the export price index in MOxLAD for twenty-four nonfuel primary commodities weighted by value shares of commodities in world trade in each year[3] **or** using the US Bureau of Labor Statistics series (hereafter BLS-textiles) on textile and wearing apparel wholesale prices (data before 1998 in Carter (2006) and later years on BLS Web site). The reason is that for some countries 'other goods' are mainly commodities, but in other cases they are dominated by assembled goods (especially textiles and clothing). Merchandise exports at constant (2000) prices are then the sum of commodity and other goods at constant (2000) prices.

Fourth, where necessary, service exports have been converted to constant prices using an index of volume based on tourist arrivals. This series is taken from WDI (1995–2008), CARICOM database (1990–4), Chernick (1978), Hope (1986), UNSY, Caribbean Tourism Organization (CTO) and national sources for other years and/or other countries. There are also data for 1980 and 1985 for all countries in Thomas (1988). Where this was not possible, service exports have been converted to constant prices using the GDP deflator derived from Tables D.18 and D.19.

Where the export price index is derived from official data based on exports of goods and services at constant prices, the data are colour-coded black. In other cases, they are colour-coded red.

Hispaniola

Haiti

There are no WDI data. There is, however, a series in UNNA that I used. CEPAL (2010) has exports of goods and services from 1990 at 2000 prices (there are also data on exports of goods and services at 1988 prices from 1980 in IDB (1990, 1991 and 1992)). Before 1970, I first estimated merchandise exports at constant (2000) prices using raw sugar, bauxite, cacao, coffee and other goods (the price for raw sugar in 2000 was taken from the Dominican Republic, because Haiti no longer exported sugar; for bauxite I constructed an index using Jamaican prices from 1960 to 1969; for other goods I used the

---

[3] Because MOxLAD finishes in 2000, I have extended the series to 2008 using the IMF nonfuel commodity series in IFS – hence the index is called MOxLAD/IFS.

BLS-textiles index because Haiti was a major exporter of apparel). For services before 1970, I used the GDP deflator to convert current to constant (2000) prices.

Dominican Republic
The WDI series covers all years.

Cuba

There are no WDI data, but there is a series in UNNA. However, this gives implausible results for 1970–84 because it is derived 'by applying the average share of the items of the following five years'. CEPAL (2010) has exports of goods and services at constant prices from 1990, so I used this instead. Before 1990, service exports were not important, so the index for earlier years can be based on merchandise exports. There is a series for merchandise exports at constant prices in Vidal and Fundora (2008). This uses an unpublished export series in constant (1997) prices from 1950 to 2005, based on data provided by ONE and Instituto Nacional de Investigación Económica (INIE), that the authors made available to me. I therefore used the export price index from 1990 to estimate exports of goods and services at 2000 prices, then spliced the ONE/INIE series to it to estimate exports of goods and services at constant prices back to 1960 and finally divided the current by constant price series to estimate the export price index before 1990.

CARICOM

Antigua
The WDI data start in 1977 and stop in 2002. There is also a series in UNNA, which I used. For the earlier years I separated merchandise and service exports. The merchandise exports are sugar, cotton, petroleum (net) and other goods. Because neither sugar or cotton were exported in 2000, I have converted to constant prices using the average CARICOM sugar price and the average Caribbean cotton price. I used the BLS-fuel index for petroleum (net) and the MOxLAD/IFS index for other goods. Service exports at constant prices are based on the volume of tourist arrivals.

The Bahamas
The WDI data start in 1989 and stop in 2004. There is also a series in UNNA that I used. For the years before 1970, merchandise exports consist of raw sugar, refined sugar (both re-exports), petroleum and other goods. To construct the constant price series, I used the sugar prices in 2000 and the BLS-fuel index. Other goods have been converted using the MOxLAD/IFS index. Service exports before 1970 have been converted to constant prices using tourist arrivals.

Barbados
The WDI data start in 1991 and end in 2003. There is also a UNNA series from 1970 to 2008 at constant prices in US dollars. From 1965 to 1970 there are data on exports of goods and services in current and constant (1976) prices in World Bank, *World Tables* (1980) and (1984). I used UNNA from 1970 to 2008 and *World Tables* from 1965 to 1970 to form an index of export prices from 1965 to 2008. For 1960–4, I separated goods and services. Goods at constant (2000) prices were estimated using raw sugar and other goods, with the latter adjusted to constant prices using the MOxLAD/IFS index. Services at constant prices were estimated using an index of tourist arrivals.

Belize
The WDI data start in 1980 and finish in 2007. There is also a UNNA series from 1970 to 2008 in 1990 US dollars. However, this gives implausible results for the 1980s because too much weight is given to re-exports. I therefore used WDI and extended it from 2007 to 2008 with UNNA. From 1960 to 1980, I used my estimates of domestic exports at constant prices (see Chapter 11) to derive an export price index for those years and spliced it to the WDI index (because service exports were such a small part of total exports in those years, it is legitimate to base the export price index on goods only).

Dominica
The WDI data start in 1977 and finish in 2006. There is also a series in UNNA that I used. For years before 1970, I separated merchandise and service exports. In the case of merchandise exports, I converted bananas and cacao exports to 2000 prices using country data on volumes and values (same sources as for Table D.5). Other goods were then converted to constant (2000) prices using the MOxLAD/IFS series. Service exports before 1970 were adjusted using the GDP deflator.

Grenada
There are no WDI data. There is, however, a series in UNNA. For earlier years, I first estimated merchandise exports at constant (2000) prices using volumes for refined sugar, bananas, cacao, cotton and nutmeg. The volume data are from the same sources as for Table D.5, except nutmeg, which is from FAOSTAT from 1961 onwards and from Table C.5 for 1960. Prices are derived from volume and value data in 2000 for Grenada, except cotton, which was no longer exported. This price is the same as used for Antigua (see above). Other merchandise exports were then converted to constant prices using the MOxLAD/IFS index. Service exports were converted to constant prices using the GDP deflator.

Guyana
The WDI series covers all years up to 2002. I used it from 1960 to 2000, and I used UNNA from 2000 to 2008.

Jamaica

There are no WDI data and no data on exports of goods and services at constant prices in ECLAC. There is, however, a series in UNNA and a series from 1965 to 1970 in World Bank, *World Tables* (1980) and (1984). For years before 1965, I converted series on sugar, molasses, bananas, tobacco leaf, citrus, cacao and coffee, petroleum (net), bauxite/alumina and other goods from current to constant (2000) values using the same sources as for Table D.5 (the price for molasses was the Caribbean average because Jamaica had stopped exporting by then; the price index for petroleum was BLS-fuel; the price index for bauxite was derived from UNYITS; the price index for other goods was MOxLAD because Jamaica was not yet a major exporter of assembled goods). For services before 1965, I used tourist arrivals.

St Kitts & Nevis

There are no WDI data and no official estimates of exports of goods and services at constant prices. There is a series in UNNA from 1970, but using it gives implausible results for the export price index (this is because of a doubling of exports of goods and services at constant prices in UNNA between 1999 and 2000 for which there is no supporting evidence). I therefore separated goods and services in all years, disaggregating merchandise exports into sugar and other goods. I adjusted sugar to constant prices using the unit value in 2000 (data on sugar are from the same sources as for Table D.5). I adjusted other goods using the MOxLAD/IFS index. Service exports were adjusted to constant prices using visitor arrivals back to 1968. Before 1968, I used the GDP deflator.

St Lucia

There are no WDI data and no official estimates of exports of goods and services at constant prices. There is a series in UNNA from 1970, but – as in the case of St Kitts & Nevis – using it gives implausible results for the export price index. I therefore separated goods and services in all years, disaggregating merchandise exports into bananas, cacao and other goods. I adjusted bananas and cacao to constant prices using the unit value in 2000 (because there were no cacao exports in 2000, I used 1998 because it was the nearest year). Data on bananas and cacao are from the same sources as for Table D.5. I adjusted other goods using the MOxLAD/IFS index. Service exports were adjusted to constant prices using visitor arrivals back to 1964. Before 1964, I assumed no change in prices.

St Vincent

The WDI series runs from 1977 to 2003. There is also a series in UNNA that I used. Before 1970, I separated merchandise exports into bananas and other goods, adjusting bananas to constant prices using the unit value in 2000. Data on bananas are from the same sources as for Table D.5. I adjusted other goods using the MOxLAD/IFS index. Service exports before 1970 were adjusted to constant prices using the GDP deflator.

Suriname
There are no data in WDI or ECLAC. There is a series in UNNA, but it is impossible to use because it is corrupted by exchange rate changes (exports of goods and services at constant prices appear to increase by 900% between 1992 and 1993, for example). However, Inter-American Development Bank (IDB), *Economic and Social Progress in Latin America* (various years) **did** estimate exports of goods and services at constant prices between 1982 and 1995. Because this includes the years when the currency was depreciating rapidly, I decided to use it. For all other years, I separated merchandise exports into bauxite/alumina, petroleum (gross), gold and other goods. The current values of the first three are taken from the same sources as Table D.5, and they were converted to constant (2000) prices using the IFS bauxite/alumina index, the MOxLAD/IFS index for petroleum and the IFS index for gold. Other goods were converted to constant prices using the MOxLAD/IFS index for nonfuel commodities. Services were adjusted to constant prices using visitor arrivals after 1975 and the GDP deflator derived from Tables D.18 and D.19 for earlier years. The estimate of exports of goods and services at constant (2000) prices was then adjusted to incorporate the IDB figures for 1982–95.

Trinidad & Tobago
The WDI series runs from 1960 to 2005. I used it to 2000. From then onwards I used the series in UNNA.

British Territories

Anguilla
There are no WDI data, but there is a complete series from 1970 in UNNA that I used (there is no need for earlier years because the Anguilla series starts in 1970). Because exports are dominated by services and GDP by exports, the series is virtually the same as the GDP deflator (as a result, the NBTT is approximately 100 in all years).

British Virgin Islands
There are no WDI data, but there is a series in UNNA from 1970 to 2008 at constant prices in US dollars. I converted this to 2000 prices and used it to derive the export price index from 1970 onwards. For earlier years, I used the GDP deflator for total exports (merchandise exports were already very small). Because exports are dominated by services and GDP by exports, the series is virtually the same as the GDP deflator (as a result, the NBTT is approximately 100 in all years).

Cayman Islands
There are no WDI data, but there is a series in UNNA from 1970 onwards. For earlier years, I converted merchandise exports to constant (2000) prices

using the MOxLAD/IFS index, and I converted service exports using the GDP deflator.

Montserrat
There are no WDI data, but there are in UNNA from 1970 onwards. This gives an implausible result in 1984, which I assume is caused by a typographical error in UNNA's constant price estimate for that year. I therefore interpolated 1984. Before 1970, I used the GDP deflator to convert total exports from current to constant prices. Because exports are dominated by services and GDP by exports, the series is virtually the same as the GDP deflator (as a result, the NBTT is approximately 100 in all years).

Turks & Caicos Islands
There are no WDI data, but there are in UNNA from 1970 onwards. For earlier years, I adjusted exports of goods and services to constant prices using the GDP deflator. Because exports are dominated by services and GDP by exports, the series is virtually the same as the GDP deflator (as a result, the NBTT is approximately 100 in all years).

French Territories

French Guiana
There are no WDI data and no official estimates of exports of goods and services at constant prices. I therefore separated merchandise exports into gold, shrimp and other goods. The gold volume data are from Table C.5 for 1960, Pétot (1986), Taubira-Delannon (n.d.), UNYITS, *Annuaire de la Guyane* and INSEE for recent years. Prices are from UNYITS and *Annuaire de la Guyane Française*, and I have used the IFS gold price index for missing years. Values are either from the sources already mentioned or are obtained by multiplying the quantity by the price. The shrimp data are in *Annuaire de la Guyane Française*, FAOSTAT (fisheries) and INSEE. Other goods have been converted to constant prices using the BLS-textile index adjusted for changes in the rate of exchange to the US dollar. Service exports were converted to constant prices using the GDP deflator.

Guadeloupe
There are no WDI data and no official estimates of exports of goods and services at constant prices. I therefore separated merchandise exports into sugar, bananas, rum and other goods. The conversion to constant prices was made with the same sources as for Table D.5 in the case of sugar and bananas using the price in 2000. For rum, I compiled a series on volume and value using UNYITS, *Annuaire Statistique de la Guadeloupe* and INSEE for more recent years, with all volume data converted to hectolitres and all values to US dollars. Because rum, sugar and bananas have separate series, other goods are essentially manufactures and are mainly sold to France (in francs/euros). I therefore converted

them to constant prices using the BLS-textile index adjusted for changes in the rate of exchange to the US dollar. Service exports were converted to constant prices using the GDP deflator.

Martinique

There are no WDI data and no official estimates of exports of goods and services at constant prices. I therefore separated merchandise exports into sugar, bananas, rum, petroleum (net) and other goods. The conversion to constant prices was made with the same sources as for Table D.5 in the case of sugar and bananas using the price in 2000 (in the case of sugar, no longer exported by then, I used the Guadeloupe price). For rum, I compiled a series on volume and value using UNYITS, *Annuaire Statistique de la Martinique* and INSEE for more recent years, with all volume data converted to hectolitres and all values to US dollars. For petroleum (net), I used the same source for current values as for Table D.5 and converted to constant prices using the BLS-fuel index. Because rum, sugar and bananas have separate series, other goods are essentially manufactures and are mainly sold to France (in francs/euros). I therefore converted them to constant prices using the BLS-textile index adjusted for changes in the rate of exchange to the US dollar. Service exports were converted to constant prices using the GDP deflator.

Dutch Territories

Dutch Antilles

There are no WDI data. There is, however, a series in UNNA from 1970. Because this excludes Aruba in all years, it is necessary to add back Aruba for 1970–85. Because the UNNA series excludes petroleum exports, I used a weighted average of the nonfuel export price index derived from UNNA and the petroleum export price index derived from the BLS-fuel index, the weights being determined by the share of refined oil (margin only) in total exports. For earlier years, I separated goods into petroleum (net) and other goods, deflating the former by the BLS-fuel index and the latter by BLS-textiles index (commodity exports were not important for the Netherlands Antilles, so the MOxLAD/IFS index is not appropriate). I adjusted service exports by the GDP deflator.

Aruba

There are no WDI data on exports of goods and services at constant prices, but there is a complete series in UNNA. The series in UNNA start in 1970, but Aruba only separated from Netherlands Antilles in 1986, so I used the series from then. Because the UNNA series excludes petroleum exports, I used a weighted average of the nonfuel export price index derived from UNNA and the petroleum export price index derived from the BLS-fuel index, the weights being determined by the share of refined oil (margin only) in total exports.

US Territories

Puerto Rico
The WDI series runs from 1971 to 2001, with a gap in 1990–1. The UNNA series cover all years from 1970, so I used it instead. For years before 1970, I separated merchandise exports into sugar, coffee, tobacco and other goods. I adjusted the first three to constant (2000) prices using the same sources as for Table D.5. Other goods were adjusted to 2000 prices using the BLS-textiles index. Service exports were adjusted to constant prices using visitor arrivals in Carter (2006), vol.5.

US Virgin Islands
There are no WDI data and no official estimates of exports of goods and services at constant prices. I therefore separated merchandise exports into petroleum (net) and other goods. I adjusted the former to constant prices using the BLS-fuel index and the latter using the BLS-textiles index. Service exports were adjusted to constant prices using visitor arrivals. These are given in Carter (2006), vol.5, up to 1997 and in USVI, Bureau of Economic Research, *Annual Tourism Indicators* for later years. Visitor arrivals include excursionists and tourists.

TABLE D.10. TOTAL EXPORTS AT 2000 PRICES

This is obtained by dividing total exports (goods and services) in Table D.8 by the price index for total exports (goods and services) in Table D.9.

TABLE D.11. MERCHANDISE IMPORTS

This table records merchandise imports (i.e. the sum of imports for domestic consumption and imports for re-export). The source for 1960 for all countries is Table C.18. In the case of those countries whose oil exports were based on imports of crude oil, I have deducted 90 per cent of the value of the gross oil exports from imports (the net oil exports – assumed to be 10% of the gross value – are derived from the sources in Table D.5). From 1961 onwards the source for Table D.11 is merchandise imports in WDI, with the following exceptions:

CARICOM

Antigua
From 1961 to 1976 the figures are taken from IFS because they are less rounded than in WDI. Imports are net of fuel imports in 1967–75, and fuel imports are assumed to be 90 per cent of fuel exports (see Table D.6 above).

Bahamas
As with merchandise exports, great care needs to be taken in constructing this series because there is no consistency in the sources in the treatment of

oil imports and imports for re-export. For 1961–68, I used WDI without adjustment, because there were no oil exports. For 1969–72, I deducted the estimated value of oil from merchandise imports in WDI, assuming imports were 90 per cent by value of oil exports. For 1973–89, I used the 1990 annual edition of IFS because it excludes oil for re-export from merchandise imports. For 1990–1, I used the balance of payments data in IFS because this excludes oil. From 1992 onwards, I used merchandise imports in WDI without adjustment because imports of oil for refined exports had ceased to be important.

Jamaica
The country starting exporting oil in 1964 based on imports of crude. Imports have therefore been adjusted by deducting 90 per cent of oil exports.

St Kitts & Nevis
For 1961–9, I used the 1985 edition of UNYITS, converting from Eastern Caribbean to US dollars. There are no data for 1962, which I therefore estimated by interpolation.

British Territories

Anguilla
Merchandise imports are in UND from 1988. For earlier years, I used the series on imports of goods and services at current US dollars in UNNA and assumed merchandise imports were the same share (80%) as in 1988.

British Virgin Islands
From 1961 to 1982, I have used UNYITS (there is a gap in 1978, which I have filled by interpolation). From 1970 there is a series on imports of goods and services (see Table D.13) in the UN database taken from the BVI national accounts, and I have assumed that merchandise imports were 75 per cent of imports of goods and services after 1982.

Cayman Islands
Merchandise imports were obtained from UNYITS for 1971–80 and from 1982 onwards from Cayman Islands, *Foreign Trade Statistics Report*. Before 1970, I used Cayman Islands (1992). The gaps (1970 and 1989) have been filled by interpolation.

Montserrat
Merchandise imports were taken from UNYITS and UND. Missing years (1966, 1969 and 1983–5) have been filled by interpolation.

Turks & Caicos Islands
Merchandise imports are in UND from 2000 onwards. For the earlier period, starting in 1973, the data are reported irregularly in the Economist Intelligence Unit, *Quarterly Report for Bahamas etc.*, but the data are too inconsistent to

be used. There is a series in UNNA on imports of goods and services from 1970. I therefore assumed that merchandise imports were the same ratio of total imports as in 2000. The gap from 1960 to 1970 was filled by interpolation, using the 1960 figure in Table C.8 as the starting point.

French Territories

French Guiana

The revised series covers 1993–2006 and is available from INSEE, but 2006 was subsequently revised again. It disaggregates merchandise and service imports. For 2006–8, merchandise imports are from *L'Année Economique et Sociale de la Guyane*. Before 1993, I have used two sources. The first series is UNYITS, which can be used until 1987. The second is Besson and Dablin (1995), which gives imports of goods and services before 1993. This is the only series consistent with the revised INSEE series. I therefore calculated services in 1987 as the difference between imports of goods and services and merchandise imports, estimated services by interpolation for 1988–92 and made merchandise imports the residual for those years.

Guadeloupe

The revised series covers 1993–2006 and is available from INSEE. For 2007–8, merchandise imports are from *L'Année Economique et Sociale de Guadeloupe*. It disaggregates merchandise and service imports. For 2007 merchandise imports are from *L'Année Economique et Sociale*, and for 2008 I have used the growth rate in order to include St Barthélemy and St Martin. Before 1993 I have used UNYITS.

Martinique

The revised series covers 1993–2006 and is available from INSEE. It disaggregates merchandise and service imports. For 2007–8, merchandise imports are from *L'Année Economique et Sociale de Martinique*. Before 1993, I have used UNYITS. I have adjusted merchandise imports for oil imports (assumed to be 90% of oil exports).

Dutch Territories

Dutch Antilles

WDI has a series on merchandise imports in all years up to 1985, from which I deducted 90 per cent of the value of gross oil exports. Imports are therefore net of crude oil imported for re-export. From 1986 onwards, the Netherlands Antilles switched to a different methodology, under which oil refining is treated as offshore. As a result, the import of goods in the balance of payments refers to non-oil imports only. This series is reported in IFS, and I used it from 1986 (this is also the year when Aruba separated from the Netherlands Antilles). In the Netherlands Antilles and Aruba retained imports are only a small part

of merchandise imports because most goods are re-exported through duty-free zones.

Aruba

The WDI series begins in 1986, after Aruba separated from the Netherlands Antilles. The merchandise imports exclude imports of oil for refining after the refinery restarted in 1991 (it had been closed in 1985). Merchandise imports are dominated by goods subsequently re-exported.

US Territories

Puerto Rico

Merchandise imports starting in fiscal 1969–70 are in UND. I have allocated the fiscal year to the later of the two calendar years (i.e. 1969–70 = 1970). For the years before 1970, there is a series in Carter (2006), vol.5. Although some merchandise imports consist of crude oil for refining and export, it is a small proportion of the total, and I have therefore made no adjustment to the series.

US Virgin Islands

There are numbers for 1980 and series starting in 1990 in US Virgin Islands, Bureau of Economic Research, *Annual Economic Indicators* (various years), which separate oil and non-oil merchandise imports. Before 1990, I used the series on merchandise imports in Carter (2006), vol. 5. I estimated fuel imports before 1980 and between 1981 and 1989 by multiplying fuel exports by 90 per cent. Net imports were then calculated as non-oil imports.

TABLE D.12. SERVICE IMPORTS

This table records commercial service imports, and the main source is WDI. However, there are many gaps in WDI because the data rarely go back before the 1970s, even for those countries for which WDI has figures. For those countries in WDI, the gaps were filled by assuming that service imports were the same share of merchandise imports in the missing years as in the first year for which they are recorded. For other countries, the procedure was as follows:

Hispaniola

Haiti

Commercial service imports are first recorded in 1971 in WDI. However, CEPAL (2009) has a series on service imports in the balance of payments starting in 1950. For those years where the two series overlap, the CEPAL series is higher. I used it to construct an index and spliced this to the 1971 value in WDI.

Dominican Republic

CEPAL (2009) has a series on service imports in the balance of payments, which I used for the years before 1968 when the WDI series begins.

Cuba

There are no commercial service imports recorded in WDI. However, CEPAL (2010) has a series on service imports in the balance of payments starting in 1990. In its annual *Economic Survey of Latin America and the Caribbean*, ECLAC from 1978 to 1987 also provided imports of services in a table on Cuba's balance of payments in freely convertible currency (the 1986 figure must be a typographical error because it is three times bigger than the previous and subsequent year; I therefore assumed it should be $832 million and not $1,832 million). I deducted interest paid from service imports and interpolated the figures for 1988–9. For the years before 1978, I assumed services were 5 per cent of imports of goods and services. There is a series on imports of goods and services at current dollars from 1970 in UNNA, but this implies implausibly large imports of services in most years (up to 50%) when merchandise imports are deducted. The year 2008 is an estimate.

CARICOM

Barbados

CEPAL (2009) has a series on service imports in the balance of payments, which I used for the years before 1970, when the WDI series begins. The year 2008 is an estimate.

Guyana

CEPAL (2009) has a series on service imports in the balance of payments, which I used for the years before 1977, when the WDI series begins.

Jamaica

CEPAL (2009) has a series on service imports in the balance of payments, which I used for the years before 1976, when the WDI series begins.

Suriname

Commercial service imports are first recorded in 1977 in WDI. However, CEPAL (2009) has a series on service imports in the balance of payments starting in 1950. For those years where the two series overlap, the CEPAL series is lower. I used it to construct an index and spliced this to the 1977 value in WDI.

Trinidad & Tobago

CEPAL (2009) has a series on service imports in the balance of payments, which I used for the years before 1975, when the WDI series begins. The year 2008 is an estimate.

British Territories

Anguilla

Imports of services are in UND from 1988 to 2006. For 2007–8, they are the difference between imports of goods and services in IFS and merchandise imports in Table D.11. From 1970 to 1987, they are the difference between total (see Table D.13) and merchandise imports.

British Virgin Islands

These are assumed to be the difference between imports of goods and services (Table D.13) and merchandise imports (Table D.11).

Cayman Islands

It is only from 2006 that the Cayman Islands Statistics Office is able to report imports of services (in Cayman Islands, *Balance of Payments Report*). This shows that services were 40 per cent of imports of goods and services. For earlier years, I assumed that services were the difference between total imports (see Table D.13) and merchandise imports in Table D.11. This gives a plausible ratio of services to total imports in most years, but in the early 1980s it is probably too low. For the years before 1970, I assumed merchandise imports were 60 per cent of total imports and used this to derive service imports as the residual.

Montserrat

There is a series on total imports of goods and services from 1970 (see Table D.13). I deducted merchandise imports in Table D.11 to derive service imports. The implied ratio of service to total imports is plausible in most years, but it is probably too low in 1972 and 1974. For years before 1970, I assumed merchandise imports were 90 per cent of total imports and derived service imports as the residual.

Turks & Caicos Islands

Service imports from 2000 are in UND. From 1970 to 1999, I used the series on total imports (see Table D.13) and derived service imports as the difference between total and merchandise imports. Before 1970, I estimated total imports assuming merchandise imports were the same proportion of the total as in 1970 and derived service imports as the residual. The year 2008 is an estimate.

French Territories

French Guiana

There are data on service imports from 1993 to 2006 in the INSEE revised national accounts. For 2007–8, I assumed they were the same proportion of merchandise imports as in 2006. From 1987 to 1992, I estimated services as stated in Table D.11 above. I then assumed that services were 10 per cent of imports of goods and services in 1960 and estimated the intervening years by

interpolation. Although Besson and Dablin (1995) and INSEE (1990) claim to have a series on imports of goods and services back to 1975, these series in fact refer to merchandise imports before 1987.

Guadeloupe
There are data on service imports from 1993 to 2006 in the INSEE revised national accounts. For 2007–8, I assumed they were the same proportion of merchandise imports as in 2006. In the absence of detailed information on service imports before 1993, I assumed that services were the same proportion of imports of goods and services as in 1993.

Martinique
There are data on service imports from 1993 to 2006 in the INSEE revised national accounts. For 2007–8, I assumed they were the same proportion of merchandise imports as in 2006. In the absence of detailed information on service imports before 1993, I assumed that services were the same proportion of imports of goods and services as in 1993.

Dutch Territories

Dutch Antilles
Commercial service imports are first recorded in 1968 in WDI. I assumed services in earlier years were the same proportion of imports of goods and services as in 1968. The year 2008 is an estimate.

Aruba
Commercial service imports are first recorded in WDI in 1986.

US Territories

Puerto Rico
Service imports from 1970 (fiscal 1969–70) are in UND. Before 1970, I assumed that services were the same proportion of imports of goods and services as in 1970.

US Virgin Islands
I assumed that services were 10 per cent of imports of goods and services in all years.

TABLE D.13. TOTAL IMPORTS

These are the sum of merchandise imports (Table D.9) and imports of services (Table D.10). In a few cases, however, imports of goods and services were obtained directly. These cases were as follows:

Anguilla. There is a series in UNNA from 1970, which I used to estimate merchandise and service imports before 1988.

British Virgin Islands. There is a series starting in 1970 in UND taken from the BVI national accounts (there are no data for 1990–4, so I have filled these years by interpolation). There is also a complete series in UNNA from 1970, but it is much lower than UND until 1995, after which the two series are the same. I used the UND series to estimate merchandise and service imports after 1982.

Cayman Islands. There is a series in UNNA from 1970, which I used to derive service imports before 2006 by deducting merchandise imports in Table D.11.

Montserrat. There is a series in UNNA from 1970, which I used to derive service imports by deducting merchandise imports in Table D.11.

Turks & Caicos Islands. There is a series in UNNA from 1970, which I used up to 2000 to derive service imports by deducting merchandise imports in Table D.11.

TABLE D.14. TOTAL IMPORTS PRICE INDEX (2000=100)

There are series on imports of goods and services at current and constant prices since 1970 for most countries in UNNA. Unfortunately, these cannot be used to derive an import price index because they are generally not independent of the export price index (this means that the implied NBTT is close to 100 in all years). There are, however, data for some countries and some years in WDI.

In the Caribbean there is a close correlation between import prices and the GDP deflator as a result of the high degree of openness of each economy to foreign trade. I therefore filled any gaps in the WDI data using the GDP deflator as a proxy for import prices. It is obtained by dividing GDP at current prices (Table D.18) by GDP at constant prices (Table D.19).

This method is not ideal, but it is the best that is available until more accurate ways can be found of measuring independently export and import prices.

The only country for which an exception was made is Cuba, because the GDP deflator is not a good proxy for the import price. I used CEPAL (2010) from 1995 onwards to derive an import price index from imports of goods and services at current and constant (2000) prices. There is a series for merchandise imports at constant prices in Vidal and Fundora (2008). This uses an unpublished import series in constant (1997) prices from 1950 to 2005, based on data provided by ONE and INIE, that the authors made available to me. I therefore used the import price index from 1995 to estimate imports of goods and services at 2000 prices, then spliced the ONE/INIE series to it to estimate imports of goods and services at constant prices back to 1960 and finally divided the current by constant price series to estimate the import price index before 1995. The ONE/INIE series and the CEPAL are very similar from 1995, but not between 1990 and 1995, which is why I only used CEPAL from 1995.

TABLE D.15. TOTAL IMPORTS AT 2000 PRICES

This is obtained by dividing total imports (goods and services) in current prices (Table D.13) by the price index for total imports (goods and services) in Table D.14.

TABLE D.16. NET BARTER TERMS OF TRADE (2000=100)

This is obtained by dividing the price index for total exports (goods and services) in Table D.9 by the price index for total imports (goods and services) in Table D.14.

TABLE D.17. INCOME TERMS OF TRADE (2000=100)

This is obtained by multiplying the NBTT in Table D.16 by an index (2000=100) formed from total exports (goods and services) at constant (2000) prices in Table D.10.

TABLE D.18. GROSS DOMESTIC PRODUCT

The main sources for GDP at current prices in US dollars are WDI, UND, UNNA and CEPAL (2009). Gaps have been filled as explained below.

Cuba

There is a series in CEPAL (2009) starting in 1985. For earlier years, I used the series, starting in 1962, in MOxLAD in local currency units and converted this to current US dollars at the official exchange rate shown in Table D.4 (in most years this was unity). I then spliced this to the CEPAL figure for 1985. There is a series at current prices from 1950 to 1958 in MOxLAD, so the problem is how to fill the missing three years (1959–61) in a way that is consistent with the earlier series. Because the percentage annual change in current GDP is roughly equal to the percentage change in real GDP plus the percentage change in prices, I took the annual growth at constant prices from Table D.19 (see below) and then assumed a value for the GDP deflator of 6.5 per cent in 1959 and 10 per cent in each year between 1960 and 1962. These figures for the GDP deflator are higher than the estimates of inflation (Mesa-Lago (2000), p. 180, gives the official estimate of annual inflation in 1959–61 as 2.0% and in 1963–5 as 5.7% (table III.4, p. 351)). However, the GDP deflator in those years is likely to have been much higher, because consumer price inflation was repressed by price controls.

CARICOM

Antigua
There is a series in WDI that starts in 1977. I then used the UNNA series back to 1974. There is a series in Chernick (1978), table SA2.6, from 1960 to 1974

in Eastern Caribbean (EC) dollars at factor cost. I converted this to GDP at market prices in US dollars using the exchange rate in Table D.4 and spliced it to the WDI/UNNA series.

Bahamas
The latest WDI series stops in 2007. I therefore used the 2007–8 growth rate in earlier versions to derive 2008.

Dominica
There is a series starting in 1970 in UNNA. There is a series in Chernick (1978), table SA2.7, from 1961 to 1970 in EC dollars at factor cost, and for 1960 the figure is in O'Loughlin (1968), p. 94. I used this to estimate GDP at market prices in US dollars.

Grenada
There is a series starting in 1977 in WDI and a series in Chernick (1978) from 1960 to 1974. I used this to calculate GDP at market prices in US dollars and filled the gap in 1975–6 by splicing to the series in UNNA. It is not possible to use UNNA for years before 1974 because the metadata in UNNA state that GDP in 1970–2 was 'derived by applying the backward trend of GDP at current prices'. This gives a figure that is far too low.

St Lucia
There is a series starting in 1979 in WDI, and this can be extended back to 1975 using CEPAL (2009) and 1973 using UNNA. There is a series in Chernick (1978) from 1961 to 1973, and for 1960 the figure is in O'Loughlin (1968), p. 94. The estimate of GDP implies a ratio of public revenue to GDP in 1960 of 27.8 per cent, which is consistent with the share of public administration in GDP given in Chernick (1978), table SA2.11, p. 293, for 1963 and in O'Loughlin (1963), p. 140, for 1961 (these are the first years in which GDP is disaggregated by sector).

Suriname
There are no gaps in the series, but the depreciation of the currency reduces the current dollar value of GDP dramatically between 1988 and 1989. Because the official devaluation was not until 1994, this means that the WDI series is based on an unofficial exchange rate after 1988. This is indeed the case, as can be seen by comparing GDP at current prices in national currency and US dollars in WDI, and this is the exchange rate I use in Table D.4.

British Territories

British Virgin Islands
There is a series in UNNA starting in 1970. From 1994 to 2008, however, I used the figures from the BVI Development Planning Unit (Web site) because they have been revised. There are no official figures for GDP before 1970, so I

proceeded as follows: I took the figure for public revenue at current dollars in 1960 (see Table C.28) and assumed that it represented 20 per cent of current GDP (this is a high ratio, but public revenue for BVI included grants-in-aid from the British government in that year). I then used exports and services in 1960 (see Table D.8) to calculate the export-to-GDP ratio in that year. This ratio is available for 1970 and is higher than in 1960 because of the rapid growth of service exports in the 1960s. I then interpolated the export-to-GDP ratio for the missing years assuming geometric growth. With this ratio it is possible to estimate GDP at current prices before 1970.

Cayman Islands

There is a series in UNNA starting in 1970. However, it does not use official figures before 1983. Instead, according to the metadata on the UNNA Web site, the figures from 1970 to 1982 are 'derived by applying the trend of GDP at current prices of the previous estimates'. This gives implausible results before 1983. I therefore took the figure for public revenue at current dollars in 1960 (see Table C.28) and assumed that it represented 20 per cent of current GDP (this is a high ratio, but public revenue for the Cayman Islands included grants-in-aid from the British government in that year). Detailed revenue figures for 1960 excluding grants-in-aid are in Cayman Islands (1992), table 6.02. I then used merchandise imports in 1960 (see Table D.11) to calculate the import-to-GDP ratio in that year. I then interpolated the import-to-GDP ratio for the missing years up to 1982, assuming geometric growth. With this ratio it is possible to estimate GDP at current prices before 1983.

Montserrat

There is a series in UNNA starting in 1970. There is also a series on GDP at factor cost starting in 1960 in Chernick (1978). I converted this to current dollars using the exchange rate in Table D.4 and spliced it to the UNNA series. The figure for 1960 implies that public revenue in 1960 (see Table C.28) was 53 per cent of GDP and the ratio of merchandise exports to GDP was only 7.5 per cent. The revenue ratio is much higher than for other countries, but most of it was grants-in-aid (see O'Loughlin (1963), pp. 152–3), so it is not implausible. Furthermore, the contribution of public administration to GDP in 1961–2 (the first years in which there is a disaggregation by sector) was very high, and that of export agriculture was very low (see Chernick (1978), table SA2.9, p. 291, and O'Loughlin (1963), p. 140).

Turks & Caicos Islands

There is a series in UNNA starting in 1970. There are no official figures for GDP before 1970, so I proceeded as follows: I took the figure for public revenue at current dollars in 1960 (see Table C.28) and assumed that it represented 20 per cent of current GDP. I then used exports and services in 1960 (see Table D.8) to calculate the export-to-GDP ratio in that year. This ratio is

available for 1970 and is higher than in 1960 because of the rapid growth of service exports in the 1960s. I then interpolated the export-to-GDP ratio for the missing years, assuming geometric growth. With this ratio it is possible to estimate GDP at current prices before 1970.

French Territories

French Guiana

The revised INSEE series runs from 1993 to 2006 and is given in euros. I converted this to current dollars (as explained in Table D.6 for merchandise exports). For 2007–8, I used the figures on GDP growth rates at current prices in *L'Année Economique et Sociale en Guyane* in INSEE and adjusted for the change in the euro/dollar rate. From 1975 to 1992, there is an earlier INSEE series in Besson and Dablin (1995), which is in French francs and consistent with the later series. I converted this to dollars and used it without further adjustment. There are no official figures before 1975. However, a series was constructed for 1952–60 in Blaise (1962) at 1958 prices. I took the 1960 figure, converted it to US dollars and made an adjustment for inflation between 1958 and 1960 using the figures in the same source. From 1960 to 1974, I assumed current GDP in dollars moved in line with current merchandise imports in Table D.11 (these were a very high proportion of GDP in this period). The figure for 1975 using this methodology is very close to the first year in the series in Besson and Dablin (1995).

Guadeloupe

The revised INSEE series starts in 1993 and is given in euros. I converted this to current dollars (as explained in Table D.6 for merchandise exports). For 2007–8, I used the figures on GDP growth rates at current prices in *L'Année Economique et Sociale en Guadeloupe* in INSEE and adjusted for the change in the euro/dollar. From 1970 to 1993 there is an earlier INSEE series in Besson and Dablin (1995), which is in French francs. I converted this to dollars and spliced this to the revised INSEE series. Before 1970, I assumed current GDP in dollars moved in line with merchandise imports in dollars (these were a very high proportion of GDP in this period).

Martinique

The revised INSEE series runs from 1993 to 2006 and is given in euros. I converted this to current dollars (as explained in Table D.6 for merchandise exports). For 2007–8, I used the figures on GDP growth rates at current prices in *L'Année Economique et Sociale en Martinique* in INSEE and adjusted for the change in the euro/dollar rate. From 1970 to 1993 there is an earlier INSEE series in Besson and Dablin (1995), which is in French francs. I converted this to dollars and spliced this to the revised INSEE series. Before 1970, I assumed current GDP in dollars moved in line with merchandise imports in dollars (these were a very high proportion of GDP in this period).

Dutch Territories

Dutch Antilles

There is a series for GDP from 1970 in UNNA (the metadata show that before 1979 the numbers were derived 'by applying the backward trend of GDP at current prices', so these figures should be treated with caution). Because this excludes Aruba, I added Aruba to the figures from 1970 to 1985. I then spliced the figures in current guilders in *Statistisch Jaarboek* for the Netherlands Antilles (converted to US dollars at the exchange rate in Table D.4) to the UNNA series. There are gaps in 1961–2 and 1969–70, which I filled assuming GDP at current prices moved in line with merchandise exports in current prices (see Table D.6). The Netherlands Antilles changed its methodology for measuring the national accounts on several occasions.

Aruba

There is a series for GDP from 1970 in UNNA, but I only used the figures from 1986 onwards when Aruba separated from the Netherlands Antilles.

US Territories

Puerto Rico

The WDI series stops in 2001. Because GDP is so much bigger than GNP in Puerto Rico and GNP is a better reflection of Puerto Rican economic performance, the *Statistical Abstract of the United States* now reports only GNP. The GDP series, however, is reported by the Puerto Rico Planning Board and can be found on the Junta de la Planificación de Puerto Rico Web site. In the interest of consistency with the rest of the Caribbean, I have used the GDP series in Table D.18. There is a series in UNNA from 1970, which gives the same results as the sources I used except that the figures are lagged by one year (e.g. UNNA in 2007 is 2008 in other source). This confusion is because of the fact that the fiscal year in Puerto Rico ends on June 30.

US Virgin Islands

There is a series in WDI, but it stops in 1993. It is taken from national sources, but it refers to Gross Territorial Product (GTP) because there were no GDP figures until recently. The GTP series was used by USVI authorities until 2006, but it was then stopped. It is available from USVI, Bureau of Economic Research, *Annual Economic Indicators*. In May 2010, the US Department of Commerce, Bureau of Economic Analysis, released the first ever figures on USVI GDP starting in 2002 and ending in 2007 (this shows that GDP was bigger than GTP in 2002 by nearly 30%). I spliced the GTP series for earlier years to the GDP figure for 2002. For 2008, I assumed that GDP moved in line with personal income, which is reported in USVI, Bureau of Economic Research, *Annual Economic Indicators*.

TABLE D.19. GROSS DOMESTIC PRODUCT (2000 PRICES)

The main sources for GDP at 2000 prices in US dollars are WDI, UNNA, UND and CEPAL (2009). The data in WDI and CEPAL are given in 2000 prices, and those in UNNA and UND are in 1990 prices. I therefore adjusted UNNA and UND data to 2000 prices. Any gaps have been filled as explained below.

The conversion of GDP in current dollars to GDP in constant dollars (2000 prices) requires the use of a GDP deflator in those years where there are no official figures. Given the stability of nominal exchange rates for most countries in the Caribbean, it is possible to use domestic inflation in local currency units (LCUs) as a proxy for the GDP deflator (see Table D.14). In those cases where the exchange rate changed significantly, however, inflation in LCUs must be adjusted for changes in the nominal exchange rate.

Cuba

There is a series in CEPAL (2009) starting in 1985. Cuba has never published GDP figures for 1959–84, but two Cuban economists have published an article (see Vidal and Fundora (2008)) making use of an unpublished GDP series in constant (1997) prices from 1950 to 2005, based on data provided by ONE and INIE, that they made available to me. I therefore used this before 1985 and spliced it to the CEPAL series (there is a very high correlation between the resulting series and the one obtained using the MOxLAD series at constant (1981) prices from 1962–2000).

CARICOM

Antigua
The series in WDI starts in 1977. I then used the UNNA series at constant (1990) prices and spliced it to the WDI series back to 1970. I then used the series on inflation in Chernick (1978), table SA11.1, to deflate the current price series in Table D.18. Because the Chernick series starts in 1962, I used the GDP deflator (derived from Tables D.18 and D.19) for the Bahamas for 1960–1.

Bahamas
The latest WDI series stops in 2007. I therefore used the 2007–8 growth rate in earlier versions to derive 2008.

Dominica
There is a series in UNNA at 1990 prices starting in 1970, which I converted to 2000 prices. I estimated the GDP deflator for earlier years using the consumer price index in Chernick (1978), p. 511. Because the Chernick series starts in 1962, I used the GDP deflator (derived from Tables D.18 and D.19) for the Bahamas for 1960–1.

Grenada

The WDI series starts in 1977. I used the series in UNNA at constant (1990) prices to splice the WDI series back to 1970. I then estimated the GDP deflator for earlier years using the inflation indices in Chernick (1978). Because the Chernick series starts in 1962, I used the GDP deflator (derived from Tables D.18 and D.19) for the Bahamas for 1960–1.

Jamaica

The WDI series starts in 1966. I estimated the GDP deflator for earlier years using the inflation indices in Chernick (1978). Because the Chernick series starts in 1962, I used the GDP deflator (derived from Tables D.18 and D.19) for the Bahamas for 1960–1.

St Kitts & Nevis

The series in WDI starts in 1977. I then used the UNNA series at constant (1990) prices and spliced the WDI series back to 1970. I then estimated the GDP deflator for earlier years using the inflation index in Chernick (1978). Because the Chernick series starts in 1962, I used the GDP deflator (derived from Tables D.18 and D.19) for the Bahamas for 1960–1.

St Lucia

There is a series starting in 1980 in WDI and a series starting in 1970 in UNNA at 1990 prices, which I converted to 2000 prices. I then estimated the GDP deflator for earlier years using the inflation index in Chernick (1978). Because the Chernick series starts in 1962, I used the GDP deflator (derived from Tables D.18 and D.19) for the Bahamas for 1960–1.

Suriname

The WDI series starts in 1975 (the year of independence). During the period before 1975, but not later, the nominal exchange rate was very stable. I therefore used the consumer price index in Table D.20 to extend the GDP deflator back to 1960.

British Territories

British Virgin Islands

There is a series in UNNA at 1990 prices starting in 1970, which I converted to 2000 prices. For earlier years I assumed that the GDP deflator in BVI was the same as in the Bahamas in view of the fact that both countries used the US dollar and were specialised in service exports. I then applied this deflator to GDP at current prices in Table D.18.

Cayman Islands

There is a series in UNNA at 1990 prices starting in 1970. I converted this to 2000 prices, but it cannot be used before 1983 for the same reasons as the series at current prices (see Table D.18 above). Before 1983, I deflated the current

price series using Cayman Islands inflation from 1980 (available in UND) and the GDP deflator for Antigua in earlier years (there are no reliable inflation figures for the Cayman Islands before 1980; there are some data on the cost of living before 1980 in Cayman Islands (1992), but not enough to form an index of consumer prices).

Montserrat

There is a series in UNNA starting in 1970 at 1990 prices, which I converted to 2000 prices. I then estimated the GDP deflator for earlier years using the inflation index in Chernick (1978). Because the Chernick series starts in 1962, I used the GDP deflator (derived from Tables D.18 and D.19) for the Bahamas for 1960–1.

Turks & Caicos Islands

There is a series in UNNA at 1990 prices starting in 1970, which I converted to 2000 prices. For earlier years I assumed that the GDP deflator in the Turks & Caicos Islands was the same as in the Bahamas in view of the fact that both countries used the US dollar and were specialised in service exports. I then applied this deflator to GDP at current prices in Table D.18.

French Territories

French Guiana

The constant price series is in general obtained from the series in current dollars in Table D.18 by use of a GDP deflator (2000=100). This deflator is the difference between the annual change in domestic prices in LCUs and the annual change in the nominal exchange rate derived from Table D.4 (INSEE gives the growth in real GDP in euros from 1994 to 2006 in its revised series and explains that this is based on deflating GDP in current prices by annual inflation in LCUs). For 2007–8, I used *L'Année Economique et Sociale en Guyane* in INSEE, which gives the growth of GDP in constant prices for these two years. Before 1993, I used the index of inflation in LCUs for French Guiana in INSEE (1990). This covers the years 1969–88, and for 1989–93, I used Bulmer-Thomas (2001a). For 1960–9, I used the GDP deflator for France in IFS.

Guadeloupe

The constant price series is obtained from the series in current dollars in Table D.18 by use of a GDP deflator (2000=100). This deflator is the difference between the annual change in domestic prices in LCUs and the annual change in the nominal exchange rate derived from Table D.4 (INSEE gives the growth in real GDP in euros from 1994 to 2006 in its revised series and explains that this is based on deflating GDP in current prices by annual inflation in LCUs). For 2007–8, I used *L'Année Economique et Sociale en Guadeloupe* in INSEE, which gives the growth of GDP in constant prices for these two

years. Before 1993, I used the index of inflation in LCUs for Guadeloupe in INSEE (1990). This covers the years 1967–88, and for 1989–93, I used Bulmer-Thomas (2001a). From 1960 to 1967, I used the GDP deflator for France in IFS.

Martinique
The constant price series is obtained from the series in current dollars in Table D.18 by use of a GDP deflator (2000=100). This deflator is the difference between the annual change in domestic prices in LCUs and the annual change in the nominal exchange rate derived from Table D.4 (INSEE gives the growth in real GDP in euros from 1994 to 2006 in its revised series and explains that this is based on deflating GDP in current prices by annual inflation in LCUs). For 2007–8, I used *L'Année Economique et Sociale en Martinique* in INSEE, which gives the growth of GDP in constant prices for these two years. Before 1993, I used the index of inflation in LCUs for Martinique in INSEE (1990). This covers the years 1966–88, and for 1989–93, I used Bulmer-Thomas (2001a). From 1960 to 1966, I used the GDP deflator for France in IFS.

Dutch Territories

Dutch Antilles
There are data at 1990 prices from 1970 in UNNA. Because these exclude Aruba, I added Aruba from 1970 to 1985. I then converted to 2000 prices. For the years before 1970. I deflated current GDP in Table D.18 using the consumer price index in various issues of *Statistisch Jaarboek*.

Aruba
There is a series in UNNA at 1990 prices from 1970. I only used the data from 1986 when Aruba separated from Netherlands Antilles. I then converted to 2000 prices.

US Territories

Puerto Rico
The WDI series stops in 2001. The GDP series at constant (1954) prices, however, is reported by the Puerto Rico Planning Board and can be found on the Junta de la Planificación de Puerto Rico Web site. I spliced this series to the World Bank series from 2000. It gives the same results as the constant price series in UNNA after 2000, provided that it is remembered that UNNA in year 't' is 't+1' in other sources.

US Virgin Islands
In May 2010, the US Department of Commerce, Bureau of Economic Analysis, released the first ever figures on USVI GDP at constant (2005) prices starting in 2002 and ending in 2007. There is a series for Gross Territorial Product (GTP)

in UND from 1970 to 1989 at 1982 prices. From 1990, the same series is reported until 2005 in USVI, Bureau of Economic Research, *Annual Economic Indicators*. In order to link the two series, it is necessary to estimate the figure for 1989, and I did this by adjusting the change in current price GDP for inflation (assumed to be the same as Puerto Rico in that year). I then converted the two series at 1982 and 2005 prices to 2000 prices. For the years before 1970, I assumed that the GDP deflator for USVI moved in line with Puerto Rico. For 2008, I assumed that GDP at constant prices moved in line with personal income at constant prices (see USVI, Bureau of Economic Research, *Annual Economic Indicators*).

TABLE D.20. ANNUAL INFLATION (%)

The main source is WDI followed by CEPAL (2009). To fill the gaps for the earlier years in the case of the former British colonies (including Montserrat) I used Chernick (1978), table SA11.1, followed by Bulmer-Thomas (2001a). For recent years in the British Overseas Territories, I used official sources, the databases of the Caribbean Development Bank and of the Eastern Caribbean Central Bank. For earlier years (except Montserrat), I used the GDP deflator derived from Tables D.18 and D.19. For the French territories, I used the consumer price index given in INSEE for each country from 1993 and Bulmer-Thomas (2001a) for earlier years. For Puerto Rico, I used Carter (2006), vol. 5, up to 1989 and the Junta de la Planificación de Puerto Rico Web site thereafter. For the US Virgin Islands, I used the GDP deflator until 2000 and USVI, Bureau of Economic Research, *Annual Economic Indicators* thereafter (a consumer price index started in 2001). For Cuba the sources are Mesa-Lago (2000), CEPAL (2010) and ECLAC (2010).

Bibliography

Electronic Sources

Anguilla (Statistics Unit). http://www.gov.ai/statistics/statistics.htm
Aruba (Central Bureau of Statistics). http://www.cbs.aw/cbs/home.do
The Bahamas (Department of Statistics). http://statistics.bahamas.gov.bs/
Barbados (Statistical Service). http://www.barstats.gov.bb/
Belize (Statistical Institute). http://www.statisticsbelize.org.bz/
Bibliography of the Netherlands Caribbean. http://opc-kitlv.oclc.org/
Bibliothèque Nationale de France. http://gallica.bnf.fr/
British Virgin Islands (Development Planning Unit). http://www.dpu.gov.vg/
Caribbean Centre for Money and Finance. http://www.ccmfuwi.org/
Caribbean Community (CARICOM) Secretariat. http://www.caricom.org/
Caribbean Development Bank (CDB). http://www.caribank.org/
Caribbean Tourism Organization (CTO). http://www.onecaribbean.org/
Cayman Islands (Economics and Statistics Office). http://www.eso.ky/
Conference Board. http://www.conference-board.org/data/economydatabase/
Cuba (Oficina Nacional de Estadísticas). http://www.one.cu/
Danish Virgin Islands. http://www.virgin-islands-history.dk/eng/
Digital Library of the Caribbean (DLOC). http://dloc.com/
Dominican Republic (Oficina Nacional de Estadísticas). http://www.one.gob.do/
Dutch Antilles (Central Bureau of Statistics). http://www.cbs.an/
Eastern Caribbean Central Bank (ECCB). http://www.eccb-centralbank.org/
Economic Commission for Latin America and the Caribbean (ECLAC/CEPAL).
    http://www.eclac.org/
Food and Agriculture Organization (FAOSTAT). http://faostat.fao.org/
Guyana (Bureau of Statistics). http://www.statisticsguyana.gov.gy/
Haiti (Institut Haitien de Statistique et d'Informatique). http://www.ihsi.ht/
Institut National de la Statistique et des Etudes Economiques (INSEE).
    http://www.insee.fr/
Inter-American Development Bank (IDB). http://www.iadb.org/
International Labour Organization (ILO) (Key Indicators of Labour Market).
    http://kilm.ilo.org/KILMnetBeta/

International Monetary Fund (IMF). http://www.imf.org/
Jamaica (Statistical Institute). http://statinja.gov.jm/
Maddison, Angus. http://www.conference-board.org/data/economydatabase
Mitchell's West Indian Bibliography. http://books.ai/10th/Bru-Buq.htm
Montevideo-Oxford Latin American Economic Database (MOxLAD). http://oxlad.qeh.
  ox.ac.uk/
Parliamentary Papers. http://www.portcullis.parliament.uk/
Puerto Rico (Junta de la Planificación de Puerto Rico). http://www.jp.gobierno.pr/
Suriname (Algemeen Bureau Voor de Statistiek). http://www.statistics-suriname.org/
Trinidad & Tobago (Central Statistical Office). http://www.cso.gov.tt/
Turks & Caicos Islands (Department of Economic Planning and Statistics).
  http://www.depstc.org/
United Nations, World Tourism Organization. http://unwto.org/en
United Nations, World Urbanization Prospects. http://esa.un.org/unup/
United Nations Conference on Trade and Development (UNCTAD).
  http://www.unctad.org/
United Nations Data (UND). http://data.un.org/
United Nations Millennium Development Goals (MDGs) Indicators.
  http://unstats.un.org/unsd/mdg/
United Nations National Accounts (UNNA).
  http://unstats.un.org/unsd/snaama/Introduction.asp
United States Bureau of Labor Statistics. http://www.bls.gov/
United States Department of Agriculture. http://www.usda.gov/
United States Department of Commerce. http://www.commerce.gov/
United States Energy Information Administration. http://www.eia.doe.gov/
United States Virgin Islands (Bureau of Economic Research). http://www.usviber.org/
World Bank, World Development Indicators (WDI). http://data.worldbank.org/

Official Sources

International Organizations

CARICOM. (2002). *Intra-Regional Trade, Volume I.* Georgetown, Guyana.
Comisión Económica para América Latina (CEPAL). (1958). *El Desarrollo económico
  de Cuba: Proyecto de investigación para el periodo 1951–1956.* Santiago.
Comisión Económica para América Latina y el Caribe (CEPAL). (1978). *Series
  Históricas del Crecimiento de América Latina.* Santiago.
Comisión Económica para América Latina y el Caribe (CEPAL). (2004). *Globalización
  y desarrollo: Desafíos de Puerto Rico frente al siglo XXI.* Mexico, DF.
Comisión Económica para América Latina y el Caribe (CEPAL). (2009). *América Lat-
  ina y el Caribe: Series históricas de estadísticas económicas 1950–2008.* Cuadernos
  Estadísticas, No. 37. Santiago.
Comisión Económica para América Latina y el Caribe (CEPAL). (2010). *Estudio
  económico de América Latina y el Caribe 2009–2010.* Santiago.
Economic Commission for Latin America (ECLA). (1966). *Statistical Bulletin for Latin
  America* 3:1. Santiago.
Economic Commission for Latin America and the Caribbean (ECLAC). (various years).
  Economic Survey of Latin America and the Caribbean. Santiago.

Economic Commission for Latin America and the Caribbean (ECLAC). (various years). *Statistical Yearbook for Latin America and the Caribbean*. Santiago.

Economic Commission for Latin America and the Caribbean (ECLAC). (2010). *Statistical Yearbook for Latin America and the Caribbean, 2010*. Santiago.

Food and Agriculture Organization (FAO). (1947). *Yearbook of Food and Agricultural Statistics*. Washington, DC.

Food and Agriculture Organization (FAO). (1961). *The World Coffee Economy*. Rome.

Food and Agriculture Organization (FAO). (various years). *Production Yearbook*. Rome.

Food and Agriculture Organization (FAO). (various years). *Trade Yearbook*. Rome.

Inter-American Development Bank (IDB). (various years). *Economic and Social Progress in Latin America*. Washington, DC.

International Bureau of the American Republics. (1893). *Haiti: a Handbook*. Washington, DC.

International Institute of Agriculture (IIA). (various years). *International Yearbook of Agricultural Statistics*. Rome.

International Monetary Fund (IMF). (various years). *Direction of Trade Statistics (DOTS)*. Washington, DC.

International Monetary Fund (IMF). (various years). *International Financial Statistics (IFS)*. Washington, DC.

League of Nations. (various years). *Statistical Yearbook*. Geneva.

Pan-American Union (PAU). (1952). *The foreign trade of Latin America since 1913*. Washington, DC.

United Nations. (1949). *Mission to Haiti*. New York.

United Nations. (2009). *International Trade Statistics*, 1900–60. New York.

United Nations Conference on Trade and Development (UNCTAD). (various years). *Handbook of Trade Statistics*. Geneva.

United Nations Yearbook of International Trade Statistics (UNYITS). (various years). New York.

World Almanac and Encyclopedia. (various years). New York: Press Pub. Co.

World Bank. (1980). *World Tables*. Baltimore: Johns Hopkins University Press.

World Bank. (1984). *World Tables*. Baltimore: Johns Hopkins University Press.

World Bank. (1989). *World Tables*. Baltimore: Johns Hopkins University Press.

World Bank. (1991). *World Tables*. Baltimore: Johns Hopkins University Press.

World Bank. (2005). *A Time to Choose: Caribbean Development in the 21st Century*. Washington, DC.

World Bank. (various years). *World Development Indicators*. Washington, DC.

Independent Countries

The Bahamas

Quarterly Statistical Digest. (various years). Nassau.

Barbados

Abstract of Statistics. (various years). Bridgetown.

Cuba

Anuario Estadístico de Cuba. (various years). Havana.
Banco Nacional de Cuba. (1957). *La Economía de Cuba, 1951–1957.* Havana.
Banco Nacional de Cuba. (1995). *Economic Report 1994.* Havana.
Oficina Nacional de Estadísticas (ONE). (2010). *Anuario Estadístico de Cuba 2009.* Havana.

Dominican Republic

Anuario Estadístico Dominicano. (various years). Santo Domingo.
Dominican Republic. (1975). *Primer censo nacional de República Dominicana, 1920.* Santo Domingo: Editora de la Universidad Autónoma de Santo Domingo.
United States, Bureau of Insular Affairs. (various years). *Report of the Dominican Customs Receivership.* Washington, DC.

Haiti

Chambres des Comptes. (1890). *La Chambre des Comptes au Sénat de la République.* Port-au-Prince.
Institut Haitien de Statistique. (1963). *Guide Economique de la République d'Haiti.* Port-au-Prince.

St Lucia

Annual Statistical Digest. (various years). Castries.

St Vincent

Digest of Statistics. (various years). Kingstown.

Trinidad & Tobago

Statistical Digest. (various years). Port of Spain.
Vision 2020. Draft National Strategic Plan. (2007). Port of Spain.

United States of America

Bureau of the Census (US). (1909). *Cuba: Population, History and Resources 1907.* Washington, DC.
Department of State. (various years). *Commercial Relations of the United States with Foreign Countries.* Washington, DC. (US Consular Reports).
Department of State. (1948). *Havana Charter for an International Trade Organization.* Washington, DC.
Department of State. (various years). *The World's Commerce.* Washington, DC.
Department of Treasury. (1984). *Tax Havens in the Caribbean Basin.* Washington, DC.
Statistical Abstract of the United States. (various years). Washington, DC.

Dependent Countries

British Territories

Blue Books. (various years for each colony). London.
Cayman Islands. (various years). *Balance of Payments Report.* George Town.
Cayman Islands. (1992). *Cayman Islands Historical Compendium of Statistics, 1774–1980.* George Town.
Cayman Islands. (various years). *Foreign Trade Statistics Report.* George Town.
Colonial Department. (1836). *Honduras: Account of the Expenses of the Government of Honduras defrayed by Taxes raised on the Inhabitants of that Settlement, from the beginning of the Year 1824 down to the present period, so far as the same can be made out.* London.
Colonial Office. (1950). *Monetary System of the Colonies.* London.
Colonial Reports. (various years for each colony). London.
Report of the British Guiana and British Honduras Settlement Commission (Evans Commission). (1948). London.
Report of the Royal Commission on trade relations between Canada and the West Indies. (1910). London.
Report of the West India Royal Commission (Norman Commission). (1897). London.
Statistical Abstract for the British Empire. (various years). London.
Statistical Abstract for the Principal and Other Foreign Countries. (various years). London.
Statistical Abstract for the several Colonial and other Possessions of the United Kingdom. (various years). London.
Statistical Tables Relating to the Colonial and other Possessions of the United Kingdom. (various years). London.
Sugar Policy: Proposals of His Majesty's Government (cmd. 4964). (1935). London.
Turks & Caicos Islands Statistics Office. (1989). *Statistical Yearbook.* Grand Turk.
West India Royal Commission, 1938–1939: Recommendations. (1940). London.
West India Royal Commission Report (Moyne Commission). (1945). London.

Dutch Territories

Algemeen Bureau voor de Statistiek Suriname. (1959). *Produktie: absolute cijfers.* The Hague.
Almanak voor de Nederlandsche West-Indische Bezittingen: En de kust van Guinea, voor het jaar 1856 (1856; 1858–1860). The Hague: Gebroeders van Cleef.
Jaarcijfers voor Suriname 1958–62. (1963). Paramaribo, Suriname.
Jaarcijfers voor Suriname 1960–65. (1966). Paramaribo, Suriname.
Statistisch Jaarboek: Nederlandse Antillen. (various years). Willemstad, Curaçao.
Statistical Yearbook: Netherlands Antilles. (various years). Willemstad, Curaçao.
Surinaamsche Almanak. (various years). Paramaribo, Suriname.

French Territories

Annuaire de la Guadeloupe. (various years). Paris.
Annuaire de la Guyane Française. (various years). Paris.

Annuaire de la Martinique. (various years). Paris.
Annuaire de la Vie Martiniquaise. (1946). Paris.
Annuaire Statistique de la Guadeloupe. (various years). Paris.
Annuaire Statistique de la Guyane Française. (various years). Paris.
Annuaire Statistique de la Martinique. (various years). Paris.
Annuaire Statistique d'Outre-Mer. (1949). Paris.
Budget des Recettes et des Dépenses pour la Guadeloupe. (various years). Point à Pitre.
Budget des Recettes et des Dépenses pour la Martinique. (various years). Fort de France.
Institut National de la Statistique et des Etudes Economiques (INSEE). (1990). *Annuaire Rétrospectif de la France, 1948–1988.* Paris.
Institut National de la Statistique et des Etudes Economiques (INSEE). (2009). *Sur Chômage aux Antilles-Guyane: des éléments d'explication.* Paris.
Ministère des Colonies. (various years). *Statistiques coloniales, etc. Renseignments généraux sur le commerce des colonies françaises et la navigation.* Paris.
Ministère des Colonies. (various years). *Statistiques coloniales, etc. Statistiques du commerce des colonies françaises.* Paris.

Scandinavian Territories

Statistisk Aarbog for Danmark. (various years). Copenhagen.
Statistiska Centralbyrån. (1863–5). 'Statistiska Upplysningar Rörande Svenska Kolonien St. Barthélemy.' *Statistisk Tidskrift Band II.* Stockholm: Norstedt & Söners, pp. 256–63.
Swedish National Archives. (various years). Stockholm.

US Territories

Annual Report of the Governor of the US Virgin Islands. (various years). Washington, DC.
Anuario Estadístico de Comercio Exterior de Puerto Rico. (various years). San Juan.
Anuario Estadístico de Puerto Rico. (various years). San Juan.
Anuario Estadístico de Puerto Rico: Estadísticas Históricas. (1959). San Juan.
Department of Commerce. (1920). *Birth and Mortality Statistics of the Virgin Islands of the United States, 1901–19.* Washington, DC.
Department of Commerce. (1931). *Mortality Statistics.* Washington, DC.
US Virgin Islands, Bureau of Economic Research. (various years). *Annual Economic Indicators.* Charlotte Amalie, St Thomas.
US Virgin Islands, Bureau of Economic Research. (various years). *Annual Tourism Indicators.* Charlotte Amalie, St Thomas.

Secondary Sources

Achéen, R. (1973). *Economie antillaise.* Fort de France: Desormeaux.
Adamson, A. H. (1972). *Sugar without slaves: The political economy of British Guiana, 1838–1904.* New Haven: Yale University Press.
Ahvenainen, J. (1996). *The history of the Caribbean telegraphs before the First World War.* Helsinki: Suomalainen Tiedeakatemia.
Aldcroft, D. H. (1993). *The European economy, 1914–1990.* 3rd ed. London: Routledge.

Alienes, U. J. (1950). *Características fundamentales de la economía cubana*. Havana: Banco Nacional de Cuba.

Alm, J. (2006). 'Assessing Puerto Rico's Fiscal Policies.' In Collins, S. M., Bosworth, B., and Soto-Class, M. A. (eds.), *The economy of Puerto Rico: Restoring growth*, pp. 319–98. San Juan: Center for the New Economy.

Ameringer, C. D. (1974). *The democratic left in exile: The antidictatorial struggle in the Caribbean, 1945–1959*. Coral Gables, Fla.: University of Miami.

Anderson, A. H., and Burdon, J. A. (1963). *Brief sketch of British Honduras*. Belize: Government Printer.

Añé Aguiloche, L. (2000). 'La Reforma Económica y La Economía Familiar en Cuba.' In Miranda, P. M. (ed.), *Reforma económica y cambio social en América Latina y el Caribe: Cuatro casos de estudio: Colombia, Costa Rica, Cuba, México*, pp. 509–36. Bogotá: TM Editores.

Angelino, A. D. A. de K. (1931). *Colonial Policy*. 2 vols. Chicago: University of Chicago Press.

Annuaire de l'économie politique. (1892). Paris: Guillaumin.

Annuaire de l'économie politique et de la statistique. (1852). Paris: Guillaumin.

Ardouin, B. (1853–60). *Etudes sur l'histoire d'Haïti; suivies de la vie du général J.-M. Borgella*. 11 vols. Paris: Dézobry et E. Magdeleine.

Argy, V. E. (1981). *The postwar international money crisis: An analysis*. London: Allen & Unwin.

Arthur, O. (2008). 'The Economic Partnership Agreement between CARIFORUM and the European Union and the Building of a Post-Colonial Economy in the Caribbean.' *Journal of Eastern Caribbean Studies* 33(2), pp. 24–44.

Ashcraft, N. (1973). *Colonialism and underdevelopment: Processes of political economic change in British Honduras*. New York: Teachers College Press.

Ashdown, P. (1979). 'Race, class and the unofficial majority in British Honduras, 1890–1949.' Ph.D. diss., University of Sussex.

Ashdown, P. (1985). 'The growth of Black Consciousness in Belize 1914–1919: The Background to the Ex-Servicemen's Riot of 1919.' *BELCAST Journal of Belizean Affairs* 2(2), pp. 1–5.

Ashdown, P. (1986). 'Race Riot, Class Warfare and Coup d'état: The Ex-Servicemen's Riot of July 1919.' *BELCAST Journal of Belizean Affairs* 3(1 & 2), pp. 8–14.

Ashdown, P. (1986a). 'The Colonial Administrators of Belize: Sir Alfred Moloney (1891–1897).' *Belizean Studies* 14(2), pp. 1–10.

Ashley, P. (1920). *Modern tariff history: Germany, United States, France*. London: J. Murray.

Aspinall, A. E. (1912). *The British West Indies: Their history, resources and progress*. London: Pitman.

Aspinall, A. E. (1929). *The Handbook of the British West Indies, British Guiana and British Honduras*. London: West India Committee.

Atkins, E. F. (1926). *Sixty years in Cuba: Reminiscences*. Cambridge: Riverside.

Atkins, G. P., and Wilson, L. C. (1998). *The Dominican Republic and the United States: From imperialism to transnationalism*. Athens: University of Georgia Press.

Bacchus, M. K. (1994). *Education as and for legitimacy: Developments in West Indian education between 1846 and 1895*. Waterloo, Ontario: Wilfrid Laurier University Press.

Bailey, T. A. (1964). *A diplomatic history of the American people*. Englewood Cliffs, N.J.: Prentice-Hall.

Baker, G. (2003). *Cuban Biotechnology.* Washington, DC: Center for Defense Information.

Baker Fox, A. (1949). *Freedom and welfare in the Caribbean: A colonial dilemma.* New York: Harcourt, Brace.

Balch, E. G. (1927). *Occupied Haiti: Being the report of a committee of six disinterested Americans representing organizations exclusively American, who, having personally studied conditions in Haiti in 1926, favor the restoration of the independence of the negro republic.* New York: Writers.

Bangou, H. (1987). *La Guadeloupe.* 3 vols. Paris: L'Harmattan.

Banque Nationale de la République d'Haiti. (n.d.). *Annual Report of the Fiscal Department for the Fiscal Year October 1947–September 1948.* Port-au-Prince.

Barberia, L. (2004). 'Remittances to Cuba: An Evaluation of Cuban and U.S. Government Policy Measures.' In Domínguez, J. I., Pérez, V. O. E., and Barberia, L. (2004), *The Cuban economy at the start of the twenty-first century,* pp. 353–412. Cambridge, Mass.: David Rockefeller Center for Latin American Studies.

Barberia, L., de Souza Briggs, X., and Uriarte, M. (2004). 'The End of Egalitarianism? Economic Inequality and the Future of Social Policy in Cuba.' In Domínguez, J. I., Pérez, V. O. E., and Barberia, L. (2004), *The Cuban economy at the start of the twenty-first century,* pp. 297–316. Cambridge, Mass.: David Rockefeller Center for Latin American Studies.

Barón Castro, R. (1945). *Españolismo y antiespañolismo en la América hispana: La población hispanoamericana a partir de la independencia.* Madrid: Atlas.

Barro, R. J., and Sala-i-Martin, X. (1995). *Economic growth.* Cambridge, Mass.: MIT Press.

Barros, J. (1984). *Haïti, de 1804 à nos jours.* 2 vols. Paris: L'Harmattan.

Bassières, E. (1900). *Notice sur la Guyane.* Paris.

Baud, M. (1995). *Peasants and tobacco in the Dominican Republic, 1870–1930.* Knoxville: University of Tennessee Press.

Beckles, H., and Shepherd, V. (eds.) (1993). *Caribbean Freedom: Society and Economy from Emancipation to the Present.* Kingston, Jamaica: Ian Randle.

Beachey, R. W. (1957). *The British West Indies sugar industry in the late 19th century.* Oxford: Blackwell.

Bellegarde, D. (1953). *Histoire du peuple haïtien, 1492–1952.* Port-au-Prince: Beauchemin.

Benjamins, H. D., and Snelleman, J. F. (1917). *Encyclopædie van Nederlandsch West-Indië.* The Hague: Nijhoff.

Bennett, J. A. (2008). *Education in Belize: A historical perspective.* Belize City: Angelus.

Benoit, P. V. (1954). *Cent cinquante ans de commerce exterieur d'Haïti, 1804–1954.* Port-au-Prince: H. Deschamps.

Benoit, P. V. (1954a). *Evolution budgetaire et développement économique d'Haïti.* Port-au-Prince: H. Deschamps.

Bergad, L. W. (1983). *Coffee and the growth of agrarian capitalism in nineteenth-century Puerto Rico.* Princeton, N.J.: Princeton University Press.

Bergad, L. W. (1983a). 'Coffee and Rural Proletarianization in Puerto Rico, 1840–1898.' *Journal of Latin American Studies* 15(1), pp. 83–100.

Berloquin-Chassany, P. (2004). *Haïti, une démocratie compromise, 1890–1911.* Paris: L'Harmattan.

Bernal, R. (2008). 'CARICOM-EU Economic Partnership Agreement Negotiations: Why and How.' *Journal of Eastern Caribbean Studies* 33(2), pp. 1–23.

Bernardin, E. A. (1999). *Histoire économique et sociale d'Haïti de 1804 à nos jours: L'état complice et la faillite d'un système.* Port-au-Prince: E. A. Bernardin.

Bernardo, R. M. (1971). *The theory of moral incentives in Cuba.* Tuscaloosa: University of Alabama Press.

Bertram, G. (2004). 'On the Convergence of Small Island Economies with their Metropolitan Patrons.' *World Development* 32(2), pp. 343–64.

Besson, D., and Dablin, J.-P. (1995). *25 ans de comptes économiques des départments d'outremer.* Paris: INSEE.

Best, L. (2010). *Economic Policy and Management Choices: A Contemporary Economic History of Trinidad and Tobago* (in collaboration with Eric St. Cyr). (mimeo).

Best, L., and Levitt, K. (2009). *Essays on the theory of plantation economy: A historical and institutional approach to Caribbean economic development.* Kingston, Jamaica: University of West Indies Press.

Bethell, L. (1970). *The abolition of the Brazilian slave trade: Britain, Brazil and the slave trade question, 1807–1869.* Cambridge: Cambridge University Press.

Billini, H. (1885). *Present condition of the Dominican Republic.* New York: Thompson & Moreau.

Blaise, René-Marie (1962). *Comptes Economiques Légers de la Guyane Française pour la Periode 1952–1960.* Paris: Société d'Etudes pour le Developpement Economique et Sociale.

Blancpain, F. (2001). *Un siècle de relations financières entre Haïti et la France, 1825–1922.* Paris: L'Harmattan.

Blérald, A. P. (1986). *Histoire économique de la Guadeloupe et de la Martinique: Du XVIIe siècle à nos jours.* Paris: Karthala.

Boletín Histórico de Puerto Rico (published from 1914 to 1927). Reprinted Barcelona: Jorge Casas Montserrat, 1971.

Bolland, O. N. (1977). *The formation of a colonial society: Belize, from conquest to crown colony.* Baltimore: Johns Hopkins University Press.

Bolland, O. N. (1981). 'Systems of Domination after Slavery: The Control of Land and Labor in the British West Indies after 1838.' *Comparative Studies in Society and History* 23(4), pp. 591–619.

Bolland, O. N. (1988). *Colonialism and resistance in Belize: Essays in historical sociology.* Benque Viejo del Carmen, Belize: Cubola Productions.

Bolland, O. N. (1995). *On the march: Labour rebellions in the British Caribbean, 1934–39.* Kingston, Jamaica: Ian Randle.

Bolland, O. N. (2001). *The politics of labour in the British Caribbean: The social origins of authoritarianism and democracy in the labour movement.* Princeton, N.J.: Markus Wiener.

Bolland, O. N. (2003). *Colonialism and resistance in Belize: Essays in historical sociology.* Benque Viejo del Carmen, Belize: Cubola Productions.

Bolland, O. N., and Shoman, A. (1977). *Land in Belize, 1765–1871.* Mona, Jamaica: Institute of Social and Economic Research, University of the West Indies.

Boorstein, E. (1968). *The economic transformation of Cuba: A first-hand account.* New York: Modern Reader.

Borah, W. W., and Cook, S. F. (1971). *Essays in population history: Mexico and the Caribbean.* Berkeley: University of California Press.

Bourdin, G. (1978). *Histoire de St. Barthélemy.* Pelham, N.Y.: Porter Henry.

Boyce, R. W. (1910). *Health progress and administration in the West Indies.* London: J. Murray.

Boyd, W. D. (1955). 'James Redpath and American Negro Colonization in Haiti, 1860–1862.' *The Americas* 12(2), pp. 169–82.

Brändström, D. (1976). 'Les Relations entre Saint-Barthélemy et la Suède entre 1784 et 1878.' *Bulletin de la Société de la Guadeloupe* 29, pp. 5–19.

Brereton, B. (1981). *A history of modern Trinidad, 1783–1962.* Kingston, Jamaica: Heinemann.

Brewster, H., and Thomas, C. Y. (1967). *The dynamics of West Indian economic integration.* Kingston, Jamaica: University of the West Indies.

Brezis, E. (2003). 'Mercantilism.' In Mokyr, J. (ed.), *The Oxford encyclopedia of economic history*, vol. 3, pp. 483–5. Oxford: Oxford University Press.

Brière, J.-F. (2006). 'L'Emprunt de 1825 dans la dette de l'indépendance haïtienne envers la France.' *Journal of Haitian Studies* 12(2), pp. 126–34.

Brière, J.-F. (2008). *Haïti et la France, 1804–1848: Le rêve brisé.* Paris: Karthala.

Bristowe, L., and Wright, P. (1890). *The Handbook of British Honduras for 1889–90.* Edinburgh: Blackwood.

Brock, H. G., Smith, P. S., and Tucker, W. A. (1917). *The Danish West Indies, their resources and commercial importance.* Washington, DC. Dept. of Commerce, Bureau of Foreign and Domestic Commerce, Special Agents Series No. 129.

Brøndsted, J. (1953). *Vore gamle tropekolonier.* 2 vols. Copenhagen: Westermann.

Brown, L. (2002). 'The Three Faces of Post-Emancipation Migration in Martinique, 1848–1865.' *Journal of Caribbean History* 36(2), pp. 310–35.

Brundenius, C. (1984). *Revolutionary Cuba, the challenge of economic growth with equity.* Boulder, Colo.: Westview.

Brundenius, C. (2002). 'Whither the Cuban Economy after Recovery? The Reform Process, Upgrading Strategies and the Question of Transition.' *Journal of Latin American Studies* 34(2), pp. 365–95.

Bryan, P. (2004). 'Proletarian Movements.' In Brereton, B. (ed.), *The Caribbean in the twentieth century*, pp. 141–73. Paris: UNESCO.

Buckley, R. N. (1998). *The British Army in the West Indies: Society and the military in the revolutionary age.* Gainesville: University Press of Florida.

Buffon, A. (1979). *Monnaie et crédit en économie coloniale: Contribution à l'histoire économique de la Guadeloupe, 1635–1919.* Basse-Terre: Société d'histoire de la Guadeloupe.

Bulletin de la Société d'histoire de la Guadeloupe. (1964–). Basse-Terre: Archives départementales.

Bulletin de l'Académie des Sciences Humaines et Sociales d'Haïti. (1983). Port-au-Prince: Université d'Haiti. 13, pp. 9–47.

Bulmer-Thomas, V. (1990). 'Nicaragua since 1930.' In Bethell, L. (ed.), *The Cambridge History of Latin America.* Vol. 7, *1930 to the Present*, pp. 317–66. Cambridge: Cambridge University Press.

Bulmer-Thomas, V. (1996). *The new economic model in Latin America and its impact on income distribution and poverty.* New York: St. Martin's.

Bulmer-Thomas, V. (2001). *Regional integration in Latin America and the Caribbean: The political economy of open regionalism.* London: Institute of Latin American Studies.

Bulmer-Thomas, V. (2001a). 'The Wider Caribbean in the 20th Century: a Long-Run Development Perspective.' *Integration & Trade* 5(15), pp. 5–56.

Bulmer-Thomas, V. (2003). *The economic history of Latin America since independence.* Cambridge: Cambridge University Press.

Bulmer-Thomas, V. (2006). 'Globalization and the New Economic Model in Latin America.' In Bulmer-Thomas, V., Coatsworth, J. H., and Cortés, C. R. (eds.), *The Cambridge economic history of Latin America*. Vol. 2, *The Long Twentieth Century*, pp. 135–68. Cambridge: Cambridge University Press.

Burdon, J. A. (1931–6). *Archives of British Honduras: Being extracts and précis from records, with maps*. 3 vols. London: Sifton, Praed & Co.

Burns, A. (1949). *Colonial Civil Servant*. London: Allen & Unwin.

Burns, A. (1965). *History of the British West Indies*. London: Allen & Unwin.

Buschkens, W. F. L. (1974). *The family system of the Paramaribo Creoles*. The Hague: Nijhoff.

Byron, M., and Condon, S. (2008). *Migration in comparative perspective: Caribbean communities in Britain and France*. New York: Routledge.

Calder, B. J. (1984). *The impact of intervention: The Dominican Republic during the U.S. occupation of 1916–1924*. Austin: University of Texas Press.

Candler, J. (1842). *Brief notices of Hayti: with its condition, resources, and prospects*. London: T. Ward.

Carey Jones, N. S. (1953). *The pattern of a dependent economy: The national income of British Honduras*. Cambridge: Cambridge University Press.

Carr, R. (1975). *Spain, 1808–1939*. Oxford: Clarendon.

Carr, R. (1984). *Puerto Rico, a colonial experiment*. New York: New York University Press.

Carranza, J., Gutiérrez, U. L., and Monreal, G. P. M. (1995). *Cuba, la restructuración de la economía: Una propuesta para el debate*. Havana: Editorial de Ciencias Sociales.

Carranza, J., Gutiérrez, U. L., Monreal, G. P. M., and University of London. (1996). *Cuba, restructuring the economy: A contribution to the debate*. London: Institute of Latin American Studies.

Carter, S. B. (2006). *Historical statistics of the United States: Earliest times to the present*. 5 vols. New York: Cambridge University Press.

Cassá, R. (1982). *Capitalismo y dictadura*. Santo Domingo: Editora de la Universidad Autónoma de Santo Domingo.

Cassá, R. (1987). *Historia social y económica de la República Dominicana*. 2 vols. Santo Domingo: Alfa y Omega.

Chalmin, P. (1990). *The making of a sugar giant: Tate and Lyle, 1859–1989*. Chur: Harwood.

Chaloner and Fleming, Mahogany and Timber Brokers. (1851). *The Mahogany Tree: its botanical characters, qualities and uses … With a map and illustrations. And an appendix*, etc. Liverpool: Rockliff & Son; London: Effingham Wilson.

Chatelain, J. (1954). *La Banque nationale: Son histoire, ses problèmes*. Port-au-Prince.

Chauleau, L. (1993). *Dans les îles du vent: La Martinique (XVIIe–XIXe siècle)*. Paris: L'Harmattan.

Chernick, S. E. (1978). *The Commonwealth Caribbean: The integration experience: report of a mission sent to the Commonwealth Caribbean by the World Bank*. Baltimore: Johns Hopkins University Press.

Cherrington, E., et al. (2010). *Forest Cover and Deforestation in Belize*. Panama: CATHALAC.

Chinea, J. L. (2005). *Race and labor in the Hispanic Caribbean: The West Indian immigrant worker experience in Puerto Rico, 1800–1850*. Gainesville: University Press of Florida.

Chomsky, A. (1996). _West Indian workers and the United Fruit Company in Costa Rica, 1870–1940_. Baton Rouge: Louisiana State University Press.

Clapham, J. H. (1968). _The economic development of France and Germany, 1815–1914_. Cambridge: Cambridge University Press.

Clarence-Smith, W. G. (2000). _Cocoa and chocolate, 1765–1914_. London: Routledge.

Clarence-Smith, W. G., and Topik, S. (2003). _The global coffee economy in Africa, Asia and Latin America, 1500–1989_. Cambridge: Cambridge University Press.

Clark, V. S. (1930). _Porto Rico and its problems_. Washington, DC: Brookings Institution.

Clegern, W. M. (1967). _British Honduras: colonial dead end, 1859–1900_. Baton Rouge: Louisiana State University Press.

Coll y Toste, C. (1899). _Reseña del estado social, económico e industrial de la isla de Puerto-Rico al tomar posesión de ella los Estados-Unidos_. Puerto Rico: 'Correspondencia'.

Collver, O. A. (1965). _Birth rates in Latin America: New estimates of historical trends and fluctuations_. Berkeley: University of California Press.

Connell-Smith, G. (1966). _The Inter-American system_. London: Oxford University Press.

Corden, W. M. (1971). _The theory of protection_. Oxford: Clarendon.

Craig-James, S. (2008). _The changing society of Tobago, 1838–1938: A fractured whole_. Arima, Trinidad & Tobago: Cornerstone.

Crassweller, R. D. (1966). _Trujillo: The life and times of a Caribbean dictator_. New York: Macmillan.

Craton, M. (1997). _Empire, enslavement, and freedom in the Caribbean_. Kingston, Jamaica: Ian Randle.

Craton, M. (2003). _Founded upon the seas: A history of the Cayman Islands and their people_. Kingston, Jamaica: Ian Randle.

Creamer, D. B., and Creamer, H. L. (1948). _Gross product of Puerto Rico, 1940–1944_. Río Piedras: University of Puerto Rico.

Crusol, J. (1980). _Economies insulaires de la Caraïbe: Aspects théoriques et pratiques du développement: Guadeloupe, Martinique, Barbade, Trinidad, Jamaïque, Puerto-Rico_. Paris: Editions Caribéennes.

Crusol, J. (2007). _Les îles à sucre: De la colonisation à la mondialisation_. Bécherel: Les Perséides.

Cuba Commission Report (1993). _A hidden history of the Chinese in Cuba: the original English-language text of 1876_. Baltimore: Johns Hopkins University Press.

Cuban Economic Research Project (CERP) (1965). _A study on Cuba: The colonial and republican periods, the socialist experiment, economic structure, institutional development, socialism and collectivization_. Coral Gables, Fla.: University of Miami Press.

Cumper, G. (1960). 'Personal Consumption in the West Indies.' In Cumper, G. E. (ed.), _The economy of the West Indies_, pp. 126–51. Kingston, Jamaica: United Printers.

Cumper, G. (1960a). 'Employment and Unemployment in the West Indies.' In Cumper, G. E. (ed.), _The economy of the West Indies_, pp. 152–80. Kingston, Jamaica: United Printers.

Curet, J. (1980). 'From slavery to 'liberto': A study on slavery and its abolition in Puerto Rico, 1840–1880.' Ph.D. diss., Columbia University.

Curtin, P. D. (1969). _The Atlantic slave trade: A census_. Madison: University of Wisconsin Press.

Cushion, S. (2010). *Cuba Popular Resistance to the 1953 London Sugar Agreement.* London: Institute for the Study of the Americas, Commodities of Empire Working Paper, No. 15.

Daniel, J. (2001). 'Economic Performance Stimulated by Public Transfers: the Experience of Martinique.' *Integration & Trade* 5(15), pp. 223–46.

Davies, O. (1984). *An analysis of Jamaica's fiscal budget (1974–1983), with special reference to the impact of the bauxite levy.* Mona, Jamaica: University of the West Indies.

de Booy, T. (1918). *The Virgin islands: Our new possessions, and the British islands.* Philadelphia: J. B. Lippincott.

de la Rosa, J. (1969). *Las Finanzas de Santo Domingo y el Control Americano.* Santo Domingo: Nacional.

de Groot, S. (1985). 'The Maroons of Surinam: Agents of their own Emancipation.' In Richardson, D. (ed.), *Abolition and its Aftermath. The Historical Context, 1790–1916.* London: Frank Cass.

Deerr, N. (1949). *The history of sugar.* 2 vols. London: Chapman.

Despachos de los cónsules norteamericanos en Puerto Rico (1982). Río Piedras: Universidad de Puerto Rico.

Dev Pandey, K., Buys, P., Chomitz, K., and Wheeler, D. (2006). 'Biodiversity Conservation Indicators: New Tools for Priority Setting at the Global Environment Facility' (2006). Data updated to 2008 (available on World Bank Web site).

Devlin, R., and Estevadeordal, A. (2001). 'What's New in the New Regionalism in the Americas?' In Bulmer-Thomas, V. (ed.), *Regional integration in Latin America and the Caribbean: The political economy of open regionalism*, pp. 17–44. London: Institute of Latin American Studies.

Díaz Soler, L. M. (1974). *Historia de la esclavitud negra en Puerto Rico.* San Juan: Universidad de Puerto Rico.

Dietz, J. L. (1986). *Economic history of Puerto Rico: Institutional change and capitalist development.* Princeton, N.J.: Princeton University Press.

Dietz, J. L. (2001). 'The "Three-Legged" Economy.' *Integration and Trade* 5(15), pp. 247–74.

Dietz, J. L. (2003). *Puerto Rico, negotiating development and change.* Boulder, Colo.: Lynne Rienner.

Dinwiddie, W. (1899). *Puerto Rico: Its conditions and possibilities.* New York: Harper & Bros.

Dobson, N. (1973). *A history of Belize.* Port of Spain: Longman Caribbean.

Dodd, T. (1974). 'Un Tratado Inconcluso entre los Estados Unidos y la República Dominicana en 1892.' *eme eme: Estudios Dominicanos*, no. 13, pp. 26–46.

Domínguez, J. J. (1986). *La dictadura de Heureaux.* Santo Domingo: Universidad Autónoma de Santo Domingo.

Dominican Republic. (1907). Washington, DC: Direction of the Department of Promotion and Public Works for the Jamestown Ter-Centennial Exposition.

Dookhan, I. (1972). 'The Virgin Islands Company and Corporation: the plan for economic rehabilitation in the Virgin Islands.' *Journal of Caribbean History* 4, pp. 54–76.

Dookhan, I. (1974). *A history of the Virgin Islands of the United States.* Epping: Caribbean Universities Press for the College of the Virgin Islands.

Dorsey, J. C. (2003). *Slave traffic in the Age of Abolition: Puerto Rico, West Africa, and the non-Hispanic Caribbean, 1815–1859.* Gainesville: University Press of Florida.

Dosman, E. J. (2008). *The life and times of Raúl Prebisch, 1901–1986.* Montreal: McGill-Queen's University Press.

Douyon, F. (2004). *Haïti, de l'indépendance à la dépendance.* Paris: L'Harmattan.

Duany, J. (2002). *The Puerto Rican nation on the move: Identities on the island & in the United States.* Chapel Hill: University of North Carolina Press.

Dumond, D. E. (1997). *The machete and the cross: Campesino rebellion in Yucatan.* Lincoln: University of Nebraska Press.

Dupont-Gonin, P. (1970). *La Guyane Française. Le pays. Les hommes. Ses problèmes et son avenir, etc.* Geneva: Librairie Droz.

Dupuy, A. (1989). *Haiti in the world economy: Class, race, and underdevelopment since 1700.* Boulder, Colo.: Westview.

Duval, J. (1864). *Les Colonies et la Politique Coloniale de la France.* Paris.

Dyde, B. (2005). *Out of the crowded vagueness: A history of the islands of St Kitts, Nevis & Anguilla.* Oxford: Macmillan Caribbean.

Dye, A. (1998). *Cuban sugar in the age of mass production: Technology and the economics of the sugar central, 1899–1929.* Stanford, Calif.: Stanford University Press.

Eckstein, S. (1994). *Back from the future: Cuba under Castro.* Princeton, N.J.: Princeton University Press.

Economist Intelligence Unit. (various years). *Quarterly Report for Bahamas etc.* London.

Eisner, G. (1961). *Jamaica, 1830–1930: A study in economic growth.* Manchester: Manchester University Press.

El-Agraa, A., and Nicholls, S. (1997). 'The Caribbean Community and Common Market.' In El-Agraa, A. (ed.), *Economic integration worldwide*, pp. 278–96. New York: St. Martin's.

Eltis, D. (1972). 'The Traffic in Slaves between the British West Indian Colonies, 1807–1833.' *Economic History Review* (n.s.) 25(1), pp. 55–64.

Eltis, D. (1987). 'The Nineteenth-Century Transatlantic Slave Trade: An Annual Time Series of Imports into the Americas Broken down by Region.' *Hispanic American Historical Review* 67(1), pp. 109–38.

Eltis, D., Behrendt, S., Richardson, D., and Klein, H. (1999). *The Trans-Atlantic Slave Trade: A Database on CD-ROM.* Cambridge: Cambridge University Press.

Emmer, P. C. (1998). *The Dutch in the Atlantic economy, 1580–1880: Trade, slavery and emancipation.* Aldershot: Ashgate.

Engerman, S. (2000). 'Slavery and its Consequences for the South in the Nineteenth Century.' In Engerman, S. L., and Gallman, R. E. (eds.), *The Cambridge economic history of the United States.* Vol 2., *The Long Nineteenth Century*, pp. 329–66. Cambridge: Cambridge University Press.

Engerman, S., and Higman, B. (1997). 'The demographic structure of the Caribbean slave societies in the eighteenth and nineteenth centuries.' In Knight, F. W. (ed.), *General history of the Caribbean.* Vol. 3, *The Slave Societies of the Caribbean*, pp. 45–104. London: UNESCO.

Espina Prieto, M. (2004). 'Social Effects of Economic Adjustment: Equality, Inequality and Trends toward Greater Complexity in Cuban Society.' In Domínguez, J. I., Pérez, V. O. E., and Barberia, L. (eds.), *The Cuban economy at the start of the twenty-first century*, pp. 209–44. Cambridge, Mass.: David Rockefeller Center for Latin American Studies.

Estrella, J. C. (1971). *La moneda, la banca, y las finanzas en la República Dominicana.* 2 vols. Santiago: Universidad Católica Madre y Maestra.

Evans, L. H. (1945). *The Virgin islands: From naval base to new deal.* Ann Arbor, Mich.: J. W. Edwards.

Farnie, D. A. (1979). *The English cotton industry and the world market, 1815–1896.* Oxford: Clarendon.

Farraudière, Y. (1987). *Ecole et Société en Guyane Française.* Paris: Sciences Education.

Fass, S. M. (1988). *Political economy in Haiti: The drama of survival.* New Brunswick, N.J.: Transaction.

Fernández, S. J. (2002). *Encumbered Cuba: Capital markets and revolt, 1878–1895.* Gainesville: University Press of Florida.

Ferriol, A. (2002). 'Explorando nuevas estrategias para reducir la pobreza en el actual contexto internacional: Experiencias de Cuba.' Talk presented at the Seminario Internacional Estrategias de Reducción de la Pobreza. Havana: CLACSO/CROP.

Figueroa, L. A. (2005). *Sugar, slavery, & freedom in nineteenth-century Puerto Rico.* Chapel Hill: University of North Carolina Press.

Firmin, J.-A. (1901). *La France et Haïti.* Paris: F. Pichon.

Firmin, J.-A. (1905). *M. Roosevelt, président des Etats-Unis et la République d'Haïti.* New York: Hamilton Bank Note Engraving and Printing Company.

Focke, H., et al. (eds.). (1855). *West-Indië:Bijdragen tot de Bevordering van de Kennis der Nederlandsch West-Indische Koloniën.* Haarlem.

Franco, F. J. (1999). *Historia económica y financiera de la República Dominicana, 1844–1962: Introducción a su estudio.* Santo Domingo: Universidad Autónoma de Santo Domingo.

Franklin, J. (1828). *The present state of Hayti (Saint Domingo): With remarks on its agriculture, commerce, laws, religion, finances, and population, etc. etc.* London: J. Murray.

French Guiana (1920). Handbook issued by Historical Section of the Foreign Office. London: Her Majesty's Stationery Office.

French Yearbook: Statistical and Historical Annual of France (1919). London: Bale; Paris: Comité du Livre.

Füllberg-Stollberg, C. (2004). 'The Caribbean in the Second World War.' In Brereton, B. (ed.), *The Caribbean in the twentieth century*, pp. 82–140. Paris: UNESCO.

Gallagher, R. (1990). *Survey of Offshore Finance Sectors in the Caribbean Dependent Territories.* London: Foreign and Commonwealth Office.

Galletti, R. (1949). *Industrial Development in the British Territories of the Caribbean.* 3 vols. London: Colonial Office.

Galloway, J. H. (1989). *The sugar cane industry: An historical geography from its origins to 1914.* Cambridge: Cambridge University Press.

Gallup, J. L., Sachs, J., Mellinger, A. D., and National Bureau of Economic Research. (1998). *Geography and economic development.* Cambridge, Mass.: National Bureau of Economic Research.

Gaztambide-Geigel, A. (1996). 'La invención del Caribe en el siglo XX: Las definiciones del Caribe como problema histórico e metodológico.' *Revista Mexicana del Caribe* 1(1), pp. 75–96.

Gereffi, G., Korzeniewicz, M., and Political Economy of the World-System Conference. (1994). *Commodity chains and global capitalism.* Westport, Conn: Greenwood.

Ghai, D. P., Kay, C., and Peek, P. (1988). *Labour and development in rural Cuba.* New York: St. Martin's.

Gibbs, A. R. (1883). *British Honduras: An historical and descriptive account of the colony from its settlement, 1670.* London: S. Low, Marston, Searle & Rivington.

Girvan, N. (1967). *The Caribbean bauxite industry*. Mona, Jamaica: University of the West Indies.

Girvan, N. (2005). 'Reinterpreting the Caribbean.' In Pantin, D. (ed.), *The Caribbean economy: A reader*, pp. 304–18. Kingston, Jamaica: Ian Randle.

Girvan, N. (2008). 'The Effect of the Economic Partnership Agreement on the CSME: The Fork in the Road.' *Journal of Eastern Caribbean Studies* 33(2), pp. 45–69.

Gleijeses, P. (2002). *Conflicting missions: Havana, Washington, and Africa, 1959–1976*. Chapel Hill: University of North Carolina Press.

Gøbel, E. (1994). 'Shipping through the Port of St. Thomas, Danish West Indies, 1816–1917.' *International Journal of Maritime History* 6(2), pp. 155–73.

Gøbel, E. (2002). *A guide to sources for the history of the Danish West Indies (U.S. Virgin Islands), 1671–1917*. Odense: University Press of Southern Denmark.

Goizueta-Mimó, F. (1987). *Bitter Cuban sugar: Monoculture and economic dependence from 1825–1899*. New York: Garland.

Gómez, L. (1979). *Relaciones de producción dominantes en la sociedad dominicana, 1875–1975*. Santo Domingo: Alfa y Omega.

González, N. L. S. (1988). *Sojourners of the Caribbean: Ethnogenesis and ethnohistory of the Garifuna*. Urbana: University of Illinois Press.

Goslinga, C. C. (1990). *The Dutch in the Caribbean and in Surinam, 1791/5–1942*. Assen, Netherlands: Van Gorcum.

Grant, C. H. (1976). *The making of modern Belize: Politics, society, & British colonialism in Central America*. Cambridge: Cambridge University Press.

Green, W. A. (1976). *British slave emancipation: The sugar colonies and the great experiment, 1830–1865*. Oxford: Clarendon.

Griffith, I. L. (2004). *Caribbean security in the age of terror: Challenge and change*. Kingston, Jamaica: Ian Randle.

Griffiths, R. T. (1980). *The Economy and politics of the Netherlands since 1945*. The Hague: Nijhoff.

Griggs, E. L. (1952). *Henry Christophe & Thomas Clarkson*. Berkeley: University of California Press.

Grilli, E. R. (1993). *The European community and the developing countries*. Cambridge: Cambridge University Press.

Guerra y Sánchez, R. (1927). *Azúcar y población en las Antillas*. Havana: Cultural.

Guevara, E. (1967). *Le socialisme et l'homme*. Paris: Maspero.

Hall, C. (2002). *Civilising subjects: Colony and metropole in the English imagination, 1830–1867*. Chicago: University of Chicago Press.

Hall, D. (1959). *Free Jamaica, 1838–1865: An economic history*. New Haven: Yale University Press.

Hall, D. (1971). *Five of the Leewards, 1834–1870*. St Lawrence, Barbados: Caribbean Universities Press.

Hall, D. (1978). 'The Flight from the Estates Reconsidered: The British West Indies, 1838–42.' *Journal of Caribbean History* 10(11), pp. 7–24.

Hall, K. O. (1988). 'The Caribbean Community.' In El-Agraa, A. (ed.), *International Economic Integration*, pp. 220–36. London: Macmillan.

Hall, K. O. (2001). *The Caribbean Community: Beyond survival*. Kingston, Jamaica: Ian Randle.

Hall, N. A. T. (1985). *The Danish West Indies, empire without dominion: 1671–1848*. Charlotte Amalie, St Thomas: Division of Libraries, Museums and Archaeological Services.

Halperín-Donghi, T. (1985). 'Economy and Society in post-Independence Spanish America.' In Bethell, L. (ed.), *The Cambridge History of Latin America*. Vol. 3, *From Independence to c.1870*, pp. 299–46. Cambridge: Cambridge University Press.

Hartog, J. (1961). *Aruba, past and present: From the time of the Indians until today*. Oranjestad, Aruba: DeWit.

Hartog, J. (1968). *Curaçao, from colonial dependence to autonomy*. Aruba: DeWit.

Hartog, J. (1975). *History of Saba*. Saba, Netherlands Antilles: Van Guilder.

Hazard, S. (1873). *Santo Domingo, past and present: With a glance at Hayti*. New York: Harper & Bros.

Henderson, W. O. (1975). *The rise of German industrial power, 1834–1914*. Berkeley: University of California Press.

Henry, P. (1985). *Peripheral capitalism and underdevelopment in Antigua*. New Brunswick, N.J.: Transaction.

Heston, T. J. (1987). *Sweet subsidy: The economic and diplomatic effects of the U.S. sugar acts, 1934–1974*. New York: Garland.

Heuman, G. J. (1994). *The killing time: The Morant Bay rebellion in Jamaica*. Knoxville: University of Tennessee Press.

Hewitt, A., and Stevens, C. (1981). 'The Second Lomé Convention.' In Stevens, C. (ed.), *EEC and the Third World: a survey-1*. London: Hodder and Stoughton.

Hibben, T., and Picó, R. (1948). *Industrial development of Puerto Rico and the Virgin Islands of the United States*. Port of Spain: Caribbean Commission.

Higman, B. W. (1984). *Slave populations of the British Caribbean, 1807–1834*. Baltimore: Johns Hopkins University Press.

Higman, B. W. (2005). *Plantation Jamaica, 1750–1850: Capital and control in a colonial economy*. Kingston, Jamaica: University of the West Indies Press.

Higman, B. W. (2011). *Concise History of the Caribbean*. Cambridge: Cambridge University Press.

Hill, R. T. (1898). *Cuba and Porto Rico, with the other islands of the West Indies: Their topography, climate, flora, products, industries, cities, people, political conditions, etc*. New York: Century.

Hiss, P. H. (1943). *Netherlands America: The Dutch territories in the West*. New York: Distributed by Duell, Sloan & Pearce.

Hoefte, R. (1998). *In place of slavery: A social history of British Indian and Javanese laborers in Suriname*. Gainesville: University Press of Florida.

Hoetink, H. (1969). *Encyclopedie van de Nederlandse Antillen*. Amsterdam: Elsevier.

Hoetink, H. (1982). *The Dominican people, 1850–1900: Notes for a historical sociology*. Baltimore: Johns Hopkins University Press.

Högström, E. O. E. (1888). *S. Barthelemy under svenkt välde*. Upsala: Almqvist & Wiksells.

Holloway, T. H. (1975). *The Brazilian coffee valorization of 1906: Regional politics and economic dependence*. Madison: State Historical Society of Wisconsin.

Holloway, T. H. (1980). *Immigrants on the land: Coffee and society in São Paulo, 1886–1934*. Chapel Hill: University of North Carolina Press.

Hope, K. R. (1986). *Economic development in the Caribbean*. New York: Praeger.

Hornby, O., and Justesen, O. (1976). *Studier i de dansk-vestindiske øers historie 1665–1976: Resultater af 21 historiestuderendes arbejde i Danmark og på øerne 1975–76*. Copenhagen.

Horsefield, J. (1969). *The International Monetary Fund, 1945–1965: Twenty years of international monetary cooperation*. 3 vols. Washington, DC: International Monetary Fund.

Howard, M. (2006). *The economic development of Barbados*. Kingston, Jamaica: University of the West Indies Press.

Huberman, L., and Sweezy, P. M. (1960). *Cuba: Anatomy of a revolution*. New York: Monthly Review Press.

Hummel, C. (1921). *Report on the Forests of British Honduras, with suggestions for a far reaching forest policy*. London: Colonial Research Committee.

Humphreys, R. A. (1961). *The diplomatic history of British Honduras, 1638–1901*. London: Oxford University Press.

Hyrenius, H. (1977). *Royal Swedish Slaves*. Gothenburg: University of Gothenburg.

Ibarra, G. J. R. (2006). *El tratado anglo-cubano de 1905: Estados Unidos contra Europa*. Havana: Editorial de Ciencias Sociales.

IBGE. (1987). *Estatísticas Históricas do Brasil*. Rio de Janeiro.

IBRD. (1952). *Report on Cuba*. Baltimore: Johns Hopkins University Press.

Instituto de Historia de Cuba. (1998). *La Neocolonia: Organización y Crisis desde 1899 hasta 1940*. Havana: Política.

Instituto de Investigaciones Estadísticas. (1988). *Los Censos de Población y Vivienda en Cuba*. Havana: Instituto de Investigaciones Estadísticas.

INTAL-IDB. (2005). *CARICOM Report, No.2*. Buenos Aires.

Inter-American Development Bank. (1971). *The IDB's first decade and perspectives for the future: [proceedings of the] Round Table, Inter-American Development Bank, Punta del Este, Uruguay, April 1970*.

Iyo, A., Tzalam, F., and Humphreys, F. (2007). *Belize, New Vision: African and Mayan Civilizations*. Belize City: Angelus.

Jacobstein, M. (1907). *The tobacco industry in the United States*. New York: Columbia University Press.

Jefferson, O. (1999). *Stabilization and stagnation in the Jamaican economy, 1972–97: Some reflections on macroeconomic policy over the past twenty-five years*. Kingston, Jamaica: Canoe.

Jenks, L. H. (1928). *Our Cuban colony: A study in sugar*. New York: Vanguard.

Jensen, P. (1983). *Dansk kolonihistorie: Indføring og studier*. Århus: Forlaget HISTORIA.

Jimeno Agius, J. (1885). *Población y comercio de la isla de Puerto Rico*. Madrid: El Correo.

Joachim, B. (1972). 'Commerce et Décolonisation: L'Expérience franco-haïtienne au XIXe siècle.' *Annales E.S.C.* 6, pp. 1497–1525.

Joachim, B. (1979). *Les racines du sous développement en Haïti*. Port-au-Prince: H. Deschamps.

Johansen, H. (1981). 'Slave Demography of the Danish West Indian Islands.' *Scandinavian Economic History Review* 29(1), pp. 1–20.

Johnson, H. (1996). *The Bahamas from slavery to servitude, 1783–1933*. Gainesville: University Press of Florida.

Jones, R. L. (1933). *The eighteenth amendment and our foreign relations*. New York: Thomas Y. Crowell.

Jordan, M. (2005). *The great abolition sham: The true story of the end of the British slave trade*. Stroud: Sutton.

Karol, K. S. (1971). *Guerrillas in power: The course of the Cuban Revolution*. London: Cape.

Kepner, C. D., and Soothill, J. H. (1935). *The banana empire: A case study of economic imperialism*. New York: Vanguard.

Kiple, K. F. (1970). "The Cuban slave trade, 1820–1862: The demographic implications for comparative studies." Ph.D. Diss., University of Florida.

Kneer, W. G. (1975). *Great Britain and the Caribbean, 1901–1913: A study in Anglo-American relations*. East Lansing: Michigan State University Press.

Knight, F. W. (1970). *Slave society in Cuba during the nineteenth century*. Madison: University of Wisconsin Press.

Knight, F. W. (1985). 'Jamaica Migrants and the Cuban Sugar Industry, 1900–34.' In Moreno, F. M., Moya Pons, F., and Engerman, S. L. (eds.), *Between slavery and free labor: The Spanish-speaking Caribbean in the nineteenth century*. Baltimore: Johns Hopkins University Press.

Knight, F. W. (1990). *The Caribbean, the genesis of a fragmented nationalism*. New York: Oxford University Press.

Knight, M. M. (1928). *The Americans in Santo Domingo*. New York: Vanguard.

Knox, J. P. (1852). *A historical account of St. Thomas, W.I.: With its rise and progress in commerce; missions and churches; climate and its adaptation to invalids; geological structure; natural history, and botany*. New York: C. Scribner.

Kuitenbrouwer, M. (1991). *The Netherlands and the rise of modern imperialism: Colonies and foreign policy, 1870–1902*. New York: Berg.

Lacerte, R. (1981). 'Xenophobia and Economic Decline: The Haitian Case, 1820–1843.' *The Americas* 37(4), pp. 499–515.

Lacerte, R. (1993). 'The Evolution of Land and Labor in the Haitian Revolution, 1791–1820.' *The Americas* 34(4), pp. 449–59.

Lammens, A. F. (1982). *Bijdragen tot de kennis van de kolonie Suriname: Dat gedeelte van Guiana hetwelk bij tractaat ten jare 1815 aan het Koningrijk Holland is verbleven, tijdvak 1816 tot 1822*. Amsterdam: Vrije Universiteit.

Lamur, H. E. (1973). *The demographic evolution of Surinam 1920–1970: A socio-demographic analysis*. The Hague: Nijhoff.

Langer, M. (2010). 'Offshore for Over 50 Years.' (mimeo).

Laurence, K. O. (1994). *A question of labour: Indentured immigration into Trinidad and British Guiana, 1875–1917*. New York: St. Martin's.

Lavallé, B., Naranjo, C., and Santamaría, A. (2002). *La América española, 1763–1898: Economía*. Madrid: Síntesis.

Lawrence, R., and Lara, J. (2006). 'Trade Performance and Industrial Policy.' In Collins, S. M., Bosworth, B., and Soto-Class, M. A. (eds.), *The economy of Puerto Rico: Restoring growth*, pp. 507–65. San Juan: Center for the New Economy.

Léger, J. N. (1907). *Haïti: Son histoire et ses détracteurs*. New York: Neale.

Lepelletier, S.-R. R. (1846). *Saint-Domingue: Etude et solution nouvelle de la question haïtienne*. Paris: A. Bertrand.

Lewis, G. K. (1972). *The Virgin Islands: A Caribbean Lilliput*. Evanston: Northwestern University Press.

Lewis, W. A. (1950). *The Industrialisation of the British West Indies*. Bridgetown, Barbados. (Reprinted in Pantin, D. (ed.), (2005), *The Caribbean economy: A reader*, pp. 5–43. Kingston, Jamaica: Ian Randle).

Lewis, W. A. (1954). 'Economic Development with Unlimited Supplies of Labour.' *Manchester School* 22(2), pp. 139–91.

Lewis, W. A. (1970). *Tropical development, 1880–1913*. Evanston: Northwestern University Press.

Lewis, W. A. (1977). *Labour in the West Indies: The Birth of a Workers' Movement*, with an Afterword, 'Germs of an Idea', by Susan Craig. London (first published by the Fabian Society as Research Series, no. 44).

Lewis, W. A. (1978). *Growth and fluctuations, 1870–1913*. London: Allen & Unwin.

Leyburn, J. G. (1941). *The Haitian people*. New Haven: Yale University Press.

Lipsey, R. E. (2000). 'US Foreign Trade and the Balance of Payments, 1800–1913.' In Engerman, S. L., and Gallman, R. E. (eds.), *The Cambridge economic history of the United States*. Vol. 2, *The Long Nineteenth Century*, pp. 685–732. Cambridge: Cambridge University Press.

Lipton, J. A. (1979). *Bauxite in Jamaica: Ownership and control in a partially nationalized industry*. Austin, Tex.: Institute of Latin American Studies.

Lloyd Jones, C. (1931). *Caribbean backgrounds and prospects*. New York: D. Appleton.

Lloyd Jones, C. (1936). *The Caribbean since 1900*. New York: Prentice-Hall.

Lluberes Navarro, A. (1978). 'Caribe, Azúcar y Migración, 1789–1944.' *eme eme: Estudios Dominicanos* 39, pp. 3–44.

Lobdell, R. (1972). 'Patterns of Investment and Credit in the British West Indian Sugar Industry.' *Journal of Caribbean History* 4, pp. 31–53.

Logan, R. W. (1930). 'Education in Haiti.' *Journal of Negro History* 15(4), pp. 401–60.

Logan, R. W. (1941). *The diplomatic relations of the United States with Haiti, 1776–1891*. Chapel Hill: University of North Carolina Press.

Look Lai, W. (1993). *Indentured labor, Caribbean sugar: Chinese and Indian migrants to the British West Indies, 1838–1918*. Baltimore: Johns Hopkins University Press.

Look Lai, W. (1998). *The Chinese in the West Indies, 1806–1995: A documentary history*. Kingston, Jamaica: University of the West Indies Press.

Looney, R. E. (1987). *The Jamaican economy in the 1980s: Economic decline and structural adjustment*. Boulder, Colo.: Westview.

López, K. (2006). 'The Chinese in Cuban History.' In Look Lai, W. (ed.), *Essays on the Chinese diaspora in the Caribbean*. Trinidad & Tobago: University of the West Indies Press.

López, R. A. (1989). 'Political Economy of U.S. Sugar Policies.' *American Journal of Agricultural Economics* 71(1), pp. 20–31.

Lundahl, M. (1979). *Peasants and poverty: A study of Haiti*. New York: St. Martin's.

Lynch, J. (2006). *Simón Bolívar: A life*. New Haven: Yale University Press.

McCloy, S. T. (1966). *The Negro in the French West Indies*. Lexington: University of Kentucky Press.

McCoy, A. W., and Block, A. A. (1992). *War on drugs: Studies in the failure of U.S. narcotics policy*. Boulder, Colo.: Westview.

MacDonald, R. (2007). *Exchange rate economics: Theories and evidence*. London: Routledge.

Mackenzie, C. (1830). *Notes on Haiti: Made during a residence in that republic*. 2 vols. London: H. Colburn and R. Bentley.

McLeish, J. (1926). 'British Activities in Yucatán and on the Moskito Shore in the Eighteenth Century.' M.A. thesis, University of London.

MacMillan, M. (2001). *Peacemakers: The Paris Conference of 1919 and its attempt to end war*. London: J. Murray.

Macmillan, W. M. (1936). *Warning from the West Indies: A tract for Africa and the Empire*. London: Faber and Faber.

McNeill, J. R. (2010). *Mosquito empires: Ecology and war in the Greater Caribbean, 1620–1914*. New York: Cambridge University Press.

Macpherson, J. S. (1947). *Development and Welfare in the West Indies 1945–46.* London: Her Majesty's Stationery Office.

Maddison, A. (2001). *The World Economy: A Millennial Perspective.* Paris: OECD.

Maddison, A. (2003). *The World Economy: Historical Statistics.* Paris: OECD.

Maddison, A. (2007). *Contours of the world economy, 1–2030 AD: Essays in macroeconomic history.* Oxford: Oxford University Press.

Madiou, T. (1988). *Histoire d'Haïti.* Port-au-Prince: H. Deschamps.

Maingot, A. (1988). 'Laundering the Gains of the Drug Trade: Miami and Caribbean Tax Havens.' *Journal of Interamerican Studies and World Affairs* 30(2/3), pp. 167–87.

Maluquer, J. (1974). 'El Mercado Colonial Antillano en el Siglo XIX.' In Nadal, J., and Tortella, C. G. (eds.), *Agricultura, comercio colonial y crecimiento económico en la España contemporánea: Actas del primer Coloquio de Historia Económica de España.* Barcelona: Ariel.

Mam-Lam-Fouck, S. (1982). *La Guyane française de la colonisation à la départementalisation: la formation de la société créole guyanaise.* Fort de France: Désormeaux.

Mam-Lam-Fouck, S. (1987). *Histoire de la Société guyanaise. Les années cruciales: 1848–1946.* Paris: Editions Caribéennes.

Mam-Lam-Fouck, S. (1999). *La Guyane française au temps de l'esclavage, de l'or et de la francisation (1802–1946).* Petit-Bourg: Ibis Rouge.

Mam-Lam-Fouck, S. (2002). *Histoire générale de la Guyane française: Des débuts de la colonisation à l'aube de l'an 2000: les grands problèmes guyanais, permanence et évolution.* Cayenne, French Guiana: Ibis Rouge.

Marcelin, L.-J. (1892). *Haïti: Ses guerres civiles – leurs causes, leurs conséquences présentes, leur conséquence future et finale. Moyens d'y mettre fin et de placer la nation dans la voie du progrès et de la civilisation. Etudes économiques, sociales et politiques.* Paris: A. Rousseau.

Marquetti, H. (1998). 'La Economía del dólar: balance y perspectivas.' *Temas*, no. 11, pp. 51–62.

Marquetti, H., and García, A. (2002). 'Cuba's Model of Industrial Growth: Current Problems and Perspectives.' In Monreal, G. P. M. (ed.), *Development prospects in Cuba: An agenda in the making*, pp. 69–95. London: Institute of Latin American Studies.

Marrero, L. (1972–90). *Cuba, economía y sociedad.* 15 vols. Río Piedras: Editorial San Juan.

Marshall, D. (2007). 'The New International Financial Architecture and Caribbean OFCs: Confronting Financial Stability Discourse.' *Third World Quarterly* 28(5), pp. 917–38.

Marshall, W. (1965). 'Metayage in the Sugar Industry of the British Windward Islands, 1838–65.' *Jamaica Historical Review* 5, pp. 28–55.

Marshall, W. (1968). 'Peasant Development in the West Indies since 1838.' *Social and Economic Studies* 17, pp. 252–63.

Marte, R. (1984). *Estadísticas y documentos históricos sobre Santo Domingo, 1805–1890.* Santo Domingo: Museo Nacional de Historia y Geografía.

Martin, R. M. (1834). *History of the British Colonies.* Vol. 2, *Possessions in the West Indies.* London: Cochrane and McCrone.

Martin, R. M. (1843). *History of the Colonies of the British Empire in the West Indies, South America, North America, Asia, Austral-Asia, Africa, and Europe.* London: Allen and Routledge.

Martínez-Fernández, L. (1994). *Torn between empires: Economy, society, and patterns of political thought in the Hispanic Caribbean, 1840–1878*. Athens: University of Georgia Press.

Maurer, B. (2001). 'Islands in the Net: Rewiring Technological and Financial Circuits in the "Offshore" Caribbean.' *Comparative Studies in Society and History* 43(3), pp. 467–501.

Meehan, M. (1927). *The Guianas: Commercial and Economic Survey*. Washington, DC: US Department of Commerce, Trade Information Bulletin, No. 516.

Meeks, B., and Girvan, N. (2010). *The thought of New World: The quest for decolonisation*. Kingston, Jamaica: Ian Randle.

Mesa-Lago, C. (1981). *The economy of socialist Cuba: A two-decade appraisal*. Albuquerque: University of New Mexico Press.

Mesa-Lago, C. (2000). *Market, socialist, and mixed economies: Comparative policy and performance: Chile, Cuba, and Costa Rica*. Baltimore: Johns Hopkins University Press.

Metzgen, M. S., and Cain, H. E. C. (1925). *The handbook of British Honduras, comprising historical, statistical and general information concerning the colony*. London: Crown Agents for the Colonies.

Millspaugh, A. C. (1929). 'Our Haitian Problem.' *Foreign Affairs* 7(4), pp. 556–70.

Mintz, S. W. (1974). *Caribbean transformations*. Chicago: Aldine.

Mintz, S. W. (1985). *Sweetness and power: The place of sugar in modern history*. New York: Viking.

Mitchell, B. R. (2007). *International historical statistics: The Americas, 1750–2005*. Houndmills: Palgrave Macmillan.

Mitchell, B. R. (2007a). *International historical statistics: Europe, 1750–2005*. Houndmills: Palgrave Macmillan.

Mitchell, H. P. (1963). *Europe in the Caribbean: The policies of Great Britain, France and the Netherlands towards their West Indian territories in the twentieth century*. Stanford, Calif.: Hispanic American Society.

Moberg, M. (1992). *Citrus, strategy, and class: The politics of development in Southern Belize*. Iowa City: University of Iowa Press.

Moberg, M. (1997). *Myths of ethnicity and nation: Immigration, work, and identity in the Belize banana industry*. Knoxville: University of Tennessee Press.

Moberg, M. (2003). 'Responsible Men and Sharp Yankees: the United Fruit Company, Resident Elites, and Colonial State in British Honduras.' In Striffler, S., and Moberg, M. (eds.), *Banana wars: Power, production, and history in the Americas*, pp. 145–70. Durham, N.C.: Duke University Press.

Modeste, N. C. (1976). *Economic instability and the monetary process of adjustment in an open economy: The experience of Guyana: 1955–1973*. Gainesville: University Press of Florida.

Moitt, B. (2001). *Women and slavery in the French Antilles, 1635–1848*. Bloomington: Indiana University Press.

Mokyr, J. (ed.). (2003). *The Oxford encyclopedia of economic history*. 5 vols. Oxford: Oxford University Press.

Monreal, G. P. M. (2002). *Development prospects in Cuba: An agenda in the making*. London: Institute of Latin American Studies.

Montague, L. L. (1940). *Haiti and the United States, 1714–1938*. Durham, N.C.: Duke University Press.

Monteith, K. E. A. (2000). 'Emancipation and Labour on Jamaican Coffee Plantations, 1838–48.' *Slavery and Abolition* 21(3), pp. 125–35.

Monteith, K. E. A. (2008). *Depression to decolonization: Barclays Bank (DCO) in the West Indies, 1926–1962*. Kingston, Jamaica: University of the West Indies Press.

Moohr, M. W. (1971). 'Patterns of change in an export economy: British Guiana, 1830–1914.' Ph.D. thesis, University of Cambridge.

Moohr, M. W. (1972). 'The Economic Impact of Slave Emancipation in British Guiana, 1832–1852.' *Economic History Review* 25(4), pp. 588–607.

Moore, B. L. (1987). *Race, power, and social segmentation in colonial society: Guyana after slavery, 1838–1891*. New York: Gordon & Breach.

Moral, P. (1961). *Le paysan haïtien: Etude sur la vie rurale en Haïti*. Paris: Maisonneuve & Larose.

Morales Carrión, A. (1974). *La abolición de la esclavitud*. San Juan: Asociación pro Democracia Española.

Mordecai, J. (1968). *Federation of the West Indies*. Evanston: Northwestern University Press.

Moreau de Jonnès, A. (1842). *Recherches statistiques sur l'esclavage colonial et sur les moyens de le supprimer*. Paris: Bourgogne et Martinet.

Moreno Fraginals, M. (1978). *El ingenio: Complejo económico social cubano del azúcar*. 3 vols. Havana: Editorial de Ciencias Sociales.

Moreno Fraginals, M., Moya Pons, F., and Engerman, S. L. (1985). *Between slavery and free labor: The Spanish-speaking Caribbean in the nineteenth century*. Baltimore: Johns Hopkins University Press.

Morris, D. (1883). *The colony of British Honduras: Its resources and prospects; with particular reference to its indigenous plants and economic productions*. London: E. Stanford.

Morris, D. (1911). *The Imperial Department of Agriculture in the West Indies*. London: Colonial Reports.

Morris, E. (2008). 'Cuba's New Relationship with Foreign Capital: Economic Policy-Making since 1990.' *Journal of Latin American Studies* 40(4), pp. 769–92.

Morrissey, M. (1981). 'Towards a Theory of West Indian Economic Development.' *Latin American Perspectives* 8(1), pp. 4–27.

Moya Pons, F. (1974). 'Nuevas consideraciones sobre la historia de la población dominicana: curvas, tasas y problemas.' *eme eme: Estudios Dominicanos*, no.15, pp. 3–29.

Moya Pons, F. (1976). 'Datos sobre la economía dominicana durante la primera república.' *eme eme: Estudios Dominicanos*, no. 24, pp. 21–44.

Moya Pons, F. (1985). 'Haiti and Santo Domingo: 1790–c.1870.' In Bethell, L. (ed.), *The Cambridge History of Latin America*. Vol. 3, *From Independence to c.1870*, pp. 237–76. Cambridge: Cambridge University Press.

Moya Pons, F. (1998). *The Dominican Republic: A national history*. Princeton, N.J.: Markus Wiener.

Moya Pons, F. (2007). *History of the Caribbean: Plantations, trade, and war in the Atlantic world*. Princeton, N.J.: Markus Wiener.

Munro, D. G. (1964). *Intervention and dollar diplomacy in the Caribbean, 1900–1921*. Princeton, N.J.: Princeton University Press.

Munro, D. G. (1974). *The United States and the Caribbean republics, 1921–1933*. Princeton, N.J.: Princeton University Press.

Murray, D. R. (1980). *Odious commerce: Britain, Spain, and the abolition of the Cuban slave trade*. Cambridge: Cambridge University Press.

Mutto, P. (1974). 'La Economía de Exportaciones de la República Dominicana.' *eme eme: Estudios Dominicanos* 3(15), pp. 67–110.

National Bank of Commerce. (1917). *The Virgin Islands: a Description of the Commercial Value of the Danish Virgin Islands*. New York.

Naylor, R. A. (1988). *Influencia británica en el comercio centroamericano durante las primeras décadas de la independencia: 1821–1851*. Antigua, Guatemala: Centro de Investigaciones Regionales de Mesoamérica.

Naylor, R. A. (1989). *Penny ante imperialism: The Mosquito Shore and the Bay of Honduras, 1600–1914: a case study in British informal empire*. Rutherford, N.J.: Fairleigh Dickinson University Press.

Nicholls, D. (1974). *Economic dependence and political autonomy: The Haitian experience*. Montreal: McGill University.

Nicholls, D. (1979). *From Dessalines to Duvalier: Race, colour, and national independence in Haiti*. Cambridge: Cambridge University Press.

Nicholls, G. (2001). 'Reflections on Economic Growth in Antigua and Barbuda.' *Integration & Trade* 5(15), pp. 105–44.

Nicholls, S. (2001). 'Panel Data Modelling of Long-Run Per Capita Growth Rates in the Caribbean.' *Integration & Trade* 5(15), pp. 57–82.

Norregaard, G. (1967). *Dansk Vestindien 1880–1917*. Copenhagen.

Nurse, K. (2004). *Diaspora, migration and development in the Caribbean*. Ottawa: FOCAL.

Nurse, K. (2008). 'The Economic Partnership Agreement and Beyond: The Case for Innovation and Industrial Policy.' *Journal of Eastern Caribbean Studies* 33(2), pp. 70–104.

Nye, J. S. (2008). *The powers to lead*. Oxford: Oxford University Press.

Nye, J. V. C. (2007). *War, wine, and taxes: The political economy of Anglo-French trade, 1689–1900*. Princeton, N.J.: Princeton University Press.

Ocampo, J., and Parra, M. (2003). 'Los términos de intercambio de los productos básicos en el siglo XX.' *Revista de la Cepal* 73, pp. 7–35.

Officer, L. H. (1982). *Purchasing power parity and exchange rates: Theory, evidence and relevance*. Greenwich, Conn.: JAI Press.

O'Loughlin, C. (1963). *A Survey of Economic Potential and Capital Needs of the Leeward Islands, Windward Islands, and Barbados*. London: Her Majesty's Stationery Office.

O'Loughlin, C. (1966). *Methods and sources of the national income statistics of the Leeward and Windward Islands*. Kingston, Jamaica: University of the West Indies.

O'Loughlin, C. (1968). *Economic and political change in the Leeward and Windward Islands*. New Haven: Yale University Press.

O'Loughlin, C., and Best, L. (1960). 'Economic Structure in the West Indies.' In Cumper, G. E. (ed.), *The economy of the West Indies*, pp. 95–125. Kingston, Jamaica: United Printers.

Olmsted, V. H., and Gannett, H. (1909). *Cuba: Population, history and resources 1907*. Washington, DC: United States Bureau of the Census.

Oranje en de Zes Caraibische Parelen: Officieel gedenkboek ter gelegenheid van het gouden regeringsjubileum van Hare Majesteit Koningin Wilhelmina, Helena, Pauline, Maria, 1898–31 Augustus–1948. (1948). Amsterdam: J. H. de Bussy.

Ortiz, F. (1940). *Contrapunteo cubano del tabaco y el azúcar*. Havana: J. Montero.

Overseas Economic Surveys. (1950). *Cuba*. London: His Majesty's Stationery Office.

Overseas Economic Surveys. (1954). *Cuba*. London: Her Majesty's Stationery Office.

Overseas Economic Surveys. (1956). *Hayti*. London: Her Majesty's Stationery Office.

Overseas Economic Surveys. (1957). *Dominican Republic*. London: Her Majesty's Stationery Office.

Paiewonsky, R. M., and Dookhan, I. (1990). *Memoirs of a governor: A man for the people*. New York: New York University Press.

Palmer, R. W. (1998). *U.S.-Caribbean relations: Their impact on peoples and culture*. Westport, Conn: Praeger.

Palmer, R. W. (2009). *The Caribbean economy in the age of globalization*. Basingstoke: Palgrave Macmillan.

Panday, R. M. N. (1959). *Agriculture in Surinam, 1650–1950: An inquiry into the causes of its decline*. Amsterdam: H. J. Paris.

Pantin, D. (2005). *The Caribbean economy: A reader*. Kingston, Jamaica: Ian Randle.

Parker, J. C. (2008). *Brother's keeper: The United States, race, and empire in the British Caribbean, 1937–1962*. Oxford: Oxford University Press.

Parry, J. H., Sherlock, P. M., and Maingot, A. P. (1987). *A short history of the West Indies*. New York: St. Martin's.

Payne, A. (1985). 'Whither CARICOM? The Performance and Prospects of Caribbean Integration in the 1980s.' *International Journal* 40(2), pp. 207–28.

Pérez, L. (1990). 'Cuba, c.1930–59.' In Bethell, L. (ed.), *The Cambridge History of Latin America*. Vol. 7, *1930 to the Present*, pp. 419–56. Cambridge: Cambridge University Press.

Pérez, V. O. E. (2002). 'Foreign Direct Investment in Cuba: Recent Experience and Prospects.' In Monreal, G. P. M. (ed.), *Development prospects in Cuba: An agenda in the making*, pp. 47–68. London: Institute of Latin American Studies.

Pérez, V. O. E. (2004). 'The Cuban Economy Today and its Future Challenges.' In Domínguez, J. I., Pérez, V. O. E., and Barberia, L. (2004), *The Cuban economy at the start of the twenty-first century*, pp. 49–90. Cambridge, Mass.: David Rockefeller Center for Latin American Studies.

Pérez de la Riva, J. (1975). *La República neocolonial*. 2 vols. Havana: Editorial de Ciencias Sociales.

Pérez de la Riva, J. (1979). *El monto de la inmigración forzada en el siglo XIX*. Havana: Editorial de Ciencias Sociales.

Pérez-López, J. F. (1987). *Measuring Cuban economic performance*. Austin: University of Texas Press.

Pérez-Stable, M. (1993). *The Cuban Revolution: Origins, course, and legacy*. New York: Oxford University Press.

Perkins, D. (1937). *The Monroe doctrine, 1867–1907*. Baltimore: Johns Hopkins University Press.

Perloff, H. S. (1950). *Puerto Rico's economic future: A study in planned development*. Chicago: University of Chicago Press.

Perloff, H. S. (1969). *Alliance for progress: A social invention in the making*. Baltimore: Johns Hopkins University Press.

Pétot, J. (1986). *L'or de Guyane: Son histoire, ses hommes*. Paris: Editions Caribéenes.

Petras, E. M. L. (1988). *Jamaican labor migration: White capital and Black labor, 1850–1930*. Boulder, Colo.: Westview.

Petty, C. L. (1991). *A handbook history of Anguilla*. Anguilla: East End.

Pim, A. (1934). *British Honduras, Financial and Economic Position* (cmd 4586). London: His Majesty's Stationery Office.

Pitkin, T. (1835). *A statistical view of the commerce of the United States of America: Including also an account of banks, manufactures and internal trade and improvements: together with that of the revenues and expenditures of the general government: accompanied with numerous tables.* New Haven: Durrie & Peck.

Plante, F. J. M. (1918). *West-Indië in het Parlement, 1897–1917: Bijdrage tot Nederland's koloniaal-politieke geschiedenis.* The Hague: Nijhoff.

Platt, D. C. M. (1971). 'Problems in the Interpretation of Foreign Trade Statistics before 1914.' *Journal of Latin American Studies* 3(2), pp. 119–30.

Platt, R. R., Wright, J. K., Weaver, J. C., and Fairchild, J. E. (1941). *The European possessions in the Caribbean area: A compilation of facts concerning their population, physical geography, resources, industries, trade, government, and strategic importance.* New York: American Geographical Society.

Pletcher, D. (1977). 'Inter-American Trade in the Early 1870s–A State Department Survey.' *The Americas* 33(4), pp. 593–612.

Pletcher, D. M. (1998). *The diplomacy of trade and investment: American economic expansion in the Hemisphere, 1865–1900.* Columbia: University of Missouri Press.

Plummer, B. G. (1988). *Haiti and the great powers, 1902–1915.* Baton Rouge: Louisiana State University Press.

Pollitt, B. (1997). 'The Cuban Sugar Economy: Collapse, Reform and Prospects for Recovery.' *Journal of Latin American Studies* 29(1), pp. 171–210.

Pollitt, B. (2004). 'The Rise and Fall of the Cuban Sugar Economy.' *Journal of Latin American Studies* 36(2), pp. 319–48.

Poole, B. L. (1951). *The Caribbean Commission: Background of cooperation in the West Indies.* Columbia: University of South Carolina Press.

Porter, R. P. (1899). *Report on the commercial and industrial condition of Cuba.* Washington, DC: Government Printing Office.

Prados de la Escosura, L. (2003). *El Progreso Económico de España (1850–2000).* Madrid: Fundación BBVA.

Prados de la Escosura, L. (2006). 'The Economic Consequences of Independence in Latin America.' In Bulmer-Thomas, V., Coatsworth, J. H., and Cortés, C. R. (eds.), *The Cambridge economic history of Latin America.* Vol. 1, *The Colonial Era and the Short Nineteenth Century*, pp. 463–504. Cambridge: Cambridge University Press.

Prest, A. R. (1960). 'Public Finance.' In Cumper, G. E. (ed.), *The economy of the West Indies*, pp. 181–222. Kingston, Jamaica: United Printers.

Price, R. (1976). *The Guiana Maroons: A historical and bibliographical introduction.* Baltimore: Johns Hopkins University Press.

Prinsen, G. H. C. (1909). *Cane sugar and its manufacture.* London: N. Rodger.

Prior, F. (2010). 'Medium-Term Economic Growth in the Caribbean.' *Social and Economic Studies* 59(3), pp. 127–40.

Proudfoot, M. M. (1954). *Britain and the United States in the Caribbean: A comparative study in methods of development.* London: Faber and Faber.

Quigley, N. (1989). 'The Bank of Nova Scotia in the Caribbean, 1889–1940.' *Business History Review* 63(4), pp. 797–838.

Ragatz, L. J. (1928). *The fall of the planter class in the British Caribbean, 1763–1833: A study in social and economic history.* New York: Century.

Ragatz, L. J. (1928a). *Statistics for the study of British Caribbean economic history, 1763–1833.* London: Bryan Edwards.

Ramsaran, R. (1984). *The monetary and financial system of the Bahamas: Growth, structure, and operation.* Mona, Jamaica: University of the West Indies.

Rangarajan, L. N. (1978). *Commodity conflict: The political economy of international commodity negotiations*. Ithaca, N.Y: Cornell University Press.

Rapley, J., Thorburn, D., King, D., and Campbell, C. (2010). *The Economic Partnership Agreement (EPA): Towards a New Era for Caribbean Trade*. CIGI: Caribbean Paper, No. 10.

Rathbone, J. P. (2010). *The sugar king of Havana: The rise and fall of Julio Lobo, Cuba's last tycoon*. New York: Penguin.

Redpath, J. (1861). *A guide to Hayti*. Boston: Haytian Bureau of Emigration.

Reed, N. A. (1964). *The Caste War of Yucatan*. Stanford, Calif.: Stanford University Press.

Renard, R. (1993). 'Labour Relations in Martinique and Guadeloupe, 1848–1870.' In Beckles, H., and Shepherd, V. (eds.), *Caribbean freedom: Society and economy from emancipation to the present*, pp. 161–68. Kingston, Jamaica: Ian Randle.

Reno, P. (1964). *The ordeal of British Guiana*. New York: Monthly Review Press.

Richardson, B. (2004). 'The Migration Experience.' In Brereton, B. (ed.), *The Caribbean in the twentieth century*. Paris: UNESCO.

Ritter, A. R. M. (2004). *The Cuban economy*. Pittsburgh: University of Pittsburgh Press.

Rivière, E. (1972). 'Labor Shortage in the British West Indies after Emancipation.' *Journal of Caribbean History* 4, pp. 1–30.

Robert, G. (1950). *La France aux Antilles de 1939 à 1943*. Paris: Plon.

Roberts, C. P., and Hamour, M. (1970). *Cuba 1968: Supplement to the Statistical abstract of Latin America*. Los Angeles: UCLA Latin American Center.

Roberts, G. W. (1960). 'Movements in Population and the Labour Force.' In Cumper, G. E. (ed.), *The economy of the West Indies*, pp. 24–47. Kingston, Jamaica: United Printers.

Roberts, G. W. (1966). 'Summary Statistics on Indenture and Associated Migration Affecting the West Indies, 1834–1918.' *Population Studies* 20(1), pp. 125–34.

Roberts, S. (1995). 'Small Place, Big Money: The Cayman Islands and the International Financial System.' *Economic Geography* 71(3), pp. 237–56.

Roberts, T. D., and Callaway, S. G. (1966). *Area handbook for the Dominican Republic*. Washington, DC: Government Printing Office.

Roberts, W. A. (1942). *The French in the West Indies*. New York: Bobbs-Merrill.

Robichek, W., and Sanson, C. (1972). 'The Balance of Payments Performance of Latin America and the Caribbean, 1966–70.' *IMF Staff Papers* 19(2), pp. 286–343.

Roca, S. (1976). *Cuban economic policy and ideology: The ten million ton sugar harvest*. Beverly Hills, Calif.: Sage.

Rodney, W. (1981). *A history of the Guyanese working people, 1881–1905*. Baltimore: Johns Hopkins University Press.

Rodríguez, J. J. C., and Vélez, C. R. (1980). *El precapitalismo dominicano de la primera mitad del siglo XIX, 1780–1850*. Santo Domingo: Universidad Autónoma de Santo Domingo.

Rodríguez, J. L., and Carriazo, M. G. (1987). *Eradicación de la pobreza en Cuba*. Havana: Editorial de Ciencias Sociales.

Roldán de Montaud, I. (1990). *La hacienda en Cuba durante la Guerra de los Diez Años, 1868–1880*. Madrid: Instituto de Cooperación Iberoamericana.

Römer, R. A. (1981). *Curaçao*. San Juan: Association of Caribbean Universities and Research Institutes, UNICA.

Romney, D. (ed.). (1959). *Land in British Honduras: Report of the British Honduras Land Use Survey team*. London: Her Majesty's Stationary Office.

Rotberg, R. I. (1971). *Haiti; the politics of squalor.* Boston: Houghton Mifflin.

Russell, R. S. (1947). *Imperial preference: Its development and effects.* London: Empire Economic Union.

Ryan, S. D. (2009). *Eric Williams: The myth and the man.* Kingston, Jamaica: University of the West Indies Press.

Sainte-Croix, C. L. F. F. R. (1822). *Statistique de la Martinique: Ornée d'une carte de cette île, avec les documens authentiques de sa population, de son commerce, de sa consommation annuelles et de ses revenus, etc., etc.* Paris: Chaumerot.

Salvucci, L., and Salvucci, R. (2000). 'Cuba and the Latin American Terms of Trade: Old Theories, New Evidence.' *Journal of Interdisciplinary History* 31(2), pp. 197–222.

Sánchez, G. (2007). *Cuba and Venezuela: An insight into two revolutions.* Melbourne: Ocean.

Sánchez-Albornoz, N. (1986). 'The Population of Latin America, 1850–1930.' In Bethell, L. (ed.), *The Cambridge History of Latin America*, Vol. 4, *c.1870–1930*, pp. 121–50. Cambridge: Cambridge University Press.

Sanger, J. P., Gannett, H., and Willcox, W. F. (1900). *Report on the census of Porto Rico, 1899.* Washington, DC: Government Printing Office.

Sanger, J. P., Gannett, H., and Willcox, W. F. (1900a). *Report on the census of Cuba, 1899.* Washington, DC: Government Printing Office.

Santamaría, G. A. (2000). 'El Crecimiento Económico de Cuba Republicana (1902–59). Una Revisión y Nuevas Estimaciones en Perspectiva Comparada.' *Revista de Indias* 60(219), pp. 505–44.

Santamaría, G. A. (2005). *Las Cuentas Nacionales de Cuba, 1690–2005.* Madrid: Instituto de Historia.

Santamaría, G. A., and García, A. A. (2004). *Economía y colonia: La economía cubana y la relación con España, 1765–1902.* Madrid: Instituto de Histora.

Scammell, W. M. (1980). *The international economy since 1945.* New York: St. Martin's.

Scarano, F. A. (1984). *Sugar and slavery in Puerto Rico: The plantation economy of Ponce, 1800–1850.* Madison: University of Wisconsin Press.

Scheler, A. (1858). *Almanach Statistique.* Brussels: A. Schnée.

Scherer, F. M. (1992). *International high-technology competition.* Cambridge, Mass: Harvard University Press.

Schmidt, H. (1971). *The United States occupation of Haiti, 1915–1934.* New Brunswick, N.J.: Rutgers University Press.

Schmidt, N. (1990). 'Les migrations de main-d'oeuvre dans la politique colonial française aux Caraïbes pendant la seconde moitié du XIXe siècle.' *Le Mouvement Social* 151, pp. 11–37.

Schnakenbourg, C. (1980). 'Statistiques pour l'Histoire de l'Economie de Plantation en Guadeloupe et Martinique.' *Bulletin de la Société d'Histoire de la Guadeloupe* 31, pp. 3–121.

Schnakenbourg, C. (1980a). *Histoire de l'industrie sucrière en Guadeloupe aux XIXe et XXe siècles.* Paris: L'Harmattan.

Schneider, J., Schwarzer, O., and Zellfelder, F. (1991). *Währungen der Welt. I, Europäische und nordamerikanische Devisenkurse 1777–1914.* 3 vols. Stuttgart: Franz Steiner.

Schoenrich, O. (1918). *Santo Domingo: A country with a future.* New York: Macmillan.

Schroeder, S. (1982). *Cuba: A handbook of historical statistics*. Boston: G. K. Hall.

Scott, R. J. (1985). *Slave emancipation in Cuba: The transition to free labor, 1860–1899*. Princeton, N.J.: Princeton University Press.

Searle, C. (1983). *Grenada, the struggle against destabilization*. London: Writers and Readers.

Serbin, A. (1994). 'Towards an Association of Caribbean States: Raising some Awkward Questions.' *Journal of Interamerican Studies and World Affairs* 36(4), pp. 61–90.

Sewell, W. G. (1861). *The ordeal of free labor in the British West Indies*. New York: Harper & Bros.

Sharma, S. D. (2004). The Promise of Monterrey: Meeting the Millennium Development Goals.' *World Policy Journal* 21(3), pp. 51–66.

Shaxson, N. (2010). *Treasure islands: Tax havens – the darkest chapter in economic history since the slave trade*. London: Bodley Head.

Shepherd, V. (2002). *Slavery without sugar: Diversity in Caribbean economy and society since the 17th century*. Gainesville: University Press of Florida.

Shoman, A. (1973). 'The Birth of the Nationalist Movement in Belize, 1950–1954.' *Journal of Belizean Affairs* 2, pp. 3–40.

Shoman, A. (2010). *Belize's independence and decolonization in Latin America: Guatemala, Britain, and the UN*. New York: Palgrave Macmillan.

Shoman, A. (2011). *13 Chapters of a history of Belize*. 2nd ed. Belize City: Angelus.

Simmons, D. C. (2001). *Confederate settlements in British Honduras*. Jefferson, N.C: McFarland.

Sircar, K. K. (1971). 'Emigration of Indian indentured labour to the Danish West Indian island of St Croix, 1863–68.' *Scandinavian Economic History Review* 19(2), pp. 134–48.

Skrubbeltrang, F. (1967). *Dansk Vestindien 1848–80*. Copenhagen.

Smith, A. (1776). *An inquiry into the nature and causes of the wealth of nations*. London: Printed for W. Strahan; and T. Cadell.

Smith, F. H. (2005). *Caribbean rum: A social and economic history*. Gainesville: University Press of Florida.

Smith, G. (2011). *George Price. A Life Revealed – The Authorized Biography*. Kingston, Jamaica: Ian Randle.

Smith, R. T. (1962). *British Guiana*. London: Oxford University Press.

Sno, I. (2008). *Enkele vormen van ongelijkheid in Suriname en mogelijke toepassingen van onder meer de Gini coëfficiënt daarbij. Bevolkingsprojecties voor de republiek Suriname 2004–2024*. The Hague: Algemeen Bureau voor de Statistiek.

Société d'Etudes pour la Colonisation de la Guyane. (1844). *Note sur la Fondation d'Une Nouvelle Colonie dans la Guyane Française*. Paris: Firmin Didot Frères.

Société Anglo-Française de Honduras. (1857). *Notice sur les acajous de la Baie de Honduras*. Paris.

Sonesson, B. (1990). *La Real Hacienda en Puerto Rico: Administración, política y grupos de presión, 1815–1868*. Madrid: Instituto de Cooperación Iberoamericana.

South American Handbook. (annual). Bath: Trade & Travel.

Spraos, J. (1980). 'The Statistical Debate on the Net Barter Terms of Trade Between Primary Commodities and Manufactures.' *Economic Journal* 90(357), pp. 107–128.

St. John, S. (1889). *Hayti: or, The black republic*. New York: Scribner & Welford.

Stallings, B., and Peres, W. (2000). *Growth, employment, and equity: The impact of the economic reforms in Latin America and the Caribbean*. Washington, DC: Brookings Institution Press.

Statesman's Yearbook. (annual). New York: Macmillan.

Stephens, J. (1974). 'La Emigración de Negros Norteamericanos en Haiti en 1824–1825.' *eme eme: Estudios Dominicanos* 14, pp. 40–71.

Striffler, S., and Moberg, M. (2003). *Banana wars: Power, production, and history in the Americas.* Durham, N.C.: Duke University Press.

Stubbs, J. (1985). *Tobacco on the periphery: A case study in Cuban labour history, 1860–1958.* Cambridge: Cambridge University Press.

Sweig, J. (2002). *Inside the Cuban Revolution: Fidel Castro and the urban underground.* Cambridge, Mass.: Harvard University Press.

Swerling, B. C. (1949). *International control of sugar, 1918–41.* Stanford, Calif.: Stanford University Press.

Székely, M., and Montes, A. (2006). 'Poverty and Inequality.' In Bulmer-Thomas, V., Coatsworth, J. H., and Cortés, C. R. (eds.), *The Cambridge economic history of Latin America.* Vol. 2, *The Long Twentieth Century*, pp. 585–646. Cambridge: Cambridge University Press.

Szulc, T. (1986). *Fidel: A critical portrait.* New York: Morrow.

Tafunell, X. (2007). *La inversión en equipo de transporte de América Latina, 1890–1930: Una estimación basada en la demanda de importaciones.* I Congreso Latinoamericano de Historia Económica, Montevideo, Uruguay.

Taitt, G. (2007). 'Domestic Food Production in Guadeloupe in World War II.' In Besson, J., and Momsen, J. H. (eds.), *Caribbean land and development revisited*, pp. 41–52. New York: Palgrave Macmillan.

Tansill, C. C. (1932). *The purchase of the Danish West Indies.* Baltimore: Johns Hopkins University Press.

Tansill, C. C. (1938). *The United States and Santo Domingo, 1798–1873: A chapter in Caribbean diplomacy.* Baltimore: Johns Hopkins University Press.

Taubira-Delannon, C. (n.d.). *L'Or en Guyane, Eclats et Artificiers.* Paris: Rapport à Monsieur le Premier Ministre.

Taussig, F. W. (1931). *The tariff history of the United States.* New York: G. P. Putnam's Sons.

Taussig, F. W. (1967). *The tariff history of the United States: Including a consideration of the tariff of 1930.* New York: A. M. Kelley.

Taylor, F. (1993). *To hell with paradise: A history of the Jamaican tourist industry.* Pittsburgh: University of Pittsburgh Press.

Tea and Coffee Trade Journal. (1935). *Two Hundred Years of Coffee in Haiti.* Vol. 68. pp. 103–5. New York: F. H. Hobbs.

Teunissen, H., and Blokker, N. (1985). 'Textile Protectionism in the 1980s: the MFA and the EEC's Bilateral Textile Agreements with Developing Countries.' In Stevens, C., and Verloren van Themaat, J. (eds.), *EEC and the Third World: A Survey 5. Pressure Groups, Policies and Development*, pp. 61–86. London: Hodder and Stoughton.

Thoby, A. (1890). *Les finances d'Haïti sous le gouvernement du Général Salomon: Le budget des recettes et les impots.* Port-au-Prince: Imprimerie de la Jeunesse.

Thomas, C. Y. (1988). *The poor and the powerless: Economic policy and change in the Caribbean.* London: Latin America Bureau.

Thomas, H. (1971). *Cuba: Or, Pursuit of freedom.* London: Eyre & Spottiswoode.

Thomas, H. (1997). *The slave trade: The story of the Atlantic slave trade, 1440–1870.* New York: Simon & Schuster.

Thomas-Hope, E. M. (2001). 'The Role of the Environment in Caribbean Economic Development.' *Integration & Trade* 5(15), pp. 83–104.

Thomas-Hope, E. M. (2002). *Caribbean Migration*. Bridgetown, Barbados: University of the West Indies Press.

Thurber, F. B. (1881). *Coffee: from plantation to cup: A brief history of coffee production and consumption*. New York: American Grocer.

Tignor, R. L. (2006). *W. Arthur Lewis and the birth of development economics*. Princeton, N.J.: Princeton University Press.

Tinker, H. (1993). *A new system of slavery: The export of Indian labour overseas 1830–1920*. London: Hansib.

Tippenhauer, L. (1893). *Die Insel Haiti*. Leipzig: Brodhaus.

Toft, P. (1982). 'Kriser og Nedgang: Den økonomiske udvikling I Dansk Vestindien 1875–1917.' *Erhvervshistorisk Arbog* 32, pp. 146–91.

Togores, V., and García, A. (2004). 'Consumption, Markets and Monetary Duality.' In Domínguez, J. I., Pérez, V. O. E., and Barberia, L. (eds.), *The Cuban economy at the start of the twenty-first century*, pp. 245–96. Cambridge, Mass.: David Rockefeller Center for Latin American Studies.

Tomich, D. W. (1990). *Slavery in the circuit of sugar: Martinique and the world economy, 1830–1848*. Baltimore: Johns Hopkins University Press.

Tooke, T. (1857). *A history of prices, and of the state of the circulation, from 1793 to 1837: Preceded by a brief sketch of the state of corn trade in the last two centuries*. London: Longman, Orme, Brown, Green, and Longmans.

Trouillot, M.-R. (1988). *Peasants and capital: Dominica in the world economy*. Baltimore: Johns Hopkins University Press.

Turnbull, D. (1840). *Travels in the West: Cuba, with notices of Porto Rico and the slave trade*. London: Longman, Orme, Brown, Green, and Longmans.

Turner, M. (1974). 'Chinese Contract Labour in Cuba, 1847–1874.' *Caribbean Studies* 14(2), pp. 66–81.

Turnier, A. (1955). *Les Etats-Unis et le marché haïtien*. Washington, DC.

Uribe, C. A. (1954). *Brown gold: The amazing story of coffee*. New York: Random House.

van Dijck, P. (2001). 'Structural Change and Long-Term Growth: the Suriname Experience.' *Integration & Trade* 5(15), pp. 275–302.

van Lier, R. A. J. (1971). *Frontier society: A social analysis of the history of Surinam*. The Hague: Nijhoff.

van Schaaijk, M. (1992). *Micromacrodataset*. The Hague: STUSECO.

van Soest, J. (1978). *Trustee of the Netherlands Antilles: A history of money, banking and the economy, with special reference to the central Bank van de Nederlandse Antillen 1828–6 February–1978*. Zutphen: Walburg Pers.

van Traa, A. (1946). *Suriname, 1900–1940*. Deventer: W. van Hoeve.

Vedovato, C. (1986). *Politics, foreign trade and economic development: A study of the Dominican Republic*. London: Croom Helm.

Vega, W. (1977). 'El Regimen Laboral y de Tierras durante la Primera República.' *eme eme: Estudios Dominicanos* 30, pp. 16–26.

Vertovec, S. (1995). 'Indian indentured migration to the Caribbean.' In Cohen, R. (ed.), *The Cambridge Survey of World Migration*, pp. 57–62. Cambridge: Cambridge University Press.

Vibaek, J. (1967). *Dansk Vestindien 1755–1848*. Copenhagen.

Victor, R. (1944). *Recensement et démographie*. Port-au-Prince: Impr. de l'état.

Vidal, P., and Fundora, A. (2008). 'Trade-Growth Relationship in Cuba: Estimation using the Kalman Filter.' *CEPAL Review* 94, pp. 97–116.

Vincent, S. (1939). *Outline of financial history of the Republic of Haiti.* Port-au-Prince: Impr. de l'état.

Wagley, C. (1960). 'Plantation America: A Culture Sphere.' In Rubin, V. D. (ed.), *Caribbean studies: A symposium.* Seattle: University of Washington.

Wallich, H. C. (1950). *Monetary problems of an export economy: The Cuban experience, 1914–1947.* Cambridge, Mass.: Harvard University Press.

Ward, J. R. (1988). *British West Indian slavery, 1750–1834: The process of amelioration.* Oxford: Clarendon.

Watts, D. (1987). *The West Indies: Patterns of development, culture, and environmental change since 1492.* Cambridge: Cambridge University Press.

Wawoe, J. (2000). 'The Impact of Development Aid on the Netherlands Antilles and Aruba.' M.Sc. thesis, Queen Mary & Westfield College, London University.

Weintraub, S. (1994). *The NAFTA debate: Grappling with unconventional trade issues.* Boulder, Colo.: Lynne Rienner.

Welch, R. E. (1985). *Response to revolution: The United States and the Cuban revolution, 1959–1961.* Chapel Hill: University of North Carolina Press.

Welles, S. (1928). *Naboth's vineyard: The Dominican Republic, 1844–1924.* 2 vols. New York: Payson & Clarke.

West Indian Commission. (1992). *Time for action: Report of the West Indian Commission.* Largo, Md.: International Development Options.

West Indies Yearbook, 1941–2. (1942). Montreal.

Westergaard, W. (1917). *The Danish West Indies under company rule (1671–1754): With a supplementary chapter, 1755–1917.* New York: Macmillan.

White, M. J. (1996). *The Cuban missile crisis.* Basingstoke: Macmillan.

Wiarda, H. J. (1969). *The Dominican Republic: Nation in transition.* New York: Praeger.

Wilkie, J. W. (1974). *Statistics and national policy.* Los Angeles: UCLA Latin American Center.

Wilkins, M. (1970). *The emergence of multinational enterprise: American business abroad from the colonial era to 1914.* Cambridge, Mass.: Harvard University Press.

Wilkins, M. (1974). *The maturing of multinational enterprise: American business abroad from 1914 to 1970.* Cambridge, Mass.: Harvard University Press.

Wilkins, M., and Schröter, H. G. (1998). *The Free-standing company in the world economy, 1830–1996.* Oxford: Oxford University Press.

Williams, E. E. (1944). *Capitalism & slavery.* Chapel Hill: University of North Carolina Press.

Williams, M. W. (1916). *Anglo-American Isthmian diplomacy, 1815–1915.* Washington, DC: American Historical Association.

Willmore, L. (1996). *Export Processing in the Caribbean: Lessons from Four Case Studies.* United Nations ECLAC Working Paper No. 42.

Wilson, S. M. (1997). *The indigenous people of the Caribbean.* Gainesville: University Press of Florida.

Winkler, M. (1928). *Investments of United States capital in Latin America.* Boston: World Peace Foundation.

Winters, A. (1990). 'The Road to Uruguay.' *Economic Journal* 100(403), pp. 1288–1303.

Winzerling, E. O. (1946). *The beginning of British Honduras, 1506–1765*. New York: North River.

Witter, M. (2005). 'The Informal Economy of Jamaica.' In Pantin, D. (ed.), *The Caribbean Economy: a Reader*, pp. 434–63. Kingston, Jamaica: Ian Randle.

Woodruff, W. (1967). *Impact of western man, a study of Europe's role in the world economy, 1750–1960*. New York: St. Martin's.

Worrell, D. L., and Bourne, C. (1989). *Economic adjustment policies for small nations: Theory and experience in the English-speaking Caribbean*. New York: Praeger.

Zabriskie, L. K. (1918). *The Virgin Islands of the United States of America: Historical and descriptive, commercial and industrial facts, figures, and resources*. New York: G. P. Putnam's Sons.

Zanetti, O., and García, A. (1976). *United Fruit Company: Un caso del dominio imperialista en Cuba*. Havana: Editorial de Ciencias Sociales.

Zanetti, O., and García, A. (1998). *Sugar & railroads: A Cuban history, 1837–1959*. Chapel Iill: University of North Carolina Press.

Zimbalist, A. S., and Brundenius, C. (1989). *The Cuban economy: Measurement and analysis of socialist performance*. Baltimore: Johns Hopkins University Press.

Index

Note: The term 'territories' has been used throughout the index as it is the most neutral word to describe the different constitutional status of British, Dutch, French, Spanish, Scandinavian and US countries in the Caribbean. The text provides differentiation between colonial, dependent and independent status. Page numbers followed by the letters *a, f, n* or *t* indicate material in appendixes, figures, notes or tables. Though both British and American English spellings appear throughout the text, British English has been used in the index.